Living with the Earth

AN INTRODUCTION TO ENVIRONMENTAL PHILOSOPHY

Kent A. Peacock
The University of Western Ontario

Harcourt Brace & Company, Canada
TORONTO MONTREAL FORT WORTH NEW YORK ORLANDO
PHILADELPHIA SAN DIEGO LONDON SYDNEY TOKYO

Canadian Cataloguing in Publication Data

Main entry under title:

Living with the Earth

ISBN 0-7747-3377-2

1. Environmental ethics. I. Peacock, Kent Alan, 1952–

GE42.I59 1996 179'.1 C95-933009-7

Publisher: Heather McWhinney
Senior Acquisitions Editor: Christopher Carson
Projects Manager: Liz Radojkovic
Developmental Editor: Laura Paterson Pratt
Director of Publishing Services: Jean Davies
Editorial Manager: Marcel Chiera
Supervising Editor: Semareh Al-Hillal
Production Editor: Laurel Parsons
Production Manager: Sue-Ann Becker
Production Co-ordinator: Sheila Barry
Copy Editor: Wayne Herrington
Cover and Interior Design: Maher Design
Typesetting and Assembly: MacTrix DTP
Printing and Binding: Hignell Printing Limited

Cover Art: Shirley Wiitasalo, *Double Shadow*, 1992, oil on canvas, 215.9 cm x 152.4 cm. Courtesy of Susan Hobbs Gallery. Photo by Cheryl O'Brien.

This book was printed in Canada. The interior was printed on recycled paper containing a minimum of 20% post-consumer waste.

1 2 3 4 5 00 99 98 97 96

To my boys, Lewis and Evan, who never let me forget
that the seventh generation is only six generations away.

PREFACE

This book is meant to be an introduction to environmental philosophy that can be used for individual reading and study or as a core or supplemental text in a first- or second-year university or college course. As explained more fully in the Introduction, environmental philosophy is not just environmental ethics; indeed, I take it to be part of my task here to show why many people believe that ethics has anything at all to do with finding a better approach, if not a solution, to our huge environmental problems. Although the issues are universal, I have cited a number of especially significant Canadian examples, and relied upon several outstanding Canadian authors, to help tell the story.

The reader will find a kaleidoscopic array of viewpoints in this anthology. Many of the authors in this text are not professional philosophers; in fact, many are not academics at all, but simply people who, out of their experience and reflection, have expressed some philosophically significant perception (or misconception!) in an especially effective or striking way. At the risk of overstating the obvious, let it be stipulated that the editor of this volume does not necessarily agree with all the authors represented here. In fact, I have deliberately set out, in many cases, to illustrate opposing or divergent views. Compare, for instance, the attitudes toward the value and preservation of forests expressed by Jamie Swift's West Coast logger and the Haida Gwaganad; it would be difficult to find a sharper contrast. Or compare William Leiss, who insists that "nothing is sacred," with Schweitzer or Naess.

In particular, this collection attempts to bridge the gap between scientific and humanistic approaches to the environment. If any activity should be transdisciplinary and **holistic**, it is the study of the environment, and yet some sort of centrifugal force seems to constantly threaten to fragment the subject into noncommunicating and even competing subdisciplines. Environmental scientists and engineers disdain "fuzzy" subjects such as ethics and politics, while ethicists and political scientists refuse to believe that questions such as *how* sustainable agriculture could actually work have anything to do with their concerns. Here the reader will find discussions of topics all along a spectrum from the mechanics of soil cultivation to the ultimate aims, if any, of human existence. It *all* counts.

If there is a message this book avowedly sets out to convey, apart from an encouragement to its readers to open their minds to the breadth, complexity, and depth of these problems, it is to direct attention to the concept of *symbiosis* and to suggest that "living with the Earth" in a truly fulfilling and sustainable way must mean setting up, somehow, a genuine symbiosis between humans and our broader earthly environment. Whether this is a vapid platitude or our last best hope I leave for the reader to decide.

A few words about the organization of the book. It is divided into six parts, each containing two to five relatively short, focussed chapters. Roughly speaking, it follows a progression, from more or less purely scientific and historical matters, through environmental ethics, to its application in questions of economics and sustainable development, and with a concluding attempt at integration. The readings vary greatly in difficulty, depth, and length. Although the material is ordered in such a way as to tell a story (partly by implication), the selections are, I hope, well enough articulated that readers and instructors should be able to pick and choose material in convenient "chunks" to suit their needs and interests. Each chapter is followed by a selection of questions for further study and some pointers to the bibliography.

The questions vary greatly in difficulty. Some are elementary, requiring little more than sensitive *explication de texte*, or clarification of some interesting factual or verbal point. (But be careful; the shortness of a question is not directly proportional to its difficulty. *No* question has one and only one correct answer; any, if pursued with sufficient curiosity and imagination, may lead the reader into unsuspected depths.) For many questions, I have no definite answer in mind; they are asked in order to provoke and stimulate or simply because I wish that I knew the answer myself. Most can be answered (at least in a preliminary way) using the resources provided in this book, although many require that the reader be able and willing to find connections among several readings. Some questions might lead the reader who demands a really satisfactory answer to do research beyond the confines of this anthology. A few questions are deep enough that they might serve as the basis of a PhD thesis, or a lifetime study.

Some books and papers are mentioned in the suggested readings for more than one part, in the hope that the added convenience for the reader will justify the slight waste of paper. (This is, of course, an all-too-typical environmental trade-off!) The sources mentioned here, as is this book itself, are no more than entry points into the vast and ever-growing literature on the science, philosophy, and history of the environment.

Acknowledgements

The author is grateful to many people for their assistance in ways great and small; this book is truly the product of a symbiosis. Chris Carson and Laura Paterson Pratt of Harcourt Brace Canada encouraged me to develop a somewhat sprawling set of course notes into a text, and enthusiastically and patiently supported the project through its first tremulous steps to maturity (and I have, indeed, tried their patience on occasion); several referees—Allen Carlson (University of Alberta), Alan Drengson (University of Victoria), and Hugh Lehman (University of Guelph)—provided invaluable advice and criticism; my wife, Sharon Simmers, deserves all credit for whatever mental equilibrium I retain after this and other momentous enterprises we have shared in recent years; Wayne Sumner and Kathleen Okruhlik provided me with opportunities to teach somewhat experimental environmental philosophy courses; Grant A. Whatmough is responsible for much of what is sound in my present philosophical outlook, as well as many specific insights into the relation between humans and their environment; and for valuable discussion or information I am grateful to Andrew Brook, Janet Cureton, Kevin Delaplante, William Fyfe, Maya Karta, Jim Ketchen, Nada Khirdaji, Hugh Lehman, Patrick Maynard, John D. Milton, William Rees, Ted Schrecker, Greg Stapleton, Michael Yeo, and numerous students in my environmental philosophy courses at the universities of Toronto and Western Ontario. I am also much indebted to the Social Sciences and Humanities Research Council of Canada for indispensable financial assistance.

A NOTE FROM THE PUBLISHER

Thank you for selecting *Living with the Earth: An Introduction to Environmental Philosophy*, by Kent A. Peacock. The authors and publisher have devoted considerable time to the careful development of this book. We appreciate your recognition of this effort and accomplishment.

We want to hear what you think about *Living with the Earth: An Introduction to Environmental Philosophy*. Please take a few minutes to fill in the stamped reader reply card at the back of the book. Your comments and suggestions will be valuable to us as we prepare new editions and other books.

CONTENTS

INTRODUCTION

What Is Philosophy?

This text is advertised as an introduction to "environmental philosophy." We all think we know what "the environment" is, but it may be useful to explain the term "philosophy," since it is very easily misunderstood.

People often think of philosophy as merely vague speculation about "life, the universe, and everything," something that is a sort of stimulating intellectual recreation if one has time for it, but is of little practical use. It is true that philosophy can be practised recreationally, but there is much more to it than that. I sometimes jokingly say that the Philosophy Department is the place that tries to deal with questions which are too ill-defined or fundamental for other, more specialized departments to handle, but which at the same time are too important to ignore. When we talk about the environment, we will run into a lot of questions like that. However, it is possible to give a more concrete definition of "philosophy" than this.

The word "philosophy" is Greek in origin and means literally "love of wisdom." It could also be construed as "study of wisdom," "search for wisdom," or something similar. What is wisdom? That is a tough question. Wisdom is certainly, among other things, a kind of knowledge, but knowledge does not always count as wisdom—for instance, knowledge of how to bake a cake or of the periodic table, no matter how useful, is not usually thought of as wisdom. Consider how we use the word "wisdom": we say that people are wise if they exhibit a sense of proportion, if they can make sound choices and give good advice, if they can get their priorities straight. Wisdom, therefore, is *knowledge of what is important.* It is mere knowledge to have the mechanical skill necessary to drive a car, but it is wisdom to know what approach to take when driving (for instance, it is wisdom to know that one should generally drive defensively and not aggressively); it is greater wisdom still to know where or even whether one should be driving at all. But what do we mean by saying that something is "important"?

Obviously, the notion of importance is meaningful only in relation to definite ends, goals, or purposes. If I say that something is just "important," you might not know what I meant, unless there was between us some implicit understanding of what it was important for. So to be wise means to have knowledge or understanding of human ends and the things that conduce to them. In fact, we reserve the name wisdom for knowledge concerned with the ends of deepest interest for human beings—issues of survival, morality, the basic principles behind our knowledge and conduct. In the *long* run, therefore, philosophy could be quite as practical as engineering or medicine, and the consequences of incompetent philosophy could be at least as disastrous as the consequences of incompetent engineering or medicine. Again: philosophy is the study of wisdom, and wisdom is an understanding of the things that are most deeply important to human beings. More sophisticated, although not necessarily more accurate, definitions of philosophy can be given, but that will do for our purposes.

When we talk about the environment, we realize that there are many forms of **life**—bacteria, whales, trees, possibly the Earth itself—which may have ends (even if not conscious purposes) that might be very different from, or in conflict with, human ends. The fact that philosophy is concerned with human ends certainly does not mean that we should not be concerned with what is important to all these other beings—in fact, one of the themes of environmental philosophy is that we must be concerned with the ends of other beings. But obviously, if we assume that philosophy is to serve as any kind of guide to the conduct of our lives, then we have to consider how the ends of other beings relate to our own. That is, we have to understand why it is important to *us* that some end is important to some other being.

There are two particular characteristics of philosophy that must be mentioned: it is *interdisciplinary* and it is often very *tentative.*

Philosophy is unavoidably interdisciplinary because, in order to accomplish its primary function, it needs to achieve an overview of the whole intellectual landscape. This makes it surprisingly difficult to practise, and this is nowhere more apparent than in environmental philosophy, in which one must have some effective grasp, at least, of a vast spectrum of subjects ranging from ozone chemistry to law to history. (In all modesty, I myself certainly do not have the kind of grasp of the number of subjects that really would do justice to the problem. But I do my best.) It can take a lifetime to become truly expert in, say, forestry or ethical theory, and you might question whether anyone has the right to venture opinions on so many diverse subjects. But we have to try; it is the only way we can get the overview we desperately need.

Philosophy is also unavoidably tentative, and many people find this to be very frustrating, both because they are impatient to get the answers they need and get on with life, and because it is somewhat frightening to discover that we often *do not have* a sufficient understanding of the matters of life and death that are of deepest concern to us. I can't offer much consolation for this; I agree, it is frustrating, but that's just the way it is. I believe very deeply that we will not get any closer to an understanding of these vital matters if we just impatiently brush off the whole inquiry, or worse still, invent and defend convenient and comforting myths that, in our inner selves, we know to be unfounded. A large part of the purpose of philosophy is to teach ourselves to live with uncertainty, by which I mean accepting that much of what we know is uncertain but not being paralysed by this fact.

Although there is a lot of academic philosophy that is, frankly, like colourless and odourless gas, rising like Freon to the stratosphere and staying there, in the long run nothing could be more important or have more far-reaching practical implications than the basic philosophy by which we conduct our lives. Philosophy is the attempt to formulate, and to continually revise in the light of experience, our most basic guidelines for thought and conduct. As humans, we all have a philosophy of life, whether we mean to or not; the only question is whether we choose to leave our philosophy in a muddled, implicit, and incomplete state, or to bring it out in the open and work on it enough that we have some idea where we stand.

So we could define *environmental philosophy*, therefore, as an attempt to find some degree of wisdom concerning the nature of the environment and our relationship to it.

"You'll Make People Fearful!"

When I first taught an environmental ethics course at the University of Toronto in 1990, an incident occurred that underlines the kind of difficulty we have in squarely facing and thinking about the environmental crisis. I had been lecturing about the interrelationships between life and the climate that sustains it, and described the then-recent paper by Shukla et al. (1990)[1] on the impact of Amazon deforestation on the Amazonian climate. Shukla and co-workers make the point that while the high rainfall in Amazonia obviously is necessary to sustain the rainforest, the reverse is also true: the rainforest helps to maintain the moist climate that makes its own continued existence possible. Computer modelling shows that if the rainforest were to be substantially removed (which might take only 50 to 100 years at current rates of deforestation), the land would degenerate to a condition of "degraded pasture" and *the high rainfall would collapse*, making it impossible to regenerate the rainforest once it was removed. Shukla et al. conclude that "the current climate and vegetation may coexist in a dynamic equilibrium," implying that each needs the other for its own continued existence. Results like these make the continued high rate of deforestation in Amazonia seem especially unwise, to say the least.

Having recounted this tale, I asked my students to think of its broader ethical implications. It is very easy for us in North America to criticize the Brazilians for their questionable practices, but how about our own forestry policies? In particular, has anyone done any studies on possible irreversible effects on the North American climate of temperate and boreal deforestation? Irreversible soil erosion is obvious to anyone who has travelled or lived in certain hard-rock regions in Ontario; no scientific studies are needed to prove that when the cover of trees is stripped in areas where shallow soil overlies the Canadian Shield, all that remains in a few years is a barren expanse of impregnable igneous rock. But what does this do to the climate? Has anyone thought to find out? Are we in North America any wiser than the Brazilians? Have we the right to criticize?

After the lecture, a student (who happened to be from the Faculty of Forestry) came up to the front to see me, fuming with anger. He insisted that I had no right to make any comparison between what happens in Canada and in Brazil. Forestry in Canada, he insisted, is practised by responsible professionals whose judgement can be trusted implicitly. To question their competence is to question their personal integrity, and threatens to undermine the whole basis of our economic prosperity. He wanted to know if I was against "progress." He raged on for some time, and then as he stalked out of the classroom, he intoned, as if it were the worst accusation that could possibly be hurled against me, "*You'll make people fearful!*" That was the last time I saw him in my class, for he promptly dropped the course.

I can only conclude that I did, indeed, make him fearful, regardless of what harm I might have done to the mental equilibrium of my other students. But why did my more or less obvious remarks, which would occur almost immediately to any dispassionate observer, touch such a sensitive nerve within him? It is true that talk of the ozone hole, climate change, **Waldsterben**, species extinctions, and the **greenhouse effect** can be very frightening and depressing—one feels so helpless!—even if one believes that these things are not going to affect us personally or immediately. But there is more to it than just that. The very tough problem we face is that apparently much of the world's environmental problems are caused precisely by ordinary human beings going about their day-to-day business, earning their living as best they can. Very often, what we humans do in order to get by is exactly what is causing many of the problems. (This is, of course, a sweeping statement; in this book we will try to understand exactly what it means.) But this means that any criticism of how humans relate to their environment can be very personal. Any one of us might become defensive if told that what we or our parents do to earn a living, and perhaps have a very strong commitment to as a profession or way of life, is causing some sort of grievous harm. We will be angry; we will want to deny the whole cogency of the criticism, and we might even attribute base motives to the critic. I have found, through my teaching, that people can get just as passionate about environmental issues as they can when debating such issues as human sexuality, abortion, or euthanasia. It strikes close to the bone in much the same way, for it forces us to examine, in a pitiless light, our whole way of life.

Let me, then, issue a gentle warning: some things discussed in this book may make some readers fearful. It can't be helped; some of these topics make me fearful, too. But the problems won't go away if we try to pretend they are not there, so let us (holding hands if necessary) press forward into the unknown. We really don't have much choice in the matter, anyway.

Are We Left, Right, or Centre?

In this book we will end up, after some preliminaries, talking about so-called *environmental ethics*. From **ethics**, it is a short distance to politics, but we will not try to travel that distance here. However, we will take the inquiry fairly close to the point at which one could begin to think of political implications. I will not say much more than the following about politics: we often tend to categorize and pigeonhole people's views as *either* left *or* right, *either* communistic *or* capitalistic, *either* liberal *or* conservative, *either* socialistic *or* free-market, so that discussions sometimes degenerate into a crossfire of slogans. (For instance, some may think that I am *necessarily* in favour of some sort of authoritarian socialism simply because I criticize the free-market system. I do not have to be, and I am not.) The problem is that these familiar categories may be irrelevant to the deep problems we consider here; an ecologically sound political and economic system just might not fit easily into our present understanding of the way political views divide up. For instance, one could argue in favour of ownership of forests by small woodlot owners and at the same time argue for strict laws governing methods of timber harvesting (say, to prevent erosion or unnecessary damage by heavy machinery). The best policy in the long run might involve a mixture of practices, some of which we might now think of as "socialistic," some of which we might now think of as "capitalistic," and some of which might not easily fit into either slot. The point of this inquiry is not to argue in favour of someone's favourite political system, but to show that there are reasons to believe that ecological considerations almost certainly demand *a rethinking from first principles on up* of our present economic and political systems; perhaps even our whole way of life.

What's the Difference between Environmental Philosophy and Environmental Ethics?

Is there really any difference between environmental *philosophy* in general and environmental *ethics* in particular? We have already attempted to describe philosophy as a search for "wisdom," whatever that may be. Ethics, loosely speaking, is the part of philosophy that is specifically concerned with the regulation or direction of conduct and questions of right and wrong or good and bad. Although all of philosophy is in a certain sense normative (i.e., tending to set or ascertain standards) or at least judgemental, there are certainly large parts of philosophy that are not *explicitly* ethical. And there are quite a lot of philosophically interesting questions one can ask about the environment that are not ethical, even if many or all of them ultimately may have a bearing on the crucial ethical problems. One can, for instance, ask essentially metaphysical questions ("What *is* the environment?"; "What are living systems?") or epistemological questions ("Is there anything special about environmental knowledge that distinguishes it from other sorts of knowledge?"; "What would count as evidence for a scientific hypothesis about the environment?"). One can argue that some of our environmental problems stem from a kind of *perceptual* or *cognitive error* quite as much as lack of an appropriate ethic; we shall see an example of this when we look at the history of the ozone hole. And much of what an environmental philosopher needs to understand about the environment would more usually be thought of as historical or scientific rather than "philosophical," or to at least lie within the fuzzily delimited border zones where philosophy overlaps with other disciplines.

I have sometimes encountered a certain impatience on the part of some students and even some other professional philosophers (especially specialists in ethical or political theory) with the more scientific and historical aspects of environmental philosophy. Let's get on to the *real* stuff, they say, such as, how should we solve the problems of distributional justice and equity in a world of increasing scarcity? or, should we accord nonhuman entities consideration as ends as well as means? However, I believe very strongly that vital questions like these cannot be sensibly answered without a thorough imaginative grasp of the environmental problem itself. One just has to *get it*; and in order to do this one must (no matter how anxious to get on with the terribly pressing problems of our time) somehow get *interested enough* in the science and the history to really get a glimmering of the big picture. Such matters as the global carbon cycle, what little we know of the behaviour of the great whales, the probable amount of solar radiation to be received by the Earth 500 million years from now, or the history of forestry in the Levant might have everything to do with how we order our priorities right now. That is why environmental philosophy does not begin just with environmental ethics, even though it inevitably ends up in that territory, and also why environmental philosophy is not entirely just what would traditionally be understood as philosophy at all.

There is another caution that should perhaps be added. It is quite fashionable these days to talk of the "social construction of reality." I suggest that such talk could be very misleading when applied to the environment. It is extremely important for us to realize that the physical environment around us is no "social construct" (i.e., a myth held in common by some social group and reinforced by linguistic practice), but a vast assemblage of living and nonliving matter and forces that is immensely older and larger than we are and from which we sprang and to which we owe our continued existence. Of course, it is inevitably the case that the concepts and terms we use in order to represent to ourselves (as best we can) whatever aspects of this larger reality we can dimly grasp are human constructs. But they are not the vibrant thing itself. Surely one of the great lessons to be learned from the current environmental crisis (not to mention from history in general) is that human survival and well-being depend in large part upon our willingness and ability to *pay attention* to the significance of factors outside the familiar human social sphere. This collection of readings is an attempt to do just that.

NOTES

1. We should note that there has been some scientific controversy as to whether anthropogenic (human-caused) destruction of vegetation can change local, regional, or even global climate. There now seems little doubt that deforestation, overgrazing, and other ecologically unsound practices can trigger climatic change at all levels, by a variety of mechanisms; and that conversely afforestation or the re-establishment of ground cover, where that is possible, can to some extent lead to the recovery of climate.

PART ONE

Is there really an environmental crisis?

... the environmental crisis derives from the entire human enterprise.
(No longer can we say, "Après nous, le déluge." Le déluge, c'est nous.)
–JOHN LIVINGSTON (1989)

It is not impossible, although a bit harder than it was a few years ago, to find people who still believe that all this talk of the environmental crisis is nothing more than what some have called the "greenhoax effect"; that is, a form of hysteria, supposedly manipulated for obscure reasons by self-serving environmentalists. If only it were so. There is, however, little reasonable doubt that the particular environmental conditions on this planet that are favourable to human and other life are facing serious and immediate threats due almost entirely to human activities. There remains much disagreement about precisely which trouble areas—soil erosion, escalating desertification, deforestation, depletion of fisheries, extinctions of plant and animal species, various forms of pollution both subtle and overt, nuclear waste and leakage, overpopulation, depletion of petroleum reserves, global warming, the ozone hole, urban and industrial garbage, loss of productive land to urbanization, stripmining and industrialization, and the ever-growing burden of human poverty—are the most urgent, and much disagreement about precisely what steps must be taken. But *that* we have a problem seems painfully clear.

It is beyond the scope of this book to attempt to present a complete and balanced picture of the earthly environment and all its various problems. Instead, in this part we present some case studies of certain key environmental problem areas that might reasonably be thought to be at, or near, a state of crisis—where by "crisis" we mean, "A turning point in the progress of an affair or of a series of events; a critical moment" (Funk and Wagnalls 1958)—and that are especially indicative and typical (in ways that will become apparent) of the broader problematic. What we want to do is to get an idea of what is *common* to all these crises and others like them. This will help us get a glimmering of the inner structure of what we might call "the human problem" itself.

For a very useful and up-to-date overview of the global environment, see the annual series *The State of the World*, edited by Lester R. Brown for the Worldwatch Institute (see, for example, Brown et al. 1990). For Canada specifically, see Environment Canada (1991), which is massive, authoritative, and pulls relatively few punches, and Israelson (1990) for a perceptive journalistic overview.

CHAPTER ONE

CRISIS IN THE SKIES: THE OZONE HOLE AND GLOBAL WARMING

There are several reasons why it is instructive to begin an overview of the global environmental crisis with a detailed study of the problem of the infamous "ozone hole."

First, many people are very frightened and puzzled by it (including this author), and we might all be glad to understand it a little better.

Second, it is indeed very serious; some (especially among those living in the Southern Hemisphere) would insist that it is the most immediately pressing environmental problem we face today.

Third, it is in certain respects relatively conceptually simple (although complicated *technically*), and the philosophical and policy imperatives that it raises are relatively clear-cut (forgive the environmental pun) although no less painful to confront than those arising out of many other issues we will consider. Most people, although certainly not all, agree about what should be done about it. There is surprisingly little scientific disagreement about the basic nature and seriousness of the ozone hole, as compared to many other highly contentious issues such as the greenhouse effect, deforestation, and nuclear safety. From the scientific and historical point of view, we know pretty well what went wrong. This makes the ozone hole quite rare among ecological problems, where disputes about the facts of the matter get inextricably entangled with disputes about values. (For instance, technical debates about the most effective methods of silviculture can hardly be resolved without some agreement on what sorts of forests it is desirable and proper to maintain.) The consensus on the ozone hole is very recent. Ten years ago the debates about the ozone hole sounded much like the debates about the greenhouse effect today.

Hence the ozone surprise is almost a "textbook" case, if there could be such a thing, of an environmental disaster. It defines a basic pattern that we will see repeated again and again in other contexts. It is also, as we shall see, replete with terrible ironies and devastating surprises.

THE OZONE SURPRISE

Kent A. Peacock

I can't go home and dump my garbage in my neighbour's backyard. The police would arrest me in five minutes. But I could take a tank of chlorofluorocarbons, put it in my backyard, turn it on and let it go into the atmosphere all day long, and no one can stop me! Somehow that's very wrong.

– Susan Solomon[1]

In the Beginning . . .

Very early in the Earth's history (more than 3 billion years ago), our planet possessed what is technically known as a "reducing" atmosphere—a mixture of compounds such as water vapour, carbon dioxide, and probably methane and ammonia, with little or no free oxygen. There was a high flux of UV (ultra-violet radiation) from the sun, at levels which would be lethal to most forms of life today. Somehow, simple life-forms appeared on the Earth that used anaer-obic processes (processes not requiring oxygen) to get their energy. (We will not here delve into the mystery of the origin of life itself.) There are many such bacteria still present on the Earth—the so-called chemoautotrophic bacteria that make iron plumbing smell of sulphur, for example.

About 3.5 billion years ago, photosynthetic forms evolved. Photosynthesis is the complex process by which organisms containing chlorophyl or similar compounds can utilize solar energy to create carbohydrates from water and carbon dioxide, releasing free oxygen in the process. Photosynthesis was the most sophisticated strategy that had yet been found for extracting energy from the environment, and these early photosynthesizers (such as the blue-green algae) eventually came to dominate the biosphere.

With the evolution of photosynthesis, the planet experienced its first pol-lution crisis, for oxygen is very toxic to most anaerobic organisms. As oxygen released by photosynthesis built up, the anaerobes declined, and now survive only in places where there is very little free oxygen, such as the bottom of the sea and our intestines. Aerobic organisms, which could use the oxygen for respiration, evolved. Respiration (which is really a highly controlled combustion process) makes much more energy available to the organism than any anaerobic process; this in turn allows respiring organisms a much higher level of activity than anaerobic organisms or photosynthesizers, and these organisms quickly took over as dominant life-forms on the planet.

As oxygen accumulated in the atmosphere, an ozone layer began to form. Ozone is a form of oxygen created by the action of high-energy ultraviolet light (UV) on oxygen. Ozone absorbs ultraviolet light (or more precisely, UV is absorbed by the creation and destruction of ozone). This protected the surface of the planet from the high-energy ultraviolet light from the Sun, which allowed more complex and delicate life-forms (like us) to evolve. Hence we could summarize this whole process by saying that *life itself helped to create the very atmospheric conditions that made its own continuance and further evolution possible.* The ozone layer is one among many important examples of components of the Earth's physical environment that are *biogenic* (meaning, created and maintained by life itself).

The ozone layer also helps to maintain the very structure of the atmosphere. The ultraviolet energies absorbed by the ozone layer are re-radiated to the upper atmosphere (the *stratosphere*) as heat, warming it and thereby causing the temperature inversion that defines the boundary between the stratosphere and the lower atmosphere (or *troposphere*).[2] The total or near-total disappearance of the ozone layer might result in atmospheric instabilities of a type never before experienced, quite apart from the destruction of most life on Earth by irradiation.

Ozone and the Ozonosphere

Ozone itself is a bluish, irritating gas with a pungent odour. It is a powerful oxidant and can be used as a bleach and sterilizing agent; in large enough concentrations it is quite toxic.

Ninety percent of the ozone in the atmosphere is normally in the stratosphere, concentrated at an altitude of around 12 to 25 kilometres. (This layer is sometimes called the *ozonosphere.*) However, in a heavy smog, ozone concentration at ground level can be as much as ten times higher than normal, causing respiratory irritation and damage to plants. One of the many ironies of the ozone story is that while we have too little where it is needed, we are often getting too much where it is not, both effects being due to different kinds of pollution.

If all the ozone that is normally present in the atmosphere were to be separated out from the air in which it is mixed, and were concentrated into a single layer at ground-level temperature and pressure, it would only be about

3 millimetres thick. The existence of all life on Earth more complex than bacteria depends on this evanescent wisp of gas.

The UV radiation that can reach the Earth's surface can be divided into two bands, usually called UV-B (the far ultraviolet) and UV-A (or the near ultraviolet). The UV that gives us a sunburn is mostly UV-A, a little bit of which can actually be good for us. The effect of ozone is to filter out most of the UV-B, the most energetic (and hence the most potentially damaging) radiation that would otherwise reach the Earth's surface. Hence the depletion of the ozone layer not only increases the intensity of the UV radiation reaching the surface, but it tends to shift the peak energy into the UV-B range. This is the kind of UV that does the most harm to sensitive biomolecules such as proteins and nucleic acids.

Ozone is constantly being created and destroyed by the action of UV on oxygen in the stratosphere. There are other natural processes that destroy ozone as well, but until recently the processes of creation and destruction were usually in balance, so that the net amount of ozone created was equal to the amount being destroyed. (This is an example of a *dynamic equilibrium.*) This happy state of affairs went on for a few billion years until about the year A.D. 1928, when a brilliant industrial chemist named Thomas Midgley, Jr., invented **CFCs** (chlorofluorocarbons). These compounds, which are rare or non-existent in the Earth's normal chemistry, break down ozone, leaving the planet's surface again at risk from ultraviolet radiation from the Sun. And this is where our story really begins.

What Are CFCs?

Midgley (who was also the creator of tetraethyl lead) was really just trying to solve what seemed to be a straightforward problem of product safety. By 1928, the refrigeration industry was expanding rapidly, but the only working fluids available for refrigerators were compounds like ammonia, methylene chloride, or sulphur dioxide, all toxic, flammable, or corrosive. Some accidental deaths from leaky refrigerators had actually occurred. It was essential to find a refrigerant that was safe, and CFCs fit the bill perfectly.

Chlorofluorocarbons are chemically very similar to methane and other simple hydrocarbons, but with the hydrogens replaced by fluorines and chlorines. They have great chemical stability, which makes them almost entirely nontoxic and nonflammable. Midgley demonstrated these desirable properties by inhaling some CFCs and then blowing out a candle flame. They also turned out to have many other useful properties—as solvents, propulsion agents for spray cans, and foaming agents in plastic manufacture. But it is precisely their stability that allows them to survive the trip to the stratosphere; most other chlorine-containing compounds break down long before then. Before CFCs, there was no mechanism that could transport significant amounts of chlorine to the stratosphere. Hence there is a considerable irony in this story: the very property of CFCs that makes them so useful is also the property that makes them so deadly. It was many years, however, before anyone became aware of this.

First Warnings

The first intimations that CFCs could be endangering the ozone layer came by an indirect route. In the late 1960s, there was considerable controversy in the United States over whether the government should support a major project to develop a fleet of commercial SSTs (supersonic transports). These would have been jet aircraft (like the Anglo-French Concorde, the only SST that eventually went into brief commercial production) that could fly high in the stratosphere at supersonic speeds, cutting international travel times to a fraction of the time required by standard subsonic commercial aircraft. Jet aircraft release nitric oxide as a combustion by-product, and it was known that nitric oxide can attack ozone. Hence a worry was born that fleets of SSTs might damage the ozone layer, and this fear may have had something to do with the eventual abandonment of the project. (Cost was likely at least as important a factor in the decision. See Roan 1989.)

It is now believed that the nitric oxide from jet exhaust would pose a minimal threat to the ozone layer. But the debate led scientists to ask if there were other industrial pollutants that might damage ozone. The first measurements of CFC concentrations in the atmosphere had been made in the early 1970s by James Lovelock. Because the amounts revealed by his measurements were so low (a few parts per trillion at that time—they are now much higher) Lovelock remarked that they posed no danger, a position he later reversed.[3] In 1973, chemist Sherwood Rowland set his postdoctoral fellow Mario Molina the problem of investigating whether CFCs could be having any effect on the ozone layer. Rowland and Molina soon discovered to their consternation that ozone can be broken down by chlorine via a *catalytic* reaction cycle—that is, a reaction in which a substance (in this case chlorine) promotes a reaction but is not used up by it.

The important point to note is that because the reaction is catalytic, a very small amount of the catalyst (chlorine) can break down a great deal of ozone, even though the concentration of CFCs in the atmosphere is at trace levels. In fact, one chlorine atom will break down between 10,000 and 100,000 ozone molecules before it finally precipitates out of the atmosphere (usually as a form of acid rain, to add environmental insult to injury). This is a good illustration of a general rule that we are gradually learning to respect: the danger posed by a pollutant may not be in simple proportion to its amount or concentration in the environment.

A check of CFC production figures convinced Rowland and Molina that CFCs could eventually (but not for several decades, they first estimated) do significant damage to the ozonosphere. It is reported that Rowland came home from the lab one day and reported to his wife, "It looks like the end of the world!"[4]

Rowland and Molina, and then many other scientists and concerned citizens, began to argue that CFCs should be restricted. In the late 1970s, a number of countries (Canada, the United States, Norway, and Sweden) introduced bans on CFC usage for aerosol sprays, and overall consumption of CFCs briefly decreased before beginning its inexorable climb again in the 1980s. However, there was, up until the mid-1980s, still no absolutely convincing evidence either that CFCs actually were breaking down ozone in the stratosphere, or that ozone was becoming depleted. In other words, it was not known with certainty that CFCs *do* harm the ozone layer, only that they *could*. The CFC industry fought back vigorously, using all the public relations powers at its disposal, and played on the scientific uncertainties to argue that the case against CFCs had not been established. The debate became at times very bitter and personal.[5]

Bit by bit, further scientific evidence accumulated that CFCs might indeed be doing exactly what Rowland and Molina had predicted they would do. But many uncertainties remained.

The Ozone Hole Appears

Since 1957 (the International Geophysical Year), a team of scientists led by James Farman had been measuring ozone levels, among other geophysical data, at the British research station in Antarctica. This was just for the sake of "pure" science, and they were close to being shut down by budget cuts on at least one occasion.

In 1984, Farman and colleagues noticed that ozone readings over the polar region had been dropping markedly since the late 1970s, with a more dramatic drop each year. It seemed that a large hole was appearing over Antarctica in the ozone layer each Antarctic spring. Farman published his results in 1985. Shortly afterward, it was discovered that an American NIMBUS weather satellite had been showing the same thing since the late 1970s, but the data from the satellite had been rejected because it was assumed that any readings that were so low must be due to instrumental error! (How many other important things have been ignored because someone assumed that they were impossible?)

In the southern spring (September to November) there is nearly 100 percent depletion of ozone in some areas of Antarctica and over the Southern Sea.

There is a loss of zero to 10 percent (and occasionally higher) in other areas of the world, even as far as the Equator. These differences are definitely greater than the normal variations in the long-run average levels. And there is a similar depletion in the Arctic each northern spring, but less severe. According to a recent report from Environment Canada:

> The most pronounced depletion [of ozone in the Northern Hemisphere] occurs during January to May. Data from the Canadian ozone network indicated that ozone levels for the first 4 months of 1993 were down by 14.8 percent. Scientists are predicting that average depletion of ozone over Canada this summer [1994] will be from 5 to 10% and will give rise to an increase in UV-B of 6-12%. Depletion is expected to be this bad or worse for the next 15 to 20 years.[6]

Intense debate sprang up on the cause of the ozone hole, and the call was renewed to ban CFCs. Several theories were proposed to account for the hole; at the time of its discovery there still was no proof (although certainly a strong suspicion) that it was due to CFCs. In 1986 and 1987, teams of scientists went to Antarctica and under conditions of some hardship studied the ozone hole intensively. Aircraft were flown through the hole to take direct samples of the air. (It was no trivial matter to fly a temperamental ER-2 aircraft at altitudes above 60,000 ft over Antarctica in the winter time. If a plane had gone down, the pilots would have had little hope of being rescued. Considerable personal courage, both physical and moral, may be needed to answer the questions that need to be answered.) By early 1988, scientists were finally convinced that they had found unmistakable evidence that CFCs were guilty: "The extensive new data leave no doubt that man-made CFCs are primarily responsible for the ozone hole."[7] Not even Rowland and Molina had imagined that so much ozone could be broken down so quickly. The situation is much worse than they had predicted.

The explanation for this lies partly in an important fact about catalytic chemistry that had not been noticed, and partly in the very unusual meteorological conditions in the Antarctic winter. I will omit most of the fascinating but very technical details.[8] Here is the essence of the matter: CFCs are broken down by energetic ultraviolet in the stratosphere, releasing chlorine, which quickly is taken up in harmless "reservoir compounds." In the Antarctic winter, a stratospheric vortex forms, a great whirlpool of air as big as the continent itself. Within the vortex, polar stratospheric clouds (PSCs) form, clouds of tiny ice crystals. This was somewhat unexpected since the stratosphere is usually too dry to form cloud. The reservoir compounds can break down into highly reactive chlorine and chlorine monoxide at a very high rate on the ice crystals;

this is the "heterogeneous" chemistry that surprised the experts. When sunlight hits the PSCs in the Antarctic spring, it stimulates the breakdown of ozone by the accumulated chlorine and chlorine monoxide, and a huge hole forms in the ozone layer. Eventually, as the polar vortex breaks up in late spring, the depleted air mixes with air at lower latitudes, causing patches of low ozone worldwide. A similar process occurs in the Northern Hemisphere, although the hole formed is less deep because the northern polar vortex is much less intense. And there is strong evidence, as well, that this process can occur anywhere in the stratosphere where dust or ice particles are available. The eruption of the volcano Pinatubo, for instance, is suspected to have provided enough stratospheric dust to contribute significantly to recent ozone depletion.[9]

The key factor that no one had originally anticipated was the ability of tiny ice crystals and dust particles to promote and accelerate the catalytic breakdown reactions. In fact, it is well known that catalytic reactions of many kinds go faster on surfaces; perhaps this possibility had not occurred even to the most vigilant of experts because of a belief (which we now know to be mistaken) in the stratosphere as a volume of pristine clean air.

The ozone story is therefore a history of surprises: first, that CFCs can decompose ozone catalytically, and second, that the decomposition can be further accelerated by the freakish "heterogeneous chemistry" that occurs on the surface of ice crystals in the Antarctic winter vortex.

One often hears of "worst case scenarios"; it is as if for CFCs every worst case scenario has, so far, come true.

Biological Effects of Ozone Depletion

For simplicity, we can divide the biological effects of ozone depletion into two sorts: effects on humans, and effects on life in general.

The effects on humans naturally get the most press. The most dramatic dangers are skin cancer and retinal burn. A 2 percent increase in UV-B reaching the ground is predicted to lead to a 6 to 8 percent increase in skin cancer in people with light skin. People in the Southern Hemisphere are especially at risk. It is estimated, for instance, that two-thirds of all Australians now living will eventually need treatment for skin cancer, while in Canada skin cancer rates have been going up 5 to 7 percent per year. There will also be an increase in sunburn and retinal burn.[10] There is also a poorly understood effect upon the human immune system; UV-B seems to suppress the activity of certain types of immune system cells. It is suspected that neither pigmentation nor sunscreen protects against this effect. For that matter, there is no epidemiological evidence that sunscreen actually protects against skin cancer either, only a presumption that it must do so because it blocks UV-B.[11]

The deepest concern, from the viewpoint of understanding the consequences of the ozone hole for the integrity of the ecosystem as a whole, is the possible effects upon animals, plants, and marine organisms. Recently, sheep near Puenta Arenas in southern Chile, an area that occasionally finds itself directly under the ozone hole,[12] have been suffering unusual tumours, cataracts, and retinal burns. While locals are convinced, there is no "scientific" proof that this is due to increased UV exposure.[13]

Much investigative work has already been done on the biological effects of UV. There is much reason to fear that ozone depletion could lead to greatly diminished growth and vitality of forests and agricultural crops. For instance, some recent studies indicate that land plant biomass can be reduced by as much as 10 to 20 percent; even a short burst of UV early in the growing season can irreversibly stunt plant growth.[14] Even more serious could be its effects on the krill (near-microscopic crustaceans, which serve as staple food for many marine mammals and birds) and marine micro-organisms such as plankton and algae. UV can penetrate sea-water to a considerable depth (sunburn is a hazard for scuba divers). The plankton and algae are the very base of the marine food chain and, furthermore, provide much of the planet's oxygen. Of course, marine organisms must already be adapted to a fair amount of UV, but they clearly have their limits. There is already evidence that UV levels 10 to 20 percent higher than normal can damage marine micro-organisms, as well as small fish. A recent detailed survey of Antarctic waters found evidence that photosynthesis by those phytoplankton regularly exposed to the ozone hole is reduced by 6 to 12 percent.[15]

No one yet knows exactly how serious the situation could become, although it appears probable that the base of the planetary food chain will, from now on, suffer some and possibly significant extra stress from UV-B, above and beyond all other stresses being imposed upon it by human action, for decades to come.

Feedback between Ozone Depletion and the Greenhouse Effect

It is not unusual for people to confuse ozone depletion with the greenhouse effect. For instance, consider the following remark by that well-known environmental expert, former U.S. Vice-President Dan Quayle:

> Now we have an international treaty, a treaty that is commonly referred to as the Montreal Treaty. [Actually, it's called the Montreal Protocol.] For the first time we are talking about the impact of CO_2 on the ozone layer. That's progress for the environment. [Quoted in *Punch*, January 12, 1990.]

Let's be clear: the ozone hole is not directly caused by carbon dioxide, but by chlorine released from CFCs and related compounds. Excess carbon dioxide and other substances (including halocarbons themselves) are believed to cause the so-called greenhouse effect, a predicted warming of the lower atmosphere, by trapping heat that would otherwise radiate back to space.

Although the mechanisms are quite different, there appears to be a complex and insidious **positive feedback** relationship between the ozone hole and the greenhouse effect. So perhaps the former vice-president knew what he was talking about after all!

Ozone depletion tends to enhance warming of the troposphere and leads to a cooling of the stratosphere by as much as 20 to 30°C, because the UV energy that should be absorbed in the stratosphere is absorbed lower down instead. So ozone depletion is an additional source of lower atmospheric heating and stratospheric cooling, on top of the greenhouse effect itself. Cooling of the stratosphere in turn enhances the heterogeneous chemistry of ozone breakdown by allowing more stratospheric ice crystals to form, and possibly by allowing the polar vortex to become deeper and more stable. Increased UV in the troposphere causes more ozone to be created in the troposphere; but ozone is itself a greenhouse gas, providing yet another means by which ozone depletion can indirectly contribute to the greenhouse effect. Atmospheric warming will release methane from permafrost. Methane is also a greenhouse gas, and in addition it oxidizes in the stratosphere to water vapour, which provides more stratospheric ice crystals and thereby further enhances ozone breakdown. Furthermore, the inhibition of photosynthesis by UV-B could lead to increased carbon dioxide (although Smith et al. 1990 emphasize that the amounts involved so far do not seem to be dangerous). And to add insult to injury, CFCs are very potent greenhouse gases themselves — about 10,000 times as potent as carbon dioxide.

In summary, there seems to be a number of positive feedback loops between the greenhouse effect and ozone breakdown, and so far no one knows what can intervene to damp them out.

Where Things Stand Now

By 1988, it was clear that there is a worldwide ozone depletion of a few percent, and between 50 percent and nearly 100 percent depletion in the Antarctic hole. This implies a significant increase in ultraviolet exposure for many parts of the world, especially in the Southern Hemisphere. Governments at last began ponderously to address the fact that this is an international emergency. In 1987, a treaty was signed in Montreal by 51 nations and the European Community, under the auspices of UNEP (United Nations Environmental Program) to limit the release of CFCs and halons. In March 1988, Dupont Corporation, a major producer (and defender) of CFCs, finally conceded the danger and said that it will phase out production of CFCs. The Montreal Protocol was strengthened in 1990 and again in 1992, with phase-out deadlines moved up, but some countries have not yet signed.

CFCs had already been banned as aerosol propellants by the late 1970s by Canada, the United States, Norway, and Sweden. This resulted in a brief drop in production of CFCs, but production rose quickly again to a peak of over a million tonnes per year in the late 1980s. Finally, production has begun to fall sharply in the mid-1990s as a consequence of the Montreal Protocol.[16] On the face of it, therefore, the worst of the crisis may have passed. Unfortunately, matters are not so simple.

The Antarctic ozone hole continues to appear every Antarctic spring and is, if anything, deepening and becoming more stable and long-lived. CFCs remain in the atmosphere for a hundred years or more, and are still being added to the atmosphere at a significant rate. All over the world, there are old refrigerators rusting in dumps, just waiting to release their loads of Freon into the atmosphere. Even given full compliance with the Montreal Protocol, the concentration of CFCs in the stratosphere is expected to double or triple over the next few years. Even if we entirely stop producing CFCs this very day, the stratospheric concentration will continue to increase for some years because it takes some time for CFCs to diffuse to the stratosphere. According to Environment Canada (1994b), "the period of maximum stratospheric ozone depletion will be around the turn of the century."

There is a little recent good news: the rate of increase of CFCs in the atmosphere is slowing from 6 percent per year to a mere 3 percent per year.[17] It is difficult to tell how much of this small improvement is due to the effects of compliance with the Montreal Protocol and how much is due to the slowdown of industrial activity coming from the economic recession of the early 1990s.

The Outlook

For decades, the biosphere will be subjected to more UV-B than normal—some areas, such as the Southern Sea, dangerously more at some times of the year. There is no question that this will have some deleterious effect on the ecosystem, as well as putting human beings themselves at higher risk in a number of ways. Exactly how much harm will be done is very difficult to say, except that it is very likely that it will get worse than it is now. It is within the bounds of possibility that UV levels over some parts of the Earth will become near-lethal, particularly in the high southern latitudes.

Best case scenario: CFCs are phased out or replaced by about the turn of the century, and life on Earth succeeds in enduring marginal UV-B stress for 100 years or so, although with a hard-to-predict overall reduction in vitality of the global ecosystem and possibly some species extinctions or at least realignment of marine ecosystems.

The worst case: use of CFCs does not stop, due to a failure to uphold effective international agreements. It is impossible to predict the result of this, but the experiment should not be tried—especially given the possibility that there could be further "surprises."

Ozone is still being created at a constant rate by sunlight, and eventually, as the CFCs finally settle out of the atmosphere, the ozone layer will "self-heal." But it will take at least a hundred years for it to return to its pre-1970s condition.

Possible Policy Responses

Few environmental scientists disagree that we must do everything we can to secure international agreement to ban CFCs and similar compounds. This is surely the first step to take, whatever else might be necessary. It will be very difficult to persuade the developing countries not to use CFCs because they won't be convinced of the danger and will believe that the West is trying to secure some sort of economic advantage over them. In fact, the Montreal Protocol has built into it provisions that allow developing countries to "catch up" to the developed countries in CFC production before they have to start their phase-outs.

A dimly hopeful point is that this disaster may teach us to co-operate on other global problems, such as control of greenhouse emissions, depletion of fisheries, etc. The fact that extraordinary political measures had to be taken even to secure a cautious and highly qualified international agreement like the Montreal Protocol highlights the uncomfortable fact that the world still remains more or less in a state of anarchy, in spite of all the talk of a "New World Order" following the end of the Cold War and the Gulf War. It is not out of the question that we will finally be forced to set up some sort of effective world government precisely because of a series of environmentally induced catastrophes.

"Lifestyle" Changes

Many parents now accept the necessity of lathering their small children with sunscreen before sending them out to play, much as sexually active adults in the 1990s now accept the grim necessity of "safe" sex. In 1987, the Reagan administration briefly dared to suggest that such "personal protection" would do in place of regulations to control CFCs. It was not made clear how sunglasses and floppy hats were expected to protect krill or field crops from UV-B. This proposal was greeted with howls of derision, and the embarrassment may have helped to persuade the United States to eventually support the Montreal Protocol.[18] It seems painfully clear that while lifestyle changes (such as wearing sunglasses regularly) are a reasonable, if not inevitable, personal response to the UV-B threat, they are hardly going to solve the problem.

Are There Technological "Fixes"?

There are a number of technical responses that could conceivably be made to the ozone crisis, ranging from the highly responsible and practicable to the far-fetched and science fictional.

A number of proposals might well come under the heading of "atmospheric engineering," a subject that so far exists primarily in the imagination. Star Fleet engineers in the twenty-sixth century A.D. might simply filter CFCs and other pollutants out of the atmosphere, but this is rather far beyond our present (and likely any conceivable) technical capabilities. One suggestion (certainly thinkable, although very expensive) was to build an ozone factory in the Antarctic and launch replacement ozone into the ozone hole with rockets or balloons. Another, more far-fetched perhaps, was to "zap" CFCs with ground- or space-based infrared lasers.[19] It is also conceivable that there could be substances that might absorb or react with CFCs or chlorine monoxide; perhaps these could be fired into the Antarctic vortex at the right time. Yet another dim possibility might be to somehow interfere with the formation of the Antarctic vortex or somehow disperse the polar stratospheric clouds in it.[20]

All such proposals would depend upon untried engineering and scientific principles and would have to be carried out on a gigantic scale in order to have any hope of being effective. Not only would their monetary cost be enormous, but they would carry with them a host of further unknown environmental risks. (What would the construction of a series of ozone factories do to the still relatively pristine Antarctic environment, for instance?) Worse still, the dubious availability of a technological bandaid over the ozone hole might lull people into the belief that we do not have to phase out CFCs after all, even though that would seem to be the only really reliable "fix" in the long run. We can all hope that ozone losses will never get so bad that we will find ourselves forced to such a desperate expedient.

Considerably more practicable and sensible are the attempts to find substitutes for CFCs. CFCs as aerosol propellants, foaming agents, and solvents can be replaced fairly easily, and for the most part this has been done already.[21] More difficult is the replacement of CFCs as refrigerants, the purpose for which they were originally developed. It can be said without too much exaggeration that modern industrial society has evolved a real dependency upon the availability of cheap, efficient refrigeration. The very shape of our cities, and the structure of our transportation systems, for instance, depend upon the ability to preserve perishable food long enough to transport it to urban centres. Industrial and commercial buildings could not be built as they are without efficient air conditioning, especially in warmer climates. Sadly, perhaps, going back to the days in which little wagons drove around delivering blocks of ice does not really seem to be a possibility. CFCs have therefore evolved far beyond being merely a dispensable convenience, even though many of their uses certainly have been frivolous (for instance, one could, at one time, purchase a clever device that cooled one's martini with a flow of Freon that, of course, escaped directly into the atmosphere).

The problem, therefore, is to find a safe substitute for CFC refrigerants without abruptly shutting down urban society as it is now structured—although this does not mean that we might not ultimately find it wise to reconsider the very architecture of urban society itself.

Accordingly, Dupont Corporation has developed a class of compounds known as HCFCs. These are similar to CFCs, except that some of the chlorine atoms have been replaced with hydrogen atoms. The hope is that these will be less dangerous to the ozone layer because they will be able to break down in the lower atmosphere. Dupont claims that such compounds are 95 per cent less harmful than CFCs, although many environmentalists are sceptical.[22]

Retrofitting and retrofilling existing air conditioning and refrigeration units—and there are tens of thousands of major air conditioning units in large buildings, let alone the millions of private refrigerators and air conditioners—is a huge task. Often, existing equipment cannot function with the replacement fluids and would have to be replaced or overhauled. A Dupont executive recently claimed that it will cost the Dupont Corporation itself 1 billion dollars to retrofit all the air conditioning units in its own factories and offices.[23] Nevertheless, in *some* countries—including Canada and the United States—the enormous effort of replacement is now underway.

An eminently practicable and environmentally benign approach is to develop recycling technologies for CFCs, since a lot of CFCs reach the atmosphere simply from being spilled during take-down and repair of refrigerators and air conditioners. A Canadian engineer, Dusanka Ognjanovic-Filipovic, is a leader in this effort. She has helped to develop a device known as the Blue Bottle™, now being marketed by Halozone Technologies of Mississauga, Ontario. This is a two-part technology—a compact, easy-to-use system that allows a technician to recover refrigerant from a unit that is being serviced, and then release the refrigerant for later use. Widespread adoption of such a device could greatly reduce CFC losses to the atmosphere. The problem, however, is getting the Blue Bottle™ to survive in the market. As Ognjanovic-Filipovic observes, ". . . since the inherent value of the CFC compound is $2–6 per pound, which is not high enough to offset recycling costs, few industries are going to recycle them until it is mandatory."[24]

Certainly, too, we should continue scientific research into the problem in spite of pressure to cut budgets — knowledge is our best guide to action. Incremental changes, such as Ognjanovic-Filipovic's recycling technology, or the introduction of *somewhat* less harmful compounds such as HCFCs will certainly help, but it is almost as if we have to rethink the whole process of cooling, invent a whole new type of technology. Or should we just make do with less technology? Could we even do this, given the number of people in many parts of the world today who are highly dependent upon refrigeration technology for the delivery and preservation of their food? It is by no means obvious which way we should turn.

Structure of the Problem

The ozone problem has the following structure, which with minor variations one sees repeated in the case of many of the technologies that human ingenuity has provided:

- *Ingenious invention of very useful product or method, done with the best of intentions.* However, no one asks if product could do long-term damage; there is a complete lack of foresight.
- *We come to depend on this product.* It becomes so useful, at least to some, that almost nothing else will do quite as well; society evolves a kind of dependency on the product, which makes it very difficult to drop it or switch to a substitute. There is a real reason why the market supports the vast trade in CFCs; it is not just corporate greed, although corporate greed is a factor in the response to the problem.
- *Experts warn of danger, but are mostly disbelieved.*
- *Evidence (often indirect) mounts, but disbelief continues.*
- *Strongest denial of warnings from those who benefit most from the product or process.* It becomes a political issue, decided in part by advertisement and lobbying.
- *Conflict between short-term economic and long-term environmental interests.*
- *Finally there is undeniable evidence that experts were right;* indeed, it is worse than they predicted, because there is a completely unexpected mechanism that enhances the effect.
- *Effort begins, maybe too little, too late.*
- *Some still can't be convinced.*

Lessons to Be Learned

It is very easy to point fingers and treat the CFC disaster as entirely a moral issue; surely, we demand, Midgely and others should have known better and perhaps were not even acting from the best of motives. But it is not as simple as that. Recall, again, the history: Midgely was simply doing his duty as an engineer, trying to solve an apparently straightforward problem of public safety, and on the face of it, he succeeded brilliantly. While some corporate executives in later years may well be open to blame in a variety of ways, it is not at all clear that the early developers of CFCs were morally culpable at all. Where, then, if anywhere, did they go wrong?

I would like to suggest that the problem is epistemological, and not just moral. Epistemology has to do with the nature and sources of knowledge and perception, questions which, at least on a first reading, go somewhat beyond purely ethical issues.[25] Midgely's failure was above all else a kind of *cognitive error*. He and others like him at the time never saw the results of their engineering work as coupled to a larger but finite physical system (which we now call the environment) that could be somehow affected in any important way by anything they could do. Of course, Midgely knew that the Freon he spilled on the shop floor had to go somewhere; and of course he knew that the atmosphere is finite in extent; but he apparently never made the cognitive connection. He and others acted precisely as if the environment were an infinitely deep sink, capable of absorbing any conceivable human waste. It is almost as if they suffered from an illusion of moral perspective. If one stands very close to a large object, it may seem to stretch off to infinity, even if in fact it does not.

If there was a failure of responsibility, it was a failure to ask the right sorts of questions. It is almost as if we have a *responsibility to be philosophical*—which in this sense means to sometimes stop and ruthlessly demand of ourselves, *have we got the right picture*?

We should note also that the ozone story raises the difficult question of burden of proof. Normally, if a person is accused of a criminal offence, the prosecution must prove *beyond all reasonable doubt* that the person was guilty before he or she can be convicted and sanctions applied. Frequently, the defenders of CFCs seemed to be insisting on a similar standard of evidence, evidence that, until recently, critics of CFCs could not supply. (And even now, it is unclear *precisely* how much biological damage will be done by ozone depletion, only that some certainly will be.) If we insist on such a standard of evidence for all environmental risks, our problems might become insoluble, and the damage they cause irreversible, before we have the absolutely irrefutable evidence we think we want. On the other hand, there clearly is a danger of overreacting to threats that eventually show themselves to be insignificant. How much evidence, how much warning, do we need before we accept that it is wise to change our ways? In fact, many of the critical decisions we have to make in our lives must inevitably be on the basis of incomplete evidence and mere probabilities, and good judgement consists in large part of being able to weigh and balance the uncertainties in order to make as reasonable as possible a choice. Clearly, human society still needs to learn the knack of good environmental judgement.

Some Further Reading

Rowland (1990) provides an excellent, authoritative, and very detailed overview of the scientific aspects of ozone depletion. Roan (1989) is still probably the best overview for the serious general reader. Nance (1991) is a bit more journalistic, but paints a vivid picture of many of the key personalities and personality conflicts involved in the ozone and greenhouse stories. Levi (1988) is an excellent hot-off-the-press review of scientific findings at the professional level. The October 1990 issue of *Ambio* (Vol. 19, No. 6–7) is devoted entirely to CFCs and the ozone layer. Environment Canada (1994b) contains an authoritative précis of recent data.

NOTES

1. Dr. Susan Solomon is one of the major players in the effort to understand the ozone hole. Her remark is quoted in Nance (1991), p. 20.
2. For more detail, see Rowland (1990), p. 282. A temperature inversion is simply a condition in which the normal tendency of temperature to decrease with altitude is reversed.
3. Lovelock now states: "The CFCs and other industrial halocarbons have increased by 500 percent since I first measured them in 1971. They were harmless then, but now there is too much halocarbon gas in the air. The first symptoms of poisoning are now felt. I now join with those who would regulate the emissions of CFCs and other carriers of chlorine to the stratosphere" (from Lovelock 1988, p. 170). For a sympathetic discussion of Lovelock's early doubts about the dangers of CFCs, see Joseph (1990), ch. VIII.
4. Roan (1989), p. 2.
5. See Dotto and Schiff (1978) for a detailed account.
6. See Environment Canada (1994b).
7. Levi (1988), p. 17.
8. For a very readable exposition, see Roan (1989). For more technical coverage, see Rowland (1990) or Levi (1988).
9. See Immen (1993) for a report on recent Canadian work on the link between ozone levels, UV-B, and Pinatubo after-effects.
10. Retinal burn is already on the rise in the United States. See Taylor (1990).
11. CBC (1992).

12. Time-lapse satellite photos of the ozone hole show it moving around restlessly and hungrily extending pseudopods like a sinister, predacious amoeba.
13. CBC (1992).
14. CBC (1992).
15. See Smith et al. (1992). Voytek (1990) and Karentz (1991) are excellent reviews, and provide a good picture of both the possible risks and the difficulties in determining those risks.
16. Environment Canada (1994b).
17. CBC (1992).
18. See Roan (1989), pp. 201–3.
19. Fisher (1990).
20. Peacock (1992).
21. An exception is the use of CFCs for medical purposes. Asthmatics, like this author, are allowed to use CFC-propelled "puffers" to inhale their medication. Alternatives to these have been developed as well, however.
22. HCFCs have a similar potential as greenhouse gases to CFCs, even if they do less ozone damage.
23. CBC (1992).
24. Quoted in Piper (1992).
25. I need to choose my words carefully here, for one can argue that the criteria by which stimuli are organized by the human mind into coherent perceptions are in part aesthetic; hence the separation between questions about value and questions about knowledge is not quite as sharp as I have suggested.

We now examine the greenhouse effect. The following excerpt from a longer article by Barbara Goss Levi comes as close as anything we have seen to illustrating what seems to be the professional scientific consensus on this subject—and also suggests some of the difficulties scientists have in giving us the advice we need.

CLIMATE MODELERS STRUGGLE TO UNDERSTAND GLOBAL WARMING

Barbara Goss Levi

In the sweltering summer of 1988 the public heard claims that global warming from the greenhouse effect had definitely begun. In the chilly winter of 1989/90 they are hearing skeptics question whether it will ever arrive. Just as temperatures fluctuate about an average value, the mean opinion on global warming falls somewhere between these extremes.

To narrow this range of uncertainties surrounding the greenhouse effect, researchers have been working for decades to simulate the highly complex and imperfectly understood atmosphere with sophisticated, three-dimensional models. They face a herculean task, with high stakes riding on their predictions. Currently the climate models estimate that a doubling of atmospheric carbon dioxide (expected in the next century) may raise global temperatures somewhere between 1.5 and 4.5 K.[1]

Skeptics have long questioned whether such model predictions are sufficiently accurate to serve as guides to making policy, and some have suggested—only qualitatively so far—factors that might keep the temperatures from rising. The climate modelers stand by their predictions that increased releases of infrared absorbers such as carbon dioxide will warm Earth's climate. They have much less confidence in the models' abilities to answer definitively by how much and by when. Nor can they reliably predict what the regional climate will be.

The greenhouse effect that the models are attempting to gauge results from atmospheric constituents that are generally transparent to short-wavelength radiation but strongly absorb long-wavelength radiation. These constituents allow solar radiation to penetrate to Earth's surface but trap the reradiated infrared. The greenhouse gases in turn emit infrared radiation. The additional infrared absorbers decrease the fraction of surface-emitted radiation that escapes to space. But the radiation to space must remain constant if Earth is at equilibrium, so the surface temperature warms as the fraction radiated to space decreases.

Water vapor is the most potent greenhouse gas, and together with CO_2, it is largely responsible for keeping our planet at the comfortable 15C average temperature rather than at the chilly –18C that would obtain without an atmosphere. However, concern focuses on carbon dioxide because its atmospheric concentration (less than 10% that of water vapor) is increasing, and hence it may be shifting the current equilibrium. Some trace gases, such as methane, chlorofluorocarbons, and nitrous oxide, have concentrations about 100 times smaller than that for CO_2, but they are growing more rapidly. Simulations of the impact of a doubling of CO_2 can also represent some radiatively equivalent mixture of CO_2 and other greenhouse gases.

A doubling of CO_2 would increase the atmospheric trapping of long-wavelength radiation by about 4 W/m^2 compared to the trapping of about 150 W/m^2 in today's atmosphere. This small change may be amplified or dampened by a variety of feedbacks.

Temperature Trends

Besides gazing into the future through a screen of computer graphics, climatologists try to peer into the past through historical temperature records. Two questions impel the search: Has the planet become warmer over the past 100 years as CO_2 concentrations have risen from preindustrial levels of 280 ppm to the current values, which exceed 350 ppm? Can the climate models reproduce the observed change? Again large uncertainties characterize the answers.

Cataloguing temperatures over the globe has been far from systematic. Instruments and techniques have varied with time and with location. Recording stations have changed locations, or the nature of the locations surrounding the stations has changed. Many of these factors average out when large numbers of stations are examined over long time periods. But one troublesome systematic effect will not average out: the tendency of stations near burgeoning cities to register increased temperatures associated with the urban heat islands. Most analysts correct for this heat-island effect in some way, but they still estimate that it may exaggerate the temperature rise over the past 100 years by about 0.1 K.

Sets of land data of course represent the temperatures for only about one third of Earth's surface. Marine-air and sea-surface temperature readings have also been collected during the past century, but they, too, are awash in uncertainties.

Using a data set that combines land and marine temperatures, Phil D. Jones, Tom Wigley, and Peter B. Wright (University of East Anglia) estimated[2] that Earth is now 0.5 K warmer than in the mid-1880s. James Hansen and Sergej Lebedeff of the NASA Goddard Institute for Space Studies, New York,[3] placed the past warming at 0.6 ± 0.2 K, based on a similar data set for land only.

Based on his temperature observations and studies with a GISS climate model, Hansen in 1988 stated to Congress that "the global warming is now sufficiently large that we can ascribe with a high degree of confidence a cause and effect relationship to the greenhouse effect. . . ." As if to temper this air of certainty, Kirby Hanson, George Maul, and Thomas Karl (National Oceanic and Atmospheric Administration [NOAA]) soon afterward published their study of climate within the contiguous U.S. over a period dating back to 1895, which indicates no overall trend in either temperature or precipitation.[4] Subsequently another group reported[5] that the temperature changes for the contiguous 48 states represented a warming rate of 0.26 K/century. Even the null result for the U.S., which covers only about 1–2% of the globe, does not necessarily contradict the estimates of worldwide temperature increases: Temperature changes do not occur uniformly over the globe.

A prevailing consensus is that Earth may have warmed by about 0.5 K in the last century—a weak signal that is not much larger than the interannual fluctuations. Current climate models have so far only simulated the temperature increase expected for a doubling of CO_2 but these results can roughly indicate what the temperature increase might have been over the past 100 years, when the CO_2 increase was only 25%. Models that predict warmings of 2 K or 3 K for a CO_2 doubling correspond to temperature increases of 0.5 K and 0.7 K, respectively, for the past century. The thermal inertia of the oceans causes the temperature response to lag behind the CO_2 forcing by some time interval which is not precisely known.

The models should not be asked to account entirely for the past climate changes because they do not include many factors besides the greenhouse gases that influence the climate. Volcanos and variations in the solar radiation certainly are among these factors. So are industrial emissions of sulfur dioxides that may alter the albedo. Wigley has estimated that the upper limit on this effect is sufficiently large that it may have significantly offset the temperature changes that have resulted from the greenhouse effect.[6] [Editor's Note: Brookes 1989, p. 100, remarks sarcastically, "Of course, it is very upsetting to an environmentalist to discover that a pollutant has a beneficial side effect."]

Jerry Mahlman, director of GFDL [Geophysical Fluid Dynamics Lab, NOAA], defends the global circulation models as central tools, which are attempting one of the most difficult calculations ever undertaken. He points to successes in simulating the very cold climate of the last glacial maximum and of the extreme temperatures found on Mars and Venus. Among the predictions to which he would assign a probability of greater than 90% are global-mean surface warming, large stratospheric cooling, global-mean precipitation increase, and enhanced winter surface warming in the northern polar regions. To address the significant deficiencies that still remain, he admits the need for more data, more computer time or speed (which can translate into finer grid spacing and better physics for the models), and more scientific talent.

NOTES

1. National Academy of Sciences, *Changing Climate: Report of the Carbon Dioxide Assessment Committee* (National Academy Press, Washington, D.C., 1983).
2. P.D. Jones, T.M.L. Wigley, P.B. Wright, *Nature* 322, 430 (1986).
3. J. Hansen, S. Lebedeff, J. Geophys. Res. 92, 13345 (1987); Geophys. Res. Lett. 15, 323 (1988).
4. K. Hanson, G.A. Maul, T.R. Karl, Geophys. Res. Lett. 16, 49 (1989).
5. J. Hansen, D. Rind, A. DelGenio, A. Lacis, S. Lebedeff, M. Prather, R. Ruedy, T. Karl, in *Proc. Second North American Conf. on Preparing for Climate Change*, Climate Institute, Washington, D.C. (1989).
6. T.M.L. Wigley, *Nature* 339, 365 (1989).

Climatic trends in recent years have been confusing. (I recall lecturing on global warming to a somewhat sceptical class in London, Ontario, in January 1994, when the temperature outside was hovering around –38°C.) Through the late

1980s, global temperatures reached levels unprecedented for centuries. However, in the early 1990s there seemed to be, in fact, a slight *cooling* trend, due probably to a factor that was not sufficiently appreciated at the time Levi's article appeared—dust. (However, Bryson and Murray emphasized the importance of dust in **anthropogenic** climate deterioration as far back as 1977.) Dust can cause cooling both by directly blocking solar radiation and by causing the formation of clouds. Mount Pinatubo in the Philippines in 1991 was the largest volcanic eruption this century in terms of the amount of dust ejected into the stratosphere, and this is believed to have had a significant short-term cooling effect. However, the major sources of dust are industry, sulphates from the burning of coal, carbon from the burning of biomass following deforestation, and soil particles stirred up by agriculture. These produce a cooling effect which may, to some degree, counterbalance global warming. It must not be thought that any cooling effect that might be contributed by these anthropogenic sources of dust really means that the emission of carbon dioxide and other greenhouse pollutants is any less serious a problem. Instead, it is simply a further destabilizing factor, increasing the likelihood of violent shifts of climate in the next decades. See Pearce (1994) for a review of recent findings on the importance of dust.

In spite of the dust from Pinatubo, which perhaps is now settling out, other evidence continues to point to a warming trend. Models of global warming predict that the Arctic and Antarctic regions will show the most dramatic temperature increases, and in fact Antarctica has indeed shown a temperature increase of 2.5°C over the past 50 years. The recent, startling break-up of the Wordie Ice Shelf has helped draw scientists' attention to the fact that Antarctic sea ice is currently disappearing at a rate of about 1.4 percent per decade. (These figures are from MacKenzie 1995.) Still, whether these changes are *definitely* due to the greenhouse effect, or are merely "natural" variations (whatever that might mean), remains to be seen.

It is instructive to look at the greenhouse problem from the perspective of different time scales. It seems fairly likely that if present trends continue, the combined effect of greenhouse emissions and deforestation in the near term—say, over the next few decades—will be to cause a net warming of the troposphere. Exactly how much warmer it may get and exactly how serious will be the attendant shifts in climate zone, sea level rise, increase in violent weather, and so forth, remain to be seen. However, the Earth's climate is so complex that we cannot say for sure if continued greenhouse emissions will always translate into a proportional degree of warming. The history of the Earth's climate in the past shows that climate regimes tend to be metastable rather than stable. This means that sudden and dramatic shifts of climatic regime are possible in some rare circumstances. (For instance, it is known now that the winding down of the last Ice Age was interrupted by a brief return to full glaciation about 10,000 years ago, which took only about *twenty-five years* to establish itself.) All we can say for sure is that we are destabilizing a system that exists in an apparent equilibrium that is probably much more precarious than we quite realize.

What about the middle term—say, over the next several centuries or few thousands of years? What should we prepare for on this time scale? A look at climatic history will help here. For about the past 2.5 million years or so, the planet has been experiencing a series of Ice Ages. There have been a dozen or more of these; each glaciation lasts as much as a hundred thousand years or more, and they are separated by warm periods called interglacials or interstades. These palmy interludes typically last perhaps ten to twenty thousand years, and then the planet begins a long slide into the next peak glaciation. There seems to be absolutely no reason to think that the pattern that has occurred with such remarkable regularity many times in the past will not be repeated again. If this is so, we are therefore currently at or near the end of our current interglacial; sooner or later, be it in a few centuries or a few millennia, the winters will relentlessly get longer and colder and icecaps will begin to form in places like central Labrador and Baffin Island. (And perhaps smart real-estate operators will take options on those sections of the continental shelf that will soon be high and dry.) Once continental glaciation gets well enough started, it is self-reinforcing by a variety of mechanisms, and eventually most of Canada, Great Britain, and northern Europe will again be crushed under ice sheets kilometres thick.

Faced with the near-inevitability of the ultimate return of the glaciers, some have argued that the greenhouse effect might be a good thing. Maybe a little extra greenhouse warming is just what we need over the next few centuries. Unfortunately, it is not quite as simple as that.

To see one reason (but not the only reason) why it might be best to avoid any further greenhouse warming, consider the *very long-term* outlook for the Earth's climate, over the next several hundred million years. If astronomers are roughly correct about the probable course of evolution of the solar system, this may be far from irrelevant to our immediate worries.

Astronomers believe that around any reasonably stable star one can define a so-called Zone of Habitability. This is the zone of distances from the star within which life as we know it could be possible, given a suitably endowed planet. Inside the Zone of Habitability it would be too hot; outside it would be too cold. Now, it is the opinion of many astronomers (although by no means all) that as a so-called Main Sequence (normal garden-variety) star like our Sun gradually ages, it tends to get steadily *hotter*. Over a time scale of hundreds of millions of years, therefore, the Zone of Habitability slowly moves outward. Given our present understanding of stellar dynamics, our Sun has quite possibly increased in luminosity by about 20 percent to 30 percent during the time that life has existed on Earth; hence, Earth must be much closer to the inner edge of the Sun's Zone of Habitability than it once was. Early in the history of the Earth, we were comfortably within the central region of the zone, with the optimal period (James Lovelock guesses; see Lovelock 1988) perhaps in the Paleozoic, 400 million years ago or so. Now, however, the outward expansion of the zone has put us *very near the inner edge*; if this picture is right (and this is a point on which experts will disagree), the Earth's real *long-term* problem is overheating!

This puts the problem of greenhouse emissions in an interesting light, for if this view is correct, then by recklessly pumping out greenhouse gases faster than the system can absorb them we are forcing the system *in exactly the opposite direction to which it needs to go*. We presently have no way of guessing whether this will provoke a gradual evolution to a much warmer and (for humans) less hospitable planet, a sudden excursion to a higher temperature regime (as Lovelock speculates it might), or even a more severe Ice Age than we might have otherwise experienced. (This is unlikely but thinkable.) But it is clearly highly destabilizing.

Many atmospheric scientists have emphasized that by pumping vast quantities of greenhouse gases into the atmosphere, humanity is in effect conducting an unprecedented *experiment* on a planetary scale. In their pioneering paper of 1957 (which emphasized the scientific difficulties of determining the actual climatic effects of increased carbon dioxide emissions), Revelle and Suess remarked that

> human beings are now carrying out a large scale geophysical experiment of a kind that could not have happened in the past nor be reproduced in the future. Within a few centuries we are returning to the atmosphere and oceans the concentrated organic carbon stored in sedimentary rocks over hundreds of millions of years. (Revelle and Suess 1957, p. 19)

Recently, Bill McKibben put it with less restraint:

> If you become an environmentalist, people will say you're a radical. But that's not the case. What is radical is saying, "Hey, let's double the amount of CO_2 in the atmosphere and see what happens." That's a really radical thought. And that's what we are doing. (Quoted in Revkin 1992, p. 115)

With these sobering considerations in mind, we turn to two short but striking readings on the greenhouse effect, which illustrate very nearly the opposite extremes in opinion on this question.

GREENHOUSE EFFECT BLAMED FOR DEATHS OF ONE MILLION IN THIRD WORLD LAST YEAR

André Picard

The greenhouse effect killed at least one million people in the Third World last year, underlining the need for developed countries to change their energy consumption habits, a French agronomist says.

"Every waste of energy is an act of murder in the Third World," René Dumont said yesterday at a conference in Montreal on **sustainable development.**

"Restraint, or death— that is the choice."

Mr. Dumont said global warming is causing drought, which in turn has resulted in food production falling behind population growth. Of the 10 million deaths he attributed to starvation last year, Mr. Dumont said at least one million were caused directly by the greenhouse effect.

Calling the greenhouse effect the greatest threat humanity has ever seen, Mr. Dumont said that the solution to global warming is for people in developed countries to alter their energy consumption habits radically.

The self-described "militant Third Worldist" said there should be an immediate tax of 17 cents on every litre of fossil fuel sold. The resulting $280-billion collected in taxes annually should be used to develop alternative energy, he said in an interview.

In addition, there should be an outright ban on all cars that consume more than 5.5 litres of fuel per 100 kilometres, and fines for all forms of energy waste— up to and including penalties on people who put up Christmas lights.

"There can be no compromise. Compromise will end in death," Mr. Dumont said. "There are two billion people living in poverty in the world and they are hostages to our greed, to our waste of energy."

Mr. Dumont said the relatively minor droughts that hit China, India, and the United States in the past two years should serve as a warning that "we are on the verge of the greatest famine in the history of humanity."

His dire predictions are particularly troubling because of his track record. In 1930, he warned that exploitation and starvation of peasants would lead to revolution in China. That same year, he began promoting birth control methods, saying the population explosion threatened the planet.

A professor at the Institut national agronomique in Paris since 1933, Mr. Dumont predicted in 1966 that Africa would experience widespread drought and famine within a generation. In 1971 he published *Ethiopia or Death*, a book that predicted the devastating famine in Ethiopia and outlined how it could be avoided.

The outspoken Mr. Dumont, now 85, said most of the world's problems are linked to an unjust economic system. "The world economy is amoral, it is immoral, and we are living with the results of an amoral, immoral economy," he said in an interview.

He becomes angry when people say his proposals are unworkable. "We live in a society that imposes conditions on all aspects of life. We already have red lights at intersections. All I want is more red lights to slow us down because we are on the road to death."

The professor places much of the blame for the wasteful consumption on transnational corporations, and assails the World Bank and International Monetary Fund for "complicity" by promoting consumerism in the Third World.

For example, Mr. Dumont said, there are now 50 million cars in the Third World, and the money spent on them "could have been used to purchase two billion bicycles, rickshaws and wheelbarrows . . . tools that will help people feed themselves instead of killing them."

He also criticized the economic policies of the Quebec government. He said the so-called "bébé-bonus"—a program that gives parents cash grants for having children—is scandalous. "Fourteen million children died of starvation last year, many more are living inhumane lives. Why should there be a premium paid to those who have children?"

Mr. Dumont denounced the Canadian government, singling out the cut in passenger rail services, and grants to Western farmers, which "promote agricultural methods that lead to soil erosion and energy waste."

MORE RESEARCH NEEDED

G. Christopher Anderson

The Bush administration, under fire from environmentalists for its reluctance to embrace global warming countermeasures, believes that two more years of research are needed before the science of climate modelling is strong enough to dictate environmental policy, said Energy Secretary James Watkins in an interview last week.

By 1992, "our national laboratories are going to have enough answers for us to get specific" about climate predictions, Watkins said. The administration reckons it will be spending half the worldwide total on climate change research in 1991; Department of Energy (DOE) research alone accounts for $66 million of the request.

Although several European countries have already begun programmes that would restrict the emission of carbon dioxide and other greenhouse gases to current levels, Watkins said recent scientific advances still cannot "economically justify taking drastic steps" to control emission in the United States. But he believes that the moderate measures already in place can have a significant impact on greenhouse gas concentrations. "We're going after all the knowns, such as acid rain, the ozone layer, and deforestation, while we wait for the science clarification" on global warming, he said; efforts such as the phasing out of chlorofluorocarbons, along with new energy-efficiency initiatives, can cut greenhouse gas emission by about a quarter in the next decade.

Speaking a week after President Bush opened a United Nations meeting on climate change by calling cautiously for more research, without accepting predictions for global warming, Watkins acknowledged that DOE's own experts do indeed forecast a global temperature rise from present predictions of the increase in carbon dioxide. "I believe that there is a greenhouse gas increase, and infrared absorption [by those gases]. The [DOE] labs clearly say that the greenhouse effect is generated under those circumstances," he said. But, he added, do "we have to destroy the industrial base and our economy for world survival?"

FURTHER READING

For an up-to-date and very accessible description of the human impact upon the climate, see Revkin (1992). Brookes (1989) presents a contrary view to the scientific consensus on the greenhouse effect. See Schneider (1989) for a senior atmospheric scientist's views on global warming, and Lovelock (1988) for a scientifically controversial but thought-provoking Gaian perspective.

QUESTIONS TO CONSIDER

1. Briefly explain what the ozone hole is and how it came about. How much of the danger might have been predictable in 1928 when CFCs were first created (given the scientific and technical knowledge available at that time) had someone asked the right sort of questions? And what would have been the right sort of questions to ask?
2. As mentioned in the text, the slight possibility exists of various "bandaid" solutions to the ozone crisis. All of these would be more or less expensive, uncertain in their effectiveness and practicability, and fraught with unknown or unpredictable hazards and side-effects. Given the seriousness of the ozone crisis, and the probability that

it will worsen before it gets better even with full implementation of existing treaties to control the use of chlorofluorocarbons, do you think that it would be wise to attempt technological emergency repairs to the ozone hole? Or would it be safer to put all our efforts into implementing more effective international agreements to cut back CFC usage, and hope that nature can eventually repair the ozone hole by itself? If efforts to secure an international agreement eventually prove unsuccessful, might it then be worth the cost and environmental risk of developing "bandaid" solutions?

3. Do you think that the engineers who developed CFCs in the 1930s and 1940s were in any way morally culpable for their apparent lack of foresight about the environmental effects of their products? In other words, did they or did they not make an "honest" mistake?
4. Former U.S. energy secretary James Watkins objected to reducing greenhouse emissions and asked, do "we have to destroy the industrial base and our economy for world survival?" Do you detect any internal contradiction in his particular choice of wording?
5. Distinguish between "amoral" and "immoral." What does René Dumont mean by saying that the economic system is amoral? Does he mean to say that it is immoral to be amoral?
6. Deforestation, especially in the tropics, is believed to contribute to the global increase in CO_2 second only to combustion of fossil fuels. How much reduction in personal fossil fuel use should an affluent North American accept before having the right to teil small farmers in Brazil that they should not clear their land for crops? Or is this comparison really fair?
7. With reference to Levi's article, or any other sources that seem relevant, do you feel that scientists have made their case for global warming?

CHAPTER TWO

EXTINCTION IS SO FINAL: THE CRISIS IN BIODIVERSITY

If there is one thing that seems to suggest that we are near a turning point, or perhaps a point of no return, it is the ever-accumulating evidence showing that the damage done to the nonhuman parts of the biosphere by pervasive human predation and encroachment is approaching a critical level. For Canadians (and many other peoples who depend heavily upon the sea for their sustenance), the crisis in the fisheries is one of the most visible faces of this tale. There is nothing theoretical about the near-total shut-down of the groundfish fishery on the Canadian East Coast. This has done more than merely put thousands of people out of work— it has ended a whole way of life that has flourished for 500 years.

It has emerged that Canada's 200-mile limit does not protect the "nose" and the "tail" of the Grand Banks, where much of the surviving stock is still being wrenched from the sea by foreign and multinational draggers. After years of looking the other way, the Canadian government has abruptly reacted, forcing an almost total shut-down of the cod fishery—and ending a way of life for thousands of Newfoundlanders. Journalist Rex Murphy presents an impassioned epitaph for the inshore cod fishery and the communities that depended upon it.

TWO EXTINCTIONS

Rex Murphy

There's a cataclysm going on, on the East Coast of this country. There are two extinctions involved: the destruction of one of the world's greatest food resources, the Newfoundland cod fishery, and the dissolution after 500 years of one of the most tenacious lifestyles on the continent, the Newfoundland outport. The scenes are tranquil enough, but there's a chill menace sweeping the coastline communities of Newfoundland. People who live in these towns have stared down hard times, bad weather, and isolation for generations. It cannot be a pleasant occupation, watching all the props of custom and livelihood slipping away. Since the ban on fishing imposed two years ago, these towns have gone still and quiet. The outharbours are silent. The signatures are everywhere of a great interruption, a falling off into retreat from the grand alliance with the sea.

The abundance of these waters has always been a wonder of the world. When the conquistadors ransacked Peru with sword and crucifix, the more fluid gold off Newfoundland's coast drew the great merchant navies of Europe to an even richer gathering: the sea was ripe with cod. It was limitless. The island of Newfoundland was a giant wharf perched conveniently over the continental shelf, one vast marina containing an extravagant, almost incomprehensible, variety and crush of sea life.

Settlement followed fish. All the early outports may be understood as a wharf surrounded by houses. The old fishery was very much an individual enterprise. It was a small-boat, land-based, family-centred operation, conducted out of the hundreds of small harbours, coves, and inlets that formed a perimeter spine of Newfoundland's 4,800 miles of coastline.

The outports had one essential recommending feature: they were places to fish from. The hitherto inconceivable collapse of the fishery carries with it one inescapable conclusion: the outports no longer have a reason to be. . . .

Spotting and finding the predators is not the problem; daily overflights, the best radar and satellite equipment map everything that moves. Detection, alas, is not enforcement. It is very difficult for people outside Newfoundland to realize the depth of animosity directed toward the offshore draggers that have been scouring the shelf for over three decades. That animosity has turned to pure white-hot rage since the imposition of the moratorium. Foreign draggers, chiefly Spanish and Portuguese, have been doing an end run on the so-called nose and tail of the Grand Banks. Those two outcroppings of the continental shelf outside the 200-mile limit. Drawn by the Gulf Stream's warm current, all of the fish that are left are on this nose and tail. . . .

Joe Smallwood argued the case for Newfoundland joining Canada and putting an end to four and a half centuries of isolation and independence. . . . What has federal control meant? Ottawa granted excessive quotas to foreign nations and ourselves. It refused to police overfishing. It refused to heed a decade of warnings from inshore fishermen. Its scientists madly overestimated the stocks, and it poured billions into the offshore when the inshore was dying.

Ottawa tolerated the vacuuming of the nose and tail, thereby greasing the skid way to extinction. Let there be no mistake, the undigested villain of this piece is the deep sea dragger, the most indiscriminate, ravaging, and relentless machine ever to rake and vacuum the oceans of the world. Underwater strip-mining. **Clear-cutting** with nets. The dragger fishery of other nations and our own worked a biological meltdown on the East Coast of Canada. This is what Chernobyl looks like when it puts to sea. . . .

The extinction of the northern cod stock may yet be seen as one of the great ecological savageries of this entire century. One of the great food resources of this planet, an incredible richness has evaporated. Yet, where has been the protest? I think cod are a damned species for two reasons: cod aren't cute. They don't give good poster. There were more reporters in Newfoundland during the seal protest than followed Tonya Harding at the Olympics, and more environmentalists that went three years ago to Rio. Fish, in general, aren't glamorous and they disappear invisibly. The calamity took place under water. They are not tigers or elephants, eagles, or owls. The Grand Banks is not a rain forest. The cod is not a dolphin. The plain codfish, however, is the central link in an ecology that binds a unique natural environment with a unique human one.

Farley Mowat tells us that "it is probably impossible for anyone now alive to comprehend the magnitude of fish life in the waters of the New World when the European invasion began" (1984, p. 166). In the early years, cod and other "groundfish" were so staggeringly numerous that at times they even "stayed the passage" of John Cabot's ships (Mowat 1984, p. 167). Eventually, as the groundfish stocks melted away, we have turned to species that in early years would have been tossed back into the sea with hardly a sniff of contempt and—disastrously—the baitfish, the smaller fish upon which the groundfish feed.

"THE SEAS ARE DYING, AS IF YOU DIDN'T KNOW"

Farley Mowat

Today, industry spokesmen and scientific advisers are extolling the potential profitability of a whole new range of species that might be fished in place of those that have been commercially exterminated. These include such deep-water and even abyssal species as the wolf fish, the probeagle (a fancy name for the mackerel shark), and a small shark called the spiny dogfish. The thorny skate is also being touted, as are the grenadiers (otherwise known as rat-tails), which live as much as three-quarters-of-a-mile down in the black deeps. New fishing techniques will be required to "harvest" these "resources," but this should pose no problem to technological men who can travel to the moon and back. It will be interesting to see under what evocative names these species will be marketed.

At this point it would be well to look at one of the major justifications advanced to excuse the fishing industry's biocidal activities. This is the contention that the industry is *duty bound* to constantly increase its landings in order to improve the supply of protein for a human population, much of which lives on the edge of starvation.

This is blatant hypocrisy. In actual fact, the fishing industry of the developed nations, which is by far the largest and most destructive, achieves just the opposite result. Most of its production goes, not to starving peoples, but to those who are already the world's best fed, and who can afford high-priced food. In order to produce high-value (and high-profit) products, usually fillets, the Western fishing industry processes its catches in such a way that as much as 40 per cent of what *could* be used as human food is either completely wasted or is downgraded to make fish meal for animal feeds or fertilizer. On top of which, of course, there is the overriding fact that, by commercially exterminating species after species of the more nutritious and abundant fishes in the sea, the modern commercial fishing industry is actually guaranteeing an increased burden of starvation for the hungry hordes who fill the human future.

This is a new phenomenon. Until 1939, the bulk of the groundfish catch from the northwestern Atlantic was processed as salt fish, a product that preserved as much as 90 per cent of the edible portion of the catch and that was sold at a price affordable to impoverished peoples, for whom it provided a staple source of protein. Profit was certainly a central motive in the industry then, but it was not the all-embracing one it has since become.

Without doubt the most numerous fishes in the seas washing the eastern coasts of North America are still the smaller kinds collectively known as baitfishes. They acquired the name not so much because they provided bait for fishermen as because they were the basic food that sustained other sea animals ranging from sea trout through salmon, cod, halibut, and tuna all the way up the scale to seals, porpoises, and whales.

Baitfishes tend to live in gigantic schools. The best-known species in the northwestern Atlantic are squid, mackerel, herring, shad, smelt, gaspereaux or alewife, and capelin. Mackerel are deep-sea breeders; herring and squid mostly spawn close inshore; some capelin spawn offshore on the banks while other populations lay their eggs on landward beaches; the remaining species ascend freshwater rivers and streams to lay their eggs.

Some indication of the prodigious abundance of the baitfishes can perhaps be derived from the following random observations spanning the period from 1600 to recent times:

> The late Monsieur de la Tour had a weir built in which were caught great numbers of these Gaspereaux which were salted down for winter. Sometimes they were caught in so great a quantity that he was obliged to break the weir and throw them into the sea, as otherwise they would have befouled the weir which would thus have been ruined.
>
> Herring abound in countless shoals. Anyone not familiar with northern water will suspect me of romancing when I say that I have seen 600 barrels taken in one sweep of a seine net. Often sufficient salt cannot be procured to save them and they are used as manure.
>
> An American schooner struck a school of mackerel . . . and before midnight, fishing with hook and line, the crew had 100 barrels caught . . . fish are destroyed and wasted in the most reckless manner, but the supply never fails. For a week in the spring, smelts run up all the rivers in an unceasing stream.
>
> When the capelin drove up on the beaches of Conception Bay to spawn we would stand up to our knees in a regular soup of them, scooping them out with buckets and filling the wagons until the horses could hardly haul them off the beaches. You would sink to your ankles in the sand, it was that spongy with capelin eggs. We took all we needed for bait and for to manure the gardens, and it was like we'd never touched them at all, they was so plenty.
>
> In the Potomac River the annual catch was 2,000,000 pounds of shad and 4,000,000 of alewives. . . . As much as two million pounds of salted shad was shipped to the United States every year from the Bay of Fundy in the 1890s.
>
> In the spring of 1953 on a herring seiner in the Gulf of St. Lawrence we caught a *million* herring in a single set of the seine — a not unusual occurrence at that time.

Although smelt, shad, and alewives were savaged on their spawning runs as well as being ruinously netted at other seasons, this may not have been the deciding factor in the decline that has now brought them down to as low as 4 or 5 per cent of their former profusion. The ultimate blow seems to have been dealt by dams, diversions, pollution, and other man-made changes to their spawning grounds. In any event, none of these three species now exists in sufficient numbers to be a significant source of profit, and their former ability to sustain vast numbers of predacious fishes in the sea has vanished, too. One ray of light in an otherwise almost unrelievedly dark scene of devastation is to be found in current efforts by U.S. authorities to restore some of their shad rivers. Preliminary results seem good. One can but hope they will continue to improve.

Before the present century began, many of the commercially important fishes in our northeastern waters depended on herring, mackerel, and capelin as the mainstays of their existence. This natural toll was greatly intensified by a human catch made first for food, and then for bait, and finally for a variety of industrial products ranging from fish oil to imitation pearl lustre produced from herring scales. Nevertheless, all three species were still enormously abundant when, in the 1960s, new ways were found to profit from them on a previously unheard-of level of destruction.

First was the mass production of fish meal for animal feed and fertilizer. The species initially selected to fuel the ominously named reduction plants that sprang up along the northeastern seaboard was the herring.[1] Early in the 1960s, at about the same time the Newfoundland Industrial Development Service was concluding that local herring stocks were "under-utilized," the herring fishery on the Pacific coast of Canada was collapsing because of overfishing. In the words of the director of the IDS: "What could be more rational than to invite the unemployed British Columbia herring seiners to go to work for us?"

The first reduction plant was built on Newfoundland's south coast in 1965 and a single B.C. seiner made the long voyage around, through the Panama Canal, to test the waters, as it were. The test was eminently successful. By 1969, fifty of the biggest, most modern B.C. seiners were working the south and west Newfoundland coasts year-round, while half-a-dozen reduction plants filled the skies with black and oily smoke. Herring landings in Newfoundland, which had previously averaged less than 4,000 tons a year, shot up to 140,000 tons. Meanwhile, annual landings from the southern Gulf of St. Lawrence increased from 20,000 to 300,000 tons.

Then, in the early 1970s, herring began to disappear. Fisheries spokesmen reassuringly explained that the little fishes had probably altered their migration patterns but would undoubtedly return before too long. The herring were not aware of these optimistic forecasts—for their once prodigious hosts have not returned as yet. There are those who doubt they ever will . . . or can.

The herring massacre was only one of several. During the 1960s, a mass fishery for mackerel began off southern New England to produce oil, fertilizer, and animal feed (including cat food). By 1972 it was landing the colossal amount of 390,000 tons a year, but shortly thereafter the mackerel mysteriously faded away. The slaughter off New England, together with several similar massacres in Canadian waters, has reduced the once-fabulous mackerel run up the northeast coast from Cape Cod to Labrador to an insignificant vestige of its former self.

In the 1960s Japanese seiners began pursuing offshore capelin on the Grand Banks. When word of this reached the Canadian Department of Fisheries, its mandarins concluded that capelin must be a money-maker and they thereupon decided to "develop a major capelin fishery." What had traditionally been an inshore fishery carried on by Newfoundland shoremen, with a catch of less than 10,000 tons a year, was now converted into an international offshore fishery with enormous quotas being granted to foreign as well as domestic fleets. The foreigners, it must be said, mostly used their catch for human food; the Canadians mostly poured theirs into the reduction plants. In 1976, the reported catch, which was almost certainly much lower than the real one, reached 370,000 tons. By the spring of 1978, the offshore capelin stocks had been effectively exhausted.

But not to worry. Inshore populations that spawned on Newfoundland beaches were still available for "development." These stocks are even now being decimated by Canadian companies, not to provide basic human food, or even fish meal, but to supply a luxury market. Although both sexes of capelin are seined in their millions, only the spawn from gravid females is processed, to be sold to the Japanese gourmet trade. The bulk of the catch is often simply dumped.

By 1983 most of the inshore capelin populations had been reduced to residual levels. Some biologists believe that this havoc has effectively blocked a recovery of groundfish stocks as well as administering what may well be a mortal blow to the few remaining large colonies of seabirds on Newfoundland's coasts—colonies that largely depend on capelin for their survival. Still other marine zoologists suspect that the mass destruction of baitfishes in general is seriously affecting the vitality of the remaining grey, harbour, and hood seal stocks together with several kinds of whales, all of which have been savagely depleted by man in recent years.

A few months ago, I asked a disaffected Fisheries biologist (of which there seems to be a growing number) what he thought about the industry practice of exhausting not only the populations of commercial fishes, but their feed stocks as well. Some of what he had to say in reply is unprintable, but the gist can be summed up in these words.

"Listen! For those bastards, there's no tomorrow. Or if there is, they'll have moved their money into something else, like maybe processing Third World human populations to make dog food. No matter what anyone in the industry, or in the Department tells you—there's just one thing on everybody's mind: make money... make as much as you can before the whole damn bottom drops out of ocean fisheries.... The seas are dying, as if you didn't know."

NOTES

1. The rationalization for fish meal production defies all logic. As animal food, about 100 pounds, live weight, of fish is required to produce one pound of beef. Two hundred pounds of fish meal used as fertilizer produces no more than three pounds of vegetable protein.

In turning from the depleted groundfish to the baitfish, we are, in effect, eating our way down the food chain. In fact, commercial harvesting of krill is now well underway, so far in quantities that are presumed to be insignificant. Will plankton be next?

The depletion of the North Atlantic fisheries leads us directly to the question of species extinctions and loss of global biodiversity. As usual, a glance back through history helps to put matters in perspective. Biologists now realize that at many times in the history of life on earth, tremendous spasms or waves of extinctions have ravaged life on the planet. Five of these massacres were so sweeping as to destroy a significant fraction of life on Earth and totally realign the future direction of evolution. The sudden end of the so-called Mesozoic era about 65 million years ago, the era of the dinosaurs, was not even the most dramatic mass extinction (that being a cataclysm of unknown provenance that occurred at the end of the Permian era 245 million years ago). Many, although perhaps not all, of these mass extinctions are associated with major meteor impacts, but other factors are apparently involved as well. (For up-to-date and very thorough coverage of recent findings about the causes of mass extinctions, see Ward 1994).

It is presently the sober opinion of many biologists that this world is currently experiencing one of the major mass extinctions in geological history—a wave of extinctions entirely, or almost entirely, due to one agent: *H. sapiens.* (See Ward 1994, Kaufman and Mallory [eds.] 1986, and especially Wilson 1992 for detailed arguments and figures in support of this view.) The ravaging of marine life described by Mowat is only a small part, though a very telling part, of the whole story. Ecologist Les Kaufman provides a thoughtful review.

WHY THE ARK IS SINKING

Les Kaufman

Human beings are the most adaptable creatures that have ever lived on Earth. Reason and insight, the chief human talents, have given us the power to forge a world increasingly fit for our own comfort. We feed voraciously on all other manner of life, from whale to lily. We have no significant predators save a diminishing roster of infectious diseases. Of course, there is also the odd shark, crocodile, or lion, but they are disappearing even faster than the diseases. We carve the planet's surface into fields and streets, shopping malls and parking lots, with little regard to what was there before, because what we replace it with offers a more immediate, short-term benefit. Never before in Earth's history has such an abundant, aggressive, industrious omnivore at the peak of the energy pyramid comprised such a large portion of the living biomass. The prognosis is clear for the five to ten million other kinds of living things that share the Earth. They are in big trouble.

The world is host to two hundred nations and what amounts to five billion rulers. The strain of catering to so many separate interests is manifest in the flow of political, economic, and social crises. All living things are affected by these crises, but humanity as a species has thus far survived them and prospered. The bounds of human habitability include nearly the whole globe, whereas the entire liveable universe of other species can vanish overnight as one river is dammed or one hillside is laid bare. As we eliminate each species that stands in our way today, we lose any hope of having it back tomorrow. Life on the planet advances irreversibly, like a ratchet, toward greater impoverishment.

The ratchet clicks faster each day. Between the years 1600 and 1900, species of mammals and birds vanished at the rate of approximately one every four years. During the twentieth century, mammals and birds have disappeared at the average rate of about one species per year. The fossil record is too poor to provide an accurate estimate of historical extinction rates for other organisms that do not preserve as well as vertebrates, but scientists can make a reasonable guess. In 1974 the extinction rate for all species was estimated to be approximately 100 per year.[1] Because mammals and birds combined comprise less than half of one percent of all living species, this estimate is probably conservative. Norman Myers projected that by the end of this century, species will be vanishing at the rate of 100 per day, due largely to the destruction of tropical rain forests.[2] On a human time scale, these rates may seem slow. On a geological time scale, however, the wheel is spinning at a blurring rate, and the disappearance of species amounts to a virtually instantaneous mass extinction.

The enormous variety of life is regarded by many as a sort of sideshow: fascinating, but dispensable, should it stand as an obstacle to human interests. This shortsighted view is finally beginning to exact its toll. Animals and plants that have been of great value to humans are disappearing forever. A piece of America's soul died along with the passenger pigeon, plains buffalo, and American chestnut. We are now quickly losing the whales, elephants, tigers, lions, bears, apes, and rhinoceroses. Imagine a world in which our own children no longer know the fantastic wealth of creatures we associate with the word "zoo." Imagine summertime with fewer birds than during the winter. The brilliant orioles, tanagers, warblers, and wading birds will be gone because their tropical wintering grounds will no longer exist. But the extinction of any one species is of only passing significance to human society. It is the longer-term cumulative effects that should have people worried.

The long-term effects of mass extinction on human society fall along four basic lines: moral, aesthetic, economic, and ecological.[3] In each of these can be found strong arguments for arresting activities that cause extinctions, but in each case the long-term benefits of species conservation must be weighed against extremely tempting short-term gains.

One consequence of perpetrating a mass extinction is that at least some of us are going to have trouble with our consciences. In human terms, other forms of life have a right to exist, and thus to extinguish them is akin to genocide. Although morals have hardly eliminated regular attempts at human genocide, by a strange twist of fate moral persuasion has often worked against practices that threaten critical habitats and charismatic species, such as songbirds and whales. But the bans of whaling and DDT resulted from conflicts between wildlife and profits. When the conflict is between wildlife and human life, the difference between right and wrong is no longer so clear. Indonesian farmers have been moved en masse into the rain forest as part of a national resettlement plan to ease population pressure. As a result they have been repeatedly harassed by displaced elephants who stomp on the settlers' crops and sit on their houses.[4] Despite valiant attempts to relocate the elephants, there is little assurance that there will always be room in Southeast Asia for both its people and its magnificent wildlife, of which elephants, tigers, and rhinoceroses are only the most conspicuous elements.

A second consequence of mass extinction is that our children might hate us for the world we took away from them. Natural diversity is critical to us aesthetically, helping to satisfy an important human need for sensory and intellectual stimulation. Edward O. Wilson calls this hunger for other life biophilia, a basic part of the human psyche.[5] The diversity of life is also the master key to the science of life—as we extinguish species, we snuff out countless lines of fruitful inquiry. But if diversity is a basic need, many people are out of touch with it. Squalid, dirty, lifeless cities make it difficult for us to feel closeness to nature. We do not foster the sense that biological diversity is a thing of value. And yet, it is in this environment that most of humanity may be finding itself in the future. In the noisy cities the aesthetic arguments for saving species fall on deaf ears.

The extinction will have economic impacts of fantastic proportions but of a sort that only a broker in futures can appreciate. This is most apparent in tropical rain forests. The sustainable yield from a rain forest through lumbering or shifting agriculture is low, so tropical industries have tended toward a "get in, get out" modus operandi. Although a few interests have gotten rich this way, new technologies have made this way of doing business increasingly stupid and wasteful. The major commodity in the world's rain forests lies dormant and largely unrecognized: It is information. Sequestered in the countless plants and insects of the forest is a vast chemical arsenal. To the organisms these chemicals are defensive and offensive weapons, but to people they offer medicines and chemical conveniences of great potential. The importance of this chemical warehouse lies not only in the substances themselves but also in the fact that for each there already exists a genetically coded blueprint. It is such a blueprint, extracted and placed in bacteria or yeast cells, that can allow us to produce huge quantities of any desired substance. The genes of rain forest organisms also contain the secrets needed to create animals and crop plants that can live effectively under moist tropical conditions. Just as the synthetic chemical industry has made oil too precious a resource to lavish on Sunday drivers, so has biotechnology made natural diversity too valuable to let it be wasted on narrow-minded, one-shot business ventures. This is one resource that can be protected only by keeping it absolutely intact.

The fourth argument for preserving biological diversity is the simplest: Our lives depend on it. We are part of a common fabric of life. Our survival is dependent on the integrity of this fabric, for the loss of a few critical threads could lead to a quick unraveling of the whole. We know that there have been previous mass extinctions, through which some life survived. As for our own chances of surviving this mass extinction, there can be no promises. If the Grim Reaper plays any favorites at all, then it would seem to be a special fondness for striking down dominant organisms in their prime. Humans are now the dominant creatures, at least in terms of their influence. So, lest history bear false witness and barring some serious conservation efforts on our part, this mass extinction could well be the last one that we will ever know about.

How Bad Is This Extinction?

One of the principal obstacles facing conservationists is a lack of public awareness of the magnitude of the extinction taking place today. By the most pessimistic accounts, the current mass extinction is more severe than the one that wiped out the dinosaurs 65 million years ago. More optimistic accounts note that we do not know how bad the problem really is because there are no comprehensive, up-to-date data on extinction rates, especially on organisms yet to be discovered. Some have gone so far as to interpret the lack of data to mean that the problem has been greatly blown out of proportion, but most scientists would reject this "know-nothing" position.

Obviously if there is to be substantive movement on this issue, a great many people have to be convinced that there is a problem. The lack of adequate data is a reality. But if we wait until there are empirical data to back our pleas, we will clearly have waited too long—the mass extinction will already be far advanced. Thus the crucial premise that we are presently experiencing a period of mass extinction must rest on inference. How solid is this inference? How strong are its supporting arguments?

Three major claims are at issue: that we are experiencing a mass extinction, that this extinction is caused by humans, and that this extinction demands immediate attention as one of the most serious problems facing the world today.

There is no doubt that a mass extinction is occurring, even though most of the evidence is inferential rather than direct. Even the historical extinction rate of one bird or mammal species per year since 1900 qualifies this as a mass extinction. The original discussions of this issue in the popular literature are those of Vinzenz Ziswiler and David Ehrenfeld, followed by the more sensational books of Norman Myers and of Paul and Anne Ehrlich.[6] It is frequently noted that news of the extinction crisis has been brought to us by the same people who brought us the population crisis (now seemingly dormant) and the nuclear winter (a hypothesis which, if ever tested, will render this book superfluous). To some people, these Cassandras, as they call themselves, are professional doomsayers, intellectual terrorists who should not be encouraged, supported, or believed. What seems to have escaped such doubters, however, is that the whole point of being a doomsayer is to agitate the world into proving you wrong or into doing something about it if you are right.

In any event, when it comes to the extinction issue, Myers and the Ehrlichs did more than review historical extinction rates. They projected such rates through the year 2000 and concluded that they would climb to 40,000 species per year—40 million times faster than the rate of extinction of the dinosaurs. This projection is based largely on certain assumptions about the rate at which tropical rain forest is being destroyed around the world, as it is in the rain forest that much of the world's diversity is sequestered.[7] According to one critic, Rodger Sedjo, a forestry economist with Resources for the Future, Myers's calculations were based on early estimates of deforestation rates that were highly inflated.[8] More recent data suggest that actual rates are less than half those first projected.[9] Furthermore, Sedjo disagrees with Myers's assumptions that the number of species lost is necessarily directly proportional to the area of rain forest destroyed per year and that a large proportion of what is being destroyed is primary rain forest.[10] In a popular article, John Tierney interpreted Sedjo's results to mean that the entire mass extinction problem has been trumped up.[11] But the new data on tropical forestation do nothing to alter the bleak scenario because a factor-of-two change in projected rates of extinction means nothing when orders of magnitude are at issue. Moreover, much of the primary rain forest land now being cut will not regenerate as rain forest.

Worse still, the relation of species lost to area of habitat destroyed could actually be higher, not lower, than a one-to-one ratio because many of the world's high-diversity habitats have been carved into little pockets where unique species are concentrated. Foose's hairy rhinoceros is limited to a tiny peninsula in the southwest corner of Java. The golden lion tamarin holds court in a narrow strip of remnant coastal rain forest in Brazil. The rain forest of northern Australia, with many endemic forms, has been reduced to a strand of small parks strung along the top of a mountain range and a few lowland areas cut up by land speculators.

A body of ecological theory, called island biogeography, predicts that extinction rates increase disproportionately when continuous habitats are transformed into archipelagoes of small biological islands.[12] Thomas Lovejoy and his associates are now examining the magnitude of this effect in the Amazon by comparing the ability of variously sized remnant patches of Amazonian rain forest to maintain their original flora and fauna.[13] It is already apparent that some of the most important biological preserves in the world are too small and too highly disturbed to hang on to their treasures: Parched Everglades and poached African game parks come immediately to mind. Some of the most interesting faunas developed their diversity within small areas that are now highly vulnerable. All such cases are, like the famous Galápagos Islands, priceless evolutionary laboratories. One example is the Hawaiian fauna, whose demise is discussed by Willams and Nowak. Lakes Tanganyika, Malawi, and Victoria in East Africa, Lake Lanao in the Philippines, Lake Baikal in Russia, and Lake Titicaca in the Peruvian Andes have all mothered astounding radiations of freshwater life, wild profusions of evolution that make the Galápagos finches look pale. All are either severely threatened or already disrupted.

The Ehrlichs may well have overstated their case. Perhaps Myers stretched his imagination a bit, or his calculator. But the only allowable interpretation of the data now at hand is that the world is indeed experiencing a mass extinction easily on a par with those of the geological past.

Mass extinction is not the sort of event we would expect to slip by unnoticed, but this one seems to be doing just that. On our own time scale, the extinctions occurring today seem scattered over many years and many miles. They do not seem so bad. Partly, however, people may be denying facts because they do not want or know how to cope with them.

Stephen Jay Gould, of Harvard University, has made a career out of demonstrating the broad chasms between what people want to believe and the truth. He maintains that people most want to see the world in terms of slow, gradual changes, whereas most of the characteristics of the world have been shaped by short-lived events that are, in retrospect, catastrophic. Gould first faced this kind of opposition when he questioned a traditional view that evolution takes place gradually and continuously, with species gracefully branching from the mother stem, as in a willow tree. With his associate Niles Eldredge, Gould countered that most evolution takes place during the geologically brief, tumultuous birth of a species.[14] Once born, a species remains relatively constant in character until it goes extinct. This notion of evolution by "punctuated equilibrium" has gained wide acceptance but only after a struggle. In a recent speech Gould postulated that the same facet of human nature that inspired people to reject the notion that species can evolve quickly and then virtually cease evolving, now has them denying that species can disappear even more quickly than they evolve, never to return.[15] The notion is, after all, rather disturbing. If other species can disappear so quickly, regardless of their strengths and weaknesses, so can we.

NOTES

1. See the article "Scientists talk of the need for conservation and an ethic of biotic diversity to slow species extinction," *Science* 184 (1974), 646–647.
2. Norman Myers, *The Sinking Ark: A New Look at the Problem of Disappearing Species* (Oxford and New York: Pergamon Press, 1979).
3. See Paul Ehrlich and Anne Ehrlich, *Extinction: The Causes and Consequences of the Disappearance of Species* (New York: Random House, 1981).
4. Catherine Caufield, *In the Rainforest* (New York: Knopf, 1985), 202.
5. Edward O. Wilson, *Biophilia* (Cambridge, Massachusetts: Harvard University Press, 1984).
6. Myers, *The Sinking Ark*; Ehrlich and Ehrlich, *Extinction*; David Ehrenfeld, *Biological Conservation* (New York: Holt, Rinehart, and Winston, 1970); Vinzenz Ziswiler, *Extinct and Vanishing Animals: A Biology of Extinction and Survival*, F. Bunnell and P. Bunnell, trans. (New York: Springer Verlag, 1967).
7. As a general rule, species richness goes up and abundance of any one species down as one approaches the equator. This is not true in all habitats: Much of the latitudinal diversity gradient owes to the stupendous species richness of two kinds of communities: rain forests and coral reefs. For good comparative discussions of diversity in temperate and tropical forests, see Caufield, *In the Rainforest*, and Rodger D. Stone, *Dreams of Amazonia* (New York: Viking Penguin, 1985).
8. Rodger A. Sedjo and M. Clawson, "How serious is tropical deforestation?" *Journal of Forestry* 81(12) (1983), 792–794.
9. Food and Agriculture Organization, Forestry Paper 30, Rome.
10. Rodger A. Sedjo, personal communication.
11. John Tierney, "Lonesome George of the Galápagos," *Science 85* 6(5) (June 1985), 50–61.
12. Robert MacArthur and Edward O. Wilson, *The Theory of Island Biogeography* (Princeton, New Jersey: Princeton University Press, 1967).

13. Thomas E. Lovejoy, R.O. Bierregaard, J.M. Rankin, and H.O.R. Schubart, "Ecological dynamics of forest fragments," in *Tropical Rain Forest Ecology and Management*, S.L. Sutton et al., eds. (Oxford: Blackwell Scientific Publications, 1983); T.E. Lovejoy and David C. Oren, "Minimum critical size of ecosystems" (Lansing, Michigan: American Institute of Biological Sciences, Michigan State University, 1977).
14. Niles Eldredge and Steven J. Gould, "Punctuated equilibria: An alternative to phyletic gradualism," in *Models in Paleobiology*, T.J.M. Schopf, ed. (San Francisco: Freeman, Cooper, 1972).
15. Gould presented this speech before the 1985 Northeast Regional meeting of the American Association of Zoological Parks and Aquaria, hosted by the New England Aquarium.

Edward O. Wilson now presents us with a controversial historical perspective on species extinctions. In a nutshell, Wilson's claim is this:

> The extinction of large mammals and flightless birds coincided closely with the arrival of humans in North America, Madagascar, and New Zealand, and less decisively earlier in Australia. In Africa, where humans and animals evolved together for millions of years, the damage was less severe. (From Wilson 1992, p. 252)

This claim can be upsetting for those who would prefer to believe that aboriginal peoples are uniquely attuned to their environments. If Wilson's claim is correct, then one could say that while many aboriginals eventually attained a remarkable degree of attunement to their natural environments as they settled and adapted to them, they were at first quite as destructive in their own way as modern industrial humans. As the reader will see, however, Wilson's charge is debatable—especially with regard to the role of North American Paleo-Indians (the so-called Clovis peoples) in the megafaunal extinctions at the end of the Pleistocene, where the fact of massive climate change and the relative paucity of paleontological evidence complicate the picture.

HUNTERS' BLITZKRIEG

Edward O. Wilson

Hidden among the western Andean foothills of Ecuador, a few kilometers from Rio Palenque, there is a small ridge called Centinela. Its name deserves to be synonymous with the silent hemorrhaging of biological diversity. When the forest on the ridge was cut a decade ago, a large number of rare species were extinguished. They went just like that, from full healthy populations to nothing, in a few months. Around the world such anonymous extinctions—call them "centinelan extinctions"—are occurring, not open wounds for all to see and rush to stanch but unfelt internal events, leakages from vital tissue out of sight.

The revelation of Centinela and a growing list of other such places is that the extinction of species has been much worse than even field biologists, myself included, previously understood. Any number of rare local species are disappearing just beyond the edge of our attention. They enter oblivion like the dead of Gray's *Elegy*, leaving at most a name, a fading echo in a far corner of the world, their genius unused.

Extinction has been much greater even among larger, more conspicuous organisms than generally recognized. During the past ten years, scientists working on fossil birds, especially Storrs Olson, Helen James, and David Steadman, have uncovered evidence of massive destruction of Pacific Island landbirds by the first human colonists centuries before the coming of Europeans. The scientists obtain their data by excavating fossil and subfossil bones wherever the dead birds dropped or were thrown, in dunes, limestone sinkholes, lava tubes, crater lake beds, and archaeological middens. On each of the islands the deposits were mostly laid down from 8,000 years ago up to nearly the present, bracketing the arrival of the Polynesians. They leave little room for doubt that in the outer Pacific in particular, from Tonga in the west to Hawaii in the east, the Polynesians extinguished at least half of the endemic species found upon their arrival.

This vast stretch of Pacific islands was colonized by the Lapita people, ancestors of the modern Polynesian race. They emigrated from their homeland somewhere in the fringing islands of Melanesia or Southeast Asia and spread steadily eastward from archipelago to archipelago. With great daring and probably heavy mortality, they traveled in single outrigger or double canoes across hundreds of kilometers of water. Around 3,000 years ago they settled Fiji, Tonga, and Samoa. Stepping from island to island they finally reached Hawaii, with Easter the most remote of the habitable Pacific islands, as recently as A.D. 300.

The colonists subsisted on crops and domestic animals carried in their boats but also, especially in the early days of settlement, whatever edible animals they encountered. They ate fish, turtles, and a profusion of bird species that had never seen a large predator and were easily caught, including doves, pigeons, crakes, rails, starlings, and others whose remains are only now coming to light. Many of the species were endemics, found only on the islands discovered by the Lapita. The voyagers ate their way through the Polynesian fauna. On Eua, in present-day Tonga, twenty-five species lived in the forests when the colonists arrived around 1000 B.C., but only eight survive today. Nearly every island across the Pacific was home to several endemic species of flightless rails before the Polynesian occupation. Today populations survive only on New Zealand and on Henderson, an uninhabited coral island 190 kilometers northeast of Pitcairn. It used to be thought that Henderson was one of the few virgin habitable islands of any size left in the world, never occupied by human beings. But recently discovered artifacts reveal that Polynesians colonized Henderson, then abandoned it, probably because they consumed the birds to less than sustainable levels. On this and other small islands lacking arable soil, birds were the most readily available source of protein. The colonists drove the populations down, erasing some species in the process, then either starved or sailed on.

Hawaii, last of the Edens of Polynesia, sustained the greatest damage measured by lost evolutionary products. When European settlers arrived after Captain Cook's visit in 1778, there were approximately fifty native species of landbirds. In the following two centuries, one third disappeared. Now we know from bone deposits that another thirty-five species identified with certainty, and very likely twenty other species less well documented, had already been extinguished by the native Hawaiians. Among those identified to date are an eagle similar to the American bald eagle, a flightless ibis, and a strange parliament of owls with short wings and extremely long legs. Most remarkable of all were bizarre flightless forms evolved from ducks but possessing tiny wings, massive legs, and bills resembling the beaks of tortoises. Helen James and Storrs Olson record that

> although they were terrestrial and herbivorous, like geese, we now know from the presence of a duck-like syringeal bulla that these strange birds were derived either from shelducks (Tadornini), or more likely from dabbling ducks (Anatini), quite possibly from the genus *Anas*. They may have had an ecological role similar to that of the large tortoises of the Galápagos and islands of the western Indian Ocean. Because we now recognize three genera and four species of these birds, and because they are neither phyletically geese nor functionally ducks, we have coined a new word, *moa-nalo*, as a more convenient general term for all such flightless, goose-like ducks of the Hawaiian islands.

The surviving native Hawaiian birds are for the most part inconspicuous relicts, small, elusive species restricted to the remnant mountain forests. They are a faint shadow of the eagles, ibises, and moa-nalos that greeted the Polynesian colonists as the Byzantine empire was born and Mayan civilization reached its zenith.

Centinelan extinctions also occurred on other continents and islands as human populations spread outward from Africa and Eurasia. Mankind soon disposed of the large, the slow, and the tasty. In North America 12,000 years ago, just before Paleo-Indian hunter-gatherers came from Siberia across the Bering Strait, the land teemed with large mammals far more diverse than those in any part of the modern world, including Africa. Twelve millennia back may seem like the Age of Dinosaurs, but it was just yesterday by geological standards. Humanity was stirring then, some eight million people alive and many seeking new land. The manufacture of hooks and harpoons for fishing was widespread, along with the cultivation of wild grains and the domestication of dogs. The construction of the first towns, in the Fertile Crescent, lay only a thousand years in the future.

In western North America, just behind the retreating glacial front, the grasslands and copses were an American Serengeti. The vegetation and insects were similar to those alive in the west today—you could have picked the same wildflowers and netted the same butterflies—but the big mammals and birds were spectacularly different. From one spot, say on the edge of riverine forest looking across open terrain, you could have seen herds of horses (the extinct, pre-Spanish kind), long-horned bison, camels, antelopes of several species, and mammoths. There would be glimpses of sabertooth cats, possibly working together in lionish prides, giant dire wolves, and tapirs. Around a dead horse might be gathered the representatives of a full adaptive radiation of scavenging birds: condors, huge condor-like teratorns, carrion storks, eagles, hawks, and vultures, dodging and threatening one another (we know from the species that survived), the smaller birds snatching pieces of meat and waiting for the body to be whittled down enough to be abandoned by their giant competitors.

Some 73 percent of the large mammal genera that lived in the late Pleistocene are extinct. (In South America the number is 80 percent.) A comparable number of genera of the largest birds are also extinct. The collapse of diversity occurred about the same time that the first Paleo-Indian hunters entered the New World, 12,000 to 11,000 years ago, and then spread southward at an average rate of 16 kilometers a year. It was not a casual, up-and-down event. Mammoths had flourished for two million years to that time and were represented at the end by three species—the Columbian, imperial, and woolly. Within a thousand years all were gone. The ground sloths, another ancient race, vanished almost simultaneously. The last known surviving population, foraging out of caves at the western end of the Grand Canyon, disappeared about 10,000 years ago.

If this were a trial, the Paleo-Indians could be convicted on circumstantial evidence alone, since the coincidence in time is so exact. There is also a strong motive: food. The remains of mammoths, bison, and other large mammals exist in association with human bones, charcoal from fires, and stone weapons of the Clovis culture. These earliest Americans were skilled big-game hunters, and they encountered animals totally unprepared by evolutionary experience for predators of this kind. The birds that became extinct were also those most vulnerable to human hunters. They included eagles and a flightless duck. Still other victims were innocent bystanders: condors, teratorns, and vultures dependent on the newly devastated populations of heavy-bodied mammals.

In defense of the Paleo-Indians, their counsel might argue the existence of another culprit. The end of the Pleistocene was a time not only of human invasion of the New World, but also of climatic warming. As the continental glacier retreated across Canada, forests and grasslands shifted rapidly northward. Changes of this magnitude must have exerted a profound effect on the life and death of local populations. Between 1870 and 1970, by way of comparison, Iceland warmed an average 2°C in the winter and somewhat less in the spring and summer. Two Arctic bird species, the long-tailed duck and the lesser auk, declined to near extinction. At the same time, lapwings, tufted ducks, and several other southern species established themselves on the island and began to breed. There are hints of similar responses during the great Pleistocene decline. Mastodons, for example, were apparently specialized for life in coniferous forests. As this belt of vegetation migrated northward, the proboscideans moved with it. In time they became concentrated along the spruce forest zone in the northeast, then disappeared. Their extinction might have stemmed not only from overkill by hunters but also from fragmentation and reduction of the populations forced by a shrinking habitat.

Let the defense now speak even more forcefully: for tens of millions of years before the coming of man, mammal genera were born and died in large numbers, with the extinction of some accompanied by the origin of others to create a rough long-term balance. The changes were accompanied by climatic shifts much like those in evidence 11,000 years ago, and perhaps they were driven by them. During the last 10 million years, David Webb has pointed out, six major extinction episodes leveled the land mammals of North America. Among them the terminating event of the Pleistocene (the Rancholabrean, named after Rancho La Brea, in California) was not the most catastrophic. The greatest, according to available records,

> was the late Hemphillian (nearly five million years ago) when more than sixty genera of land mammals (of which thirty-five were large, weighing more than 5 kg) disappeared from this continent. The late Rancholabrean extinction pulse (about 10,000 years ago) was the next greatest; over forty genera became extinct, of which nearly all were large mammals. . . . Some evidence shows that these extinction

episodes were correlated with terminations of glacial cycles, when climatic extremes and instability are thought to have reached their maxima. [David Webb as quoted in Martin and Klein 1984.]

In at least two of the great extinction spasms, the large browsing mammals were destroyed as the climate deteriorated and the broad continental savannas gave way to steppes. At the end of the Hemphillian, even grazing mammals such as horses, rhinos, and pronghorns precipitously declined.

It may seem that the debate between experts who favor overkill by humans and those who favor climatic change resembles a replay, in a different theater, of the debate over the end of the Age of Dinosaurs. The Paleo-Indians have replaced the giant meteorite in this new drama. Circumstantial evidence is countered by other circumstantial evidence, while both sides search for a smoking gun. The dispute is the product of neither ideology nor clashing personalities. It is the way science at its best is done.

That said, I will lay aside impartiality. I think the overkill theorists have the more convincing argument for what happened in America 10,000 years ago. It seems likely that the Clovis people spread through the New World and demolished most of the large mammals during a hunters' blitzkrieg spanning several centuries. Some of the doomed species hung on here and there for as long as 2,000 years, but the effect was the same: swift destruction, on the scale of evolution that measures normal lifespans of genera and species in millions of years.

There is an additional reason for accepting this verdict provisionally. Paul Martin, who revived the idea in the mid-1960s (a similar proposal had been made a century earlier for the Pleistocene mammals of Europe), called attention to this important circumstance: when human colonists arrived, not only in America but also in New Zealand, Madagascar, and Australia, and whether climate was changing or not, a large part of the megafauna—large mammals, birds, and reptiles—disappeared soon afterward. This collateral evidence has been pieced together by researchers of various persuasions over many years, and it points away from climate and toward people.

Before the coming of man around A.D. 1000, New Zealand was home to moas, large flightless birds unique to the islands. These creatures had ellipsoidal bodies, massive legs, and long necks topped by tiny heads. The first Maoris, arriving from their Polynesian homeland to the north, found about thirteen species ranging in size from that of large turkeys to giants weighing 230 kilograms or more, the latter among the largest birds ever evolved. There had in fact been a moa radiation, filling many niches. It was of the kind normally occupied by medium-sized and large mammals, of which there were Indian hunters. How, Diamond pressed, did Australia's reptiles manage to survive the prehistoric human invasions better, as did the smaller mammals and birds? And, finally, why did such large forms as the marsupial wolf and giant kangaroos disappear about the same time from both Australia's arid interior and rain forests, as well as from nearby New Guinea's wet mountain forests?

> Quaternary extinctions were selective in space and time because they appear to have occurred at those places and times where naive animals first encountered humans. It is further argued that they were selective in taxa and in victim size because human hunters concentrate on some species (e.g., large mammals and flightless birds) while ignoring other species (e.g., small rodents). It is argued that Quaternary extinctions befell species in all habitats because humans hunt in all habitats, and human hunters help no species except as an incidental consequence of habitat changes and of removing other species.

"Human hunters help no species." That is a general truth and the key to the whole melancholy situation. As the human wave rolled over the last of the virgin lands like a smothering blanket, Paleo-Indians throughout America, Polynesians across the Pacific, Indonesians into Madagascar, Dutch sailors ashore on Mauritius (to meet and extirpate the dodo), they were constrained by neither knowledge of endemicity nor any ethic of conservation. For them the world must have seemed to stretch forever beyond the horizon. If fruit pigeons and giant tortoises disappear from this island, they will surely be found on the next one. What counts is food today, a healthy family, and tribute for the chief, victory celebrations, rites of passage, feasts. As the Mexican truck driver said who shot one of the last two imperial woodpeckers, largest of all the world's woodpeckers, "It was a great piece of meat."

REFERENCES

Diamond, Jared. 1989. *Journal of Archeological Science* 16, 167–175.
Dye, Tom, and Steadman, D.W. 1990. *American Scientist* 78, 207–215.
Martin, Paul S., and Klein, Richard G. (eds.). 1984. *Quaternary Extinctions: A Prehistoric Revolution*. Tucson: University of Arizona Press.
Olson, Storrs L., and James, Helen F. 1991. *Ornithological Monographs* 45, 1–88; 46, 1–88.
Plimpton, George. 1977. "Un gran pedazo de carne," *Audobon Magazine* 79, 10–25.
Steadman, David W. 1989. *Journal of Archeological Science* 16, 177–205.

Roughly speaking, humans bring about the demise of other life by three means: habitat disruption (when our roads, farms, and buildings supplant forest, field, and marsh); pollution; and what might be loosely described as "overharvesting" or "overhunting." Sometimes excessive predation is motivated by short-sighted commercial aims (see Freedman on the demise of the great auk, below, for instance), and sometimes we kill for no other reason than sheer perverse delight in cruelty. (For painful documentation of this fact, see Mowat 1972.) Often our predation stems simply from the necessity of seeking basic subsistence, even though it all too often ironically undercuts the foundations of that very subsistence. And as our population grows, the pressure we exert on diminishing environmental resources will increase inexorably. Paleontologist Peter Ward concludes a long discussion of the causes and significance of extinctions past and present with a revealing personal confession that highlights the stark conflict of priorities we all face.

A PARENT'S NIGHTMARE

Peter Ward

I have a son. He is tall and gangly, with a face speckled by a galaxy of freckles. He is mischievous and playful, willful and happy, the normal mix of boyish hopes, dreams, and emotions. He is precious to me beyond belief.

I keep having this vision, of living with him in the Amazon rain forest, where we exist in a small hovel no different from that inhabited by a fifth of humanity. And in this dream, my son is hungry. Behind our house sits one last patch of forest, and in that pristine copse is the nest of a beautiful bird, the last nest, it so happens, of that species. This vision is a nightmare to me, because even knowing that these birds are the last of their race, I don't have the slightest doubt what my actions would be: To feed my son, to keep him alive, I would do whatever I had to do, including destroying the last of another species.

Anyone who thinks he or she might do otherwise is probably not a parent. There are a great number of parents currently on the earth, and many more on the way.

As a final footnote we present Bill Freedman's short, sad, and ironic story of the great auk—a formerly abundant species driven into extinction purely and simply by overexploitation. For more detail on the unfortunate auk, see the chapter entitled "Spearbill" in Mowat (1984).

Is there an environmental crisis? For the great auk, and many other forms of life unlucky enough to have proven either especially useful or nutritious to humans, or to have simply gotten in the way, the environmental crisis was over a long time ago—for the auk specifically, on June 4, 1844.

"WHAT DO YOU MEAN THE GREAT AUK'S EXTINCT?"

Bill Freedman

The first well-described anthropogenic extinction of an animal whose range was at least partly North American was that of a seabird, the great auk (*Pinguinus impennis*). . . . In memoriam to this unfortunate species, the journal of the American Ornithological Union has been named "The Auk." The great auk was commonly known to mariners as the original "pennegoin," although it is a member of the Alcidae, and not related to the superficially similar southern hemisphere penguin family, Spheniscidae.

Originally, the great auk had an amphi-Atlantic distribution. It bred on a few Northern Atlantic islands off eastern Newfoundland, in the Gulf of St. Lawrence, around Iceland, and north of Scotland. Because the great auk bred on only a few islands, it was vulnerable to extirpation by uncontrolled hunting. Although the great auk was initially abundant on its breeding islands, it was easy to catch or club because it was flightless, and therefore it could be killed in large numbers.

For many centuries, the great auk had been exploited by aboriginal Newfoundlanders and European fishermen as a source of fresh meat, eggs, and oil. However, when its feathers became a valuable commodity for the stuffing of mattresses in the mid-1700s, a systematic and relentless exploitation began that quickly caused the extinction of the species. A harvesting and processing operation was described in 1785 at one of the largest breeding colonies of the great auk and other alcids, on Funk Island off eastern Newfoundland (from Nettleship and Evans 1986): "It has been customary of late years, for several crews of men to live all summer on that island, for the sole purpose of killing birds for the sake of their feathers, the destruction of which they have made is incredible. If a stop is not soon put to that practice, the whole breed will be diminished to almost nothing, particularly the penguins." The slaughter of great auks and other seabirds on Funk Island was so great in the late 1700s that much of the soil that presently occurs there has been formed from their carcasses. . . . About 85 years after the extirpation of the great auk from Funk Island, the common puffin . . . began to breed there. This seabird requires soil that is sufficiently deep for the excavation of a nesting burrow. On Funk Island, the auk-derived soil was apparently suitable, and today puffins can sometimes be observed carrying bones of the extinct great auk out of their excavations.

The great auk became extinct on Funk Island in the early 1800s. The last known individuals of this species were killed on June 4, 1844, on the island of Eldey Rock, by three Icelanders who were searching for specimens for a bird "collector" in Reykjavik. They killed the only two adult birds they saw, and smashed the only egg they found, because it had been cracked and therefore was not a good specimen. They were reputed to have said, "What do you mean the great auk's extinct? We just killed two of them!"

REFERENCES

Nettleship, D.N., and Evans, P.G.H. 1986. "Distribution and Status of the Atlantic Alcidae." In *The Atlantic Alcidae* (D.N. Nettleship and T. R. Birkhead, eds.), pp. 54–154. New York: Academic Press.

FURTHER READING

See Mowat (1984) and Will (1992) for further perspective on the fisheries collapse. There is a huge literature on species extinctions and loss of biodiversity. See some of the sources cited by Kaufman. Regenstein's *Politics of Extinction* (1975) is basic reading in this field. Moorehead (1959) is a sensitive exploration of the dynamics that seem to lead almost inevitably to the wipeout of wildlife by humans. Wilson (1992) is more recent, and Shiva (1993) provides a valuable alternative perspective. On threatened Canadian species, see Burnett et al. (1989).

QUESTIONS TO CONSIDER

1. Given the disastrous situation of the fishery as it now stands, where would you assign priorities for the Canadian government? Should the inshore communities be written off as a lost cause, or could they be rehabilitated?
2. Do you think that there may be too much of a tendency to blame "foreign" fishermen for the overfishing of the Grand Banks?
3. Will (1992) and many others have argued that the Canadian inshore fishery could be "sustainable" if it were not for the vast quantities of fish being taken by draggers, and the destruction done by those draggers when they do their work. What does it mean to say that a fishery could be sustainable, given that any human predation whatsoever must impose some stress upon an ecosystem?
4. Freedman notes that the *coup de grâce* was administered to the highly vulnerable great auk by a period of intense commercial exploitation in the late eighteenth century. Presumably the industry that processed auk down employed many persons at that time. Suppose that someone in the auk industry argued that there should be no restrictions on the auk "harvest" because jobs would be lost. How might you, with the benefit of your historical perspective, answer this statement?
5. Kaufman says, "If the Grim Reaper plays any favorites at all, then it would seem to be a special fondness for striking down dominant organisms in their prime." What does it mean to say that a species is dominant? Are we humans really dominant in this sense?
6. Which of Kaufman's arguments for preserving biodiversity seems most compelling? Can you think of others? Are there any arguments for *not* worrying about the loss of biodiversity caused by human activities?

CHAPTER THREE

THE HUMAN CRISIS: WAR, DISEASE, POVERTY, AND OVERPOPULATION

". . . behold a pale horse; and his name that sat on him was Death . . ."
—REVELATION 6:8

Are we humans, as Les Kaufman suggests, within sight of "the last extinction"—our own? Apocalyptic visions are a common feature of many eras, cultures, and religious traditions. For those of us in Canada who grew up in the post–Second World War "baby boom" generation of the 1950s and 1960s, the cloud that loomed over all our dreams was mushroom-shaped. I well remember nuclear-attack drills in my Grade 6 class in 1961. Our school happened to be a few kilometres west of Toronto (presumably Ground Zero), with our classroom windows facing toward the city. Our teacher told us that if the alert came (and we knew that we would have no more than ten or fifteen minutes' warning), we should huddle under the windows so as not to be shredded by flying glass when the shock wave hit. (There was little point in mentioning that at that proximity the concrete-block walls would likely be pulverized also.) This makes an impression upon a 9-year-old. Most of us of that generation were sure that a catastrophic nuclear exchange between the United States and the Soviet Union was almost inevitable, and would lead to the utter destruction of civilization and possibly all vertebrate life on Earth.

Since those days, many surprising things have happened—and few more surprising than the fall of the Berlin Wall and the sudden collapse of European authoritarian communism. (The Chinese version remains alive and well.) Now, although there still remains a very real danger that the mushroom cloud will again blossom in some vicious regional conflict, the sort of Strangelovean total nuclear exchange we feared in the 1960s seems very unlikely. Other fears have come to the fore, notably "resource wars," overpopulation, and disease.

Let us first look at the problem of emergent diseases, which has received much recent media attention. Richard Preston ponders the ecological significance of the irruption of the deadly Ebola virus and other tropical pathogens.

THE EARTH RESPONDS

Richard Preston

The emergence of AIDS, Ebola, and any number of other rainforest agents appears to be a natural consequence of the ruin of the tropical biosphere. The emerging viruses are surfacing from ecologically damaged parts of the earth. Many of them come from the tattered edges of tropical rainforest, or they come from tropical savanna that is being settled rapidly by people. The tropical rainforests are the deep reservoirs of life on the planet, containing most of the world's plant and animal species. The rainforests are also its largest reservoir of viruses, since all living things carry viruses. When viruses come out of an ecosystem, they tend to spread in waves through the human population, like echoes from the dying biosphere. . . .

In a sense, the earth is mounting an immune response against the human species. It is beginning to react to the human parasite, the flooding infection of people, the dead spots of concrete all over the planet, the cancerous rot-outs in Europe, Japan, and the United States, thick with replicating primates, the colonies enlarging and spreading and threatening to shock the biosphere with mass extinctions. Perhaps the biosphere does not "like" the idea of five billion humans. Or it could also be said that the extreme amplification of the human race, which has occurred only in the past hundred years or so, has suddenly produced a very large quantity of meat, which is sitting everywhere in the biosphere and may not be able to defend itself against a life form that might want to consume it. Nature has interesting ways of balancing itself. The rainforest has its own defenses. The earth's immune system, so to speak, has recognized the presence of the human species and is starting to kick in. The earth is attempting to rid itself of an infection by the human parasite. Perhaps AIDS is the first step in a natural process of clearance.

While we are understandably terrified by exotic viruses such as HIV and Ebola, we should not forget that the most lethal epidemic in the last 100 years was the great outbreak in the years 1918 to 1921 of common influenza. This swept the world like wildfire, killing tens of millions of people, including many thousands in Canada. The disease was highly transmissible and often felled its victims in two to three days. One should certainly not downplay the tragic significance of AIDS, but it could well be that the ordinary flu virus—easily transmitted, fast acting, highly mutable, essentially incurable, and abundant in reservoirs of domestic and wild animals all over the world—could well be the most likely agent of Preston's hypothetical "natural process of clearance."

Others have argued, however, that the danger of an outbreak of disease wiping the human slate clean is highly exaggerated. Malcolm Gladwell (1995) does not deny that ecological and demographic upheavals may release new diseases from their natural reservoirs and stir them at random into the human population. But he believes this will lead only to many relatively localized outbreaks, no doubt causing great suffering, but not erupting into one vast plague that wipes out the species. He quotes a prominent virologist who has said that the human race is like the chickens of Pennsylvania that in 1983 died helplessly in millions from avian influenza; Gladwell, however, insists that we differ from chickens in "our ability to understand a threat and act accordingly" (1995, p. 46).

Perhaps Gladwell is a little too optimistic. History shows that human population, until the twentieth century, has often been kept in check by disease, and that occasionally (as with the Black Death in medieval Europe, and the disastrous impact of European disease on North and South American Natives) disease can have catastrophic effects on major human population groups (see McNeill 1976). However, we need not look to exotic disease or nuclear war for possible agents of human extinction. Simple exhaustion of resources will do it. We turn now to a very sobering report from Jared Diamond, who summarizes and evaluates recent archeological work on Easter Island.

EASTER'S END

Jared Diamond

Among the most riveting mysteries of human history are those posed by vanished civilizations. Everyone who has seen the abandoned buildings of the Khmer, the Maya, or the Anasazi is immediately moved to ask the same question: why did the societies that erected those structures disappear?

Their vanishing touches us as the disappearance of other animals, even the dinosaurs, never can. No matter how exotic those lost civilizations seem, their framers were humans like us. Who is to say we won't succumb to the same fate? Perhaps someday New York's skyscrapers will stand derelict and overgrown with vegetation, like the temples at Angkor Wat and Tikal.

Among all such vanished civilizations, that of the former Polynesian society on Easter Island remains unsurpassed in mystery and isolation. The mystery stems especially from the island's gigantic stone statues and its impoverished landscape, but it is enhanced by our associations with the specific people involved: Polynesians represent for us the ultimate in exotic romance, the background for many a child's, and an adult's, vision of paradise. My own interest in Easter was kindled over 30 years ago when I read Thor Heyerdahl's fabulous accounts of his *Kon-Tiki* voyage.

But my interest has been revived recently by a much more exciting account, one not of heroic voyages but of painstaking research and analysis. My friend David Steadman, a paleontologist, has been working with a number of other researchers who are carrying out the first systematic excavations on Easter intended to identify the animals and plants that once lived there. Their work is contributing to a new interpretation of the island's history that makes it a tale not only of wonder but of warning as well.

Easter Island, with an area of only 64 square miles, is the world's most isolated scrap of habitable land. It lies in the Pacific Ocean more than 2,000 miles west of the nearest continent (South America), 1,400 miles from even the nearest habitable island (Pitcairn). Its subtropical location and latitude—at 27 degrees south, it is approximately as far below the equator as Houston is north of it—help give it a rather mild climate, while its volcanic origins make its soil fertile. In theory, this combination of blessings should have made Easter a miniature paradise, remote from problems that beset the rest of the world.

The island derives its name from its "discovery" by the Dutch explorer Jacob Roggeveen on Easter (April 5) in 1722. Roggeveen's first impression was not of a paradise but of a wasteland: "We originally, from a further distance, have considered the said Easter Island as sandy; the reason for that is this, that we counted as sand the withered grass, hay, or other scorched and burnt vegetation, because its wasted appearance could give no other impression than of a singular poverty and barrenness."

The island Roggeveen saw was a grassland without a single tree or bush over 10 feet high. Modern botanists have identified only 47 species of higher plants native to Easter, most of them grasses, sedges, and ferns. The list includes just two species of small trees and two of woody shrubs. With such flora, the islanders Roggeveen encountered had no source of real firewood to warm themselves during Easter's cool, wet, windy winters. Their native animals included nothing larger than insects, not even a single species of native bat, land bird, land snail, or lizard. For domestic animals, they had only chickens.

European visitors throughout the eighteenth and early nineteenth centuries estimated Easter's human population at about 2,000, a modest number considering the island's fertility. As Captain James Cook recognized during his brief visit in 1774, the islanders were Polynesians (a Tahitian man accompanying Cook was able to converse with them). Yet despite the Polynesians' well-deserved fame as a great seafaring people, the Easter Islanders who came out to Roggeveen's and Cook's ships did so by swimming or paddling canoes that Roggeveen described as "bad and frail." Their craft, he wrote, were "put together with manifold small planks and light inner timbers, which they cleverly stitched together with very fine twisted threads. . . . But as they lack the knowledge and particularly the materials for caulking and making tight the great number of seams of the canoes, these are accordingly very leaky, for which reason they are compelled to spend half the time in bailing." The canoes, only 10 feet long, held at most two people, and only three or four canoes were observed on the entire island.

With such flimsy craft, Polynesians could never have colonized Easter from even the nearest island, nor could they have traveled far offshore to fish. The islanders Roggeveen met were totally isolated, unaware that other people existed. Investigators in all the years since his visit have discovered no trace of the islanders' having any outside contacts: not a single Easter Island rock or product has turned up elsewhere, nor has anything been found on the island that could have been brought by anyone other than the original settlers or the Europeans. Yet the people living on Easter claimed memories of visiting the uninhabited Sala y Gomez reef 260 miles away, far beyond the range of the leaky canoes seen by Roggeveen. How did the islanders' ancestors reach that reef from Easter, or reach Easter from anywhere else?

Easter Island's most famous feature is its huge stone statues, more than 200 of which once stood on massive stone platforms lining the coast. At least 700 more, in all stages of completion, were abandoned in quarries or on ancient roads between the quarries and the coast, as if the carvers and moving crews had thrown down their tools and walked off the job. Most of the erected statues were carved in a single quarry and then somehow transported as far as six miles—despite heights as great as 33 feet and weights up to 82 tons. The abandoned statues, meanwhile, were as much as 65 feet tall and weighed up to 270 tons. The stone platforms were equally gigantic: up to 500 feet long and 10 feet high, with facing slabs weighing up to 10 tons.

Roggeveen himself quickly recognized the problem the statues posed: "The stone images at first caused us to be struck with astonishment," he wrote, "because we could not comprehend how it was possible that these people, who are devoid of heavy thick timber for making any machines, as well as strong ropes, nevertheless had been able to erect such images." Roggeveen might have added that the islanders had no wheels, no draft animals, and no source of power except their own muscles. How did they transport the giant statues for miles, even before erecting them? To deepen the mystery, the statues were still standing in 1770, but by 1864 all of them had been pulled down, by the islanders themselves. Why then did they carve them in the first place? And why did they stop?

The statues imply a society very different from the one Roggeveen saw in 1722. Their sheer number and size suggest a population much larger than 2,000 people. What became of everyone? Furthermore, that society must have been highly organized. Easter's resources were scattered across the island: the best stone for the statues was quarried at Rano Raraku near Easter's northeast end; red stone, used for large crowns adorning some of the statues, was quarried at Puna Pau, inland in the southwest; stone carving tools came mostly from Aroi in the northwest. Meanwhile, the best farmland lay in the south and east, and the best fishing grounds on the north and west coasts. Extracting and redistributing all those goods required complex political organization. What happened to that organization, and how could it ever have arisen in such a barren landscape?

Easter Island's mysteries have spawned volumes of speculation for more than two and a half centuries. Many Europeans were incredulous that Polynesians—commonly characterized as "mere savages"—could have created the statues or the beautifully constructed stone platforms. In the 1950s, Heyerdahl argued that Polynesia must have been settled by advanced societies of American Indians, who in turn must have received civilization across the Atlantic from more advanced societies of the Old World. Heyerdahl's raft voyages aimed to prove the feasibility of such prehistoric transoceanic contacts. In the 1960s the Swiss writer Erich von Däniken, an ardent believer in Earth visits by extraterrestrial astronauts, went further, claiming that Easter's statues were the work of intelligent beings who owned ultramodern tools, became stranded on Easter, and were finally rescued.

Heyerdahl and von Däniken both brushed aside overwhelming evidence that the Easter Islanders were typical Polynesians derived from Asia rather than from the Americas and that their culture (including their statues) grew out of Polynesian culture. Their language was Polynesian, as Cook had already concluded. Specifically, they spoke an eastern Polynesian dialect related to Hawaiian and Marquesan, a dialect isolated since about A.D. 400, as estimated from slight differences in vocabulary. Their fishhooks and stone adzes resembled early Marquesan models. Last year DNA extracted from 12 Easter Island skeletons was also shown to be Polynesian. The islanders grew bananas, taro, sweet potatoes, sugarcane, and paper mulberry—typical Polynesian crops, mostly of Southeast Asian origin. Their sole domestic animal, the chicken, was also typically Polynesian and ultimately Asian, as were the rats that arrived as stowaways in the canoes of the first settlers.

What happened to those settlers? The fanciful theories of the past must give way to evidence gathered by hardworking practitioners in three fields: archeology, pollen analysis, and paleontology.

Modern archeological excavations on Easter have continued since Heyerdahl's 1955 expedition. The earliest radiocarbon dates associated with human activities are around A.D. 400 to 700, in reasonable agreement with the approximate settlement date of 400 estimated by linguists. The period of statue construction peaked around 1200 to 1500, with few if any statues erected thereafter. Densities of archeological sites suggest a large population; an estimate of 7,000 people is widely quoted by archeologists, but other estimates range up to 20,000, which does not seem implausible for an island of Easter's area and fertility.

Archeologists have also enlisted surviving islanders in experiments aimed at figuring out how the statues might have been carved and erected. Twenty people, using only stone chisels, could have carved even the largest completed statue within a year. Given enough timber and fiber for making ropes, teams of at most a few hundred people could have loaded the statues onto wooden sleds, dragged them over lubricated wooden tracks or rollers, and used logs as levers to maneuver them into a standing position. Rope could have been made from the fiber of a small native tree, related to the linden, called the hauhau. However, that tree is now extremely scarce on Easter, and hauling one statue would have required hundreds of yards of rope. Did Easter's now barren landscape once support the necessary trees?

That question can be answered by the technique of pollen analysis, which involves boring out a column of sediment from a swamp or pond, with the most recent deposits at the top and relatively more ancient deposits at the bottom. The absolute age of each layer can be dated by radiocarbon methods. Then begins the hard work: examining tens of thousands of pollen grains under a microscope, counting them, and identifying the plant species that produced each one by comparing the grains with modern pollen from known plant species. For Easter Island, the bleary-eyed scientists who performed that task were John Flenley, now at Massey University in New Zealand, and Sarah King of the University of Hull in England.

Flenley and King's heroic efforts were rewarded by the striking new picture that emerged of Easter's prehistoric landscape. For at least 30,000 years before human arrival and during the early years of Polynesian settlement, Easter was not a wasteland at all. Instead, a subtropical forest of trees and woody bushes towered over a ground layer of shrubs, herbs, ferns, and grasses. In the forest grew tree daisies, the rope-yielding hauhau tree, and the toromiro tree, which furnishes a dense, mesquite-like firewood. The most common tree in the forest was a species of palm now absent on Easter but formerly so abundant that the bottom strata of the sediment column were packed with its pollen. The Easter Island palm was closely related to the still-surviving Chilean wine palm, which grows up to 82 feet tall and 6 feet in diameter. The tall, unbranched trunks of the Easter Island palm would have been ideal for transporting and erecting statues and constructing large canoes. The palm would also have been a valuable food source, since its Chilean relative yields edible nuts as well as sap from which Chileans make sugar, syrup, honey, and wine.

What did the first settlers of Easter Island eat when they were not glutting themselves on the local equivalent of maple syrup? Recent excavations by David Steadman, of the New York State Museum at Albany, have yielded a picture of Easter's original animal world as surprising as Flenley and King's picture of its plant world. Steadman's expectations for Easter were conditioned by his experiences elsewhere in Polynesia, where fish are overwhelmingly the main food at archeological sites, typically accounting for more than 90 percent of the bones in ancient Polynesian garbage heaps. Easter, though, is too cool for the coral reefs beloved by fish, and its cliff-girded coastline permits shallow-water fishing in only a few places. Less than a quarter of the bones in its early garbage heaps (from the period 900 to 1300) belonged to fish; instead, nearly one-third of all bones came from porpoises.

Nowhere else in Polynesia do porpoises account for even 1 percent of discarded food bones. But most other Polynesian islands offered animal food in the form of birds and mammals, such as New Zealand's now extinct giant moas and Hawaii's now extinct flightless geese. Most other islanders also had domestic pigs and dogs. On Easter, porpoises would have been the largest animal available—other than humans. The porpoise species identified at Easter, the common dolphin, weighs up to 165 pounds. It generally lives out at sea, so it could not have been hunted by line fishing or spearfishing from shore. Instead, it must have been harpooned far offshore, in big seaworthy canoes built from the extinct palm tree.

In addition to porpoise meat, Steadman found, the early Polynesian settlers feasted on seabirds. For those birds, Easter's remoteness and lack of predators made it an ideal haven as a breeding site, at least until humans arrived. Among the prodigious numbers of seabirds that bred on Easter were albatross, boobies, frigate birds, fulmars, petrels, prions, shearwaters, storm petrels, terns, and tropic birds. With at least 25 nesting species, Easter was the richest seabird breeding site in Polynesia and probably in the whole Pacific.

Land birds as well went into early Easter Island cooking pots. Steadman identified bones of at least six species, including barn owls, herons, parrots, and rail. Bird stew would have been seasoned with meat from large numbers of rats, which the Polynesian colonists inadvertently brought with them; Easter Island is the sole known Polynesian island where rat bones outnumber fish bones at archeological sites. (In case you're squeamish and consider rats inedible, I still recall recipes for creamed laboratory rat that my British biologist friends used to supplement their diet during their years of wartime food rationing.)

Porpoises, seabirds, land birds, and rats did not complete the list of meat sources formerly available on Easter. A few bones hint at the possibility of breeding seal colonies as well. All these delicacies were cooked in ovens fired by wood from the island's forests.

Such evidence lets us imagine the island onto which Easter's first Polynesian colonists stepped ashore some 1,600 years ago, after a long canoe voyage from eastern Polynesia. They found themselves in a pristine paradise. What then happened to it? The pollen grains and the bones yield a grim answer.

Pollen records show that destruction of Easter's forests was well under way by the year 800, just a few centuries after the start of human settlement. Then charcoal from wood fires came to fill the sediment cores, while pollen of palms and other trees and woody shrubs decreased or disappeared, and pollen of the grasses that replaced the forest became more abundant. Not long after 1400 the palm finally became extinct, not only as a result of being chopped down but also because the now ubiquitous rats prevented its regeneration: of the dozens of preserved palm nuts discovered in caves on Easter, all had been chewed by rats and could no longer germinate. While the hauhau tree did not become extinct in Polynesian times, its numbers declined drastically until there weren't enough left to make ropes from. By the time Heyerdahl visited Easter, only a single, nearly dead toromiro tree remained on the island, and even that lone survivor has now disappeared. (Fortunately, the toromiro still grows in botanical gardens elsewhere.)

The fifteenth century marked the end not only for Easter's palm but for the forest itself. Its doom had been approaching as people cleared land to plant gardens; as they felled trees to build canoes, to transport and erect statues, and to burn; as rats devoured seeds; and probably as the native birds that had pollinated the trees' flowers and dispersed their fruit died out. The overall picture is among the most extreme examples of forest destruction anywhere in the world: the whole forest gone, and most of its tree species extinct.

The destruction of the island's animals was as extreme as that of the forest; without exception, every species of native land bird became extinct. Even shellfish were overexploited, until people had to settle for small sea snails instead of larger cowries. Porpoise bones disappeared abruptly from garbage heaps around 1500; no one could harpoon porpoises anymore, since the trees used for constructing the big seagoing canoes no longer existed. The colonies of more than half of the seabird species breeding on Easter or on its offshore islets were wiped out.

In place of these meat supplies, the Easter Islanders intensified their production of chickens, which had been only an occasional food item. They also turned to the largest remaining meat source available: humans, whose bones became common in late Easter Island garbage heaps. Oral traditions of the islanders are rife with cannibalism; the most inflammatory taunt that could be snarled at an enemy was "The flesh of your mother sticks between my teeth." With no wood available to cook these new goodies, the islanders resorted to sugarcane scraps, grass, and sedges to fuel their fires.

All these strands of evidence can be wound into a coherent narrative of a society's decline and fall. The first Polynesian colonists found themselves on an island with fertile soil, abundant food, bountiful building materials, ample lebensraum, and all the prerequisites for comfortable living. They prospered and multiplied.

After a few centuries, they began erecting stone statues on platforms, like the ones their Polynesian forebears had carved. With passing years, the statues and platforms became larger and larger, and the statues began sporting ten-ton red crowns—probably in an escalating spiral of one-upmanship, as rival clans tried to surpass each other with shows of wealth and power. (In the same way, successive Egyptian pharaohs built ever-larger pyramids. Today Hollywood movie moguls near my home in Los Angeles are displaying their wealth and power by building ever more ostentatious mansions. Tycoon Marvin Davis topped previous moguls with plans for a 50,000-square-foot house, so now Aaron Spelling has topped Davis with a 56,000-square-foot house. All that those buildings lack to make the message explicit are ten-ton red crowns.) On Easter, as in modern America, society was held together by a complex political system to redistribute locally available resources and to integrate the economies of different areas.

Eventually Easter's growing population was cutting the forest more rapidly than the forest was regenerating. The people used the land for gardens and the wood for fuel, canoes, and houses—and, of course, for lugging statues. As forest disappeared, the islanders ran out of timber and rope to transport and erect their statues. Life became more uncomfortable—springs and streams dried up, and wood was no longer available for fires.

People also found it harder to fill their stomachs, as land birds, large sea snails, and many seabirds disappeared. Because timber for building seagoing canoes vanished, fish catches declined and porpoises disappeared from the table. Crop yields also declined, since deforestation allowed the soil to be eroded by rain and wind, dried by the sun, and its nutrients to be leached from it.

Intensified chicken production and cannibalism replaced only part of all those lost foods. Preserved statuettes with sunken cheeks and visible ribs suggest that people were starving.

With the disappearance of food surpluses, Easter Island could no longer feed the chiefs, bureaucrats, and priests who had kept a complex society running. Surviving islanders described to early European visitors how local chaos replaced centralized government and a warrior class took over from the hereditary chiefs. The stone points of spears and daggers, made by the warriors during their heyday in the 1600s and 1700s, still litter the ground of Easter today. By around 1700, the population began to crash toward between one-quarter and one-tenth of its former number. People took to living in caves for protection against their enemies. Around 1700 rival clans started to topple one another's statues, breaking the heads off. By 1864 the last statue had been thrown down and desecrated.

As we try to imagine the decline of Easter's civilization, we ask ourselves, "Why didn't they look around, realize what they were doing, and stop before it was too late? What were they thinking when they cut down the last palm tree?"

I suspect, though, that the disaster happened not with a bang but with a whimper. After all, there are those hundreds of abandoned statues to consider. The forest the islanders depended on for rollers and rope didn't simply disappear one day—it vanished slowly, over decades. Perhaps war interrupted the moving teams; perhaps by the time the carvers had finished their work, the last rope snapped. In the meantime, any islander who tried to warn about the dangers of progressive deforestation would have been overridden by vested interests of carvers, bureaucrats, and chiefs, whose jobs depended on continued deforestation. Our Pacific Northwest loggers are only the latest in a long line of loggers to cry, "Jobs over trees!" The changes in forest cover from year to year would have been hard to detect; yes, this year we cleared those woods over there, but trees are starting to grow back again on this abandoned garden site here. Only older people, recollecting their childhoods decades earlier, could have recognized a difference. Their children could no more have comprehended their parents' tales than my eight-year-old sons today can comprehend my wife's and my tales of what Los Angeles was like 30 years ago.

Gradually trees became fewer, smaller, and less important. By the time the last fruit-bearing adult palm tree was cut, palms had long since ceased to be of economic significance. That left only smaller and smaller palm saplings to clear each year, along with other bushes and treelets. No one would have noticed the felling of the last small palm.

By now the meaning of Easter Island for us should be chillingly obvious. Easter Island is Earth writ small. Today, again, a rising population confronts shrinking resources. We too have no emigration valve, because all human societies are linked by international transport, and we can no more escape into space than the Easter Islanders could flee into the ocean. If we continue to follow our present course, we shall have exhausted the world's major fisheries, tropical rain forests, fossil fuels, and much of our soil by the time my sons reach my current age.

Every day newspapers report details of famished countries — Afghanistan, Liberia, Rwanda, Sierra Leone, Somalia, the former Yugoslavia, Zaire — where soldiers have appropriated the wealth or where central government is yielding to local gangs of thugs. With the risk of nuclear war receding, the threat of our ending with a bang no longer has a chance of galvanizing us to halt our course. Our risk now is of winding down, slowly, in a whimper. Corrective action is blocked by vested interests, by well-intentioned political and business leaders, and by their electorates, all of whom are perfectly correct in not noticing big changes from year to year. Instead, each year there are just somewhat more people, and somewhat fewer resources, on Earth.

It would be easy to close our eyes or to give up in despair. If mere thousands of Easter Islanders with only stone tools and their own muscle power sufficed to destroy their society, how can billions of people with metal tools and machine power fail to do worse? But there is one crucial difference. The Easter Islanders had no books and no histories of other doomed societies. Unlike the Easter Islanders, we have histories of the past — information that can save us. My main hope for my sons' generation is that we may now choose to learn from the fates of societies like Easter's.

Is Jared Diamond right that the tragic story of Easter Island could be simply a miniature version, a test run, of what is happening on the Earth as a whole? Are we are headed for destruction and maybe even extinction "not with a bang but a whimper"? (This famous phrase is from T.S. Eliot's poem "The Hollow Men." See Eliot 1958.) If this is correct, then it won't be a fiery nuclear conflagration or a hyper-virulent mutant virus that sweeps humanity from the globe — just an accelerating decline into starvation, political and administrative fragmentation and chaos, poverty, vicious and destructive bickering over the remaining scraps of ecological bounty, and perhaps ultimately cannibalism. Are we, ultimately, just so many "chickens" after all? Or is there some crucial and saving difference between Easter Island and the global island other than merely scale?

Many argue that all of these problems — resource exhaustion and the threat of war and disease — are caused purely and simply by human overpopulation. Let us briefly examine this very difficult problem.

We won't call this item a "case study" because to do so would be to trivialize the suffering of millions. The facts are brutal. The human population at this writing stands at around 5.7 billion persons, and increases by about 90 million per year. No other single species of comparable body mass has ever existed in such numbers. No other species has ever appropriated so much of the Earth's biological productivity to itself. (It is estimated, for instance, that we use 20 to 40 percent of the products of all the photosynthesis by land plants on the planet; Wilson 1992, p. 272.) And yet, in spite of our overwhelming numerical dominance of the biosphere, which (if numbers were all that mattered) might be accounted a sign of great reproductive success, at least one billion humans are chronically malnourished, so poor that they can almost never get enough to eat, rarely know where their next meal is going to come from, and suffer from all the medical and developmental problems that malnutrition brings.

Only about a fifth or less of the world's population lives as well as the average Canadian (and many in Canada as well live in terrible poverty). Hundreds of millions of people can, in any given day, have only one concern: to somehow scratch out the bare necessities in the way of food and firewood to get them through that particular day. No matter that they might have been born with the talents of a Mozart or Marie Curie, that is all that their day, and their life, can be. And the problem relentlessly worsens: in virtually every country in the world, not only are the absolute numbers of poor increasing, but the economic gap between rich and poor steadily deepens.

Indira Gandhi called poverty the worst form of pollution; certainly, even if "pollution" is not quite the right term, the deepening crisis of poverty and the social disintegration that seems to go with it are glaringly symptomatic of the unbalanced, if not pathological state of the human **ecology**. It seems bitterly ironic that we enjoy this enormous reproductive dominance while at the same time a large percentage of our own supposedly "dominant" species cannot enjoy the basic necessities of life, let alone any sort of prosperity that might permit the full enjoyment and exercise of their capacities. What irony! "You call this reproductive success?" a sceptical Martian biologist might demand.

Many authors have argued that the human population "bomb" is close to bursting, if not already past the point of no return. Canadian writer Carolyn Garlich (1994) states, "While most people still talk of the population bomb as though it were timed to go off in the future, there is mounting evidence that it has already exploded. . . . Our numbers as a species are already in excess of the earth's carrying capacity." Garlich cites figures from the United Nations Fund for Population Activities, which strongly suggest that we have "overshot." (To **overshoot** is to exploit an ecosystem beyond its long-term **carrying capacity**—the population that a particular ecosystem is capable of supporting—resulting usually in a reduction in long-term carrying capacity.) Right now, for instance, in spite of the vaunted "green revolution," world population is increasing at roughly twice the rate of the food supply, while cropland is decreasing due to various sorts of anthropogenic degradation (such as soil erosion). At current rates, by A.D. 2000 there will be only about half the cropland per person in the world as in 1950. Garlich argues that because of this, current human numbers cannot possibly be sustained and must inevitably fall; the only question is how drastically and painfully this will occur.

Whether or not this bleak prediction is correct, many people are quite understandably inclined to blame all our environmental problems on overpopulation, and accordingly advocate simplistic measures such as authoritarian enforcement of birth control and "ecotriage"—ecological **triage**. In practice, this essentially means cutting one's losses by restricting immigration and refusing to give aid to starving countries. (See the discussion by Ynestra King in Chapter Thirteen. For a defence of the **lifeboat ethic**, see Hardin 1974.) Indeed, as overpopulation becomes increasingly desperate, it is hard to see how one could avoid such drastic measures.

Such views ignore the fact that throughout history environmental degradation has very often *preceded* the stage at which a region is overtly overpopulated. It is not just the numbers of us living but somehow the very way we live that seems to be the problem. All too often, humans have recklessly squandered resources even when population densities were quite low (see Wilson's discussion of Pleistocene extinctions in Chapter Two); often, the more abundant resources were in relation to the population density, the more wastefully they were squandered. (Think of the European pioneers in the North American West who slaughtered buffalo for their tongues, or simply for fun.) Often the rising curve of population has met a descending curve of carrying capacity, a curve dragged downward by greed, carelessness, and ignorance. Simply blaming the human tendency to reproduce may be beside the point; or perhaps mistaking the symptom for the disease.

It is perfectly true that human population growth in historic times is **exponential**. Mathematically, it resembles nothing so much as the growth curve that one might expect if one stirred a heaping spoonful of nutrients into a beaker containing some yeast. In such a case, the yeast population would indeed bloom exponentially—and then crash when some limiting factor (such as the nutrient running out or a toxic waste product reaching lethal levels) suddenly imposed itself. (See David Dehaas's account of the "cycles of **boom and crash**" experienced by beaver in Chapter Twelve, and also Catton 1988.) If the yeast could somehow be wise enough to limit its reproduction before critical limits were exceeded, its growth curve would level out to a gentle **logistic**.

Indeed, one can draw a compelling analogy between the human race and our hypothetical jar of yeast. Human beings were few in number to begin with, a marginal offshoot of anthropoid evolution. For reasons yet unaccountable, our ancestors experienced peculiar neurological developments that permitted *language* and *technological ingenuity*, traits that enable us to rapidly adapt to and overcome environmental challenges. We have been able to find an infinite variety of ways to exploit the stupendous store of physical and biological "resources" built up in the natural world. Minerals, petroleum, vast forests, and huge populations of fish and animals were converted to human use, often very wastefully.

If we are to be compared to the beaker of yeast, then it is we ourselves who made the spoon, and the nutrients stirred in are simply the vast quantities of animal flesh, timber, plant matter, coal, minerals, and petroleum that our technological ingenuity has allowed us to appropriate. (Note that, with the exception of most but not all minerals, this treasure trove of "resources" we have exploited was *biologically produced*. We are thus in a fundamentally predatory or parasitical relationship to the rest of the biosphere. See Chapter Seven for further discussion of this point.)

And, of course, if we are this much like that beaker of yeast, is there any reason to think that we would not suffer essentially the same kind of fate—a catastrophic crash just at the point at which overt *numerical* dominance makes sudden extinction or near-extinction the hardest turn of events to imagine?

However, this parallel between humans and yeast, accurate enough in itself, fails to display the fact that humans are behaviourally much more complex than yeast. In particular, as Gladwell and Diamond indicate, we are capable (at least under certain hard-to-reproduce conditions) of something called *learning*. In fact, one could say that it is precisely our capacity to learn both that has gotten us into so much trouble and which is the only thing that could get us out of it, if anything could. But much more needs to be said than this. Learning of what, and by whom, might solve the problem?

Some statistics from the United Nations Fund for Population Activities provide a clue, and a gleam of hope to relieve the general gloom presented in this chapter. It emerges that the one demographic factor that correlates most strongly and positively with low infant mortality and moderate birthrate in many countries is *not*, as some might expect, the per capita income or Gross National Product of a given country, but simply *women's literacy* (Sadik 1989). Perhaps this should not be surprising; few women, one would think, if given the power and knowledge to choose (which in many countries they are not), would willingly accept the burden of a crowded, malnourished family as opposed to a family of comfortable size in which each child has a good chance to survive infancy and receive decent care. But this demographic fact adds a new dimension to the famous remark by H.G. Wells: "Human history becomes more and more a race between education and catastrophe" (Wells 1920).

FURTHER READING

A recent controversial article by Robert D. Kaplan (1994) highlights the connection between poverty, political disintegration, and environmental degradation. Kaplan insists that environmental stress will inevitably be the driving factor in human history in the decades to come; that most existing political boundaries and organizations will disintegrate under the pressure of people desperately trying to survive; that disease will again become rampant, and crime will become indistinguishable from endless internecine warfare. Canadian scholar Thomas Homer-Dixon (Soto 1993) argues that increasing resource scarcity will lead to political chaos. Catton (1980) explicitly attempts to link sociological and political pathologies to environmental overload, citing Nazi Germany and the violent implosion of the Easter Island culture as instances in which the veneer of civilization cracks when a supporting ecosystem is pushed beyond its limits of sustainability. Paul and Anne Ehrlich are among the most articulate exponents of the dangers of overpopulation; see, for instance, their 1973 study and Paul Ehrlich's 1971 book. A notable dissenting voice is economist Julian Simon (1981), who claims that human ingenuity is the "ultimate resource," and that natural resources are not limited "in any economic sense." Catton (1988) presents a grim view of the prospects for human "lemmings," and Meadows et al. (1972) and (1992) are controversial studies of the consequences of running into environmental limits.

QUESTIONS TO CONSIDER

1. Kaplan, Homer-Dixon, and others like them have been criticized and even derided for their pessimistic predictions of environmentally caused upheaval, which some feel to be unwarranted if not actually harmful. Given what we know of the rapidly growing human impact on the environment, and the great uncertainties often involved in predicting its effects, do you think that such dire predictions are well enough grounded to be taken seriously?
2. As Diamond tells us, environmental degradation often creeps up so slowly and insidiously that no one feels alarmed and warnings from the far-sighted are not taken seriously. Try to work out some *general* principles according to which you might be able to decide when a probable threat (environmental or otherwise) would be serious enough to force you to change your way of life. How probable would such a threat have to appear to be?
3. Not even Julian Simon would deny that resources *at any given time* are finite. To what extent can human ingenuity be relied upon to find or generate new resources? Bear in mind that many of the resources we require for our continued existence—including the very oxygen we breathe—are biological products.
4. Are there any steps the early Easter Islanders could have taken that might have made it possible for them to live sustainably on the island? If not, why not?
5. Is Easter Island really "Earth writ small," as Diamond puts it? Or is this a false analogy? If so, why?

PART TWO

"Those who cannot remember the past . . ."

Those who cannot remember the past are condemned to repeat it.
— GEORGE SANTAYANA (1948)

In part, the purpose of this section is merely to provide the reader with useful and interesting background to some of the problems we face today. But we also want to show that our environmental problems are not simply the product of the Industrial Age, even though they are undoubtedly far worse now, both in quantity and kind, than they have ever been throughout history. We will see that, as already suggested by our discussion of species extinctions, they have been going on for thousands of years — perhaps for as long as there have been people.

Much of human evolutionary history remains shrouded in mystery, since there are huge gaps in the fossil record. Nevertheless, it seems clear that modern *Homo sapiens* emerged, perhaps rather suddenly and probably in Africa, from earlier prehuman hominids such as Neanderthal Man between fifty and a hundred thousand years ago. (Research keeps pushing the date further and further back.) By about thirty thousand years ago, all other hominids were extinct. Although we do not know why this happened, it seems possible if not likely that our ancestors had a hand in their demise. Perhaps we warred with them, perhaps we simply hunted them. (I emphasize that there is no actual paleontological evidence for this — only that our evolutionary cousins disappeared abruptly at our appearance, just as did so many other competing and prey mammals at the end of the Pleistocene.) If this is so, then we may have begun our evolutionary career with an act of genocide.

This is speculation, of course. But what is not speculation is the fact that humans have been drastically altering their environment for a long time, sometimes for the better, often for the worse. Not all of these alterations have been destructive, but the bad ones do tend to stand out in the historical record—and provide object lessons, if only we will learn.

CHAPTER FOUR

SOILS AND FORESTS

We turn now to some views of the interlinked histories of forests and soils. John Perlin's book *A Forest Journey* (1989) demonstrates that there is much truth in the statement that the history of civilization is the history of deforestation. Cultures rose where there were rich forests and fertile topsoil; civilizations grew using the products of the forest for building, manufacturing, and fuel, and often fell if their forests were exhausted. Shipbuilding was crucial: many maritime powers such as Venice and Phoenicia were founded in regions where there was abundant shipbuilding timber. Early industry, such as it was, was powered largely by combustion of wood.

What is especially interesting to note, in the following excerpts from Perlin's book, is the striking fact that even the earliest cultures that we know much about were acutely aware of their dependency upon the forests. The story of Gilgamesh has an air of tragedy; Gilgamesh seemed to know that he could not help but destroy the very thing from which he drew his power. Later, in Greek, Roman, and medieval times, we see attempts to practise conservation, to switch to solar heating, and to reforest. We even see the beginnings of a very modern-sounding "ecological conscience." The debate between Cicero and one Servillius Rullus sounds very familiar: change the names and details slightly, and it would not be out of place on the opinion pages of *The Globe and Mail*.

A FOREST JOURNEY

John Perlin

The Epic of Gilgamesh

With wood so high a priority on the list of past civilizations' needs, it should not surprise us that our first written account of timber procurement and subsequent deforestation originates from the site where Western civilization first emerged, the Fertile Crescent. The following story comes from an episode in the *Epic of Gilgamesh* known as "The Forest Journey." It shows an understanding of ecological processes and the consequences of human action on the earth that anticipates current ecological work.

The story takes place about 4,700 years ago in Uruk, a city-kingdom in southern Mesopotamia. Uruk's ruler at that time, Gilgamesh, wished to make for himself "a name that endures" by building up his city. To realize his goal, he had to have at his disposal large amounts of timber for his ambitious construction plans.

Fortunately for Gilgamesh a great primeval forest lay before him. It extended over such a great area of land that no one in Uruk knew its true size. That such vast tracts of timber grew near southern Mesopotamia might seem a flight of fancy considering the present barren condition of the land, but before the intrusion of civilizations an almost unbroken forest flourished in the hills and mountains surrounding the Fertile Crescent.

To penetrate this forest was not a simple task. Its foliage was so dense that the sun could barely shine through. So hazardous was a trip into this forest that the citizens of Uruk shuddered in fright when Gilgamesh announced to them his intention of going in and cutting down its cedars.

Before Gilgamesh's day, no civilized person had ventured into these woods. To ensure that no one entered, Enlil, the chief Sumerian deity, appointed the ferocious demigod Humbaba "to safeguard the cedar forest." Enlil entrusted Humbaba to protect the interests of nature, and hence of the gods, against the needs of civilization. This god knew too well the ambitions of civilized human beings and did not doubt that once in the forest, they would hack away at the gods' bountiful garden. No matter how religious they might profess to be, they would destroy such divine beauty where "the cedars raise aloft their luxuriance."

Civilization has never recognized limits to its needs, and Gilgamesh, an early representative, would not be deterred from attempting to conquer the cedar forest even under threat of death. "I will fell the cedars!" he boldly announced in reply to his countrymen's warnings about the dangers of Humbaba, whose roar "is the storm flood," whose mouth "is fire," and whose breath "is death."

Armed for their conquest with tools of the lumberjack—"mighty adzes" and "axes of three talents"—Gilgamesh and his companions headed to the cedar forest with the intention of ridding it of Humbaba. With Humbaba dead, the forest would become accessible to the civilized world, which then might fell timber to its heart's content.

The beauty or holiness of the cedar forest distracted Gilgamesh briefly from the task he had set out to accomplish, but not for long. After a moment of enjoying the beauty of "the abode of the gods," Gilgamesh and his companions proceeded to fell cedars and chop their branches and trunks into transportable portions. The timber felling continued until the noise of all this work aroused Humbaba. He naturally became incensed that humans would dare to come where they were forbidden and, worst, were tampering with the trees. Humbaba ordered the intruders to stop their destructive activities. A fight ensued for control of this precious resource. In the end civilization won the battle, and the mighty forest demigod lost his head.

With the guardian of the cedar forest dead and with Gilgamesh now reigning as master of the forest, the cedars wailed in fear. "For two miles you could hear the sad song of the cedars." True to the worst fears of Enlil and the trees, the men cut down the cedars, "stripping the mountains of their cover," leaving bare rock in their wake. When Enlil, who must forever watch over the well-being of the earth, learned of the destruction of the cedar forest, he sent down a series of ecological curses on the offenders: "May the food you eat be eaten by fire; may the water you drink be drunk by fire."

The writers of the *Epic of Gilgamesh* knew that once civilization gained access to the forests trees would be vulnerable. They also knew that droughts naturally follow deforestation, and so ended the tale, lamenting the soon-to-be sorry state of southern Mesopotamia, as well as the many other civilizations bent on destroying their forests. Thus, the epic transcends time, foreshadowing events to come. Gilgamesh's war against the forest has been repeated for generations in every corner of the globe in order to supply building and fuel stocks needed for each civilization's continual material growth.

The Legacy of Gilgamesh

During the latter part of the third millennium B.C. many rulers of southern Mesopotamian city-states made tree-felling expeditions to the cedar forest. Gudea, one of these potentates, reigned over Lagash, a city-state not too distant from Uruk, during the twenty-second century B.C. Like Gilgamesh, he wished to leave his name to posterity by developing Lagash to heights never before attained. To carry out his building plans, Gudea had to obtain large quantities of cedar timber as well as other sorts of wood. He thus "made a path into the cedar mountain . . . and cut its cedars with great axes."

Once cut, the cedar logs were made into rafts and floated southward, eventually arriving at Lagash where they became the cornerstone of Gudea's grandiose schemes. Lumber workers turned some of the cedar into planks with which shipwrights built cargo ships. On their cedar decks, a wide variety of imports—timber from Arabia and India, barley, metals, and building stones—was imported to enrich Gudea's city. He also used cedar wood to build a great temple and was given the title of "Temple Builder" and "Priest of Ningirsu," fulfilling his desire for lasting fame.

Lagash before Gudea

Gudea's predecessors on the throne of Lagash also needed large amounts of wood for the smooth running of their monarchies. Uru-Ka-Gina, who ruled Lagash about 150 years before Gudea came to power, decided that for the good of his kingdom the supply of and demand for essential goods should be kept well balanced. He therefore established an administrative position to oversee all acquisitions and outlays of important materials, one of them being wood, and chose Enigal for this office.

Whenever wood was needed Enigal made sure that the city had ample supplies. How crucial this role was to the well-being of Lagash can be seen in Enigal's relationship with the city's canal diggers. The city could not exist without canals and their continued maintenance since the farmers depended on these waterways for irrigation and the merchants depended on them for the transport of most of their commodities. The canal diggers, however, could not do their work without wooden handles for their tools. To ensure that they always had enough tool handles, Enigal arranged for a sufficient inventory of wood.

Third Dynasty at Ur, 2100 B.C.

Lagash, despite its magnificence and splendor, paled in significance when compared with the Third Dynasty of Ur. Here we see Sumeria at its greatest. The widespread use of bronze tools such as axes, hammers, hoes, and sickles facilitated common work, but it also drastically increased the need for wood to fuel foundry furnaces.

The records of carpentry shops tell of other needs for wood. Tables were popular and they were usually built from wood. The chairs that surrounded them were also of wood as were the bowls and dishes placed on top.

The Exploitation of Local Forests

Wood from local forests was exploited as much as possible. Foresters had three varieties from which to choose: the Euphrates poplar, the willow, and a hardwood whose identification eludes ancient Near Eastern scholars. From these species woodsmen made logs, roof beams, levers, pegs, rungs for ladders, posts, rods for reed buckets, planks, boards, wooden boards for baskets, boats' ribs, hoes, hoe blades, plow shares, sickle handles, and keels. They also collected branches and twigs to make charcoal as well as long, cylindrical bundles used to reinforce the banks of canals and rivers.

The Importation of Wood

Other varieties of wood had to be imported. In Gudea's time, for instance, cedars came from the Ammanus mountains, northwest of Lagash in what is now southwest Turkey. Oak wood was sent to Lagash from the southeast Arabian peninsula. "Boats full of wood" also sailed from northern Arabia and India to Lagash so that Gudea could complete his temple. From what is presently northern Syria, Gudea "collected trunks of juniper, large firs, sycamores," and other types of trees to furnish his buildings with beams.

The Increased Value of Wood

During periods of accelerated growth, wood was in such demand that its value approached that of precious metals and stones. When the kingdom of Akkad blossomed as a powerful state in the twenty-fourth century, its ruler, Naram-Sin, pillaged for wood as greedily as he did for gold, silver, and jewelry. Certain woods in Gudea's city were so valuable that they were held in the royal treasury, which could only be opened with the royal seal. Wood was so valuable to Naram-Sin, Gudea, and Sargon, the founder of the dynasty of Akkad, that each mountain where wood grew carried the name of the dominant usable species of tree.

Timber and Foreign Policy

The high value placed on wood by rulers of this region is also illustrated by the influence its procurement played in foreign policy. When cedars grew just east of Sumer, the reigning prince of Lagash, Enannatum, overthrew the ruler of this area and in the process acquired its timberlands. After the timber supply on the eastern frontier had dwindled, Sargon and Naram-Sin struck northwestward with their troops "as far as the Cedar Forest" and "overpowered the Ammanus, the Cedar Mountain."

To assure access to the northwestern highlands where a plethora of wood awaited the axe, Naram-Sin slew the king of Ebla, who ruled over this area. The conquest of Ebla by Naram-Sin freed vast tracts of timber land for

Mesopotamian exploitation. Soon logs began flowing southward. For the continued prosperity of southern Mesopotamia, Sumerian control of the main watercourses of the Near East became imperative to ensure safe passage of timber down the Euphrates, Tigris, and Karun rivers.

Problems Due to Excessive Silt

Once the southerners began felling large quantities of trees near the banks of the upper courses of the Euphrates, Tigris, and Karun rivers and tributaries, salt and silt as well as timber filled the waters heading south. The exposure of steep hillsides directly to sun, wind, and rain accelerated erosion and large quantities of soil found its way into the Mesopotamian watershed. Coinciding with peak deforestation in the north, silt accumulated in the south at a dangerous pace, forever threatening to clog up the irrigation canals. Without constant vigilance, water for irrigation would have been in short supply and ships would have been unable to navigate to the important urban centers. Increased siltation therefore required almost constant dredging. When Ur-Nammu, the first king of the Third Dynasty of Ur, took over Ur, he made dredging the canals a high priority. His action helped revive agriculture and allowed ships from abroad to call at Ur's docks as they had in earlier times.

Problems Due to Salinity

Deforestation also exposed salt-rich sedimentary rocks of the northern mountains to erosion. Mineral salts in abnormally large quantities were consequently carried downstream and accumulated in the irrigated farmlands of southern Mesopotamia. After 1,000 to 1,500 years of very successful farming, a serious salinity problem suddenly developed. Increased salinization of the alluvial soils of Sumeria coincided with the onset of Mesopotamian control of northern timberlands and their exploitation. Unlike the siltation problem, salinization proved nonreversible and worsened as time went on, causing a progressive decline in crop yields.

Field records of the time show the slow disintegration of Sumerian agriculture. Harvests at Girsu, an important agricultural area in the south, averaged 2,537 liters of barley per hectare around 2400 B.C., which compares well with current yields in the United States and Canada. Three hundred years later, yields had dropped by 42 percent. In 1700 B.C. farmers at nearby Larsa could produce only 897 liters of barley per hectare, or only 35 percent of the barley produced at Girsu 700 years earlier.

The Decline of Sumerian Civilization

The rise and decline of the cultural, economic, and political domination of the Near East by southern Mesopotamia closely followed the vicissitudes of barley production. By 2000 B.C., when barley yields were in steady decline, the last Sumerian empire had collapsed. Three hundred years later, as barley production dropped further, the center of power moved northward to Babylonia, which was unaffected by salinization. Most of the great cities of Sumeria disappeared or dissipated into mere villages. Declining food production due to increased salinity was one of the factors that contributed to the fall of Sumerian civilization. Without surpluses of barley—the staple food of the Mesopotamians—the superstructure of administrators, traders, artisans, warriors, and priests that comprised this civilization could not survive. Unwittingly, the building schemes of mighty kings, begun by Gilgamesh, brought on the destruction of the civilization they had worked so hard to build.

Ecological Condition of Athens after Its Defeat, 404 B.C.

The condition of the environment surrounding Athens was as depressed as the mood right after the news of Athens' defeat. Deforestation during the years of growth and war had left its nearby mountains with "nothing but food for bees." Where wolves once roamed, hunters could not even find a single rabbit to spear. When rain fell, the water could not penetrate the ground but flowed off the bare land into the sea, doing considerable damage to the meager soil still available to Athenian farmers. One landholder, the son of Tesias, explained that after a heavy downpour, a torrent surged down a local road and when its path was blocked, water and mud overflowed upon the neighboring farms, eroding their land. In such fashion all the rich, soft topsoil washed away, leaving little besides rock. What remained could not absorb and store rainwater for the dry season. Shrines testified to the erstwhile locations of springs, but these natural aquifers no longer held water. Farmers, using agricultural techniques that had been successful in the past when the soil was more fertile, could now expect no more return on their planting than the seed originally sown.

A New Ecological Consciousness

In earlier days when trees grew everywhere, men of letters wrote about them in a purely pragmatic fashion, as Homer and Hesiod did, or as nuisances, since they often stood in the way of cultivation and settlement. The eighth century B.C. poet Archilochos, who came to Thasos as a pioneer, took the latter approach. Like other settlers, he found the island's virgin state ugly, describing its landscape as standing "like the backbone of an ass, crowned with savage wood."

When wood became scarce at the end of the fifth century B.C., intellectuals began to emphasize its importance. Aristotle considered accessibility to timber for building as one of the prerequisites of his ideal state. Plato also gave forests a major role in his utopia. In his vision of what Attica looked like in its pristine state, "the country was unimpaired . . . it had much forest land in its mountains . . . and besides," he added, "there were many lofty trees of cultivated species. . . . " The canopy of the woodlands protected the rich earth covering these hills from the erosive action of deluges prevalent at the time, the philosopher argued, allowing the soil of Attica to be "enriched by the yearly rains from Zeus . . . " and providing all the surrounding "districts with abundant springs and streams. . . . "

New Techniques for Survival: Farming, Solar Design, and Smelting

Plato's portrayal of the ideal conditions that flourished in his well-wooded paradise served as a yardstick to demonstrate to the public the extent of deterioration that had taken place. New methods were developed for survival in the less-than-perfect environment of fourth century B.C. Greece. Xenophon, a student of Socrates, wrote a treatise on agriculture to help farmers succeed in working soils robbed of their fertility as a consequence of deforestation and erosion. Xenophon compared the present Greek soil to a worn-out sow, arguing that it was just as difficult for her to suckle a large litter to adulthood as it would be to produce large yields of healthy wheat by continually planting in exhausted soil. Plowing the shoots of one's first crop into the soil instead would enrich the land, according to Xenophon, and guarantee satisfactory harvests. Tesias's son described a strategy to fight soil loss. His father had built a retaining wall, he claimed, to prevent torrents from washing away topsoil.

To help heat houses without recourse to scarce wood-based fuel, Aristotle suggested the following method already in vogue in Athens. "For the comfort of inhabitants," Aristotle advocated, "the house must be sunny in winter and well sheltered from the north"—the direction from which the cold winter winds would most likely come. In the fourth century B.C. the adoption of passive solar design spread to many sections of the Greek world and interest in it continued unabated for several centuries to come. Entire cities, such as the new city of Priene, were planned so that every citizen could receive solar heat. First, urban planners laid out Priene's streets in a checkerboard pattern despite its hilly location. Its major streets ran east–west so every house would have a southern exposure. Then all houses at Priene, no matter what size, were designed according to what the excavator of Priene called "the solar building principle." On the island of Delos, during its most populated era when charcoal was at its greatest demand, the principles of solar architecture played a major role in house design. Most of the important houses built in this period had their principal porticos facing the winter sun.

The scarcity of wood in Attica forced fourth century B.C. metallurgists at Laurion to change their methods of operation. They moved their furnaces to locations on the coast so they could easily receive imported fuel brought by ship, and cut the amount of charcoal used in the smelting process, resulting in slag high in lead but poor in silver. Thus, mostly silver remained in the furnace. Some modern technologists criticize the fourth-century Greeks' smelting method as inefficient since much lead was lost, but unlike silver, lead was not worth very much and could not be easily sold. On the other hand, the money saved on fuel with this technique far outweighed the value of the lead that was wasted. These changes made possible the revival of large-scale silver mining at Laurion after the Peloponnesian War, which helped to revivify Athens' economy by providing a means of exchange to finance trade.

Secular and Sacred Regulation of Wood Use

The conservation of wood, Aristotle felt, was a matter too important to be left to voluntary compliance. He therefore recommended that the state employ magistrates "to watch over the forest." Many city-states followed the spirit of his advice and adopted laws to protect forests and regulate the use of wood and to see to their enforcement.

The section of the Athenian judiciary that handled capital cases also tried defendants who tampered with Attica's remaining trees. Lysias, a famous fourth century B.C. orator, appeared before this court, charged with destroying an olive stump on his property. An enemy accused Lysias of standing by while slaves chopped it into pieces and loaded the wood onto a wagon, presumably taking it to sell for fuel. If found guilty, he faced exile, a stiff penalty for a seemingly insignificant act. But his alleged felling violated an Attic law stipulating that lease holders could not destroy shoots or stumps or turn wood into charcoal. In this time of scarcity, the community had to deal harshly to save whatever trees remained. Fortunately for Lysias, the court acquitted him.

Decrees with the same intent as the one enforced in Attica were passed by the ruling clans on the island of Chios. One of their laws forbade herdsmen to take their flocks grazing into those parts of the forest where saplings were growing. Another decree kept the populace from felling young trees. These two laws encouraged the regeneration of forests. A third decree stipulated the amount of wood per year that any leaseholder could cut.

The government of Delos passed legislation to control the sale of wood and charcoal on the island. Its regulation coincided with the popularization of solar architecture there, no doubt a similar response to the same problem, the scarcity of wood. The law stipulated that wood and charcoal importers had to declare to customs the prices for which they planned to sell their products and had to stick to these prices — neither raising nor lowering them — at the marketplace, and they were also forbidden to sell their wood and charcoal to middlemen.

These provisions aimed at protecting consumers. The first provision prevented dealers from undervaluing the price of their wood products at customs and then either raising prices or selling at reduced rates to larger buyers, leaving the little customer to do without. Forbidding middlemen kept a lid on prices as well, and avoided the possibility that any single group or individual would corner the wood and charcoal market. Delian regulation of the wood and charcoal trade shows that authorities regarded these commodities as too essential, scarce, and valuable to be controlled solely by merchants.

Government and religious authorities also sought to protect sacred groves from the axe. The spirits of divinities were thought to live in sacred groves, which were therefore dedicated to them. Until the end of the fifth century B.C. this sacred status protected the groves and they came to resemble our national parks as the last vestiges of pristine nature in otherwise developed areas.

Although the Greeks worshipped the trees in the groves, believed profoundly in their sanctity, and considered the mere cutting of a bough to be an act of sacrilege, the nearby populace used the trees as a last resort when other sources no longer provided building material or fuel. Therefore authorities could no longer rely merely on the spiritual sanction of impiety to stop the felling of trees, but had to impose stiff secular penalties for their protection.

One of the first decrees protecting sacred groves, taking effect during the late fifth century B.C., came from the island of Kos. The decree stipulated that anyone cutting down cypress trees would be fined one thousand drachmas, which was an extremely large sum in those days, about three years' pay for the average worker. Religious and secular leaders probably felt that a severe fine was the only way to stop people from violating the sanctity of the grove to secure a commodity so necessary yet so scarce. Unfortunately, a loophole in the decree permitted logging if done for public work. Apparently this caveat allowed the community to cut down large numbers of trees and by the fourth century B.C. the grove was threatened with extinction. To save the remaining trees Philstos, son of Aeschines, moved that "no president is to propose for debate or put to the vote any motion, nor is any individual to express an opinion, to the effect that the cypress wood be used up [for timber]."

From the fourth century B.C. on, as the deforestation of Greece accelerated, laws for the protection of sacred groves became even more numerous. Three of these dating to this period protected groves in Attica. Those who rented land at a sacred grove dedicated to Poseidon at Sounion, bordering the Laurion silver-mining region, had to sign contracts not to cut down any trees. A sanctuary by the Port of Athens prohibited the collection of wood on its property. Those caught with wood belonging to the sanctuary were to be punished according to "the old laws on the book." The transgressors were probably the poorer citizens of the harbor trying to get free fuel. Another sacred grove in Attica forbade "cutting [timber] in the sanctuary and carrying away wood or twigs. . . ." A slave caught violating this decree would receive fifty lashes while a freeman would have to pay a fine of fifty drachmas. In addition to penalties and fines, the name of either slave or freeman had to be reported to civil authorities. The involvement of both religious and secular groups in the protection of the grove's timber indicates the great concern for its safety. That the decree had to proscribe removing even twigs suggests just how scarce wood had become around Athens. Similar laws protected sacred groves at Andania in central Messenia, Euboea, and Samos.

Wood Resources and the Rise of Macedonia, Fourth Century B.C.

Despite attempts by the Greeks to cut down on their consumption of wood, they still needed huge quantities. Silver smelting at Laurion alone burned more than 24 million pines or over 52 million oaks. The largest outlays of fuel for Laurion occurred during the two most active periods of the mines, from 482 to 404 B.C. and from the second decade of the fourth century B.C. until its end. The surrounding area could supply only a fraction of Laurion's fuel. The Athenians therefore had to import wood for this and other purposes. In the fourth century B.C., Athens had to depend on Macedonia as its "timber yard" since Athens was never able to reclaim its "wood-lot" at Amphipolis even though the Spartans had promised its return at the end of the Peloponnesian War.

Wood from abroad was indeed very expensive. A single log cost the Athenians as much as 177½ drachmas, or about eighty-eight times the daily wage of a master mason at the start of the fourth century B.C. The dearth of wood in Athens brought fortunes to those who still had trees growing on their land in Attica. A law case in Athens during the fourth century B.C. demonstrates this. The proceedings revealed that the defendant, Phaenippus, had a "very considerable source of revenue: six asses carry off wood the whole year through and he receives more than twelve drachmae a day." More revealing was the fact that Phaenippus found the wood business so profitable even though his donkeys carried the wood daily from his Kytheron estate to Athens, a distance of over forty miles. The jury was also informed that Phaenippus "sold cut timber," making more than 3,000 drachmas by the sale.

Athenians who needed wood also resorted to the most dastardly acts to acquire supplies. The high cost of wood led a naval commander, Medias, to desert his duty. Medias was to have used his ship to help escort the Athenian fleet home from war in Euboea. Instead, he lagged behind to load "his ship with timber [for] fences . . . door posts for his own house and pit props for his silver mines."

The Macedonians, in contrast, had so much wood to spare that Philip played upon its scarcity in lands he wished to conquer by offering their leaders gifts of timber in exchange for their loyalty and their help in overthrowing their respective governments. Demosthenes argued that once the Olynthian politician Lasthenes "had roofed his house with timber [which was] sent as a present from Macedonia, nothing could save" the Olynthians from losing their independence to Philip. Demosthenes likewise charged that Philip had seduced certain Athenian envoys to sign a peace treaty and make an alliance with him by giving them generous supplies of timber. Timber, in fact, had become the most notorious bribe used by Macedonia to induce betrayal.

Macedonia's forests were one of two main sources of the state's wealth and military strength, and it was therefore no coincidence that when the Macedonians used their trees for their own development rather than allowing other states to exploit them, Macedonia became the premier power of Greece and of much of the known world.

The Romans were well aware of the role wood had played in Macedonia's rise to greatness. After conquering Macedonia in 167 B.C., Rome prohibited Macedonians from cutting their timber. This policy was adopted as a precautionary measure with the objective of ensuring that Macedonia could never again develop into a power that might rival Rome's.

A Leading Roman Citizen's Concern

Cicero, one of late Republican Rome's most eloquent statesmen, expressed concern over the decline of Rome's woodlands in a Senate debate. Servillius Rullus, Tribune of the People, asked the Senate to sell an important state forest to the private sector. Cicero saw Rullus's proposal as the latest example of the cupidity of land management policies that favored development over preservation. He lambasted the trend, arguing, "He is a luxurious rake who sells his forest before his vineyards." Before the Senate he appealed to the national interests to defeat Rullus's proposal. Cicero equated the loss of an important forest with robbing the Roman people of material to wage war.

Toward Self-Sufficiency

Deprived of their principal sources of wood, the Egyptian rulers of the eleventh century, in the fashion of their predecessors, the Ptolomies, made the cultivation of trees a national priority. They planted numerous trees in southern Egypt on both sides of the Nile and dug many canals to irrigate these plantations, which occupied about forty square miles. This was a significant amount of land, considering the narrowness of the Nile valley and the small amount of available arable land, much of which had to be reserved for growing crops to feed Egypt's huge population.

Ibn Mamati, who lived at the time the Egyptians were compelled to conserve wood, attested to the importance the government placed on forestry: "Orders were constantly given by the rulers to guard the forests, to protect and defend them against deprivations." According to Mamati, the government did not leave anything to chance: it oversaw every aspect, from the trees' growth in the plantations to the arrival of the wood at the Cairo docks. Egyptian authorities also prioritized wood use. "Forest guards were told," Mamati related, "not to allow the cutting of trees suitable for the building of the fleet." They also had orders "only to permit the use of fallen branches" and wood unsuitable for anything else for firewood. When the fuel merchant took possession of his allotted portion, the forest guardian issued a certificate indicating the amount purchased. Upon arriving in Cairo, an employee of the central government would inspect the load. If he found wood suitable for shipbuilding, he would confiscate it. If not, he weighed the firewood and checked to see that it corresponded with the forest guard's computations.

Those in charge of the forests also sold wood to local people and delivered wood to merchants in Cairo for construction, to make sugarcane presses, sugar mills, and olive mills. Ship timber, however, was so highly valued that it traveled in barges escorted by guards. The government took these precautions to make sure such prized cargo went straight to the shipyards.

Care for the forests degenerated over time, reaching its nadir in the middle of the thirteenth century. The governor of Faiyum, who administered a region southwest of Cairo, complained bitterly that the forests "have not escaped vast spoilage." He took to task consumers "who frequently cut for the needs of their housing, their sugar mills or other construction or for fuel." Farmers were also to blame, according to the governor, as they would chop down trees "whose shade interfered with planting" or to supplement their income so they could buy a new ox to replace an animal that had died. Lax enforcement by officials and corruption of those in government responsible for the implementation of forest policy permitted such "cuttings, even though the trees were the exclusive property of the public," the governor charged. He pointed his accusing finger at his fellow governors in the provinces who looked the other way when farmers rid their land of trees and wood merchants bribed forest officers "by means of small gifts."

Although such malfeasance "resulted in a large number of wealthy people," the governor observed, those living in the highly populated north suffered, as did the navy. The needs of people in Cairo became so acute that they ravaged trees growing on plantations near the city until all of them disappeared. Next to go were neighboring woods. In one forest, "four thousand trees were cut in a few days and since then even more," lamented this concerned official.

Dealing with the Infidels

As local forests disappeared but the need for wood remained, the Egyptians of the thirteenth century had to rely more heavily on the few foreign sources still available to them. Egyptian wood merchants could still bid for teak wood from India in the markets of Oman, where they paid approximately thirty dinars for each log, an amount comparable to the cost of an exceptional black slave.

According to an Arab commentator of the thirteenth century, there were "enormous forests" in Venetian territory, but Muslims could not consider seizing the wood since the Christians had once again become "the masters of the sea." Instead, the Muslims had to pay exorbitant prices to obtain such timber.

Wood and the Balance of Payments

Wood merchants returned home well remunerated for the risks they took. So much gold passed from Muslims to Europeans in payment for wood, other commodities, and slaves that the balance of payments tipped in favor of Europe. Egypt's economic downturn reflected the change that the early-fifteenth-century Egyptian historian al-Maqrizi linked to the vicissitudes of its wood supply. When forests abounded, keeping Egypt well stocked, the nation prospered, Maqrizi argued. But in his day, Maqrizi claimed that buildings languished in disrepair as "it is practically impossible to find any wood."

Many people might find it difficult to picture the fact that the area of the world now known as Lebanon, or the Levant, was once graced with some millions of acres in timber, the famous Cedars of Lebanon. As Carter and Dale describe in the following selection, these forests, and the rich topsoil that supported them, provided the foundation for the relatively brief but brilliant flourishing of the Phoenician civilization. At the height of its period of prosperity, Phoenicia had 150,000 forestry workers in its employ!

Take particular note of Carter and Dale's observations about the well-known ecological dangers of goat herding. Countrysides severely degraded by goats are sometimes called "goatscapes." Goat herding tends naturally to arise as the fertility of an area breaks down, because goats can survive under very harsh conditions. But they can denude the land of all vegetation that may be still struggling to survive, even climbing trees to strip them of their last leaves. Nevertheless, it can prove to be very difficult to persuade people in such regions to restrain or give up their goats, since these animals are often the main wealth the people possess. This example illustrates how difficult it can be to break out of the cycle of environmental degradation, which, like poverty itself, tends to be self-reinforcing.

The example of the Levant is surprisingly relevant to the Canadian context, because of the geographical similarities with the British Columbia coast. As in British Columbia, the Levant was steeply sloped, with a very similar climate and dense coniferous forest cover. The soil in both regions tends to erode easily when the forest cover is stripped. Is it out of the question that Canada's West Coast might not suffer a similar fate, if deforestation goes on long enough? At least one can say that goat herding has not become widespread in British Columbia yet.

LUMBERJACKS IN LEBANON

Vernon Gill Carter and Tom Dale

The Phoenicians, who borrowed most of their culture from Mesopotamia, Egypt, and Crete, probably settled the country now known as Lebanon between 2500 and 2000 B.C. Apparently never great creators, they were great imitators and distributors of civilization. The Phoenicians were primarily responsible for disseminating the alphabet over most of the Mediterranean region. They possibly learned navigation from the Minoans, whom they soon surpassed in this skill, and became the foremost merchants, traders, and seafaring people of the known world from about 1000 to 500 B.C. They were the first people of the Mediterranean to venture out into the Atlantic Ocean, sailing as far as Britain seven hundred years before Caesar, and circumnavigating the continent of Africa two thousand years before DaGama of Portugal gained fame for accomplishing that feat.

The homeland of the Phoenicians consisted of a relatively narrow strip of coastal plain, the back of which was another strip of foothills that rose steeply into the Lebanon Mountains. The coastal plain and foothills undoubtedly had fertile soil when these people settled there, and enough rain falls there to produce excellent yields of grain, grapes, olives, and most other crops grown by the ancients. Before crops were grown by man, nature grew lush crops of grass and forests, including the famed "Cedars of Lebanon." The chief trouble was that the amount of easily tilled land was definitely limited by the mountain range.

The Lebanon Mountains gave the Phoenicians considerable protection from warlike inland tribes. They were not overrun by conquering armies as often as were most of the other peoples of the eastern Mediterranean region. But the mountains also served to hem in the Phoenicians as well as keep out their enemies. It seems logical to assume that their population grew faster than that of most other peoples surrounding them because of the protection against war that the mountains afforded. Hence, we may assume that the Phoenicians literally pushed themselves out into the Mediterranean Sea, and probably became sailors and merchants more from necessity than from choice.

Early in their history, the Phoenicians found that they had an easily marketed product, timber, growing in their homeland. The people of the treeless plains of Egypt and Mesopotamia were hungry for timber; building with stone and clay alone has its limitations. So the Phoenicians, using bronze axes, started lumbering off the forests. They used what wood they needed for their buildings and ships and exported the surplus.

But the Phoenicians found it necessary to eat. The narrow coastal plain between the sea and the hills soon became inadequate for the expanding population. With only one way to go, cultivated fields began to creep up the cleared slopes. Hill farms took over the formerly forested land as rapidly as the trees were cut. Erosion began almost at once when the winter rains came. Most of the slopes were steep, ranging up to 75 per cent (about 34 degrees). Generally speaking, soil conservationists in the United States consider slopes of more than 20 to 25 per cent unfit for cultivation; such sloping land should be kept covered with forests or grass.

Food was always a problem. Lumber was traded to Egypt and Mesopotamia for grain, but it was seldom enough. The Phoenicians, having an abundance of timber and a driving need, expanded their export trade, while villages of lumberjacks sprang up in the mountains. Palestine, to the south, became another good market for timber. King Solomon was a very good customer in the tenth century. Some 150,000 men labored in the Lebanon forests to supply timber for his palaces and temples and for homes for other wealthy Hebrews.

We do not know whether the forests were cut primarily to get the timber and hill farms were the by-product, or whether the clearing was done mainly to get more farm land and timber was the by-product; but the two went together—deforestation and hill farming. Both continued at an increasing rate, while soil erosion accelerated rapidly.

The Phoenicians were not easily defeated in their fight against nature. They had plenty of stone on the cleared hillsides, and they made unique and profitable use of it. They constructed rock walls across the slopes and made the first bench terraces known to history. They built some of these rock-wall terraces probably as early as the fifteenth century B.C. In time, they terraced thousands of acres in this way.

The construction of such terraces requires a tremendous amount of labor and is undertaken only by people faced with starvation. The cost of labor alone to terrace a single acre would amount to at least $5,000 if figured at current American wages. Some of these terraces are still cultivated today, more than three thousand years after they were built, and the ruins of many others are still visible. Faulty engineering, the power of cloudbursts, and the lack of repairs led to the failure of many of the formerly terraced slopes, which are now eroded to bare rock.

Where terracing was established as a community habit, the farmers, at least, had food, but they probably produced little surplus since the cost, in labor, of constructing and maintaining such terraces limited cultivation to rather small areas and thus prevented the production of any large yields. Yet the food production might have been adequate to maintain a moderately prosperous civilization if all the land had been terraced, but only a small part of the deforested hillsides was so treated.

The Phoenicians were probably a nomadic tribe originally, and most individuals were not inclined to the hard labor of terrace agriculture. Goat herds were favored by many as a source of livelihood. As the two thousand square miles of forest were slowly cut and herbaceous plants appeared, the goats took over. Stories told about the indestructible digestive systems of goats are not without foundation—a goat can eat almost any type of vegetation, including young trees; it can go almost anywhere to get food, even to the most inaccessible crag; and it can even climb certain types of trees and eat the leaves or fruits.

It seems certain that the desolation which is Lebanon today can in part be traced to the goats. Where the forests might have recovered to protect the soil, prevent floods, and provide a continuing economic asset, the goats prevented such recovery. Seedling trees, starting from windblown seed, were eaten and killed as fast as they appeared. Deforestation and the scavenger goats brought on most of the erosion which turned Lebanon into a well-rained-on desert.

By the ninth century B.C., the Phoenicians found that their lumbering, industry, commerce, and meager agriculture were inadequate to support their growing population. Colonization of other lands became almost imperative. They began by founding colonies along the coast of North Africa and eventually colonized all the poorly defended lands along the coast of the western Mediterranean. Carthage and other points along the North African coast, Sardinia, Sicily, Spain, and other colonies, soon became the breadbasket for Lebanon. The Phoenicians in Lebanon shipped manufactured products to the colonies in exchange for food, and not only did this trade supply food for the cities in Lebanon, but it also stimulated commerce and industry. According to custom, the colonists usually paid the high shipping charges both ways, while the Lebanese merchants exacted fat profits on all transactions.

Furthermore, the enterprising merchants of Lebanon opened trade relations with the people of practically all ports of the Mediterranean, and some of them even traded with the barbarians of Atlantic ports, especially with the Britons. They also traded overland with Mesopotamia and far eastern countries. By the end of the eighth century B.C., they had almost a monopoly on shipping in the Mediterranean.

From the eighth through the sixth centuries B.C., the Phoenicians had their golden age. Lumbering continued, and both industry and trade prospered, but the prosperity was mainly confined to the port cities. The land of Lebanon was by now so poor that it afforded little more than subsistence living for the farmers and goatherders who occupied it. When an occasional conquering army came through the passes of the Lebanon Mountains, it paid little attention to the farmers. Tribute levied on Tyre, Sidon, Byblos, and the other rich cities was paid mainly by taxes assessed against the wealthy merchants and shipowners. Fortunately, such conquerors did not come too often during this prosperous period.

The Phoenician prosperity had definite limitations because it depended on ever-expanding industry and trade, which, in turn, depended on sea power. In this last area the Greeks began to challenge them during the sixth century B.C. By the time of the Greek and Persian wars, the Greeks had become such formidable competitors that the Phoenicians gladly sent a large fleet to fight with the Persians. Then the Greeks defeated the combined fleets of the Phoenicians and other Persian satrapies at Salamis in 480 B.C. This was the beginning of the end of progressive Phoenician civilization. Commerce declined rapidly, and the decline of industry followed. Lebanon became more and more dependent on her colonies, especially Carthage, which still dominated the western Mediterranean.

After Alexander conquered all Lebanon, destroyed the principal city of Tyre, and killed or sold into slavery that city's inhabitants in 332 B.C., Phoenicia was never again an important factor in eastern Mediterranean civilization. And after Rome destroyed Carthage in 146 B.C., the Phoenicians, like the Minoans, were soon forgotten.

By the time of Alexander's conquest, there were few resources left in Lebanon. Most of the forests were gone, and the remaining trees disappeared within a few centuries under Greek and Roman axes. Most of the topsoil was gone from the hills, lowlands were covered with erosional debris, harbors were silting up with mud from the eroding highlands, and river deltas were marshy pestholes infested with malaria-bearing mosquitoes. Civilization in Lebanon could not rise again, as it had in Mesopotamia and Egypt, because the resources were no longer there to support it. The total life span of progressive civilization in Lebanon was little more than fifteen hundred years (about fifty or sixty generations).

It seems logical that during the 2,300 years that have since passed nature would have repaired most of the damage done to the land—and nature doubtless would have done so if given a chance—but Lebanon has been kept down mainly by man and his goats. Much of the former forest land, now reduced to four small groves, is so severely eroded that only geologic weathering can build a new soil, a process that will require thousands of years and no goats.

Some of the Phoenicians made a valiant effort toward saving their land. A small minority, whose insight or need led them to the root of the evil, built bench terraces, regardless of cost and hardship, and attempted to insure for themselves and their descendants a permanent basis for survival. The majority, however, in their ignorance, greed, laziness, or preoccupation with shekels and commerce, ignored what was happening to the land. Apparently they never considered sustained-yield forestry, which might have given them a continuing export trade in lumber. If they did think of it, their goats prevented them from practicing it. In other words, their conservation efforts were both too little and too late.

The following two selections require very little comment. They illustrate nearly totally opposite views as to the value of the West Coast forest. The statement by Gwaganad of the Haada Gwaii (the Queen Charlotte Islands) was made before Justice Harry McKay (Kilsli, as she addresses him) on November 6, 1985. Gwaganad was opposing the attempt of a logging company to get an injunction to prohibit Haida blocking of logging roads.

"THAT'S ALL TREES ARE FOR . . ."

Jamie Swift

Gordon Gibson is a member of an endangered species in the Canadian forest industry. He is a pioneer logger whose successful family business was based on "hands-on management" and a hard-working, hard-nosed approach to the business of getting the logs out of the bush. The self-styled "Bull of the Woods" has been a merchant, a sailor, and a politician as well as a logging boss. Gibson and his three brothers ran logging operations up and down the west coast of Vancouver Island for sixty years, starting out by felling cedar trees forty-five feet in circumference directly into Clayoquot Sound. The Gibson family eventually sold out to a powerful international forest corporation based in Denmark.

This Horatio Alger of Canadian logging brought what might be called an old fashioned approach to the modern forest industry: a perspective closer to that of an old Ottawa Valley timber baron than a modern forest industry executive. "Logging will always be done best where the owner puts on his caulk boots[1] and goes where he's logging," Gibson once stated. "How can we expect efficient logging with the owner in New York—someone who can't tell a hemlock from a cedar?"

Gibson's story, told in his rambling autobiography, reads like an ode to the virtues of honest, hard work and rugged individualism, a sharp contrast to the new era he saw coming in, when the multinational forest firm and the notion of sustained yield forest management were taking firm root. Gibson, the no-nonsense, do-it-yourself logging operator, had no use for the new ways of the forest business which characterized the sixties and seventies.

In 1960, while still a sprightly fifty-six years of age, Gordon Gibson sat down with C.D. Orchard, who had just retired as B.C.'s Chief Forester, to discuss the state of the woods and the changes both men had seen in their long careers. As head of the B.C. Forest Service (BCFS), Orchard had been the civil servant chiefly responsible for administering the transformation of provincial forest policy in the wake of the report of the first Sloan Commission. It had been Orchard's job to initiate the system of forest management licences, the basis of the new-look postwar policy of intensive forestry in Canada's premier forest jurisdiction.

The former B.C. Chief Forester was understandably miffed when confronted with Gibson's adamant rejection of a concept that Orchard himself regarded as sacrosanct: the idea that forests cut down had to be replaced through the active intervention of forest managers. Orchard asked Gibson what they were here for, if not to grow trees? "To cut down the ones we've got, make a living out of them and maybe make a fortune," replied Gibson. "The trees are no more important than the pleasure they give the human race out of using them. That's all trees are for."

Clearly, the logging operator and the forester could scarcely see eye to eye when it came to a discussion of the way the forest should be treated. Orchard was well aware that the province's overwhelming dependence on the forest industry would continue into the twenty-first century. He asked incredulously, "Aren't you preaching now that we have no responsibility to posterity?"

Gibson was forthright. "Absolutely none at all. . . . We have to cut trees. The more we cut, the better it is."

The irascible businessman, who knew the timber trade from the end of a cross-cut saw on Clayoquot Sound to the halls of the legislature down the coast of Victoria, maintained that the risk of running out of timber was the same as any other business risk. As for the government's modern-day policy of managing the forest to assure a sustained yield in the future, he said: "I'm not much of a believer in a country as big as B.C. talking yet about planting, thinning or pruning. It's too costly. . . . I don't think we can afford it."

NOTES

1. Caulk boots (pronounced cork) are the spiked boots worn by B.C. loggers in order to stay upright working on the wet, fallen timber of the coastal region.

SPEAKING FOR THE EARTH: THE HAIDA WAY

Gwaganad

Kilsli, Kilsligana, Kiljadgana, Taaxwilaas. Your Honour, chiefs, ladies held in high esteem, friends. I thank you for this opportunity to speak today. I was aware that I could get a lawyer, but I feel you lose if you go through another person.

My first language is Haida. I feel through another person, a lawyer, they also speak another language, and I would have lost what I hope to help Kilsli understand and feel.

Since the beginning of time—I have been told this through our oral stories—since the beginning of time the Haidas have been on the Queen Charlotte Islands.

That was our place, given to us.

We were put on the islands as caretakers of this land.

Approximately two hundred years ago foreigners came to that land. The Haida are very hospitable people. The people came. They were welcomed. We shared. They told us that perhaps there is a better way to live, a different religion, education in schools. The Haida tried this way. The potlatches were outlawed. In many schools my father attended in Kokalitza, the Haida language was not allowed to be spoken. He was punished if he used his language. To this day, Watson Price, my father, understands every word of the Haida language, but he doesn't speak it.

So the people came. We tried their way. Their language. Their education. Their way of worship. It is clear to me that they are not managing our lands well. If this continues, there will be nothing left for my children and my grandchildren to come. I feel that the people governing us should give us a chance to manage the land the way we know how it should be.

It seems that the other cultures don't see trees. They see money. It's take and take and take from the earth. That's not the way it is in my mind.

On Lyell Island—I want to address Lyell Island and South Moresby, the injunction being served on us. I want to say why that concerns me. To me it is a home of our ancestors. As Lily stated, our ancestors are still there. It is my childhood. Every spring come March my father and mother would taken me down to Burnaby Narrows. We stayed there till June. It's wonderful memories I had. I am thankful to my parents for bringing me up the traditional way. There was concern on the Indian agent's part that I missed too much school. But how can you tell them that I was at school?

Because of that upbringing, because I was brought down to Lyell Island area, Burnaby Narrows and living off the land—that's why I feel the way I do about my culture and the land.

In those early years the first lesson in my life that I remember is respect. I was taught to respect the land. I was taught to respect the food that comes from the land. I was taught that everything had a meaning. Every insect had a meaning and none of those things were to be held lightly. The food was never to be taken for granted. In gathering the food—the nearest I can translate—I can say to gather food is a spiritual experience for me.

We are a nation of people at risk today. They say that to make a culture the language is important. I am proud to say I speak my language, but not too many more people in my age do. So you can say in a sense, if this keeps up, the language is going fast. In the past the culture was in very much jeopardy when the potlatching was outlawed. We almost lost ourselves as a people. That culture has been revived in the past few years. There is pride in being a Haida, pride in being a native. The only thing we can hold onto to maintain that pride and dignity as a people is the land. It's from the land we get our food, it's from the land we get our strength. From the sea we get our energy. If this land such as Lyell Island is logged off as they want to log it off—and they will go on logging. We have watched this for many years. I have read records that our forefathers fought in 1913. It's been an ongoing fight. But no one is really hearing us. They said they wouldn't log Lyell Island at first and now I hear they are going to go ahead. So today I am here because pretty soon all we are going to be fighting for is stumps. When Frank Beban and his crew are through and there are stumps left on Lyell Island, they got a place to go. We, the Haida people, will be on the Island. I don't want my children and my future grandchildren to inherit stumps. They say, "Don't be concerned, we're planting trees again. Wait for the second growth. It will be just like before." I travel all around the Island a lot with my family. I see lots of things. This summer I got to see second growth coming. I saw twenty-year-old second growth around Salt Lagoon. They were planted so close that the trees couldn't grow big. They were small and there was no light getting into them. They couldn't grow. You could see and you could feel that they could not grow. Therefore, I don't feel too hopeful when I hear second growth.

I want to touch now on another very important area in my life as a food gatherer. It is my job, my purpose, to insure that I gather certain food for my husband and my children, and I want to share one part. It's called *gkow*. That's herring roe on kelp. In the spring the herring come and they spawn on kelp. For many years now I have been harvesting that and putting it away for the winter. But so far I haven't heard what—why is food gathering spiritual?

It's a spiritual thing that happens. It doesn't just happen every year. You can't take that for granted. We can't take that for granted because everything in the environment has to be perfect. The climate has to be perfect, the water temperature, the kelp have to be ready and the herring have to want to spawn.

But I want to share what goes on in my spiritual self, in my body, come February. And I feel it's an important point. That's what makes me as a Haida different from you, Kilsli. My body feels that it's time to spawn. It gets ready in February. I get a longing to be on the sea. I constantly watch the ocean surrounding the island where the herring spawn. My body is kind of on edge in anticipation.

Finally the day comes when it spawns. The water gets all milky around it. I know I am supposed to speak for myself, but I share this experience with all the friends, the lady friends, that we pick together this wonderful feeling on the day that it happens, the excitement, the relief that the herring did indeed come this year. And you don't quite feel complete until you are right out on the ocean with your hands in the water harvesting the kelp, the roe on kelp, and then your body feels right. That cycle is complete.

And it's not quite perfect until you eat your first batch of herring roe on kelp. I don't know how to say it well, but your body almost rejoices in that first feed. It feels right. If you listen to your body it tells you a lot of things. If you put something wrong in it, your body feels it. If you put something right in it, your body feels it. Your spiritual self feels it. In order to make me complete I need the right food from the land. I also need to prepare it myself. I have to harvest it myself. The same things goes for fish, the fish that we gather for the winter. But I wanted to elaborate on the harvesting of kelp to give you an idea of how it feels as Haida to harvest food.

So I want to stress that it's the land that helps us maintain our culture. It is an important, important part of our culture. Without that land, I fear very much for the future of the Haida nation. Like I said before, I don't want my children to inherit stumps. I want my children and my grandchildren to grow up with pride and dignity as a member of the Haida nation. I fear that if we take that land, we may lose the dignity and the pride of being a Haida. Without that there is no — there is no way that I can see that we could carry on with pride and dignity. I feel very strongly — that's why I came down to express my concern for my children and grandchildren.

So today, if that injunction goes through and the logging continues — and there is a saying up there, they say, "Log it to the beach." Then what? What will be left and who will be left? We can't go anywhere else but the Island.

I study a lot about our brothers on the mainland, the North American Plains Indians in their history. They moved a lot because they were forced to. Some moved north, south, east, west, back up against the mountains and back again.

We as Haida people can't move anymore west. We can go over into the ocean is all. So when the logging is gone, is done, if it goes through and there is stumps left, the loggers will have gone and we will be there as we have been since the beginning of time. Left with very little to work with as a people.

Again I want to thank you, Kilsli, for this opportunity to speak and share my culture. Thank you very much.

We now explore a chapter of Canadian environmental history that, like many significant chapters in Canadian history, has been almost entirely forgotten—the reclamation of the Palliser Triangle region of Saskatchewan from desert during the Dust Bowl years of the 1930s.

SUMMERFALLOWING: THE LESSON UNLEARNED

Kent A. Peacock

In the following, I rely heavily on the very valuable book *Men against the Desert* by James H. Gray (Gray 1967). This is an account of the Dust Bowl years in the Canadian Prairies and especially in that region known as the Palliser Triangle, which lies in the southern portion of the province of Saskatchewan.

To understand this story, we need to know the meaning of the term *summerfallow*. In general, to let land lie fallow is to leave it unharvested for a year or more in order to allow it to recover its fertility. Summerfallowing is a type of fallowing developed in Western Canada (indeed, to meet the needs of farming in the Palliser Triangle) in the 1880s. It is a way of conserving soil moisture (some might say a way of cheating nature) that sometimes makes possible bumper crops of wheat in low rainfall areas.

A good crop of wheat requires around 20 inches of rainfall. However, in the Palliser region, annual precipitation is typically only about 15 inches per year. It was discovered that if a farmer leaves a field fallow for a year but prevents, by cultivation or other means, all plant growth on that field, enough soil moisture may build up that a good crop of wheat is possible every second year. The idea is that by keeping down weeds and grass one prevents them from using up soil moisture by evaporation and transpiration.

The essence of the method, as it was practised in the early years of the century, was frequent, assiduous cultivation of the fallow field, in order to kill weeds and keep the surface bare. Farmers prided themselves on how smooth and black they could keep the "dust mulch" on their fields. Even though this worked at first (for reasons I will explain below), it was a prescription for disaster.

What happened in the Dust Bowl of the 1930s seems to have been the result of synergy between two factors: the depletion of soil fertility caused by two to three decades of incompetent soil cultivation and a prolonged drought cycle (which itself, as far as we know, was caused by factors outside human agency). Huge areas of fertile land in Canada and the United States turned to powder and "blew out of control," as the saying went. As Gray reports, on May 12, 1934, a gigantic black cloud of dust was sighted over the Atlantic Ocean, as a vast "black blizzard" ravaged the Plains and scoured away hundreds of millions of tons of topsoil in one day alone.

> Each year the disaster area had expanded until it now [1938] embraced 250 municipalities and 18,000,000 acres [7,300,000 hectares]—a quarter of all the arable land in Canada. . . . It threatened the social and economic survival of 900,000 people. If prairie agriculture could not be saved, if the desert could not be contained and then reclaimed, the cities that lived off agriculture could not survive. And without productive and prosperous and populated prairie provinces, could Canada itself survive? This was the unasked question on everyone's mind. (Gray 1967, p. 3)

With the dust storms came plagues of grasshoppers and other insect pests, in quantities that stagger the imagination. More than once farmers in the Palliser region would have a crop off to a good start only to have it totally destroyed in a few hours by clouds of grasshoppers, who would eat not only the crops but fenceposts, shovel handles, and literally the shirts off people's backs if they were unlucky enough to be outside at the time.

Farley Mowat (1984) points out a little-noticed connection between locust plagues and the near-extinction of a migratory bird species called the Eskimo curlew. This omnivorous bird travelled in vast flocks from North to South America and back again, apparently timing its arrival in a region with the appearance of some especially plentiful foodsource. It appears that the curlews would migrate northwards through the Great Plains at just about the same time that grasshopper larvae were hatching in the millions, and would feast upon them. The Eskimo curlews were slaughtered indiscriminately wherever their flight paths brought them within shotgun range of farmers and hunters, and in a few decades they, like the passenger pigeon, were wiped out. (The species is not "officially" extinct, since a handful of individual birds have been sighted in the last sixty years or so. See Freedman 1989.) It seems quite likely (although perhaps it could never be proven) that the multiplication of grasshopper hordes by the turn of the century may have been brought about in part by the pointless extirpation of their chief predator.

While one can cite specific local factors that contributed to the disaster—summerfallowing, possibly the destruction of the Eskimo curlew—Gray sees the Canadian Dust Bowl as part of a larger historical pattern:

> And how had all this come to pass, in a land that had been broken to the plow for less than two generations? Essentially, the disaster in Saskatchewan was part of a much larger whole which extended backwards to the dawn of time. . . . It began, possibly, when the first cave man domesticated the first goats which over-grazed and trampled out the grass on the hillsides to open the soil for wind and water erosion. Archaeologists in Mesopotamia have uncovered the village of Khorsabad which was buried in 15 feet of soil blown over it 2600 years ago. . . . The Romans destroyed Carthage, and then took only 200 years to turn the rich soils of North Africa into a desert wasteland. . . . People everywhere have tended to follow the same pattern—cut, burn, plant, destroy, move on.

Apart from this grim overall historical lesson, there are three points of special relevance to take from Gray's story.

First, even though the defeat of the desert by the huge combined efforts of agronomists, government workers, and thousands of farmers and their families is one of the remarkable success stories in Canadian history, it is almost totally marginalized and forgotten. Perhaps success, like good health, is taken for granted when one has it; one just moves on to something else. I must leave it for the reader to decide whether or not this phenomenon is somehow typically Canadian.

Second, Gray makes it clear that successful farming on dry Prairie soils depends very much on having the right sort of equipment—powerful enough tractors to do the work quickly enough, and new types of cultivation implements that had never been used before and had to be improvised with much trial and error. This suggests that technology could have a very positive role to play in the achievement of sustainability.

The third, and perhaps the most philosophically interesting, point to note is that Gray repeatedly emphasizes that the culprit in the whole story, the one clearly identifiable technical mistake made by virtually all farmers in the region (and indeed throughout the Great Plains) was the practice of summerfallowing. (The "universal practice of maintaining a black summerfallow throughout the summer was the primary cause of soil erosion and farm abandonment" Gray 1967, pp. 187–88.) This method of conserving soil moisture can be very effective, but only when the soil has what pedologists (soil scientists) call good "structure," and that is primarily a consequence of a sufficient content of humus and organic matter. In the beginning, there was plenty of this to go around. Prairie soils belong to the class of soils called "chernozems." These are deep, fertile topsoils based on limestone-rich loess (fine wind-blown sediments laid down in the glacial epoch). The soils of the steppes of Eastern Europe are also chernozemic. When the settlers first arrived on the Prairies, the deep, rich humus supported grasses that were often so tall and thick they could hide a rider on horseback.

When the almost impenetrable virgin sod was first broken, Prairie soils had a very high organic matter content, and so for a few years farmers could get away with summerfallowing. However, after repeated plowing, with exposure to sun and wind, and with crops being taken off but not much organic matter being put back into the soil, the organic matter in the soil disintegrates and oxidizes. The topsoil, which is a symbiotic association of plants, invertebrates, and micro-organisms, literally dies. The soil particles (the "peds," as they are called) lose their cohesion, and the soil crumbles into a largely mineral powder. Combine this with a drought period and, in only a few years, one has turned some of the most productive land in the world into desert. So if there is any one lesson to be learned from the Dust Bowl, it is this: don't summerfallow!

A great part of Gray's book describes the intense efforts of agronomists, farmers, and mechanics to devise means of cultivating the land that would tend to build up rather than deplete the organic content of the soil and protect its structure from wind and sun. Eventually, methods of plowless fallowing were developed. These involved leaving a so-called stubble mulch or trash mulch of crop residue on the land after the grain had been taken off. Trash mulching went against all the better farmers' instincts, since it seemed so sloppy and unworkmanlike, and it took some effort to re-educate their standards of beauty.

The mistake the early Prairie farmers made was to think of grain growing as primarily a problem in water management, when in fact this is only a part of the farmer's job. The heart of any successful method of soil cultivation (on the Prairies or anywhere else) is the maintenance of enough organic matter in the soil to nourish the soil microfauna. The farmer is first and foremost a farmer of bacteria, actinomycetes, fungi, and earthworms. In effect, the farmer's main job is to establish a kind of rough-and-ready **symbiosis** with the soil organisms. This is what the farmers of the Palliser region eventually learned to try to accomplish with trash mulching, although they might not have said in so many words that this was what they were doing. With flourishing soil microfauna comes good soil structure; with good soil structure comes good water retention; and with good water retention any number of schemes for water conservation might be workable.

Note that even Gray misreads the issue:

> . . . the whole of the northern Great Plains was little more than a gigantic evaporation basin left over from the ice age. On its surface, the sun and air would evaporate twice the amount of free water the land received from the rain and snow that fell. It was therefore necessary to use the moisture of two years to grow one crop of grain. But by keeping the stubble standing upright on the surface of the soil . . . the hot winds could not reach down to suck out the moisture. (Gray 1967, p. 238)

It is perfectly true that one of the main benefits of stubble mulch is to prevent wind from drying the soil. But the statement that it takes two years of moisture to grow one crop of grain misses the point that before the sod was broken one year's precipitation sufficed to support a fabulously luxuriant plant growth. Could there be something wrong-headed about our whole technique of farming, which focusses on stripping off existing plant cover and forcing a monoculture food crop?

This raises questions that we cannot answer here; and in any case, there is no question that the practical techniques developed during the Dust Bowl years—stubble mulching and innovative cultivation—were an enormous improvement from an ecological point of view. But are we really that much wiser than the ancient Romans and Mesopotamians?

One might think that the lessons learned from an ecological disaster that nearly permanently destroyed a major portion of Canada's agricultural breadbasket would be branded in memory. But, in fact, many Prairie farmers still practise summerfallowing, in spite of strenuous efforts by Agriculture Canada to convince them not to. At this writing, *the amount of land in summerfallow is still in the millions of hectares.* (A difference today, however, is that herbicides would often be used to control weed growth in summerfallowing, instead of relying entirely on cultivation. This would be less immediately damaging to soil structure, but questionable in other ways; in particular because of the damage that the herbicides may do to soil microfauna.) So far, we have not yet had another drought cycle quite as severe as the one that devastated the West in the 1930s, although we came close to it in the late 1980s (and then the land did begin to blow again). So far . . .

But why don't we remember what we have so painfully and expensively been forced to learn?

FURTHER READING

The importance of cultivation techniques in agriculture was stressed by many pioneer "organic" farmers, such as Edward Faulkner (1943) and Louis Bromfield (1950). Carter and Dale (1974) and Perlin (1989) trace the effect of soil erosion and deforestation throughout history. Swift (1983) provides a critical history of Canadian forestry. Worster (1979) gives an overview of the whole phenomenon of the Dust Bowl, with particular attention to its ecological aspects. Gray (1967) recounts the reclamation of the Palliser Triangle region of Saskatchewan in the Dust Bowl years of the 1930s. Sears (1980[1935]) and Thirgood (1981) are classic studies of historical land degradation by humans. Runnels (1995) recounts recent findings on ancient Greece.

QUESTIONS TO CONSIDER

1. John Perlin notes that many cultures in ancient times practised techniques of soil conservation and afforestation, and developed an "ecological conscience" not unlike that of today. Why were almost all these early efforts at environmental protection ultimately unsuccessful? (Students frequently respond to this question with the answer, "Greed, greed, it was all greed." Does this really explain anything? If you think it does, be sure to define "greed.")
2. Can the needs of civilization for wood ever be reconciled with the needs of indigenous people who dwell within the forests?

CHAPTER FIVE

SEEKING A PERSPECTIVE

In the twentieth century, we see a dramatic acceleration of the human impact upon nature. It seems natural, therefore, for us to think of the environmental crisis as a peculiarly modern phenomenon. And given the fact that certain tendencies in Western civilization seem to be especially conducive to environmental destruction (see White's famous paper of 1967, for instance), it is natural to blame the crisis entirely on these historically recent and culturally specific elements. But, as always, history shows us that matters are not so simple.

The fact is that environmental destruction by humans goes a long way back. We already have before us the debatable role of early humans in Pleistocene extinctions, and the very clear role of early civilizations in deforestation and soil erosion. George Perkins Marsh, in a pioneering work on the human impact on the environment written over a century ago, provides, in rolling nineteenth-century prose, a sobering perspective.

THE RAVAGES OF MAN

George Perkins Marsh

... If we compare the present physical condition of the countries of which I am speaking, with the descriptions that ancient historians and geographers have given of their fertility and general capability of ministering to human uses, we shall find that more than one half of their whole extent—including the provinces most celebrated for the profusion and variety of their spontaneous and their cultivated products, and for the wealth and social advancement of their inhabitants—is either deserted by civilized man and surrendered to hopeless desolation, or at least greatly reduced in both productiveness and population. Vast forests have disappeared from mountain spurs and ridges; the vegetable earth accumulated beneath the trees by the decay of leaves and fallen trunks, the soil of the alpine pastures which skirted and indented the woods, and the mould of the upland fields, are washed away; meadows, once fertilized by irrigation, are waste and unproductive, because the cisterns and reservoirs that supplied the ancient canals are broken, or the springs that fed them dried up; rivers famous in history and song have shrunk to humble brooklets; the willows that ornamented and protected the banks of the lesser watercourses are gone, and the rivulets have ceased to exist as perennial currents, because the little water that finds its way into their old channels is evaporated by the droughts of summer, or absorbed by the parched earth, before it reaches the lowlands; the beds of the brooks have widened into broad expanses of pebbles and gravel, over which, though in the hot season passed dryshod, in winter sealike torrents thunder; the entrances of navigable streams are obstructed by sandbars, and harbors, once marts of an extensive commerce, are shoaled by the deposits of the rivers at whose mouths they lie; the elevation of the beds of estuaries, and the consequently diminished velocity of the streams which flow into them, have converted thousands of leagues of shallow sea and fertile lowland into unproductive and miasmatic morasses.

Besides the direct testimony of history to the ancient fertility of the regions to which I refer—Northern Africa, the greater Arabian peninsula, Syria, Mesopotamia, Armenia, and many other provinces of Asia Minor, Greece, Sicily, and parts of even Italy and Spain—the multitude and extent of yet remaining architectural ruins, and of decayed works of internal improvement, show that at former epochs a dense population inhabited those now lonely districts. Such a population could have been sustained only by productiveness of soil of which we at present discover but slender traces; and the abundance derived from that fertility serves to explain how large armies, like those of the ancient Persians, and of the Crusaders and the Tartars in later ages, could, without an organized commissariat, secure adequate supplies in long marches through territories which, in our times, would scarcely afford forage for a single regiment.

It appears, then, that the fairest and fruitfulest provinces of the Roman Empire, precisely that portion of terrestrial surface, in short, which, about the commencement of the Christian era, was endowed with the greatest superiority of soil, climate, and position, which had been carried to the highest pitch of physical improvement, and which thus combined the natural and artificial conditions best fitting it for the habitation and enjoyment of a dense and highly refined and cultivated population, is now completely exhausted of its fertility, or so diminished in productiveness, as, with the exception of a few favored oases that have escaped the general ruin, to be no longer capable of affording sustenance to civilized man. If to this realm of desolation we add the now wasted and solitary soils of Persia and the remoter East, that once fed their millions with milk and honey, we shall see that a territory larger than all Europe, the abundance of which sustained in bygone centuries a population scarcely inferior to that of the whole Christian world at the present day, has been entirely withdrawn from human use, or, at best, is thinly inhabited by tribes too few in numbers, too poor in superfluous products, and too little advanced in culture and the social arts, to contribute anything to the general moral or material interests of the great commonwealth of man. . . .

The following paper by Yi-Fu Tuan is frequently cited but infrequently reprinted. His main intent is to raise with exquisite tact the huge question of the discrepancy between our good intentions and what we really do. We will see that this is a recurrent theme throughout the history of the interaction between humans and the environment.

DISCREPANCIES BETWEEN ENVIRONMENTAL ATTITUDE AND BEHAVIOUR: EXAMPLES FROM EUROPE AND CHINA

Yi-Fu Tuan

Discrepancy between stated ideal and reality is a worrisome fact of our daily experience: in the political field one learns to discriminate between an orator's fulsome profession and what he can or will, in fact, carry out. The history of environmental ideas, however, has been pursued as an academic discipline largely in detachment from the question of how—if at all—these ideas guide the course of action, or how they arise out of it. Needless to say, there are many paradigmatic views of nature, such as those of science, that have great explicatory power and may, once they are applied, affect the lives of many people; but in themselves they do not enjoin a specific course of action. In contrast, the acceptance of certain specific environmental ideas can have a definite effect on decision and on behaviour. If it is widely held, for example, that a dry and sunny climate is a great restorer of health, we may suppose that an appreciable number of people will seek out these areas for health. But what of less specific ideas? We may believe that a world-view which puts nature in subservience to man will lead to the exploitation of nature by man; and one that regards man as simply a component in nature will entail a modest view of his rights and capabilities, and so lead to the establishment of a harmonious relationship between man and his natural environment. But is this correct? And if essentially correct, how direct or tenuous is the link? These are some of the questions I wish to explore with the help of examples from Europe and China. The discrepancies are noted here; their resolution must await another occasion.

I

To the question, what is a fundamental difference between the European and the Chinese attitude towards nature, most people with any opinion at all will probably make some such reply: that the European sees nature as subordinate to him whereas the Chinese sees himself as a part of nature. Taken as a broad generalization and with a grain of salt there is much truth in this distinction; a truth illustrated with diagrammatic force when one compares the formal European garden of the seventeenth century with the Chinese naturalistic garden. The geometric contrast reflects fundamental differences in environmental evaluation. The formal European garden in the style of the Le Nôtre was designed to produce a limited number of imposing prospects. It can be appreciated to the full only at a limited number of favoured spots where the onlooker is invited by the garden's design to gaze at distant vistas. Or, seen in another way, the European garden is a grandiose setting for man; in deference to him, nature is straitjacketed in court dress. The Chinese garden, on the other hand, is designed to produce almost constantly shifting scenes: there are no set prospects. The nature of the garden requires the perceiver to move along a winding path and to be more than visually involved with the landscape. It is not nature that is required to put on court dress in deference to man; rather, it is man who must lay aside his formalistic pretensions in order to enter nature.

This widely recognized distinction is valid and important. On the other hand, by the crude test of the total tonnage of earth removed there may not be so very much difference between the European formal and the Chinese naturalistic garden. Both are human artifacts. It is not widely known that some of the famous scenic areas of China are works of man rather than of geologic processes. The West Lake of Hang-chou, for example, was celebrated by T'ang and Sung poets and it remains to this day an adornment of China. To the casual visitor, the West Lake region may appear to be a striking illustration of how the works of man can blend modestly into the magistral context of nature. However, the pervasiveness of nature is largely an illusion induced by art. Some of the islands in the lake are man-made. Moreover, the lake itself is artificial and has to be maintained with care. In the thirteenth century, military patrols, under the command of specially appointed officials, looked after its policing and maintenance; it was forbidden, for example, to throw any rubbish into it or to plant in it lotuses or water-chestnuts. Peasants were recruited to clear and enlarge the lake, to keep it from being cluttered up by vegetation and silt.[1] Hang-chou's environs, then, owe much of their calm, harmonious beauty to human art and effort. The sense of open nature in Hang-chou is enhanced by its scale: the West Lake region is a cluster of public and semi-public parks. In the much smaller compass of the private garden the illusion of pervasive nature is far more difficult to achieve; nevertheless the aim of the Chinese gardener was to achieve it with cleverly placed, water-worn limestone whose jagged outlines denoted wildness, and by means of winding footpaths that give the stroller an illusion of depth and space. In this line the Oriental's ultimate triumph is symbolized by the miniature garden, where wild nature is reduced to the scale of a dwarf landscape that can be fitted into a bowl. Complete artifice reigns: in the narrow confines of a bowl, shrubs are tortured by human skill into imitating the shape and posture of pines, the limbs of which may have been deformed by winds that swept the China Seas.

II

I have begun with a contrast and then proceeded to suggest that, from another perspective, the contrast is blurred. The publicized environmental ethos of a culture seldom covers more than a fraction of the total range of environmental behaviour. It is misleading to derive the one from the other. Simplifications that can mislead have at times been made. For example, Professor Lynn White has recently said: "What people do about their ecology depends on what they think about themselves in relation to things around them. Human ecology is deeply conditioned by beliefs about our nature and destiny—that is, by religion."[2] He goes on to say that the victory of Christianity over paganism was the greatest psychic revolution in Western culture. In his view, despite all the talk of "the post-Christian age" and despite evident changes in the forms of modern thinking, the substance often remains amazingly akin to that of the Christian past. The Western man's daily habits of action are dominated by an implicit faith in perpetual progress which was unknown either to Greco-Roman antiquity or to the Orient. It is rooted in, and is indefensible apart from, Judeo-Christian teleology. Peoples of the Western world continue to live, as they have lived for about 1700 years, very largely in a context of Christian beliefs. And what has Christianity told people about their relations with the environment? Essentially that man, as something made in God's image, is not simply a part of nature; that God has planned the universe for man's benefit and rule. According to White, Christianity is the most **anthropocentric** religion the world has seen. It has not only established a dualism of man and nature but has also insisted that it is God's will that man exploit nature for his proper ends.[3]

To press the theme further, it is said that Christianity has destroyed antiquity's feeling for the holiness of landscapes and of natural things. The Greek religious tradition regarded the land not as an object to be exploited, or even as a visually pleasing setting, but as a true force which physically embodied the powers that ruled the world. Vincent Scully, the architectural historian, has argued that not only were certain landscapes regarded by the ancient Greeks as holy and expressive of specific gods, but also that the temples and the subsidiary buildings of their sanctuaries were so formed in themselves and so placed in the landscapes and to each other as to enhance, develop, and complement the basic meaning of the landscape.[4]

Martin Heidegger, a modern philosopher whose insights have been greatly influenced by early Greek philosophy, characterized the Greek temple as disclosing the earth on which it stands. The whiteness of the temple discloses the darkness and the strength of the rock underneath; it reveals the height and blueness of the sky, the power of the storm, and the vastness of the sea.[5] In the Christian tradition, on the other hand, holiness was invested not in landscapes but in man-made altars, shrines, churches, and basilicas that dominated the landscapes. Constantine and Helen are said to have built basilicas over caves in the Holy Land to celebrate the triumph of Christianity over the "cave cultus" of the pagan world. In the Christian view it was not emanation from the earth but ritual that consecrated the site; man not nature bore the image of God and man's work, the hallowed edifice, symbolized the Christian cosmos. In pagan antiquity, at the level of the common people, each facet of nature had its own guardian spirit. Before one ventured to cut a tree, mine a mountain, or dam a brook, it was important to placate the spirit in charge of that particular situation, and to keep it placated. By destroying animistic beliefs, Christianity made it possible to exploit nature in a mood of indifference to the feeling of natural objects.

Much of this is now Western folklore and Lynn White is among the more recent writers to give it eloquent expression. The thesis, then, is that Christianity has introduced a fundamentally new way of evaluating the environment, and that this new evaluation has strongly affected Western man's traffic with the natural objects around him. The generalization is very useful, although one should take note of facts that appear to contradict it. As Clarence Glacken has demonstrated, in the ancient world there was no lack of interest in natural resources and their quick exploitation. Economic activities such as mining, the various ways of obtaining food, canal building, and drainage are clear proof of man's incessant restlessness in changing the earth about him.[6] Glacken points out that in Sophocles' *Antigone* there are lines which remind one of the eulogies of science in the eighteenth century, and of contemporary enthusiasm for man's control over nature. At one point in the play the chorus declares how the earth has felt man's ungentle touch:

> Oh, Earth is patient, and Earth is old,
> And a mother of Gods, but he breaketh her,
> To-ing, froing, with the plough teams going,
> Tearing the soil of her, year by year.[7]

The tearing of soil has led to erosion. In Plato's *Critias* there is the well-known passage in which he describes how the soils of Attica have been washed down to the sea. "And, just as happens in small islands, what now remains compared with what then existed is like the skeleton of a rich man, all the fat and soft earth have wasted away, and only the bare framework of the land being left." Plato then describes the former arable hills, fertile valleys, and forested mountains "of which there are visible signs even to this day." Mountains which today have food only for bees could, not so long ago, grow trees fit for the largest buildings. Cultivated trees provided pasturage for flocks, and the soil was well watered and the rain was "not lost to it, as now, by flowing from the bare land to the sea."[8] Plato's comments sound remarkably modern; they remind us almost of the lamentations of latter-day conservationists.

If there is evidence of man's awareness of his power to transform nature—even destructively—in the time of Sophocles and Plato, there is evidence of much greater awareness of the almost limitless capabilities of man in Hellenistic times. Agriculture and related occupations such as cattle-breeding were then the most important source of wealth in the ancient world. Land reclamation was not a haphazard affair but one based on the science of mechanics and on practical experience with canal-digging, irrigation, and swamp drainage. It was a time of faith in progress. But far more than the Greeks, the Romans have imposed their will on the natural environment. And perhaps the most dramatic example of the triumph of the human will over the irregular lineaments of nature is the Roman grid method of dividing up the land. As Bradford puts it, centuriation well displayed the arbitrary but methodical qualities in Roman government. With absolute self-assurance and great technical competence, the Romans have imposed the same formal pattern of land division on the well-watered alluvium of the Po Valley as on the near-desert of Tunisia. Even today the forceful imprint of centuriation can be traced across some thousands of square miles on both sides of the central Mediterranean, and it can still stir the imagination by its scale and boldness.[9]

Against this background of the vast transformations of nature in the pagan world, the inroads made in the early centuries of the Christian era were relatively modest. Christianity teaches that man has dominion over nature. St. Benedict himself had cut down the sacred grove at Monte Cassino because it was a survival of pagan worship. And the story of how monks moved into the forested wilderness, and by a combination of work and prayer, had transformed them into cloistered "paradises" is a familiar one. But for a long time man's undisputed power over nature was more a tenet of faith than a fact of experience: to become a realized fact Europe had to wait for the growth of human numbers, for the achievement of greater administrative centralization, and for the development and wide application of new technological skills. Fields that were cleared in heavy forests testified to the mediaeval farmer's great capacity for changing his environment: it was a change, however, that must continually be defended against the encroachments of nature. Farmsteads and arable lands multiplied through the Middle Ages at the expense of forests and marshes, but these man-made features lacked the permanence, the geometric order, and the prideful assertion of the human will that one can detect more readily in the Roman road system, aqueducts, and centuriated landholdings. The victory of Christianity over paganism may well have been, as Lynn White says, the greatest psychic revolution in Western culture; but for lack of real, as distinct from theologically postulated, power the full impact of that revolution on ecology was postponed.

III

As to China, Western humanists commonly show bias in favour of that country's Taoist and Buddhist traditions. They like to point out the virtues of the Oriental's quiescent and adaptive approach towards nature in contrast to the aggressive masculinity of Western man. Support for the quiescent view is easily found in the Taoist classics. The *Tao Tê Ching*, for example, has a rather cryptic message of seven characters (*wei wu wei, tzu wu pu chih*) which James Legge has translated as: "When there is this abstinence from action, good order is universal." And Joseph Needham has recently interpreted it to mean: "Let there be no action (contrary to Nature), and there is nothing that will not be well regulated."[10] It is easy to see how these words might appeal to the modern man, who finds in his own environment the all-too-evident consequences of human action "contrary to nature." In another influential Taoist book of much later date (*T'ai shang kan ying p'ien*), one finds the belief that "even insects and crawling things, herbs and trees, may not be injured." These Taoist texts have been much translated into European languages; the latter, with its injunction against injuring even insects and crawling things, is believed to have had some influence on the thought of Albert Schweitzer.[11]

Another aspect of Chinese attitude towards nature, which has found favour among some Western humanists, is embodied in the concept of *feng-shui* or geomancy. This concept has been aptly defined as "the art of adapting the residences of the living and the dead so as to co-operate and harmonize with the local currents of the cosmic breadth."[12] If houses and tombs are not properly located, evil effects would injure the inhabitants and the descendants of those whose bodies lay in the tombs. On the other hand, good siting would favour wealth, health, and happiness. Good siting involves, above all, taking proper note of the forms of hills and directions of watercourses since these are themselves the outcome of the moulding influences of winds and waters, that is, of *feng-shui*; but in addition one must also consider the heights and forms of buildings, the directions of roads and bridges. A general effect of the belief in *feng-shui* is to encourage a preference for natural curves—for winding paths and for structures that seem to fit into the landscape rather than to dominate it; and at the same time it promoted a distaste for straight lines and geometrical layouts. In this respect it is of interest to note the short life of China's first railway. This was built in 1876 and connected Shanghai with its port of Wu-sung. Although the venture was at first well received, the mood of the local people turned sour after a native was killed by the locomotive. The people in their hostility thought that the railway had offended the principle of *feng-shui*. On 20 October, 1877, the Chinese government closed the railway, and so a symbol of Western progress was temporarily sacrificed to the local currents of the cosmic breadth.[13]

An adaptive attitude towards nature has ancient roots in China. It is embodied in folklore, in the philosophical-ethical precepts of Taoism, and later, Buddhism, and it draws support from practical experience: the experience that uncontrolled exploitation of timber, for example, brings hurtful results. In ancient literature one finds here and there evidence of a recognition for the need to regulate the use of resources. Even as early as the Eastern Chou period (eighth century–third century B.C.), deforestation necessitated by the expansion of agriculture and the building of cities seems to have led to an appreciation of the value of trees. In that ancient compendium of songs the *Shi Ching*, we find the sentiment expressed in lines such as these:

> On the hill were lovely trees,
> Both chestnut-trees and plum trees.
> Cruel brigands tore them up;
> But no one knew of their crime.

Trees were regarded as a blessing. As another poem put it,

> So thick grow those oaks
> That the people never look for firewood.
> Happiness to our lord!
> May the spirits always have rewards for him.[14]

In the *Chou Li*—a work which was probably compiled in the third century B.C., but may well include earlier material—we find mentioned two classes of officials whose duties were concerned with conservation. One was the *Shan-yu*, inspector of mountains, and the other the *Lin-heng*, inspector of forests. The inspectors of mountains were charged with the care of forests in the mountains. They saw to it that certain species were preserved, and in other ways enforced conservation practices. Thus trees could only be cut by the common people at certain times: those on the south side in the middle of winter and those on the north side in the middle of summer. At other seasons the people were permitted to cut wood in times of urgent need, such as when coffins had to be made or dykes strengthened, but even then certain areas could not be touched. The inspectors of forests (in the *Lin-heng* office) had similar duties. Their authority covered the forests that lay below the mountains.[15] Another ancient literary reference to conservation practice was in the *Mencius*. The sage advised King Huai of Liang that he would not lack for wood if he allowed the people to cut trees only at the proper time.[16]

Through Chinese history, perspicacious officials have from time to time warned against the dire consequences of deforestation. A scholar of the late Ming dynasty reported on Shan-hsi, a province in North China: "At the beginning of the reign of Chia-ching" (1522–66), he wrote, "people vied with each other to build houses, and wood from the southern mountains was cut without a year's rest. The natives took advantage of the barren mountain surface and converted it into farms. . . . If heaven sends down a torrent, there is nothing to obstruct the flow of water. In the morning it falls on the southern mountains; in the evening, when it reaches the plains, its angry waves swell in volume and break embankments causing frequent changes in the course of the river."[17]

Deforestation was deplored by the late Ming scholars not only because of its effect on stream flow and on the quality of the soil in the lowlands, but also—interestingly enough—because of their belief that the forests on mountain ridges were effective in slowing down the horse-riding barbarians. As one scholar put it, "I saw the fact that what the country relies on as strategically important is the mountain, and what the mountain relies on as a screen to prevent advance are the trees."[18] There was also recognition of the aesthetics of forested mountains. Wu-tai mountains in northern Shan-hsi, for example, were famous everywhere. But the question was asked: since they have become almost bare, what remained to keep them famous?

These brief notes suggest that there existed in China an old tradition of forest care. Officials encouraged the practice but the people engaged in it on their own initiative when it did not conflict with the urgent needs of the moment. Nearly forty years ago, the American conservationist W.C. Lowdermilk noted how thousands of acres in An-hui and Ho-non were planted with pine from local nurseries, a practice he recognized as ancient and independent of the modern forestry movement. Lowdermilk also found that the North China plain "actually exports considerable quantities of logs of *Paulownia tomentosa* to Japan and poplar (*Populus tomentosa*) to match factories. It is true that no forests are to be found in this plain, but each village has its trees, which are grown according to a system."[19]

In Communist China trees are extensively planted to control soil erosion, in answer to pressing economic needs but also for aesthetic reasons. Roadside planting, a practice dating back to the Eastern Chou period, uses the "traditional" trees (*Populus simonii, Pinus tabulaeformis, Salix babylonica, S. matsudana, Aesculus chinensis, Ulmus parvifolia*), but in particular the poplars. Afforestation proceeds in villages, and most conspicuously, in cities, new suburbs, and industrial districts where the trees hide a great deal of the raw ugliness of new construction.[20]

IV

Thus far I have sketched what may indeed be called the "official" line on Chinese attitude towards environment; it is widely publicized and commonly accepted. There is, however, another strain: the enlightened memorials to the emperor on the need for the conservation of resources are in themselves clear evidence of the follies that have already been committed. Unlike the Western man of letters the geographer is usually aware of China's frequent mistreatment of nature. He perceives that country, not through the refined sentiments of Taoist philosophy, Neo-Confucianism, and Oswald Siren, but through the bleak reports of Mallory, Lowdermilk, and Thorp. Deforestation and erosion on the one hand, the building of cities and rice terraces on the other are the common foci of his attention rather than landscape painting or poetry contests in the cool precincts of a garden. The two images of reality complement each other: in an obvious but not trite sense, civilization is the exercise of human power over nature, which in turn may lead to the aesthetic appreciation of nature. Philosophy, nature poetry, gardens, and orderly countryside are products of civilization, but so equally are the deforested mountains, the clogged streams, and, within the densely packed, walled cities, the political intrigue.

If animistic belief and Taoist nature philosophy lie at the back of an adaptive attitude towards nature, what conceptions and ideals—we may ask—have encouraged the Chinese, through their long history, to engage in gigantic transformation of environment—whether this be expressed positively in huge works of construction or negatively in deforested mountains? Several ancient beliefs and conceptions may be recognized and they, individually or together, have allowed the Chinese to express the "male" principle in human nature. Consider, for example, the fact that one of the greatest culture heroes of China was Yu, the legendary founder of the Hsia dynasty. He was famed primarily for his magnificent deeds: He "opened up the rivers of the Nine Provinces and fixed the outlets of the nine marshes"; he brought peace and order to the lands of Hsia and his achievements were of an enduring kind which benefited succeeding dynasties.[21] Chinese rulers were bidden to imitate the ancient culture heroes, and one way to imitate them was to ensure order and prosperity by large-scale engineering works. Another ancient idea of importance to the "male" principle of dominance was to see in the earthly environment a model of the cosmos. The regular motions of the stars were to be translated architecturally and ritually to space and time on earth. The walled city oriented to the cardinal directions, the positioning of the twelve city gates, the location of the royal compound, and the alignment of the principal axial street were given a geometric pattern that reflected the order to be found in heaven. The key concept was built on the related notions of rectilinearity, order, and rectitude. This key concept acquired architectural and social forms which were then imposed on earth, for the earth itself lacked paradigms of perfect order. Indeed the experience of mountains and waters has led to such unaggressive prescriptions as the need to observe and placate the spirits of the earth, the need for man to understand the balance of forces in nature, to contemplate this harmony and to adapt himself to it. By contrast, the observation of the stars has inspired such masculine attitudes as geometric order, hierarchy, and authoritarian control over earth and men.

The two outlooks—celestial and terrestrial, masculine and feminine—are not easy to reconcile. Events in heaven affect events on earth but not in any obvious or dependable way: abnormal floods and droughts have traditionally been taken as warnings by those who derive their power from astronomy. Tension, if not contradiction, is also revealed when these two ideas find architectural and geographical substance. The construction of Ch'ang-an in the Sui and T'ang dynasties illustrates the triumph of the cosmic principle of order and rectilinearity over the earth principle of complex harmony and natural lines. Ch'ang-an was laid on new ground and on an unprecedented scale. The site in the Wei Ho valley was chosen for functional reasons but also because of its great historical links: the site received the sanction of the great men and deeds in the past. Geomantic properties of the site were studied; however, unlike villages and rural roads the topographical character of the region seems to have made little impact on the city's fundamental design. Astronomers had an important role in the laying out of the city: they measured the shadow of the noon sun on successive days and observed the North Star by night in order to arrive at accurate alignments of the city walls to the four directions.[22] In the course of building

Ch'ang-an, which had an enclosed area of 31 square miles, villages were levelled and trees uprooted; broad straight avenues were laid out and then rows of trees planted. Thus, despite the geomantic gestures, in Ch'ang-an the superposition of man's and heaven's order on natural terrain was complete. Or rather not quite complete, if we accept the charming story of why one great old locust tree was not in line. It had been retained from the old landscape because the chief architect had sat under it as he supervised the construction, and a special order from the emperor in honour of his architect spared it from being felled.[23]

V

The natural environment of both Mediterranean Europe and China has been vastly transformed by man: constructively in the building of cities and roads, in the extension of arable land and the introduction of new crops; destructively in deforestation and erosion. Of any long-settled, thoroughly civilized part of the world, we can draw up a list of forces and the motives for their use that would more or less account for the transformation of the biotic mantle. Such lists may well agree in fundamentals: fire is widely used to clear vegetation; the forest is cleared to create more grazing and arable land; timber is needed for the construction of palaces, houses, and ships, for domestic and industrial fuel, or as raw material for paper mills. Then again the forest is pushed back because it may shelter dangerous wild animals or provide hiding places for bandits. Naturally, the means at hand and the motives for using them vary from region to region: in contrast to the Mediterranean world, for example, China's vegetation suffered less from sheep and goats, and less from the enormous demands of shipbuilding which flourished with the Mediterranean maritime powers. China's forests, on the other hand, suffered more from the demands of city building and the need for domestic fuel.

To illustrate further the kinds of force that work against conservation practices in China, consider some of the causes of deforestation. One is the ancient practice of burning trees in order to deprive dangerous animals of their hiding places. There exists a passage in the *Mencius* of how in ancient times the luxuriant vegetation sheltered so many wild beasts that men were endangered. The great minister Shun of legendary repute ordered Yih to use fire, and "Yih set fire to, and consumed the forests and vegetation on the mountains and in the marshes, so that the birds and beasts fled away to hide themselves."[24] Even in the early decades of the twentieth century non-Chinese tribes in Kuang-hsi and Kuei-chou provinces were known to burn forests to drive away tigers and leopards; and in North China, in such long-settled areas as central Shen-hsi province, fires were ostensibly started by Chinese farmers for no other purpose. It is not always easy to establish the real reason for setting fire to forest. When asked, the farmers may say that it is to clear land for cultivation, although the extent of burning far exceeds the need for this purpose; or it is to leave fewer places in which bandits may hide; or to encourage the growth of small-sized sprouts in the burnt over area, which would then save the farmers the labour of splitting wood![25] The last reason tends to upset any residual illusion we may have of the Chinese farmer's benign attitude towards nature. A fire can of course also be started accidentally. A risk that is special to the Chinese is the forest fire caused by the burning of paper money at the grave mounds, which, in the rugged parts of the South, are commonly located beyond the fields and at the edge of the forested hills.

Forests in North China were depleted in the past for the making of charcoal as an industrial fuel. Robert Hartwell has shown how, from the tenth century onward the expanding metallic industries had swallowed up many hundreds of thousands of tons of charcoal each year, as did the manufacture of salt, alum, bricks, tiles, and liquor.[26] By the Sung dynasty (A.D. 960–1279) the demand for wood and charcoal as both household and industrial fuel had reached a level such that the timber resources of the country could no longer meet it; the result was the increasing substitution of coal for wood and charcoal.

An enormous amount of timber was needed in the construction of the old Chinese cities, probably more than that required in building Western cities of comparable size. One reason for this lies in the dependence of traditional Chinese architecture on timber as the basic structural material. Mountains may be stripped of their cover in the construction of a large palace.[27] And if a large palace required much timber, a whole city would require much more, especially if it were of the size of Ch'ang-an, capital of T'ang dynasty, and Hang-chou, capital of the southern Sung dynasty. Both had populations of more than a million people. The great expansion in the size of Hang-chou in the nineteenth century led to the deforestation of the neighbouring hills for construction timber. The demand for timber was such that some farmers gave up rice cultivation for forestry.[28] Cities in which houses were so largely made of wood ran the constant danger of demolition by fire; and this was especially true of the southern metropolises where the streets tended to be narrow. The necessity of rebuilding after fire put further strain on timber resources. But of even greater consequence than the accidental burning of parts of cities was the deliberate devastation of whole cities in times of upheaval, when rebels or nomadic invaders toppled a dynasty. The succeeding phase of reconstruction was normally achieved in quick time by armies of men who made ruthless inroads upon the forest.

VI

The theme we have yet to trace is the involved interplay between environmental attitude and environmental behaviour, between the philosophy identified with a people and the actions that people may undertake. Besides the more glaring contradictions of professed ideal and actual practice, there exist also the unsuspected ironies: these derive from the fact that benign institutions of a complex society, no less than the exploitative, are not always able to foresee all the consequences of their inherent character and action. For example, Buddhism in China is at least partly responsible for the preservation of trees around temple compounds, for the islands of green in an otherwise denuded landscape; on the other hand, Buddhism introduced to China the idea of the cremation of the dead; and from the tenth to the fourteenth century the practice of cremation was sufficiently common in the southeastern coastal provinces to have had an effect on the timber resources of that area.[29] The research of E.H. Schafer provides us with another illustration of irony in Chinese life; for it would seem that the most civilized of arts was responsible for the deforestation of much of North China. The art was that of writing, which required soot for the making of black ink. The soot came from burnt pine. And, as Schafer put it, "Even before T'ang times, the ancient pines of the mountains of Shan-tung had been reduced to carbon, and now the busy brushes of the vast T'ang bureaucracy were rapidly bringing baldness to the T'a-hang Mountains between Shansi and Hopei."[30]

VII

I began by noting the contrast between the European formal garden and the Chinese naturalistic garden, and then suggested that these human achievements probably required comparable amounts of nature modification. To compare artworks and construction projects on the basis of the quantitative changes made on the environment is a useful exercise in so far as we wish to emphasize the role of man as a force for change along with other geophysical forces; but it is only the beginning in the interpretation of the meaning of these works and how they reflect cultural attitudes. It seems valid to me to see the European garden as an extension of the house: in the development of the European garden some of the formality and values of the house are taken outdoors in the form of courtyards, terraces, formal parterres, and avenues, and now the smooth, carpet-like lawn. The lawn displays the house; its sloping surfaces are a pedestal for the house. The Chinese garden, on the other hand, reflects a totally different philosophy from the orthogonal rectitude of the traditional Chinese house. In stepping through a circular gate, from the rectangular courtyard into the curvilinear forms of the garden, one enters a different world. Perhaps something of the difference in attitude towards outdoor spaces is retained to the present day. Simone de Beauvoir notes how a French family picnic is often an elaborate affair involving the transportation of a considerable portion of the household goods outdoors: it is not always a harmonious event for whatever tension that may exist in the house is carried to the less organized natural environment where it is exacerbated by entanglement with flies, fishing rods, and spilled strawberry jam. In Communist China, de Beauvoir spent an afternoon (1955) in the playgrounds of the Summer Palace outside Peking. She captures the peace of the scene with an anecdote: "In the middle of the lake I see a little boat: in it a young woman is lying down peacefully asleep while two youngsters are frisking about and playing with the oars. Our boatman cups his hands. 'Hey!' he calls. 'Look out for those kids!' The woman rubs her eyes, she smiles, picks up the oars, and shows the children how they work."[31]

NOTES

1. Gernet, Jacques, *Daily Life in China on the Eve of the Mongol Invasion 1250–1276* (London, 1962), pp. 51–52.
2. White, Lynn, "The Historical Roots of our Ecologic Crisis," *Science*, CLV (1967), 1205.
3. Ibid.
4. Scully, Vincent, *The Earth, The Temple, and The Gods* (New Haven, 1962), p. 3.
5. Vycinas, Vincent, *Earth and Gods: An Introduction to the Philosophy of Martin Heidegger* (The Hague, 1961), p. 13.
6. Glacken, Clarence, *Trace on the Rhodian Shore* (Berkeley and Los Angeles, 1967), p. 118.
7. Sophocles, *Antigone*, transl. by Gilbert Murray in Arnold Toynbee, *Greek Historical Thought* (New York, 1952), p. 128.
8. Plato, *Critias*, transl. by Arnold Toynbee, *Greek Historical Thought*, pp. 146–47.
9. Bradford, John, *Ancient Landscapes* (London, 1957), p. 145.
10. Needham, Joseph, *Science and Civilisation in China*, vol. II (Cambridge, 1956), p. 69.
11. Schafer, E.H., "The Conservation of Nature under the T'ang dynasty," *Journ. Econ. and Soc. Hist. of the Orient*, V (1962), 282.
12. Chatley, H., "Feng shui" in *Encyclopaedia Sinica*, ed. by S. Couling (Shanghai, 1917), p. 175. See also Andrew March, "An Appreciation of Chinese Geomancy," *Journ. Asian Studies*, XXVII (1968), 253–67.
13. *Encyclopaedia Sinica*, p. 470.
14. *Shi Ching*, transl. by Arthur Waley as *The Book of Songs* (New York, 1960), pp. 138, 213.
15. *Chou Li*, transl. by E. Biot as *Le Tcheou-li* (Paris, 1851), vol. I, 371–74.
16. *Mencius*, Bk. I, pt. 1, 3:3.
17. Chi, Ch'ao-ting, *Key Economic Areas in Chinese History* (New York, 1963), p. 22.
18. Gazetteer (1596) written by Chen Teng and translated by W.C. Lowdermilk, and D.R. Wickes, *History of Soil Use in the Wu T'ai Shan Area*, Monog., Roy. Asiatic Soc., NCB, 1938, p. 8.
19. Lowdermilk, W.C., "Forestry in Denuded China," *Ann., Amer. Acad. Pol. Soc. Sci.*, CLII (1930), 137.

20. Richardson, S.D., *Forestry in Communist China* (Baltimore, 1966), pp. 152–53.
21. Ssu-ma Ch'ien, *Shi Chi*, chap. 29.
22. Wright, A.F., "Symbolism and Functions: Reflections on Changan and Other Great Cities," *Journ. Asian Studies*, XXIV (1965), 670.
23. Wu, N.I., *Chinese and Indian Architecture* (New York, 1963), p. 38.
24. *Mencius*, Bk. III, pt. 1, 4:7.
25. Reported by A.N. Steward and S.Y. Cheo in "Geographical and ecological notes on botanical explorations in Kwangsi province, China," *Nanking Journ.*, V (1935), 174.
26. Hartwell, R., "A Revolution in the Chinese Iron and Coal Industries during the Northern Sung, 960–1126 A.D.," *Journ. Asian Studies*, XXI (1962), 159.
27. See L.S. Yang, *Les aspects économiques des travaux publics dans la Chine impériale*, Collège de France, 1964, p. 37.
28. Gernet, (n. 1), p. 114.
29. Moule, A.C., *Quinsai* (Cambridge, 1957), p. 51.
30. Schafer, (n. 11), pp. 299–300.
31. De Beauvoir, Simone, *The Long March* (Cleveland, 1958), p. 77.

In the final part of this anthology, James Lovelock will tell us more about the English landscape, which is one of the more outstanding examples of what we shall call an **artifactual ecology**. Here, historian W.G. Hoskins laments the ruination of this sensitively crafted ecosystem, and gives us an impression of its rich history. A striking point to note is Hoskins's sense of historical continuity; what went on down the laneway a thousand years ago seems to have been done only yesterday, by people that one knew personally.

THE LANDSCAPE TODAY

W.G. Hoskins

The industrial revolution and the creation of parks around the country houses have taken us down to the later years of the nineteenth century. Since that time, and especially since the year 1914, every single change in the English landscape has either uglified it or destroyed its meaning, or both. Of all the changes in the last two generations, only the great reservoirs of water for the industrial cities of the North and Midlands have added anything to the scene that one can contemplate without pain. It is a distasteful subject but it must be faced for a few moments.

The country houses decay and fall: hardly a week passes when one does not see the auctioneer's notice of the impending sale and dissolution of some big estate. The house is seized by the demolition contractors, its park invaded and churned up by the tractors and trailers of the timber merchant. Down comes the house; down come the tall trees, naked and gashed lies the once beautiful park. Or if it stands near a town, the political planners swarm into the house, turn it into a rabbit-warren of black-hatted officers of This and That, and the park becomes a site for some "overspill"—a word as beastly as the thing it describes. We may indeed find the great house still standing tidily in a timbered park: but it is occupied by what the villagers describe detachedly as "the atom men," something remote from the rest of us, though not remote in the sense they themselves like to think. And if the planners are really fortunate, they fill the house with their paper and their black hats, and open-cast mining of coal or iron ore simultaneously finishes off the park. They can sit at their big desks and contemplate with an exquisite joy how everything is now being put to a good use. Demos and Science are the joint Emperors.

Beyond the park, in some parts of England such as East Anglia, the bulldozer rams at the old hedges, blots them out to make fields big and vacant enough for the machines of the new ranch-farming and the business-men farmers of five to ten thousand acres. Fortunately, the tractor and the bulldozer cannot easily destroy the great hedgebanks and stone walls of the anciently enclosed parts of England; nor is it worth doing, for the good farmer knows the value of these banks and walls as shelter, and of the hedges for timber. Much of the old field pattern therefore remains, with its tangle of deep lanes and thick hedges.

What else has happened in the immemorial landscape of the English countryside? Airfields have flayed it bare wherever there are level, well-drained stretches of land, above all in eastern England. Poor devastated Lincolnshire and Suffolk! And those long gentle lines of the dip-slope of the Cotswolds, those misty uplands of the sheep-grey oolite, how they have lent themselves to the villainous requirements of the new age! Over them drones, day after day, the obscene shape of the atom-bomber, laying a trail like a filthy slug upon Constable's and Gainsborough's sky. England of the Nissen hut, the "pre-fab," and the electric fence, of the high barbed wire around some unmentionable devilment; England of the arterial by-pass, treeless and stinking of diesel oil, murderous with lorries; England of the bombing-range wherever there was once silence, as on Otmoor or the marshlands of Lincolnshire; England of battle-training areas on the Breckland heaths, and tanks crashing through empty ruined Wiltshire villages; England of high explosives falling upon the prehistoric monuments of Dartmoor. Barbaric England of the scientists, the military men, and the politicians: let us turn away and contemplate the past before all is lost to the vandals.

The view from this room where I write these last pages is small, but it will serve as an epitome of the gentle unravished English landscape. Circumscribed as it is, with tall trees closing it in barely half a mile away, it contains in its detail something of every age from the Saxon to the nineteenth century. A house has stood on this site since the year 1216, when the bishop of Lincoln ordained a vicarage here, but it has been rebuilt over and over again, and last of all in 1856. Down the garden, sloping to the river, the aged and useless apple trees are the successors of those that grew here in the time of Charles I, when the glebe terrier of 1634 speaks of "one orchard, one backside, and two little gardens." Beyond the apple trees and within a few feet of the river is a large raised platform, visible in winter before its annual submergence in weeds, part of a vanished building, and there are clear lines of stone walls adjoining it. Almost certainly this is the site of one of the three water-mills recorded on the estate in Domesday Book. Below it flows the Dorn, known to the Saxons as the Milk, from the cloudiness of its water after rain: and one still sees it as the Saxons saw it a thousand years ago, as I saw it a few minutes ago in the thin rain drifting down from the Cotswolds.

Across the stream, tumbling fast on its way to Glyme and Evenlode, one sees a wide sedgy hollow planted with willow saplings, from which flocks of goldfinches rise with a flash of wings on sunny mornings. This hollow, enclosed by a massive earthen bank, was the fishpond begun by the lord of the manor before his death in 1175, and completed by his son: "Ode de Berton grants to Roger de St John the land between the garden of Roger and the road to the bridge together with the moor where Thomas de St John began to make his fishpond, rendering yearly a pair of spurs or twopence."

This was about the year 1200 (the charter is undated), but there is the fishpond today. And there is the lane dropping down to the stone bridge that was rebuilt in 1948, but unquestionably on the site of the stone bridge which is mentioned as a landmark in an even earlier charter. And "the moor" is the description of the scene before it had been claimed for cultivation. We catch a sight of an earlier world in the bare words of this charter.

Beyond the fishpond, the ground rises to form the other side of the valley, fields with their broken hedges of twisted hawthorns. What age are these hedges? They were not here in 1685, when another glebe terrier shows that the parish still had its open fields. But they were probably made before 1750, by which date the enclosure had apparently been accomplished. One or two hedge-banks are, however, medieval in origin, for the St Johns had a separate enclosed pasture called Grascroft from the early 1200s onwards, and this ancient field comes into the view also.

A little to the right, on the other side of the lane, the eye dwells upon a small park, with a boating-lake catching the light, and some modest landscaping; and through the bare winter trees one sees the chimneys of a seemly Victorian "big house." The house and park were made as late as the 1870s. It must be one of the last parks to be made in England, for landowners began to feel the pinch of falling rents soon after that. The house, in fact, is older, for the work of the 1870s, though apparently a complete rebuilding, is merely a stone casing around a house originally built by a successful merchant of the Staple, whose inscription is still over the door: "*Thinke and Thanke Anno 1570*." Three hundred years later this house was remodelled by another successful bourgeois — this time a wealthy Oxford brewer.

But this was an old, long-cultivated estate when John Dormer the merchant stapler acquired it, with a history stretching back to pre-Conquest days, when it was one of the demesne-farms of the Anglo-Saxon kings. When they hunted in Woodstock Park, five miles away, in the tenth and eleventh centuries, they called upon the produce of this large estate (about seven thousand acres then) to feed their household; and one can walk, after a morning's writing, along the broad green lane that was first made to connect the estate with the hunting-park. It was a royal estate in Saxon times, but how far back into that age? What was it when the Saxons captured Eynsham, not many miles away, in the year 571? We do not yet know, but here in this room one is reaching back, in a view embracing a few hundred acres at the most, through ten centuries of English life, and discerning shadowy depths beyond that again.

By opening the window and leaning out, the parish church comes into view across the lane, a lonely building now, empty and cold and bare except for one hour each week. It was rebuilt about the year 1300, when the village was large and flourishing: this was the high farming period of the Middle Ages. But the font is of the twelfth century, so there was a church here then; and deep in the churchyard to the east of the chancel is a buried wall which is perhaps the east wall of a Saxon church. For though it stands so isolated today from human kind, St Mary's church was a mother-church for a wide area round about, as befitted the spiritual centre of a royal estate; and we do not know how far back a building stood on this site. A Roman coin came from under the tower at the restoration of 1855, but one cannot make too much of that.

And then, finally, out of sight but only fifty or sixty yards from this room, in the field next the garden, there lies buried the main street of the old village that was wiped out by the Black Death. One walks between the banks that show where the houses stood, marking how blocks of squared masonry thrust in one place out of the turf (a more important building than most of them), and how the tree-roots twist among the rubble footings of the peasant dwellings; and one picks up pieces of twelfth- and thirteenth-century pottery — mere sherds, bits of rim, or sides, of bases, but all dateable: nothing later than the Black Death, when the great silence descended.

Not every small view in England is so full of detail as this, upon the oolite of north Oxfordshire, for this was a rich and favoured countryside that was beloved of owners of Roman villas, even in places of Bronze Age men. The cultural humus of sixty generations or more lies upon it. But most of England is a thousand years old, and in a walk of a few miles one would touch nearly every century in that long stretch of time.

> Know most of the rooms of thy native country before thou goest over the threshold thereof. Especially seeing England presents thee with so many observables.

Here follows a brief but incisive observation by Harry M. Caudill, long one of the most sensitive and acute observers of the human significance of environmental depletion.

THE MYTH OF SUPERABUNDANCE

Harry M. Caudill

The most deadly aspect of American life is the profligacy growing out of the persistent myth of superabundance. In the beginning there was so much of everything that everything was squandered. Land was cheap, so men plowed and planted, and when the land failed, they moved on. Trees were an omnipresent nuisance, so they were consumed or destroyed by the tens of millions. Wild creatures were pestilent and uncountable vermin, and as such were destroyed beyond number. For a generation natural gas from the abundant oil wells of Texas, Oklahoma, and Louisiana was "flared off" as a worthless and undesirable by-product—wasting enough fuel to heat constellations of great cities. The story was the same with iron ore, copper, water, coal, and even the atmosphere. In disposing of the unwanted we lost all sense of frugality. The far-seeing have long known that an accounting must some day be rendered, but even they have fallen victim to a kindred illusion, the supposition that there is still an abundance of time.

The next item is presented as a historical footnote. To some it may be painful. However, it is quite important to realize how easy it is to mythologize the past. We might think of a myth as a story people so fervently feel ought to be true that they relax normal standards of critical perception and allow themselves to believe that it is.

THE GOSPEL OF CHIEF SEATTLE IS A HOAX

The Editor, *Environmental Ethics*

It has been informally known for several years that Chief Seattle's famous environmental speech—sometimes known as the "Fifth Gospel," and considered by many to be the best statement ever made on behalf of nature—is actually a work of fiction. Unfortunately, however, the facts behind this matter have been slow in being published and came largely unnoticed into print, even though I was watching for it. As a result, scholars still regularly quote from the spurious speech, and magazines and newspapers continue to reprint the speech in full all around the world.

Chief Seattle really did make a speech sometime in 1853, 1854, or 1855, in connection either with negotiations associated with the Port Elliott Treaty of 1855 or with the actual signing of that treaty. The chief spoke Duwamish and his words were translated into English by a Dr. Henry Smith, who happened to be on the scene. How accurate the translation is a matter of speculation. This speech, which has been given the title "The Indian's Night Promises to be Dark," and laments the untimely decay and impending passing of the Red Man, can be found in W.C. Vanderwerth, ed., *Indian Oratory: Famous Speeches by Noted Indian Chieftains* (Norman: University of Oklahoma Press, 1971, pp. 118–22). There are various authentic versions of this speech, but all are derived from this one speech. Chief Seattle never wrote a letter to President Franklin Pierce.

The famous environmental speech was written more than one hundred years later by Ted Perry, a screen writer, for a film called *Home*, produced by the Southern Baptist Convention, using a version of the original speech as a model. The words were written in the winter of 1971/72 and the film was shown on national television in 1972. Although Perry was not himself trying to perpetrate a fraud, he nevertheless "made the mistake of using Chief Seattle's name in the body of the text." As Perry recounts it, "I don't remember why this was done: my guess is that it was just a mistake on my part. In writing a fictional speech I should have used a fictional name." Although Perry expected to be given credit for writing the speech, the producer left the credit out because "he thought the text might seem more authentic if there were no 'written by' credit given." Since then this environmental oration has circulated around the globe from country to country and from newspaper to newspaper as a prophetic environmental statement by Chief Seattle himself.

The full details behind this unfortunate situation can be found in an article by Rudolf Kaiser, "'A Fifth Gospel, Almost': Chief Seattle's Speech(es): American Origins and European Reception," in Christian F. Feest, ed., *Indians and Europe: An Interdisciplinary Collection of Essays* (Aachen: Rader Verlag, 1987), pp. 505–26. A shorter discussion can also be found in an article by J. Baird Callicott, "American Indian Land Wisdom? Sorting Out the Issues," *Journal of Forest History* 33, no. 1 (January 1989): 35–42. (Callicott uncovered the truth about the Perry script after Kaiser had discovered it, but before Kaiser's paper was published, thereby relegating him to the role of Wallace to Kaiser's Darwin as far as credit for the discovery is concerned.)

In addition to inserting middle-twentieth-century pop ecology statements into Chief Seattle's speech, Perry also substituted language that sometimes disagreed with the original text, for example, replacing "Your God loves your people and hates mine. . . . The white man's God cannot love his red children" with "Our God is the same God. . . . He is the God of man, and His compassion is equal for the red man and the white." There are historical inaccuracies as well—for example, the slaughter of the buffalo occurs twenty years too early.

Troubled with the idea of declaring the Perry text a fraud or hoax, given the positive impact it has had on environmentalists around the world, Kaiser concludes his paper by saying, "This text does not represent the mind of the old Chief, but the mind of a sensitive Euro-American, worried about our ecological situation and the general dualism in our culture. Not the text of the speech is, therefore, spurious, but the headline which names Chief Seattle as the author." Callicott in contrast worries that "we may expect as a matter of course, sooner or later, a backlash repudiation of the image of traditional American Indians as native environmentalists. It will be sooner, rather than later, if Rudolf Kaiser's expose . . . becomes widely known in this country."

The Perry text is a hoax, not perpetrated by Perry directly, but indirectly by the unnamed producer of *Home*, who wanted a more "authentic" effect. Although it is a powerful statement, most certainly much of its force depends on the *false* belief that the words are those of a farsighted non-Western critic of Western civilization. To avoid a backlash, it would be best in the future to refer mostly to Indians who really did make proto-environmental remarks and when reciting the Perry text, if indeed it must be recited, to present it as the work of a twentieth-century script writer—who is not an American Indian.

The following famous remarks by Mr. (later Sir) Winston Churchill were not, of course, made with reference to the environmental crisis. But they do seem to set forth with painful accuracy the stages through which responses to an impending crisis all too often pass. The first statement in particular seems to have been made in an unusual mood of exasperation. (For an account of the actual occasions, see Manchester 1988.)

WINSTON CHURCHILL ON CRISIS MANAGEMENT

When the situation was manageable it was neglected, and now that it is thoroughly out of hand, we apply too late the remedies which might then have effected a cure. There is nothing new in the story. It is as old as the Sibylline books. It falls into that long dismal catalogue of the fruitlessness of experience and the confirmed unteachability of mankind. Want of foresight, unwillingness to act when action would be simple and effective, lack of clear thinking, confusion of counsel until the emergency comes, until self-preservation strikes its jarring gong — these are the features which constitute the endless repetition of history.

–May 2, 1935

When you are drifting down the stream of Niagara, it may easily happen that from time to time you run into a reach of quite smooth water, or that a bend in the river or a change in the wind may make the roar of the falls seem far more distant. But your hazard and your preoccupation are in no way affected thereby.

–March 26, 1936

I have nothing to offer but blood, toil, tears, and sweat . . .

–May 13, 1940

FURTHER READING

See White (1962) for more on the insufficiently known history of the development of technology in Europe. (Find out, for instance, why the invention of stirrups made such a geopolitical difference.) Yi-Fu Tuan (1974) is a sensitive exploration of the relationship between humans and their environments. On the English landscape, see Hoskins (1955) and Shoard (1980). The excerpt by Caudill is taken from his 1976 work, a sweeping and perceptive overview of the ecological rape of the American Appalachians and the consequent degradation of its people; see also his 1963 study.

QUESTIONS TO CONSIDER

1. Churchill refers to the "confirmed unteachability of mankind." Is it really true that we are unteachable? Or could it be otherwise? By the way, what were the Sibylline books?
2. Can you explain the discrepancy between apparent Chinese environmental attitudes and actual behaviour cited by Yi-Fu Tuan? How typical is this of other civilizations?
3. Yi-Fu Tuan cites Lynn White's view that "Christianity is the most anthropocentric religion the world has seen," a religion that insists that "it is God's will that man

exploit nature for his proper ends." Do you think this is a fair and accurate "knock" against Christianity?

4. In view of Yi-Fu Tuan's observations, is it possible for a culture to have a professed set of environmental values that is actually in harmony with its practices?

PART THREE

What is the environment?

In the Introduction to this collection, we hinted that it might not be entirely obvious just what the "environment" really is, much less what is the nature of the relationship of humans to it. (In fact, it turns out that to answer one of these questions is, in part, to answer the other.) The science that attempts to understand these questions is called "ecology"—a word whose root is a Greek term (*oikos*) that literally means "home." Paul B. Sears (quoted in McIntosh, p. 1) has called ecology the "subversive subject" because it forces us to question many cherished assumptions, especially, as Robert P. McIntosh puts it, the fond presumption that "human civilizations, particularly of advanced technological cultures, were above or outside the limitations, or 'laws,' of nature" (McIntosh 1985, p. 1). Here we present several views of our environmental "home" and its workings that seem to be especially illuminating or provoking. The key factor that emerges time and again is *interdependency*—between climate and the biosphere, and between the biosphere and humans. And the coupled problems we face are the failure of humans to respect this fact of interdependency, and the inadequacy of our understanding of how we could and should respect it.

What is the proper relationship between humans and the general planetary ecosystem? Where do we fit in? Or can we fit in? Are we, as John Livingston (1989) suggests, a "large mammal gone amok," or as Murray Bookchin (1990) and James Lovelock (Chapter Eight) argue, a creature that may even have the capacity (inadequately demonstrated so far) of making a unique constructive contribution to the planetary ecosystem? Or are we both? These are questions that, although philosophical, carry with them a certain urgency not attached to many other intellectual problems.

CHAPTER SIX

SOME VIEWS OF THE ECOSYSTEM

Our first excerpt is concerned with what we might call the nuts and bolts of ecology—basic concepts and terminology that will serve us throughout our investigations. A point to note in particular is Odum's description of holistic "levels of organization," and his insistence that what pertains to one level cannot always be fully explained by, or reduced to, what pertains to other levels of analysis.

SOME BASICS

Eugene P. Odum

Ecology and the Ecosystem

The word "ecology" is derived from the Greek *oikos*, meaning "house" or "place to live." Literally, ecology is the study of organisms "at home." Usually ecology is defined as the study of the relation of organisms or groups of organisms to their environment, or the science of the interrelations between living organisms and their environment. Because ecology is concerned especially with the biology of *groups* of organisms and with *functional* processes on the lands, in the oceans, and in fresh waters, it is more in keeping with the modern emphasis to define ecology as the study of the structure and function of nature, it being understood that humankind is part of nature. One of the definitions in Webster's Unabridged Dictionary seems especially appropriate for the closing decades of the 20th century, namely, "*the totality or pattern of relations between organisms and their environment.*" In the long run the best definition for a broad subject field is probably the shortest and least technical one, as, for example, "environmental biology." . . .

Living organisms and their nonliving (abiotic) environment are inseparably interrelated and interact upon each other. Any unit that includes all of the organisms (i.e., the "community") in a given area interacting with the physical environment so that a flow of energy leads to clearly defined trophic structure, biotic diversity, and material cycles (i.e., exchange of materials between living and nonliving parts) within the system is an ecological system or *ecosystem*. From the trophic (fr. *trophe* = nourishment) standpoint, an ecosystem has two components (which are usually partly separated in space and time); an *autotrophic component* (autotrophic = self-nourishing), in which fixation of light energy, use of simple inorganic substances, and buildup of complex substances predominate; and a *heterotrophic component* (heterotrophic = other-nourishing), in which utilization, rearrangement, and decomposition of complex materials predominate. . . .

From the functional standpoint an ecosystem may be conveniently analyzed in terms of the following: (1) energy circuits, (2) food chains, (3) diversity patterns in time and space, (4) nutrient (biogeochemical) cycles, (5) development and evolution, and (6) control (cybernetics).

The ecosystem is the basic functional unit in ecology, since it includes both organisms (biotic communities) and abiotic environment, each influencing the properties of the other and both necessary for maintenance of life as we have it on the earth. . . .

Since no organism can exist by itself or without an environment, our first principle may well deal with the "interrelation" and the principle of "wholeness" that are part of our basic definition of ecology. . . . The term "ecosystem" was first proposed by the British ecologist A.G. Tansley in 1935, but, of course, the concept is by no means so recent. Allusions to the idea of the unity of organisms and environment (as well as the oneness of man and nature) can be found as far back in written history as one might care to look. . . .

The concept of the ecosystem is and should be a broad one, its main function in ecological thought being to emphasize obligatory relationships, interdependence, and causal relationships, that is, the coupling of components to form functional units . . . parts are operationally inseparable from the whole. . . . Ecosystems may be conceived of and studied in various sizes. A pond, a lake, a tract of forest or even a laboratory culture (microecosystem) provide convenient units of study. As long as the major components are present and operate together to achieve some sort of functional stability, even if only for a short time, the entity may be considered an ecosystem. A temporary pond, for example, is a definite ecosystem with characteristic organisms and processes even though its active existence is limited to a short period of time. . . .

Levels of Organization

Perhaps the best way to delimit modern ecology is to consider it in terms of the concept of *levels of organization* visualized as a sort of "biological spectrum." Community, population, organism, organ, cell, and gene are widely used terms for several major biotic levels . . . in hierarchical arrangement from large to small. . . . Interaction with the physical environment (energy and matter) at each level produces characteristic functional systems. By a system we mean just what Webster's Collegiate Dictionary defines as "regularly interacting and interdependent components forming a unified whole." Systems containing living components (biological systems or biosystems) may be conceived at any level in the hierarchy . . . or at any intermediate position convenient or practical for analysis. For example, we might consider not only gene systems, organ systems, and so on, but also host-parasite systems as intermediate levels between population and community.

Ecology is concerned largely with . . . the system levels beyond that of the organism. In ecology the term *population*, originally coined to denote a group of people, is broadened to include groups of individuals of any one kind of organism. Likewise, *community* in the ecological sense (sometimes designated as "biotic community") includes all of the populations occupying a given area. The community and the nonliving environment function together as an ecological system or *ecosystem. Biocoenosis* and *biogeocoenosis*, terms frequently used in the European and Russian literature, are roughly equivalent to community and ecosystem respectively. The largest and most nearly self-sufficient biological system we know about is often designated as the *biosphere* or *ecosphere*, which includes all of the earth's living organisms interacting with the physical environment as a whole so as to maintain a steady-state system intermediate in the flow of energy between the high energy input of the sun and the thermal sink of space.

It is important to note that no sharp lines or breaks were indicated in the above spectrum, not even between the organism and the population. Since in dealing with man and higher animals we are accustomed to think of the individual as the ultimate unit, the idea of a continuous spectrum may seem strange at first. However, from the standpoint of interdependence, interrelations, and survival, there can be no sharp break anywhere along the line. The individual organism, for example, cannot survive for long without its population any more than the organ would be able to survive for long as a self-perpetuating unit without its organism. Similarly, the community cannot exist without the cycling of materials and the flow of energy in the ecosystem.

. . . In the long run, no one level is any more or less important or any less deserving of scientific study than any other level. Some attributes, obviously, become more complex and variable as we proceed [through the hierarchy], but *it is an often overlooked fact that other attributes become less complex and less variable as we go from the small to the large unit.* Because homeostatic mechanisms, that is, checks and balances, forces and counter forces, operate all along the line, a certain amount of integration occurs as smaller units function within larger units. For example, the rate of photosynthesis of a forest community is less variable than that of individual leaves or trees within the community, because when one part slows down another may speed up in a compensatory manner. *When we consider the unique characteristics which develop at each level,* there is no reason to suppose that any level is more difficult or any easier to study quantitatively. For example, growth and metabolism may be effectively studied at the cellular level or at the ecosystem level by using technology and units of measurement of a different order of magnitude. Furthermore, the findings at any one level *aid in the study of another level, but never completely explain the phenomena occurring at that level.* This is an important point because persons sometimes contend that it is useless to try to work on complex populations and communities when the smaller units are not yet fully understood. If this idea was pursued to its logical conclusion, all biologists would concentrate on one level, the cellular, for example, until they solved the problems of this level; then they would study tissues and organs. Actually, this philosophy was widely held until biologists discovered that each level had characteristics which knowledge of the next lower level explained only *in part.* In other words, not all attributes of a higher level are predictable if we know only the properties of the lower level. Just as the properties of water are not predictable if we know only the properties of hydrogen and oxygen, so the characteristics of ecosystems cannot be predicted from knowledge of isolated populations; one must study the forest (i.e., the whole) as well as the trees (i.e., the parts). . . .

Homeostasis of Ecosystems

Ecosystems are capable of self-maintenance and self-regulation as are their component populations and organisms. Thus, *cybernetics* (fr. *kybernetes* = pilot or governor), the science of controls, has important application in ecology especially since man increasingly tends to disrupt natural controls or attempts to substitute artificial mechanisms for natural ones. ***Homeostasis*** (*homeo* = same; *stasis* = standing) is the term generally applied to the tendency for biological systems to resist change and to remain in a state of equilibrium. . . .

Control depends on *feedback*, which occurs when output (or part of it) feeds back as input. When this feedback input is positive (like compound interest, which is allowed to become part of the principal), the quantity grows. *Positive feedback* is "deviation-accelerating" and, of course, necessary for growth and survival of organisms. However, to achieve control—as, for example, to prevent overheating a room or cancerous overgrowth of a population — there must also be *negative feedback*, or "deviation-counteracting" input. . . . Mechanical feedback mechanisms are often called servomechanisms by engineers; biologists use the phrase homeostatic mechanisms to refer to living systems. . . .

As critics of human society are pointing out with increasing frequency . . . the positive feedback involved in the expansion of knowledge, power, and productivity threatens the quality of human life and environment unless adequate negative feedback controls can be found. The science of controls, or cybernetics, thus becomes one of the most important subjects to be studied, understood, and practiced. . . .

[Homeostasis exists at various levels of biological organization.] Homeostasis at the organism level is a well-known concept in physiology as outlined, for example, by Walter B. Cannon in his readable little book entitled *The Wisdom of the Body* (1932). We find that equilibrium between organisms and environment may also be maintained by factors which resist chance in the system as a whole. Much has been written about this "balance of nature," but only with the recent development of good methods for measuring rates of function of whole systems has a beginning been made in the understanding of the mechanisms involved.

. . . Some populations are regulated by density, which "feeds back" by way of behavioral mechanisms to reduce or increase the reproductive rate (the "effector") and thus maintain the population size (the "controlled quantity") within set limits. Other populations do not seem to be capable of self-limitation but are controlled by outside factors (this may include man . . .). Control mechanisms operating at the ecosystem level include those which regulate the storage and release of nutrients and the production and decomposition of organic substances. *The interplay of material cycles and energy flows in large ecosystems generates a self-correcting homeostasis with no outside control or set-point required.*

It is important to note . . . that homeostatic mechanisms have limits beyond which unrestricted positive feedback leads to death. . . . As stress increases, the system, although controlled, may not be able to return to the exact same level as before. . . . CO_2 introduced into the atmosphere by man's "industrial volcanoes" is largely, but not quite, absorbed by the carbonate system of the sea; as the input increases, new equilibrium levels are slightly higher. In this case even a slight change many have far-reaching effects. We shall also have many occasions to note that *really good homeostatic control comes only after a period of evolutionary adjustment.* New ecosystems (such as a new type of agriculture) or new host-parasite assemblages tend to oscillate more violently and to be less able to resist outside perturbation as compared with mature systems in which the components have had a chance to make mutual adjustments to each other.

As a result of the evolution of the central nervous system, mankind has gradually become the most powerful organism, as far as the ability to modify the operation of ecosystems is concerned. So important is man's role becoming as "a mighty geological agent" that Vernadsky (1945) has suggested that we think of the "noosphere" (from Greek *noos*, mind) or the world dominated by the mind of man, as gradually replacing the biosphere, the naturally evolving world which has existed for billions of years. This is dangerous philosophy because it is based on the assumption that mankind is now not only wise enough to understand the results of all his actions but is also capable of surviving in a completely artificial environment. When the reader has finished with this book I am sure he will agree that we cannot safely take over the management of everything!

The idea of the ecosystem and the realization that mankind is a part of, not apart from, complex "biogeochemical" cycles with increasing power to modify the cycles are concepts basic to modern ecology and are also points of view of extreme importance in human affairs generally. Conservation of natural resources, a most important practical application of ecology, must be built around these viewpoints. Thus, if understanding of ecological systems and moral responsibility among mankind can keep pace with man's power to effect changes, the present-day concept of "unlimited exploitation of resources" will give way to "unlimited ingenuity in perpetuating a cyclic abundance of resources." . . .

It is man the geological agent, not so much as man the animal, that is too much under the influence of positive feedback, and, therefore, must be subjected to negative feedback. Nature, with our intelligent help, can cope with man's physiological needs and wastes, but she has no homeostatic mechanisms to cope with bulldozers, concrete, and the kind of agroindustrial air, water, and soil pollution that will be hard to contain as long as the human population itself remains out of control.

Susanna Hecht and Alexander Cockburn provide the one dimension missing in many accounts of the ecology of the tropical rainforest—its human inhabitants.

MAN-MADE NATURE

Susanna Hecht and Alexander Cockburn

Just as the fantasies visited upon the Amazon by the pioneers and naturalists governed their observations and behavior, so too do the scientific models described in these pages have practical consequences. Those whose view of the

Amazon is informed by the idea of an ur-forest, stable since the beginning of time with man as a late interloper in the natural epic, tend to take a catastrophist attitude to any form of human intervention. Their solution to the destruction of the forest tends to the creation of large set-asides: natural preserves from which man is excluded. Thus for example the Tropical Rain Forest Action developed by bodies including the United Nations Environmental Program and the World Resources Institute recommends a vigorous forest conservation policy that "will set aside substantial areas of remaining tropical forests as ecological reserves to be protected from all forms of encroachment." The same is often true of those whose palaeo-ecology rests on the notion of refuges.

In the conservation model based on the "refugia," areas of especially high diversity are protected and essentially become evolutionary museums. Extrapolating from theories of island biogeography, the conservationists suggest that about twenty parks, located in areas of high diversity and suitably buffered, would be capable of safeguarding about 20 per cent of the species in the Amazon. Quite aside from the fact that this accepts extinction of the other 80 per cent, these reserves are once again Edens under glass from which the local populations are excluded, denied any role in the sustaining of the ecosystem. With very few exceptions—such as the Cuyabeno Park in Ecuador and Kuna Indian Park in southern Panama (essentially native reserves coupled with "adventure tourism")—few conservation areas incorporate local populations, an approach which can be traced back to John Muir's Yosemite National Park which inaugurated its career with the expulsion of the Miwok Indians who had previously made their homes there.

Overlooked in virtually all the accounts of the distribution of species and the structure of forests is the role of humanity. There is in fact a growing body of knowledge on how indigenous and local populations manage their natural resources and sustain them over time. Amplified by the dynamic view of the region's ecological history, described above, this knowledge permits an understanding of the forest as the outcome of human as well as biological history, and hence the view that humans can continue to make their history in the forest, sustaining and sustained. Thus is the Amazon extricated from the fantasies of the *bandeirante*, the romantic, the curator, and the speculator.

Unsurprisingly, the areas that supported the densest native populations were those that had experienced the most productive natural disturbances—the floodplains. Here were fertile sediments, new oxbow lakes teeming with game and fish, water-saturated land where productive palms could flourish in good soils, excellent planting areas for the annuals and tree crops of native agronomy. In the early years, explorer after explorer "opening" an area to the European consumers of his adventures wrote effusively of the agricultural productivity of the ample populations thronging the shores. When Herndon, Bates, and Wallace trekked through similar areas of the Amazon in the nineteenth century, they saw detribalized Indians and half-breeds engaged in what they viewed as deficient agricultural practices. The Amazon of the great native populations — the societies with rich pottery that rivaled the craftsmanship of the Inca, the vast interregional trading networks of salt, seeds, and medicines — was purged from memory. As populations fled, died, or were enslaved, the banks and interiors of the great rivers became mute green walls, revealing little of their history. The agricultural bounty of native production gave way to the paltry yields of the white man's plantations. The vision of the Amazon forest as a purely biological entity began to hold sway.

Travelers today, as over the last four centuries, believe they are observing "natural" forest, but this forest is most likely the product of human decisions of the past and even today. *Caboclos* in the Amazon's estuary have developed intensively-managed systems to provide timber, palm hearts, palm fruit, cocoa, and rubber for local and international markets. *Ribeirinhos*, those who dwell along rivers near Iquitos in the Peruvian Amazon, create complex cultivation strategies, orchards of fruit and food trees. These modern resource managers use techniques derived from indigenous practice. Virtually all the crops are native. In a *caboclo* or *mestizo* backwoodsman still reside centuries of accumulated knowledge.

Wherever one turns, the landscape almost invariably bears the imprint of human agency, starting with fire. Charcoal has been found in numerous areas when soil pits are dug. Many of these ash deposits are the outcome of natural fires, but the use of burning by Indians as part of agricultural and forest management cycles is very well documented. Pot shards are found extensively throughout the basin. The existence of Indian "black earths"— kitchen midden, rich in organic matter and residua from earlier occupation — have been found in innumerable upland sites from Colombia to the mouth of the Amazon.

The impact of human activity on the biogeography and structure of plant and animal communities in the tropics has been given short shrift by many biologists and agronomists, but the fact is that there are vast tracts of forests created by man. Those of the babassu palm cover hundreds of thousands of acres on the eastern and southern flanks of the basin. Such palm forests, initially viewed as natural, are now clearly discerned and documented as the consequence of human action. Large areas along the rivers that again appear to be natural *várzca* forest are the consequence of careful choices. Indeed much of the Amazon's forests may very well reflect the intercessions of man.

Research in several areas of Latin America, such as Janice Alcorn's landmark study on the Huastec, suggests that the range of interventions in forest ecosystems is much greater than has been realized. Both *caboclos* and native peoples planted and protected forest species. In perhaps the longest running study of natural resource management by native people, the North American anthropologist Darrell Posey has been able to document substantial amounts of forest manipulation by the Kayapó Indians, with direct planting of useful species, such as *Caryocar guinanensis*— the Piqui tree — and upland plantings of *Euterpe* palms in the forest's under-story. He also suggests that they have been active in reforesting open grassland areas. The Kayapó have shifted plant material — valuable medicinals, ritual plants, and other useful species — to locations that are easier to reach. They have described to Posey how they have collected germ plasm over a region roughly the size of western Europe and planted it in areas of interest to them. They place plants along trekking trails, in forest gaps, in camping sites, in favored hunting areas, and near gardens. These produce "resource islands," areas of useful plants not necessarily located close to the village but important to the large human community and regional ecology. These fruit and food plants also serve to attract and maintain populations of wild animals, a highly prized food source for the Kayapó.

Traditional Kayapó lands were about the size of France, so a more spacious view of their agricultural systems should replace the parochial concept of tropical forest cultivation localized only in the agricultural field. Indeed numerous scholars have shown that after "abandonment" agricultural fields remain sites of planting and manipulation within forest areas. Studies throughout Latin America increasingly suggest that rural populations are actively manipulating numerous vegetation types well beyond the agricultural sites, showing once more that our concepts of agriculture may be entirely deficient for understanding the basis of resource management and production by peoples.

The portrayal of native peoples as Rousseauian creatures of the forest has served several functions. It has permitted a view of them as children, incapable of wise decisions or the exercise of adult responsibilities. Until recently the official Brazilian view is that they are wards of the state, unable to participate in political life. To perceive native peoples as stone-age remnants who lie in the same relationship to nature as a tapir or a deer has made it easy to claim that these people's contribution to modern societies amounts to little. The enormous economic contribution to the First World of their domesticated plants has been disregarded. These peoples are accomplished environmental scientists and, contrary to patronizing supposition, indigenous groups have been involved in market activities for decades. Many native economies have been shaped by such market pressures and have often adapted well, at least enough to keep the forest and many features of their societies intact.

The eyes of the intruders saw the forests as primeval and empty. They missed the innumerable trails and portages, just as they missed the trading networks of the upper Xingu, or the salt routes that extended from the Atlantic to the Andes, or the connection between Central America and the Amazon via the Orinoco to the Casiquiare to the Rio Negro. The focus of traditional anthropology on the "primitive" and its emphasis on tribal forest inhabitants fostered the illusion of sparse settlement, and made it appear that a few Indians in a state of nature were the region's only occupants, along with some tough backwoodsmen, flotsam of the long past rubber boom. But more than two million people make their living in the forest through forms of petty extraction. The patronizing eye sees nothing of this and the image of the forest as a wild biological entity secluded from human intervention remains, making it easier to envisage forest clearance as the only rational form of development. And so the forests began to fall and shrouds of smoke covered the Amazon.

Indian Lessons: Ashes and Life

In most sustainable agricultural systems in the Amazon and indeed throughout the Latin American tropics, fire has an integral and sensible role in making the land productive for human use. Fire is coupled with activities that compensate for its potentially destructive effects. Forests are cut at the beginning of the dry season, in April or May, depending on location. Indigenous peoples such as the Kayapó use a number of biological indicators such as the flowering of particular trees, migration of animals, and astronomy as signals for the beginning of the cutting period. Logs are then left to dry until late August or September when the fires are set. The period of burning is carefully monitored by shamans with particular skills in fire management. The flowering of the Piqui tree, the constellations, and movements of fish dictate the ritual cycle that culminates in carefully timed burning. Fires are set with prudent attention to weather and timing so that they burn thoroughly the small and moderate trunks and lianas, but still remain under control. Weeks prior to burning, the Kayapó women who own the fields plant varieties of sweet potato, manioc, and yam that begin to sprout almost immediately after the fires have cooled, thus quickly initiating the agricultural succession. They then plant short-cycle crops such as corn, beans, melons, and squash that rapidly cover large areas, along with longer-cycle crops that can be harvested anywhere from six months to two years after the planting. In their use of short-cycle, light-tolerant species that gradually give way to woody fruits, the principles of succession are maintained. The grasses, corn, the fast growing vines, the squashes, sweet potatoes, and melons all mirror the types of plant families found in early succession. The role of the weedy *solanum* is taken on by their domesticated cousins—peppers.

Domesticated beans mimic the wild vetches and legumes. The ubiquitous euphorbia of successional vegetation find their analogs in manioc.

The Kayapó also gather charred branches and debris, and set a second fire, called *coivara* in Portuguese, which provides particularly fertile "hot spots" within the field. Sweet potatoes, which thrive on the potassium from ash, are continuously planted and replanted on these open sites. To prevent soil compaction women till and loosen the soil with their machetes. Around the perimeters of the field, ash and branches will once again be piled and burned. Here, yams—to be harvested several years hence—are planted with papayas, pineapples, the *urucu* tree (the source of a beautiful red body paint and an excellent food coloring, annatto), and other useful ritual, medicinal, and food plants. The Kayapó prepare food in the fields, and their cooking fires and ash are moved around so that fresh nutrients from the ashes are distributed where necessary.

In areas where sweet potatoes are regularly grown, harvested, and replanted, the Kayapó set harvest residue aflame to supply nutrients to the new crops, to reduce pest problems on the younger plants, and to control weeds. Most unusual is the practice of the Kayapó of burning substantial portions of the crop field while their crops are still on the ground. Many of the cultivars—the types of crop plants—are fire tolerant, and the Kayapó practise a form of highly specific, controlled "cool" burns, so that seed stocks in the ground, and the root crops on which their subsistence is based, are not destroyed by fire. When the plot ceases to be a central area for the production of root crops it will become a source of perennial crops and of game. By planting shrubs and trees which provide fruits of interest to wildlife, the secondary successional stages become "animal gardens."

What the Kayapó are doing can easily be interpreted within the terms of First World science. The Kayapó stimulate forest succession in their fallows by making sure that their agricultural sites incorporate the necessary elements to recuperate forests, which are often as valuable to them as the agriculture. This includes the creation of suitable environmental conditions and the manipulation of successional processes themselves. In tropical forests, as we have seen, most of the nutrients are held in the plants themselves. To make these nutrients available for crop growth the forest must be cut and burned. In natural fires and native agriculture, seeds already in the ground or crops planted prior to or immediately after the burn begin to grow almost as soon as the ground has cooled. Thus plants begin to take up the available nutrients rapidly and store them in their tissues. The rapid uptake of nutrients by plants that root to different depths and have life cycles of different lengths mimics what happens in plant succession in the tropics. Short-lived plants are gradually replaced with longer-lived species. The soil is not compacted because it is carefully worked, always has a cover of vegetation, and is thus protected from rainfall — which is the main agent of soil compaction — so that forest seedlings can establish themselves fairly easily. The relatively small size of the plots (although some Kayapó ceremonial agricultural sites can be more than two hundred acres in size) results in a microclimate that is influenced by the forest surrounding it. The parching conditions so characteristic of Amazonian pastures are not found in these indigenous agricultural zones. Moreover, animals and seeds from the adjacent forest can easily arrive in the field.

Manipulation of the fallows is central to the process of forest regeneration. The forests that arise from "abandoned" agricultural plots are only as "natural" as European mixed orchards with sheep browsing underneath the shade. The Kayapó work the fallow in several ways: by weeding out some plants, protecting others such as palms, planting particularly cherished trees and shrubs, transplanting, pruning, and fertilizing them with bones, ash, and mulch. They carry out these activities at different intensities, but they always enhance the regeneration process through the introduction of species whose seeds and seedlings may have been destroyed in the burning. This fosters species and spatial diversity in the plot, thereby helping to confound the seed and seedling predators. Also, by planting and protecting plant species whose fruit are eaten by animals, they attract into the plot a diversity of wildlife and game.

About three-quarters of all tropical forest trees have fleshy fruits. A Tembé Indian conversing with the anthropologist and ethnobotanist William Balée informed him that nearly 90 per cent of the fruits produced by trees in a two-and-a-half acre plot in Maranhão were consumed by game animals. The Kayapó also plant more than sixteen species that bear fruits enjoyed not only by them but also by game. Scholars like Kent Redford who focus on wildlife interactions have demonstrated that nine out of eleven favored game animals and the seven most favored game birds eat fruit, and that more than sixty genera of fruit-bearing plants consumed by game are to be found in the Amazon gardens. Planted fruit trees are likely to attract more game into the fields which in turn introduce seeds of other fruit or forest trees through their droppings. Making gardens attractive to wildlife is an essential part of the recuperation process.

Thus do agriculture and fallow management ensure that rich and useful forests will follow cultivation. In comparison with natural succession, indeed, this manipulation can increase the diversity of species on a given site. Study after study has shown that even when tribes move these sites are anything but abandoned.

In recent years, the concept of TEK (Traditional Ecological Knowledge) has become a buzzword among academic and government environmental researchers and policy-makers. The following article is a perspective on TEK by a native leader, Chief Robert Wavey of the Fox Lake First Nation of northern Manitoba. This was Chief Wavey's keynote address to the International Workshop on Indigenous Knowledge and Community-Based Resource Management delivered in Winnipeg at the University of Manitoba in September 1991.

ACCEPT WHAT IS OBVIOUS

Chief Robert Wavey

Recently, academics, scientific researchers, and others have "discovered" that the knowledge which indigenous people hold of the earth, its ecosystems, the wildlife, fisheries, forests, and other integrated living systems is extensive and extremely accurate. On the eve of the 500th anniversary of Christopher Columbus having stumbled upon North America, it is appropriate to provide comments from the perspective of an indigenous person in North America on what the concept of "discovery" means to us.

At the time Europeans first contacted Aboriginal peoples, the quality of our environment was such that our communities had access to ample supplies of clean water, timber and wood, berries and medicinal plants, beaver, muskrat, moose, caribou, geese, and other wildlife.

The laws and customs of First Nations guided the sharing and management of resources, and ensured that our people could continue to enjoy, on a sustained basis, the resources which provided the needs of our families. These laws and customs are based on generations of observation and knowledge. Our laws and customs respecting land and resources also form the binding foundation of Aboriginal nations and systems of governance.

Europeans came to a resource-rich continent after millennia of management and stewardship of that continent by Aboriginal people. After 500 years of continuous exploitation and development, guided by science and technological discovery, non-aboriginal management systems have created an era of unprecedented opportunity for widespread ecological catastrophe.

As was the case with Columbus, "discovery" is in the eye of the beholder. It may be more accurate to state that the dominant European-based society, after 500 years, has finally stopped ignoring our traditional knowledge, laws, and customs.

As indigenous people, we spend a great deal of our time, through all seasons of the year, travelling over, drinking, eating, smelling, and living with the ecological system which surrounds us. Aboriginal people often notice very minor changes in quality, odour, and vitality long before they become obvious to government enforcement agencies, scientists, or other observers of the same ecological system.

Governments have begun to view indigenous people and their knowledge of the land as an early warning system for environmental change, perhaps in much the same way as miners once viewed canaries. The difference is that a canary does not know why it died, or what was wrong; indigenous people do. The canary can not propose solutions or provide an example of lifestyles and ethics to restore ecological balance; indigenous people can. The canary does not foretell environmental change, but indigenous people accurately predict ecological disturbance, based on multi-generational accumulations of knowledge and experience.

The United Nations World Commission on Environment and Development found in 1987 that:

> Social discrimination, cultural barriers, and the exclusion of [indigenous peoples] from national political processes makes these groups vulnerable and subject to exploitation. . . . They become the victims of what could be described as cultural extinction. . . .

In Canada, the process of acquiring Aboriginal lands for agriculture, forestry, mining, and settlements was rooted in an official policy of cultural extermination which continued for several generations. In concert with the churches, Aboriginal children were removed from our communities year after year for the entire school season. We were prevented from speaking our languages and we were prevented from practising our ceremonies in respect for Mother Earth and our ancestors. Separating the children from the grandparents and elders resulted in many of our people losing touch with traditional resource uses and knowledge of the land.

The Government of Canada did not succeed. The traditions, cultures, languages, institutions, and beliefs of our people live on and grow stronger every day.

Two important things have kept the Aboriginal people of Canada strong and together. The first is our tremendous sense of community and family. Our traditional means of teaching—with the grandparents teaching the young while the parents provide for the family—remains today within our communities; it has ensured that the young people recover, restore, and revitalize their traditions, their languages, and their way of life. The second is that *most Aboriginal people in Canada still have the land.* Without the land, our knowledge of the land, and the respect that we hold for the land, our communities and our way of life would not exist because *the land and the people are one.* A land base and extensive traditional ecological knowledge have ensured the cultural survival of Aboriginal people in Canada.

The boreal forest in Manitoba is almost roadless and is home to more than 33,000 treaty Aboriginal people living in some 30 communities. To Manitoba's northern people, there are no frontiers, wilderness, or empty lands; the forest is the First Nations homeland. Manitoba's boreal forest region is almost completely interconnected by trails, rivers, lakes, and portages. The region also contains hundreds of spring, summer, and winter hunting, fishing, gathering, and trapping encampments. The boreal forest provides considerable direct economic value to the communities, values which are largely invisible to resource developers, managers, and politicians. In addition to the teaching of skills, each elder maintains continuity and links to the community resource area by transferring a highly detailed oral "map" and inventory of resource values and land use locations. These individual and family maps knit together into a rich and complete mosaic which provides integrated knowledge of the ecosystems within the community's traditional resource area.

Therefore, major ecological disturbances such as hydroelectric development and large-scale forestry activities have profound cultural impacts by obliterating the reference points and actual resources that these maps are intended to share. Resource developments convert highly valued and sought-after family and community knowledge into memories. The UN World Commission describes the disappearance of indigenous cultures as "a loss for the larger society, which could learn a great deal from their traditional skills in managing very complex ecological systems." The same is true for the loss of traditional ecological knowledge.

If the concept of ecosystems includes those habitats extensively modified by humans, then traditional ecological knowledge is used by everybody every day of their lives; many are just not aware of it. In the cities of the world, for example, urban survival knowledge is a form of traditional knowledge. People must use their adaptive instincts to survive on the streets, in the school yards, in the factories, and in the office towers. Urban families accumulate "street smarts" which change to meet the times. Detailed knowledge of the urban environment is essential for survival.

There is a major difference between traditional ecological knowledge, which is an instinctive adaptation taking place within a few short years, and the body of traditional ecological knowledge, which is accumulated for specific lands and handed down over many generations. For example, many resource developers and government planners often assume that Aboriginal people are highly adaptive and can survive the abrupt relocations and changes in the resource base caused by hydroelectric development. Traditional ecological knowledge related to current areas of land use, occupancy, and habitation is often incorrectly assumed to allow for an instant knowledge of new or altered hunting and gathering locations. This attitude was evident during the diversion of the Churchill River and the extensive damming of the Nelson River system in northern Manitoba. Although forcibly relocated Aboriginal people may survive in the end, their well-being will be affected for many generations while the patterns of experience and observations develop into detailed knowledge of the altered localized ecology.

When the international pulp and paper giant REPAP announced the purchase of a Forest Management Licence covering 108,000 square kilometres of northern Manitoba, an area the size of Guatemala, the Chiefs of northern Manitoba were determined to protect the traditional resource areas of the First Nations affected by documenting the oral and land use maps of resource users in the REPAP cutting area.

Earlier experience with the massive hydroelectric projects in northern Manitoba had proven that non-aboriginal developers and government considered impacts to Aboriginal land uses too general to quantify accurately using existing techniques. As a result, they were effectively ignored. The Chiefs were determined in the REPAP case to combine traditional ecological knowledge with science by developing an independent capacity to document detailed land use, managing the considerable map data with an automated geographic information system (GIS), and overlaying this data with maps of the REPAP cutting plans.

Under Manitoba's Environment Act, a joint Federal-Provincial Review of the REPAP forestry expansion and bleached kraft proposals is a mandatory requirement. The terms of reference for the environmental impact statement include a detailed assessment of the impacts of logging and roads on Aboriginal land use. However, the Chief of Northern Manitoba has refused to provide this information directly to consultants working for REPAP. Such land use information is the private property of the resource users and the community. It is strictly confidential and may be released only with the consent of the resource user and community involved.

Through its Natural Resources Secretariat, the Council of Manitoba Northern Chiefs, the Manitoba Keewatinowi Okimakanak (MKO), negotiated an agreement-in-principle to have MKO First Nations conduct the land use mapping which was related to the environmental assessment process. Partly as a result of the REPAP agreement, MKO installed a geographic information system (GIS) supported by a system to display and analyze remotely-sensed images to ensure that First Nations benefit in future from the information collected as part of the assessment of forestry impacts.

The MKO GIS Development Project achieved several important objectives. Firstly, the proprietary nature of much of the resource and land use information of individuals was protected. Use, occupancy, and habitation maps are often used during land entitlement selection and settlement, mitigation program assessment, and other claims negotiations. In addition, impacts could be created by making specific details of land use public through publishing maps of prime hunting and fishing sites, gravesites, and former community locations. Second, control of the raw land-use information allows the communities to optimize the acknowledged value of this information through skills development, contracted projects, employment, and other means. And finally, MKO now has a comprehensive, computer-based geographic information system to incorporate existing and future land use mapping data, allow overlay and comparison of resource inventories and economic activity, and enable effective modelling of possible alternative patterns of development.

Maintaining complex indigenous control of traditional land use information is a cornerstone in developing a link between traditional ecological knowledge and science. This ensures that indigenous people develop the skills and capacity to benefit from the growing interest in traditional ecological knowledge. Development of the capacity for indigenous people to independently respond to and directly participate in the resource management activities arising from the application of traditional ecological knowledge is also required.

For example, biologists and chemists working in field analysis acknowledge that a human being can often detect changes in taste, water, tissue, and other substances, at levels below that of contemporary testing equipment. Aboriginal resource harvesters near the Ruttan copper-zinc mine in northern Manitoba have refused to drink water and eat fish and beaver from lakes which are not related to the licensed discharges from the mill. These changes in taste have developed over the past two years. A recent field sampling program designed by the MKO and Environmental Protection Laboratories identified sample sites and sample types on the basis of interviews with the principal resource harvesters. The field sampling technicians confirmed the significance of the 13 sampling sites suggested by an 83-year-old Cree trapper and others using the area. Work is now underway to develop a permanent First Nations capacity to link traditional ecological knowledge-based environmental monitoring with a sampling and laboratory analysis program directed and operated by Aboriginal people in northern Manitoba.

I have often been asked for some positive examples of First Nations management of natural resources. The question implies that First Nations management is something that is either new or developing through agreements with governments. First Nations in Canada have never surrendered the role of managing the natural resources protected by Aboriginal rights. In fact, the use of resources by Aboriginal people and the stewardship of resources have always been tied together. Many specific sites have been continuously used by our communities for generations, indicating the success of the existing direct management and continued stewardship by the communities.

Although government seeks to regulate lands and natural resources, the ability of government to manage these vast lands directly has always been limited. The government ability to actually manage resources is even more limited now with reductions in budgets and changes in government priorities.

When government and corporate managers fly into remote regions to set up camps for fieldwork, watching them pass overhead are a good number of Aboriginal faces turned to the sky. Aboriginal people watch as exploration camps are built, cut lines made, hydro sites selected, timber harvested, and resource roads constructed.

The people retain a record of what the land and the resources have provided for generations, and Aboriginal people are the first to see the changes. The Aboriginal resource users are the principal managers of resources who also bear the burden of the long term impacts. Aboriginal people must develop unique strategies for adjusting to and accommodating these impacts to continue our direct use of the lands and resources.

First Nations intend to ensure a quality of the environment so that our traditional pursuits are maintained. First Nations recognize the influence over decisions concerning natural resources management and the quality of the environment is directly tied to the social, cultural, and economic future of Aboriginal people. Ultimately the difference between poverty and prosperity is determined in large measure by the extent to which Aboriginal people directly manage and control the nature, scale, and type of development within our traditional lands.

Traditional resource management structures can continue to provide effective stewardship for lands and ecosystems which are not significantly disrupted by development and all the related ecological pressures. The need for linking non-traditional, science-based environmental technologies and management approaches with traditional ecological knowledge increases in relation to the extent of ecological disruption. This is particularly apparent, for example, when identifying problems related to hazardous wastes and industrial pollution. However, an identified need for applying science-based environmental technologies to a disrupted ecosystem does not mean that traditional ecological knowledge and Aboriginal stewardship should be replaced with science-based, non-aboriginal government authority. Traditional ecological knowledge is an important cornerstone of Aboriginal self-government. I agree with the UN World Commission findings that:

> . . . the recognition of traditional rights must go hand in hand with measures to protect the local institutions that enforce responsibility in resource use. And this recognition must also give local communities a decisive voice in the decisions about resource use in their area.

In Canada, the entrenchment of Aboriginal and treaty rights in the Constitution, as well as the recent reinforcement of resource rights by the Supreme Court of Canada, provides for a mandatory role for First Nations in the management of natural resources. The role remains unfulfilled.

For science to effectively support traditional ecological knowledge and indigenous resource management in Canada and elsewhere, you must place the highest priority on supporting the development of permanent technical, scientific, and support capacity under the control and direction of indigenous peoples. There is no question that increased access to traditional ecological knowledge will allow non-indigenous managers a means for refining and focusing environmental regulation and management. However, I am concerned that science-based management approaches will use the improved ecological database not to focus on development-related ecological impacts, but to impose additional regulations and restrictions on the resource uses of indigenous peoples.

Science has never been neutral in relation to indigenous peoples, lands, resources, and development. The struggle to control lands and resources to facilitate development is the principal feature of the relationship between indigenous peoples and governments worldwide. Science is based on discovery, and has provided the foundation for the industrialization of the earth and the concentration of wealth in the hands of those nations with the greatest scientific capacity. Traditional ecological knowledge is not another frontier for science to discover.

When you contemplate the linking of traditional ecological knowledge and science in order to support the healing of Mother Earth, I ask you to resist seeking to discover. I urge you instead to accept what is obvious.

Traditional ecological knowledge is based on mutual well-being and sharing. In our severely disrupted global environments, traditional ecological knowledge is now essential for our mutual survival. The benefits of traditional ecological knowledge can be shared when there is respect, understanding, the recognition of traditional rights, and the recognition of existing indigenous stewardship of many regions of the earth.

Noted Harvard University geneticist Richard Lewontin throws out a challenge to the familiar conception that the environment is first and foremost something to be "preserved."

THERE IS NO "ENVIRONMENT"

Richard C. Lewontin

What is so extraordinary about the view of an external environment set for us by nature, and essentially unchangeable except in the sense that we might ruin it and destroy the delicate balance that nature has created in our absence, is that it is completely in contradiction to what we know about organisms and environment. When we free ourselves of the ideological bias of atomism and **reductionism** and look squarely at the actual relations between organisms and the world around them, we find a much richer set of relations, relations that have very different consequences for social and political action than are usually supposed, for example, by the environmental movement.

First, there is no "environment" in some independent and abstract sense. Just as there is no organism without an environment, there is no environment without an organism. Organisms do not experience environments. They create them. They construct their own environments out of the bits and pieces of the physical and biological world and they do so by their own activities. Are the stones and the grass in my garden part of the environment of a bird? The grass is certainly part of the environment of a phoebe that gathers dry grass to make a nest. But the stone around which the grass is growing means nothing to the phoebe. On the other hand, the stone is part of the environment of a thrush that may come along with a garden snail and break the shell of the snail against the stone. Neither the grass nor the stone are part of the environment of a woodpecker that is living in a hole in a tree. That is, bits and pieces of the world outside of these organisms are made relevant to them by their own life activities. If grass is used to make a nest, then grass is part of the environment. If stones are used to break snails on, then stones are part of the environment.

There is an infinity of ways in which parts of the world can be assembled to make an environment, and we can know what the environment of an organism is only by consulting the organism. Not only do we consult the organism, but when we describe the environment we describe it in terms of the organism's behavior and life activities. If you are in any doubt of this, you might try asking a professional ecologist to describe the environment of some bird. He or she will say something like the following. "Well, the bird builds its nest three feet off the ground in hardwoods. It eats insects part of the year but then may switch to seeds and nuts when insects are no longer available. It flies south in the winter and comes back north in the summer, and when it is foraging for its food it tends to stay in the higher branches and at their outer tips," and so on. Every word uttered by the ecologist in describing the environment of a bird will be a description of the life activities of the bird. That process of description reflects the fact that the ecologist has learned what the environment of the bird is by watching birds.

A practical demonstration of the difficulty of describing an environment without having seen an organism that determined and defined it is the case of the Mars Lander. When the United States decided to send a landing module to Mars, biologists wanted to know if there was any life there. So the problem was to design a machine to detect life on Mars. There were several interesting suggestions. One was to send a kind of microscope with a long sticky tongue that would unroll on the planet's surface and then roll back up and put whatever dust it found under the microscope. If there was anything that looked like a living organism, we would see it in the images sent back to Earth. One might call this the morphological definition of life. If it looks right and it wiggles, then it is alive.

What appears to be a more sophisticated approach was taken. Instead of asking whether things on Mars look alive, it was decided to ask whether they have the metabolism of living things. So the Mars Lander contained what was essentially a long hose attached to a vacuum cleaner inside of which was a container of radioactive growth medium. When the Lander got to Mars, it would suck up some dust into the medium and if there were any living organisms in the dust, they would break down the medium as bacteria do on Earth, radioactive carbon dioxide would be produced, and a detector in the machine would signal the presence of this gas. And that is exactly what happened. When the Mars Lander sucked up the dust, radioactive carbon dioxide was produced in a pattern that had everyone convinced that there was life on Mars fermenting the medium. But then suddenly the process shut down and there was no further fermentation. This was not what living organisms were supposed to do, and the consequence was scientific confusion. After a debate among those concerned with the experiment, it was decided that there was no life on Mars. Instead, it was postulated that there was a kind of chemical reaction on finely divided clay particles catalyzed by the particles, which were not ordinarily seen on Earth. Later, this reaction was successfully mimicked in the laboratory, so everybody has now agreed that they decided correctly and that there is no life on Mars.

The problem with this experiment arises precisely from the fact that organisms define their own environment. How can we know whether there is life on Mars? We present Martian life with an environment and see whether it can live in it. But how can we know what the environment of Martian life is unless we have seen Martian organisms? All that the experiment of the Mars Lander showed was that there is no Earth-like bacterial life on Mars. We may know the temperature, the gas content of the atmosphere, the humidity, and something about the soil on Mars, but we do not know what a Martian environment is like because the environment does not consist of temperature, gas, moisture, and soil. It consists of an organized set of relationships among bits and pieces of the world, which organization has been created by living Martian organisms themselves.

We must replace that adaptationist view of life with a constructionist one. It is not that organisms find environments and either adapt themselves to the environments or die. They actually *construct* their environment out of bits and pieces. In this sense, the environment of organisms is coded in their DNA and we find ourselves in a kind of reverse Lamarckian position. Whereas Lamarck supposed that changes in the external world would cause changes in the internal structures, we see that the reverse is true. An organism's genes, to the extent that they influence what that organism does in its behavior, physiology, and morphology, are at the same time helping to construct an environment. So, if genes change in evolution, the environment of the organism will change too.

Consider the immediate environment of a human being. If one takes motion pictures of a person, using schlieren optics that detect differences in the refractive index of the air, one can see that a layer of warm, moist air completely surrounds each one of us and is slowly rising from our legs and bodies and going off the top of our heads. In fact, every living organism including trees has this boundary layer of warm air that is created by the organism's metabolism. The result is that we are encapsulated in a little atmosphere created by our own metabolic activities. One consequence is what is called the wind-chill factor. The reason that it gets much colder when the wind blows across us is because the wind is blowing away the boundary layer and our skins are then exposed to a different set of temperatures and humidities. Consider a mosquito feeding on the surface of the human body. That mosquito is completely immersed in the boundary layer that we have constructed. It is living in a warm, moist world. Yet one of the most common evolutionary changes for all organisms is a change in size, and over and over again organisms have evolved to be larger. If the mosquito species begins to evolve to a larger size, it may in fact find itself with its back in the "stratosphere" and only up to its knees in the warm, moist boundary layer while it is feeding. The consequence will be that the mosquito's evolution has put it into an entirely different world. Moreover, as human beings early in their evolution lost hair and the distribution of sweat glands over their bodies changed, the thickness of the boundary layer changed and so changed the micro-world that they carry with them, making it rather less hospitable for fleas, mosquitoes, and other parasites that live on hairy animals. The first rule of the real relation between organisms and environment is that environments do not exist in the absence of organisms but are constructed by them out of bits and pieces of the external world.

The second rule is that the environment of organisms is constantly being remade during the life of those living beings. When plants send down roots, they change the physical nature of the soil, breaking it up and aerating it. They exude organic molecules, humic acids, that change the soil's chemical nature as well. They make it possible for various beneficial fungi to live together with them and penetrate their root systems. They change the height of the water table by removing water. They alter the humidity in their immediate neighborhood, and the upper leaves of a plant change the amount of light that is available to the lower leaves. When the Canadian Department of Agriculture takes weather records for agricultural purposes, they do not set up a weather station in an open field or on the roof of a building. They take measurements of temperature and humidity at various levels above the ground in a field of growing plants because the plants are constantly changing the physical conditions that are relevant to agriculture. Moles burrow in the soil. Earthworms through their castings completely change the local topology. Beavers have had at least as important an effect on the landscape in North America as humans did until the beginning of the last century. Every breath you take removes oxygen and adds carbon dioxide to the world. Mort Sahl once said, "Remember, no matter how cruel and nasty and evil you may be, every time you take a breath you make a flower happy."

Every living organism is in a constant process of changing the world in which it lives by taking up materials and putting out others. Every act of consumption is also an act of production. And every act of production is an act of consumption. When we consume food, we produce not only gases but solid waste products that are in turn the materials for consumption of some other organism.

A consequence of the universality of environmental change induced by the life activity of organisms is that every organism is both producing and destroying the conditions of its existence. There is a great deal of talk about how we as human beings are destroying the environment. But we are not unique in the fact that our life processes are recreating the world in a way that is in part hostile to the continuation of our own lives. Every bacterium uses up food material and excretes waste products that are toxic to it. Organisms ruin the world not only for their own lives but for their children as well.

The entire vegetational landscape of New England is a consequence of that process. The primeval forest in New England consisted of a mixture of hardwoods, pines, and hemlocks. As agriculture spread at the end of the eighteenth and through the nineteenth century, all these forests were cut down and replaced by farms. Then, just before and after the Civil War, there were wholesale migrations out of the rocky soils of New England, where one could barely plant a crop, to the deep and productive soils of the Middle West. As a result, farms were abandoned and plants started to infiltrate these old fields. The first thing that came in was a variety of weeds and herbs. These were replaced later by white pines. White pines can form an almost pure stand in an old field and many such pure white pine stands could be seen in New England earlier in this century. However, they do not last. The pines make a dense shade that is inhospitable to the growth of their own seedlings, and so they cannot replace each other. As the pines die or if, as in New England, they are cut wholesale, what comes in are hardwoods, whose seedlings have been waiting around for a little opening. The white pines disappear forever with the exception of an occasional old tree, and a composition similar to the prehistoric virgin forest appears. This old-field white pine to hardwood succession is a consequence of the conditions of light and soil being changed by the pine trees in such a way that their own offspring cannot succeed them. The generation gap is not simply a human phenomenon.

So, we must put away the notion that out there there is a constant and fixed world that human beings alone are disturbing and destroying. We are certainly changing it, as all organisms do, and we certainly have a power that other organisms do not have, both to change the world extremely rapidly and, by willful activity, to change the world in various ways that we may think beneficial. Nevertheless, we cannot live without changing the environment. That is the second law of the relationship between organism and environment.

Third, organisms determine the statistical nature of the environment at least as far as it has an influence on themselves. Organisms are capable of averaging over time and buffering out the fluctuations in physical factors. An important example is the way animals and plants store sunlight. Even though the conditions for growth and good nutrition do not exist all year around in a temperate zone, it is not only farmers who make hay while the sun shines. Potatoes are the storage organs of potato plants and acorns form the storage for oak trees. Other organisms, in turn, use these storage devices for their own storage. Squirrels store away acorns for use in the winter and human beings store away potatoes. As human beings, we have even a further level of averaging: money. Money is the way in which, through futures contracts, fluctuations in the availability of natural products are ironed out for the market, and savings banks are where we put money for a rainy day. So organisms do not, in fact, perceive at a physiological level much of the fluctuation that goes on in the external world.

Conversely, organisms have techniques of reacting to the rates of change of the external world rather than the actual levels of resources. Water fleas are sometimes sexual and sometimes asexual. They change from nonsexual reproduction to sexual reproduction when a drastic change occurs in the environment, say, the change in the amount of oxygen in the water in which they live or a change in its temperature or a change in food availability. They do not alter from nonsexual to sexual when the temperature is high or when it is low but when it changes rapidly in either direction. They are detectors of change pure and simple. Our visual system is also a sensitive detector of change. Our central nervous system, by complex processing of images, enables us to see differences in intensity of light across edges in a way that is superior to what physical and electronic devices can do. We accomplish this by magnifying differences across small distances. Thus, we have greater visual acuity than optical scanning machinery. The third rule of organism and environment, then, is that fluctuations in the world matter only as organisms transform them.

Finally, organisms actually change the basic physical nature of signals that come to them from the external world. As the temperature in a room rises, my liver detects that change, not as a rise in temperature, but as a change in the concentration of sugar in my blood and the concentration of certain hormones. What begins as a change in the rate of a vibration of air molecules—a change in temperature—becomes converted inside the body into a change in the concentration of certain chemical substances. The nature of that conversion is a consequence of the action of genes, which have a strong influence on anatomy and physiology. When I am out in the desert doing my field work and I hear and see a rattlesnake, those rarefactions of the air that impinge on my eardrums and those photons of light that come into my eye are changed by my central nervous system into a chemical signal and suddenly my adrenaline starts to flow. But these vibrations and photons would be changed to a very different chemical signal in the body of another snake that is receiving exactly the same sights and sounds, especially if it were a snake of the opposite sex. This difference in transformation of one signal into another is coded in the difference between human genes and the genes of a snake. The last rule of the relation between organism and environment is that the very physical nature of the environment as it is relevant to organisms is determined by the organisms themselves.

It may be objected that such an interactive picture of organism and environment is all very well but it ignores some obvious aspects of the external world over which organisms have no control. A human being may have *discovered* the law of gravitation, but he certainly did not *pass* it. You cannot fight gravity. But that, in fact, is not true. A bacterium living in liquid does not feel gravity because it is so small and its buoyant properties free it from what is essentially a very weak force. But the size of a bacterium is a consequence of its genes, and so it is the genetic difference between us and bacteria that determines whether the force of gravitation is relevant to us.

On the other hand, bacteria feel a universal physical force that we do not, the force of Brownian motion. Precisely because bacteria are so small, they are battered from one side to the other by the motion of molecules in the liquid in which they are suspended. We, fortunately, are not constantly reeling from one side of the room to the other under the influence of that bombardment because we are so large. All forces of nature depend for their influence on size, distance, and time duration. How large an organism is, how rapidly it alters its state and position, how far it is from other organisms of different sizes and kinds are all deeply influenced by the organisms' genes. So, in a very important sense, the physical forces of the world, insofar as they are relevant to living beings, are encoded in those beings' genes. Just as we cannot talk about living organisms as just products of their genes but must recognize that the genes interact with the environment in producing the organism in its development and activity, so reciprocally we cannot make the mistake of saying that organisms confront an autonomous external world. The environment influences organisms only through interaction with their genes. The internal and the external are inextricably bound up with each other.

The facts of the relationship between organism and environment have important consequences for current political and social movements. There is a widespread perception that in many ways the world is becoming a rather less pleasant and more threatening place to live in, and there is a good possibility that it may grow catastrophically unpleasant in the not too distant future. It may get a lot warmer. A good deal more ultraviolet light may strike us than now does. The world does not smell very good. There are all sorts of noxious substances that are the agents of illness and even death, and we recognize all these changes as the consequences of human activity. It is entirely correct that human beings should want to make a world in which they can live happy, healthful, and reasonably long lives. But we cannot do that under the banner of "Save the Environment," because this slogan assumes that there is *an* environment that has been created by nature and that we in our foolishness are destroying. It assumes, too, that there is such a thing as the balance of nature, that everything is in a balance and harmony that is being destroyed only by the foolishness and greed of human beings.

There is nothing in our knowledge of the world to suggest there is any particular balance or harmony. The physical and biological worlds since the beginning of the earth have been in a constant state of flux and change, much of which has been far more drastic than anyone can now conceive. Indeed, much of what we conceive of as the environment has been the creation of living organisms. The atmosphere that we all breathe and that we hope we can continue to breathe is about 21 percent oxygen and a fraction of a percent of carbon dioxide. But that atmosphere was not on earth before living organisms. Most of the oxygen was bound up in chemicals. Oxygen is a very unstable compound and does not exist stably in free form. There was, however, a high concentration of free carbon dioxide. The carbon dioxide was removed from the atmosphere and deposited in limestone and chalk by the action of algae and bacteria during the early history of the earth and in oil and coal by plants somewhat later. The oxygen, which was not present at all, was put into the atmosphere by the activity of plants, and then animals evolved in a world made for them by the earlier organisms. Only 60,000 years ago, Canada was completely under ice, as was the middle of the United States. *The* environment has never existed and there has never been balance or harmony. Fully 99.999 percent of all species that have ever existed are already extinct, and in the end all will become extinct. Indeed, life is about half over. Our estimates are that the first living organisms appeared on earth in the order of 3 to 4 billion years ago, and we know from stellar evolution that our sun will expand and burn up the earth in another 3 to 4 billion years, putting an end to everything.

So any rational environmental movement must abandon the romantic and totally unfounded ideological commitment to a harmonious and balanced world in which the environment is preserved and turn its attention to the real question, which is, how do people want to live and how are they to arrange that they live that way? Human beings do have a unique property not shared by other organisms. It is not the destructive property but the property that they can plan the changes that will occur in the world. They cannot stop the world from changing, but they may be able with appropriate social organization to divert those changes in a more beneficial direction, and so, perhaps, even postpone their own extinction for a few hundred thousand years.

Our DNA is a powerful influence on our anatomies and physiologies. In particular, it makes possible the complex brain that characterizes human beings. But having made that brain possible, the genes have made possible human nature, a social nature whose limitations and possible shapes we do not know except insofar as we know what human consciousness has already made possible. In Simone de Beauvoir's clever but deep apothegm, a human being is "*l'être dont l'être est de n'être pas*," the being whose essence is in not having an essence.

History far transcends any narrow limitations that are claimed for either the power of genes or the power of the environment to circumscribe us. Like the House of Lords that destroyed its own power to limit the political development of Britain in the successive Reform Acts to which it assented, so the genes, in making possible the development of human consciousness, have surrendered their power both to determine the individual and its environment. They have been replaced by an entirely new level of causation, that of social interaction with its own laws and its own nature that can be understood and explored only through that unique form of experience, social action.

We conclude with an excerpt from Rachel Carson's influential book *Silent Spring* (1962). Carson's immediate concern in this book was the poisoning of the environment by chemical pesticides, and in her final chapter she discusses what is now known as Integrated Pest Management (IPM), the use of biological agents rather than synthetic chemicals to control insect pests. Her remarks, however, clearly have important implications beyond her immediate context.

THE OTHER ROAD

Rachel Carson

We stand now where two roads diverge. But unlike the roads in Robert Frost's familiar poem, they are not equally fair. The road we have long been traveling is deceptively easy, a smooth superhighway on which we progress with great speed, but at its end lies disaster. The other fork of the road—the one "less traveled by"—offers our last, our only chance to reach a destination that assures the preservation of our earth.

The choice, after all, is ours to make. If, having endured much, we have at last asserted our "right to know," and if, knowing, we have concluded that we are being asked to take senseless and frightening risks, then we should no longer accept the counsel of those who tell us that we must fill our world with poisonous chemicals; we should look about and see what other course is open to us.

A truly extraordinary variety of alternatives to the chemical control of insects is available. Some are already in use and have achieved brilliant success. Others are in the stage of laboratory testing. Still others are little more than ideas in the minds of imaginative scientists, waiting for the opportunity to put them to the test. All have this in common: they are *biological* solutions, based on understanding of the living organisms they seek to control, and of the whole fabric of life to which these organisms belong. Specialists representing various areas of the vast field of biology are contributing—entomologists, pathologists, geneticists, physiologists, biochemists, ecologists—all pouring their knowledge and their creative inspirations into the formation of a new science of biotic controls.

Through all these new, imaginative, and creative approaches to the problem of sharing our earth with other creatures there runs a constant theme, the awareness that we are dealing with life—with living populations and all their pressures and counterpressures, their surges and recessions. Only by taking account of such life forces and by cautiously seeking to guide them into channels favorable to ourselves can we hope to achieve a reasonable accommodation between the insect hordes and ourselves.

The current vogue for poisons has failed utterly to take into account these most fundamental considerations. As crude a weapon as the cave man's club, the chemical barrage has been hurled against the fabric of life—a fabric on the one hand delicate and destructible, and on the other miraculously tough and resilient, and capable of striking back in unexpected ways. These extraordinary capacities of life have been ignored by the practitioners of chemical control who have brought to their task no "high-minded orientation," no humility before the vast forces with which they tamper.

The "control of nature" is a phrase conceived in arrogance, born of the Neanderthal age of biology and philosophy, when it was supposed that nature exists for the convenience of man. The concepts and practices of applied entomology for the most part date from that Stone Age of science. It is our alarming misfortune that so primitive a science has armed itself with the most modern and terrible weapons, and that in turning them against the insects it has also turned them against the earth.

FURTHER READING

There is a huge literature on ecology, of course. Odum (1963) and (1971) are sound texts (the first very concise) by a pioneer in the field. Worster (1990) is a recent dissenting voice to Odum's view. Worster (1977) is an excellent and original view of the history of ecology, and McIntosh (1985) a valuable and detailed overview of the field. Hecht and Cockburn (1989) is one of the finest and most informative books available on the Amazon. Andrew Revkin's book (1990) on the struggle to preserve the Amazon rainforest is especially valuable. On rainforests in general, see also Jacobs (1987) and Myers (1992). The excerpt by Lewontin is from his 1991 work. Evernden (1985) is a thoughtful exploration of some concerns about the science of ecology, and many related issues by an eminent Canadian philosopher. Jacobs (1987) is a learned and perceptive study of the ecology of the rainforest.

QUESTIONS TO CONSIDER

1. Chief Wavey urges us to "accept what is obvious." Try to express in your own words what seem to be the most obvious and important truths about the relationship of humans and their ecosystems.
2. Lewontin argues that we must abandon the "romantic and totally unfounded" commitment to environmental preservation. What does he believe to be the alternative to mere environmental preservation? Do you agree? (In a way, it is unfair to ask this question at this point, since in a sense this entire book is an attempt to answer it. But it is worth thinking about now.)
3. Explain carefully the difference between what Rachel Carson called "cautiously" guiding life forces into "channels favorable to ourselves" and "control of nature," which she characterized as belonging to the "Neanderthal" age of science.

4. Does the manipulation by fire and cultivation described by Hecht and Cockburn count as the sort of cautious guidance of life forces advocated by Carson?
5. What does Odum mean by "man the geological agent"?
6. Explain in your own words what Chief Wavey meant by his statement that "science has never been neutral in relation to indigenous peoples, lands, resources, and development."

CHAPTER SEVEN

SYMBIOSIS, PARASITISM, AND COMMENSALISM

We now introduce a key set of concepts that will be central from now on to our discussion—those having to do with the many ways in which organisms can interact with each other.

VARIETIES OF SYMBIOSIS

Edward O. Wilson

To the forces that increase biodiversity, add predators. In a celebrated experiment on the seacoast of Washington state, Robert Paine discovered that carnivores, far from destroying their prey species, can protect them from extinction and thereby salvage diversity. The starfish *Pisaster ochraceus* is a keystone predator of mollusks living in rock-bound tidal waters, including mussels, limpets, and chitons. It also attacks barnacles, which look like mollusks but are actually shell-encased crustaceans that remain rooted to one spot. Where the *Pisaster* starfish occurred in Paine's study area, fifteen species of the mollusk and barnacle species coexisted. When Paine removed the starfish by hand, the number of species declined to eight. What occurred was unexpected but in hindsight logical. Free of the depredations of *Pisaster*, mussels and barnacles increased to abnormally high densities and crowded out seven of the other species. In other words, the predator in this case was less dangerous than the competitors. The assembly rule is this: insert a certain predator, and more species of sedentary animals can invade the community later.

Still another dimension of complexity is added by symbiosis, defined broadly as the intimate association of two or more species. Biologists recognize three classes of symbiosis. In **parasitism**, the first, the symbiont is dependent on the host and harms but does not kill it. Put another way, parasitism is predation in which the predator eats the prey in units of less than one. Being eaten one small piece at a time and surviving, often well, a host organism is able to support an entire population of another species. It can also sustain many species simultaneously. A single unfortunate and unmedicated human being might, theoretically at least, support head lice (*Pediculus humanus capitis*), body lice (*Pediculus humanus humanus*), crab lice (*Pthirus pubis*), human fleas (*Pulex irritans*), human bot flies (*Dermatobia hominis*), and a multitude of roundworms, tapeworms, flukes, protozoans, fungi, and bacteria, all metabolically adapted for life on the human body. Each species of organism, especially each kind of larger plant or animal, is host to such a customized fauna and flora of parasites. The gorilla, for example, has its own crab louse, *Pthirus gorillae*, which closely resembles the one on *Homo sapiens*. A mite has been found that lives entirely on the blood it sucks from the hind feet of the soldier caste of one kind of South American army ant. Tiny wasps are known whose larvae parasitize the larvae of still other kinds of wasps that live inside the bodies of the caterpillars of certain species of moths that feed on certain kinds of plants that live on other plants.

Raising diversity still more are the **commensals**, symbiotic organisms that live on the bodies of other species or in their nests but neither harm nor help them. Without any awareness of the fact, most human beings carry around on their foreheads two kinds of mites, slender creatures with wormlike bodies and spidery heads so small as to be almost invisible to the naked eye. One (*Demodex folliculorum*) dwells in the hair follicles, the other (*Demodex brevis*) in the sebaceous glands. You can get to know your own forehead mites the following way: stretch the skin tight with one hand, carefully scrape a spatula or butter knife over the skin in the opposite direction, squeezing out traces of oily material from the sebum glands. (Avoid using too sharp an object, such as a glass edge or sharpened knife.) Next scrape the extracted material off the spatula with a cover slip and lower the slip face down onto a drop of immersion oil previously placed on a glass microscope slide. Then examine the material with an ordinary compound microscope. You will see the creatures that literally make your skin crawl.

People would never notice their forehead mites in any other way. These acarines and other commensals slip the thin wedge in, sip small amounts of nutrients and energy virtually useless to their hosts, and live secure lives of flawless modesty. Their biomass is small to microscopic, their diversity immense. They are everywhere, but it takes a special eye to find them. On the leaves of trees in the tropical rain forests grow flat, centimeter-wide gardens of lichens, mosses, and liverworts. Among the epiphylls—plants that live on the leaves—thrive a host of tiny mites, springtails, and barklice. Some of the animals browse on the epiphylls, others prey on the epiphyll browsers. Thus a single leaf of a tree, often composing less than one part in 10,000 of that single large organism, is home to an entire miniaturized fauna and flora.

The tightest bond of all among species, the one that gives the word *community* more than metaphorical meaning, is mutualism. This third kind of relationship, often considered the true symbiosis and employed that way in less formal prose, is an intimate coexistence of two species benefiting both. A large part of dead wood is decomposed by termites—not by the termites really, but by protozoans and bacteria that live in the hind guts of the termites. And not entirely by these microorganisms either, since they need the termites to provide them a home and a steady stream of wood chewed into digestible pulp. So the right way to put the original phrase is: a large part of wood is decomposed by the termite-microorganism symbiosis. The termites harvest the wood but cannot digest it; the microorganisms digest the wood but cannot harvest it. It might be said that over millions of years the termites domesticated the microorganisms to serve their special needs. That, however, would be big-organism chauvinism. It is equally correct to say that termites have been harnessed to the needs of the microorganisms. Such is the nature of mutualistic symbiosis: to attain the highest level of intimacy, the partners are melded into a single organism.

Mutualistic symbioses are more than simply curiosities for the delectation of biologists. Most life on land depends ultimately on one such relationship: the mycorrhiza (literally from the Greek for fungusroot), the intimate and mutually dependent coexistence of fungi and the root systems of plants. Most kinds of plants, from ferns to conifers and flowering plants, harbor fungi that are specialized to absorb phosphorus and other chemically simple nutrients from the soil. The mycorrhizal fungi give up part of these vital materials to their plant hosts, and the plants repay them with shelter and a supply of carbohydrates. Plants deprived of their fungi grow slowly; many die.

According to species, the fungi either enter the outer root cells of their plant hosts or envelop the entire roots to form dense webs. A plant pulled up almost anywhere in the world reveals a tangle of delicate fibers clutching masses of soil particles. Some of the extensions are likely to be rootlets of the plant, but others are the moldlike hyphae of the symbiotic fungi. In many kinds of plants, fungal hyphae have completely replaced the rootlets during evolution.

Without the plant-fungus partnership, the very colonization of the land by higher plants and animals, 450 to 400 million years ago, probably could not have been accomplished. The barren, rain-lashed soil of that time was not hospitable to organisms more complex than bacteria, simple algae, and mosses. The earliest vascular plants were leafless, seedless forms that superficially resembled modern-day horsetails and quillworts. By allying themselves with fungi, they took hold of the land. Some of the pioneers evolved into the lycophyte trees and seed ferns of the great Paleozoic coal forests. They also gave rise to the ancestors of modern conifers and flowering plants, whose vegetation came in the fullness of time to harbor the largest array of animal life that has ever existed. Today the tropical rain forests, which may contain more than half the species of plants and animals on earth, grow on a mat of mycorrhizal fungi.

Coral reefs, the marine equivalents of rain forests, are also built on a platform of mutualistic symbiosis. The living coral organisms, which cover the carbonaceous bulk of the reef, are the polyps, close relatives of the jellyfish. Like the jellyfish and other coelenterates, they use feathery tentacles to capture crustaceans and other small animals. They also depend on the energy provided by single-celled algae, which they shelter within their tissues and to which they donate some of the nutrients extracted from their prey. In most coral species, each individual polyp lays down a skeletal container of calcium carbonate that surrounds and protects its soft body. Coral colonies grow by the budding of individual polyps, with the skeletal cups being added one on another in a set geometric pattern particular to each species. The result is a lovely, bewildering array of skeletal forms that mass together to make the whole reef—a tangled field of horn corals, brain corals, staghorn corals, organ pipes, sea fans, and sea whips. As the colony grows, the older polyps die, leaving their calcareous shells intact beneath; and in time the living members form a layer on top of a growing reef of skeletal remains. These massive remains, many of which are thousands of years old, play a major role in the formation of tropical islands, in particular the fringing reefs of volcanic islands and the atolls left behind when the volcanoes erode away. They create the physical basis and photosynthetic energy for tightly packed communities of thousands of species, from sea hornets and mantis shrimps to carpet sharks.

As a footnote to Wilson's account, we should note that there is some variation in terminology. Wilson speaks of mutualism, parasitism, and **commensalism** as varieties of symbiosis. Often, however, people use the term "symbiosis" to denote what Wilson means by "mutualism"—a mutually beneficial, and possibly highly obligate, relationship between two or more organisms. In the following, we shall use "symbiosis" and "mutualism" more or less interchangeably as the context seems to dictate.

An important point to note is Wilson's brief discussion of the role of predators in enhancing biodiversity. Predation, in other words, is not necessarily parasitism when viewed in proper context!

In the next selection, Anne Fausto-Sterling argues that symbiosis needs to be given the attention it deserves in our understanding of natural processes.

IS NATURE REALLY RED IN TOOTH AND CLAW?

Anne Fausto-Sterling

Recently, while flipping through the TV channels, I stumbled across an advertisement for a nature series entitled *The Trials of Life*. The language of the ad, which promised "uncensored, shocking, explicit footage" and scenes of a "savage and untamed realm," made the series sound like an X-rated flick. Watching it—so claimed the ad—would make me change how I looked at myself and nature. I would find out why we call our biological kin (and presumably ourselves?) animals.

I was astounded. True, ever since Darwin, Western European and American scientists have perceived nature as fiercely competitive—"red in tooth and claw," in the lurid words of Alfred, Lord Tennyson. Modern textbooks still like to talk of cutthroat competition, of the survival of the fittest, as the overriding force that drives evolution and determines the way species interact. Yet research in the past two decades shows that cooperation among species plays at least as big a role as violent struggle. "Symbioses are the rule rather than the exception; organisms . . . are always associated with other organisms," according to Betsey Dyer, a biologist at Wheaton College in Massachusetts. Without considerable collaboration, life on Earth as we know it would not have existed, let alone flourished.

The neglect of nature's cooperative side is all the more surprising when you consider that even the most extreme form of togetherness—the symbiotic alliance of two entirely different species—was recognized well over a century ago. (The Greek word *symbiosis*—meaning "to live together"—was first used in biology by German botanist Heinrich Anton de Bary in 1879.) Yet for reasons that had less to do with science than with history, most scientists and thinkers chose to ignore the phenomenon. Strikingly, those who did appreciate the degree of cooperation going on in the natural world were often those who espoused a vision of cooperation in human society—notably the gentle nineteenth-century Russian revolutionary Pyotr Kropotkin, the German socialist Friedrich Engels, and, in the 1940s, the American Quaker Warder C. Allee. Scientists live in the real world, not in ivory towers, and their ideas develop in a social context. Perhaps that's why a more cooperative view of life is making a comeback. The flower children of the 1960s are the working scientists of the 1990s. The cold war is over. The fragile state of our planet is uniting us in alarm. And suddenly, it seems, you can find cooperation in plants and animals wherever you look—suggesting a whole new view of evolution and interdependence among all forms of life.

Symbiosis and mutualism (for the purposes of this article, we can safely ignore the technical distinctions between them) both refer to instances in which organisms live together and help one another out. The organisms can be of vastly differing species, such as an anemone and a hermit crab, or reef-building corals and algae. Many of these arrangements are truly astonishing, and it's tempting to dwell on the most dramatic. How can I not mention the flashlight fish, which lures luminescent bacteria into chambers inside its body and then uses the cultures to light its way through the dark ocean and signal other flash-lighters about sex and danger?

But such showy examples of symbiosis are probably not as important as some of the less visible ones. The most extensive symbiotic interactions occur underground. Here one encounters a vast subterranean network of relationships between fungi and the root systems of higher plants. The technical term is mycorrhizal symbiosis (*myco* means fungal, and *rhizal* refers to the roots). Work in the past decade suggests that at least 6,000 fungal species can interact with more than 300,000 types of higher plants; indeed, at least 70 percent (and some believe 100 percent) of all trees, grasses, shrubs, and flowers thrive because of lifelong underground interactions with one or sometimes several fungi. These fungi may grow on the root surfaces or penetrate deep into the plant's root cells. They also send fruiting bodies—which we recognize as mushrooms—up above the ground.

What do the plants give to the fungi? Green plants engage in photosynthesis: they take carbon dioxide from the air and convert it into organic carbon, the stuff of which we are all built. To carry out this rather neat trick of making food from thin air, they use structures called chloroplasts within their cells. Fungi, though, have no chloroplasts and hence cannot make their own carbon compounds. But by living in the plant's root system they can use some of what the plant makes. Traditional ecology teaches that the mushrooms that grow on the forest floor get their carbon from decaying vegetable matter. Students of symbiosis, however, have shown that most of these fungi get their organic goodies more directly—from the roots of the living plants they inhabit.

That's great for the fungi, but what's in it for the plants? A plant uses its roots to take in water and nutrients, such as minerals and trace elements found in the soil that are essential to healthy growth. The larger the spread of their roots, the bigger the area they can feed off. In times of drought, for example, a plant with a widespread root system will do better than one that covers only a small area. Enter the fungi. They live underground, forming vast threadlike nets that can cover miles of territory; their association with plant roots extends the area the roots can use, improving a plant's nutrient uptake. There are also fungi that stimulate plants by producing growth hormone. In addition, fungi protect plants by sopping up potential toxins. Some varieties even defend the root system against small roundworms, using their filament nets to trap and digest them.

Just how beneficial is this relationship? In 1990 a group headed by F.T. Last, a biologist at the University of Edinburgh, showed that conifer seedlings with few fungi in their roots grew only two inches in two years, whereas those provided with 10,000 fungi reached ten inches—a fivefold improvement.

Occasionally symbiotic relationships involve dozens of interacting organisms. Like other animals, termites can't digest cellulose, the major component of wood. So how do they manage to digest the wood chewed out of your house or a decaying tree stump? They get by with a little help from their friends—as many as 40 different species of bacteria, spirochetes (long, mobile bacteria), and protozoa (single-cell creatures) living inside the termite gut. These bacterial and protozoan symbionts convert cellulose into sugar to feed both themselves and their termite hosts. Without their helpers, termites could chomp wood ad nauseam, but they'd starve to death.

Even more fascinating, the termite symbionts have symbionts. One of the most prominent residents of the termite gut is a large protozoan called a polymastigote. This beast has thousands of spirochetes attached to its surface, giving it the appearance of a shaggy-dog cell. Propelled by these spirochetes, the polymastigote swims about the gut, scooping up and digesting wood fragments. Other tiny, rodlike bacteria live on the surface near the spirochete attachment points, possibly providing the chemical energy needed for all this motion, but the actual role of these and many other termite gut organisms is still speculative. The polymastigote, for example, also has bacteria and spirochetes living *inside* its single-celled body, but what their metabolic functions might be is anyone's guess.

The termite system for digesting the indigestible may also shed light on the forces that shaped the insects' social behavior. Many termites live in large nests, in a complex colony headed by an egg-laying queen. Egg laying, however, presents a problem for them. The egg is sterile; none of the gut symbionts are inside. To avoid starvation the new larvae must get a dose of gut microorganisms by licking the anuses of their caretakers—more mature larvae destined to become soldiers, workers, and reproducers. This vital communication between colony members of different ranks may have been the starting point for all the complex behaviors that keep everyone in the group doing the right things at the right time. In other words, social behavior may have evolved because of the need to transfer essential microorganisms from one generation to the next.

The polymastigote, made hairy by its coat of many spirochetes, also hints at how the cells of higher organisms developed in the first place. The idea that our cells are colonies of microbes was first suggested in the 1920s by the American biologist Ivan Wallin. Now, largely because of the advocacy of University of Massachusetts biologist Lynn Margulis, the idea has gained a foothold in contemporary thought. (Indeed, her marshaling of the evidence transformed Wallin from scientific crank into visionary.) The story goes something like this: In the beginning there was almost no free oxygen in Earth's atmosphere. The first bacteria to evolve were thus anaerobic—able to survive without oxygen. Next some bacteria developed photosynthesis. They used energy from sunlight to make organic carbon from gases in the atmosphere, releasing oxygen in the process. Eventually other bacteria used oxygen to breathe. The diversity and talents of bacterial species increased. Some became excellent swimmers by developing whiplike flagella, which act like propellers, while others crept around like amoebas, extending pseudopodia ("false feet") to pull themselves along.

The future of higher plants and animals, however, depended on a major new evolutionary step. Bacteria are relatively simple cells—sometimes likened to bags of enzyme soup with genetic material floating in it—but the cells of higher organisms are far more complicated. Just as our bodies have organs such as the heart, lungs, and stomach, our cells have minuscule organelles. They include the nucleus (containing chromosomes packed full of genes), sausage-shaped mitochondria (charged with the task of respiration), and versatile, tubelike structures called centrioles. Centrioles form the templates for making the long flagella and short, undulating cilia that cells use for locomotion. And they play a vital part in a cell's reproduction: they help chromosomes divide accurately when the cell splits in two, thus ensuring the faithful transfer of genetic information to the next generation. Plant cells have another organelle besides. This is the chloroplast, the structure mentioned earlier that carries out photosynthesis, converting atmospheric carbon to the organic building blocks on which life depends.

How did these more complex cells evolve from primordial bacteria? Margulis explains it using the "serial endosymbiotic theory" of cell evolution. In the early 1970s she proposed that way back when, some oxygen-breathing bacteria might have invaded some anaerobic amoebalike bacteria and struck a deal—we'll breathe for you if you will creep out into new high-oxygen-containing places to find food. There's little doubt left that these oxygen-breathing bugs are the ancestors of our mitochondria.

The new hybrid then hooked up with some tubular spirochetes. Margulis thinks the friendship looked something like the one that developed between the termite polymastigote and its spirochete pals. The nimble spirochetes helped their partners navigate and find the best feeding spots and even helped gather food into their mouths. Eventually they became permanent fixtures. They helped the cell make flagella and cilia. In addition, they lost most of their own genetic material and instead helped their hosts reproduce. The original amoeba-like bacterium, now composed of three organisms living in cozy symbiosis, became the cell (with a nucleus, mitochondria, and centrioles) now found in higher animals. Some of these originally single-celled creatures evolved into the multicellular organisms we know today as animals and fungi. Others acquired a photosynthetic bacterium and became algae: single-celled organisms that—like higher plants—harness the sun's energy to make carbon.

Although some of Margulis's ideas remain controversial, there's mounting evidence from many laboratories that supports this symbiotic scenario. Indeed, since the mid-1970s scientific research into every aspect of mutualism and symbiosis has increased dramatically. Yet their importance is taking an astonishingly long time to sink in. The 1991 edition of a standard college biology textbook, *An Introduction to Evolutionary Ecology*, lists eight entries on competition in its index but only two on mutualism and none on symbiosis. A section entitled "Why are there so many species?" devotes four paragraphs to the role of competition but never mentions the idea that the acquisition of new symbionts plays a major role in the evolution of new species.

What is going on here? Why has cooperation been ignored by so many scientists for more than a century? And why has it been especially derided in the capitalist West? Has the vision of our economic and social world as a dog-eat-dog sort of place prevented us from giving mutualism its due?

History certainly suggests this is the case. During the late 1880s and early 1890s, for example, a debate between the British evolutionist T.H. Huxley and the Russian revolutionary and scientist Kropotkin spilled over into the pages of a London magazine called *The Nineteenth Century*. Huxley believed that competition was the driving progressive force of nature and that there was little sense in looking to nature for moral guidance. "From the point of view of the moralist," he wrote, "the animal world is on about the same level as a gladiators' show." Kropotkin—in articles later gathered into a popular book called *Mutual Aid*—argued that Huxley was distorting Darwin's original ideas. His keen observations of animals struggling to survive the harsh Siberian climate convinced him that mutualism was a major influence in nature: far from relentlessly competing against one another, most animals cooperated in the interest of survival. Ultimately these observations led him to reject the exploitative brand of capitalism that had brought poverty and despair to many in his beloved prerevolutionary Russia.

For Kropotkin, biology pointed to a better way of life. But Huxley's view of biology was widely taken to mean that capitalism—whatever its inequities—was simply following nature's law. (To be fair to Huxley, though, he himself thought humans should rise above such nasty, brutish behavior.) Among the intellectuals preoccupied with this question was the Marxist socialist Engels. "The whole Darwinian theory of the struggle for existence," he believed, was a "transference from society to organic nature." Once thinkers transferred the idea of struggle from capitalist culture onto nature, he felt, it was only a matter of time before they moved "these theories back again, from natural history to the history of society." To Engels's mind, scientific theory grew from social belief and then was used to reinforce it.

The sparring between Huxley and Kropotkin mirrored an intense social-policy debate about competition and struggle in nineteenth-century Europe. That debate was framed, of course, by the effects of the industrial revolution, which had created undeniable wealth for some but had also caused tremendous hardship for others. In general, management tended to embrace the rawest competitive view of the world. Laborers, meanwhile, responded to the upheaval by forming unions and mutual-aid societies.

By the 1940s interest in mutualism had spread to the United States. One of its chief proponents was biologist Warder C. Allee, a Quaker who wanted to use his knowledge of zoology to build a world without war, and who, in 1949, wrote the influential book *Principles of Animal Ecology*; in contrast to current books, this text had multiple index entries under the topics of mutualism and symbiosis. But by the mid-1950s (the era of the cold war, McCarthyism, and anticommunist witchhunts) the tide had turned. A quite different vision of ecology had once more taken hold—one in which organisms competed for resources.

It apparently took the turmoil of the late sixties and seventies, the years of flower power, antiwar marches, and civil rights activism, to open up some intellectual space for the revival of interest in mutualism and symbiosis. A bit of research by Douglas Boucher, a biologist and historian at the University of Quebec, illuminates the progression. In 1985 he searched for publications describing a particular mathematical model of mutualistic interactions. The first, published in 1935, had no companions until two more appeared in the mid-1960s. During the 1970s there were 17 publications, and the increased pace kept up throughout the 1980s.

Even so, acceptance is not coming nearly fast enough to satisfy Brown University biologist Mark Bertness. Bertness studies the interaction between various species that inhabit New England's salt marshes. In benign conditions, these organisms compete, but under stressful conditions, he's found, they behave in mutually beneficial ways. To wrest a toehold from the sea, for example, large numbers of ribbed mussels settle in among the small marsh grasses growing on exposed coastal mud flats. The mussels use threads to attach to the marsh grasses, which in turn help anchor the soil and other less hardy grasses. In addition, they nourish the plants by defecating right above their root systems. "It's a perfect case of mutualism," says Bertness. The mud flats are also home to legions of fiddler crabs. Like thousands of John Deere tractors, the crabs plow through the soil, aerating it and making it easier for grass roots to establish themselves. "If you take them away," says Bertness, "grass production drops by about 50 percent in one growing season."

Bertness's general message is that when the going gets tough, the tough cooperate. But his message meets with a lot of flak. His critics argue that findings about mussels, crabs, and marsh plants are not applicable to other ecological systems, such as forest and grassland. "It's a mind-set," says Bertness, convinced that what a scientist already believes conditions what he or she looks for. "These kinds of interactions are going to be common in forests and grasslands too," he insists. "It's all dependent on the physical regime—benign or harsh."

Where does this leave us? First, a strong case can be made for viewing nature as a socialist cooperative ("green in root and flower," as Boucher has written to counteract Tennyson's "red in tooth and claw"). I suspect that eventually a balanced view will emerge—of organisms influenced as much by cooperation as by struggle. But it will not happen because we suddenly discover mutualism and symbiosis. We already know a lot about these processes, and it is clear that they are widespread and of great importance in ecology and evolution. Only a change in social ambience will permit these already existing ideas to be incorporated into the mainstream of biological thought.

Scientific knowledge does not, after all, grow in a vacuum. It does not simply bubble forth from the wellsprings of nature. Nor is it driven forward by the sheer force of ideas. Instead we construct it with whatever tools of thought are available in our particular culture and moment in history. Perhaps, if we ever really do become a kinder, gentler nation, mutualism and symbiosis will be given the place in scientific theory that they surely deserve.

In our next selection, we take a sweeping look through human history. The following are excerpts from historian William McNeill's book *Plagues and Peoples*, an ambitious attempt to view human history in ecological terms. McNeill makes an interesting distinction between what he calls "microparasitism," the parasitism of micro-organisms upon other forms of life, and "**macroparasitism**," the parasitism of large-bodied predators (in particular, humans) upon each other and their general surroundings. He analyses history in terms of the dynamic balances between micro- and macroparasitism, and points out that from an abstract point of view the parasitism of one group of humans upon another obeys much the same functional dynamics as the parasitism of, say, bacteria upon their hosts. Pay special attention to his characterization of the overall impact of humans upon the general biota.

MACROPARASITISM AND THE HUMAN PROBLEM

William H. McNeill

A Few Key Concepts

Before proceeding with the story, a few remarks about parasitism, disease, pestilential infection, and related concepts may help to avoid confusion.

Disease and parasitism play a pervasive role in all life. A successful search for food on the part of one organism becomes for its host a nasty infection or disease. All animals depend on other living things for food, and human beings are no exception. Problems of finding food and the changing ways human communities have done so are familiar enough in economic histories. The problems of avoiding becoming food for some other organism are less familiar, largely because from very early times human beings ceased to have much to fear from large-bodied animal predators like lions or wolves. Nevertheless, one can properly think of most human lives as caught in a precarious equilibrium between the microparasitism of disease organisms and the macroparasitism of large-bodies predators, chief among which have been other human beings.

Microparasites are tiny organisms — viruses, bacteria, or multicelled creatures as the case may be — that find a source of food in human tissues suitable for sustaining their own vital processes. Some microparasites provoke acute disease and either kill their host after only a brief period of time, or provoke immunity reactions inside his body that kill them off instead. Sometimes, too, one of these disease-causing organisms is somehow contained within a particular host's body so that he becomes a carrier, capable of infecting someone else without being noticeably sick himself. There are, however, other microparasites that regularly achieve more stable relations with their human hosts. Such infections no doubt take something away from their host's bodily energies, but their presence does not prevent normal functioning.

Macroparasites exhibit similar diversity. Some kill at once, as lions and wolves must do when feeding on human or any other kind of flesh; others allow the host to survive indefinitely.

In very early times, the skill and formidability of human hunters outclassed rival predators. Humanity thus emerged at the very top of the food chain, with little risk of being eaten by predatory animals any more. Yet for a long time thereafter cannibalism almost certainly remained a significant aspect of the interaction of adjacent human communities. This put the successful human hunters exactly on a level with a pride of lions or a pack of wolves.

Later, when food production became a way of life for some human communities, a modulated macroparasitism became possible. A conqueror could seize food from those who produced it, and by consuming it himself become a parasite of a new sort on those who did the work. In specially fertile landscapes it even proved possible to establish a comparatively stable pattern of this sort of macroparasitism among human beings. Early civilizations, in fact, were built upon the possibility of taking only a part of the harvest from subjected communities, leaving enough behind to allow the plundered community to survive indefinitely, year after year. In the early stages the macroparasitic basis of civilization remained harsh and clear; only later and by slow degrees did reciprocal services between town and countryside develop importance enough to diminish the one-sidedness of tax and rent collection. To begin with, though, the hardpressed peasantries that supported priests and kings and their urban hangers-on received little or nothing in return for the food they gave up, except for a somewhat uncertain protection from other, more ruthless and shortsighted plunderers.

The reciprocity between food and parasite that has undergirded civilized history is matched by parallel reciprocities within each human body. The white corpuscles, which constitute a principal element in defenses against infection, actually digest intruders. Organisms they are unable to digest become parasites, digesting in their turn whatever they find nourishing within the human body.

This is, however, only one facet of the exceedingly complex processes that affect the success or failure of any particular organism in invading and proliferating within a particular human being. In fact, despite all the advances of medical research in the past hundred years or so, no one fully understands their interaction. At every level of organization—molecular, cellular, organismic, and social—one confronts equilibrium patterns. Within such equilibria, any alteration from "outside" tends to provoke compensatory changes throughout the system so as to minimize over-all upheaval, though there are always critical limits which, if transgressed, result in the breakdown of the previously existing system. Such a catastrophic event may involve dissolution into simpler, smaller parts, each with equilibrium patterns of its own; or, on the contrary, may involve incorporation of smaller parts into some larger or more complex whole. The two processes may in fact combine, as in the familiar case of animal digestion, whereby the feeder breaks down the cells and proteins of its food into simpler parts only to combine them into new proteins and the cells of its own body.

Simple cause-and-effect analysis is inadequate for such systems. Since many variables are simultaneously at work, interacting constantly and altering their magnitudes at irregular rates, it is usually misleading to concentrate attention on a single "cause" and try to attribute a particular "effect" to it. Study of simultaneity among multiple processes is presumably a better way to approach an understanding. But the conceptual and practical difficulties here are enormous.

Recognition of patterns, and observation of their endurance or dissolution is, at most levels of organization, about as much as people are capable of; and at some levels, including the social, there is profound uncertainty and dispute about which patterns are worth attending to, or can, in fact, be reliably detected. Divergent terminologies direct attention to different patternings; and finding a logically convincing test, acceptable all around, that can determine whether one such system of terms is superior to its rivals, is often impossible.

Yet the slow processes of evolution presumably apply to human societies and their symbolic systems as much as to human bodies, so that when logic cannot decide, survival eventually will. Terms that direct attention to the critically useful facets of a situation clearly do have enormous survival value for human beings. It is this aspect of our capacity to communicate with one another that has allowed *Homo sapiens* to become such a dominant species. Yet no system of terms is ever likely to exhaust or completely comprehend all aspects of the reality around us. We have to do the best we can with the language and concepts we inherit, and not worry about obtaining a truth that will satisfy everyone, everywhere, and for all time to come.

Man the Hunter

Before fully human populations evolved, we must suppose that like other animals our ancestors fitted into an elaborate, self-regulating ecological balance. The most conspicuous aspect of this balance was the food chain, whereby our forebears preyed upon some forms of life and were, in their turn, preyed upon by others. In addition to these inescapable relations among large-bodied organisms, we must also suppose that minute, often imperceptible parasites sought their food within our ancestors' bodies, and became a significant element in balancing the entire life system of which humanity was a part.

As long as the biological evolution of humankind's ancestors kept pace with the evolution of their parasites, predators, and prey, no very important alteration in this sort of tightly woven web of life could occur. Evolutionary development, proceeding through genetic variation and selection, was so slow that any change in one partner was compensated for by changes in the other partner's respective genetic and/or behavioral patternings. When humankind began to respond to another sort of evolution, however, elaborating learned behavior into cultural traditions and systems of symbolic meaning, these age-old biological balances began to confront new sorts of disturbances. Cultural evolution began to put unprecedented strains upon older patterns of biological evolution. Newly acquired skills made humanity increasingly capable of transforming the balance of nature in unforeseen and far-reaching ways. Accordingly, the disease liability of emerging humankind also began to change dramatically.

The first discernible upheaval of this kind resulted from the development of skills and weapons suitable for killing the sorts of large-bodied herbivores that abounded on the grasslands of the African savanna (and perhaps in similar landscapes in Asia). No definite date can be offered for this transition: it may have begun as much as four million years ago.

The first pre-human primates who came down from the trees and started to prey upon the antelope and related species probably could catch only the weak or very young. They may have had to compete with hyenas and vultures for carrion left by more efficient predators like lions. Among such pre-human primate populations hovering around the fringes of a concentrated food resource like that offered today by the vast herds of herbivores on the African savanna, any genetic change that improved hunting efficiency was sure to pay off handsomely. Enormous reward awaited any group possessing muscular and mental skills that permitted more effective co-operation in the hunt. Emergent humanity reaped these rewards by developing patterns of communication that allowed increasingly effective mutual support in moments of crisis, and by elaborating tools and weapons to augment an unimpressive musculature and puny teeth and claws. In such circumstances, new traits that paid off cumulated rapidly—rapidly, that is, by the spacious standards of biological evolution. Any fresh variation, permitting more of what had begun to work well already, enlarged the food supply and increased chances for survival.

This sort of evolutionary spurt is known among biologists as "orthogenic," and is often associated with a transition to a new ecological niche. No one can expect to disentangle all the genetic changes that this process provoked among pre-human populations. When variations could be so extravagantly successful, however, displacement of one humanoid population by another even more effective group of hunters must have occurred frequently. Survival was more likely for the more formidable in battle as well as for the more efficient in the hunt.

A major landmark in the resulting evolutionary development was the elaboration of language. Genetic changes governing the formation of brain, tongue, and throat were necessary to open the way for articulated language; language in turn allowed vastly improved social co-ordination. Talking things over and thereby enacting and re-enacting roles allowed human beings to practice and perfect skills ahead of time, so as to achieve otherwise unattainable precision in hunting and in other co-operative activities. With language, systematic teaching of the arts of life to others became possible, while those arts themselves became susceptible to extraordinary elaboration, since words could be used to classify things, order them, and define appropriate reactions to all sorts of circumstances. Language, in short, made hunters fully human for the first time, inaugurating a new dimension of social-cultural evolution which soon put vast and hitherto unmatched strains upon the ecological balance within which humanity arose.

It is not absurd to class the ecological role of humankind in its relationship to other life forms as a disease. Ever since language allowed human cultural evolution to impinge upon age-old processes of biological evolution, humankind has been in a position to upset older balances of nature in quite the same fashion that disease upsets the natural balance within a host's body. Time and again, a temporary approach to stabilization of new relationships occurred as natural limits to the ravages of humankind upon other life forms manifested themselves. Yet sooner or later, and always within a span of time that remained minuscule in comparison with the standards of biological evolution, humanity discovered new techniques allowing fresh exploitation of hitherto inaccessible resources, thereby renewing or intensifying damage to other forms of life. Looked at from the point of view of other organisms, humankind therefore resembles an acute epidemic disease, whose occasional lapses into less virulent forms of behavior have never yet sufficed to permit any really stable, chronic relationship to establish itself.

In conclusion, we turn again to Eugene P. Odum, who raises a challenge that so far remains unanswered.

A CHALLENGE FOR HUMANS

Eugene P. Odum

Lichens, as is well known, are an association of specific fungi and algae that is so intimate in terms of functional interdependence and so integrated morphologically that a sort of third kind of organism is formed which resembles neither of its components. Lichens are usually classified as single "species" even though they are composed of two unrelated species. While the components can often be cultured separately in the laboratory, the integrated unit is difficult to culture despite the fact that it is able to exist in nature under harsh conditions (lichens are often the dominant plant on bare rock or in the arctic). Lichens are also interesting because within the group one sees evidence of an evolution from parasitism to mutualism; in some of the more primitive lichens, for example, the fungi actually penetrate the algal cells . . . and are thus essentially parasites of the algae. In the more advanced species, the fungal mycelia or hyphae do not break into the algal cells, but the two live in close harmony. . . . The "lichen model" . . . is perhaps a symbolic one for man. Until now man has generally acted as a parasite on his autotrophic environment, taking what he needs with little regard to the welfare of his host. Great cities are planned and grow without any regard for the fact that they are parasites on the countryside which must somehow supply food, water, air, and degrade huge quantities of waste. Obviously it is time for man to evolve to the mutualism stage in his relations with nature since he is a dependent heterotroph and his culture is even more dependent and increasingly demanding of resources. If man does not learn to live mutualistically with nature, then, like the "unwise" or "unadapted" parasite, he may exploit his host to the point of destroying himself.

If the sort of ecologically and biologically based description of the human condition outlined by Odum and McNeill is correct, then our problem is this: Precisely what sort of behaviour on our part would constitute the establishment of a mutualism or symbiosis (pick your favourite term) between humans and the general planetary ecosystem? The answer is by no means obvious.

FURTHER READING

The selections from McNeill are from his 1976 book. Odum (1971) presents a very precise discussion of the varieties of symbiosis. Sapp (1994) is a superb study of the history of the concept of symbiosis.

QUESTIONS TO CONSIDER

1. William McNeill says, "It is not absurd to class the ecological role of humankind in its relationship to other life forms as a disease." Could this be literally true or merely metaphorically true? Do you think that it is a fair "knock" against the human race?
2. Do you agree with Fausto-Sterling's contention that there is some sort of cultural prejudice against taking seriously the importance of symbiosis in biology and ecology?
3. Odum points out that in various species of lichen one can observe a gradation from parasitism to mutualism. Does the evolutionary move to mutualism represent "progress" in some sense, or would that be purely an arbitrary human evaluation?

CHAPTER EIGHT

THE GAIA HYPOTHESIS

The **Gaia hypothesis** is one of the most ambitious and imaginative scientific hypotheses of recent years, and for many as well it serves as an inspiring metaphor. James Lovelock, who is not averse to its uses as a metaphor, insists, however, that it is first and foremost a scientific hypothesis and must stand or fall on its explanatory and predictive merits like any other scientific theory.

We first present (shorn of equations and tables) one of the early papers by Lovelock and biologist Lynn Margulis, setting forth the basic idea in concise terms.

ATMOSPHERIC HOMEOSTASIS BY AND FOR THE BIOSPHERE: THE GAIA HYPOTHESIS

James E. Lovelock and Lynn Margulis

It is widely believed that the abundance of the principal gases N_2 and O_2 is determined by equilibrium chemistry. One of the larger problems in the atmospheric sciences is that of reconciling this belief with the uncomfortable fact that these same gases are cycled by the biosphere with a geometric mean residence time measured in thousands of years. The more thoroughly the inventory of an individual gas is audited, the more certain it seems that inorganic equilibrium or steady state processes determine its atmospheric concentration but the same audit frequently further reveals the extent of its biological involvement. . . .

This paper presents a new view of the atmosphere, one in which it is seen as a component part of the biosphere rather than as a mere environment for life. In this new context the incompatibilities of biological cycles and inorganic equilibria are seen as more apparent than real.

A starting point is the consideration of the profoundly anomalous composition of the Earth's atmosphere when it is compared with that of the expected atmosphere of a planet interpolated between Mars and Venus. Thus on Earth the simultaneous presence of O_2 and CH_4 at the present concentrations is a violation of equilibrium chemistry of no less than 30 orders of magnitude. Indeed, so great is the disequilibrium among the gases of the Earth's atmosphere that it tends towards a combustible mixture, whereas the atmospheres of Mars and Venus are close to chemical equilibrium and are more like combustion products. . . .

Given the chemical composition of a planetary atmosphere, it is possible to infer the presence or absence of life. . . . To do this the entire ensemble of reactive gases constituting the atmosphere needs to be considered, and when this is done information is made available which is otherwise inaccessible when each gas is considered separately in isolation. This approach, applied to the present problem of the anomaly of the chemical distribution of the gases in the atmosphere, offers a strong suggestion that the Earth's atmosphere is more than merely anomalous; it appears to be a contrivance specifically constituted for a set of purposes.

This paper examines the hypothesis that the total ensemble of living organisms which constitutes the biosphere can act as a single entity to regulate chemical composition, surface pH, and possibly also climate. The notion of the biosphere as an active adaptive control system able to maintain the Earth in homeostasis we are calling the Gaia hypothesis. . . . Hence forward the word Gaia will be used to describe the biosphere and all of those parts of the Earth with which it actively interacts to form the hypothetical new entity with properties that could not be predicted from the sum of its parts.

Theoretical Basis

The fundamental problem underlying the formal recognition of an unfamiliar living association, such as Gaia, it that of recognizing life itself. We are so preprogrammed to recognize life instinctively that the logical basis of the recognition is rarely questioned. Thus the discovery of a member of new and bizarre animal species raises the question, what is it?, never the question, what is life? This instinctive recognition passes beyond organisms to systems provided that they are not too big to be seen. Thus a bees' nest is recognized as a purposeful structure, quite different from a cluster of non-social insects.

The intricate organization of an ecosystem such as a tropical rain forest, however, was not recognized until the evidence of the interdependence of its parts and the economy of the cycling of essential elements was discovered. With the total ecosystem, Gaia, apart from the shadowy evidence of those primitive beliefs in her reality, we are dependent upon physical rather than biological evidence. There is little doubt that living things are elaborate contrivances. Life as a phenomenon might therefore be considered in the context of those applied physical sciences which grew up to explain inventions and contrivances, namely thermodynamics, cybernetics, and information theory.

The first cautious approach to a classification of life reached general agreement as follows: "Life is one of a member of the class of phenomena which are open or continuous reaction systems able to decrease their **entropy** at the expense of free energy taken from the environment and subsequently rejected in a degraded form" (Bernal, 1951; Wigner, 1961). . . .

This classification is broad and includes also phenomena such as vortices and flames and many others. Life differs from such primitive processes of the abiological steady state in the singularity, persistence, and size of the entropy reduction it sustains. Although limited, this phenomenological description of the class of process, which includes life, is helpful in our search for proof of the existence of Gaia in two ways. Firstly by serving to define the boundary of the internal region where entropy is reduced, and secondly by suggesting that the recognition of a living entity can be based upon the extent of its physical and chemical disequilibrium from the background environment.

On the matter of boundaries, it is obvious that a man, as an example of a living entity, takes in free energy in the form of the chemical potential difference between food and oxygen and sustains a low internal entropy through excretion of waste chemicals and heat. To a man, the environment in which entropy is discarded includes the atmosphere and his boundary is therefore his skin. It might seem pointless therefore on Earth to seek the existence of a general living system. Gaia, in terms of entropy reduction within the atmosphere . . . clearly for some species is a sink for degraded products and energy, but this neglects the fact that photosynthetic life uses premium radiation direct from the sun to sustain a high chemical potential gradient within the atmosphere on a planetary scale. For a tree, the boundary within which entropy is reduced is not its surface in contact with the atmosphere, but rather the interface between the sun with the atmosphere as an extension of the tree. The tree produces not only food for consumers but also the equally important gas, oxygen, which does not accumulate within the tree waiting to be eaten.

When the whole assembly of life is so seen, it is clear that the true boundary is space. The outgoing entropy flux from the Earth, indeed from Gaia "if she exists," is long wavelength infrared radiation to space. This then, is the physical justification for delineating the boundary of life as the outer reaches of the atmosphere. There is also to a lesser extent an inner boundary represented by the interface with those inner parts of the Earth as yet unaffected by surface processes. We may now consider all that is encompassed by the bounds as putative life. Whether or not Gaia is real will depend upon the extent to which the entropy reduction within a compartment such as the atmosphere is recognizably different from the abiological steady state background. . . .

By examining the extent to which the atmosphere is in chemical and physical disequilibrium both within itself and with the surface of the Earth, we have a measure of the extent to which it is recognizable as a separate identity against a neutral background equilibrium state. Whether or not it is seen to be a component part of Gaia will depend upon the size of the disequilibrium revealed.

Thermodynamic Evidence

We can determine the degree of departure from a conceivable abiological steady state atmosphere of the Earth by two means: firstly, by comparing the Earth's atmosphere with Mars and Venus, which may be taken as representative of lifeless planets, and secondly by comparing the present atmosphere with the atmosphere to be expected if life were deleted from Earth. . . .

The simultaneous and large fluxes of N_2, CH_4, NH_3, N_2O, and O_2 are all inconsistent with an abiological model. The degree of departure from equilibrium expectations is to be measured in 10's of orders of magnitude. In these circumstances there is almost a certainty that the atmosphere is a part of the biosphere, for nowhere but in living systems is so intensive and constant a disequilibrium revealed. Conversely there is a negligible possibility that the atmosphere is a neutral background source of materials which life merely recycles.

The Atmosphere as a Contrivance

If we assume the Gaia hypothesis, and regard the atmosphere as a contrivance, then it is reasonable to ask what is the function of the various component gases. Outside the Gaia hypothesis such a question would rightly be condemned as circular and illogical, but in its context such questions are no more unreasonable than asking, for example, what is the function of fibrinogen in the blood. The function of oxygen and nitrogen in sustaining the cycle of raw material and energy is evident. Less obvious is the function, for example, of CH_4. This gas is made on a scale requiring the shunting of as much as 5% of the photosynthetic energy of the entire biosphere. In the Gaia context it must surely have an important purpose [since] biology is normally efficient and parsimonious over waste.

Such a possible important function for methane . . . is . . . a kind of molecular hydrogen balloon whose purpose is to carry excess hydrogen to the upper atmosphere where it can escape and thus sustain the present oxygen tension of the Earth. . . .

As with CH_4 the biosphere uses a great amount of energy for NH_4 production. When the total production of acids by the oxidation of nitrogen and sulphur is taken into account, the ammonia production by the biosphere is found to be just sufficient to sustain a rainfall pH near 8, the optimum for life. One penalty of oxidising environments is the tendency to low pH as the elements such as carbon, nitrogen, and sulphur oxidise. The huge biological ammonia production conveniently answers this need. Can it be accidental and have always been so? Other atmospheric gases and vapours, for example, dimethyl sulphide, dimethyl selenide, and methyl iodide, may serve in the mass transfer of essential elements between the land and the sea.

A gas wholly in disequilibrium, a biological product on a grand scale, is nitrous oxide. It is made by soil microorganisms and some penetrates to the stratosphere where it reacts to give NO_x. By the Gaia hypothesis it must have an important atmospheric purpose; could this be concerned with the regulation of the position or density of the ozone layer? In summary, there is overwhelming evidence that the atmosphere apart from its content of noble gases is a biological product. It may also be a biological contrivance; not living but as essential a part of the biosphere as is the shell to a snail or the fur to a mink.

Systems Analysis

One set of tests which can be applied to prove the existence of a control system are those which make changes in the variables thought to be controlled. It is possible to show, for example, that the core temperature of a man remains constant when the environmental temperature ranges between 0°C and 45°C. With the Earth it is reasonable to suspect that at least the following variables may be controlled: (1) Atmospheric, oceanic, and soil chemical composition. (2) Surface temperatures in the "core" region, i.e., between 45° N and 45° S latitudes. (3) Surface and ocean pH.

It is not usually possible to vary the global environment as a test, but perturbations affecting these variables have accompanied the evolution of the solar system. Since life began, 3.5×10^9 years ago, the solar output has probably increased between 30 and 100% (Sagan and Mullen, 1972). . . . The other major environmental change is that of redox potential. At its formation the Earth was highly reducing with hydrogen as a predominant atmospheric gas. It is suggested that 3.5×10^9 years ago the Earth's pE was −5 at which gases such as CH_4, NH_3, H_2S, etc., would be stable in their own chemical right. Hydrogen would be escaping to space but for some time there would be sufficient to regenerate the hydrides dissociated by solar UV. Such an atmosphere could according to Sagan and Mullen (1972) effectively retain heat. It would permit surface temperatures similar to those present in spite of a much reduced solar output. This is due principally to the radiative properties of gases such as ammonia and the others mentioned above. These were probably the conditions under which life evolved.

Soon after the evolution of life and possibly because of it . . . the pace of hydrogen loss accelerated. By 3.2×10^9 years ago the pE had risen above -4 at which level NH_3 is no longer stable in its own right. . . . Had the laws of physics and chemistry operated soon after this time, NH_3 and other polyatomic reducing gases would have vanished leaving an atmosphere of nitrogen and CO_2 at a concentration not substantially different from the present. If we assume that the solar output was in fact lower at this time, such an atmosphere could not possibly have sustained present day temperatures. The short term equilibrium temperature would have been [between] –5 and –16°C. . . .

The geological record and the fact of the persistence of life provide strong evidence that at no time in the past 3.5×10^9 years did the oceans freeze or the mean temperature rise above 50°C. Indeed the evidence suggests that apart from glacial episodes, the temperature has always been constant. . . .

Sagan and Mullen (1972) propose that the continuous biological synthesis of ammonia before oxygen appeared gave an atmospheric concentration of ammonia sufficient to sustain by its greenhouse effect equable and tolerable temperatures. This is supported by the fact that the current biological ammonia production, which is 2×10^9 tons per year, might in a neutral or reducing atmosphere have sustained the concentration of ammonia said to be needed to provide the desired radiative properties. . . . However, if we assume that the solar output was indeed lower in remote time, the mere blind production of a gas such as NH_3 by the biosphere would not have been likely to suffice in the control of surface temperatures by its radiative properties. With the reduced solar output and the possibility of positive feedback on cooling, any failure of the ammonia harvest or the evolution of a vigorous NH_3 consumer, of which there are many today, would have set in train a course for catastrophic irreversible cooling. A mechanism which plausibly can oppose an unfavourable trend is not enough; there must also be a system able to sense the trend and actively control the means for its opposition. It must be observed that there are other "greenhouse" gases than NH_3. CO_2 at high concentrations could have performed a similar function as could other polyatomic gases. To sustain a constant temperature for 3.5×10^9 years in the face of chemical and physical environmental changes strongly implies the presence of an **active process** for thermostasis. Life at its origin can be considered to have fed on the blanket of gas which kept it warm. Its continued survival required the early development of the capacity to recognize potentially adverse changes and of processes which could oppose such changes. . . . Our purpose is to stress that the present knowledge of the early environment suggests strongly that a first task of life was to secure the environment against adverse physical and chemical change. Such security could only come from the active process of homeostasis in which unfavourable tendencies could be sensed and counter measures operated before irreversible damage had been done.

In addition to the possibility of remorseless environmental change set by the evolution of the sun, there were also many changes in the chemical environment. These were caused in part by the evolution of life itself, but they also reflected upon the physical environment through the change in atmospheric composition. Prominent amongst these changes must have been the first appearance of free oxygen in the atmosphere which is thought to have taken place between 1 and 2×10^9 years ago. It is worth digressing a moment to consider what a catastrophic air pollutant oxygen must have been. Its presence in the air must have destroyed a vast range of species and driven underground into anaerobic muds others from which prison they have never returned. Not only was the appearance of oxygen itself a biological crisis, but also the rapid reduction of pH which inevitably would accompany oxidation of nitrogen and sulphur compounds and the increased rate of removal of ammonia must have posed other serious problems. Firstly in the maintenance of pH itself and secondly in sustaining a sufficient concentration of ammonia as this gas was depleted by its new role of neutralising acidity. Again the details of the atmospheric changes of this time are not known although it is conceivable that the CO_2 concentration rose as the pH fell and to some extent offset the loss of NH_3. It is unlikely, however, that this alone would have been sufficient to sustain tolerable temperatures at this period when the solar output may have been at least 10 and possibly 40% less than now. Nevertheless, sufficiently constant temperatures were sustained and life persisted. Even today the regulation of oxygen concentration may represent an important task. . . . Blind adaptation to change seems to have been unlikely to have been enough.

Conclusions

We have presented some of the evidence concerning the Gaia hypothesis. The hard core geochemist will still no doubt argue that the cycling of gases through the biosphere is a passive process and does not determine atmospheric composition. He may compare it with the cycling of water from the oceans to the land. The delivery of rain to the land surfaces involves a disequilibrium of gravitational and osmotic potential and is driven by solar energy. The vegetation merely borrows the rain and repays at the rate of borrowing. We think that it is all a matter of degree. Sunlight may distil water from the sea later to fall as rain on the land, but sunlight does not spontaneously at the Earth's surface split oxygen from water and drive reactions leading to the synthesis of intricate compounds and structures. The disequilibrium characteristic of water cycling is minor when compared with that of cycling of the atmospheric gases.

To those who are convinced that the atmospheric gases are biological products but are reluctant to accept the notion of homeostasis, we say: if life has merely a passive role in cycling the gases of the air then the concentrations will be set by equilibrium chemistry; in fact they most certainly are not. If life actively cycles the gases, then we ask how could such a system be stable in the long run without homeostasis?

The purpose of this paper is to introduce the Gaia hypothesis at least for entertainment and for the induction of new questions about the Earth. Proof of Gaia's existence may never approach certainty, but further evidence is more likely to come from the study of the contemporary Earth. Astronomical evidence is notoriously fickle, and although geological evidence is rather more certain, one learns less about a person from the study of his grandfather's bones than from talking to him face to face.

REFERENCES

Bernal, J.D. 1951. *The Physical Basis of Life*. Routledge and Kegan Paul, London.

Sagan, C., and Mullen, G. 1972. *Science* 177, 52–56.

Schrödinger, E. 1944. *What is Life?* Cambridge University Press.

Wigner, E.P. 1961. *The Logic of Personal Knowledge*. Routledge and Kegan Paul, London.

The next item is a very clear overview of the Gaia hypothesis, and contains some thought-provoking speculations about the possible role of humans in the Gaian system.

THE QUEST FOR GAIA

James Lovelock and Sidney Epton

Consider the following propositions:

1. Life exists only because material conditions on Earth happen to be just right for its existence.
2. Life defines the material conditions needed for its survival and makes sure that they stay there.

The first of these is the conventional wisdom. It implies that life has stood poised like a needle on its point for over 3500 My. If the temperature or humidity or salinity or acidity or any one of a number of other variables had strayed outside a narrow range of values for any length of time, life would have been annihilated.

Proposition (2) is an unconventional view. It implies that living matter is not passive in the face of threats to its existence. It has found means, as it were, of driving the point of the needle into the table, of forcing conditions to stay within the permissible range. This article supports and develops this view.

The Sun, being a typical star of the main sequence, has evolved according to a standard and well established pattern. A consequence of this is that during the Earth's existence the Sun's output of energy has increased substantially. The Earth now receives between 1.4 and 3.3 times more energy than it did just after its formation 4000 My ago. The Earth's surface temperature at the time when life began has been calculated. These calculations take into account the solar input, the radiative properties of the surface and the composition of the atmosphere. At that time, the atmosphere probably contained ammonia and other complex molecules which acted like the glass in a greenhouse, that is, by reducing the radiation of heat and long-wave infra-red radiation from Earth. The calculations show that the surface temperature could indeed have been within the range we now know to be needed to start life off.

Once life began, it fed on the atmospheric blanket. Unless some means had existed for restoring to it heat-retaining gases such as ammonia, or of altering the Earth's surface to make it more heat retentive, the planet would surely have become uniformly icebound and lifeless. The rate of increase of solar energy would have been too small to compensate. Yet the fossil record and the continuity of life gives no support to this conclusion. At the time of supposed emergence from glaciation, that is, when the radiation from the more active Sun had made up for the radiation loss due to loss of the heat-retaining gases, and when only the feeble beginnings of a new life should have been possible, complex multi-celled organisms had already evolved. Life must have found a way of keeping the temperature of the Earth's surface within the critical range of 15–30°C for hundreds of millions of years in spite of drastic changes of atmospheric composition and a large increase in the mean Solar flux. The calculations were wrong because they left out the effect of the defence mechanism that life uses to protect itself.

Extinction through glaciation was not the only danger. Overproduction of ammonia and other heat-retaining gases could have resulted in the opposite effect, known as the "runaway greenhouse," that is, to a rapidly increasing surface temperature that would have scorched the Earth and left it permanently lifeless, as is the planet Venus now. The evidence that this did not happen is plain — we would not have written these words nor would you be reading them.

Has life been able to control other conditions of existence besides the surface temperature of the Earth? A most significant fact about the Earth is the composition of its atmosphere. Almost everything about its composition seems to violate the laws of chemistry. If chemical thermodynamics alone mattered, almost all the oxygen and most of the nitrogen in the atmosphere ought to have ended up in the sea combined as nitrate ions. The air we breathe cannot be a very fortunate once-off emanation from the rocks; it can only be an artefact maintained in a steady state far from chemical equilibrium by biological processes.

The significance of this was first realised some years ago when one of us, in association with Dian Hitchcock, took up the problem of deciding whether it would be possible to detect life on Mars by the use only of spectroscopic observations on its atmosphere. Our suggestion was to look for any combination of constituents that was far from chemical equilibrium; if such was found life might exist there. (So far no such combination has been detected on either Mars or Venus.)

Gaia

It appeared to us that the Earth's biosphere was able to control at least the temperature of the Earth's surface and the composition of the atmosphere. *Prima facie*, the atmosphere looked like a contrivance put together cooperatively by the totality of living systems to carry out certain necessary control functions. This led us to the formulation of the proposition that living matter, the air, the oceans, the land surface were parts of a giant system which was able to control temperature, the composition of the air and sea, the pH of the soil, and so on, so as to be optimum for survival of the biosphere. The system seemed to exhibit the behaviour of a single organism, even a living creature. One having such formidable powers deserved a name to match it; William Golding, the novelist, suggested Gaia — the name given by the ancient Greeks to their Earth goddess.

The past three years have been spent in exploring and elaborating the Gaia hypothesis (in collaboration with Lynn Margulis) and checking its implications against fact. It has proved to be fruitful. It has led us along many paths and by-paths, and valuable insights have been gained especially about the consequences of Man's interaction with the biosphere. The following is a selection of some of the interesting things we have found on the way.

Atmospheric Constituents

If Gaia is a living entity we have the right to ask questions such as "what purpose does constituent X serve in the atmosphere?" As an example, the biosphere produces about 1000 million tons of ammonia a year. Why?

As already pointed out, in early times, when the Sun was cooler than it is now, ammonia served to keep the Earth warm. At the present time, the need for ammonia is different and just as important, because we believe that ammonia keeps the soil near to pH8 which is an optimum value for living processes. It is needed because a consequence of having nitrogen- and sulphur-containing substances in the air in the presence of a vast excess of oxygen is their tendency to combine to produce strongly acid materials — thunderstorms produce tons of nitric acid and if there were no regulator such as ammonia the soil would become sour and hostile to most organisms.

Another of our beliefs is that one of the purposes of the small but definite amount of methane in the atmosphere is to regulate the oxygen content. Methane is a product of anaerobic fermentation in soil and sea. Some of the methane rises into the stratosphere where it oxidises to carbon dioxide and water, so becoming the principal source of water vapour in the upper air. The water rises further into the ionosphere and is photolysed to oxygen and hydrogen. Oxygen descends and hydrogen escapes into space. In effect, methane production is a way of transporting hydrogen from the Earth's surface to the stratosphere in sufficient quantity to maintain oxygen concentration in the lower atmosphere.

We have also found interesting and unexpected trace gases in the atmosphere, such as dimethyl sulphide, methyl iodide, and carbon tetrachloride. There is no doubt that the first two are biological emissions and they may well serve to transport the essential elements, sulphur and iodine, from the sea to the land. Carbon tetrachloride does not seem to have a biological source but its uniform distribution in the atmosphere, showing no difference between the northern and southern hemispheres, and other evidence suggest that it is not a man-made pollutant either. Its origins are an intriguing puzzle as is the question of its function, if any.

For more than 3500 My in the face of a big increase of Solar output, the mean temperature of the Earth's surface must have remained within the range of 15–30°C. How did Gaia do this? She must have used several ways to keep surface temperatures so constant. Before there was a significant amount of oxygen in the air, the emission and absorption of ammonia by simple organisms may have been the control process, so making use of its heat-absorbing and heat-retaining properties. Variations of the concentration of ammonia in the air would therefore be a means of temperature control.

There must have been other ways as well, for the failure of only one year's crop of ammonia would have led to a self-accelerating temperature decline and extinction of life. One can envisage advantage being taken of the ability of certain algae to change colour from light to dark, thereby influencing the emissivity and the albedo of the surface. Later, when photosynthesising and respiring organisms existed and oxygen became a major constituent of the air, the control of the concentration of carbon dioxide, which is also a heat-absorbing and heat-retaining gas, may have been used to play a role in stabilising temperature.

Gaia and Man

Gaia is still a hypothesis. The facts and speculations in this article and others that we have assembled corroborate but do not prove her existence but, like all useful theories, right or wrong, Gaia suggests new questions which may throw light on old ones. Let us ask another. What bearing has she on pollution, population, and Man's role in the living world?

Gaia has survived the most appalling of all atmospheric pollutants, namely oxygen, which was put into the atmosphere in substantial quantity about 2000 My ago when the photosynthesisers had completed their task of oxidising the surface and the atmosphere. Whole ranges of species must have been killed off or driven into dark, oxygen-free prisons from which they have never been released; the appearance of the whole planetary surface and its chemistry were completely changed. To appreciate the impact of oxygen, think of what would happen to us if a marine organism began to photosynthesise chlorine and was successful enough to replace oxygen in the air with chlorine. This is science fiction, but oxygen was as poisonous to the primitive ferments as chlorine would be to us today.

Man's present activity as a polluter is trivial by comparison and he cannot thereby seriously change the present state of Gaia let alone hazard her existence. But there is an aspect of Man's activities more disturbing than pollution. If one showed a control engineer the graph of the Earth's mean temperature against time over the past million years, he would no doubt remark that it represented the behaviour of a system in which serious instabilities could develop but that had never gone out of control. One of the laws of system control is that if a system is to maintain stability it must possess an adequate variety of response, that is, have at least as many ways of countering outside disturbances as there are outside disturbances to act on it. What is to be feared is that Man-the-farmer and Man-the-engineer are reducing the total variety of response open to Gaia.

The growing human population of the Earth is leading us to use drastic measures to supply this population with resources, of which food has prime importance. Natural distributions of plants and animals are being changed, ecological systems destroyed, and whole species altered or deleted. But any species or group of species in an ecological association may contribute just that response to an external threat that is needed to maintain the stability of Gaia.

We therefore disturb and eliminate at our peril; long before the world population has grown so large that we consume the entire output from photosynthesisers, instabilities generated by lack of variety of response could intervene to put this level out of reach.

Finally, a brief prospective look at the relation between man and Gaia, which also sums up the implications of this article. Socially organised Man has the ability possessed by no other species to collect, store, and process information and then to use it to manipulate the environment in a purposeful and anticipatory fashion. When our forebears became farmers they set themselves on a path, which we are still beating out, that must have had an impact on the rest of Gaia almost as revolutionary as that of the evolution of photosynthetic organisms millennia before. The area of the outside world that we, as a species, are capable of regulating to our short-term advantage has gradually expanded from the immediate locality of a settlement to vast geographical regions. This path could take us finally to the point at which the area of manipulation becomes the whole world. What happens then?

Nineteenth-century technocracy would say that we would then have won the final victory in the battle against Nature. The Earth would be our spaceship, we the passengers and crew, the rest of Nature, living and dead, our life-support system. But the price of victory might well be that we should have immobilised Gaia's control systems which she had established to keep the conditions on our planet at the level necessary for her and therefore our survival. The responsibility for the task of maintaining system stability would pass to us alone and it would be dauntingly difficult. As well as carrying technical burdens, we should also have to make agonising social and moral decisions, such as how many passengers the spaceship could afford to carry and whom to throw overboard to make room.

A Need to Survive

The easier path is to rid ourselves of nineteenth-century technocratic thinking, to reject the idea that human existence is necessarily a battle against nature. Let us make peace with Gaia on her terms and return to peaceful co-existence with our fellow creatures. Thirty thousand years ago some of our ancestors did something like this. They abandoned primitive hunting and took up what has been called the transhumane way of life. Men lived and migrated with the animal herds, defended them against other predators, and systematically culled them for food. This ensured them a more plentiful and regular supply of animal products than the random hunting mode that it superseded. But our first priority as a species is to choose from the numerous technically feasible means of limiting our own population those that are socially acceptable in social and moral terms.

Now for one more speculation. We are sure that Man needs Gaia but could Gaia do without Man? In Man, Gaia has the equivalent of a central nervous system and an awareness of herself and the rest of the Universe. Through Man, she has a rudimentary capacity, capable of development, to anticipate and guard against threats to her existence. For example, Man can command just about enough capacity to ward off a collision with a planetoid the size of Icarus. Can it then be that in the course of Man's evolution within Gaia we have been acquiring the knowledge and skills necessary to ensure her survival?

It is interesting to note that although the Gaia hypothesis really amounts to the claim that the planet's organisms function in a tightly bound mutualism or symbiosis, Lovelock himself does not seem to have used these terms.

As the selection by Lovelock and Epton suggests, the Gaia hypothesis is considerably more optimistic in tone than many other ecologically inspired views of humanity, which tend to picture us as inevitably at odds with the best interests of life in general. We conclude with a brief but illuminating passage from Lovelock (1988), which indicates that this optimism should be guarded:

> A frequent misunderstanding of my vision of Gaia is that I champion complacence, that I claim feedback will always protect the environment from any serious harm that humans might do. It is sometimes more crudely put as "Lovelock's Gaia gives industry the green light to pollute at will." The truth is almost diametrically opposite. Gaia, as I see her, is no doting mother tolerant of misdemeanours, nor is she some fragile and delicate damsel in danger from brutal mankind. She is stern and tough, always keeping the world warm and comfortable for those who obey the rules, but ruthless in her destruction of those who transgress. Her unconscious goal is a planet fit for life. If humans stand in the way of this, we shall be eliminated with as little pity as would be shown by the micro-brain of an intercontinental ballistic nuclear missile in full flight to its target. (Lovelock 1988, p. 212)

FURTHER READING

Lovelock's first book on the Gaia hypothesis was published in 1979. His 1988 book is very accessible and attempts to answer several criticisms of earlier versions of the theory. Joseph (1990) offers a sensitive overview. Schneider and Boston (1991) contains the proceedings of an interesting scientific conference on the Gaia hypothesis.

QUESTIONS TO CONSIDER

1. Evaluate Lovelock and Epton's suggestion that human society might eventually come to function as, in effect, the memory, nervous system, and perceptual system of Gaia.

2. Does the Gaia hypothesis offer only an inspiring vision? Or would it, with suitable elaboration perhaps, have practical consequences for how we should conduct ourselves ecologically?
3. The Gaia hypothesis has been criticized as excessively teleological, meaning that it attempts to explain certain natural phenomena in terms of purposes rather than biophysical causation. Is it necessarily scientifically illegitimate to speak of "purpose" or "function" in nature? Hint: consider the sense in which an organ in one's body has a "purpose" in the economy of the body.

PART FOUR

Environmental ethics at last

We arrive at last at environmental ethics proper — although it should be quite apparent by now that considerations of ethics and value arise almost automatically from the very beginning of any investigation into the environment. If we were to try to understand the importance of ethics from an ecological point of view — even though not all environmental ethicists want to do this — we might say that for humans, possessed of conscious choice and the technical ingenuity and social organization cited by McNeill, which free us from most of the biological constraints that limit the expansion of other organisms, the only way we can hope to come to some sort of desirable equilibrium with our environment is through appropriate *self*-regulation at both the social and individual level. And this seems to imply that the construction of an effective environmental ethic is an essential step on the road to ecological citizenhood for the human race.

For those who wish a more thorough introduction to the very large literature on environmental ethics, there now exist several excellent anthologies, among which are Gaard (1993), Regan (1984), Westphal and Westphal (1994), Zimmerman et al. (1993), VanDeVeer and Pierce (1986) and (1994), and Armstrong and Botzler (1993). See Beauchamp (1991) or Rachels (1986) for sound introductions to ethical theory in general.

CHAPTER NINE

WHERE ECOLOGY MEETS PHILOSOPHY

Professional ethicists are fond of pointing out that an "is" by itself never entails an "ought"; the fact that leaves are green, as pleasing to the eye as it may be, does not seem to imply that they are obliged to be so — at least in any sense of obligation that is pertinent to human choice. To argue otherwise would be to commit what is known as the **naturalistic fallacy**. But, as usual, ecology threatens to transcend such analytic distinctions. Both of the authors in this chapter are concerned with feeling out the way in which value seems to emerge automatically or implicitly from nature itself (Bookchin) or ecological imperatives (Leopold).

We open with a selection from Murray Bookchin's *Ecology of Freedom* (1982). Bookchin has for over 40 years been a controversial and outspoken champion of the environment in numerous books and papers, and is the founder of the influential stream of environmental thought known as **social ecology**.

THE IMMANENCE OF ETHICS

Murray Bookchin

My point here is that substance and its properties are not separable from life. Henri Bergson's conception of the biosphere as an "entropy-reduction" factor, in a cosmos that is supposedly moving toward greater entropy or disorder, would seem to provide life with a cosmic rationale for existence. That life forms may have this function need not suggest that the universe has been exogenously "designed" by a supernatural demiurge. But it does suggest that "matter" or substance has inherent self-organizing properties, no less valid than the mass and motion attributed to it by Newtonian physics.

Nor is there so great a lack of data, by comparison with the conventional attributes of "matter," as to render the new properties implausible. At the very least, science must *be* what nature really *is*; and in nature, life *is* (to use Bergsonian terminology) a counteracting force to the **second law of thermodynamics**—or an "entropy-reduction" factor. The self-organization of substance into ever-more complex forms—indeed, the importance of form itself as a correlate of function and of function as a correlate of self-organization—implies the unceasing activity to achieve stability. That stability as well as complexity is a "goal" of substance; that complexity, not only inertness, makes for stability; and finally, that complexity is a paramount feature of organic evolution and of an ecological interpretation of biotic interrelationships—all these concepts taken together are ways of understanding nature as such, not mere mystical vagaries. They are supported more by evidence than are the theoretical prejudices that still exist today against a universe charged with meaning, indeed, dare I say, with *ethical* meaning.

This much is clear: we can no longer be satisfied with a passive "dead" matter that fortuitously collects into living substance. The universe bears witness to an ever-striving, *developing*—not merely a "moving"—substance, whose most dynamic and creative attribute is its ceaseless capacity for self-organization into increasingly complex forms. Natural fecundity originates primarily from growth, not from spatial "changes" of location. Nor can we remove form from its central place in this developmental and growth process, or function as an indispensable correlate of form. The orderly universe that makes science a possible project and its use of a highly concise logic—mathematics—meaningful presupposes the correlation of form with function. From this perspective, mathematics serves not merely as the "language" of science but also as the *logos* of science. This scientific *logos* is above all a workable project because it grasps a *logos* that inheres in nature—the "object" of scientific investigation.

Once we step beyond the threshold of a purely instrumental attitude toward the "language" of the sciences, we can admit even more attributes into our account of the organic substance we call life. Conceived as substance that is perpetually self-maintaining or metabolic as well as developmental, life more clearly establishes the existence of another attribute: symbiosis. Recent data support the view that Peter Kropotkin's mutualistic **naturalism** not only applies to relationships within and among species, but also applies morphologically—within and among complex cellular forms. As William Trager observed more than a decade ago:

> The conflict in nature between different kinds of organisms has been popularly expressed in phrases like "struggle for existence" and "survival of the fittest." Yet few people realize that mutual cooperation between different kinds of organisms — symbiosis — is just as important, and that the "fittest" may be the one that most helps another to survive.

Whether intentional or not, Trager's description of the "fittest" is not merely a scientific judgment made by an eminent biologist; it is also an ethical judgment similar to the one Kropotkin derived from his own work as a naturalist and his ideals as an anarchist. Trager emphasized that the "nearly perfect" integration of "symbiotic microorganisms into the economy of the host . . . has led to the hypothesis that certain intracellular organelles might have been originally independent microorganisms." Accordingly, the chloroplasts that are responsible for photosynthetic activity in plants with *eukaryotic*, or nucleated, cells are discrete structures that replicate by division, have their own distinctive DNA very similar to that of circular bacteria, synthesize their own proteins, and are bounded by two-unit membranes.

Much the same is true of the eukaryotic cell's "powerhouse," its mitochondria. The most significant research in this area dates back to the 1960s and has been developed with great elan by Lynn Margulis in her papers and books on cellular evolution. The eukaryotic cells are the morphological units of all complex forms of animal and plant life. The protista and fungi also share these well-nucleated cell structures. Eukaryotes are aerobic and include clearly formed subunits, or organelles. By contrast, the *prokaryotes* lack nuclei; they are anaerobic, less specialized than the eukaryotes, and according to Margulis they constitute the evolutionary predecessors of the eukaryotes. In fact, they are the only life forms that could have survived and flourished in the early earth's atmosphere, with its mere traces of free oxygen.

Margulis has argued and largely established that the eukaryotic cells consist of highly functional symbiotic arrangements of prokaryotes that have become totally interdependent with other constituents. Eukaryotic flagella, she hypothesizes, derive from anaerobic spirochetes; mitochondria, from prokaryotic bacteria that were capable of respiration as well as fermentation; and plant chloroplasts, from "blue-green algae," which have recently been reclassified as cyanobacteria. The theory, now almost a biological convention, holds that phagocytic ancestors of what were to become eukaryotes absorbed (without digesting) certain spirochetes, protomitochondria (which, Margulis suggests, might have invaded their hosts), and, in the case of photosynthetic cells, coccoid cyanobacteria and chloroxybacteria. Existing phyla of multicellular aerobic life forms thus had their origins in a symbiotic process that integrated a variety of microorganisms into what can reasonably be called a colonial organism, the eukaryotic cell. **Mutualism**, not predation, seems to have been the guiding principle for the evolution of the highly complex aerobic life forms that are common today.

The prospect that life and all its attributes are *latent* in substance as such, that biological evolution is rooted deeply in symbiosis or mutualism, indicates how important it is to reconceptualize our notion of "matter" as *active* substance. As Manfred Eigen has put it, molecular self-organization suggests that evolution "appears to be an inevitable event, given the presence of certain matter with specified autocatalytic properties and under the maintenance of the finite (free) energy flow [that is, solar energy] necessary to compensate for the steady production of entropy." Indeed, this self-organizing activity extends beyond the emergence and evolution of life to the seemingly inorganic factors that produced and maintain a biotically favorable "environment" for the development of increasingly complex life forms. As Margulis observes, summarizing the Gaia hypothesis that she and James E. Lovelock have developed, the traditional assumption that life has been forced merely to adapt to an independent, geologically and meteorologically determined "environment" is no longer tenable. This dualism between the living and the nonliving world (which is based on accidental point mutations in life forms that determine what species will evolve or perish) is being replaced by the more challenging notion that life "makes much of its own environment," as Margulis observes. "Certain properties of the atmosphere, sediments, and hydrosphere are controlled by and for the biosphere."

By comparing lifeless planets such as Mars and Venus with the Earth, Margulis notes that the high concentration of oxygen in our atmosphere is anomalous in contrast with the carbon dioxide worlds of the other planets. Moreover, "the concentration of oxygen in the Earth's atmosphere remains constant in the presence of nitrogen, methane, hydrogen, and other potential reactants." Life, in effect, exerts an active role in maintaining free oxygen molecules and their relative constancy in the Earth's atmosphere. The same is true of the alkalinity and the remarkable degree of moderate temperature levels of the Earth's surface. The uniqueness and anomalies of the Earth's atmosphere

> are far from random. At least the "core," the tropical and temperate regions, surface and atmosphere [temperatures] are skewed from the values deduced by interpolating between values for Mars and Venus, and deviations are in directions favored by most species of organisms. Oxygen is maintained at about 20 percent, the mean temperature of

> the lower atmosphere is about 22°C, and the pH is just over 8. These planet-wide anomalies have persisted for very long times; the chemically bizarre composition of the Earth's atmosphere has prevailed for millions of years, even though the residence times of the reactive gases can be measured in months and years.

Margulis concludes that it

> is highly unlikely that chance alone accounts for the fact that temperature, pH, and the concentration of nutrient elements have been for immense periods of time just those optimal for life. It seems especially unlikely when it is obvious that the major perturbers of atmospheric gases are organisms themselves—primarily microbes. . . . It seems rather more likely that energy is expended by the biota actively to maintain these conditions.

Finally, the Modern Synthesis, to use Julian Huxley's term for the neo-Darwinian model of organic evolution in force since the early 1940s, has also been challenged as too narrow and perhaps mechanistic in its outlook. The image of a slow pace of evolutionary change emerging from the interplay of small variations, which are selected for their adaptability to the environment, is no longer as supportable as it seemed by the actual facts of the fossil record. Evolution seems to be more sporadic, marked by occasional rapid changes, often delayed by long periods of stasis. Highly specialized genera tend to speciate and become extinct because of the very narrow, restricted niches they occupy ecologically, while fairly generalized genera change more slowly and become extinct less frequently because of the more diversified environments in which they can exist. This "Effect Hypothesis," advanced by Elizabeth Vrba, suggests that evolution tends to be an immanent striving rather than the product of external selective forces. Mutations appear more like intentional mosaics than small, scratch-like changes in the structure and function of life forms. As one observer notes, "Whereas species selection puts the forces of change on environmental conditions, the Effect Hypothesis looks to internal parameters that affect the rates of speciation and extinction."

The notion of small, gradual point mutations (a theory that accords with the Victorian mentality of strictly fortuitous evolutionary changes) can be challenged on genetic grounds alone. Not only a gene but a chromosome, both in varying combinations, may be altered chemically and mechanically. Genetic changes may range from "simple" point mutations, through jumping genes and transposable elements, to major chromosomal rearrangements. It is also clear, mainly from experimental work, that permutations of genetically determined morphological shifts are possible. Small genetic changes can give rise to either minor or major morphological modifications; the same holds true for large genetic changes.

Trager's observation that the "fittest" species may well be "the one that most helps another to survive" is an excellent formula for recasting the traditional picture of natural evolution as a meaningless competitive tableau bloodied by the struggle to survive. There is a rich literature, dating back to the late nineteenth century, that emphasizes the role played by intraspecific and interspecific cooperation in fostering the survival of life forms on the planet. Kropotkin's famous *Mutual Aid* summarized the data at the turn of the century, and apparently added the word "mutualism" to the biological vocabulary on symbiosis. The opening chapters of the book summarize the contemporary work on the subject, his own observations in eastern Asia, and a sizable array of data on insects, crabs, birds, the "hunting associations" of mammalian carnivores, rodent "societies," and the like. The material is largely intraspecific; biological "mutualists" of a century ago did not emphasize the interspecific support systems that we now know to be more widespread than Kropotkin could have imagined. Buchner has written a huge volume (1953) on the endosymbiosis of animals with plant microorganisms alone; Henry has compiled a two-volume work, *Symbiosis*, that brings the study of this subject up to the mid-1960s. The evidence for interspecific symbiosis, particularly mutualism, is nothing less than massive. Even more than Kropotkin's *Mutual Aid*, Henry's work traces the evidence of mutualistic relationships from the interspecific support relationships of rhizobia and legumes, through plant associations, behavior symbiosis in animals, and the great regulatory mechanisms that account for homeostasis in planet-wide biogeochemical relationships.

"Fitness" is rarely biologically meaningful as mere species survival and adaptation. Left on this superficial level, it becomes an almost personal adaptive enterprise that fails to account for the need of all species for life support systems, be they autotrophic or heterotrophic. Traditional evolutionary theory tends to abstract a species from its ecosystem, to isolate it, and to deal with its survival in a remarkably abstract fashion. For example, the mutually supportive interplay between photosynthetic life forms and herbivores, far from providing evidence of the simplest form of "predation" or heterotrophy, is in fact indispensable to soil fertility from animal wastes, seed distribution, and the return (via death) of bulky organisms to an ever-enriched ecosystem. Even large carnivores that prey upon large herbivores have a vital function in selectively controlling large population swings by removing weakened or old animals for whom life would in fact become a form of "suffering."

Neither pain, cruelty, aggression, nor competition satisfactorily explain the emergence and evolution of life. For a better explanation we should also turn to mutualism and a concept of "fitness" that reinforces the support systems for the seemingly "fittest." If we are prepared to recognize the self-organizing nature of life, the decisive role of mutualism as its evolutionary impetus obliges us to redefine "fitness" in terms of an ecosystem's supportive apparatus. And if we are prepared to view life as a phenomenon that can shape and maintain the very "environment" that is regarded as the "selective" source of its evolution, a crucial question arises: Is it meaningful any longer to speak of "natural selection" as the motive force of biological evolution? Or must we now speak of "natural interaction" to take full account of life's own role in creating and guiding the "forces" that explain its evolution? Contemporary biology leaves us with a picture of organism interdependencies that far and away prove to be more important in shaping life forms than either a Darwin, a Huxley, or the formulators of the Modern Synthesis could ever have anticipated. Life is necessary not only for its own self-maintenance but for its own self-formation. "Gaia" and subjectivity are more than the effects of life; they are its integral attributes.

The grandeur of an authentic ecological sensibility, in contrast to the superficial environmentalism so prevalent today, is that it provides us with the ability to generalize in the most radical way these fecund, supportive interrelationships and their reliance on variety as the foundation of stability. An ecological sensibility gives us a coherent outlook that is explanatory in the most meaningful sense of the term, and almost overtly *ethical*.

From the distant Hellenic era to the early Renaissance, nature was seen primarily as a source of ethical orientation, a means by which human thought found its normative bearings and coherence. Nonhuman nature was not external to human nature and society. To the contrary, the mind was uniquely part of a cosmic *logos* that provided objective criteria for social and personal concepts of good and evil, justice and injustice, beauty and ugliness, love and hatred—indeed, for an interminable number of values by which to guide oneself toward the achievement of virtue and the good life. The words *dike* and *andike*—justice and injustice—permeated the cosmologies of the Greek nature philosophers. They linger on in many terminological variations as part of the jargon of modern natural science—notably in such words as "attraction" and "repulsion."

The fallacies of archaic cosmology generally lie not in its ethical orientation but in its dualistic approach to nature. For all its emphasis on speculation at the expense of experimentation, ancient cosmology erred *most* when it tried to cojoin a self-organizing, fecund nature with a vitalizing force alien to the natural world itself. Parmenides' Dike, like Henri Bergson's *élan vital*, are substitutes for the self-organizing properties of nature, not motivating forces within nature that account for an ordered world. A latent dualism exists in monistic cosmologies that try to bring humanity and nature into ethical commonality—a *deus ex machina* that corrects imbalances either in a disequilibriated cosmos or in an irrational society. Truth wears an unseen crown in the form of God or Spirit, for nature can never be trusted to develop on its own spontaneous grounds, any more than the body politic bequeathed to us by "civilization" can be trusted to manage its own affairs.

These archaisms, with their theological nuances and their tightly formulated teleologies, have been justly viewed as socially reactionary traps. In fact, they tainted the works of Aristotle and Hegel as surely as they mesmerized the minds of the medieval Schoolmen. But the errors of classical nature philosophy lie not in its project of eliciting an ethics from nature, but in the spirit of domination that poisoned it from the start with a presiding, often authoritarian, Supernatural "arbiter" who weighed out and corrected the imbalances or "injustices" that erupted in nature. Hence the ancient gods were there all the time, however rationalistic these early cosmologies may seem; they had to be exorcised in order to render an ethical continuum between nature and humanity more meaningful and democratic. Tragically, late Renaissance thought was hardly more democratic than its antecedents, and neither Galileo in science nor Descartes in philosophy performed this much-needed act of surgery satisfactorily. They and their more recent heirs *separated* the domains of nature and mind, recreating deities of their own in the form of scientistic and epistemological biases that are no less tainted by domination than the classical tradition they demolished.

Today, we are faced with the possibility of permitting nature—not Dike, Justitia, God, Spirit, or an *élan vital*—to open itself to us ethically on its *own* terms. Mutualism is an intrinsic good by virtue of its function in fostering the evolution of natural variety. We require no Dike on the one hand or canons of "scientific objectivity" on the other to affirm the role of community as a desideratum in nature and society. Similarly, *freedom* is an **intrinsic** good; its claims are validated by what Hans Jonas so perceptively called the "inwardness" of life forms, their "organic identity" and "adventure of form." The clearly visible effort, venture, indeed self-recognition, which every living being exercises in the course of "its precarious metabolic continuity" to preserve itself reveals—even in the most rudimentary of organisms—a sense of identity and selective activity which Jonas has very appropriately called evidence of "germinal freedom."

Finally, from the ever-greater complexity and variety that raises subatomic particles through the course of evolution to those conscious, self-reflexive life forms we call human beings, we cannot help but speculate about the existence of a broadly conceived *telos* and a latent subjectivity in substance itself that eventually yields mind and intellectuality. In the reactivity of substance, in the sensibility of the least-developed microorganisms, in the elaboration of nerves, ganglia, the spinal cord, and the layered development of the brain, one senses an evolution of mind so coherent and compelling that there is a strong temptation to describe it with Manfred Eigen's term, "inevitable." It is hard to believe that mere fortuity accounts for the capacity of life forms to respond neurologically to stimuli; to develop highly organized nervous systems; to be able to foresee, however dimly, the results of their behavior and later conceptualize this foresight clearly and symbolically. A true history of mind may have to begin with the attributes of substance itself; perhaps in the hidden or covert efforts of the simplest crystals to perpetuate themselves, in the evolution of DNA from unknown chemical sources to a point where it shares a principle of replication already present in the inorganic world, and in the speciation of nonliving as well as living molecules as a result of those intrinsic self-organizing features of reality we call their "properties."

Hence our study of nature—all archaic philosophies and epistemological biases aside—exhibits a self-evolving patterning, a "grain," so to speak, that is implicitly ethical. Mutualism, freedom, and subjectivity are not strictly human values or concerns. They appear, however germinally, in larger cosmic and organic processes that require no Aristotelian God to motivate them, no Hegelian Spirit to vitalize them. If social ecology provides little more than a coherent focus to the unity of mutualism, freedom, and subjectivity as aspects of a cooperative society that is free of domination and guided by reflection and reason, it will remove the taints that blemished a naturalistic ethics from its inception; it will provide both humanity and nature with a common ethical voice. No longer would we have need of a Cartesian—and more recently, a neo-Kantian—dualism that leaves nature mute and mind isolated from the larger world of phenomena around it. To vitiate community, to arrest the spontaneity that lies at the core of a self-organizing reality toward ever-greater complexity and rationality, to abridge freedom—these actions would cut across the grain of nature, deny our heritage in its evolutionary processes, and dissolve our legitimacy and function in the world of life. No less than this ethically rooted legitimation would be at stake—all its grim ecological consequences aside—if we fail to achieve an ecological society and articulate an ecological ethics.

Mutualism, self-organization, freedom, and subjectivity, cohered by social ecology's principles of unity in diversity, spontaneity, and non-hierarchical relationships, are thus ends in themselves. Aside from the ecological responsibilities they confer on our species as the self-reflexive voice of nature, they literally define us. Nature does not "exist" for us to use; it simply legitimates us and our uniqueness ecologically. Like the concept of "being," these principles of social ecology require no explanation, merely verification. They are the elements of an ethical *ontology*, not rules of a game that can be changed to suit one's personal needs.

A society that cuts across the grain of this ontology raises the entire question of its very reality as a meaningful and rational entity. "Civilization" has bequeathed us a vision of otherness as "polarization" and "defiance," and of organic "inwardness" as a perpetual "war" for self-identity. This vision threatens to utterly subvert the ecological legitimation of humanity and the reality of society as a potentially rational dimension of the world around us. Trapped by the false perception of a nature that stands in perpetual opposition to our humanity, we have redefined humanity itself to mean strife as a condition for pacification, control as a condition for consciousness, domination as a condition for freedom, and opposition as a condition for reconciliation. Within this implicitly self-destructive context, we are rapidly building the Valhalla that will almost certainly become a trap rather than a fortress against the all-consuming flames of Ragnarok.

Yet an entirely different philosophical and social dispensation can be read from the concept of otherness and inwardness of life—one that, in spirit at least, is not unlike that of the Wintu and Hopi. Given a world that life itself made conducive to evolution—indeed, benign, in view of a larger ecological vision of nature—we can formulate an ethics of complementarity that is nourished by variety rather than one that guards individual inwardness from a threatening, invasive otherness. Indeed, the inwardness of life can be seen as an expression of equilibrium, not as mere resistance to entropy and the terminus of all activity. Entropy itself can be seen as one feature in a larger cosmic metabolism, with life as its anabolic dimension. Finally, selfhood can be viewed as the result of integration, community, support, and sharing without any loss of individual identity and personal spontaneity.

Thus, two alternatives confront us. We can try to calm the antagonistic Bronze-Age warrior spirit of Odin, pacify him and his cohorts, and perhaps ventilate Valhalla with the breath of reason and reflection. We can try to mend the tattered treaties that once held the world together so precariously, and work with them as best we can. In the fullness of time, Odin might be persuaded to put aside his spear, cast off his armor, and lend himself to the sweet voice of rational understanding and discourse.

Or our efforts can take a radical turn: to overthrow Odin, whose partial blindness is evidence of a hopelessly aborted society. We can abandon the contractual myths that "harmonized" an inherently divided world, which the Norse epic held together with chains and banishments. It will then be our responsibility to create a new world and a new sensibility based on a self-reflexivity and an ethics to which we are heirs as a result of evolution's relentless thrust toward consciousness. We can try to reclaim our legitimacy as the fullness of mind in the natural world—as the rationality that *abets* natural diversity and integrates the workings of nature with an effectiveness, certainty, and directedness that is essentially incomplete in nonhuman nature.

"Civilization" as we know it today is more mute than the nature for which it professes to speak and more blind than the elemental forces it professes to control. Indeed, "civilization" lives in hatred of the world around it and in grim hatred of itself. Its gutted cities, wasted lands, poisoned air and water, and mean-spirited greed constitute a daily indictment of its odious immorality. A world so demeaned may well be beyond redemption, at least within the terms of its own institutional and ethical framework. The flames of Ragnarok purified the world of the Norsemen. The flames that threaten to engulf our planet may leave it hopelessly hostile to life—a dead witness to cosmic failure. If only because this planet's history, including its human history, has been so full of promise, hope, and creativity, it deserves a better fate than what seems to confront it in the years ahead.

Aldo Leopold was a professor of forestry whose philosophical musings on the relationship between humans and the environment (or simply the "land," as he called it) appeared posthumously in his *Sand County Almanac* (1966). Here is his very influential statement of the "land ethic."

THE LAND ETHIC

Aldo Leopold

When god-like Odysseus returned from the wars in Troy, he hanged all on one rope a dozen slave-girls of his household whom he suspected of misbehavior during his absence.

This hanging involved no question of propriety. The girls were property. The disposal of property was then, as now, a matter of expediency, not of right and wrong.

Concepts of right and wrong were not lacking from Odysseus' Greece: witness the fidelity of his wife through the long years before at last his black-prowed galleys clove the wine-dark seas for home. The ethical structure of that day covered wives, but had not yet been extended to human chattels. During the three thousand years which have since elapsed, ethical criteria have been extended to many fields of conduct, with corresponding shrinkages in those judged by expediency only.

The Ethical Sequence

This extension of ethics, so far studied only by philosophers, is actually a process in ecological evolution. Its sequences may be described in ecological as well as in philosophical terms. An ethic, ecologically, is a limitation on freedom of action in the struggle for existence. An ethic, philosophically, is a differentiation of social from anti-social conduct. These are two definitions of one thing. The thing has its origin in the tendency of interdependent individuals or groups to evolve modes of co-operation. The ecologist calls these symbioses. Politics and economics are advanced symbioses in which the original free-for-all competition has been replaced, in part, by co-operative mechanisms with an ethical content.

The complexity of co-operative mechanisms has increased with population density, and with the efficiency of tools. It was simpler, for example, to define the anti-social uses of sticks and stones in the days of the mastodons than of bullets and billboards in the age of motors.

The first ethics dealt with the relation between individuals; the Mosaic Decalogue is an example. Later accretions dealt with the relation between the individual and society. The Golden Rule tries to integrate the individual to society; democracy to integrate social organization to the individual.

There is as yet no ethic dealing with man's relation to land and to the animals and plants which grow upon it. Land, like Odysseus' slave-girls, is still property. The land-relation is still strictly economic, entailing privileges but not obligations.

The extension of ethics to this third element in human environment is, if I read the evidence correctly, an evolutionary possibility and an ecological necessity. It is the third step in a sequence. The first two have already been taken. Individual thinkers since the days of Ezekiel and Isaiah have asserted that the despoliation of land is not only inexpedient but wrong. Society, however, has not yet affirmed their belief. I regard the present conservation movement as the embryo of such an affirmation.

An ethic may be regarded as a mode of guidance for meeting ecological situations so new or intricate, or involving such deferred reactions, that the path of social expediency is not discernible to the average individual. Animal instincts are modes of guidance for the individual in meeting such situations. Ethics are possibly a kind of community instinct in-the-making.

The Community Concept

All ethics so far evolved rest upon a single premise: that the individual is a member of a community of interdependent parts. His instincts prompt him to compete for his place in that community, but his ethics prompt him also to co-operate (perhaps in order that there may be a place to compete for).

The land ethic simply enlarges the boundaries of the community to include soils, waters, plants, and animals, or collectively, the land.

This sounds simple: do we not already sing our love for and obligation to the land of the free and the home of the brave? Yes, but just what and whom do we love? Certainly not the soil, which we are sending helter-skelter down-river. Certainly not the waters, which we assume have no function except to turn turbines, float barges, and carry off sewage. Certainly not the plants, of which we exterminate whole communities without batting an eye. Certainly not the animals, of which we have already extirpated many of the largest and most beautiful species. A land ethic of course cannot prevent the alteration, management, and use of these "resources," but it does affirm their right to continued existence, and, at least in spots, their continued existence in a natural state.

In short, a land ethic changes the role of *Homo sapiens* from conqueror of the land-community to plain member and citizen of it. It implies respect for his fellow-members, and also respect for the community as such.

In human history, we have learned (I hope) that the conqueror role is eventually self-defeating. Why? Because it is implicit in such a role that the conqueror knows, *ex cathedra*, just what makes the community clock tick, and just what and who is valuable, and what and who is worthless, in community life. It always turns out that he knows neither, and this is why his conquests eventually defeat themselves.

In the biotic community, a parallel situation exists. Abraham knew exactly what the land was for: it was to drip milk and honey into Abraham's mouth. At the present moment, the assurance with which we regard this assumption is inverse to the degree of our education.

The ordinary citizen today assumes that science knows what makes the community clock tick; the scientist is equally sure that he does not. He knows that the biotic mechanism is so complex that its workings may never be fully understood.

That man is, in fact, only a member of a biotic team is shown by an ecological interpretation of history. Many historical events, hitherto explained solely in terms of human enterprise, were actually biotic interactions between people and land. The characteristics of the land determined the facts quite as potently as the characteristics of the men who lived on it.

Consider, for example, the settlement of the Mississippi valley. In the years following the Revolution, three groups were contending for its control: the native Indian, the French and English traders, and the American settlers. Historians wonder what would have happened if the English at Detroit had thrown a little more weight into the Indian side of those tipsy scales which decided the outcome of the colonial migration into the cane-lands of Kentucky. It is time now to ponder the fact that the cane-lands, when subjected to the particular mixture of forces represented by the cow, plow, fire, and axe of the pioneer, became bluegrass. What if the plant succession inherent in this dark and bloody ground had, under the impact of these forces, given us some worthless sedge, shrub, or weed? Would Boone and Kenton have held out? Would there have been any overflow into Ohio, Indiana, Illinois, and Missouri? Any Louisiana Purchase? Any transcontinental union of new states? Any Civil War?

Kentucky was one sentence in the drama of history. We are commonly told what the human actors in this drama tried to do, but we are seldom told that their success, or the lack of it, hung in large degree on the reaction of particular soils to the impact of the particular forces exerted by their occupancy. In the case of Kentucky, we do not even know where the bluegrass came from—whether it is a native species, or a stowaway from Europe.

Contrast the cane-lands with what hindsight tells us about the Southwest, where the pioneers were equally brave, resourceful, and persevering. The impact of occupancy here brought no bluegrass, or other plant fitted to withstand the bumps and buffetings of hard use. This region, when grazed by livestock, reverted through a series of more and more worthless grasses, shrubs, and weeds to a condition of unstable equilibrium. Each recession of plant types bred erosion; each increment to erosion bred a further recession of plants. The result today is a progressive and mutual deterioration, not only of plants and soils, but of the animal community subsisting thereon. The early settlers did not expect this: on the ciénegas of New Mexico some even cut ditches to hasten it. So subtle has been its progress that few residents of the region are aware of it. It is quite invisible to the tourist who finds this wrecked landscape colorful and charming (as indeed it is, but it bears scant resemblance to what it was in 1848).

This same landscape was "developed" once before, but with quite different results. The Pueblo Indians settled the Southwest in pre-Columbian times, but they happened *not* to be equipped with range livestock. Their civilization expired, but not because their land expired.

In India, regions devoid of any sod-forming grass have been settled, apparently without wrecking the land, by the simple expedient of carrying the grass to the cow, rather than vice versa. (Was this the result of some deep wisdom, or was it just good luck? I do not know.)

In short, the plant succession steered the course of history; the pioneer simply demonstrated, for good or ill, what successions inhered in the land. Is history taught in this spirit? It will be, once the concept of land as a community really penetrates our intellectual life.

The Ecological Conscience

Conservation is a state of harmony between men and land. Despite nearly a century of propaganda, conservation still proceeds at a snail's pace; progress still consists largely of letterhead pieties and convention oratory. On the back forty we still slip two steps backward for each forward stride.

The usual answer to this dilemma is "more conservation education." No one will debate this, but is it certain that only the *volume* of education needs stepping up? Is something lacking in the *content* as well?

It is difficult to give a fair summary of its content in brief form, but, as I understand it, the content is substantially this: obey the law, vote right, join some organizations, and practice what conservation is profitable on your own land; the government will do the rest.

Is not this formula too easy to accomplish anything worthwhile? It defines no right or wrong, assigns no obligation, calls for no sacrifice, implies no change in the current philosophy of values. In respect to land-use, it urges only enlightened self-interest. Just how far will such education take us? An example will perhaps yield a partial answer.

By 1930 it had become clear to all except the ecologically blind that southwestern Wisconsin's topsoil was slipping seaward. In 1933 the farmers were told that if they would adopt certain remedial practices for five years, the public would donate CCC labor to install them, plus the necessary machinery and materials. The offer was widely accepted, but the practices were widely forgotten when the five-year contract period was up. The farmers continued only those practices that yielded an immediate and visible economic gain for themselves.

This led to the idea that maybe farmers would learn more quickly if they themselves wrote the rules. Accordingly the Wisconsin Legislature in 1937 passed the Soil Conservation District Law. This said to farmers, in effect: *We, the public, will furnish you free technical service and loan you specialized machinery, if you will write your own rules for land-use. Each county may write its own rules, and these will have the force of law.* Nearly all the counties promptly organized to accept the proffered help, but after a decade of operation, *no county has yet written a single rule.* There has been visible progress in such practices as strip-cropping, pasture renovation, and soil liming, but none in fencing woodlots against grazing, and none in excluding plow and cow from steep slopes. The farmers, in short, have selected those remedial practices which were profitable anyhow, and ignored those which were profitable to the community, but not clearly profitable to themselves.

When one asks why no rules have been written, one is told that the community is not yet ready to support them; education must precede rules. But the education actually in progress makes no mention of obligations to land over and above those dictated by self-interest. The net result is that we have more education but less soil, fewer healthy woods, and as many floods as in 1937.

The puzzling aspect of such situations is that the existence of obligations over and above self-interest is taken for granted in such rural community enterprises as the betterment of roads, schools, churches, and baseball teams. Their existence is not taken for granted, nor as yet seriously discussed, in bettering the behavior of the water that falls on the land, or in the preserving of the beauty or diversity of the farm landscape. Land-use ethics are still governed wholly by economic self-interest, just as social ethics were a century ago.

To sum up: we asked the farmer to do what he conveniently could to save his soil, and he has done just that, and only that. The farmer who clears the woods off a 75 per cent slope, turns his cows into the clearing, and dumps its rainfall, rocks, and soil into the community creek, is still (if otherwise decent) a respected member of society. If he puts lime on his fields and plants his crops on contour, he is still entitled to all the privileges and emoluments of his Soil Conservation District. The District is a beautiful piece of social machinery, but it is coughing along on two cylinders because we have been too timid, and too anxious for quick success, to tell the farmer the true magnitude of his obligations. Obligations have no meaning without conscience, and the problem we face is the extension of the social conscience from people to land.

No important change in ethics was ever accomplished without an internal change in our intellectual emphasis, loyalties, affections, and convictions. The proof that conservation has not yet touched these foundations of conduct lies in the fact that philosophy and religion have not yet heard of it. In our attempt to make conservation easy, we have made it trivial.

Substitutes for a Land Ethic

When the logic of history hungers for bread and we hand out a stone, we are at pains to explain how much the stone resembles bread. I now describe some of the stones which serve in lieu of a land ethic.

One basic weakness in a conservation system based wholly on economic motives is that most members of the land community have no economic value. Wildflowers and songbirds are examples. Of the 22,000 higher plants and animals native to Wisconsin, it is doubtful whether more than 5 per cent can be sold, fed, eaten, or otherwise put to economic use. Yet these creatures are members of the biotic community, and if (as I believe) its stability depends on its integrity, they are entitled to continuance.

When one of these non-economic categories is threatened, and if we happen to love it, we invent subterfuges to give it economic importance. At the beginning of the century songbirds were supposed to be disappearing. Ornithologists jumped to the rescue with some distinctly shaky evidence to the effect that insects would eat us up if birds failed to control them. The evidence had to be economic in order to be valid.

It is painful to read these circumstances today. We have no land ethic yet, but we have at least drawn nearer the point of admitting that birds should continue as a matter of biotic right, regardless of the presence or absence of economic advantage to us.

A parallel situation exists in respect of predatory mammals, raptorial birds, and fish-eating birds. Time was when biologists somewhat overworked the evidence that these creatures preserve the health of game by killing weaklings, or that they control rodents for the farmer, or that they prey only on "worthless" species. Here again, the evidence had to be economic in order to be valid. It is only in recent years that we hear the more honest argument that predators are members of the community, and that no special interest has the right to exterminate them for the sake of a benefit, real or fancied, to itself. Unfortunately this enlightened view is still in the talk stage. In the field the extermination of predators goes merrily on: witness the impending erasure of the timber wolf by fiat of Congress, the Conservation Bureaus, and many state legislatures.

Some species of trees have been "read out of the party" by economics-minded foresters because they grow too slowly, or have too low a sale value to pay as timber crops: white cedar, tamarack, cypress, beech, and hemlock are examples. In Europe, where forestry is ecologically more advanced, the non-commercial tree species are recognized as members of the native forest community, to be preserved as such, within reason. Moreover, some (like beech) have been found to have a valuable function in building up soil fertility. The interdependence of the forest and its constituent tree species, ground flora, and fauna is taken for granted.

Lack of economic value is sometimes a character not only of species or groups, but of entire biotic communities: marshes, bogs, dunes, and "deserts" are examples. Our formula in such cases is to relegate their conservation to government as refuges, monuments, or parks. The difficulty is that these communities are usually interspersed with more valuable private lands; the government cannot possibly own or control such scattered parcels. The net effect is that we have relegated some of them to ultimate extinction over large areas. If the private owner were ecologically minded, he would be proud to be the custodian of a reasonable proportion of such areas, which add diversity and beauty to his farm and to his community.

In some instances, the assumed lack of profit in these "waste" areas has proved to be wrong, but only after most of them had been done away with. The present scramble to reflood muskrat marshes is a case in point.

There is a clear tendency in American conservation to relegate to government all necessary jobs that private landowners fail to perform. Government ownership, operation, subsidy, or regulation is now widely prevalent in forestry, range management, soil and watershed management, park and wilderness conservation, fisheries management, and migratory bird management, with more to come. Most of this growth in governmental conservation is proper and logical, some of it is inevitable. That I imply no disapproval of it is implicit in the fact that I have spent most of my life working for it. Nevertheless the question arises: What is the ultimate magnitude of the enterprise? Will the tax base carry its eventual ramifications? At what point will governmental conservation, like the mastodon, become handicapped by its own dimensions? The answer, if there is any, seems to be in a land ethic, or some other force which assigns more obligation to the private landowner.

Industrial landowners and users, especially lumbermen and stockmen, are inclined to wail long and loudly about the extension of government ownership and regulation to land, but (with notable exceptions) they show little disposition to develop the only visible alternative: the voluntary practice of conservation on their own lands.

When the private landowner is asked to perform some unprofitable act for the good of the community, he today assents only with outstretched palm. If the act costs him cash this is fair and proper, but when it costs him forethought, open-mindedness, or time, the issue is at least debatable. The overwhelming growth of land-use subsidies in recent years must be ascribed, in large part, to the government's own agencies for conservation education: the land bureaus, the agricultural colleges, and the extension services. As far as I can detect, no ethical obligation toward land is taught in these institutions.

To sum up: a system of conservation based solely on economic self-interest is hopelessly lopsided. It tends to ignore, and thus eventually to eliminate, many elements in the land community that lack commercial value, but that are (as far as we know) essential to its healthy functioning. It assumes, falsely, I think, that the economic parts of the biotic clock will function without the uneconomic parts. It tends to relegate to government many functions eventually too large, too complex, or too widely dispersed to be performed by government.

An ethical obligation on the part of the private owner is the only visible remedy for these situations.

The Land Pyramid

An ethic to supplement and guide the economic relation to land presupposes the existence of some mental image of land as a biotic mechanism. We can be ethical only in relation to something we can see, feel, understand, love, or otherwise have faith in.

The image commonly employed in conservation education is "the balance of nature." For reasons too lengthy to detail here, this figure of speech fails to describe accurately what little we know about the land mechanism. A much truer image is the one employed in ecology: the biotic pyramid. I shall first sketch the pyramid as a symbol of land, and later develop some of its implications in terms of land-use.

Plants absorb energy from the sun. This energy flows through a circuit called the biota, which may be represented by a pyramid consisting of layers. The bottom layer is the soil. A plant layer rests on the soil, an insect layer on the plants, a bird and rodent layer on the insects, and so on up through various animal groups to the apex layer, which consists of the larger carnivores.

The species of a layer are alike not in where they came from, or in what they look like, but rather in what they eat. Each successive layer depends on those below it for food and often for other services, and each in turn furnishes food and services to those above. Proceeding upward, each successive layer decreases in numerical abundance. Thus, for every carnivore there are hundreds of his prey, thousands of their prey, millions of insects, uncountable plants. The pyramidal form of the system reflects this numerical progression from apex to base. Man shares an intermediate layer with the bears, raccoons, and squirrels which eat both meat and vegetables.

The lines of dependency for food and other services are called food chains. Thus soil-oak-deer-Indian is a chain that has now been largely converted to soil-corn-cow-farmer. Each species, including ourselves, is a link in many chains. The deer eats a hundred plants other than oak, and the cow a hundred plants other than corn. Both, then, are links in a hundred chains. The pyramid is a tangle of chains so complex as to seem disorderly, yet the stability of the system proves it to be a highly organized structure. Its functioning depends on the co-operation and competition of its diverse parts.

In the beginning, the pyramid of life was low and squat, the food chains short and simple. Evolution has added layer after layer, link after link. Man is one of thousands of accretions to the height and complexity of the pyramid. Science has given us many doubts, but it has given us at least one certainty: the trend of evolution is to elaborate and diversify the biota.

Land, then, is not merely soil; it is a fountain of energy flowing through a circuit of soils, plants, and animals. Food chains are the living channels which conduct energy upward; death and decay return it to the soil. The circuit is not closed; some energy is dissipated in decay, some is added by absorption from the air, some is stored in soils, peats, and long-lived forests; but it is a sustained circuit, like a slowly augmented revolving fund of life. There is always a net loss by downhill wash, but this is normally small and offset by the decay of rocks. It is deposited in the ocean and, in the course of geological time, raised to form new lands and new pyramids.

The velocity and character of the upward flow of energy depend on the complex structure of the plant and animal community, much as the upward flow of sap in a tree depends on its complex cellular organization. Without this complexity, normal circulation would presumably not occur. Structure means the characteristic numbers, as well as the characteristic kinds and functions, of the component species. This interdependence between the complex structure of the land and its smooth functioning as an energy unit is one of its basic attributes.

When a change occurs in one part of the circuit, many other parts must adjust themselves to it. Change does not necessarily obstruct or divert the flow of energy; evolution is a long series of self-induced changes, the net result of which has been to elaborate the flow mechanism and to lengthen the circuit. Evolutionary changes, however, are usually slow and local. Man's invention of tools has enabled him to make changes of unprecedented violence, rapidity, and scope.

One change is in the composition of floras and faunas. The larger predators are lopped off the apex of the pyramid; food chains, for the first time in history, become shorter rather than longer. Domesticated species from other lands are substituted for wild ones, and wild ones are moved to new habitats. In this world-wide pooling of faunas and floras, some species get out of bounds as pests and diseases; others are extinguished. Such effects are seldom intended or foreseen; they represent unpredicted and often untraceable readjustments in the structure. Agricultural science is largely a race between the emergence of new pests and the emergence of new techniques for their control.

Another change touches the flow of energy through plants and animals and its return to the soil. Fertility is the ability of soil to receive, store, and release energy. Agriculture, by overdrafts on the soil, or by too radical a substitution of domestic for native species in the superstructure, may derange the channels of flow or deplete storage. Soils depleted of their storage, or of the organic matter which anchors it, wash away faster than they form. This is erosion.

Waters, like soil, are part of the energy circuit. Industry, by polluting waters or obstructing them with dams, may exclude the plants and animals necessary to keep energy in circulation.

Transportation brings about another basic change: the plants or animals grown in one region are now consumed and returned to the soil in another.

Transportation taps the energy stored in rocks, and in the air, and uses it elsewhere; thus we fertilize the garden with nitrogen gleaned by the guano birds from the fishes of seas on the other side of the Equator. Thus the formerly localized and self-contained circuits are pooled on a world-wide scale.

The process of altering the pyramid for human occupation releases stored energy, and this often gives rise, during the pioneering period, to a deceptive exuberance of plant and animal life, both wild and tame. These releases of biotic capital tend to becloud or postpone the penalties of violence.

This thumbnail sketch of land as an energy circuit conveys three basic ideas:

1. That land is not merely soil.
2. That the native plants and animals kept the energy circuit open; others may or may not.
3. That man-made changes are of a different order than evolutionary changes, and have effects more comprehensive than is intended or foreseen.

These ideas, collectively, raise two basic issues: Can the land adjust itself to the new order? Can the desired alterations be accomplished with less violence?

Biotas seem to differ in their capacity to sustain violent conversion. Western Europe, for example, carries a far different pyramid than Caesar found there. Some large animals are lost; swampy forests have become meadows or plowland; many new plants and animals are introduced, some of which escape as pests; the remaining natives are greatly changed in distribution and abundance. Yet the soil is still there and, with the help of imported nutrients, still fertile; the waters flow normally; the new structure seems to function and to persist. There is no visible stoppage or derangement of the circuit.

Western Europe, then, has a resistant biota. Its inner processes are tough, elastic, resistant to strain. No matter how violent the alterations, the pyramid, so far, has developed some new *modus vivendi* which preserves its habitability for man, and for most of the other natives.

Japan seems to present another instance of radical conversion without disorganization.

Most other civilized regions, and some as yet barely touched by civilization, display various stages of disorganization, varying from initial symptoms to advanced wastage. In Asia Minor and North Africa diagnosis is confused by climatic changes, which may have been either the cause or the effect of advanced wastage. In the United States the degree of disorganization varies locally; it is worst in the Southwest, the Ozarks, and parts of the South, and least in New England and the Northwest. Better land-uses may still arrest it in the less advanced regions. In parts of Mexico, South America, South Africa, and Australia a violent and accelerating wastage is in progress, but I cannot assess the prospects.

This almost world-wide display of disorganization in the land seems to be similar to disease in an animal, except that it never culminates in complete disorganization or death. The land recovers, but at some reduced level of complexity, and with a reduced carrying capacity for people, plants, and animals. Many biotas currently regarded as "lands of opportunity" are in fact already subsisting on exploitative agriculture, i.e., they have already exceeded their sustained carrying capacity. Most of South America is overpopulated in this sense.

In arid regions we attempt to offset the process of wastage by reclamation, but it is only too evident that the prospective longevity of reclamation projects is often short. In our own West, the best of them may not last a century.

The combined evidence of history and ecology seem to support one general deduction: the less violent the man-made changes, the greater the probability of successful readjustment in the pyramid. Violence, in turn, varies with human population density; a dense population requires a more violent conversion. In this respect, North America has a better chance for permanence than Europe, if she can contrive to limit her density.

This deduction runs counter to our current philosophy, which assumes that because a small increase in density enriched human life, an indefinite increase will enrich it indefinitely. Ecology knows of no density relationship that holds for indefinitely wide limits. All gains from density are subject to a law of diminishing returns.

Whatever may be the equation for men and land, it is improbable that we as yet know all its terms. Recent discoveries in mineral and vitamin nutrition reveal unsuspected dependencies in the up-circuit: incredibly minute quantities of certain substances determine the value of soils to plants, of plants to animals. What of the down-circuit? What of the vanishing species, the preservation of which we now regard as an esthetic luxury? They helped build the soil; in what unsuspected ways may they be essential to its maintenance? Professor Weaver proposes that we use prairie flowers to reflocculate the wasting soils of the dust bowl; who knows for what purpose cranes and condors, otters and grizzlies may some day be used?

Land Health and the A-B Cleavage

A land ethic, then, reflects the existence of an ecological conscience, and this in turn reflects a conviction of individual responsibility for the health of the land. Health is the capacity of the land for self-renewal. Conservation is our effort to understand and preserve this capacity.

Conservationists are notorious for their dissensions. Superficially these seem to add up to mere confusion, but a more careful scrutiny reveals a single plane of cleavage common to many specialized fields. In each field one group

(A) regards the land as soil, and its function as commodity-production; another group (B) regards the land as a biota, and its function as something broader. How much broader is admittedly in a state of doubt and confusion.

In my own field, forestry, group A is quite content to grow trees like cabbages, with cellulose as the basic forest commodity. It feels no inhibition against violence; its ideology is agronomic. Group B, on the other hand, sees forestry as fundamentally different from agronomy because it employs natural species, and manages a natural environment rather than creating an artificial one. Group B prefers natural reproduction on principle. It worries on biotic as well as economic grounds about the loss of species like chestnut, and the threatened loss of the white pines. It worries about a whole series of secondary forest functions: wildlife, recreation, watersheds, wilderness areas. To my mind, Group B feels the stirrings of an ecological conscience.

In the wildlife field, a parallel cleavage exists. For Group A the basic commodities are sport and meat; the yardsticks of production are ciphers of take in pheasants and trout. Artificial propagation is acceptable as a permanent as well as a temporary recourse—if its unit costs permit. Group B, on the other hand, worries about a whole series of biotic side-issues. What is the cost in predators of producing a game crop? Should we have further recourse to exotics? How can management restore the shrinking species, like prairie grouse, already hopeless as shootable game? How can management restore the threatened rarities, like trumpeter swan and whooping crane? Can management principles be extended to wildflowers? Here again it is clear to me that we have the same A-B cleavage as in forestry.

In the larger field of agriculture I am less competent to speak, but there seem to be somewhat parallel cleavages. Scientific agriculture was actively developing before ecology was born; hence a slower penetration of ecological concepts might be expected. Moreover the farmer, by the very nature of his techniques, must modify the biota more radically than the forester or the wildlife manager. Nevertheless, there are many discontents in agriculture which seem to add up to a new vision of "biotic farming."

Perhaps the most important of these is the new evidence that poundage or tonnage is no measure of the food-value of farm crops; the products of fertile soil may be qualitatively as well as quantitatively superior. We can bolster poundage from depleted soils by pouring on imported fertility, but we are not necessarily bolstering food-value. The possible ultimate ramifications of this idea are so immense that I must leave their exposition to abler pens.

The discontent that labels itself "organic farming," while bearing some of the earmarks of a cult, is nevertheless biotic in its direction, particularly in its insistence on the importance of soil flora and fauna.

The ecological fundamentals of agriculture are just as poorly known to the public as in other fields of land-use. For example, few educated people realize that the marvelous advances in technique made during recent decades are improvements in the pump, rather than the well. Acre for acre, they have barely sufficed to offset the sinking level of fertility.

In all of these cleavages, we see repeated the same basic paradoxes: man the conqueror *versus* man the biotic citizen; science the sharpener of his sword *versus* science the searchlight on his universe; land the slave and servant *versus* land the collective organism. Robinson's injunction to Tristram may well be applied, at this juncture, to *Homo sapiens* as a species in geological time:

> Whether you will or not
> You are a King, Tristram, for you are one
> Of the time-tested few that leave the world,
> When they are gone, not the same place it was.
> Mark what you leave.

The Outlook

It is inconceivable to me that an ethical relation to land can exist without love, respect, and admiration for land, and a high regard for its value. By value, I of course mean something far broader than mere economic value; I mean value in the philosophical sense.

Perhaps the most serious obstacle impeding the evolution of a land ethic is the fact that our educational and economic system is headed away from, rather than toward, an intense consciousness of land. Your true modern is separated from the land by many middlemen, and by innumerable physical gadgets. He has no vital relation to it; to him it is the space between cities on which crops grow. Turn him loose for a day on the land, and if the spot does not happen to be a golf links or a "scenic" area, he is bored stiff. If crops could be raised by hydroponics instead of farming, it would suit him very well. Synthetic substitutes for wood, leather, wool, and other natural land products suit him better than the originals. In short, land is something he has "outgrown."

Almost equally serious as an obstacle to a land ethic is the attitude of the farmer for whom the land is still an adversary, or a taskmaster that keeps him in slavery. Theoretically, the mechanization of farming ought to cut the farmer's chains, but whether it really does is debatable.

One of the requisites for an ecological comprehension of land is an understanding of ecology, and this is by no means co-extensive with "education"; in fact, much higher education seems deliberately to avoid ecological concepts. An understanding of ecology does not necessarily originate in courses bearing ecological labels; it is quite as likely to be labeled geography, botany, agronomy, history, or economics. This is as it should be, but whatever the label, ecological training is scarce.

The case for a land ethic would appear hopeless but for the minority which is in obvious revolt against these "modern" trends.

The "key-log" which must be moved to release the evolutionary process for an ethic is simply this: quit thinking about decent land-use as solely an economic problem. Examine each question in terms of what is ethically and esthetically right, as well as what is economically expedient. A thing is right when it tends to preserve the integrity, stability, and beauty of the biotic community. It is wrong when it tends otherwise.

It of course goes without saying that economic feasibility limits the tether of what can or cannot be done for land. It always has and it always will. The fallacy the economic determinists have tied around our collective neck, and which we now need to cast off, is the belief that economics determines *all* land-use. This is simply not true. An innumerable host of actions and attitudes, comprising perhaps the bulk of all land relations, is determined by the land-users' tastes and predilections, rather than by his purse. The bulk of all land relations hinges on investments of time, forethought, skill, and faith rather than on investments of cash. As a land-user thinketh, so is he.

I have purposely presented the land ethic as a product of social evolution because nothing so important as an ethic is ever "written." Only the most superficial student of history supposes that Moses "wrote" the Decalogue; it evolved in the minds of a thinking community, and Moses wrote a tentative summary of it for a "seminar." I say tentative because evolution never stops.

The evolution of a land ethic is an intellectual as well as emotional process. Conservation is paved with good intentions which prove to be futile, or even dangerous, because they are devoid of critical understanding either of the land, or of economic land-use. I think it is a truism that as the ethical frontier advances from the individual to the community, its intellectual content increases.

The mechanism of operation is the same for any ethic: social approbation for right actions; social disapproval for wrong actions.

By and large, our present problem is one of attitudes and implements. We are remodeling the Alhambra with a steamshovel, and we are proud of our yardage. We shall hardly relinquish the shovel, which after all has many good points, but we are in need of gentler and more objective criteria for its successful use.

Leopold's concept of the land ethic informs much of modern thought on environmental ethics, but his views have also sparked annoyance and controversy. His writing is all too often sketchy if not telegraphic, and he sometimes gets details wrong. (It was Telemachus, for instance, not Odysseus, who slew the slave-girls.) Leopold was no professional philosopher or historian; he roughs in a sweeping view of human history and the place of ethics in it with a broad brush, and has little patience for, or even awareness of, the niceties of philosophic argument. (He was, after all, a forester and farmer, not a professional philosopher.) A student of mine once objected eloquently and bitterly to Leopold's remark that ethical systems are for the guidance of the "average individual." Who are these exceptional and far-seeing persons, my student wondered, who will frame the ethics needed so that the rest of us ordinary folk will not get into too much trouble? Noted Canadian ethicist Wayne Sumner, fearing that individual rights would be trampled if the land ethic were followed, remarks that the land ethic is "not only nonsense, but dangerous nonsense." Marti Kheel (1993) criticizes Leopold's ethics as focussed too excessively on the modulation of aggression rather than on the positive fostering of care.

Nevertheless, whatever Leopold's failings may have been, he articulated a very important guiding idea—namely, that some sort of ethic that modulates human behaviour with respect to other humans *and* the environment is a necessary component of a vital human symbiosis. It is puzzling that even some of his most sympathetic critics (such as Callicott 1987) have failed to pick up the fact that Leopold's argument starts from a consideration of what would be required for a symbiosis. Furthermore, his radical suggestion that *all* ethics is ecologically based deserves far more comment and analysis than it has received. Leopold's essay is seminal, and any discussion of environmental ethics in recent years needs to place it somewhere near the beginning.

FURTHER READING

See Bookchin (1982), the source from which our excerpt was taken, and his 1987 article for more complete statements of his views. Eckersley (1989) and Fox (1989) criticize Bookchin; in his 1990 article he offers a spirited defence. See also Callicott (1989) for another interesting view of the way in which value may emerge from ecology. For more on Leopold, see Callicott (1987), Meine (1988), and Flader (1974).

QUESTIONS TO CONSIDER

1. Bookchin argues that it is a mistake to think of the particular way the physical universe and the life within it have evolved as purely an accident, and yet at the same time he rejects any notion of an external creator, designer, or Demiurge. How does he resolve this apparent contradiction?
2. Leopold states that "An ethic may be regarded as a mode of guidance for meeting ecological situations so new or intricate, or involving such deferred reactions, that the path of social expediency is not discernible to the average individual." Precisely what does this mean? Note that Leopold does not seem to be speaking of *environmental* ethics explicitly. Do you agree with his view of the nature of ethics?
3. What does Leopold mean by his statement that most advances in agricultural technique are "improvements in the pump, rather than the well"?

CHAPTER TEN

IS ANYTHING SACRED?

In this chapter, we present two thinkers who argue for the necessity of an ethical attitude toward both nonhuman and human life, but from very different directions, and a philosopher who insists, on the contrary, that such a thing is not only unnecessary but an impossibility.

First, Albert Schweitzer—a winner of the Nobel Peace Prize and one of the great polymaths of the twentieth century, but regrettably almost forgotten today. We present his statement of his ethic of reverence for life first because of its simplicity, power, and directness. Ethicists might say that Schweitzer's ethic is an especially sophisticated form of what is known as "ethical intuitionism," a view that recognizing the good is almost like recognizing a particular colour—a process that seems to have a direct, unmediated quality.

REVERENCE FOR LIFE

Albert Schweitzer

When I was forbidden to work in the hospital, I thought at first that I would proceed with the completion of my book on Paul. But at once another subject forced itself upon me, one about which I had thought for many years and which became a timely issue because of the war: the problem of our civilization. So on the second day of my internment, still quite amazed at being able to sit down at my writing table early in the morning as in the days before I took up medicine, I set to work on *The Philosophy of Civilization*.

The idea of pursuing this subject had first come to me in the summer of 1899 at the house of Ernst Curtius in Berlin. Hermann Grimm and others were conversing there one evening about a session of the academy from which they had just come when suddenly one of them—I forget who it was—exclaimed, "So we are all nothing but epigones!" This pronouncement struck me like a bolt of lightning, because it put into words what I myself felt.

Since my first years at the university I had grown to doubt increasingly the idea that mankind is steadily moving toward improvement. My impression was that the fire of its ideals was burning out without anyone noticing or worrying about it. On a number of occasions I had seen public opinion failing to reject officially proclaimed theses that were barbaric; on the contrary, it approved inhumane conduct whether by governments or individuals. What was just and equitable seemed to be pursued with only lukewarm zeal. I noticed a number of symptoms of intellectual and spiritual fatigue in this generation that is so proud of its achievements. It seemed as if I were hearing its members trying to convince one another that their previous hopes for the future of mankind had been placed too high, and that it was becoming necessary to limit oneself to striving for what was attainable. The slogan of the day, "Real-politik," meant approval of a shortsighted nationalism and a pact with the forces and tendencies that had hitherto been resisted as enemies of progress. One of the most visible signs of decline seemed to be the return of superstition, long banished from the educated circles of society.

Toward the end of the nineteenth century, when people began to review their past achievements in order to measure the progress that had been made, they displayed an optimism that I found incomprehensible. It was assumed everywhere not only that we had made progress in inventions and knowledge but that in the intellectual and ethical spheres we lived and moved at a height that had never before been attained and should never be questioned. My own impression was that in our intellectual and spiritual life not only had we sunk below the level of past generations, but we were in many respects merely living on their achievements, and that not a little of this heritage was beginning to melt away in our hands.

And now, here was someone expressing the criticism that I myself had silently and half unconsciously leveled against our age! After that evening at Professor Curtius's house, along with my other work I always considered writing a book with the title "Wir Epigonen" (We Inheritors of a Past).

When I discussed these thoughts with my friends, they usually took them to be interesting paradoxes and manifestations of a fin-de-siècle pessimism. After that, I kept my ideas strictly to myself. Only in my sermons did I express my doubts concerning our culture and spirituality.

Now war had broken out as a result of the collapse of our civilization. "We Inheritors of a Past," then, had lost its meaning. The book had been conceived as a criticism of civilization. It was meant to demonstrate its decadence and to draw attention to its inherent dangers. But since the catastrophe had already come about, what good could come of deliberating about the causes?

I thought of writing for my own sake this book, which had thus become out of date. But could I be certain that the manuscript would not be taken from a prisoner of war? Was there any prospect of my returning to Europe again? In this spirit of complete detachment I set to work and went on with it even after I was allowed to go about and devote myself to the sick again.

Many a night I sat thinking and writing, overcome with emotion as I thought of those who at that very hour were lying in the trenches.

At the beginning of the summer of 1915 I awoke from some kind of mental daze. Why only criticize civilization? Why limit myself to analyzing ourselves as *epigones*? Why not work on something constructive?

I then began to search for the knowledge and convictions that comprise the will to civilization and the power to realize it. "We Inheritors of a Past" expanded into a work dealing with the restoration of civilization.

As I worked along, the connection between civilization and our concept of the world became clear to me. I recognized that the catastrophe of civilization stemmed from a catastrophe in our thinking.

The ideals of true civilization had lost their power because the idealistic attitude toward life in which they are rooted had gradually been lost. All the events that occur within nations and within mankind can be traced to spiritual causes stemming from the prevailing attitude toward life.

But what is civilization?

The essential element in civilization is the ethical perfecting of the individual as well as society. At the same time, every spiritual and every material step forward has significance for civilization. The will to civilization is, then, the universal will to progress that is conscious of the ethical as the highest value. In spite of the great importance we attach to the achievements of science and human prowess, it is obvious that only a humanity that is striving for ethical ends can benefit in full measure from material progress and can overcome the dangers that accompany it. The present situation was terrible proof of the misjudgment of the generation that had adopted a belief in an immanent power of progress realizing itself, naturally and automatically, and which thought that it no longer needed any ethical ideals but could advance toward its goals by means of knowledge and work alone.

The only possible way out of chaos is for us to adopt a concept of the world based on the ideals of true civilization.

But what is the nature of that concept of the world in which the will to general progress and the will to ethical progress join and are linked together?

It consists in an ethical affirmation of the world and of life.

What is affirmation of the world and of life?

To us Europeans and to people of European descent everywhere, the will to progress is something so natural and so much a matter of course that it never occurs to us that it is rooted in a concept of life and springs from an act of the spirit. But if we look around us, we soon notice that what we take for granted is not at all natural everywhere.

In Indian thought all efforts to acquire knowledge and power and to improve the living conditions of man and society as a whole are considered mere folly. It teaches that the only wise attitude for a person is to withdraw entirely into himself and to concern himself with the perfecting of his inner life. What may become of human society and of mankind does not concern the individual. The meditation of the inner life in Indian thought consists of man's submission to the idea of giving up his will to live; it reduces his earthly existence to abstinence from all action and to negation of life in order to achieve a state of nonbeing.

It is interesting to trace the origin of this unnatural idea of negation of the world. At first it had nothing whatever to do with any concept of the world, but was a magical idea of the Brahmin priests of early times. They believed that by detachment from the world and from life they could become supernatural beings and obtain magical powers. The experience of ecstasy has contributed to the growth of this idea.

In the course of time this rejection of the world and of life, which was originally the privilege of the Brahmin, was developed into a system of thought that claimed to be valid for all men.

Whether the will to progress is present or not depends, then, on the prevailing concept of the world and of life. A concept that negates this world excludes progress, while affirmation demands it. Among primitive and semiprimitive peoples, who have not yet faced the problem of acceptance or rejection of the world, there is also no will to progress. Their ideal is the simplest life with the least possible trouble.

We Europeans have only arrived at our will to progress in the course of time and through a change in our conception of the world. In antiquity and in the Middle Ages we can find the first attempts. Greek thinking does try to establish an affirmative attitude toward the world and toward life, but it fails in the attempt and ends in resignation. The attitude of the Middle Ages is determined by the ideas of primitive Christianity brought into harmony with Greek metaphysics. It is fundamentally a rejection of the world and of life because Christianity focused on the world beyond, rather than on life on this earth. What manifests itself as affirmation of the world in the Middle Ages is inspired by the active ethic contained in the preaching of Jesus, and it is made possible through the creative forces of fresh and unspoiled peoples on whom Christianity had imposed a concept of the world that was in contradiction to their nature.

Gradually, the affirmation of life, already latent among the European peoples as a result of the Great Migration, begins to manifest itself. The Renaissance proclaims its freedom from the medieval negation of the world and of life. An ethical character is given to this new world-accepting attitude by incorporating the ethic of love taught by Jesus. This, as an ethic of action, is strong enough to reject the negative concept of the world from which it had issued, and to arrive at the new affirmative attitude toward the world and life. In this way it attained the ideal realization of a spiritual and ethical world within the natural.

The striving for material and spiritual progress that characterizes the people of modern Europe, therefore, has its source in the worldview at which these people had arrived.

As heir to the Renaissance and the spiritual and religious movements connected with it, man gains a new perspective of himself and of the world. A need awakens to create spiritual and material values that would bring about change in individuals and in mankind. The modern European is not only enthusiastic about progress to his personal advantage. He is less concerned about his own fate than about the happiness of future generations. Enthusiasm for progress has taken possession of him. Impressed by his discovery that the world is created and sustained by forces according to a definite design, he wills himself to become the active, purposeful force in the world. He looks with confidence toward the new and better times that will dawn for mankind. He learns by experience that ideas held and acted upon by the masses can gain power over circumstances and transform them.

It is upon this will to material progress, acting in conjunction with the will to ethical progress, that modern civilization is founded.

There is an essential relationship between the modern European attitude of ethical affirmation toward the world and life and that of Zarathustra and of Chinese thought, as we encounter it in the writings of Cong-tse, Meng-tse, Mi-tse, and the other great ethical thinkers of China.

In each of these we can see the striving to remold the circumstances of peoples and of mankind to achieve progress, even if the efforts are not as strong as those of modern Europe. In areas under the religious influences of Zarathustra and the Chinese, a life-affirming civilization actually emerged. But they both met with a tragic end. The neo-Persian civilization based on the philosophy of

Zarathustra was destroyed by Islam. The Chinese civilization is hampered in its natural development and threatened with decay by the pressure exerted upon it by European ideas and problems and by confusion caused by the country's political and economic disorder.

In modern European thought the tragedy is that the original bonds uniting the affirmative attitude toward the world with ethics are, by a slow but irresistible process, loosening and finally breaking apart. They will end in disintegration. European humanity is being guided by a will to progress that has become merely external and has lost its bearings.

By itself the affirmation of life can only produce a partial and imperfect civilization. Only if it turns inward and becomes ethical can the will to progress attain the ability to distinguish the valuable from the worthless. We must therefore strive for a civilization that is not based on the accretion of science and power alone, but which cares most of all for the spiritual and ethical development of the individual and of humankind.

How could it come about that the modern concept of the world and of life changed its original ethical character to a nonethical one?

The only possible explanation is that the ethical was not really founded on thought. The thought out of which it arose was noble and enthusiastic but not deep. The intimate connection between the ethical and the affirmative attitude toward life was a matter of intuition and experience, but was not based on proof. It proclaimed the affirmation of life and ethical principles without having penetrated to their essence and their inner connection.

This noble and valuable concept of the world was based on belief in, rather than consistent thought about, the real nature of things; thus it was destined to fade with time and to lose its power over man's mind.

All subsequent thinking about the problems of ethics and man's relation to his world could not but expose the weak points of view. Thus, in spite of the original intention to defend this concept, it hastened its demise. It never succeeded in replacing an inadequate with an adequate foundation. Again and again attempts to build new foundations proved too weak to support the superstructure.

With my apparently abstract yet absolutely practical thinking about the connection of civilization with philosophy, I had come to see the decay of civilization as a consequence of the continuous weakening of the ethical affirmation of life within modern worldviews. It had become clear to me that, like so many other people, I had clung to that concept of decay from inner necessity, without asking myself to what extent it could be supported by thought.

I had got thus far during the summer of 1915. What was to come next? Could the difficulty be solved that until now had seemed insoluble? Was it imaginable that the worldview that alone had made civilization possible was an illusion destined to stir our minds but always remain hidden? To continue to hold this illusion up to our generation seemed to me absurd and degrading. Only if it offers itself to us as something arising from thought can it become our own spirituality.

Fundamentally I remained convinced that ethics and the affirmation of life are interdependent and the precondition for all true civilization. A first step out of this impasse seemed imperative: to attain, through new, sincere, and direct contemplation, that truth we have hoped for in the past and which sometimes even seemed to be real.

In undertaking this I felt like someone who has to replace a rotten boat that is no longer seaworthy with a new and better one, but does not know how to proceed.

For months on end I lived in a continual state of mental agitation. Without the least success I concentrated—even during my daily work at the hospital—on the real nature of the affirmation of life and of ethics and on the question of what they have in common. I was wandering about in a thicket where no path was to be found. I was pushing against an iron door that would not yield.

All that I had learned from philosophy about ethics left me dangling in midair. The notions of the Good that it had offered were all so lifeless, so unelemental, so narrow, and so lacking in content that it was impossible to relate them to an affirmative attitude.

Moreover, philosophy never, or only rarely, concerned itself with the problem of the connection between civilization and concepts of the worldview. The affirmation of life in modern times seemed so natural that no need was felt to explore its meaning.

To my surprise I recognized that the central province of philosophy into which my reflections on civilization and the worldview had led me was virtually unexplored territory. Now from this point, now from that, I tried to penetrate to its interior, but again and again I had to give up the attempt. I saw before me the concept that I wanted, but I could not catch hold of it. I could not formulate it.

While in this mental state I had to take a long journey on the river. I was staying with my wife on the coast at Cape Lopez for the sake of her health—it was in September 1915—when I was called out to visit Madame Pelot, the ailing wife of a missionary, at N'Gômô, about 160 miles upstream. The only transportation I could find was a small steamer, which was about to leave, towing two overloaded barges. In addition to myself, only Africans were on board, among them my friend Emil Ogouma from Lambaréné. Since I had been in too much of a hurry to arrange for enough provisions for the journey, they invited me to share their food.

Slowly we crept upstream, laboriously navigating—it was the dry season—between the sandbanks. Lost in thought I sat on the deck of the barge, struggling to find the elementary and universal concept of the ethical that I had not discovered in any philosophy. I covered sheet after sheet with disconnected sentences merely to concentrate on the problem. Two days passed. Late on the third day, at the very moment when, at sunset, we were making our way through a herd of hippopotamuses, there flashed upon my mind, unforeseen and unsought, the phrase "reverence for life." The iron door had yielded. The path in the thicket had become visible. Now I had found my way to the principle in which affirmation of the world and ethics are joined together!

I was at the root of the problem. I knew that the ethical acceptance of the world and of life, together with the ideals of civilization contained in this concept, has its foundation in thought.

What is Reverence for Life, and how does it develop in us?

If man wishes to have a clear idea about himself and his relation to the world, he must turn away from the various concepts created by his reason and knowledge and reflect upon his own consciousness, the elemental, the most immediate reality. Only if he starts from this given fact can he arrive at a thoughtful concept.

Descartes begins with the sentence "I think, therefore I am" (*Cogito, ergo sum*). With his beginning thus chosen, he pursues the road to the abstract. Out of this act of thinking, which is without substance and artificial, nothing concerning the relation of man to himself and to the universe can come. In reality, however, the most immediate act of consciousness has some content. To think means to think something. The most immediate fact of man's consciousness is the assertion "I am life that wills to live in the midst of life that wills to live," and it is as will to live in the midst of will to live that man conceives himself at every moment that he spends meditating on himself and the world around him.

As my will to live includes an ardent desire to perpetuate life and the mysterious exaltation of the will to live, which we call happiness, and while there is fear of destruction and of the mysterious damage of the will to live, which we call pain, so too is this will to live in those around me, whether it expresses itself to me or remains mute.

Man must now decide how he will live in the face of his will to live. He can deny it. But if he wants to change his will to live into the will not to live, as is the case in Indian and indeed in all pessimistic thought, he creates a contradiction with himself. He builds his philosophy of life on a false premise, something that cannot be realized.

Indian thought, like that of Schopenhauer, is full of contradictions because it cannot help but make concessions over and over again to the will to live, which persists in spite of all negation of the world, though it will not admit that these are concessions. Negation of the will to live is only consistent with itself if it decides to put an end to physical existence.

If man affirms his will to live, he acts naturally and sincerely. He confirms an act, which has already been accomplished unconsciously, by bringing it to his conscious thought.

The beginning of thought, a beginning that continually repeats itself, is that man does not simply accept his existence as something given, but experiences it as something unfathomably mysterious.

Affirmation of life is the spiritual act by which man ceases to live thoughtlessly and begins to devote himself to his life with reverence in order to give it true value. To affirm life is to deepen, to make more inward, and to exalt the will to live.

At the same time the man who has become a thinking being feels a compulsion to give to every will to live the same reverence for life that he gives to his own. He experiences that other life in his own. He accepts as good preserving life, promoting life, developing all life that is capable of development to its highest possible value. He considers as evil destroying life, injuring life, repressing life that is capable of development. This is the absolute, fundamental principle of ethics, and it is a fundamental postulate of thought.

Until now the great weakness in all ethical systems has been that they dealt only with the relations of man to man. In reality, however, the question is, What is our attitude toward the universe and all that it supports? A man is ethical only when life as such is sacred to him—the life of plants and animals as well as that of his fellow men—and when he devotes himself to helping all life that is in need of help.

Only the universal ethic of growing responsibility for all that lives—only that ethic can be founded solidly in thought. The ethic of the relation of man to man is nothing but a fragment of the universal ethic.

The ethic of Reverence for Life, therefore, comprehends within itself everything that can be described as love, devotion, and compassion in suffering, the sharing of joy and common endeavors.

The world, however, offers us the horrible drama of will to live divided against itself. One existence holds its own at the cost of another; one destroys another. Only in the thinking man has the will to live become conscious of other wills to live and desirous of solidarity with them. This solidarity, however, he cannot completely bring about, because man is subject to the puzzling and horrible law of being obliged to live at the cost of other life and to incur again and again the guilt of destroying and injuring life. But as an ethical being he strives to escape whenever possible from this necessity, and as one who has become knowing and merciful, he tries to end this division of the will to live insofar as it is in his power. He aspires to prove his humanity and to release others from their sufferings.

Reverence for Life arising from the will to live that is inspired by thought contains the affirmation of life and ethics inseparably combined. It seeks to create values and to make progress of various kinds that will serve the material, spiritual, and ethical development of the individual and of mankind.

While the unthinking modern affirmation of life vacillates between its ideals of science and those of power, a reflective affirmation of life proposes the spiritual and ethical perfecting of mankind as the highest ideal, an ideal from which alone all other ideals of progress receive their real value.

Through ethical affirmation of the world and of life, we reach a deeper comprehension of life that enables us to distinguish between what is essential in civilization and what is not. The absurd pretension of considering ourselves civilized loses its power over us. We confront the truth that, with so much progress in knowledge and power, it has become not easier but more difficult to attain true civilization.

The problem of the mutual relationship between the spiritual and the material dawns on us. We know that we all have to struggle with circumstances to preserve our own humanity. We must do all we can so that the desperate struggle that many fight in order to preserve their humanity amid unfavorable social circumstances will become a battle that has a chance of success.

A deepened ethical will to progress that springs from thought will lead us back, then, out of our poor civilization with its many faults to true civilization. Sooner or later the true and final renaissance must dawn, which will bring peace to the world.

In the next selection, noted Canadian environmental philosopher John Livingston invites us to see beyond our thoughtless conception of the natural world as a mere bundle of "resources."

MORAL CONCERN AND THE ECOSPHERE

John A. Livingston

The concept of *ecosphere* involves a film of biologic being that envelops planet Earth. No doubt there are ecospheres surrounding uncountable other planets, but this is the only one we know. There are no others at hand for comparative purposes. This is a stern limitation to our understanding; a sample of one, as it were. Impoverishment of data makes classification difficult, and perhaps explains the variety of perceptions and interpretations of ecosphere that swirl about the human community, to say nothing of those that may be entertained in other sentient reflections.

The concept of ecosphere was given striking dimension by the extraordinary colour photographs that came out of the human invasion of the moon. The picture of the blue planet with its encircling cloud banks set against the total blackness beyond, gave vivid presence to the "Spaceship Earth" metaphor, which had been coined earlier. Portraits of Earth allowed us to actually *experience* the loneliness of the planet, and to feel in some very personal and intimate way the imperative self-sufficiency that such loneliness implies.

Resourcism

There can be no doubt of the overwhelming importance, both in our society and others, of what has been called the *resourcist* view of nature.[1] Peter Singer has discussed ***speciesism***—"a prejudice or attitude of bias toward the interests of members of our own species against those of members of other species."[2] **Resourcism** suggests an even wider and more inclusive *proprietary* bias: it adds, over and above all nonhuman species, not merely soils, waters, rocks and minerals, gases and chemical compounds, landscapes and landforms, but also the very processes of which these phenomena are both the agents and the creations. Resourcism sees the nonhuman world, which is *all* external to man and his structures, as raw material dedicated without reservation to the human purpose. A number of years ago, Paul Shepard observed that "Nature is usually synonymous with either natural resources or scenery, the great stereotypes in the minds of middle class, college-educated Americans."[3] Since that time, "scenic resources" have been commodified as well, and we are left with the single concept of "resource" for all that is not human. (This is not entirely accurate. "Human resources" have become a major part of the modern technocratic apparatus, apparently in the service of something that transcends even the human "component"—the technostructure itself.)

It will not be necessary here to elaborate the evolution of the traditional resourcist perspective at length. Its long history has been traced to at least and no doubt beyond the Greeks and the Torah and the Old Testament, through Francis Bacon, René Descartes and the Renaissance, through Calvinism and the Pilgrim Fathers, through the ages of colonialism, through the Industrial Revolution and the Protestant ethic, through the emergence of modern science and technology to multinational resource "imperialism" and the industrial growth society of our own time.[4]

One can characterize the resourcist perspective in a number of ways. It is usual to see resourcism described as interwoven with other essential elements in what is called the "dominant social paradigm" or the "consensus of perception," which is the array of beliefs, assumptions, values, and expectations ("realities") that are generally shared across a society and through which the society perceives the world.[5] The "realities" we perceive, in other words, are socially and culturally constructed.[6] One such "reality" is the total dedication of nature to the human purpose. All of nature is one vast bank of raw materials, exclusively earmarked for the human enterprise. The metaphor becomes the reality.

That, in the history of human affairs, is not a new or unique perception: it has been with us for a very long time, albeit in different forms. Up to the latter part of the nineteenth century in North America, however, it was cast and expressed largely in frontier or pioneer or rural terms, in its relationship to the advancement of settlement across the western part of the continent. In the present century, however, the focus has narrowed somewhat, and we now perceive nature chiefly in the service of *industrial* man, not preindustrial or nonindustrial or subsistence or aboriginal man. The dedication of nature is to the industrial growth society.

For the industrial society, growth is both goal and means. Since growth is measured chiefly in the production and consumption of commodities, the perceived role of nature is to subsidize an increasing flow of fabricated products. The products themselves range from the most basic essentials to the most preposterous luxuries. In this role, nature is itself a commodity. It has no meaning other than in terms of industrial use. That is the picture of nature as viewed through the shared perception or the dominant social paradigm of our society.

Hereunder, for the sake of brevity, are subsumed such industries as recreation, which commodifies wildlife (blood "sports," nature tourism, etc.) and relentlessly "resourcizes" even scenery. In this connection, the classification of land "capability" sheds revealing light on the resourcist perspective. Even wildlands are "evaluated" in our industrially biased inventories.

A resource is perceived as having intrinsic human utility. The moment a human use is perceived in any thing, that thing becomes a resource. Although there are still very many natural phenomena in the world that have not yet revealed their industrial utility, the *expectation* of utility allows the entire aggregate of nonhuman entities to be viewed as "resources for the future." The entire planet is so viewed. Recently, anxious resourcist eyes have begun to turn outward, toward space.

It was about one hundred years ago that the North American wildlife bloodbath, as epitomized by the passenger pigeon and the bison, reached its zenith. At approximately the same time, although there had been isolated and relatively unconnected murmurings for a good two hundred years, the "conservation" movement began to take form. With one or two notable individual exceptions in those early days, such as Henry David Thoreau and John Muir, the conservation movement in North America was and remains exceedingly difficult to distinguish from the mainstream of resourcism. Its core argument was and is the self-interest of human society.

Over the years, the human self-interest has been argued in a variety of ways, many of which are still in common currency. I have reviewed these in detail in a recent book, and shall briefly summarize some of them here.[7]

Wise Use: Resources for the Future

At the most simplistic level, the individual and collective conservation interest is served by the reminder, "If we can't be good, at least we can be prudent." Commonsense prudence dictates the *wise use* of resources; we must use them but we must not use them up. We must husband them. Resources, including wildlife, are there for our benefit, to be used in our best interests. If we treat them badly or stupidly, we will pay for it; if we treat them well, they are ours from which to benefit in perpetuity.

Of course we as individuals will not always be around, but our descendants will be—forever. It thus behooves us to see ourselves as *stewards* of resources, temporary custodians only; we have a duty to pass those resources on to future generations, and not to deplete them in our generation. This is a matter of common morality. Of course the morality is toward future generations of people, not toward nature.

Stewardship is also suggested in the "sustainable *harvest*" argument. In this case, it having been noticed that species of wildlife tend to deliver annually more young than their environment can support, and that many of those young do not usually survive, nature was seen as providing an annual "harvest" of wildlife that can be taken either for amusement or for profit without the taker eating into capital. Indeed if it were not taken it would be "wasted." (This is sometimes known as "dividend" conservation.) The harvest metaphor is widely used, in spite of the knowledge that there is no waste in nature, and that in years when there is surplus population of a species, that surplus is naturally "recycled" and serves to support other interdependent elements of the biological community. The fact that the arrogant concept of wildlife "harvest" is still in everyday use in our own time is testimony to the power of the resourcist paradigm, to the level of critical appraisal to which it has been put, and perhaps also to the level of critical capacity to which the resource "professions" have been trained.

The notions of husbandry, stewardship, and sustainable harvest as advanced by the conservation movement in both historical and contemporary times are all contained in the more general appeal to the self-interest which is expressed as "resources for the future." This is the central and controlling theme in modern resource "management." (In the context of wildlife at least, the latter term is singularly inappropriate. Wildlife "management" consists very largely of the setting and enforcing of upper limits to the number of animals that may be killed in a given season for fun or gain. It manages killing, not wildlife. In many cases it supplies wildlife for the killing.)

The most contemporary of conservation appeals is couched in terms of the values of nature to the advancement of science. (What is actually meant is the advancement of technology.) If we were to permit some aspect of nature to be depleted or destroyed in our own time, who knows to what extent future science may thereby have been deprived? Science might have found a use for it. Also, if we permit natural "ecosystems" to be destroyed before science has discovered how they work, then the greater endeavour of applied ecology will suffer in future. This assumes, with some good reason, that the chief goal of applied ecology is to find out how ecosphere works in order that it may then be "safely" manipulated in the interests of human progress. Here the self-interest comes into sharp relief. The safety of ecosphere is the future interest of human industrial society.

Such are some of the forms in which "wise use" conservation is advanced. The "bottom line" is the human self-interest. Treated wisely and intelligently, ecosphere can benefit both today's and tomorrow's users. Our right of access is unquestioned, but it is accompanied by a duty—not to ecosphere but to future generations of agriculturists, stewards, scientists, technicians, industrial workers, etc. The careful exploitation of ecosphere is thus not only prudent but also obligatory, in an ethical sense. Resources are human assets. There is not the slightest intrinsic interest on the part of the resources themselves, because they are human commodities.

The style of the resourcist approach being what it is, it is not surprising that the investment/dividend and waste/bankruptcy arguments are also used to call attention to the self-interest of the "non-consumptive" user of Earth resources. Also, there has emerged broad interest in "quality of life," ranging from breathable air and uncluttered scenic vistas to urban greenbelts and organized wilderness trips. Here the payoff is presented not so much in dollar or other quantitative terms, but rather in those of qualitative or experiential benefits. It is possible that in this form of conservation expression there may be room for some factor other than human self-interest, but at least in the language of conventional conservation, the resourcist perspective remains firm, as exemplified in "recreation planning" and in "heritage preservation." The proprietary bias is unchanged.

The Development Ethic

Resourcism, however, is more than the mere perception of ecosphere in a certain way. Running through the industrial growth society in its relationship with nature is the *development imperative.* This is related in a number of ways to the "necessity" of growth in the production and consumption of commodities, but its roots are very much deeper. The development "ethic" is concerned not merely with the commodification of nature, but also with its *improvement.*[8] The development ethic is about the enhancement of the planet by the hand of God through human instruments. Or, it can be seen as the necessary *domestication* of ecosphere so that all of it may be brought into fruitful and obedient production, as part of the human community. There is an inescapable fervour here, very like that which may be seen in the closely related *technology* imperative. As George Grant says, the drive is so strong because "it is carried on by men who still identify what they are doing with the liberation of mankind."[9]

The salvationist underpinnings of the development ethic are profoundly important. Ecosphere, like the individual human being, is seen as sinful, and as requiring redemption—or at the very least, as requiring "improvement" over the savage, brutish, and primitive state in which it exists without the enhancement made possible by industrial man.[10] This is the message that is drummed daily into the world's underprivileged, "underdeveloped" nations. If perceived resources are not developed to their fullest extent, then that would not only be a waste to the industrial growth society, but also it would be to have denied those parts of ecosphere their appointed destiny in the service of man, and we would have fallen short in our unique mission. Like other aspects of the resourcist paradigm, as a motivating orthodoxy, it has great power.

The development ethic is "*environment-intolerant.*" Since its sole purpose is resource consumption and its sole means is also resource consumption, its survival depends ultimately on environmental inappropriateness. Environmental "fittingness" would destroy it; fittingness implies both flexibility and compliance with things as they are or as they become. Industrial production is totally inflexible, for it can do nothing other than to consume. The mission of the development ethic, for its advancement, depends ultimately on the systematic dismantling of ecosphere.

Much of the modern rhetoric of resource conservation involves such expressions as "appropriate development," which is internally contradictory, and "eco-development," short for "ecological development." Ecology is the science of the relationships between beings and their environments; "ecological development" is quite without meaning. It is in such terms, however, that the necessary enhancement of ecosphere by the industrial growth society is justified in our time.

There is yet another aspect of the notion of "development" which has special relevance in our discussions today. Since at least Aristotelian times it has been assumed by mankind that there are greater and lesser, or higher and lower, levels of "development" in sentient beings. It is out of such assumptions that evolutionary taxonomies, and the classification process that accompanies them, are made. In a very approximate way, the assumed ladder of relative "perfection" parallels the sequence in which living beings seem to have arisen in ecosphere. Among animals, first there were invertebrates, then fishes, then amphibians and reptiles, then birds, then mammals, including man. Each stage is seen to be more "highly" developed than its predecessor.

There are echoes here of the development ethic. There are notions of perfectibility, enhancement, improvement, and (at least by implication) liberation, to say nothing of purposefulness, which latter aspect cannot be pursued here. The essence of the assumption is that the "higher" a being finds itself on the evolutionary scale, the "better" it is than those below it. An arbitrary hierarchy of relative "development" is readily translated into a hierarchy of relative *importance* in ecosphere. Again, metaphor becomes reality.

One may not be stretching the point by observing that there are on planet Earth millions upon millions of human beings who are oppressed by powerful tyrants. Most human societies are organized on principles of hierarchical power relationships. Yet no rational mind could for a moment assume that the tyrants of the world are "better" than their subordinates—at least not on the available evidence. The tyrant, however, very probably *believes* that he is superior, in some absolute sense, to his underlings.

From the moral point of view, there is little if any difference between despotism in human political affairs and the assumed hierarchy of absolute worth in ecosphere. Both conceptual and actual structures are kept in place by naked *power*, which power was in various ways either seized or assumed, but in neither instance, so far as one can determine, was the arrangement the result of relative or absolute "superiority." Both assumptions are the gratuitous fabrications of those who happen to hold the power.

Fabrication or not, however, violent and indifferent treatment of both plant life and animal life has always proceeded from this justification. Indeed, violent and indifferent treatment of some forms of human life has also proceeded from the assumption of absolute differences between races of mankind. The latter derives from a conceptual-perceptual trick known as "pseudospeciation," in which one race is viewed by another as being of a different, usually "lower" species, in precisely the same way that both races would view, for example, a dog.[11] Pseudospeciation again underscores the role of speciesism in human-nonhuman relationships.

Speciesism appears to be at the root of conceptual hierarchies of relative worth. It manifests itself in many ways, but one in particular is especially alarming. This is the assumption that "higher" forms on the evolutionary scale have more "highly developed" sensory gifts, greater sentience, deeper sensitivity.

There is of course no way of demonstrating the validity of such an assumption. No human being has yet experienced the sensory universe of a trout or a bullfrog or a grouse and returned to tell about it.

These of course are not mammals; they are fishes and amphibians and birds. Mammals are assumed to be more "highly developed," more sophisticated, more sensitive. However, in order to maintain the conceptual pyramid of relative worth it becomes necessary to subdivide the mammal class into two: man, and all others. Nonhuman mammals are thereupon deemed to have *more limited access to sensory and other experience* than the species man.[12] The logic is grotesque, the conclusion is nonsensical, and the reason for the exercise is deeply vulnerable on moral grounds.

All of these, and related perceptual-conceptual problems, flow from the cultural assumption of absolutes about the role and position of man in ecosphere. A familiar manifestation is the *necessary* "sacrifice" of nonhuman beings to the human purpose. From the same assumption of absolutes flow most of the issues with which humane societies, animal welfare associations, and nature preservationists are most concerned.

Ecophilosophy

As pointed out earlier, there has emerged an actively growing field of study loosely called "ecophilosophy." It is concerned in major part with the historical and cultural roots, and the evolutionary path, of the dominant social paradigm, including the phenomenon we have called resourcism. Ecophilosophy searches for an alternative to the prevailing shared paradigm, and it searches in particular for threads in existing human traditions which might be retrieved towards a more appropriate and more morally defensible relationship between man and ecosphere. What it must do at the outset, however, is try to describe the presently dominant consensus of perception sufficiently well to be able to understand its structure and its processes.

Many individuals have chosen to enter the problem by way of study of the "environmental" or "ecology" movement of relatively recent times. In 1973 the Norwegian philosopher Arne Naess discerned not one but two movements, which he characterized as the **"shallow" ecology** movement and the **"deep"** or long-range **ecology** movement.[13] There are elements of both in contemporary affairs, and obviously they overlap, but they constitute "two great streams of environmentalism in the twentieth century."[14] The shallow stream is seen as "reformist," the deep stream as "revolutionary." Other adjectives have been used. Shallow or reformist environmentalism has also been described as "dividend"; deep or revolutionary environmentalism as "foundational." Whatever the language, the distinction is clear. Shallow environmentalism is concerned with fine-tuning or adjusting or tinkering with, but not significantly changing, current ways of seeing things; deep environmentalism is concerned with accomplishing a fundamental "paradigm shift"—a new consensus of reality, a more environmentally appropriate way of culturally perceiving the relationship between man and nature.

One element within shallow environmentalism has already been discussed as "resource conservation." Brief mention has also been made of "resource management" and "applied ecology," as aspects of resourcism. I should like to elaborate on this briefly. A dominant paradigm is even more than a shared perceptual filter that allows most members of a society to apprehend things in essentially similar ways. It is also a *projector*. It allows a society to project upon external phenomena—as for example ecosphere—a "model" in context of which those external phenomena may then be seen and thus explained. Three models of ecosphere were offered at the outset; it may be seen as "support system," as "being," or as "home." It may then be understood in terms of those projected models. Another model that is projected upon living nature is the hierarchical pyramid of relative importance. There are more.

One of the more interesting of these, because it is intimately related to the "resource development" imperative, is the *economic* model of nature. This is one of the important tools of resource "management." By seeing ecosphere as functioning in ways analogous to a human economy, it then becomes possible to perceive all of nature as a *natural* and *necessary* element of the human economy. This process can be described as "economic outreach," an extension into ecosphere of the apparatus of the industrial growth society.[15]

In this generation, the economic model of nature has come to dominate studies of biological communities and environments. "Input-output" models abound. Donald Worster described the New Ecology, as he puts it, as emphasizing "the quantitative study of energy flows and 'ecological efficiency' in nature, using the ecosystem idea. Other terms, such as 'producers' and 'consumers,' give the New Ecology a distinctly economic cast."[16]

There are few widely-used ecology texts that do not dwell at length upon the interpretation of ecosphere as an economic community. In addition to the central importance of the "system" approach, and the ubiquitous production-consumption metaphor, we find a cost-benefit machine driven by competition, we find "strategies of ecosystem development," and such economically loaded terms as "efficiency," "productivity," and "maximization." Even the concept of "niche," which is about the role or "function" of a "component" species in an ecosystem, depends for its logical support upon the prior assumption of a competitive natural marketplace, the currency of which is energy. Again we see the relationship between metaphor and reality.

This approach to ecology, which is obviously the natural ally of resource "development" and "management," is highly visible in such enterprises as "environmental assessment" and "eco-development," among others. It is shallow environmentalism, as defined. The projection of a competitive economic "system" upon ecosphere allows the dominant paradigm to foreclose all perceptual options but one. It is an approach, as Worster says, that may well be "an alienating force, always trying to reduce nature to a mechanistic or physiochemical system with which only an economic relation is conceivable."[17]

The deep or long-range ecology movement, on the other hand, suggests that there are perceptual options, and therefore that there is potential for "paradigm shift."[18] Let me suggest just one example. It is an essential plank in the edifice of belief that evolution is now over. All of that competition and elbowing and cut-and-thrust towards "survival of the fittest" did go on in the past, to be sure. But it is now over. The purpose of evolution has now been achieved. Darwinian selection played its role in bygone days, but now we have a new situation. The old rules no longer apply. As Pierre Teilhard de Chardin mused, if the goal and the purpose of evolution were to produce mankind, then it would be irrational for the ultimate creation to thereupon become extinct.[19] That would contradict the rationale for the entire life process.

The competitive economic model of ecosphere would suggest that to have become extinct is to have been a loser. Our society has a long list of losers—the dinosaur, the dodo, Neanderthal, pagan animism, the Roman Empire, and so on. All must have been "born" losers, because all declined and fell. All became extinct. Or did they?

There are two ways of becoming extinct. One is to vanish utterly and without trace. The other is, as gracefully and compliantly as possible, to change into something new, something more appropriate and fitting to newly prevailing environmental circumstances. (This is of course another way of describing "paradigm shift.") To vanish utterly and without trace is no doubt quite unthinkable in any human society. Human societies, at any point in their careers, presumably assume that they have arrived at the pinnacle of perfection in the here and now, or at the very least that they are on the verge of it. Just one more breakthrough. To become extinct *now* would simply not make sense.

The second option—to gracefully and compliantly evolve into something more fitting to the time—seems to be almost equally repellent. At root here is the radical fear of change. It is possible to speculate that fear of change is especially prevalent in the industrial growth society because it is the society in which the imperative of *control* has reached its historic apogee.[20] The "management" ethos, a major preoccupation of our time, is about nothing so much as it is about control. What evolution seems to be about, however, is *change*—

change in directions indicated by external forces and events. Compliance with external forces and events, however, would be seen in our present society as passive submission, which is not decently thinkable within the prevailing competitive paradigm, of which the essential nucleus is the human domination of nature.

Ecospheric Egalitarianism

Yet everyone knows that change is coming. There is an exploding literature having to do with the post-industrial society, and much of deep ecology is concerned with the social and cultural options that are now beginning to be revealed. As a society we have the choice of either fighting against inevitable change or complying with it. It has been pointed out that if we do not move voluntarily to more environmentally appropriate ways, then either human totalitarianism or environmental backlash will do it for us — forcibly.[21] Such is the Hobson's choice that an unrelenting resourcist paradigm is creating for us. (Note that even this scenario says nothing of the morality of our bringing the temple down with us.)

We devote enormous time and effort to the rationalizing of our activities. Many of our most bizarre and even vicious doings — strip-mining, clear-cutting, killing for recreation, killing for frivolous products — are rationalized in terms of the greater human interest. That greater interest can be expressed in any number of ways, but its most common trappings are economic, and economic rationalizations are persuasive in our society. Certainly the law, for example, has always tended to come down firmly on the side of traditional economic freedoms. But even those can change.

The current Canadian constitutional experience is illustrative. The Charter of Rights, it is said, will force the Supreme Court of Canada to no longer restrict itself to the interpretation of existing law. In view of the new Charter, it is now going to have to *make* law. And it will have to make law on *moral* grounds, because morality is what the Charter is all about. That is going to represent a basic and fundamental shift in the perception of the relationship between moral and legal principles in Canada.

Morality, in other words, can and does play a part in public affairs. And it is a shift towards morality — albeit on a much more significant scale — that deep ecology suggests. The shift must be away from resourcism and despotism, and towards *ecospheric egalitarianism*. Just as legislation of any Charter of Rights must await the development of a widely-based public moral consciousness with respect to individual human freedoms, so the shift towards ecospheric egalitarianism must await a widely-based human *ecological consciousness* with respect to the morality of individual species freedoms.[22]

The intellectual and philosophical frameworks for ecological consciousness exist, as demonstrated by historic and more recent thinking. The moral implications of course take longer to enter the social interpretation of reality, and the legal consequences take very much longer still, but the foundation has been laid, and awaits the scaffolding. What the scaffolding is going to have to look like is less uncertain than it used to be.

NOTES

1. "Resourcism" has been widely discussed of late, together with its close kin "scientism." See especially Theodore Roszak, *Where the Wasteland Ends* (Garden City: Doubleday, 1972); David Ehrenfeld, *The Arrogance of Humanism* (New York: Oxford University Press, 1978).
2. Peter Singer, *Animal Liberation* (New York: Avon Books, 1977).
3. Paul Shepard and Daniel McKinley (eds.), *The Subversive Science* (Boston: Houghton Mifflin, 1969), p. 7.
4. Two of the earlier contributions were: William Leiss, *The Domination of Nature* (New York: Brazilier, 1972); John A. Livingston, *One Cosmic Instant* (Toronto: McClelland and Stewart, 1973). A very considerable body of literature is developing. See especially: *Ecophilosophy* newsletter [published by Professor George Sessions, Philosophy Department, Sierra College, Rocklin, California, USA 95677], and Bill Devall, "The Deep Ecology Movement," *Natural Resources Journal*, vol. 20, no. 2 (April 1980).
5. Problems of the social "paradigm" and "paradigm shift" have been widely discussed since the exploration of the nature of scientific change in Thomas Kuhn, *The Structure of Scientific Revolutions*, 2nd edition (Chicago: University of Chicago Press, 1970).
6. Peter L. Berger and Thomas Luckmann, *The Social Construction of Reality* (Garden City: Doubleday, 1966).
7. John A. Livingston, *The Fallacy of Wildlife Conservation* (Toronto: McClelland and Stewart, 1981), pp. 24–63.
8. The "development ethic" is discussed in John A. Livingston, *Arctic Oil* (Toronto: Canadian Broadcasting Corporation, 1981), pp. 118–123. In its relation to technology, see George Grant, *Technology and Empire* (Toronto: House of Anansi, 1969).
9. Grant, op. cit., p. 27.
10. Livingston, *Arctic*, op. cit., p. 120.
11. Joseph W. Meeker, *The Comedy of Survival* (New York: Charles Scribner's Sons, 1974), pp. 70–72, 143. The term "pseudospeciation" was coined in Eric Erikson, "The Ontogeny of Ritualization in Man," *Philosophical Transactions of the Royal Society*, 772 (1966), 251B, pp. 337–349, and is discussed in Konrad Lorenz, "Knowledge, Belief, and Freedom," in Paul Weiss, *Hierarchically Organized Systems* (New York: Hafner, 1971), p. 248.
12. This "argument" is the assumption that underlies virtually all rationalizations in the defence of vivisection, "factory farming," wildlife "harvests," and other activities

involving the physical and psychological suffering of nonhuman sentient beings, at any scale.

13. Arne Naess, "The Shallow and the Deep, Long-Range Ecology Movements: A Summary," *Inquiry* (Oslo), vol. 16, 1973, pp. 95–100.
14. Devall, op. cit.
15. Livingston, *Arctic*, op. cit., p. 124.
16. Donald Worster, *Nature's Economy: The Roots of Ecology* (Sierra Club Books, 1977).
17. Worster, op. cit., p. 314.
18. Devall, op. cit.
19. The thought runs through much of Teilhard's work. See Pierre Teilhard de Chardin, *The Phenomenon of Man* (New York: Harper and Row, 1959), and *Man's Place in Nature* (New York: Harper and Row, 1966).
20. The problem of control is discussed in Livingston, *Fallacy*, op. cit., pp. 68–87.
21. William Ophuls, *Ecology and the Politics of Scarcity* (San Francisco: W.H. Freeman, 1977).
22. George Sessions, "Ecological Consciousness and Paradigm Change," in Michael Tobias (ed.), *Humanity and Radical Will* (Avant Books, 1981).

In our final selection, Canadian philosopher William Leiss demurs. What makes this short and outspoken piece so interesting is the very clear and incisive way in which Leiss states a number of objections to the whole idea of environmental ethics that one suspects must be held, though not so articulately, by many people. Note the interesting point that Leiss does not seem to be especially pleased at finding himself forced to advocate his particular position.

INSTRUMENTAL RATIONALITY, THE DOMINATION OF NATURE, AND WHY WE DO NOT NEED AN ENVIRONMENTAL ETHIC

William Leiss

These remarks will be a counterpoint to John Livingston's. I used to hold views similar to his, but no longer—although I would *rather* hold such views. The views expressed here differ considerably from those I published a couple of years ago, including an essay that sought to derive an ethic of conservation from the concept of caring.[1]

I will state these points in the form of theses, so as to emphasize their provisional nature. The first thesis is that the purpose of enlightened action on environmental matters is to preserve and enhance the quality of life for human agents and human agents alone. The first sub-thesis is that perceived human interests are the sole criteria for action; for although it can be shown, I believe, as a matter of rational insight, that other entities *have* inherent or intrinsic interest, i.e., interests of their own, it is impossible for us to know what they are or to be able to represent them. The second sub-thesis is that pristine physical environments as well as existing plant and animal species will be preserved only to the extent that they are perceived to be important to the quality of human life—as the requirements for maintaining it are understood at any particular moment—and not for their own sake.

The second thesis follows from what I understand the meaning of an environmental ethic to be, and the thesis is that we do not need an environmental ethic. (My thesis is dependent on my understanding of what is implied by the term "ethic"; I must confess that the study of ethics was not one of my strong points during the years leading to my doctorate in philosophy.) I understand an environmental ethic to entail necessarily some conception of a community of beings, or community of interests, encompassing more than the human species alone—for example, a community of beings based on the property of sentience. I have trouble with this notion because—as I understand ethical systems—they require, for the most part, a reciprocal mutual recognition by moral agents of the rights and obligations shared by them (excepting only special cases, such as infants in human societies). Such reciprocal acknowledgement of equal ethical standing is impossible for any group of beings wider than the human species.

I *do not* conclude from this that it would be a matter of indifference whether or not, for example, we inflict unnecessary suffering on nonhuman species. But I don't believe that there is any sensible way to say that our duty to refrain from inflicting unnecessary suffering on nonhuman species is based upon a reciprocal obligation of the same nature. I do not see the sense in saying that we owe any obligation to nature as such, for example, the duty to "enhance the beautiful" or to implement the principle of functional diversity—except as anything of this sort is of importance to us in terms of human interest. This is because I accept, because I think we must accept, the fundamental axiom of modern society, the axiom of instrumental rationality and all that follows from it.

From the viewpoint of our modern, science-based civilization, nothing is sacred and nothing can be sacred. *Everything* is instrumental. Now of course there are and have been other human societies based on radically different axioms; many do and did function on the basis of some belief in a community of beings that was wider than the members of the human species itself, including for example animal spirits, the spirits of place, and so on. Those are very worthy forms of existence, and perhaps the grave troubles experienced now by the human species began when it departed from such modes of existence. But we cannot follow that route. In other words, we cannot suddenly elect to reinstate what is fundamentally inconsistent with a science-based civilization. With reference to the "oceanic feeling," I think, yes, it is certainly still with us today, either in the collective subconscious or some other part of our being. I agree with John Livingston in this respect, that it is still here, still present; but our science and technology are at war with it and will do their very best to extirpate it — and may very well succeed in doing so.

Yet if thesis number one — that the purpose of enlightened action in environmental matters is to preserve and enhance the quality of life in human agents — is accepted, how can it be achieved? By the triumph of economism — I hate to say it, since it upsets the conclusions of one of my earlier books, *The Limits to Satisfaction*[2] — by the triumph of economism, the triumph of benefit-cost analysis; by rationalizing all interests, by bargaining among them and by achieving trade-offs, in the only way one can include all interests, namely by quantifying all of them.

I wrote a paper some time ago in which I reviewed the literature on landscape assessment, wherein the aesthetic appreciation of natural scenery is quantified as a variable in landscape planning.[3] It's a very interesting way of dealing with environmental issues, including the preservation of endangered species. From this standpoint environmental issues will be addressed when and if, and to the extent to which, they affect perceived human interests as they are articulated and made potent by various social groups. This is the mode of decision-making by revealed preference. Thus we will protect natural environments and other species if, for whatever reason, there are some citizens willing to pay for doing so.

Here I must enter a caveat. I don't believe that a society dominated by economistic decision-making based on revealed preference is an eternal or the best form of society, as the Chicago School seems to believe, or indeed that it is a stable social formation in the long run. On the contrary, I believe that it is highly unstable, and it is certainly not going to last indefinitely. And I think I know why this is the case: because economism destroys, of necessity, all the interpersonal bonds on which human beings depend in a very fundamental sense. If you know something about the Chicago School of Economics, you know that they have extended the concept of revealed-preference to things like marriage, developing a conception of marriage based on the principle of exchange of services, including sexual services, as a way of exploring the allocation of time among family members.

It's a powerful theory, once one gets past its somewhat bizarre assumptions. What follows from recognizing the power of economism is that we should not try to exempt one class of issues, in this case environmental issues, from the general framework of revealed-preference behaviour. For example, attempting to use the concept of the beautiful in opposition to benefit-cost analysis for environmental protection will prove unworkable. An environmental ethic based on an aesthetic concept of the beautiful cannot fit into our general system of decision-making. But I don't think that this is a problem for us. I think we can achieve a very fine level of environmental protection by fully incorporating preferences about natural entities into a system of revealed preferences and bargaining among social interests.

If we thought it would be a good way of accomplishing this, we could use the concept of rights. We could follow up on a suggestion made ten years ago by Christopher Stone to confer rights on all natural entities. The legal system already has, he suggested, through the principle of guardianship, the means by which we can do this, if we think we can get a better decision-making forum in this way.[4] It's not an insuperable obstacle. But we shouldn't pretend that we have anything other than human interests in mind when we are doing so. So, for example, in the famous case of the TVA Tellico dam and the possible extinction of the snail darter fish species in the U.S., it would be very easy to achieve enhanced environmental protection by this means. One may in the end conclude that the TVA has to have its dam, since it has a preponderant interest, but the TVA may have to build a separate stream for the snail darter somewhere else. The fish species doesn't have a right to its original habitat—nothing has a right to its original habitat—but it may have a right to exist, if we decide to confer that right on it.

At the basis of technological civilization, of course, there is a specific conception of the relation of nature and humanity, and that conception is the domination of nature. It means that in principle nothing in nature can resist the human will, that we should strive systematically to manipulate and stimulate desired conditions in ecosystems for the satisfaction of perceived interests and needs. This is the core program of a science-based society.

In concluding my remarks I would like to refer to "Norman," the basset hound in the Sony television advertisement. (In the ad Norman is ordered repeatedly to change functions on a VTR until at the behest of its master, recumbent in an armchair a short distance away; displaying increasing annoyance and some insouciance, Norman finally fetches a remote control device for the master, thus resolving the antagonism between them.) For me the ad is a sign or emblem of our fundamental condition, namely the replacement (for humanity) of mediations through natural processes by mediations through technological processes. The Sony ad is an excellent illustration of a general process whereby we seek to wrap ourselves ever more securely within our technological blanket, insulating ourselves as individuals and societies from the play of natural conditions which affect all other species. I believe this is the fundamental imperative of our society.

Some extreme versions of these tendencies are worked out in imaginary situations in the science fiction literature, where the remnants of humanity huddle inside their cities, surrounded by a devastated natural environment which is heavily polluted and unfit for habitation anymore. There is a kernel of truth in this representation of a kind of fundamental antagonism between humanity and nature. Because in a fundamental sense this domination of nature and this technological blanket are consistent with our profound sense of individual development and the dignity of the person — specifically, the feeling that we should seek security of life conditions over our lifespan, including an environment that facilitates the development of our moral and intellectual faculties.

Consider the matter in this way: Think of the long development of the human mind and sensibility from childhood onwards, over a period of twenty, thirty, or more years, as it absorbs and utilizes the heritage of civilization. This is a precious and deeply satisfying aspect of existence. Now think of the natural setting. Some creature is sunning itself with great pleasure and suddenly a predator pounces on it and gobbles it up. Think of this in relation to the long development of human sensibility: For thirty or forty years one has worked on the development of a cultured sensibility, and then one goes out for a walk and becomes some other creature's evening repast. It doesn't make sense; it isn't right. The natural conditions affecting all other species are unacceptable to us, and we should say so. I regard consciousness and nature as irreconcilably antagonistic entities. I expect that we will seek to distance ourselves even further from the natural order. This will be our fundamental striving, namely that through technological advance we will seek to simulate and redesign to our liking all biological processes, so that we may achieve ever more control over the conditions of life — so that we are not dependent on Norman anymore.

This is the fundamental intention of technological civilization, namely to distance ourselves from the natural order and from the natural conditions affecting all other species, to wrap ourselves as securely as possible in a technological blanket. Whether we can succeed in developing a peaceful and enduring civilization on this basis is quite another matter. For the species as a whole, competing for space and resources in the thermonuclear age, to secure its technological civilization and to avoid destroying itself and its habitat utterly is a wager with long odds.

NOTES

1. Wm. Leiss, "A Value Basis for Conservation Policy," in *Policy Analysis: Basic Concepts and Methods*, ed. Wm. Dunn, JAI Press Inc. (Greenwich, Conn., 1986).
2. Wm. Leiss, *The Limits of Satisfaction*, Marion Boyars Pub. Ltd. (London, 1978).
3. Wm. Leiss, "Nature as Commodity: Landscape Assessment and the Theory of

Reification," in *Boston Studies in the Philosophy of Science*, ed. R.S. Cohen and M.W. Wartofsky (Dordrecht, Holland: Reidel), forthcoming.

4. C. Stone, *Should Trees Have Standing? Towards Legal Rights for Natural Objects*, Avon Books (New York, 1975).

FURTHER READING

Our first selection is from Schweitzer's autobiography (1990 [1933]). He believed that his concept of reverence for life was the key to restructuring civilization, and in his 1955 book he works this out with great thoroughness. John Livingston's recent book *Rogue Primate* (1994) is, as the title suggests, a critical examination of **humanism** itself. Another author who disputes the meaningfulness of "environmental ethics" is Janna Thompson (1990).

QUESTIONS TO CONSIDER

1. What, exactly, is "instrumental rationality"? Do you agree with Leiss that we must inevitably guide our actions by this and this alone?
2. Why is it that Schweitzer's ethic of reverence for life, in spite of its simplicity and power, has not been more influential?
3. Leiss argues that any ethical system necessarily involves "reciprocal mutual recognition by moral agents of the rights and obligations shared by them." What is a simpler way of saying this? Do you agree?
4. How can we prevent the "cautious guiding of natural forces into channels favorable to ourselves" advocated by Rachel Carson from slipping into the "arrogant resourcism" criticized by Livingston?
5. What is an "epigone"? What was the point of the remark, "We are all nothing but epigones!" quoted by Schweitzer?

CHAPTER ELEVEN

"DEEP" AND "SHALLOW" ECOLOGY

Discussions of environmental priorities among philosophers often devolve to the following question: Should we protect the environment for the sake of the environment itself, because we perceive it to have intrinsic value, or do we protect it only because it has **extrinsic value**, a value only insofar as it bears on human welfare? If the former, then we protect the environment out of a sense of duty, love, or compassion; if the latter, we protect the environment out of enlightened self-interest. And these distinctions could make a practical difference, for if we regard the environment as having value in and for itself we might be prepared to give up quite a bit more for its sake than if we regard it as having only instrumental value.

Noted Norwegian philosopher Arne Naess distinguishes these two approaches, and in so doing coins the now-familiar terms "deep" and "shallow" ecology.

IDENTIFICATION AS A SOURCE OF DEEP ECOLOGICAL ATTITUDES

Arne Naess

The Shallow and the Deep Ecological Movement

In the 1960s two convergent trends made headway: a deep ecological concern, and a concern for saving deep cultural diversity. These may be put under the general heading "deep ecology" if we view human ecology as a genuine part of general ecology. For each species of living beings there is a corresponding ecology. In what follows I adopt this terminology which I introduced in 1973 (Naess 1973).

The term *deep* is supposed to suggest explication of fundamental presuppositions of valuation as well as of facts and hypotheses. Deep ecology, therefore, transcends the limit of any particular science of today, including systems theory and scientific ecology. *Deepness of normative and descriptive premises questioned* characterize the movement.

The difference between the shallow and deep ecological movement may perhaps be illustrated by contrasting typical slogans, here formulated very roughly:[1]

Shallow Ecology	Deep Ecology
Natural diversity is valuable as a resource for us.	Natural diversity has its own (intrinsic) value.
It is nonsense to talk about value except as value for mankind.	Equating value with value for humans reveals a racial prejudice.
Plant species should be saved because of their value as genetic reserves for human agriculture and medicine.	Plant species should be saved because of their intrinsic value.
Pollution should be decreased if it threatens economic growth.	Decrease of pollution has priority over economic growth.
Third World population growth threatens ecological equilibrium.	World population at the present level threatens ecosystems but the population and behavior of industrial states more than that of any others. Human population is today excessive.
"Resource" means resource for humans.	"Resource" means resource for living beings.
People will not tolerate a broad decrease in their standard of living.	People should not tolerate a broad decrease in the quality of life but in the standard of living in overdeveloped countries.
Nature is cruel and necessarily so.	Man is cruel but not necessarily so.

Deep ecological argumentation questions both the left-hand and the right-hand slogans. But tentative conclusions are in terms of the latter.

The shallow ecological argument carries today much heavier weight in political life than the deep. It is therefore often necessary for tactical reasons to hide our deeper attitudes and argue strictly homocentrically. This colors the indispensable publication *World Conservation Strategy*.[2]

As an academic philosopher raised within analytic traditions it has been natural for me to pose the questions: How can departments of philosophy, our establishment of professionals, be made interested in the matter? What are the philosophical problems explicitly and implicitly raised or answered in the deep ecological movement? Can they be formulated so as to be of academic interest?

My answer is that the movement is rich in philosophical implications. There has, however, been only moderately eager response in philosophical institutions.

The deep ecological movement is furthered by people and groups with much in common. Roughly speaking, what they have in common concerns ways of experiencing nature and diversity of cultures. Furthermore, many share priorities of life style, such as those of "voluntary simplicity." They wish to live "lightly" in nature. There are of course differences, but until now the conflicts of philosophically relevant opinion and of recommended politics have, to a surprisingly small degree, disturbed the growth of the movement.

In what follows I introduce some sections of a philosophy inspired by the deep ecological movement. Some people in the movement feel at home with that philosophy or at least approximately such a philosophy; others feel that they, at one or more points, clearly have different value priorities, attitudes, or opinions. To avoid unfruitful polemics, I call my philosophy "Ecosophy T," using the character *T* just to emphasize that other people in the movement would, if motivated to formulate their world view and general value priorities, arrive at different ecosophies: Ecosophy "A," "B," . . . , "T," . . . , "Z."

By an "ecosophy" I here mean a philosophy inspired by the deep ecological movement. The ending *-sophy* stresses that what we modestly try to realize is wisdom rather than science or information. A philosophy, as articulated wisdom, has to be a synthesis of theory and practice. It must not shun concrete policy recommendations but has to base them on fundamental priorities of value and basic views concerning the development of our societies.[3]

Which societies? The movement started in the richest industrial societies, and the words used by its academic supporters inevitably reflect the cultural provinciality of those societies. The way I am going to say things perhaps reflects a bias in favor of analytic philosophy intimately related to social science, including academic psychology. It shows itself in my acceptance in Ecosophy T of the theory of thinking in terms of "gestalts." But this provinciality and narrowness of training does not imply criticism of contributions in terms of trends or traditions of wisdom with which I am not at home, and it does not imply an underestimation of the immense value of what artists in many countries have contributed to the movement.

Selected Ecosophical Topics

The themes of Ecosophy T which will be introduced are the following:

- The narrow self (ego) and the comprehensive Self (written with capital *S*)
- Self-realization as the realization of the comprehensive Self, not the cultivation of the ego
- The process of identification as the basic tool of widening the self and as a natural consequence of increased maturity
- Strong identification with the whole of nature in its diversity and interdependence of parts as a source of active participation in the deep ecological movement
- Identification as a source of belief in intrinsic values. The question of "objective" validity.[4]

Self-Realization, Yes, but Which Self?

When asked about *where* their self, their "I," or their ego is, some people place it in the neighborhood of the *larynx*. When thinking, we can sometimes perceive movement in that area. Others find it near their eyes. Many tend to feel that their ego, somehow, is inside their body, or identical with the whole of it, or with its functioning. Some call their ego spiritual, or immaterial and not within space. This has interesting consequences. A Bedouin in Yemen would not have an ego nearer the equator than a whale-hunting eskimo. "Nearer" implies space.

William James (1890: Chapter 10) offers an excellent introduction to the problems concerning the constitution and the limits of the self.

> The Empirical Self of each of us is all that he is tempted to call by the name of *me*. But it is clear that between what a man calls *me* and what he simply calls *mine* the line is difficult to draw. We feel and act about certain things that are ours very much as we feel and act about ourselves. Our fame, our children, the work of our hands, may be as dear to us as our bodies are, and arouse the same feelings and the same acts of reprisal if attacked. And our bodies, themselves, are they simply ours, or are they *us*?

> The body is the innermost part of *the material Self* in each of us; and certain parts of the body seem more intimately ours than the rest. The clothes come next. . . . Next, our immediate family is a part of ourselves. Our father and mother, our wife and babes, are bone of our bone and flesh of our flesh. When they die, a part of our very selves is gone. If they do anything wrong, it is our shame. If they are insulted, our anger flashes forth as readily as if we stood in their place. Our *home* comes next. Its scenes are part of our life; its aspects awaken the tenderest feelings of affection.

One of his conclusions is of importance to the concepts of self-realization: "We see then that we are dealing with a fluctuating material. The same object being sometimes treated as a part of me, at other times is simply mine, and then again as if I had nothing to do with it all."

If the term *self-realization* is applied, it should be kept in mind that "I," "me," "ego," and "self" have shifting denotations. Nothing is evident and indisputable. Even *that* we are is debatable if we make the question dependent upon answering *what* we are.

One of the central terms in Indian philosophy is *ātman*. Until this century it was mostly translated with "spirit," but it is now generally recognized that "self" is more appropriate. It is a term with similar connotations and ambiguities as those of "self"— analyzed by William James and other Western philosophers and psychologists. Gandhi represented a *maha-ātman*, a *mahatma*, a great (and certainly very wide) self. As a term for a kind of metaphysical maximum self we find *ātman* in *The Bhagavadgita*.

Verse 29 of Chapter 6 is characteristic of the truly great *ātman*. The Sanskrit of this verse is not overwhelmingly difficult and deserves quotation ahead of translations.

> *sarvabhūtastham ātmānam*
> *sarvabhutāni cā'tmani*
> *Itsate yogayuktātmā*
> *sarvatra samadarśanah*

Radhakrisnan: "He whose self is harmonized by yoga seeth the Self abiding in all beings and all beings in Self; everywhere he sees the same."

Eliot Deutsch: "He whose self is disciplined by yoga sees the Self abiding in all beings and all beings in the Self; he sees the same in all beings."

Juan Mascaró: "He sees himself in the heart of all beings and he sees all beings in his heart. This is the vision of the Yogi of harmony, a vision which is ever one."

Gandhi: "The man equipped with *yoga* looks on all with an impartial eye, seeing *Atman* in all beings and all beings in *Atman*."

Self-realization in its absolute maximum is, as I see it, the mature experience of oneness in diversity as depicted in the above verse. The minimum is the self-realization by more or less consistent egotism—by the narrowest experience of what constitutes one's self and a maximum of alienation. As empirical beings we dwell somewhere in between, but increased maturity involves increase of the wideness of the self.

The self-realization maximum should not necessarily be conceived as a mystical or meditational state. "By meditation some perceive the Self in the self by the self; others by the path of knowledge and still others by the path of works (*karma-yoga*) [*Gita*: Chapter 13, verse 24]. Gandhi was a *karma-yogi*, realizing himself through social and political action.

The terms *mystical union* and *mysticism* are avoided here for three reasons: First, strong mystical traditions stress the dissolution of individual selves into a nondiversified supreme whole. Both from cultural and ecological point of view diversity and individuality are essential. Second, there is a strong terminological trend within scientific communities to associate mysticism with vagueness and confusion.[5] Third, mystics tend to agree that mystical consciousness is rarely sustained under normal, everyday conditions. But strong, wide identification *can* color experience under such conditions.

Gandhi was only marginally concerned with "nature." In his *ashram* poisonous snakes were permitted to live inside and outside human dwellings. Anti-poison medicines were frowned upon. Gandhi insisted that trust awakens trust, and that snakes have the same right to live and blossom as the humans (Naess, 1974).

The Process of Identification

How do we develop a wider self? What kind of process makes it possible? One way of answering these questions: There is a process of ever-widening identification and ever-narrowing alienation which widens the self. The self is as comprehensive as the totality of our identifications. Or, more succinctly: Our Self is that with which we identify. The question then reads: How do we widen identifications?

Identification is a spontaneous, non-rational, but not irrational, process through which *the interest or interests of another being are reacted to as our own interest or interests*. The emotional tone of gratification or frustration is a consequence carried over from the other to oneself: joy elicits joy, sorrow sorrow. Intense identification obliterates the experience of a distinction between *ego* and *alter*, between me and the sufferer. But only momentarily or intermittently: If my fellow being tries to vomit, I do not, or at least not persistently, try to vomit. I recognize that we are different individuals.

The term *identification, in the sense used here*, is rather technical, but there are today scarcely any alternatives. "Solidarity," and a corresponding adjective in German, "solidarisch," and the corresponding words in Scandinavian languages are very common and useful. But genuine and spontaneous solidarity with others already presupposes a process of identification. Without identification, no solidarity. Thus, the latter term cannot quite replace the former.

The same holds true of empathy and sympathy. It is a necessary, but not sufficient condition of empathy and sympathy that one "sees" or experiences something similar or identical with oneself.[6]

A high level of identification does not eliminate conflicts of interest: Our vital interests, if we are not plants, imply killing at least some other living beings. A culture of hunters, where identification with hunted animals reaches a remarkably high level, does not prohibit killing for food. But a great variety of ceremonies and rituals have the function to express the gravity of the alienating incident and restore the identification.

Identification with individuals, species, ecosystems, and landscapes results in difficult problems of priority. What should be the relation of ecosystem ethics to other parts of general ethics?

There are no definite limits to the broadness and intensity of identification. Mammals and birds sometimes show remarkable, often rather touching, intraspecies and cross-species identification. Konrad Lorenz tells of how one of his bird friends tried to seduce him, trying to push him into its little home. This presupposes a deep identification between bird and man (but also an alarming mistake of size). In certain forms of mysticism, there is an experience of identification with every life form, using this term in a wide sense. Within the deep ecological movement, poetical and philosophical expressions of such experiences are not uncommon. In the shallow ecological movement, intense and wide identification is described and explained psychologically. In the deep movement this philosophy is at least taken seriously: reality consists of wholes which we cut down rather than of isolated items which we put together. In other words: there is not, strictly speaking, a primordial causal process of identification, but one of largely unconscious alienation which is overcome in experiences of identity. To some "environmental" philosophers such thoughts seem to be irrational, even "rubbish."[7] This is, as far as I can judge, due to a too narrow conception of irrationality.

The opposite of *identification* is *alienation*, if we use these ambiguous terms in one of their basic meanings.[8]

The alienated son does perhaps what is required of a son toward his parents, but as performance of moral duties and as a burden, not spontaneously, out of joy. If one loves and respects oneself, identification will be positive, and, in what follows, the term covers this case. Self-hatred or dislike of certain of one's traits includes hatred and dislike of the beings with which one identifies.

Identification is not limited to beings which can reciprocate: Any animal, plant, mountain, ocean may induce such processes. In poetry this is articulated most impressively, but ordinary language testifies to its power as a universal human trait.

Through identification, higher level unity is experienced: from identifying with "one's nearest," higher unities are created through circles of friends, local communities, tribes, compatriots, races, humanity, life, and, ultimately, as articulated by religious and philosophic leaders, unity with the supreme whole, the "world" in a broader and deeper sense than the usual. I prefer a terminology such that the largest units are not said to comprise life *and* "the not living." One may broaden the sense of "living" so that any natural whole, however large, is a living whole.

This way of thinking and feeling at its maximum corresponds to that of the enlightened, or yogi, who sees "the same," the *atman*, and who is not alienated from anything.

The process of identification is sometimes expressed in terms of loss of self and gain of Self through "self-less" action. Each new sort of identification corresponds to a widening of the self, and strengthens the urge to further widening, furthering Self-seeking. This urge is in the system of Spinoza called *conatus in suo esse perseverare*, striving to persevere in oneself or one's being (*in se, in suo esse*). It is not a mere urge to survive, but to increase the level of *acting out* (ex) *one's own nature or essence*, and is not different from the urge toward higher levels of "freedom" (*libertas*). Under favorable circumstances, this involves wide identification.

In western social science, self-realization is the term most often used for the competitive development of a person's talents and the pursuit of an individual's specific interests (Maslow and others). A conflict is foreseen between giving self-realization high priority and cultivation of social bonds, friends, family, nation, nature. Such unfortunate notions have narrow concepts of self as a point of departure. They go together with the egoism-altruism distinction. Altruism is, according to this, a moral quality developed through suppression of selfishness, through sacrifice of one's "own" interests in favor of those of others. Thus, alienation is taken to be the normal state. Identification precludes sacrifice, but not devotion. The moral of self-sacrifice presupposes immaturity. Its relative importance is clear, in so far we all are more or less immature.

Wideness and Depth of Identification as a Consequence of Increased Maturity

Against the belief in fundamental ego-alter conflict, the psychology and philosophy of the (comprehensive) Self insist that the gradual maturing of a person *inevitably* widens and deepens the self through the process of identification.

There is no need for altruism toward those with whom we identify. The pursuit of self-realization conceived as actualization and development of the Self takes care of what altruism is supposed to accomplish. Thus, the distinction egoism-altruism is transcended.

The notion of maturing has to do with getting out what is latent in the nature of a being. Some learning is presupposed, but thinking of present conditions of competition in industrial, economic growth societies, specialized learning may inhibit the process of maturing. A competitive cult of talents does not favor Self-realization. As a consequence of the imperfect conditions for maturing as persons, there is much pessimism or disbelief in relation to the widening of the Self, and more stress on developing altruism and moral pressure.

The conditions under which the self is widened are experienced as positive and are basically joyful. The constant exposure to life in the poorest countries through television and other media contributes to the spread of the voluntary simplicity movement (Elgin, 1981). But people laugh: What does it help the hungry that you renounce the luxuries of your own country? But identification makes the efforts of simplicity joyful and there is not feeling of moral compulsion. The widening of the self implies widening perspectives, deepening experiences, and reaching higher levels of activeness (in Spinoza's sense, not as just being busy). Joy and activeness make the appeal to Self-realization stronger than appeal to altruism. The state of alienation is not joyful, and is often connected with feelings of being threatened and narrowed. The "rights" of other living beings are felt to threaten our "own" interests.

The close connection between trends of alienation and putting duty and altruism as a highest value is exemplified in the philosophy of Kant. Acting morally, we should not abstain from maltreating animals because of their sufferings, but because of its bad effect on us. Animals were to Kant, essentially, so different from human beings, that he felt we should not have any moral obligations toward them. Their unnecessary sufferings are morally indifferent and norms of altruism do not apply in our relations to them. When we decide ethically to be kind to them, it should be because of the favorable effect of kindness on us—a strange doctrine.

Suffering is perhaps the most potent source of identification. Only special social conditions are able to make people inhibit their normal spontaneous reaction toward suffering. If we alleviate suffering because of a spontaneous urge to do so, Kant would be willing to call the act "beautiful," but not moral. And his greatest admiration was, as we all know, for stars and the moral imperative, not spontaneous goodness. The history of cruelty inflicted in the name of morals has convinced me that increase of identification might achieve what moralizing cannot: beautiful actions.

Relevance of the Above for Deep Ecology

This perhaps rather lengthy philosophical discourse serves as a preliminary for the understanding of two things: first, the powerful indignation of Rachel Carson and others who, with great courage and stubborn determination, challenged authorities in the early 1960s, and triggered the international ecological movement. Second, the radical shift (see Sahlins, 1972) toward more positive appreciation of nonindustrial cultures and minorities — also in the 1960s, and expressing itself in efforts to "save" such cultures and in a new social anthropology.

The second movement reflects identification with threatened cultures. Both reactions were made possible by doubt that the industrial societies are as uniquely progressive as they usually had been supposed to be. Former haughtiness gave way to humility or at least willingness to look for deep changes both socially and in relation to nature.

Ecological information about the intimate dependency of humanity upon decent behavior toward the natural environment offered a much needed rational and economic justification for processes of identification which many people already had more or less completed. Their relative high degree of identification with animals, plants, landscapes, were seen to correspond to *factual relations* between themselves and nature. "Not man apart" was transformed from a romantic norm to a statement of fact. The distinction between man and environment, as applied within the shallow ecological movement, was seen to be illusory. Your Self crosses the boundaries.

When it was made known that the penguins, of the Antarctic might die out because of the effects of DDT upon the toughness of their eggs, there was a widespread, *spontaneous* reaction of indignation and sorrow. People who never see penguins, and who would never think of such animals as "useful" in any way, insisted that they had a right to live and flourish, and that it was our obligation not to interfere. But we must admit that even the mere appearance of penguins makes intense identification easy.

Thus, ecology helped many to know more *about themselves*. We are living beings. Penguins are too. We are all expressions of life. The fateful dependencies and interrelations which were brought to light, thanks to ecologists, made it easier for people to admit and even to cultivate their deep concern for nature, and to express their latent hostility toward the excesses of the economic growth societies.

Living Beings Have Intrinsic Value and a Right to Live and Flourish

How can these attitudes be talked about? What are the most helpful conceptualizations and slogans?

One important attitude might be thus expressed: "Every living being has a *right* to live." One way of answering the question is to insist upon the value in themselves, the autotelic value, of every living being. This opposes the notion that one may be justified in treating any living being as just a means to an end. It also generalizes the rightly famous dictum of Kant "never use a person solely as a means." Identification tells me: if *I* have a right to live, *you* have the same right.

Insofar as we consider ourselves and our family and friends to have an intrinsic value, the widening identification inevitably leads to the attribution of intrinsic value to others. The metaphysical maximum will then involve the attribution of intrinsic value to all living beings. The right to live is only a different way of expressing this evaluation.

The End of the Why's

But why has *any* living being autotelic value? Faced with the ever returning question of "why?," we have to stop somewhere. Here is a place where we well might stop. We shall admit that the value in itself is something shown in intuition. We attribute intrinsic value to ourselves and our nearest, and the validity of further identification can be contested, and *is* contested by many. The negation may, however, also be attacked through series of "whys?" Ultimately, we are in the same human predicament of having to start somewhere, at least for the moment. We must stop somewhere and treat where we then stand as a foundation.

The use of "Every living being has a value in itself" as a fundamental norm or principle does not rule out other fundamentals. On the contrary, the normal situation will be one in which several, in part conflicting, fundamental norms are relevant. And some consequences of fundamental norms *seem* compatible, but in fact are not.

The designation "fundamental" does not need to mean more than "not based on something deeper," which in practice often is indistinguishable from "not derived logically from deeper premises." It must be considered a rare case, if somebody is able to stick to one and only one fundamental norm. (I have made an attempt to work with *a model* with only one, Self-realization, in Ecosophy T.)

The Right to Live Is One and the Same, but Vital Interests of Our Nearest Have Priority of Defense

Under symbiotic conditions, there are rules which manifest two important factors operating when interests are conflicting: vitalness and nearness. The more vital interest has priority over the less vital. The nearer has priority over the more remote—in space, time, culture, species. Nearness derives its priority from our special responsibilities, obligations, and insights.

The terms used in these rules are of course vague and ambiguous. But even so, the rules point toward ways of thinking and acting which do not leave us quite helpless in the many inevitable conflicts of norms. The vast increase of consequences for life in general, which industrialization and the population explosion have brought about, necessitates new guidelines.

Examples: The use of threatened species for food or clothing (fur) may be more or less vital for certain poor, nonindustrial, human communities. For the less poor, such use is clearly ecologically irresponsible. Considering the fabulous possibilities open to the richest industrial societies, it is their responsibility to assist the poor communities in such a way that undue exploitation of threatened species, populations, and ecosystems is avoided.

It may be of vital interest to a family of poisonous snakes to remain in a small area where small children play, but it is also of vital interest to children and parents that there are no accidents. The priority rule of nearness makes it justifiable for the parents to remove the snakes. But the priority of vital interest of snakes is important when deciding where to establish the playgrounds.

The importance of nearness is, to a large degree, dependent upon vital interests of communities rather than individuals. The obligations within the family keep the family together; the obligations within a nation keep it from disintegration. But if the nonvital interests of a nation, or a species, conflict with the vital interests of another nation, or of other species, the rules give priority to the "alien nation" or "alien species."

How these conflicts may be straightened out is of course much too large a subject to be treated even cursorily in this connection. What is said only points toward the existence of rules of some help (for further discussion, see Naess [1979]).

Intrinsic Values

The term "objectivism" may have undesirable associations, but value pronouncements within the deep ecological movement imply what in philosophy is often termed "value objectivism" as opposed to value subjectivism, for instance, "the emotive theory of value." At the time of Nietzsche there was in Europe a profound movement toward separation of value as a genuine aspect of reality, on a par with scientific, "factual" descriptions. Value tended to be conceived as something projected by man into a completely value-neutral reality. The *Tractatus Philosophico-Logicus* of the early Wittgenstein expresses a well-known variant of this attitude. It represents a unique trend of *alienation of value* if we compare this attitude with those of cultures other than our technological-industrial society.

The professional philosophical debate on value objectivism, which in different senses—according to different versions, posits positive and negative values independent of value for human subjects—is of course very intricate. Here I shall only point out some kinds of statements within the deep ecological movement which imply value objectivism in the sense of intrinsic value:

- Animals have value in themselves, not only as resources for humans.
- Animals have a right to live even if of no use to humans.
- We have no right to destroy the natural features of this planet.
- Nature does not belong to man.
- Nature is worth defending, whatever the fate of humans.
- A wilderness area has a value independent of whether humans have access to it.

In these statements, something *A* is said to have a value independent of whether *A* has a value for something else, *B*. The value of *A* must therefore be said to have a value inherent in *A*. *A* has *intrinsic value*. This does not imply that *A has* value for *B*. Thus *A* may have, and usually does have, both intrinsic and extrinsic value.

Subjectivistic arguments tend to take for granted that a subject is somehow implied. There "must be" somebody who performs the valuation process. For this subject, something may have value.

The burden of proof lies with the subjectivists insofar as naive attitudes lack the clear-cut separation of value from reality and the conception of value as something projected by man into reality or the neutral facts by a subject.

The most promising way of defending intrinsic values today is, in my view, to take gestalt thinking seriously. "Objects" will then be defined in terms of gestalts, rather than in terms of heaps of things with external relations and dominated by forces. This undermines the subject-object dualism essential for value subjectivism.

Outlook for the Future

What is the outlook for growth of ecological, relevant identification and of policies in harmony with a high level of identification?

A major nuclear war will involve a setback of tremendous dimensions. Words need not be wasted in support of that conclusion. But continued militarization is a threat: It means further domination of technology and centralization.

Continued population growth makes benevolent policies still more difficult to pursue than they already are. Poor people in megacities do not have the opportunity to meet nature, and shortsighted policies which favor increasing the number of poor are destructive. Even a small population growth in rich nations is scarcely less destructive.

The economic policy of growth (as conceived today in the richest nations of all times) is increasingly destructive. It does not *prevent* growth of identification but makes it politically powerless. This reminds us of the possibility of significant *growth* of identification in the near future.

The increasing destruction plus increasing information about the destruction is apt to elicit strong feelings of sorrow, despair, desperate actions, and tireless efforts to save what is left. With the forecast that more than a million species will die out before the year 2000 and most cultures be done away with, identification may grow rapidly among a minority.

At the present about 10% to 15% of the populace of some European countries are in favor of strong policies in harmony with the attitudes of identification. But this percentage may increase without major changes of policies. So far as I can see, the most probable course of events is continued devastation of conditions of life on this planet, combined with a powerless upsurge of sorrow and lamentation.

What actually happens is often wildly "improbable," and perhaps the strong anthropocentric arguments and wise recommendations of *World Conservation Strategy* (1980) will, after all, make a significant effect.

NOTES

1. For survey of the main themes of the shallow and the deep movement, see Naess (1973); elaborated in Naess (1981). See also the essay of G. Sessions in Schultz (1981) and Devall (1979). Some of the 15 views as formulated and listed by Devall would perhaps more adequately be described as part of "Ecosophy D" (D for Devall!) than as parts of a common deep ecology platform.
2. Commissioned by The United Nations Environmental Programme (UNEP) which worked together with the World Wildlife Fund (WWF). Published 1980. Copies available through IUNC, 1196 Gland, Switzerland. In India: Department of Environment.
3. This aim implies a synthesis of views developed in the different branches of philosophy—ontology, epistemology, logic, methodology, theory of value, ethics, philosophy of history, and politics. As a philosopher the deep ecologist is a "generalist."
4. For comprehensive treatment of Ecosophy T, see Naess (1981, Chapter 7).
5. See Passmore (1980). For a reasonable, unemotional approach to "mysticism," see Stahl (1975).
6. For deeper study more distinctions have to be taken into account. See, for instance, Scheler (1954) and Mercer (1972).

7. See, for instance, the chapter "Removing the Rubbish" in Passmore (1980).
8. The diverse uses of the term *alienation* (*Entfremdung*) has an interesting and complicated history from the time of Rousseau. Rousseau himself offers interesting observations of how social conditions through the process of alienation make *amour de soi* change into *amour propre.* I would say: How the process of maturing is hindered and self-love hardens into egotism instead of softening and widening into Self-realization.

REFERENCES

Elgin, Duane. 1981. *Voluntary Simplicity*, New York: William Morrow.

James, William. 1890. *The Principles of Psychology*. New York: Chapter 10: The Consciousness of Self.

Köhler, W. 1938. *The Place of Value in a World of Facts.* New York: On thinking in terms of gestalts.

Meeker, Joseph W. 1980. *The Comedy of Survival.* Los Angeles: Guild of Tutor's Press.

Mercer, Philip. 1972. *Sympathy and Ethics.* Oxford: The Clarendon Press. Discusses forms of identification.

Naess, A. 1973. "The Shallow and the Deep, Long Range Ecology Movement," *Inquiry* 16: (95–100).

———. 1974. *Gandhi and Group Conflict.* 1981, Oslo: Universitetsforlaget.

———. 1979. "Self-realization in Mixed Communities of Humans, Bears, Sheep and Wolves," *Inquiry*, Vol. 22 (pp. 231–241).

———. 1981. *Ekologi, samhälle och livsstil. Utkast til en ekosofi.* Stockholm: LTs förlag.

Passmore, John. 1980. *Man's Responsibility for Nature.* 2nd ed., London: Duckworth.

Rodman, John. 1980. "The Liberation of Nature," *Inquiry* 20: (83–145).

Sahlins, Marshall. 1972. *Stone Age Economics.* Chicago: Aldine.

Scheler, Max. 1954. *The Nature of Sympathy*. London: Routledge & Kegan Paul.

Schultz, Robert C. and J.D. Hughes (eds.). 1981. *Ecological Consciousness.* University Press of America.

Schumacher, E.F. 1974. *The Age of Plenty: A Christian View*. Edinburgh: Saint Andrew Press.

Sessions, George. 1981. *Ecophilosophy* (mimeo), Department of Philosophy, Sierra College, Rocklin, CA. Survey of literature expressing attitudes of deep ecology.

Stahl, Frits. 1975. *Exploring Mysticism*. Berkeley: University of California Press.

Stone, Christopher D. 1974. *Should Trees Have Standing?* Los Altos, CA: Kaufmann.

World Conservation Strategy. 1980. Prepared by the International Union for Conservation of Nature and Natural Resources (IUCN).

Indian ecologist Ramachandra Guha suggests that the deep/shallow distinction may be essentially beside the point. Guha's paper has evoked some controversy.

RADICAL AMERICAN ENVIRONMENTALISM AND WILDERNESS PRESERVATION: A THIRD WORLD CRITIQUE

Ramachandra Guha

Even God dare not appear to the poor man except in the form of bread.
– Mahatma Gandhi

I. Introduction

The respected radical journalist Kirkpatrick Sale recently celebrated "the passion of a new and growing movement that has become disenchanted with the environmental establishment and has in recent years mounted a serious and sweeping attack on it—style, substance, systems, sensibilities and all."[1] The vision of those whom Sale calls the "New Ecologists"—and what I refer to in this article as deep ecology—is a compelling one. Decrying the narrowly economic goals of mainstream environmentalism, this new movement aims at nothing less than a philosophical and cultural revolution in human attitudes toward nature. In contrast to the conventional lobbying efforts of environmental professionals based in Washington, it proposes a militant defence of "Mother Earth," an unflinching opposition to human attacks on undisturbed wilderness. With their goals ranging from the spiritual to the political, the adherents of deep ecology span a wide spectrum of the American environmental movement. As Sale correctly notes, this emerging strand has in a matter of a few years made its presence felt in a number of fields: from academic philosophy (as in the journal *Environmental Ethics*) to popular environmentalism (for example, the group Earth First!).

In this article I develop a critique of deep ecology from the perspective of a sympathetic outsider. I critique deep ecology not as a general (or even a foot soldier) in the continuing struggle between the ghosts of Gifford Pinchot and John Muir over control of the U.S. environmental movement, but as an outsider to these battles. I speak admittedly as a partisan, but of the environmental movement in India, a country with an ecological diversity comparable to the U.S., but with a radically dissimilar cultural and social history.

My treatment of deep ecology is primarily historical and sociological, rather than philosophical, in nature. Specifically, I examine the cultural rootedness of a philosophy that likes to present itself in universalistic terms. I make two main arguments: first, that deep ecology is uniquely American, and despite superficial similarities in rhetorical style, the social and political goals of radical environmentalism in other cultural contexts (e.g., West Germany and India) are quite different; second, that the social consequences of putting deep ecology into practice on a worldwide basis (what its practitioners are aiming for) are very grave indeed.

II. The Tenets of Deep Ecology

While I am aware that the term *deep ecology* was coined by the Norwegian philosopher Arne Naess, this article refers specifically to the American variant.[2] Adherents of the deep ecological perspective in this country, while arguing intensely among themselves over its political and philosophical implications, share some fundamental premises about human-nature interactions. As I see it, the defining characteristics of deep ecology are fourfold:

First, deep ecology argues that the environmental movement must shift from an "anthropocentric" to a "**biocentric**" perspective. In many respects, an acceptance of the primacy of this distinction constitutes the litmus test of deep ecology. A considerable effort is expended by deep ecologists in showing that the dominant motif in Western philosophy has been anthropocentric—i.e., the belief that man and his works are the center of the universe—and conversely, in identifying those lonely thinkers (Leopold, Thoreau, Muir, Aldous Huxley, Santayana, etc.) who, in assigning man a more humble place in the natural order, anticipated deep ecological thinking. In the political realm, meanwhile, establishment environmentalism (shallow ecology) is chided for casting its arguments in human-centered terms. Preserving nature, the deep ecologists say, has an intrinsic worth quite apart from any benefits preservation may convey to future human generations. The anthropocentric-biocentric distinction is accepted as axiomatic by deep ecologists, it structures their discourse, and much of the present discussion remains mired within it.

The second characteristic of deep ecology is its focus on the preservation of unspoilt wilderness—and the restoration of degraded areas to a more pristine condition—to the relative (and sometimes absolute) neglect of other issues on the environmental agenda. I later identify the cultural roots and portentous consequences of this obsession with wilderness. For the moment, let me indicate three distinct sources from which it springs. Historically, it represents a playing out of the preservationist (read *radical*) and utilitarian (read *reformist*) dichotomy that has plagued American environmentalism since the turn of the century. Morally, it is an imperative that follows from the biocentric perspective; other species of plants and animals, and nature itself, have an intrinsic right to exist. And finally, the preservation of wilderness also turns on a scientific argument—viz., the value of biological diversity in stabilizing ecological regimes and in retaining a gene pool for future generations. Truly radical policy proposals have been put forward by deep ecologists on the basis of these arguments. The influential poet Gary Snyder, for example, would like to see a 90 percent reduction in human populations to allow a restoration of pristine environments, while others have argued forcefully that a large portion of the globe must be immediately cordoned off from human beings.[3]

Third, there is a widespread invocation of Eastern spiritual traditions as forerunners of deep ecology. Deep ecology, it is suggested, was practiced both by major religious traditions and at a more popular level by "primal" peoples in non-Western settings. This complements the search for an authentic lineage in Western thought. At one level, the task is to recover those dissenting voices within the Judeo-Christian tradition; at another, to suggest that religious traditions in other cultures are, in contrast, dominantly if not exclusively "biocentric" in their orientation. This coupling of (ancient) Eastern and (modern) ecological wisdom seemingly helps consolidate the claim that deep ecology is a philosophy of universal significance.

Fourth, deep ecologists, whatever their internal differences, share the belief that they are the "leading edge" of the environmental movement. As the polarity of the shallow/deep and anthropocentric/biocentric distinctions makes clear, they see themselves as the spiritual, philosophical, and political vanguard of American and world environmentalism.

III. Toward a Critique

Although I analyze each of these tenets independently, it is important to recognize, as deep ecologists are fond of remarking in reference to nature, the interconnectedness and unity of these individual themes.

(1) Insofar as it has begun to act as a check on man's arrogance and ecological hubris, the transition from an anthropocentric (human-centered) to a biocentric (humans as only one element in the ecosystem) view in both religious and scientific traditions is only to be welcomed.[4] What is unacceptable are the radical conclusions drawn by deep ecology, in particular, that intervention in nature should be guided primarily by the need to preserve biotic integrity rather than by the needs of humans. The latter for deep ecologists is anthropocentric, the former biocentric. This dichotomy is, however, of very little use in understanding the dynamics of environmental degradation. The two fundamental ecological problems facing the globe are (i) overconsumption by the industrialized world and by urban elites in the Third World and (ii) growing militarization, both in a short-term sense (i.e., ongoing regional wars) and in a long-term sense (i.e., the arms race and the prospect of nuclear annihilation). Neither of these problems has any tangible connection to the anthropocentric-biocentric distinction. Indeed, the agents of these processes would barely comprehend this philosophical dichotomy. The proximate causes

of the ecologically wasteful characteristics of industrial society and of militarization are far more mundane: at an aggregate level, the dialectic of economic and political structures, and at a micro-level, the life style choices of individuals. These causes cannot be reduced, whatever the level of analysis, to a deeper anthropocentric attitude toward nature; on the contrary, by constituting a grave threat to human survival, the ecological degradation they cause does not even serve the best interests of human beings! If my identification of the major dangers to the integrity of the natural world is correct, invoking the bogy of anthropocentricism is at best irrelevant and at worst a dangerous obfuscation.

(2) If the above dichotomy is irrelevant, the emphasis on wilderness is positively harmful when applied to the Third World. If in the U.S. the preservationist/ utilitarian division is seen as mirroring the conflict between "people" and "interests," in countries such as India the situation is very nearly the reverse. Because India is a long settled and densely populated country in which agrarian populations have a finely balanced relationship with nature, the setting aside of wilderness areas has resulted in a direct transfer of resources from the poor to the rich. Thus, Project Tiger, a network of parks hailed by the international conservation community as an outstanding success, sharply posits the interests of the tiger against those of poor peasants living in and around the reserve. The designation of tiger reserves was made possible only by the physical displacement of existing villages and their inhabitants; their management requires the continuing exclusion of peasants and livestock. The initial impetus for setting up parks for the tiger and other large mammals such as the rhinoceros and elephant came from two social groups, first, a class of ex-hunters turned conservationists belonging mostly to the declining Indian feudal elite and second, representatives of international agencies, such as the World Wildlife Fund (WWF) and the International Union for the Conservation of Nature and Natural Resources (IUCN), seeking to transplant the American system of national parks onto Indian soil. In no case have the needs of the local population been taken into account, and as in many parts of Africa, the designated wildlands are managed primarily for the benefit of rich tourists. Until very recently, wildlands preservation has been identified with environmentalism by the state and the conservation elite; in consequence, environmental problems that impinge far more directly on the lives of the poor — e.g., fuel, fodder, water shortages, soil erosion, and air and water pollution — have not been adequately addressed.[5]

Deep ecology provides, perhaps unwittingly, a justification for the continuation of such narrow and inequitable conservation practices under a newly acquired radical guise. Increasingly, the international conservation elite is using the philosophical, moral, and scientific arguments used by deep ecologists in advancing their wilderness crusade. A striking but by no means atypical example is the recent plea by a prominent American biologist for the takeover of large portions of the globe by the author and his scientific colleagues. Writing in a prestigious scientific forum, the *Annual Review of Ecology and Systematics*, Daniel Janzen argues that only biologists have the competence to decide how the tropical landscape should be used. As "the representatives of the natural world," biologists are "in charge of the future of tropical ecology," and only they have the expertise and mandate to "determine whether the tropical agroscape is to be populated only by humans, their mutualists, commensals, and parasites, or whether it will also contain some islands of the greater nature—the nature that spawned humans, yet has been vanquished by them." Janzen exhorts his colleagues to advance their territorial claims on the tropical world more forcefully, warning that the very existence of these areas is at stake: "if biologists want a tropics in which to biologize, they are going to have to buy it with care, energy, effort, strategy, tactics, time, and cash."[6]

This frankly imperialist manifesto highlights the multiple dangers of the preoccupation with wilderness preservation that is characteristic of deep ecology. As I have suggested, it seriously compounds the neglect by the American movement of far more pressing environmental problems within the Third World. But perhaps more importantly, and in a more insidious fashion, it also provides an impetus to the imperialist yearning of Western biologists and their financial sponsors, organizations such as the WWF and IUCN. The wholesale transfer of a movement culturally rooted in American conservation history can only result in the social uprooting of human populations in other parts of the globe.

(3) I come now to the persistent invocation of Eastern philosophies as antecedent in point of time but convergent in their structure with deep ecology. Complex and internally differentiated religious traditions—Hinduism, Buddhism, and Taoism—are lumped together as holding a view of nature believed to be quintessentially biocentric. Individual philosophers such as the Taoist Lao Tzu are identified as being forerunners of deep ecology. Even an intensely political, pragmatic, and Christian influenced thinker such as Gandhi has been accorded a wholly undeserved place in the deep ecological pantheon. Thus the Zen teacher Robert Aitken Roshi makes the strange claim that Gandhi's thought was not human-centered and that he practiced an embryonic form of deep ecology which is "traditionally Eastern and is found with differing emphasis in Hinduism, Taoism and in Theravada and Mahayana Buddhism."[7] Moving away from the realm of high philosophy and scriptural religion, deep ecologists make the further claim that at the level of material and spiritual practice "primal" peoples subordinated themselves to the integrity of the biotic universe they inhabited.

I have indicated that this appropriation of Eastern traditions is in part dictated by the need to construct an authentic lineage and in part a desire to present deep ecology as a universalistic philosophy. Indeed, in his substantial and quixotic biography of John Muir, Michael Cohen goes so far as to suggest that Muir was the "Taoist of the [American] West."[8] This reading of Eastern traditions is selective and does not bother to differentiate between alternate (and changing) religious and cultural traditions; as it stands, it does considerable violence to the historical record. Throughout most recorded history the characteristic form of human activity in the "East" has been a finely tuned but nonetheless conscious and dynamic manipulation of nature. Although mystics such as Lao Tzu did reflect on the spiritual essence of human relations with nature, it must be recognized that such ascetics and their reflections were supported by a society of cultivators whose relationship with nature was a far more *active* one. Many agricultural communities do have a sophisticated knowledge of the natural environment that may equal (and sometimes surpass) codified "scientific" knowledge; yet, the elaboration of such traditional ecological knowledge (in both material and spiritual contexts) can hardly be said to rest on a mystical affinity with nature of a deep ecological kind. Nor is such knowledge infallible; as the archaeological record powerfully suggests, modern Western man has no monopoly on ecological disasters.

In a brilliant article, the Chicago historian Ronald Inden points out that this romantic and essentially positive view of the East is a mirror image of the scientific and essentially pejorative view normally upheld by Western scholars of the Orient. In either case, the East constitutes the Other, a body wholly separate and alien from the West; it is defined by a uniquely spiritual and nonrational "essence," even if this essence is valorized quite differently by the two schools. Eastern man exhibits a spiritual dependence with respect to nature—on the one hand, this is symptomatic of his prescientific and backward self, on the other, of his ecological wisdom and deep ecological consciousness. Both views are monolithic, simplistic, and have the characteristic effect—intended in one case, perhaps unintended in the other—of denying agency and reason to the East and making it the privileged orbit of Western thinkers.

The two apparently opposed perspectives have then a common underlying structure of discourse in which the East merely serves as a vehicle for Western projections. Varying images of the East are raw material for political and cultural battles being played out in the West; they tell us far more about the Western commentator and his desires than about the "East." Inden's remarks apply not merely to Western scholarship on India, but to Orientalist constructions of China and Japan as well:

> Although these two views appear to be strongly opposed, they often combine together. Both have a similar interest in sustaining the Otherness of India. The holders of the dominant view, best exemplified in the past in imperial administrative discourse (and today probably by that of "development economics"), would place a traditional, superstition-ridden India in a position of perpetual tutelage to a modern, rational West. The adherents of the romantic view, best exemplified academically in the discourses of Christian liberalism and analytic psychology, concede the realm of the public and impersonal to the positivist. Taking their succour not from governments and big business, but from a plethora of religious foundations and self-help institutes, and from allies in the "consciousness industry," not to mention the important industry of tourism, the romantics insist that India embodies a private realm of the imagination and the religious which modern, western man lacks but needs. They, therefore, like the positivists, but for just the opposite reason, have a vested interest in seeing that the Orientalist view of India as "spiritual," "mysterious," and "exotic" is perpetuated.[9]

(4) How radical, finally, are the deep ecologists? Notwithstanding their self-image and strident rhetoric (in which the label "shallow ecology" has an opprobrium similar to that reserved for "social democratic" by Marxist-Leninists), even within the American context their radicalism is limited and it manifests itself quite differently elsewhere.

To my mind, deep ecology is best viewed as a radical trend within the wilderness preservation movement. Although advancing philosophical rather than aesthetic arguments and encouraging political militancy rather than negotiation, its practical emphasis — viz., preservation of unspoilt nature — is virtually identical. For the mainstream movement, the function of wilderness is to provide a temporary antidote to modern civilization. As a special institution within an industrialized society, the national park "provides an opportunity for respite, contrast, contemplation, and affirmation of values for those who live most of their lives in the workaday world."[10] Indeed, the rapid increase in visitations to the national parks in postwar America is a direct consequence of economic expansion. The emergence of a popular interest in wilderness sites, the historian Samuel Hays points out, was "not a throwback to the primitive, but an integral part of the modern standard of living as people sought to add new 'amenity' and 'aesthetic' goals and desires to their earlier preoccupation with necessities and conveniences."[11]

Here, the enjoyment of nature is an integral part of the consumer society. The private automobile (and the life style it has spawned) is in many respects the ultimate ecological villain, and an untouched wilderness the prototype of ecological harmony; yet, for most Americans it is perfectly consistent to drive a thousand miles to spend a holiday in a national park. They possess a vast, beautiful, and sparsely populated continent and are also able to draw upon the natural resources of large portions of the globe by virtue of their economic and political dominance. In consequence, America can simultaneously enjoy the material benefits of an expanding economy and the aesthetic benefits of unspoilt nature. The two poles of "wilderness" and "civilization" mutually coexist in an internally coherent whole, and philosophers of both poles are assigned a prominent place in this culture. Paradoxically as it may seem, it is no accident that Star Wars technology and deep ecology both find their fullest expression in that leading sector of Western civilization, California.

Deep ecology runs parallel to the consumer society without seriously questioning its ecological and socio-political basis. In its celebration of American wilderness, it also displays an uncomfortable convergence with the prevailing climate of nationalism in the American wilderness movement. For spokesmen such as the historian Roderick Nash, the national park system is America's distinctive cultural contribution to the world, reflective not merely of its economic but of its philosophical and ecological maturity as well. In what Walter Lippman called the American century, the "American invention of national parks" must be exported worldwide. Betraying an economic determinism that would make even a Marxist shudder, Nash believes that environmental preservation is a "full stomach" phenomenon that is confined to the rich, urban, and sophisticated. Nonetheless, he hopes that "the less developed nations may eventually evolve economically and intellectually to the point where nature preservation is more than a business."[12]

The error which Nash makes (and which deep ecology in some respects encourages) is to equate environmental protection with the protection of wilderness. This is a distinctively American notion, borne out of a unique social and environmental history. The archetypal concerns of radical environmentalists in other cultural contexts are in fact quite different. The German Greens, for example, have elaborated a devastating critique of industrial society which turns on the acceptance of environmental limits to growth. Pointing to the intimate links between industrialization, militarization, and conquest, the Greens argue that economic growth in the West has historically rested on the economic and ecological exploitation of the Third World. Rudolf Bahro is characteristically blunt:

> The working class here [in the West] is the richest lower class in the world. And if I look at the problem from the point of view of the whole of humanity, not just from that of Europe, then I must say that the metropolitan working class is the worst exploiting class in history. . . . What made poverty bearable in eighteenth or nineteenth-century Europe was the prospect of escaping it through exploitation of the periphery. But this is no longer a possibility, and continued industrialism in the Third World will mean poverty for whole generations and hunger for millions.[13]

Here the roots of global ecological problems lie in the disproportionate share of resources consumed by the industrialized countries as a whole *and* the urban elite within the Third World. Since it is impossible to reproduce an industrial monoculture worldwide, the ecological movement in the West must begin by cleaning up its own act. The Greens advocate the creation of a "no growth" economy, to be achieved by scaling down current (and clearly unsustainable) consumption levels.[14] This radical shift in consumption and production patterns requires the creation of alternate economic and political structures — smaller in scale and more amenable to social participation — but it rests equally on a shift in cultural values. The expansionist character of modern Western man will have to give way to an ethic of renunciation and self-limitation, in which spiritual and communal values play an increasing role in sustaining social life. This revolution in cultural values, however, has as its point of departure an understanding of environmental processes quite different from deep ecology.

Many elements of the Green program find a strong resonance in countries such as India, where a history of Western colonialism and industrial development has benefited only a tiny elite while exacting tremendous social and environmental costs. The ecological battles presently being fought in India have as their epicenter the conflict over nature between the subsistence and largely rural sector and the vastly more powerful commercial-industrial sector. Perhaps the most celebrated of these battles concerns the **Chipko** (Hug the Tree) **movement**, a peasant movement against deforestation in the Himalayan foothills. Chipko is only one of several movements that have sharply questioned the nonsustainable demand being placed on the land and vegetative base by urban centers and industry. These include opposition to large dams by displaced peasants, the conflict between small artisan fishing and large-scale trawler fishing for export, the countrywide movements against commercial forest operations, and opposition to industrial pollution among downstream agricultural and fishing communities.[15]

Two features distinguish these environmental movements from their Western counterparts. First, for the sections of society most critically affected by environmental degradation—poor and landless peasants, women, and tribals—it is a question of sheer survival, not of enhancing the quality of life. Second, and as a consequence, the environmental solutions they articulate deeply involve questions of equity as well as economic and political redistribution. Highlighting these differences, a leading Indian environmentalist stresses that "environmental protection per se is of least concern to most of these groups. Their main concern is about the use of the environment and who should benefit from it."[16] They seek to wrest control of nature away from the state and the industrial sector and place it in the hands of rural communities who live within that environment but are increasingly denied access to it. These communities have far more basic needs, their demands on the environment are far less intense, and they can draw upon a reservoir of cooperative social institutions and local ecological knowledge in managing the "commons"—forests, grasslands, and the waters—on a sustainable basis. If colonial and capitalist expansion has both accentuated social inequalities and signaled a precipitous fall in ecological wisdom, an alternate ecology must rest on an alternate society and polity as well.

This brief overview of German and Indian environmentalism has some major implications for deep ecology. Both German and Indian environmental traditions allow for a greater integration of ecological concerns with livelihood and work. They also place a greater emphasis on equity and social justice (both within individual countries and on a global scale) on the grounds that in the absence of social regeneration environmental regeneration has very little chance of succeeding. Finally, and perhaps most significantly, they have escaped the preoccupation with wilderness preservation so characteristic of American cultural and environmental history.[17]

IV. A Homily

In 1958, the economist J.K. Galbraith referred to overconsumption as the unasked question of the American conservation movement. There is a marked selectivity, he wrote, "in the conservationist's approach to materials consumption. If we are concerned about our great appetite for materials, it is plausible to seek to increase the supply, to decrease waste, to make better use of the stocks available, and to develop substitutes. But what of the appetite itself? Surely this is the ultimate source of the problem. If it continues its geometric course, will it not one day have to be restrained? Yet in the literature of the resource problem this is the forbidden question. Over it hangs a nearly total silence."[18]

The consumer economy and society have expanded tremendously in the three decades since Galbraith penned these words; yet his criticisms are nearly as valid today. I have said "nearly," for there are some hopeful signs. Within the environmental movement several dispersed groups are working to develop ecologically benign technologies and to encourage less wasteful life styles. Moreover, outside the self-defined boundaries of American environmentalism, opposition to the permanent war economy is being carried on by a peace movement that has a distinguished history and impeccable moral and political credentials.

It is precisely these (to my mind, most hopeful) components of the American social scene that are missing from deep ecology. In their widely noticed book, Bill Devall and George Sessions make no mention of militarization or the movements for peace, while activists whose practical focus is on developing ecologically responsible life styles (e.g., Wendell Berry) are derided as "falling short of deep ecological awareness."[19] A truly radical ecology in the American context ought to work toward a synthesis of the appropriate technology, alternate life style, and peace movements.[20] By making the (largely spurious) anthropocentric-biocentric distinction central to the debate, deep ecologists may have appropriated the moral high ground, but they are at the same time doing a serious disservice to American and global environmentalism.[21]

NOTES

1. Kirkpatrick Sale, "The Forest for the Trees: Can Today's Environmentalists Tell the Difference," *Mother Jones* 11, no. 8 (November 1986): 26.
2. One of the major criticisms I make in this essay concerns deep ecology's lack of concern with inequalities *within* human society. In the article in which he coined the term *deep ecology*, Naess himself expresses concerns about inequalities between and within nations. However, his concern with social cleavages and their impact on resource utilization patterns and ecological destruction is not very visible in the later writings of deep ecologists. See Arne Naess, "The Shallow and the Deep, Long-Range Ecology Movement: A Summary," *Inquiry* 16 (1973): 96 (I am grateful to Tom Birch for this reference).
3. Gary Snyder, quoted in Sale, "The Forest for the Trees," p. 32. See also Dave Foreman, "A Modest Proposal for a Wilderness System," *Whole Earth Review*, no. 53 (Winter 1986–87): 42–45.
4. See, for example, Donald Worster, *Nature's Economy: The Roots of Ecology* (San Francisco: Sierra Club Books, 1977).
5. See Centre for Science and Environment, *India: The State of the Environment 1982: A Citizens Report* (New Delhi: Centre for Science and Environment, 1982): R. Sukumar, "Elephant-Man Conflict in Karnataka," in Cecil Saldanha, ed., *The State of Karnataka's Environment* (Bangalore: Centre for Taxonomic Studies, 1985). For Africa, see the brilliant analysis by Helge Kjekshus, *Ecology Control and Economic Development in East African History* (Berkeley: University of California Press, 1977).
6. Daniel Janzen, "The Future of Tropical Ecology," *Annual Review of Ecology and Systematics* 17 (1986): 305–06; emphasis added.

7. Robert Aitken Roshi, "Gandhi, Dogen, and Deep Ecology," reprinted as appendix C in Bill Devall and George Sessions, *Deep Ecology: Living as if Nature Mattered* (Salt Lake City: Peregrine Smith Books, 1985). For Gandhi's own views on social reconstruction, see the excellent three volume collection edited by Raghavan Iyer, *The Moral and Political Writings of Mahatma Gandhi* (Oxford: Clarendon Press, 1986–87).
8. Michael Cohen, *The Pathless Way* (Madison: University of Wisconsin Press, 1984), p. 120.
9. Ronald Inden, "Orientalist Constructions of India," *Modern Asian Studies* 20 (1986): 442. Inden draws inspiration from Edward Said's forceful polemic, *Orientalism* (New York: Basic Books, 1980). It must be noted, however, that there is a salient difference between Western perceptions of Middle Eastern and Far Eastern cultures respectively. Due perhaps to the long history of Christian conflict with Islam, Middle Eastern cultures (as Said documents) are consistently presented in pejorative terms. The juxtaposition of hostile and worshiping attitudes that Inden talks of applies only to Western attitudes toward Buddhist and Hindu societies.
10. Joseph Sax, *Mountains Without Handrails: Reflections on the National Parks* (Ann Arbor: University of Michigan Press, 1980), p. 42. Cf. also Peter Schmitt, *Back to Nature: The Arcadian Myth in Urban America* (New York: Oxford University Press, 1969), and Alfred Runte, *National Parks: The American Experience* (Lincoln: University of Nebraska Press, 1979).
11. Samuel Hays, "From Conservation to Environment: Environmental Politics in the United States since World War Two," *Environmental Review* 6 (1982): 21. See also the same author's book entitled *Beauty, Health and Permanence: Environmental Politics in the United States, 1955–85* (New York: Cambridge University Press, 1987).
12. Roderick Nash, *Wilderness and the American Mind*, 3rd ed. (New Haven: Yale University Press, 1982).
13. Rudolf Bahro, *From Red to Green* (London: Verso Books, 1984).
14. From time to time, American scholars have themselves criticized these imbalances in consumption patterns. In the 1950s, William Vogt made the charge that the United States, with one-sixteenth of the world's population, was utilizing one-third of the globe's resources. (Vogt, cited in E.F. Murphy, *Nature, Bureaucracy and the Rule of Property* [Amsterdam: North Holland, 1977, p. 29]). More recently, Zero Population Growth has estimated that each American consumes thirty-nine times as many resources as an Indian. See *Christian Science Monitor*, 2 March 1987.
15. For an excellent review, see Anil Agarwal and Sunita Narain, eds., *India: The State of the Environment 1984–85: A Citizens Report* (New Delhi: Centre for Science and Environment, 1985). Cf. also Ramachandra Guha, *The Unquiet Woods: Ecological Change and Peasant Resistance in the Indian Himalaya* (Berkeley: University of California Press, 1990).
16. Anil Agarwal, "Human-Nature Interactions in a Third World Country," *The Environmentalist* 6, no. 3 (1986): 167.

17. One strand in radical American environmentalism, the bioregional movement, by emphasizing a greater involvement with the bioregion people inhabit, does indirectly challenge consumerism. However, as yet bioregionalism has hardly raised the questions of equity and social justice (international, intranational, and intergenerational) which I argue must be a central plank of radical environmentalism. Moreover, its stress on (individual) *experience* as the key to involvement with nature is also somewhat at odds with the integration of nature with livelihood and work that I talk of in this paper. Cf. Kirkpatrick Sale, *Dwellers in the Land: The Bioregional Vision* (San Francisco: Sierra Club Books, 1985).
18. John Kenneth Galbraith, "How Much Should a Country Consume?" in Henry Jarrett, ed., *Perspectives on Conservation* (Baltimore: Johns Hopkins Press, 1958), pp. 91–92.
19. Devall and Sessions, *Deep Ecology*, p. 122. For Wendell Berry's own assessment of deep ecology, see his "Amplications: Preserving Wildness," *Wilderness* 50 (Spring 1987): 39–40, 50–54.
20. See the interesting recent contribution by one of the most influential spokesmen of appropriate technology—Barry Commoner, "A Reporter at Large: The Environment," *New Yorker*, 15 June 1987. While Commoner makes a forceful plea for the convergence of the environmental movement (viewed by him primarily as the opposition to air and water pollution and the institutions that generate such pollution) and the peace movement, he significantly does not mention consumption patterns, implying that "limits to growth" do not exist.
21. In this sense, my critique of deep ecology, although that of an outsider, may facilitate the reassertion of those elements in the American environmental tradition for which there is a profound sympathy in other parts of the globe. A global perspective may also lead to a critical reassessment of figures such as Aldo Leopold and John Muir, the two patron saints of deep ecology. As Donald Worster has pointed out, the message of Muir (and, I would argue, of Leopold as well) makes sense only in an American context; he has very little to say to other cultures. See Worster's review of Stephen Fox's *John Muir and His Legacy*, in *Environmental Ethics* 5 (1983): 277–81.

FURTHER READING

Zimmerman et al. (1993) presents a good selection of papers on deep ecology and offers a rejoinder to Guha without, however, reprinting his paper. Tobias (1985) contains a fascinating selection of papers, but is unfortunately hard to find now; the paper by Naess above comes from this source. See also Devall and Sessions (1985), which is very influential. Passmore (1980) is a scholarly and carefully reasoned statement of a "shallow" position that emphasizes human *responsibility*. Manes (1990) is a thorough and clear statement of the radical deep position. Lewis (1992) is an outspoken critique of radical environmentalism. See Callicott and Ames (1989) for discussions of environmental philosophy from an Asian perspective.

QUESTIONS TO CONSIDER

1. Must we really hope for enough people to identify with nonhuman nature before there is any real chance of it being saved?
2. Precisely why does Guha insist that it is an error to equate environmental protection with wilderness protection?
3. Guha cites militarism as one of the two major ecological problems we face. As an exercise, find reliable estimates for the amounts of money (roughly, of course) spent worldwide in a year on arms and on education; compare the two figures.
4. Guha quotes the following statement by Gandhi: "Even God dare not appear to the poor man except in the form of bread." What does this statement mean? (Based on classroom experience, I would say that this question is more difficult than it appears.) Why is it so suitable at the head of Guha's paper?
5. Is Leopold's land ethic a "deep" view in the sense that Naess intends?
6. Does Guha's critique of American deep ecology apply to the version of deep ecology proposed by Naess?

CHAPTER TWELVE

HUNTING, TRAPPING, AND ANIMAL RIGHTS

In this chapter, we present two contrasting views of an ethical problem that for many is very acute, the ethics of hunting and trapping. In our first selection, noted Canadian ethicist L.W. Sumner sets forth a careful analysis of the ethical propriety of the seal hunt.

THE CANADIAN HARP SEAL HUNT: A MORAL ISSUE

L.W. Sumner

The harp seal, *pagophilus groenlandicus*, is the only member of one of the thirteen genera of *phocidae* or true seals. The second most numerous seal species in the world, it is divided into three distinct breeding populations centred respectively on the White Sea, the northeast coast of Greenland, and the northwest Atlantic. The last of these three populations, by far the largest, summers in the Arctic waters of Canada and west Greenland. In the autumn it begins to migrate southward ahead of the advancing ice pack. By late December or early January the seals reach the coast of Labrador and Newfoundland, and the Gulf of St. Lawrence. In late February or early March the adult females climb onto the ice pack to give birth to their young. The pups remain on the ice for about a month before they are weaned, moult, and take to the water. During this month both the pups and the more mature seals are extensively hunted for their pelts and, to a lesser degree, their oil and meat.

Although other seal species are hunted in Canada, and although harp seals are hunted at other times of the year, the scope and resulting publicity of this annual event have given it the status of the Canadian seal hunt. The hunt is managed by the Canadian Department of Fisheries and Oceans which imposes quotas on the annual catch and enforces the provisions of the (somewhat inappropriately titled) Seal Protection Regulations.

Sealing on the east coast of Canada has a continuous history of some four centuries, but the harp seal hunt has attracted its present level of attention for only about the past two decades. During this period it has become the catalyst of an increasingly hostile annual confrontation between sealers and government officials on the one side and protesters on the other.

The propaganda war has thus far been won by neither side: the hunt continues but so do the protests. The Canadian government still maintains that the hunt does not differ materially from other common practices which elicit no comparable moral objection, while the protesters remain convinced that it is a brutal and barbaric spectacle which shames Canada in the eyes of the civilized nations.

More propaganda from either side will not break this stalemate. What is needed at this stage of the debate is an objective and rational assessment of the hunt, one which will take into account and weigh as impartially as possible all of the complex factors which bear upon its moral status. That is my project in this article. My conclusion will be that the hunt is unjustifiable and ought to be ended.

The scope of the discussion to follow will be limited to the annual harp seal hunt on the ice of the Labrador and Newfoundland coast ("the Front") and the Gulf of St. Lawrence. It will not concern itself with, and cannot be extrapolated to cover, any other seal hunt, whether it be the hunting of other species of seal (in Canada or elsewhere), the hunting of other breeding populations of harp seal, or the hunting of this breeding population at other times or in other places (e.g., by native peoples). It will also be silent on the justifiability of practices which are similar in some respects to the seal hunt: the trapping or farming of terrestrial fur-bearing animals and the rearing of domestic livestock. Each one of these further raises important moral questions of its own, questions which cannot be evaded by a nation concerned to ensure that its treatment of non-human animals is responsible and decent. But this article will address none of them.

Morality and Objectivity

Seal hunt abolitionists have tended to see the hunt in moral terms; for them it is an evil to be combatted. Retentionists have by and large been more reluctant to concede that a moral issue is involved. When they have acknowledged this fact, moreover, they have tended to make two connected mistakes, which I shall call *separatism* and *subjectivism*.

Separatism is the practice of first detaching the moral aspect of the hunt from its economic, sociological, and ecological aspects, and then treating it as just another factor to be balanced against the rest. When the various dimensions of the hunt are separated in this way the moral issue usually comes to be equated with the humaneness issue. This practice in turn encourages the conclusion that to make the hunt morally respectable it is necessary only to render its conduct more humane.

Subjectivism is the habit of labelling moral objections to the hunt as "merely subjective" or emotional. The intended contrast is between the moral dimension of the hunt and its scientific dimensions: whereas the latter are susceptible to evidence and rational argument, the former (it is assumed) is a matter only of opinion or attitude.

Separatism and subjectivism are mutually reinforcing. Once the morality of the hunt has been detached from its various factual dimensions, the way is clear for doubts about the former's objectivity. Conversely, general background suspicions concerning the rationality of moral beliefs provide a supporting reason for just such a detachment.

Separatism mislocates the moral issue of the hunt and misconstrues the structure of moral argument about the hunt. To oppose the hunt is, typically, to hold that it is morally unacceptable *because of* its relatively trivial economic contributions, its marginal role in the folkways of the fishing outports, its potentially serious impact on the harp seal population, and the suffering which it inflicts on its victims. Likewise, to defend the hunt it, typically, to hold that it is justifiable *because of* its economic and social benefits, its sound conservationist practices, and the humaneness of its slaughter techniques. In both cases a moral conclusion about the hunt is drawn from the facts of the hunt, and much of the moral controversy consists of disagreement about these facts.

The hunt's morality is thus not a further special aspect of it on the same logical footing as its scientific aspects. The partial points of view furnish the materials on which a moral assessment of the hunt, whether favourable or unfavourable, must be grounded. The moral point of view includes and supersedes all of the lower-order special points of view. The hunt does not contain a moral issue; it *is* a moral issue.

Subjectivism, on the other hand, rests on a strict dichotomy of values and facts which it then misapplies to the issues of the hunt. The misapplication emerges easily when we confine ourselves to any of the special points of view. The economic issue, for example, is not exhausted by figures concerning pelts landed, capital investment, and returns to labour. These figures are merely the materials on which we must base a judgement of the economic importance of the hunt, and *importance* is (if we accept the dichotomy) a matter of value rather than of brute fact. Likewise, statistics concerning the present size and growth rate of the breeding population confirm conclusions concerning the *overexploitation* of the population, and these too are judgements of value. Each of the special points of view generates its own special assessment of the hunt. These special assessments furnish in their turn the materials for a global moral assessment. But they are already value judgements; it cannot therefore be a distinctive feature of the moral point of view that it introduces such values.

Nor does the fact that much opposition to the hunt is indeed emotional impugn the objectivity of the moral issue. Moral problems easily engage our passions because they usually touch our lives in deep and significant ways. But the fact that we readily become emotional about such issues goes no way toward showing that they are "merely emotional" issues — whatever that could mean. There are those on both sides of the debate who present their case in a "merely emotional" manner, that is, by foregoing objective analysis and argument in favour of distortion of the facts and direct appeal to our sensibilities. But emotionalism of this sort is a feature of the presentation of the issues, not of the issues themselves.

On the contrary, there is an intimate connection between the moral point of view and the ideal of objectivity. If a moral evaluation of the hunt requires an overview which incorporates and transcends all of the special points of view, then that overview must be as balanced and impartial as possible. The subjectivist may wish to claim that in morality this ideal of objectivity is unattainable and that our belief that we sometimes attain it, or at least approach it, is an illusion. But this claim is a mere dogma until itself supported by evidence, and it is in any case a weapon which a hunt retentionist cannot safely deploy, for retentionism is itself a moral position. The most decisive response to the retentionist who takes refuge in subjectivism is, however, to show how a reasonable and considered case may be made for the abolition of the hunt.

A Moral Framework

The seal hunt, though a large-scale and complex phenomenon, is not different in kind from other human activities calling for moral assessment. In all such cases, a reasonable assessment requires adopting an impartial and objective standpoint. The requirements of such a standpoint will partially define a general evaluation procedure. Once we have such a procedure, the seal hunt becomes simply another particular case to which it can be applied. In the absence of such a general procedure we have no reason for confidence in any position on the morality of the hunt.

The requirements of impartiality are divisible into two distinct states: at the first we identify and include in our assessment all of the morally relevant features of the hunt, while at the second we combine all of these factors into an overall evaluation of the hunt. We may begin by assuming that a feature of the hunt is morally relevant if it affects the welfare of any individual or group of individuals. At this initial stage of collecting the relevant data impartiality requires that we not restrict ourselves to the hunt's implications for human welfare. Let us call *humanism* the view that in assessing the morality of a practice we need look only to its effects on human interests. Impartiality then requires that we reject humanism. The seal hunt demonstrably affects the interests of human beings, but it also demonstrably affects the interests of the seals. No moral evaluation of the hunt can count as impartial which from the outset excludes either set of effects.

Including a creature's welfare in our moral evaluation procedure is one way of recognizing the moral standing of that creature.[1] It is to treat the creature as counting or mattering in its own right, and not only because direct effects on its welfare are indirect effects on ours. It is, in one sense of that elastic notion, to assign the creature intrinsic rather than merely instrumental value. If morality has to do, at least in part, with the causing of benefits and harms then impartiality demands that we extend moral standing to all creatures capable of being benefited or harmed by our activities. Already this basic requirement is at odds, however, with the Canadian government's policy concerning the "management" of seals:

> The Canadian government's policy on seals and sealing is consistent with its policies on the management of other fishery resources. Seals are considered a natural resource available to be humanely harvested like many other species. The harvesting of this resource is permitted only within the limits of sound conservation principles, taking into account their role in the ecosystem. The government's objective is to gain the maximum socioeconomic benefits for Canadians in general and those who depend directly on the resource in particular.[2]

The objective set out in the final sentence is a clear example of humanism: the impact of sealing policy *on the seals themselves* has here dropped entirely from sight. Likewise, the policy's treatment of seals as a "natural resource" to be "managed" reduces them to the status of fossil fuels or minerals—that is, to the status of *things*. In selecting an energy policy we do not consider ourselves bound to consult the interest of oil or natural gas in addition to the human interests which will be affected. Likewise, in selecting a sealing policy (so the government is telling us) we need not consult the interests of the seals. (We might also pause here to mourn that bureaucratic debasement of the language that enables us to redescribe the slaughter of sentient animals as a "harvest.")

To be fair, the government's policy does include two constraints on the "harvesting" of seals: it must be humane and it must be "within the limits of sound conservation principles." The latter requirement presumably means that the numbers of seals killed must not endanger the species, or the breeding population. Both constraints may reflect some recognition of the independent moral standing of the seals. The conservation constraint is ambiguous on this point, since its justification might be that it would be bad *for us* if the seals became extinct, just as it might be bad for us to exhaust any non-renewable resource. The policy does not clearly acknowledge that extinction would also be bad *for the seals*, and that this fact counts against it. Only the humaneness constraint unambiguously recognizes that seals are creatures capable of suffering, and that this capacity itself imposes limits on the ways in which we may treat them. The government's policy does therefore contain some concession of the moral standing of the seals, but this concession is a minor countercurrent running against its humanist mainstream.

Impartiality requires that we include all interests, human and non-human in our moral evaluation procedure. It also requires that we assign equal weight to equal interests, human and non-human. But when *are* the interests of different species equal? A precise answer to this question may not be possible, but it is helpful to recall that, by and large, members of more developed species lead richer and fuller lives than members of less developed species. The capacity for such lives is indeed part at least of what we mean by calling some species more developed than others. It is also the principal reason most of us have for preferring to be human rather than bovine or piscine: we assume that on some absolute scale our lives are more worth living than that of cattle or fish. It follows that in determining when the interests of different species are equal we must take into consideration *inter alia* the sorts of species they are, and especially their level of development. Thus, *de facto* but not *de jure*, the interests of more developed species will count for more in the moral scales than the interests of less developed species. Vertebrates will therefore typically count for more than invertebrates, mammals for more than vertebrates, primates for more than other mammals, and human beings the most of all.

Seals are marine animals, a biological category which they share with cetaceans (whales, dolphins, porpoises), sea lions, walruses, and other related species. They are decidedly *not* fish. Yet the Canadian government persists in speaking of the "seal fishery" and in justifying its sealing policy as "consistent with its policies on the management of other fishery resources," as though seals were some exotic breed of cod or flounder. This misclassification is not as egregious as grouping seals with forest products or ferrous metals, but it is nonetheless a denial of their proper weight in the moral scales. In assessing the morality of the seal hunt we must assign the interests of seals roughly the weight which we would give in comparable cases to the interests of their closest terrestrial counterparts: dogs, wolves, otters, and bears.

The first stage of impartiality requires that we identify and include all of the interests affected by the practice whose morality is in question. Where we exploit animals the benefits of the practice are typically ours and the costs typically theirs. In the case of the seal hunt, therefore, we need to locate its principal human benefits and non-human costs. These appear to be the following:

Human Benefits
Economic: The returns to those employed in the sealing industry; benefits to consumers from the use of the seal products; the protection of the cod fishery.
Social: The role of the hunt in outport communities.

Animal Costs
Ecological: The impact of the hunt on the seal population.
Humanitarian: The suffering caused by the "harvesting" methods.

These four categories of benefits and costs capture what are commonly taken to be the main aspects of the hunt, and underline the earlier contention that these special aspects provide the materials on which a moral assessment of the hunt must be grounded.

We want to know how beneficial the seal hunt is for us and how costly it is for the seals. In reckoning the quantity of a benefit or cost—in any of the four categories—some guidelines must be kept in mind. The simplest is that it is *net* benefit or cost which matters. This is most obvious in the economic category. No economic activity is costless; from its gross returns we therefore must deduct expenses before we have an accurate measure of net gain (or loss). Luckily in this category we have a common medium in terms of which all gains and losses can be reckoned.

The quantity of a benefit or cost will in general vary with two dimensions which we may call *intensity* and *extent*. Intensity measures the importance or seriousness of the benefit or cost in the life of the individual who experiences it. Since we have no general measure of intensity, some examples will have to suffice. A principal income is generally more important than an income supplement, and necessities are generally more important than luxuries. Likewise, being killed is generally more serious than being confined, and intense suffering is more serious than mild discomfort. Extent, on the other hand, is a function of the number of individuals who experience the benefit or cost. It is, therefore, more beneficial overall to provide a given income to many individuals rather than a few, and more costly overall to kill many individuals rather than a few.

The first stage of our moral methodology has required reckoning the main benefits and costs of the seal hunt. The second stage requires balancing the former against the latter. The question at this stage is whether we are justified in obtaining these benefits (for ourselves) at these costs (for another species). In order to answer such a question we need a standard which will enable us to move from the cost/benefit balance of a practice to a moral conclusion concerning it.

This discussion will employ a standard which we may call that of *minimal decency*. A practice involving the treatment of animals *falls below* this standard if it satisfies all of the following conditions: (1) its human benefits are relatively low; (2) its animal costs are relatively high; and (3) there are alternative ways of producing comparable benefits without comparable costs.

These conditions are imprecise in their employment of qualifiers like "relatively" and "comparable," but they are exact enough for us to classify some practices as clearly rising above the standard and others as clearly falling below it. The former category contains such practices as the use of guide dogs for the blind where substantial human benefits are purchased at the price of minimal animal costs and the latter contains such practices as the poaching of rhinoceroses for the supposed aphrodisiac power of their horn, where limited (or nonexistent) human benefits are purchased at the price of high animal costs.

The moral requirement that a practice be minimally decent is very weak. A considerably stronger requirement, one which would offer a good deal more protection to animals, doubtless could be justified. It is the very weakness of the requirement, however, which gives it its force, since any practice which fails to meet it stands plainly condemned before the bar of morality. Such a practice is not one which a civilized society will wish to tolerate.

The analysis to follow will apply the standard of minimal decency to the seal hunt. The relatively indeterminate requirement of moral objectivity has thus been shaped into a reasonably clear question: Is the seal hunt minimally decent? It should now be clear why the conclusions of this discussion cannot be extrapolated to cover any other practice. The balancing required by morality must be done separately for every case, and the differences among cases may be morally relevant. It is common to hear retentionists argue that opponents of the hunt must also be opposed, say, to the rearing of domestic animals as food. This *ad hominem* rests on the assumption that the two practices are similar in all morally relevant respects. But this assumption can be neither confirmed nor disconfirmed until each practice has been analyzed in its own right. In advance of these separate inquiries we are entitled to no assumptions about connections among different cases. No such assumptions will, therefore, be made here: ours will be the modest aim of deciding what we ought to believe about one particular case.

The Hunt: Economic and Social Aspects

The economic benefits generated by the seal hunt are enjoyed primarily by two groups: employees of the sealing industry (and their dependants) and consumers of seal products. The industry is standardly divided into primary ("harvesting") and secondary (processing and marketing) sectors.[3] The primary sector employs the sealers themselves. Because the seal hunt is a seasonal event no one is a full-time sealer; the main occupation for most sealers is the east coast fishery. Sealing generates at most an income supplement for its primary participants, rather than a principal income.

In the five-year period from 1976 through 1980 the number of sealers participating in the hunt varied year to year from 5,000 to more than 7,000. Total gross income for all participants varied from $3 million to $5 million and the average return varied from $400 to $700. Sealers worked an average of about four weeks on the hunt, which contributed in 1976 an average of about seven per cent of their annual income.

These global figures, however, conceal the maldistribution of income derived from the seal hunt. Sealers are standardly divided into three groups: those working from large vessels (over 65 feet in length), those working from small vessels (between 35 and 65 feet), and landsmen. Incomes are distributed unevenly both across and within these groups. During the same five-year period large vessel sealers earned the highest average income ($2,400–$4,800, depending on the year) but formed the smallest group (190–250, about four per cent of all participants). Small vessel sealers earned average incomes varying from $1,300 to $1,900, but their numbers were also comparatively small (450–800, about nine per cent of all participants). The number of active landsmen fluctuated from 4,000 to 6,600, but they normally made up nearly 90 per cent of all participants. Their average return varied from $230 to $450.

Income is also unevenly distributed within these groups. The 1976 economic survey revealed that of the small vessel sealers (average income $1,256) over a quarter earned $200 or less while another quarter earned over $1,000. Likewise, among the landsmen (average income $232) nearly two-thirds earned $100 or less.[4] Thus while the annual totals may seem impressive, at the individual level a small number of sealers are earning a significant return while the rest gain relatively little.

These income figures are, moreover, gross rather than net. In order to gain a more accurate picture of the economic payoffs, we must therefore deduct costs incurred in the process of participating in the hunt. Again the results of the 1976 economic survey are illuminating.[5] Deduction of expenditures lowers the average of small vessel hunters by 30 per cent and those of landsmen by 50 per cent. Collectively, the small vessels actually operated at a loss.[6]

Economic returns in the secondary sector are inherently more difficult to calculate. This sector consists of such activities as the buying of landed pelts, the initial processing of pelts, the rendering of blubber into oil, and the processing of seal meat. Final processing of pelts is done outside the country. In 1976 these operations provided employment for a total of 260 people for periods ranging from three weeks to three months. In the five-year period from 1976 through 1980 total gross income in the secondary sector varied from $2.5 million to $4.2 million. No analysis of the distribution of this income is currently available.

The *added value* of the seal hunt is computed as the sum of the gross incomes which it generates in the primary and secondary sectors. This figure has varied from $5.5 million to $9.5 million during this period.[7] Most of the added value from both sectors accrues in Newfoundland, although some is realized elsewhere in the Atlantic provinces, especially in Nova Scotia. By way of some perspective on these figures, the value added annually by the seal hunt amounts to less than one-half of one per cent of the total value added annually by goods-producing industries in Newfoundland.[8] The economic returns of the industry would of course be higher if final processing of pelts were done in Canada. However, as matters now stand sealing makes only a minor marginal contribution to the economy of the province in which most of its gains are realized.

Against the economic contributions of the seal hunt must be set the costs of managing it. The Canadian government has estimated these costs as approximately $700,000 for the fiscal year 1976–77.[9] This total includes funding of research on seals, enforcement of the Seal Protection Regulations by Fisheries Officers, preparation of publications "to correct misinformation and erroneous statements about the management of Canadian seals," and headquarters costs in Ottawa. It does not include such additional costs as subsidies to the sealing industry, the operating expenses of the Committee on Seals and Sealing (which advises the government on sealing policy), the policing of coastal communities during the annual period in which sealers and protesters confront one another, and the funding of public relations campaigns designed to defend the hunt. The hunt's total costs, direct and indirect, are impossible to estimate with accuracy. If we reckon them conservatively at $1 million per annum then the economic benefits of the hunt must correspondingly be reduced by that amount.

Reckoning the gains of consumers of seal products demands some information on the nature of these products.[10] Three commodities are recovered from the bodies of the seals: pelts, blubber, and meat. Processed seal pelts are ultimately marketed as either fur or fine leather. Blubber is rendered into oil which is eventually used as lubricant or as an ingredient in soaps, cosmetics, and a variety of foodstuffs. Meat, including flippers, is either consumed fresh or marketed in frozen or canned form. Historically seals were hunted primarily for their oil, but today they are valued chiefly for their pelts. In 1976 the pelts accounted for 77 per cent of the gross receipts from landings, oil 9 per cent, and meat 14 per cent.[11] Because of quotas imposed on the hunt, and also because blubber is routinely separated from pelts during initial processing, the quantity of pelts and oil produced annually is fairly constant. Seal meat, by contrast, is decidedly a by-product of the hunt. Most of the meat recovered is consumed or sold privately; the market for frozen or canned seal meat, and for flippers, is confined to Newfoundland and is understandably limited. At least two-thirds of all carcasses are left on the ice.[12] Besides the limited commercial value of the meat, the main reason for this wastage is that seal meat is recoverable only from animals over three months old (although flippers may be removed from pups). Approximately three-quarters of the seals killed annually are, however, pups.[13] They are killed primarily for their white coats and secondarily for their blubber. Overall, it is safe to say that if there were no market for seal pelts there would be no seal hunt.

In addition to the economic benefits already canvassed, it is sometimes argued that the seal hunt aids the cod fishery by keeping the harp seal population under control. Seals do not themselves feed much on cod, but they do feed on smaller fish such as capelin which are also part of the staple diet of cod. Thus, the argument runs, the seals compete for a limited food supply and if their numbers were to expand the cod fishery would be adversely affected. Since the fishery is undeniably important to the economy of the Atlantic provinces, these adverse effects could be significant.

We will consider separately the role of the hunt in "managing" the harp seal population. Meanwhile we need only note that the fishery argument enjoys little scientific support. After a careful review of the evidence, one marine biologist reached the following conclusion:

> In reality, then, if there is a threat to the northwest Atlantic ecosystem it is not the harp seal's competing with man and cod for capelin. The most insidious threat would appear to be the possibility that rapid development of a capelin fishery . . . will adversely affect cod, harp seals and whales. . . . [14]

The alleged social benefits of the hunt derive entirely from its place in the seasonal activities of the fishing communities. The seal hunt occurs toward the end of a winter of reduced activity and before the opening of the fishing season. It thus provides an outlet for repressed energies, and for this reason has long been a tradition in some rural communities. It is impossible to quantify these contributions and difficult to separate them from the economic returns of sealing. In communities with few available opportunities even those with limited payoff may take on an importance out of proportion to their cash value. The social benefits of the hunt, like its economic benefits, are strictly relative to other opportunities available. If more such opportunities develop, as may occur with the impending oil exploration, then the importance of the hunt within the lives of these communities will correspondingly decline.

The Hunt: Ecological and Humanitarian Aspects

The task of reckoning the human benefits yielded by the hunt is facilitated by the fact that at least many of them can be measured in monetary terms. The hunt's cost for the seals themselves cannot be quantified in this way. Nonetheless, we can identify and classify these costs and also go some way toward estimating them.

To begin with the obvious, the hunt causes its victims two distinct evils: death and suffering. The death toll is the most palpable consequence. It is, indeed, a misnomer to label this event a hunt at all. It is in fact an organized slaughter, a vast open-air abbatoir. Until 1961 the slaughter was entirely unregulated; quotas were not imposed until 1971. Since 1977 the hunt has been conducted entirely under Canadian jurisdiction and the annual Total Allowable Catch (TAC) for the Front and Gulf areas remained from 1978 through 1981 at a level of 170,000 animals (it has been raised for 1982). Actual catches have been at or near the TAC in every year, and in 1981 overran it by more than 20,000 animals.

The overall quantity of a cost (or a benefit) distributed over a group of individuals is a function of its intensity and its extent. Death, unlike suffering, does not at first appear to admit of degrees of intensity. However, this appearance is misleading. Death is the loss of life; the dimension of the loss for a particular individual is determined by the quantity and quality of life which the individual would otherwise have enjoyed.[15] The average life expectancy of the harp seal is 25–30 years.[16] The younger the seal at the time of its death the more of its potential life it loses. It follows that the cost of killing a seal pup—the cost, that is, *to the victim*—must be greater, other factors equal, than the cost of killing an adult. As was noted earlier, about three-quarters of the seals killed annually are pups.

Seal lives are not human lives, but they are the lives of mammals who in sentience and intelligence are comparable to dogs or cats. While such lives may not count for as much as human lives, the impartiality which partly defines the moral point of view requires that they count for something. The extent of this loss of life is of course given by the number of victims. The seal hunt is a slaughter on an immense scale. Large numbers tend to defeat our imagination, but when we remember that each life is the life of a distinct individual then we ought to reckon the overall loss—the loss to that group as a whole—as the algebraic sum of the individual losses. In that case, the cost of the annual slaughter, in terms of death alone, is the cost of an average killing (whatever finite quantity we assign to that) multiplied by 170,000.

Killing large numbers of an animal species introduces a further consideration, for it may affect the ability of the species to maintain its numbers, and ultimately to survive. If we mean by an endangered species one threatened with imminent extinction then harp seals are not an endangered species, and the northwest Atlantic breeding population is not an endangered population. The position of the Canadian government has been that the annual TAC has been set below the level of sustainable yield, so that the breeding population will increase at a modest rate.[17] On this view, the seal hunt is consistent with "sound conservation principles" for the "management" of a wildlife species.

This claim, like most concerning the hunt, is controversial and has been hotly challenged by abolitionists. What is perhaps most impressive to a lay observer of this ecological controversy is just how little is yet known of this much-studied species.[18] A population which is both mobile and aquatic admits of no accurate census, and thus there are no reliable empirical data on the present size of the northwest Atlantic breeding population, nor on whether that population is increasing, stabilizing, or decreasing. Further, while the harp seal is not technically endangered it does possess some biological characteristics which render it vulnerable: it is a large predator with narrow habitat tolerances which reproduces once a year at a rate of one pup per dam and whose young take four or more years to reach sexual maturity. A species with these natural features cannot easily reverse a downward population spiral. Whatever its present numbers may be, everyone agrees that they are a fraction of the stock that existed before hunting began on a large scale. These facts conspire to urge a "management" policy (if we accept the legitimacy of this notion in the first place) which is cautious and conservative. They therefore suggest that the present TAC may indeed be set too high.

While the conservation issue is important, it should not be allowed to dominate our attention entirely. Its appeal is based on the fact that it takes to be an evil only what virtually everyone would concede as one, namely the extinction of a species (or a breeding population). But a species is a collection of individuals and the extinction of a species is an evil only if the lives of its individual members are goods. If those lives *are* goods then killing members of the species produces a cost regardless of whether the species is threatened with extinction. Exterminating the species of course precludes the possibility of *any* lives of this particular sort being lived again; it is a great evil in part because of its irreversibility. But it is only the extreme case which, though undeniably dramatic, should not lead us to conclude that killing animals in numbers which will not endanger the species requires no justification.

Death is but one of the two evils which the hunt imposes on its victims; the other is the suffering which may occur in the process of dying. The Seal Protection Regulations specify the methods which may be used to kill seals; among the authorized instruments those which are most popular at present are the club and hakapik. The regulations require that a seal must be rendered unconscious by a blow on the skull before it is killed by exsanguination and subsequently skinned. Signs of unconsciousness include the absence of a blinking reflex when the eye is touched. When the regulations are fully complied with the process appears to be relatively humane.[19]

How extensive, however, is full compliance? Fisheries Officers who enforce the regulations are empowered to suspend the licence of any sealer observed to be breaking them. In addition, representatives of animal welfare organizations have been allowed to observe the conduct of the hunt and have regularly reported their observations. Unfortunately, these reports conflict dramatically. According to some observers 95 per cent of all killings comply with the regulations, while according to others violations are common. Faced with this contradictory evidence, it is difficult for an outsider to determine just how humane the hunt is.

However, it is obvious that the hunt is inherently difficult to regulate. A handful of Fisheries Officers and authorized observers cannot adequately monitor the activities of six or seven thousand sealers distributed over hundreds or thousands of square miles of open ice. As was shown in the 1981 hunt, the landsmen are particularly difficult to oversee. Working conditions on the ice are far from ideal and the sealers must often work very rapidly. Under these conditions it would be miraculous if shortcuts were not taken, especially when there is slight chance of being observed. Even under the most optimistic estimate of compliance, it should be remembered, thousands of seals are skinned every year while quite possibly still conscious.

One other dimension of suffering must be noted, namely the impact on the dam of having her pup killed. Again relatively little is known about the dam-pup relationship in the harp seal, and therefore about the extent, if any, to which dams grieve the loss of their pups. Most dams flee at the approach of the sealer rather than defending the pup, and many do not return to the spot where the pup was abandoned. But some do not flee and some do return to search for the pup. We cannot therefore discount the possibility that, at least for these dams and possibly for all, the killing of their pups is a distressing experience.

Conclusions

It remains only to balance the hunt's benefits against its costs. The hunt will fail to be minimally decent if its human benefits are relatively low, its animal cost relatively high, and there are available means of generating comparable benefits without comparable costs. The incomes of sealers are both low on average and unevenly distributed, so that only a small number of workers earn a significant return. Even for the fortunate few, this is but a supplement to a primary income earned elsewhere. The sealing industry as a whole provides employment for a limited number of workers and makes a very slight contribution to the economy of the Atlantic provinces. The principal seal products, for whose sake the hunt is actually conducted, are luxuries rather than necessities, serving a market for fine furs and leathers. For the uses of seal oil as lubricants and ingredients in consumer products there are in general adequate substitutes. Seal meat, meanwhile, is not extensively recovered. The hunt is unnecessary as a "cull" to protect the east coast cod fishery. And its social benefits appear to be the product of necessity rather than genuine choice; given any viable alternative employment opportunity the outports would nicely survive without the hunt.

By any reasonable measure the hunt's animal costs are substantial. Its high annual death toll is not only a great evil in itself for the seals; it may also have adverse long-term effects on the breeding population. Further, a good deal of suffering appears to be an unavoidable by-product of the hunt. The first two conditions, therefore, are readily satisfied.

The third is less clearcut. There would, to be sure, be no serious costs to consumers if harp seal products vanished entirely from the market. We are left, therefore, with the position of those who derive an income from the hunt.[20] For many sealers there are at present few alternative employment opportunities at that time of the year. Whether the oil rigs and oil-related development will begin to furnish such opportunities is not yet clear. As matters now stand the burden of abolition of the hunt would be borne principally by the sealers themselves. Although this burden may be offset somewhat by increased unemployment benefits, it cannot be entirely ignored. Instead of immediate abolition, therefore, there may be a case for phasing the hunt out gradually over a period of a few years, reducing the TAC annually until it reaches zero. This winding down of the hunt would give those who now profit from it, however minimally, a longer lead time to seek out an alternative source of income supplement.

The seal hunt fails to meet even the weak standard of minimal decency. It exacts a high toll in death and suffering from a developed animal species for relatively slight human gains. Collectively we can forgo it at little cost to ourselves. It is therefore indecent to continue it. Canadians pride themselves on being a decent people. They refrain from other indecent practices, such as invading small and defenceless nations, waging genocidal campaigns against racial minorities, and using terror as a political weapon. In these respects they belong to a distinct minority among the world's nations. The seal hunt is not a practice in which such decent people will wish to indulge.

The case which has been made for the abolition of the hunt differs in important respects from some common abolitionist arguments. It makes no appeal whatever to the fact that harp seal pups are cuddly and attractive, or that they are innocent and defenceless, or that the sight of their blood on the ice is repellent and disturbing. These considerations have all been dismissed by retentionists as aesthetic rather than moral, or sentimental rather than rational; they have in any case played no role in the argument of this paper.[21] The argument has also rested little weight on the humaneness issue. Whether the slaughter techniques are humane, ideally or in practice, is certainly not unimportant, but the main question to ask about the hunt is not *how* the seals are killed but *why*. There can be good reasons for killing animals, perhaps even for killing large numbers of animals. But the servicing of a luxury market is the wrong reason for killing hundreds of thousands of animals. We cannot remedy the moral deficiencies of the slaughter by rendering it more humane, for its basic and irremediable fault is its very existence.

The argument has rested squarely on the assumption that in the moral scales the lives and well-being of animals must be given some weight. The immediate implication of this assumption is that the killing of animals, especially their large-scale slaughter, is a practice which requires moral justification. That justification must take the form of pointing to human benefits which are sufficiently great to offset these costs. If there are none then the practice stands condemned. The case for the abolition of the seal hunt has rested on an objective balancing of its benefits and costs. The case can be defeated only at the price of denying that animals count for something in their own right—only, that is, by reducing them to the status of things. And that is a price which no decent person will be willing to pay.

NOTES

1. For further analysis of the notion of moral standing, See L.W. Sumner, *Abortion and Moral Theory* (Princeton University Press, 1981), Sections 5 and 23.

2. Department of Fisheries and Oceans (Canada), *Canada's Policy on Seals and Sealing* (I-HQ-81-01E), p. 1.
3. The economic profile which follows has been drawn principally from John Barzdo, *International Trade in Harp and Hooded Seals* (Fauna and Flora Preservation Society, 1980); Department of Fisheries and Oceans (Canada), *The Economic Value of the Atlantic Seal Hunt* (I-HQ-80-009E) and *Historical and Sociological Perspective of Sealing* (I-HQ-81-05E); and D.L. Dunn, *Canada's East Coast Sealing Industry 1976: A Socio-Economic Review* (Fisheries and Marine Service Industry Report No. 98, 1977).
4. Dunn, op. cit., Table 2.3.
5. Ibid., Table 2.4.
6. Ibid., Tables 2.5 and 4.1.
7. I have here discarded the 1980 figure of $10.7 million value added, given in Fisheries and Oceans, *Historical and Sociological Perspective of Sealing*, p. 5, which appears to be mistaken.
8. Source for total value added: *Canada Year Book*. For the purpose of this calculation I have treated all added value from the seal hunt as though it were being realized in Newfoundland.
9. In a Briefing Note issued by the (then) Department of Fisheries and the Environment.
10. See Barzdo, op. cit.
11. Dunn, op. cit., p. 24. The 1980 figures are 76 per cent, 10 per cent, and 14 per cent respectively; see Fisheries and Oceans, *Historical and Sociological Perspective of Sealing*, p. 5.
12. Dunn, op. cit., p. 110. It should be noted that a carcass counts here as having been utilized if any part of it, including only the flippers, has been recovered.
13. Barzdo, op. cit., Tables 3 and 4.
14. D.M. Lavigne, "The Harp Seal Controversy Reconsidered," *Queen's Quarterly* 85:3 (1978), p. 382.
15. See Sumner, op. cit., Section 24.
16. David J. Coffey, *Dolphins, Whales and Porpoises: An Encyclopedia of Sea Mammals* (New York: Collier Books, 1977), p. 148.
17. Department of Fisheries and Oceans (Canada), *Harp Seal Population Assessment* (I-HQ-81-02E).
18. See Lavigne, op. cit.
19. Department of Fisheries and Oceans (Canada), *Humane Aspects of the Harp Seal Hunt* (I-HQ-81-03E).
20. The economic cost of abolishing the hunt cannot simply be identified with the value added by the hunt, since some at least of the resources presently occupied by the hunt would be reallocated to other economic activities.
21. On the other hand it is unclear why the fact that harp seals are beautiful creatures should not matter to the moral status of the hunt. Is destroying something beautiful not worse than destroying something ugly?

Discussions of ethics by professional philosophers tend to become very theoretical, perhaps excessively so at times. In the following reading, Canadian trapper David Dehaas forthrightly presents his workaday philosophy, explaining why he believes it is right and proper for him to intervene in the natural cycles of life and death. This article never fails to provoke discussion.

THE BEAVERS OF STARVATION CREEK

David Dehaas

"Let's make another pass low and down the middle," I shouted into the pilot's ear.

After a quick check through the ice-streaked window at the outside fuel gauge, he put the little plane into a tight bank that sent us thundering down the valley again.

With only a few metres between us and the unbroken undulations of snow below, the two huge beaver houses were at first hardly discernible spots in the distance, then loomed large and near for a split second before flashing past. But I'd seen what I half expected: the dark circles of vent holes indicating that these were indeed occupied houses.

"Okay?" shouted the pilot.

"Okay," I replied, waving a circle with my hand and pointing south in the general direction of the airstrip. That would do for today. We had covered in two hours all the remote and inaccessible streams and potholes shown on the topographical maps, an area that would have taken two weeks to cover on snowshoes.

As we climbed into the bright January sunshine and headed for home, the image of those two beaver houses burned in my mind, and the story they told was one of despair.

For that little valley, as far as the eye could see, showed only the tottering hulks of dead and dying trees where the water had backed up behind the dams in large stagnant ponds. On the land only the endless terraced ranks of pine and spruce climbed away from the creek's edge. Not a single white trunk stood out against the evergreens. Not a single birch or poplar was left. There could be no doubt that the inhabitants of the two beaver houses had entered into the final stage of the life cycle of the beaver colony.

They were alive, but starving to death.

I am a trapper. I love animals.

Many people find it hard to equate those two statements, and when they ask me about it, I tell the story of the beavers in that sad little five-kilometre-long stream that I've marked on my map as Starvation Creek.

I could tell the story of the muskrat swamp—where every year without fail eight out of every 10 die when the swamp freezes solid to the bottom, from epidemics that regularly sweep the lodges, from fierce territorial fighting, or simply when the food runs out. I could tell the story of the lynx I once found curled up tight in a ball under a balsam tree, dead, dead from the cold when slow starvation had eaten away its resistance to the –40s of January. I could talk about the horrors of rabies rampant in a peak fox population.

But the beavers of Starvation Creek represent perhaps the best illustration of the trapper's role in the scheme of wilderness life.

The trapline I was working in the Chapleau district lies in the very heart of Northern Ontario, about 750 kilometres north of Toronto. Its roughly rectangular boundaries enclose an area of about 150 square kilometres of some of the most rugged terrain the province has to offer. There are parts of two rivers—the Shawmere and the Ivanhoe—half a dozen fair-sized lakes, and any number of potholes, creeks, streams, and swamps.

Beaver are a major crop on the line, and because of their prolific building and breeding habits, they are also the species requiring the closest attention and most careful management.

There was every indication, however, that the territory had not been diligently or wisely worked for a good many years. That fact—and a persistent suspicion of what I might find—had set off my aerial survey. Now it was easy, very easy, to put together the whole depressing story of the beavers of Starvation Creek, a story that would end when I returned with the snowmobile and a dozen of the big new number 330 Conibear traps.

It was seven or eight, perhaps nine, years ago that a pair of young beavers had found themselves unwelcome in their home lodges. Perhaps they were forced out by the crush of new young; perhaps all the building sites had been colonized by previous generations. It could have been dwindling food, an overly aggressive male, or even an outbreak of disease. In any case and for whatever reason, they had left their natal waters to set out in search of a new home.

The migration likely took place at the spring flood when streams are rivers and gullies are streams, but there was still the better part of three kilometres of high, dry, and hostile ground to waddle across. They would have smelled the little creek in the valley and sought it out as a haven from the dangers that beset an aquatic animal on dry land.

What they found was a small and insignificant creek, its banks only a metre or two apart, which wound a few kilometres along the bottom of the valley. Alders and dogwood lined its banks and the dry ground stood thick with young poplars. The beavers plunged with relief into the safety of the stream, and, finding none of the scent posts by which beavers claim their territory, they set up a temporary home in a hollow in the bank. If the ragged outline of an ancient dam snaked across the valley, and if the rotting humps of long-dead lodges stood oddly high and dry, the ghosts were silent and no warning was taken.

Through that first summer they worked to build the dam that would turn their section of the creek into a large pond. This would serve not only as a moat to keep them safe from predators, it would also raise the water level high enough to keep the winter freeze from locking them into the lodge, and it would make large new areas of the forest accessible from the relative safety of the water.

Next came the building of a lodge, a large elevated structure in the middle of the pond, a home and a fortress for the three or four kits that would be produced in the spring.

The following year, as the kits took to the water, the dam grew higher and stronger, and ever longer. More trees were flooded out, more poplars and birch brought within reach. Then ducks came to paddle in the pond and moose paused there for the first time in many generations.

A year later another brood of young arrived, and a new lodge was built as the yearlings set out on their own. Perhaps there was a new dam downstream too.

Over the next few years the population increased rapidly, and the little stream and its valley flourished. Many birds came to nest and to feed, muskrat appeared as if from thin air, frogs sang from the verges, and all the while the beavers kept up their feverish pace—building, flooding, ever expanding.

In the sixth or seventh year, when as many as two dozen beavers called the pond their own, and the halcyon days of the little valley seemed assured and endless, the weight of change began to shift imperceptibly, the system started to overbalance, and the end became inevitable.

With the coming of the next crop of kits, the change suddenly became clear. The beavers found their room for expansion was gone. New food supplies could not be reached, the old was nearly gone. At the same time, the water in the ponds started to stagnate as the trees it had encroached upon began to rot. The ducks left; the muskrat retreated.

When in late summer the instinctive urge to pile up food for winter came, the beavers' situation was at once desperate. Some combed the banks. Every tiny sapling, every previously discarded branch, even half-chewed sticks from the dams were diligently hauled away to augment the winter hoard. But the work was unrewarding, and perilously slow. A few beavers tried to haul their feed from as far as half a kilometre away, a few others sensed the danger and set off in search of sanctuary.

Then one night, with the store of food only a fraction of that required, the ice came and all work had to cease. Five months of captivity had started, and for the beavers there was no hope.

* * *

The bottom end of Starvation Creek, where it peters out into the big swamp, lay some 25 kilometres from my base camp on the Shawmere River, and this meant that the trip in was a major expedition. It was January in the north woods where the temperature regularly dips into the −40s, and the snow lay waist-deep over the wild terrain. So I packed my gear with care onto the big sleigh: a dozen 330 Conibear traps, chainsaw, axe, tent, bedroll, food, spare gas and, just in case, the snowmobile repair kit.

I set out early in the morning. The first 10 or 12 kilometres were easy going along the well-packed trails of my regular line, but from there the route took a swing to the northwest and the going got tough. Though the snowmobile plowed through astonishing amounts of snow over terrain that would have been difficult even to walk, the trip was an arduous one. Every hill had to be snowshoed to make a trail for the snowmobile, endless tag alders had to be cut, and the chainsaw rang out at what seemed like a hundred deadfalls.

Thus the sun was already low in the western sky when the machine finally broke out of the bush and bounded ahead with a roar as it bit into the snow of the creek.

Leaving the sleigh near the first of the occupied beaver houses, I made a quick patrol up the length of the creek: no more live houses, but two rounded mounds with undisturbed snow covers that probably signalled newly dead houses. There was no point speculating on whether they were abandoned or starved out.

At the occupied houses I set to work clearing the snow, chopping holes in the ice and setting out traps in a race with the rapidly declining sun.

On a well-managed line the trapper would approach his beaver houses in a much different manner. A survey in the summer, a careful study of the amount of water, height of dams, size of houses, amount of accessible feed and even the amount of branches being wasted by the beavers would give him the information he would need to manage the beaver colony. He might decide to leave the beavers alone to expand, or he might see population pressure building and decide to remove a whole house, the breeding pair, or just the dominant male. There is no difficulty taking exactly those beavers whose removal is desired: the oldest buck is the one who investigates a breach in the dam, the breeding pair approaches the feed bed in a straight line from the lodge, the young ones circle around from behind. Simple trap placement determines the catch.

But none of these considerations concerned me. There was no question of "managing" a starving population. I was there to trap them all, except for perhaps a single pair of kits.

In two hours I had eight baited traps set beneath the half-metre ice, four at each lodge. I had scraped and frayed the sweet-smelling bark of the poplar-sapling bait cut from a hillside a kilometre away. It would draw the hungry beavers from their lodges in short order.

One by one they would enter the traps. And as they touched the triggers, the steel arms would slam around with deadly force, strike the animals squarely across the back, snap the spinal cords and write a clean, quick finish to what would otherwise have been a story of slow starvation.

Over the next two weeks I took 11 beavers from the two lodges: four adults, three yearlings, and four kits, all badly undernourished, their fur off prime and worth very little.

Why does the trapper interfere? Why did I interfere?

Man, the trapper, is a natural predator in the woods, even as the eagle and the wolf. But when the trapper roams his wilderness territory, he is more than an ordinary predator. He can decide what is right to take, and stabilize the cruel cycles of boom and crash. And he can leave the woods a better place for his coming.

Quite simply, it is the only way we know to look after the beaver.

FURTHER READING

For more on animal rights, see Singer, ed. (1985). Singer himself advocates a utilitarian basis for animal liberation. Callicott (1980) distinguishes between holistic ethics such as the land ethic, which places the whole ecosystem itself as of the highest value, and **atomistic** ethics such as Regan's, which assigns highest value to the individual animals and persons within the biological community.

QUESTIONS TO CONSIDER

1. Many readers have noted a glaring omission in Dehaas's description of the lives of the beavers, namely the complete lack of mention of the role of the normal predators of the beaver. What animals would normally prey on beaver? (This would likely vary in different regions of Ontario.) Do the beaver suffer exaggerated cycles of "boom and crash" because humans (perhaps like Dehaas) have killed off too many of the beavers' natural predators? If so, would this make any difference to Dehaas's attempt to justify his own predation?
2. Nonhuman predators such as lions and wolves can effectively be in a symbiotic relationship with their prey species even though they kill and consume individual animals, since their predation helps to maintain the prey population roughly at a level that the general environment can support. Would the kind of judicious predation advocated by Dehaas place humans in a symbiotic or mutualistic relationship with their prey? Or is this, perhaps, a sort of domestication?
3. Try to apply Sumner's method of analysis to the hunting of beaver.

CHAPTER THIRTEEN

ECOFEMINISM

One of the most vigorous and diverse approaches to the environment is the ecofeminist movement. We present here two significant but very different statements from this movement.

Ynestra King's brief but pointed critique of the deep ecologists is perhaps one of the best pieces of philosophical invective in recent years. But she has a positive point to make as well, which is to stress the urgency of her commitment to justice.

A SENSE OF URGENCY

Ynestra King

To the uninformed, "deep ecology" merely sounds like a philosophy that is more radical than "shallow environmentalism." In fact . . . deep ecologists emphasize sensibility over structure and, in a move rather like that of the ex-Marxist academic postmodernists, they reject subject, history, and human agency as inherently anti-ecological. **Ecofeminism** shares the project of other feminisms, which seek to draw on women's unarticulated (up until now) life experience to reconstitute the subject, and history, and a nondomineering agency rather than totally discard these modern (and problematic) concepts. The commitment to an ecological humanism is a crucial difference between ecofeminism and deep ecology.

Deep ecology is called by its founder, Arne Naess, "a religious and philosophical movement."... [It] ignores the structures of entrenched economic and political power within society, concentrating exclusively on self-realization and cultural transformation, taking the side of nature over culture, thereby insisting that human beings conform to the laws of nature as understood by deep ecologists. This dualistic thinking is opposed by ecofeminism and by social ecology, both of which assert that the domination of women in society precedes the domination of nonhuman nature and that we must challenge domination within society in order not only to free ourselves but to achieve our ecological objectives.

Deep ecologists have inverted the relationship of domination of people over nature into one of nature over people (which they call "biocentrism"), or, as its political arm says, "Earth First!" This maintains the idea that human beings and nonhuman nature are natural enemies. They completely ignore the fact that human beings are part of nature and evolve out of nonhuman nature, and that human beings have lived in harmony and mutual aid with one another and with nonhuman nature.

In fact . . . the ecology movement does . . . have a Malthusian wing, which claims deep ecology (with its assertion of authoritarian natural laws) as its philosophy and "Earth First!" as its practice. I would like to see [those] who uphold deep ecology address explicitly the deep insensitivity to human suffering expressed by David Foreman, a leader of the organization Earth First! in an interview with leading deep ecologist Bill Duvall. Here Foreman asserts, with no refutation from Duvall or any other deep ecologist that I know of, "The human race could go extinct and I for one would not shed any tears." He follows with, "The worse thing we could do in Ethiopia is give aid—the best thing would be to just let nature seek its own balance, to let the people there just starve there."

And if eco-triage is not enough, he sides with the Reagan Administration against Central American refugees, saying, "Likewise, letting the USA be an overflow valve for problems in Latin America is not solving a thing. It's just putting more pressure on the resources we have in the USA. It is just causing more destruction of our wilderness, more poisoning of water and air, and it isn't helping the problems in Latin America."

This resurgence of social Darwinism, recycled as eco-triage, is advocated by a bunch of guys who have set themselves up as the self-appointed protectors of another virgin—the virgin wilderness. While romancing the wild (they're very fond of backpacking in to where no man has gone before) they claim it as their own. The offensive interview cited above supposedly took place on top of a peak that had been visited by only four other persons in five years. (Obviously the fact that he could get up there gave Foreman's interview greater ecological credibility.) Foreman and his macho crowd (all self-proclaimed deep ecologists) represent nothing more than the Daniel Boone mentality in ecological drag.

The *Earth First!* newspaper, edited by Foreman, also saw fit to print an article called "Population and AIDS" (cutely written by Miss Ann Thropy) which asserts, "If radical environmentalists were to invent a disease to bring human population back to ecological sanity, it would probably be something like AIDS. . . . The only real hope of the continuance of diverse ecosystems on this planet is an enormous decline in human population" and a return to a "hunter-gatherer way of life." It goes on to say that "barring a cure, the possible benefits of this to the environment are staggering. More significantly, just as the Plague contributed to the demise of feudalism, AIDS has the potential to end industrialism, which is the main force behind the environmental crisis." The article concludes, "If the AIDS epidemic didn't exist, radical environmentalists would have to invent one."

Here one sees the political implications of a philosophy utterly bereft of compassion for human beings, with no analysis of U.S. imperialism, corporate capitalism, the debt of the Third World to the First and the enforced growing of cash crops to pay our banks as the causes of famine in the Third World and enormous suffering in Central America. And around the world, feminist research has shown that birth rates are lowest in societies with low child mortality rates, where women have economic and social power. It is pernicious and fascistic to talk about the "population problem" before one addresses the radical social, racial, and economic inequities around the world. . . .

[Ecofeminism is not] a sentimentalizing religion of earth mothers [but] rather . . . an urgent, angry critical feminist movement propelled by a powerful sense of historical urgency to end the domination of human over human in order to end the domination of people over nonhuman nature and make possible the continuation of life on earth. Our view is not that we should abolish science but that we should do it in the way that it has been done by the great women scientists Barbara McClintock and Rachel Carson, who demonstrate that there is a connection between loving and knowing—we cannot know nature or ourselves without loving both.

Stephanie Lahar's article is included here not only because it is a very fine piece of writing and analysis, but because she emphasizes the fact of the human impact on the environment, and brings out the possibility of what she calls "reciprocity"—which is perhaps what we have been calling elsewhere symbiosis or mutualism.

ROOTS: REJOINING NATURAL AND SOCIAL HISTORY

Stephanie Lahar

Social history, political history, and natural history are the three horses pulling the chariot of the study of human sociology and its relationship with the natural world.
–Richard White, *Land Use, Environment, and Social Change*

There is not a place in the world that does not reveal the touch and bear the consequences of human hands and minds—not Antarctica, not the deepest equatorial jungle, and certainly not Tokyo or New York City. At the same time, there are no people who have not been shaped by the effects of landscape and water, the climate and natural features of the area in which they live. These effects are seldom an explicit part of social and political histories, but they are readable by signs. Environments influence survival activities, necessitate closed or open constructions of shelter, which shape social interactions, and prompt understandings of connections with other life forms through predator/prey and interdependent relationships. They contain natural forces, phenomena, and objects that become the basis of religious and cultural symbols, and offer other opportunities for expressions of human creativity through interactions with the nonhuman environment. Nations and cultures have particular characters and cosmologies: compare the intense inward, religious, and artistic focus of the people of Bali, living on a small volcanic island for century after century, with individualist and acquisition-orientated white Americans, expanding their frontiers across great tracts of land ranging from coastal flats and mountains to open prairies.

Many Americans of European heritage still believe in "wilderness" and the open spaces that marked their earlier history. Seen from an airplane, however, the United States looks like a crazy quilt, with regular checkerboards of agricultural lands and planned urban areas, irregular polygons marking other urban and suburban areas and ownership boundaries, and spaghettilike swaths trailing down mountains. There are almost no areas empty of transportation corridors and dividing lines laid down by human hands with technological assistance. We do not realize how extensive the effects of our tenure on the land have been.

History has been divided into pieces like the landscape, and it is abstract and apart from us. "Natural history" is a discipline studied by environmental scientists, and "history" is an account of human events both social and political, with notable omissions of women's herstories and the cultural pasts of many other categories of people. Feminists and theorists from the relatively new and interdisciplinary fields of human ecology and environmental history have questioned and criticized from different angles the historical accounts that we have and their underlying value systems, which have written a few people, events, and ecological contexts into historical accounts and written most others out. But will reclaiming what has been left out give us a more meaningful understanding of the past? Can an ecofeminist perspective, which attempts to integrate concepts of ecology with a feminist analysis of interconnected forms of domination, contribute insights that will bring history close enough to our personal and collective experience so that lessons from the past might guide decisions that we have to make now? I believe that an integrated ecological/social context for understanding history can help change the way we think about the past and the present in necessary ways, especially if we include ourselves in the stories — embodied in a time and a place, with the past unfurling behind us and our hands and faces in the future.

Whose Social History?

If natural and social history have been divided, how has history told the stories of human beings? The major feminist critique that has been offered is that women have been made insignificant if not absent from history. Gerda Lerner explains:

> Historical scholarship, up to the most recent past, has seen women as marginal to the making of civilization and as unessential to those pursuits defined as having historical significance. . . . Thus, the recorded and interpreted past of the human race is only a partial record, in that it omits the past of half of humankind, and it is distorted, in that it tells the story from the viewpoint of the male half of humanity only.[1]

Not only have historians been men, but they have been particularly privileged men who have generally recorded events from the point of view of a small elite group. Women are not the only ones who are missing from their accounts. People of color in the West, non-Western peoples, and poor people are also absent as historical subjects. Women's invisibility as a group has, however, been central to modern critiques of history introduced by feminist theory. Many feminists have also extended a critique that starts from the absence of women's herstories to a broader socialist criticism. Adrienne Rich says that "as a woman, as a Jew, as a lesbian, I am pursued by questions of historical process, of historical responsibility, questions of historical consciousness and ignorance and what these have to do with power."[2]

What *do* these questions have to do with power and dominant value systems? Oppression and repression are sustained by individuals and institutions that are also most often sexist and heterosexist, racist and classist, as well as exploitative of the natural world. Radical feminists see the original problem as sexism; the Old and New Left see the problem as economics and government; and other progressive movements and theories point to various "isms" that interconnect, negating and distorting the past—as well as the present—in a way that is damaging to us all.

No matter what the specific focal point of the analysis, most viewpoints critical of mainstream history intersect and are complementary in making one point: history has rendered women and most non-European, nonprivileged people invisible or despicable, destroying identities and cultures. Invisibility and violence are strangely and intimately related; refusing to perceive or acknowledge another person is one end of a continuum whose other is murder and genocide. When Europeans began massive migrations in the seventeenth century into North America, Argentina, Australia, and South Africa, they did not regard the aboriginal peoples of those lands as any real obstacle to their settlement of the "New World." The indigenous people, indeed, "disappeared" through death and assimilation in a vast population replacement resulting from a complex web of ecological and social factors in which the cultural narcissism that characterized European consciousness was one part. This narcissism is not so far away as we might think: most of us can remember movie images of cowboys and Indians from our childhoods in America, and most of us cheered for the cowboys. How many socially sensitive political progressives and feminists even now know much about Native American history and culture, save for some appropriated pop ideas about Native American religion and cosmology?

We are *all* impoverished by the loss of cultural histories. When a people's past is lost, everyone's identity is diminished, paths of human possibilities are closed, reservoirs of knowledge vanish. During the Burning Times of the witch-hunts in Europe from 1300 to 1700, most of the priceless traditional knowledge about plants, healing, and folk medicine in the West died with thousands of women and men who were murdered precisely because they were the holders of this knowledge.[3]

Alongside human and cultural negations and extinctions runs the parallel of animal and plant extinctions and exploitation. Exploitation is a one-way, nonreciprocal relationship. It is exemplified in "green revolution" intensive agriculture that ruins soils, in the ivory trade's decimation of African elephants for luxury items, and in such subtle everyday practices as discharging sewage into streams and turning scarce wildlife habitat into lawns. Human exploitation of nonhuman communities is not a phenomenon confined to the modern age; the earliest major impacts of humans on the North American continent occurred in prehistoric times. Ian McHarg attributes these effects to "a tool more powerful than required, beyond [human] power to control and of enormous consequence"—huge prairie fires set to drive bison, deer, mammoth, and mastodon into closed valleys or over precipices: "It is thought that it was the combination of human hunters and a hostile climate that resulted in the extinction of this first great human inheritance in North America, the prairie herbivores. Firelike the grasses spread, firelike the herds of grazing animals swept to exploit the prairies—and it was the fire of the aboriginal hunter that hastened or accomplished their extinction."[4]

The original tool that human hunters used to alter an ecosystem is causing global alterations today as millions of acres of tropical rainforest are burned daily. Have we come so far? The quantity, scope, and consequences of contemporary environmental devastation create a situation of global crisis that is radically different from times past. Carolyn Merchant presents the ecological and social history of New England as a microcosm as she examines the compression of natural and social processes in her book *Ecological Revolutions*. What "took place in 2,500 years of European development through social evolution came to New England in a tenth of that time through revolution. . . . Today, capitalist ecological revolutions are occurring in many developing countries in a tenth of New England's transformation time."[5]

Although practices we could define as exploitative were present in very early societies, many if not most of the agricultural, hunting, and other human activities in the aboriginal cultures of North America and elsewhere seem to have been reciprocal in nature.[6] Some of the reciprocity was simply a biological byproduct of small human populations. Richard White notes how human occupation of a site often leads to enrichment of the soil: "The shells and bones, the plant refuse, the ashes from fires, the excrement of humans and animals gradually rotted and provided the surrounding soils with significant amounts of potash, phosphorous, and nitrogen."[7]

Some of the reciprocity, however, was socially structured by cosmologies, religious beliefs, and traditions that limited the taking of plants and animals and promoted practices that sustained ecological communities. For example, in the Salish Indian culture of what is now western Washington, the association of human powers with particular animals blurred the boundaries of human and animal identity, a common phenomenon in pre-modern societies. Hunting rules among the Salish included sanctions against killing young animals, killing more than could be used, and wasting meat. "Fraught not only with economic but also with religious significance, animals were not to be lightly persecuted,"

White comments. "They were to be treated with respect and were not even to be laughed at, let alone tormented or killed without need."[8]

It is tempting to conclude that aboriginal peoples, exquisitely cognizant of their place in an ecological web, possessed an intersubjective awareness of themselves and of nonhuman life that offers an alternative to the highly self-aware, blind-to-others consciousness that characterizes the most dangerous forms of modern identity. In a way this is true, but there seem to be other differences between pre-modern and modern configurations of consciousness in addition to their different relations to nature, and it would be simply impossible to return atavistically to an earlier mental attitude. There is, for example, evidence that styles and types of consciousness that developed in tribal societies were more focused on collective than individual identities. According to Donald Worster, "most who have studied ecosystem people [tribal societies subsisting on hunting, gathering, and minimal agriculture] believe that the balance between human populations and the resources of their environment is not maintained through conscious decision or overall awareness on the part of individuals."[9] Instead, sustainable relations with the nonhuman environment result from a more collective locus of identity and strong, even rigid, customs and traditions that serve to keep the group in a homeostatic relation to its environment. Sometimes stability and traditions are maintained at the cost of resilience and adaptability. This cost may be one of a complex of biological/social factors that have caused aboriginal peoples to fare so poorly when confronted with "modern" cultures from other lands.

History's Distortions from an Ecofeminist Perspective

Those who are written out of history are those who suffer at the hands of dominant groups. Invisibility and, ultimately, violence happen most easily within a short-sighted and fragmentary mindset that is isolated from the existence and needs of others, qualities that characterize a modern, reductionist, and patriarchal intellectual and scientific tradition. Modern economic systems, including but not limited to capitalism, feed cycles of alienation and abstraction as living things become commodities, monstrously erasing life and feeling. Within this tradition, pornography and vivisection are products and practices that make up our "entertainment" and routine scientific research.

Ecofeminism sees as destructive not only the perceptual distancing and isolation of different peoples from each other, but also the habits of dualistic thought that separate human society from nature. The human/nature dualism is crucial to address and redress, since it is so fundamental, underlying and undermining our relations to the world around us and to that which is embodied and unmediated within ourselves. When we set ourselves apart from nature, we disembody human experience and sever it from an organic context. This means that we stop being aware of the shapings and natural containments that a particular environment places around human practices and social structures. But of course environmental effects do not cease to exist. Instead, society is shaped by a fractured relation to the ecosystem(s) it inhabits, losing both characteristic bioregional contours and a sensibility for natural limits. Additionally, I suggest that separating ourselves from our natural heritage, which has been a central project of human civilization, also has profound psychological and social implications as it supports our nonperception of others. When we cut off a part of ourselves that we share with all other human beings and, by extension, all of life, it is easier to deny that others, or a particular other, exists.

Is it important to place *when* in the ancient past human beings began to experience personal and collective identities separately from the surrounding environment? We may read clues about the genesis of self-awareness in our cultural myths, which are fraught with ambivalence and religious fear—for example, the "fall" from grace, with its accompanying separation from a divine source of sustenance and from nature. Riane Eisler, in her popular work *The Chalice and the Blade*, suggests that the myth of the garden of Eden indicates an ancient cultural past in which people lived in nondominating partnerships with each other, cutting across gender and other differences, as well as in greater harmony with nature.[10] But perhaps the myth of the fall points to an ancient memory of our phylogeny as a species, emerging out of the oceans and savannahs; or to some primal symbolism we all derive from a sense of separation at birth. Perhaps it is the trace of a decision to take a particular path in the development of human experience made by an archaic and collective subjectivity that is the precursor of what we now recognize as our personalized consciousness.

Is there a way to know whether there were ever times and places when human beings lived in easy cooperation with each other and the nonhuman environment, without the sexist, oppressive, and exploitative complex of power relations we call patriarchy? Is seeking such times and places useful in empowering women today, by portraying model societies in which women either shared or held primary power? There has been a strong initiative in popular feminist thought to do just this, represented most prominently by the writings of Monica Sjöö and Barbara Mor, Riane Eisler and Merlin Stone. In their work a few comparatively recent societies have been presented as models, such as the Native American Iroquois nation, in which women's status in political and tribal life seems to have been near or equal to that of men. But the major focus of this search has been prehistoric human settlements in the Neolithic period.[11]

The Neolithic, or New Stone Age, was marked by the first villages, the development of animal husbandry, and the grinding and polishing of stone weapons.

Sjöö and Mor, in *The Great Cosmic Mother*, go so far as to say that the "Neolithic revolution, occurring circa 10,000 B.C., was the creation of women."[12] These authors depend heavily on interpretations of James Mellaart's archeological excavations of the city of Çatal Hüyük (c. 6500–5650 B.C.) in what is now western Turkey, and Marija Gimbutas' excavations of Vinca settlements (c. 5300–4000 B.C.) in what is now Yugoslavia. Their archeological studies yielded icons, symbols, and statues of female and woman/animal deities, and burials of women in these settlements show evidence of care and ritual treatment. Artifacts or built structures that might indicate war or defense are lacking.[13]

Feminist interpreters of Neolithic history conclude that societies were basically matriarchal (with women having power over men, the reverse of patriarchy) or matricentric (fundamentally egalitarian, but placing great value on women's activities and reproductive functions, with kinship lines traced through women). This line of thinking sees the matricentricity of Neolithic culture as a social arrangement that is not only good for women but also directly related to positive societal characteristics such as peacefulness, cooperation, and benign relations with the natural world.

"Unquestionably," says Janet Biehl, "some Neolithic societies were relatively egalitarian and organic. They may also have been matrilineal, although so far this has been impossible to prove."[14] But shaky conclusions of matriarchy based on the finding of female icons rest on an even shakier assumption: that women's higher status resulted from a belief that women were related in a special and superior way to the earth and to divine power through their childbearing capacity. There are at least two problematic leaps here. First, female religious symbols are not indicative of the status of women in daily life: in Mexico today, for example, extremely sexist social arrangements coexist with local forms of Christianity that center on and revere the Virgin Mary. In fact, the elevation of the Virgin Mary to divine archetype may even help to justify the mistreatment of ordinary, mortal women in such a culture. Gerda Lerner also points to this phenomenon, noting that because of "the coexistence of symbolic idolatry of women and the actual low status of women such as the cult of the Virgin Mary in the Middle Ages [similar to what exists today in Mexico and Central America], the cult of the lady of the plantation in antebellum America, or that of the Hollywood star in contemporary society, one hesitates to elevate such evidence to historical proof."[15]

Second, the beliefs and attitudes of Neolithic peoples toward women's childbearing capacity are unknown to us. Our projections of its enormous importance probably say more about a modern elevation/repression of sexuality and reproduction, in an age when we are alienated from natural functions, than they do about Neolithic sensibilities. Clearly Neolithic peoples celebrated and ritualized birth as well as death and other passages and transitions, as we still do today. Even if many of them did respond to childbearing with mystified awe—and one can imagine that they were very much in tune with a spirit of wonder—speculation that feelings about childbearing and its symbolization were the primary force behind establishing social and political structures is an enormous leap. It supposes that Neolithic peoples simply reversed the biological determinism that is a modern rationale for domination and asserted that "women are better/stronger" instead of "women are inferior/weaker." To attribute power-over relations to the mystification of childbearing, and men's subsequent jealousies and fears of it, is to reduce problems of domination to sexism. This trivializes other forms of privilege and oppression. New feminist theories, including ecofeminism, must continue to outgrow this categorical exclusivity. Furthermore, by looking only to human subjectivity and symbol systems as explanations for cultural arrangements, we fail to see the full range of natural forces and environmental factors that act through and upon them. By dividing the social and the natural in our understandings of human evolution, we are applying a Cartesian framework, marked by our own modern alienation from nature, to prehistoric peoples.

The human/nature and other dualisms described by Cartesian philosophy are, and were, destructive in their implications. Reinforced by exploitative social and economic systems, the results of such conceptual and cultural splits are human projects that are unsustainable, devoid of reciprocity with the nonhuman environment. Because history has made the nonhuman environment invisible, we do not understand the ecological impact of our social choices, nor how they will come back to haunt us. The invisibility of entire human and animal communities and cultures permits exclusionary and oppressive practices and projects, causing unnecessary and unacceptable suffering. It is, therefore, morally abhorrent. Those on both privileged and undervalued sides of cultural hierarchies are also deprived of models of character, action, and empowerment emerging from lives that have been hidden—darkened, muted, and placed out of our reach. The painstaking work of recovering what has been hidden historically is a critical project, and also one that is particularly susceptible to the biases of privilege. It is not surprising that some of the most powerful work about the recovery of previously invisible lives has been done by African-American women, including Alice Walker and Patricia Hill Collins. In their writing we discover models and inspiration not in an ancient, mythical, and irretrievable past, but in those who have lived just ahead of us and in those who are living now.[16]

How do we, especially those of us who are of European-American descent, escape from our biases in order to understand the past more fully and live better in the present? History is an absolutely subjective human construction or telling. Our purpose cannot be simply to render the accounts "complete" and "objective" by adding on people of non-European descent, women's herstories, and an ecological context. Simply adding on pieces leaves intact the polarized underpinnings of our view and our ways of looking, as well as perpetuating the myth of an "objective" view. In a search for fuller personal, cultural, and natural histories, we must expect and actively seek changes in our own consciousness, as we incorporate our growing understandings of the past and give them expression. To think about the past differently is to burst through the confines of rational analysis; thinking, feeling, and sensing viscerally the presence and movement of molecules, blood, and ideas that physically link us to those of many colors, cultures, and physical forms, even over millennia. This affirms history as an ongoing process. We must take our social analysis down to the nub — beginning with each person's, and humanity's, emergence from and containment within biological existence.

An Ecological Context

The miracle of our origins is enough to create a sense of awe in us today. The earth, in its 4.5 billion year history, has known human-like inhabitants only in the last 2 million years, a period known as the Quaternary.[17] Our evolution and revolutions are far from finished, and the conscious memory we have of our past, relative to the period of evolution, is extremely short. It is hard to imagine the configurations of body, mind, emotion, and spirit our direct ancestors lived in, and even harder to imagine the bodily and subjective experience of their nonhuman ancestors, tracing back through an evolutionary lineage that in its earliest, recognizably animal form begins with an unsegmented worm.[18] We piece together relics and fragments of ancient peoples and the objects they made and lived with, assisting shadows of memories with deductive logic and imaginative speculation — both colored heavily with our current perceptual biases and values. We are now a species with a number of recognizable genetic races, subgroups, and combinations populating every planetary land mass and ecosystem, and traveling across the seas. This is the context that we cannot forget in our telescoped views of human events and historical trends.

One way to approach history is to begin with a particular event or phenomenon and follow its paths backward and forward, exploring nonhuman and human forces that acted upon and resulted from it. These can range from global climatic changes to the intentional act of a single human being. I would like to follow this approach to examine a historical phenomenon of extraordinary significance to the modern world.

In the years between 1600 and 1900, massive migrations of European Caucasians to temperate regions around the globe changed the patterns by which humans inhabited the earth, and also significantly changed their genetic mix. According to Alfred Crosby, "European whites were all recently (before 1700) concentrated in Europe, but in the last few centuries have burst out . . . and have created vast settlements of their kind in the South Temperate Zone and North Temperate Zone (except Asia, a continent already and irreversibly tenanted)."[19] In a period of about three hundred years—about four human lifetimes, moments in the life of a glacier, an instant in the life of a mountain—Europeans entered North America, sections of South America, Australia, New Zealand, and South Africa, becoming the predominant human inhabitants of most of these areas. Crosby, in *Ecological Imperialism: The Biological Expansion of Europe*, names the totality of these migrations the "Great Demographic Takeover." Crosby's approach is unique because he maintains an ecological frame of reference throughout his exploration of European colonization, providing an excellent counterpoint to social analyses. His work contributes to an integration of biological and social factors that helps us to make sense of the migrations as a whole.

In the centuries before the mass European migrations, social arrangements, patterns of human inhabitation, and human-environmental relations were very different in Europe and in what was to be called the "New World." If we compare, for example, England and New England in the late Middle Ages, we find a system of intensive agriculture versus a combination of hunting and gathering plus light agriculture; settlements clustered around huge estates or manors whose boundaries had changed little for centuries versus tribal communities that often moved seasonally; a feudal system of governance and economics versus communal sharing of resources and political guidance by tribal elders and councils; a population whose numbers dramatically rose and dropped versus a relatively stable population. In England, the primeval forests had long since been pushed back: a good estimate is that at the dawn of the twelfth century, 7 to 8 million acres were in cultivation, equal to the area under the plow early in this century.[20] In New England, 95 percent of the land was covered with forest canopy.[21]

The pressures and impetuses for the modern outflow of European migrants were clearly developing by the late Middle Ages. It is impossible to categorize them as strictly "biological" or "social." Between the Norman invasion and the end of the thirteenth century, England's population tripled to about 6 million inhabitants.[22] Graham Nicholson and Jane Fawcett observe that in a good agricultural year, existing cultivation and fishing practices, along with patterns of land tenure, were probably able to support this larger population, in part because the climate was both drier and warmer than today. But by 1300 the climate became wetter and colder, steadily shortening the growing season. The bioclimatic change in this period is indicated by the rapid decline in English vineyards, the extinction of the Nordic population in Greenland, the cessation of corn growing in Iceland, and documented changes in ice conditions in Scandinavian waters and in rivers on the continent.[23] According to the Swedish oceanographer Otto Pettersson, the climate deteriorated uninterruptedly until the middle of the fifteenth century, perhaps because of the effect on the tides of the positions of the moon and the sun in relation to the earth—a configuration that occurs cyclically about every eighteen hundred years.[24]

The resulting famines weakened the population and intensified class stratifications. Landless peasants were in the worst position, with women being the poorest of the poor, a situation recapitulated in many developing nations today. The following fourteenth-century account vividly describes the misery that many endured:

> The poorest folk are our neighbors . . . in their hovels, overburdened with children, and rack-rented by landlords. For whatever they save by spinning they spend on rent, or on milk and oatmeal to make gruel and to fill the bellies of their children who clamour for food. And they themselves are often famished with hunger, and wretched with the miseries of winter—cold, sleepless nights, when they get up to rock the cradle cramped in a corner, and rise before dawn to card and comb the wool, to wash and scrub and mend, and wind yarn and peel rushes for their rushlights. The miseries of these women who dwell in hovels are too pitiful to read or describe in verse.[25]

In 1349 the Black Death, or bubonic plague, broke out among the weakened populace. By the end of the last outbreak in 1377, 40 to 50 percent of the population in England had been wiped out, and up to a third of the entire population of the continent.[26] There were immediate effects on land tenure and loyalty to the roles and traditions that had supported a manorial economy. People's faith that they would be taken care of by their lord and the land, in exchange for their labor and loyalty, had been shaken to the core. With land available and traditions undermined, there was no basis for obedience to a manorial lord. Many people who had had no land, or little, under feudalism were able to claim enough to grow food for their own comfortable subsistence and have surpluses, to gather materials for housing, and even to experience some leisure. The massive depopulation established a context for the breaking of traditions and alliances in the feudal system and an age of more individual interests and of nuclear families versus manorial families and kingdoms. It also sowed the seeds of a modern European consciousness that spread globally several hundred years later.

It was not until the sixteenth century that the European population had recovered from the losses caused by the Black Death. Population pressures rose again in the context of new patterns of land tenure and the dawn of the industrial and scientific revolutions, with their concurrent changes in knowledge, symbol systems, and awareness of self and others. Between 1500 and 1800 the numbers more than doubled, escalating into rates of population increase that were unparalleled in the world and approached only by China.[27]

Population booms are obvious contributors to social tension and environmental pressures. Historically they are often portrayed as uncontrollable natural phenomena, by-products of unconscious and unintentional sexuality which then prompt a social response. Thus, they sit on the dividing line between the conceptualized worlds of nature and humanity. But there is ample evidence that humans have deliberately shaped their numbers from the most ancient societies to the present, either through social rewards for having many children or through contraception, abortion, infanticide, and other population controls.[28] Although the burgeoning of Europe's population was certainly the result of many interacting forces, values, and institutions, it is of more than passing interest that the period of greatest population increase in Europe coincided with the upsurge of Christianity, which encouraged unlimited reproduction, and the persecution of "witches"— midwives, herbalists, and healers — who knew best how to prevent and abort unwanted pregnancies.

In addition to noting the social forces that are part of population booms, it is important to confront the mistaken assumption that more people equal more pressure on the environment in a simple numerical correlation. Deep ecologists talk about a "carrying capacity" of humans for a region, as if there were a universal increment that could be determined in a value-free and monocultural way. The reality is that pressures on the environment have more to do with human systems of production, reproduction, and consumption than with numbers of people. For example, a tiny proportion of people today consume most of the earth's "resources." The enormous consumption of Americans and other Westerners is the product of knotted practices and institutions: a capitalist economy bent on expansion; a meat-based diet that requires up to twenty times as much land as grain- and vegetable-based diets, and whose supporting industries deplete topsoil and fresh water; and the politics of global imperialism.[29]

The pressures that European peoples faced in past centuries were due not simply to increasing numbers and land scarcity, but to an interaction of particular social values, practices, and institutions with the environment. As a result, European peoples swarmed to other temperate lands along with their domesticated animals, such as horses and cattle, and such "varmints" as European rats. The animals that the immigrants brought with them accomplished their own population replacements. Usually we think of changes in animal habitation during this period as livestock replacing herds of buffalo and bison, but the changes reached into every ecological niche. One of the most successful imports, for example, was the honeybee, a native of the Mediterranean and the Middle East. The first hive in Tasmania swarmed sixteen times in the summer of 1832.[30]

Crosby's thesis is that the European migrations were an ecological phenomenon in which the interaction of humans, animals closely associated with them, weeds, pathogens, and microorganisms brought about a monumental transformation of environments and cultures. He notes that all of these different organisms "accomplished demographic takeovers of their own in the temperate, well-watered regions of North and South America, Australia and New Zealand."[31]

From an ecological standpoint, it is important to note the failures as well as the remarkable successes of the European migrations. The hardiness and adaptability of European people and their entourage of related organisms extended only to temperate regions. In neither Africa nor tropical America did European crops or animals proper. Crosby writes that "in tropical Africa, until recently, Europeans died in droves of the fevers, in tropical America they died almost as fast of the same diseases, plus a few native American additions."[32]

To the widespread regions in which they were successful, however, Europeans brought intensive forms of agriculture as well as foreign plant and animal species that transformed forests and clearings into networks of fields. This disrupted the subsistence methods of the natives, who then became more receptive to European land-use and social practices. William Cronon recounts the words of a speech given by the Narragansett sachem Miantonomo in 1642, just a few years after the arrival of English colonists near his people's villages: "Our fathers had plenty of deer skins, our plains were full of deer, as also our woods, and of turkies, and our coves full of fish and fowl. But these English having gotten our land, they with scythes cut down the grass, and with axes fell the trees; their cows and horses eat the grass, and their hogs spoil our clam banks, and we shall all be starved."[33]

Even more devastating than European land-use patterns to the culture and subsistence of the native peoples were the Old World diseases—smallpox, measles, chicken pox, influenza, plague, and tuberculosis. According to Cronon, mortality rates in the initial onslaughts of these diseases "were seldom less than 80 or 90 percent, and it was not unheard of for an entire village to be wiped out. . . . A long process of depopulation set in, accompanied by massive social and economic disorganization."[34] During the first part of the seventeenth century, certain areas such as Vermont and New Hampshire "were virtually depopulated as the western Abenaki declined from perhaps 10,000 to fewer than 500."[35] These diseases also left their mark on American Indian history and folklore. Crosby writes of a legend from the southern Plains Indians in which a Kiowa meets Smallpox on the plain, riding a horse: The man asks, "Where do you come from and what do you do and why are you here?" Smallpox answers, "I am one with the white men — they are my people as the Kiowas are yours. . . . My breath causes children to wither like young plants in spring snow. The strongest of warriors go down before me. No people who have looked on me will ever be the same."[36]

Cronon's *Changes in the Land: Indians, Colonists, and the Ecology of New England*, like Merchant's *Ecological Revolutions*, examines the mutual transformations of lands and peoples in New England. Merchant's use of the Marxist/socialist categories of production and reproduction as vectors of analysis also helps to amplify gender roles as an explicit factor in, and result of, ecological and social transformations in New England. By primarily viewing history through categories of production and reproduction that are centered in human society and implicitly partake of a nature/culture duality, Merchant's analysis approaches but does not really become an ecofeminist perspective. Her analysis of production and reproduction during the European demographic takeover in New England, and its cultural postscripts, is nevertheless helpful to ecofeminists in sorting out and integrating multiple sites of historical change.

Merchant defines production simply as "the extraction, processing and exchange of natural resources." On the other hand, reproduction is the "biological and social process through which humans are born, nurtured, socialized and governed. Through reproduction sexual relations are legitimated, population sizes and family relationships are maintained, and property and inheritance practices are reinforced."[37]

Merchant traces how biological processes and social traditions of production and reproduction interacted in the colonization of New England, shaping its perpetually expansionist character. For example, European patterns of inheritance and family life meant that each son should, ideally, be given a farmstead large enough to be nearly self-sufficient. As immigration continued, very high birthrates were maintained, and lifespans increased, this became impossible. She explains:

> It was rural New England's failure to reproduce its system of production that initiated the capitalist ecological revolution. Pushed by ecological degradation and stimulated by market opportunities, ordinary farmers took up more quantitative methods of management during the nineteenth century. Urged by elite scientists, improvers, clergy and

> doctors to abandon their old ways and become entrepreneurs, they were drawn into the mechanistic approach to nature. A participatory consciousness dominated by vision changed to the analytic consciousness required by capitalist agriculture.[38]

Both Merchant and Cronon present the changes that occurred in New England as a gradual but inexorable revolution that permanently altered the landscape and deeply affected both of the human cultures involved, but especially and most obviously the Native Americans. Additionally, Merchant traces how, as colonial subsistence agriculture changed to capitalism, male and female spheres of activity in white society, which had overlapped and intersected, were increasingly pulled apart. As men began to transport their surplus goods to market and work away from their homesteads, women's responsibilities became more and more domestic, contributing to the particular constellation of gender arrangements that has become our modern inheritance.

The case history of New England enables us to see profound changes in a particular place telescoped in time, but changes over larger parts of the globe were just as dramatic and significant in their totality. Only a few centuries after the first Old World arrivals, whites of European heritage amount to nearly 90 percent of the population in Canada and the United States, 95 percent in Argentina and Uruguay, 98 percent in Australia, and 90 percent in New Zealand.[39] As overwhelming as these statistics are, the transformations that took place between 1600 and 1900 were much more extensive than the human demographics show. In Argentina and Uruguay, for example, only a quarter of the plants growing wild in the pampa (prairie) are native. In an "inundation" of animals from the Old World, "horses, cattle, sheep, goats, and pigs have for hundreds of years been among the most numerous of the quadrupeds"—in lands that before the migrations had never seen such animals.[40] Crosby concludes:

> The demographic triumph of Europeans in the temperate colonies is one part of a biological and ecological takeover which could not have been accomplished by human beings alone, gunpowder notwithstanding. . . . The human invaders have consulted their egos, rather than ecologists, for explanations of their triumphs. But the human victims, the aborigines of the Lands of the Demographic Takeover, knew better, knew they were only one of many species being displaced and replaced; knew they were victims of something more irresistible and awesome than the spread of capitalism or Christianity.[41]

Revisiting the European Migrations from an Ecofeminist View

Ecofeminism seeks to develop an integrated—but not reductionist—perceptual experience and conceptual view of nature and society. It seeks to move beyond a purely "socialist" analysis (viewing the world primarily as the result of the production and reproduction of human cultures and commodities) or a purely "ecological" analysis (in the sense of a science-based description of organic and inorganic links). It also aims to establish an ethic of responsible action. Part of the way that ecofeminism does this is to emphasize multiple factors in and relations among different phenomena and events. In my definition, ecofeminism does not privilege a single vector of analysis and make other axes of change into secondary effects, as Marxism privileges economic forces of production, for example, and radical feminism privileges gender relations. Thus, an ecofeminist perspective draws from social and ecological contexts in an effort to develop open and evolving, rather than "finished," explanations.

In ecofeminist terms what I have presented as an ecological context for understanding the "great demographic takeover" of white Europeans needs to be further elaborated to adequately confront conceptual dualisms and the effects of power-over relations, but even by itself an ecological framework is expansive and challenges us in several ways. It stretches existing definitions of "social" and "biological" factors and helps us to integrate them. It also makes appallingly clear the simple ecological lessons from the past that have not been incorporated in the meetings of different cultures and ecosystems in the twentieth century—and therefore the degree to which history, unexamined and partial, repeats its failures. We can no longer afford to ignore how fragile, specific, and precious different ecosystems are, including their human inhabitants, and how easily devastated. Diversity in peoples and ecosystems is a natural condition. Temperate regions are not the tropics, Europe is not New England, and the once fertile soils on the banks of the Ganges River in India, ruined by green revolution technology, are not like either of those Western lands. There is no connection between the ability of a particular group of people and/or entourage of organisms to dominate or prevail against others, and the value or sustainability of their culture or tenure upon the land.

An ecological context also brings up difficult questions of historical responsibility that ecofeminism can help us examine more closely. We know that life on the planet comprises phenomena and processes that are perpetually changing, but the influences of human actions on the earth are much greater than those of any other form of life. Does our ability as human beings to wreak radical and irreversible changes in land, sea, and the organic world impart a particularly human responsibility for the earth and its life (including the well-being or suffering of other human beings), or is this capacity a morally neutral by-product of natural and human evolution? Is there a difference between a succession of red cedar and hemlock replacing an old fir forest, a swarm of African bees replacing Mediterranean honeybees, and the European demographic takeover of 1600–1900?

Let us look first at the dualistic way in which we are conditioned to think about these questions. In a world view in which nature and humanity are discontinuous, cedar trees and bees do not partake of any type of subjectivity or consciousness but are driven, without intention or choice, by biological forces. And, of course, since they are both other-than-human and therefore part of a big mossy entity called "nature," there are no significant differences between them. Continuing to think divisively, we would understand human society, in contrast, as independent of nature and its forces, completely intentional and free in its actions. In a historical framework that is *either* natural *or* social, we can choose to collapse the European migrations into the category of a "natural" phenomenon, seeing the trees, bees, and human players as equally unconscious and biologically driven. Or we can choose a social (and by implication anti-natural) perspective, in which the migrations would have to be understood as an intentional choice made by human beings out of at least relative freedom, particularly freedom from biological needs and pressures. "Humanity" also becomes an undifferentiated entity in this case, without distinctions between privileged ruling elite and poor and hungry European peasants, or those who were oppressed on the basis of their ethnicity, religious affiliation, or gender. When humanity is undifferentiated, it is easy to see the European migrants as wholly to blame for decimating peoples and ecosystems in temperate latitudes, and also to see indigenous peoples, animals, and ecosystems wholly as victims. In our historical view this makes some people more powerful than they actually were, some less powerful, and all but a few invisible. Dualistic thinking guides us into polarities in thinking about the European migrations: either the complete absolution of responsibility (in the image of an unconscious swarm) or total blame (the evil empire).

Human beings are not trees or bees, however—whichever species we consider diminished by such analogies. There are meaningful and critical differences in consciousness and intentionality among humans, and among all forms of life.[42] Neither is history, though, the story of a masterminded plan for human civilization independent of the rest of nature. The differences among forest succession, bee swarms, and human migrations can certainly be explored, but not by viewing them through reductionist categories such as nature and culture. Ecofeminism is unique in deconstructing the nature/culture dualism from both sides, unlike such progressive movements as deep ecology and, to a lesser extent, bioregionalism (the latter is less developed as an overall theory). Deep ecology, for example, redefines nature to include humanity and presents environmental degradation as an abhorrent symptom of our alienation from the "wild" parts of ourselves. But in using a universal "we" that is powerful, privileged, and historically alienated from natural processes, it fails to see human diversity (including diversity in human-environmental relations) and abuses of power played out in ethnocentric, classist, and sexist acts and institutions. Therefore, overpopulation and the lack of a proper reverence for nature become the causes of the "environmental crisis" to which social dislocations and human suffering are secondary or incidental.[43] Clearly an ecofeminist examination of history shows that we cannot reduce complex realities in this way.

But let us return to one particular and difficult question. Can and should the European migrants be held morally responsible for the ways in which their mass migrations and individual actions were destructive and caused suffering for others? I would answer this question with an equivocal yes and no — not because I am waffling, but because the question itself is too simple. We must first examine the idea of moral responsibility. It contains two concepts that each have many layers: first, an equation with power, the capacity to effect physical and subjective changes in living and nonliving things and processes; and, second, a relation to a system of ethics that establishes ideals and criteria to distinguish good and evil.

The relative power that different European migrants had to determine their own lives and to affect lives and landscapes around them was extremely varied, as was the power of indigenous peoples and other life forms to shape their surroundings and to resist changes not of their own making. The degree of power that a particular individual could exercise also changed greatly in some cases and very little in others as Europeans traveled to the New World. For example, most women who arrived in North America from Europe found that their surroundings and conditions had changed, but their social position and influence remained much the same, as Old World family cultures were continued and replicated. On the other hand, some minor European lords suddenly controlled huge tracts of land and colonies in the New World, which gave them much greater social status and influence, and convicted criminals imprisoned in European countries became free men in places like Australia.

To consider moral dimensions of responsibility for the flourishing of some people and forms of life and the suffering of others, we must add ethical judgments to an understanding of unequal and changing power relations. But we must also understand the ethical systems that we use as historical in their own right. As Murray Bookchin has observed in his studies in the political history of philosophy, ethics that define individual and collective good usually (if not always) develop partly as a construction of, or as a reaction to, particular political forms and structures. For example, the ethics of Socrates and Aristotle, foundational to Western thought, emerged with and reflect the rise and heyday of the Greek polis, that civic structure which sought to institutionalize a form of democratic governance based on both individual fulfillment and collective well-being *for its elite members*. The polis explicitly excluded women, slaves, non-Greeks, and resident aliens.[44] In the last quarter-century, feminist theorists and activists have accumulated sufficient voice to confront the critical ethical assumption supporting not only the Greek polis but also most Western political, religious, and social institutions in our written history. This assumption is that one group (specifically white male elites) can, through the manipulation of abstract and universal principles such as democracy and justice, provide the greatest good for a society or the world.

Some feminists have sought to define an alternative ethical orientation that is more accountable to women's experience. They have projected an ideal based in a personal sense of relationship and mutual responsibility, a caring for human and nonhuman others described by some as a characteristic of women's personalities.[45] Early descriptions of such an alternative ethic—for example, Carol Gilligan's *In a Different Voice*—emphasize the difference from the traditional ethic that elevates self-fulfillment to the top of a hierarchy of values. Instead, an almost symmetrically opposite ethic of care and relation to others is portrayed as desirable. More recent treatments, especially those with an ecofeminist focus, emphasize a dialectical relationship between individual needs, compassion for others, and collective memberships and realities as a source for ethics.[46]

From ecofeminist guidelines developed by myself, Marti Kheel, and others, I would define an ethical position most simply as this: acting to the best of one's ability from a sensibility that simultaneously knows and values oneself as an individual; is compassionate through identification with human and nonhuman others and caring about others' lives and well-being; and is creative, undergoing self-transformation through cultivating a relation to collectives ranging from human families to the planetary community. I believe that an ethical position becomes a basis for morally responsible action when a person, through the particular form of nature's subjectivity that is human consciousness, fully accepts and exercises her or his personal power to shape lives and events—and also accepts and exercises the *limits* to that power that emerge through mediating one's multiple alliances. The definitions of ethics and moral responsibility I have developed are useful to me in guiding trivial and large decisions, but they would probably not be wholly meaningful to either Native Americans or European migrants several hundred years ago. My definitions, framed in a vernacular that is a product of a specific and contemporary experience, may be a better measure of the quality of the actions I take in my own life than they are of historical events. I would argue that the moral responsibility of individuals and groups in the past depends on their access to power and also on whose ethical standards we use to make such judgments. This means that it is impossible to establish absolute, unmediated accountability, or blame, for historical events. This does not preclude compassion for or identification with people and other living beings in history, and emotional responses to their experience — anger, sadness, joy, hope; nor does it prevent us from passing judgments on historical events and actions. But it does require that we acknowledge that the criteria we are using arise out of our own experience, which both connects with and differs from the experiences of people in other places and times. This is particularly important for white, wealthy, heterosexual, or otherwise privileged ecofeminists, who through refraining from fixing absolute blame may more easily find points of identification with privileged historical groups, as well as those that have been oppressed. This can help us examine more honestly the ways we may be causing suffering through consciously or unconsciously exploiting our own privilege, and explore the combinations and intersections of oppression and privilege that our ethical systems and world views grow from.

Bringing the Past into the Present

Issues today present choices that mirror those of times past. These give us the opportunity to notice how we have changed — or stayed the same. In Quebec and New England, for example, a controversy has raged over the last several years about the proposed expansion of an already huge hydroelectric dam project, involving on the one hand descendants of the European colonists in New England and Quebec and, on the other, Native Americans. The backdrop to the economic debate (which has, in keeping with mainstream social values and the concerns of current political systems, emerged as the primary focus of public dialogue and media attention) is the face-off of two different cultural constructs and attendant value systems. Additionally, the future of a large ecosystem in anything like its present form is at stake. If the Canadian provincial utility company, Hydro-Quebec, implements the next proposed phase of its project, it will add thousands of square miles to the 4,600 that have already been flooded in the James Bay region of Quebec, which includes the home territory of the Cree and Inuit people as well as a multitude of plant and animal communities.[47] If the project is not implemented, some consumers of electricity in Quebec, New England, and New York may need either to find alternative supplies of energy, each with their own environmental and social impacts, or to restructure radically their needs for and consumption of electricity.

In New England, recent events have shown that citizens and policy-makers have been split in their alliances. Early in 1990 Maine's Public Service Commission rejected the purchase of power from Hydro-Quebec and directed its largest utility to pursue conservation programs instead. Later that year Vermont's Public Service Board approved a contract under which that state's twenty-four electric utilities would buy power from Hydro-Quebec over a period of thirty years. Yet in a special election in October 1991, citizens of Burlington, Vermont's largest city, voted not to authorize its utility's participation in the contract.[48]

What is involved in making choices like the ones that citizens and public officials have faced in this controversy? In the case of Hydro-Quebec, a major (and inconclusive) part of the debate has hinged on economics and whether or not needs for additional power have been accurately assessed. But human rights and environmental impacts have clearly been another key part of the public dialogue and decision-making processes, and these require a different type of consideration. To ignore these latter issues would be to make the Cree and Inuit peoples, the animals, and the environment of the James Bay region invisible, and to cut them off from citizens' and officials' sense of themselves and their communities. This reveals the kind of narrow identifications based on political boundaries and cultural groupings that have enabled the appropriation of "natural resources" throughout history. The choice to perceive and to incorporate indigenous peoples and the nonhuman environment into one's own sense of self and community, as the European colonists of 1600–1900 did not, is a choice to face personal and cultural change oneself. To stand against a project such as Hydro-Quebec's expansion on the basis of its concomitant destruction of human cultures and the environment is an active response to history and the effects of human choices in the past.

To take a morally responsible position means holding a compassionate awareness of others and an understanding of a whole in which one is a part, along with an affirmation of one's own individual integrity. It requires a willingness to undergo self-transformation. Traditionally, in the West, "moral" choices have been regarded as something to be expected only of the most privileged individuals, those educated or gifted in rarefied forms of reason and capable of holding the abstract ideas regarded as necessary to act with more than the most selfish interests in mind. This attitude has both reinforced the classic nature/culture dualism and justified political institutions in which only elites can make large-scale decisions. But in fact the impetus to act in what I have defined as a morally responsible way may be traced to impulses and emotions that are both biological and social by our usual definitions. Emotional experiences similar to what we, in a specific human culture, name compassion, grief, and love are clearly present in some (but not all) animal communities, as well as specifically cultivated in some (but not all) human communities. Abstract reasoning may be one culturally specific path to a sensibility I am portraying as an ecofeminist perspective, and as a morally responsible position. But there are other paths, including some that may be simpler and more direct, to help us live and act in ways that approach a wholly embodied and inspirited state—that of a fully *sensible* human being.

To transform our relationship to the past by learning to understand the interactions and continuity of what has been divided into natural and social history, to establish a personal relation and place in it, is to develop roots—a metaphor that expresses grounding in both the organic world and social communities. This is riskier, more confusing, more exciting, and more transformative than adding on pieces to a purely social construction of history. It involves experiencing viscerally and intuitively, as well as rationally, the genesis of the human body and its organic and subjective evolution out of the oceans and savannahs, as well as through the social milieus of our grandmothers and grandfathers. We simultaneously arrive from the past and depart for the future in each encounter with history and with the decisions that we must make today.

NOTES

1. Gerda Lerner, *The Creation of Patriarchy* (New York: Oxford University Press, 1986), 4.
2. Adrienne Rich, "Resisting Amnesia," *Woman of Power* 16 (Spring 1990): 15.
3. Herbal healing and the practice of midwifery were clear signs of heresy and witchcraft, according to the *Malleus Maleficarum*, or "Hammer of Witches." I have not been able to find reliable statistics on the number of people burned or hanged as witches. In Rosemary Ellen Guiley, *The Encyclopedia of Witches and Witchcraft* (New York: Facts on File, 1989), estimates range from 30,000 to 100,000 in Germany alone, and I have seen estimates elsewhere of up to 9 million in all of Europe.
4. Ian McHarg, *Design with Nature* (Garden City, N.Y.: Doubleday/Natural History Press, 1969), 67.
5. Carolyn Merchant, *Ecological Revolutions: Nature, Gender, and Science in New England* (Chapel Hill and London: University of North Carolina Press, 1989), 2.
6. Ester Boserup draws on the work of Frank Hole to speculate about evidence of overgrazing and the cultivation of steep hillsides, which resulted in erosion and desertification in southwestern Asia, in periods from 8000 to 4000 B.C.: see "Environment, Population and Technology in Primitive Societies," in *The Ends of the Earth*, ed. Donald Worster (Cambridge: Cambridge University Press, 1988), 28. Evidence has also been found for the extinction of native species through human activities in prehistoric times in New Zealand and Madagascar.

7. Richard White, *Land Use, Environment, and Social Change: The Shaping of Island County, Washington* (Seattle: University of Washington Press, 1980), 20.
8. Ibid., 29.
9. Donald Worster, "Doing Environmental History," in Worster, *The Ends of the Earth*, 279.
10. Riane Eisler, *The Chalice and the Blade* (San Francisco: Harper & Row, 1988).
11. In addition to Eisler, see Monica Sjöö and Barbara Mor, *The Great Cosmic Mother: Rediscovering the Religion of the Earth* (San Francisco: Harper & Row, 1987); and Merlin Stone, *When God Was a Woman* (New York: Dial Press, 1976).
12. Sjöö and Mor, *The Great Cosmic Mother*, 88.
13. Ibid., 88–92.
14. Janet Biehl, "Goddess Mythology in Ecological Politics," *New Politics*, no. 2, (1989): 91. See Biehl's article and her book *Rethinking Ecofeminist Politics* (Boston: South End Press, 1991), for an in-depth critique of the scholarship and popular texts about goddess worship in Neolithic cultures. I disagree with key elements of Biehl's critique from the left, especially her elevation of reason and denigration of feeling, intuition, and other modes of human knowing. I also feel that her polemical attempt to discredit ecofeminism as a whole in *Rethinking Ecofeminist Politics* is misguided; nevertheless, her exposure of logical fallacies in feminist revisionings of the Neolithic period is well formulated and valuable.
15. Lerner, *The Creation of Patriarchy*, 28–29.
16. Patricia Hill Collins collects pieces of a rich intellectual tradition among African-American women in *Black Feminist Thought* (Boston: Unwin Hyman, 1990). Jamaica Kincaid's and Alice Walker's novels, as well as Walker's edited collection of Zora Neale Hurston's work, offer multiple models of powerful women living under oppressive conditions. See Jamaica Kincaid, *Lucy* (New York: Farrar Straus Giroux, 1990), and *Annie John* (New York: Farrar Straus Giroux, 1985); and Alice Walker, *The Color Purple* (New York: Harcourt Brace Jovanovich, 1982).
17. Andrew Goudie, *Environmental Change* (Oxford: Clarendon Press, 1983; New York: Oxford University Press, 1983), 1.
18. See Richard Grossinger, *Embryogenesis: From Cosmos to Creature—The Origins of Human Biology* (San Francisco: North Atlantic Books, 1986).
19. Alfred Crosby, "Ecological Imperialism: The Overseas Migration of Western Europeans as a Biological Phenomenon," in Worster, *The Ends of the Earth*, 104.
20. Graham Nicholson and Jane Fawcett, *The Village in England* (New York: Rizzoli, 1988), 14.
21. Merchant, *Ecological Revolutions*, 31.
22. Nicholson and Fawcett, *The Village in England*, 45.
23. These signs are described in Gustaf Utterstrom, "Climatic Fluctuations and Population Problems in Early Modern History," in Worster, *The Ends of the Earth*, 42, and also in Nicholson and Fawcett, *The Village in England*, 46.
24. Utterstrom, "Climatic Fluctuations," 41.
25. *Piers Plowman*, quoted in Nicholson and Fawcett, *The Village in England*, 11. For

additional material on gender and other inequities in the Middle Ages, see Carolyn Merchant, *The Death of Nature: Women, Ecology and the Scientific Revolution* (San Francisco: Harper & Row, 1980). Merchant promotes the view that medieval societies held a more "organismic" view of the world than moderns do, seeing themselves as part of a larger whole. This did not mean, however, that preindustrial society in Europe was egalitarian in either social or human-environmental relations. The feudal system was at least in part justified by the philosophy/cosmology of Aristotle's great chain of being (*scala natura*), in which there was a hierarchy in the heavens and a hierarchy on earth. The pope and then the king were at the top, peasants were at the bottom, and women were below the men of their particular status group.

26. These estimates are from Nicholson and Fawcett, *The Village in England*, 46, and Donald Worster, "The Vulnerable Earth: Toward a Planetary History," in Worster, *The Ends of the Earth*, 9.
27. Worster, "The Vulnerable Earth," 9.
28. See Dianne Fenton, "Looking at Issues of Abortion Through an Ecofeminist Perspective," senior thesis, University of Vermont, 1990; Norman Himes, *Medical History of Contraception* (New York: Gamut Press, 1963); Rosalind Petchesky, "Reproductive Choice in the Contemporary United States: A Social Analysis of Female Sterilization," in *And The Poor Get Children: Radical Perspectives on Population Dynamics*, ed. Karen Michaelson (New York and London: Monthly Review Press, 1981). In addition to evidence of early population control in human societies, note that many other animals appear to regulate their population through their behavior (including infanticide) as well as through "unconscious" fluctuations in reproductive capacities.
29. Statistics on resource consumption attributable to a meat-centered diet and its industries are from "Realities 1990: Facts," excerpted from John Robbins, *Diet for a New America* (Walpole, N.H.: Stillpoint, 1987).
30. Crosby, "Ecological Imperialism," 109.
31. Ibid., 116.
32. Ibid., 104–5.
33. William Cronon, *Changes in the Land: Indians, Colonists, and the Ecology of New England* (New York: Hill and Wang, 1983), 162.
34. Ibid., 86.
35. Ibid., 89.
36. Crosby, "Ecological Imperialism," 112. Also see Alfred Crosby, *Ecological Imperialism: The Biological Expansion of Europe 900–1900* (Cambridge: Cambridge University Press, 1986), in which he describes legends about smallpox that arose in other indigenous cultures colonized by Old World societies. For example, "the Yukaghirs, who in the 1630's occupied vast areas of Siberia from the Lena basin east, and of whom there were only 1500 at the end of the nineteenth century, have a legend that the Russians were not able to conquer them until the intruders brought smallpox in a box and opened the box. Then the land was filled with smoke, and the people began to die" (39).

37. Merchant, *Ecological Revolutions*, 11, 14.
38. Ibid., 113.
39. Crosby, "Ecological Imperialism," 114.
40. Ibid., 114.
41. Ibid., 116.
42. Hans Jonas, *The Phenomenon of Life: Toward a Philosophical Biology* (Chicago and London: University of Chicago Press, 1982), provides a fascinating and well-reasoned account of phases in the evolution of plants and animals, and the subjectivity of living organisms.
43. See Bill Devall and George Sessions, *Deep Ecology: Living As If Nature Mattered* (Salt Lake City: Gibbs Smith, 1985), esp. 69–76.
44. Murray Bookchin, *The Rise of Urbanization and the Decline of Citizenship* (San Francisco: Sierra Club Books, 1987), 41.
45. See especially Carol Gilligan, *In a Different Voice: Psychological Theory and Women's Development* (Cambridge: Harvard University Press, 1982); Mary Belenky et al., *Women's Ways of Knowing* (New York: Basic Books, 1986).
46. I have introduced parameters describing and defining ecofeminism, including its moral dimensions, at greater length in Stephanie Lahar, "Ecofeminist Theory and Grassroots Politics," *Hypatia* 6 (Spring 1991): 28–45. Also see Marti Kheel, "Ecofeminism and Deep Ecology: Reflections on Identity and Difference," in *Reweaving The World: The Emergence of Ecofeminism*, ed. Irene Diamond and Gloria Feman Orenstein (San Francisco: Sierra Club Books, 1990), 128–37; Marti Kheel, "The Liberation of Nature: A Circular Affair," *Environmental Ethics* 7 (1985): 135–49.
47. Paul Markowitz, "Energy Efficiency: Vermont's Most Promising Power Source," *Vermont Environmental Report* (Summer 1988): 11.
48. The Burlington special election in October 1991 reversed a March 1990 vote that had been declared invalid because literature supporting Hydro-Quebec had been placed inside voting booths.

FURTHER READING

Vandana Shiva is the author of several important books on women, the environment, and development. See Shiva (1989a, 1989b) and especially her *Monocultures of the Mind* (1993), which treats in some detail the conditions for a human/land symbiosis and points out the crucial connection between symbiosis and biodiversity. Shiva has been very active in women's and ecological movements in her native India. See also Mies and Shiva (1993). For more views of ecofeminism, see Gaard, ed. (1993), Plant, ed. (1989), and the sections on ecofeminism in Zimmerman et al., eds. (1993) and VanDeVeer and Pierce, eds. (1994).

QUESTIONS TO CONSIDER

1. Evaluate King's claim that "the domination of women in society precedes the domination of nonhuman nature." Should this be construed as a purely historical claim?
2. Try to explain King's notion of a connection between "knowing and loving."
3. Explain the connection between "invisibility" and violence cited by Lahar.

PART FIVE

The environment and the economy

It seems ironic that there have been so many conflicts between economic and environmental priorities, especially since the two terms stem from the same Greek root—*oikos*, meaning home or household—and since one might well see ordinary economics (concerned with the dynamics of exchange and investment) as essentially just a branch of human ecology in general. In fact, there is a tremendous conceptual revolution under way now, as economists attempt to rewrite their subject to take into account our emerging understanding of the importance of ecology. Conventional economic theory tends to refer to such things as soil erosion, the disappearance of species, or disease as "externalities," meaning something that impinges from *outside* upon the pure human economy. One could briefly summarize the paradigm shift going on now as a recognition that there are no "externalities"; that human activities are so tightly linked to the functioning of the ecosystem that we might as well take anything that bears on ecological functioning as in some way part of, or coupled to, the "economy."

Here, obviously, we can do little more than point a finger to some of the huge issues currently being debated. A few references are given at the end of each chapter that will lead the reader further.

CHAPTER FOURTEEN

SHOULD WE LET THE MARKET DECIDE?

We begin this chapter with a brisk exchange of opinion that appeared in the University of Western Ontario *Gazette* in 1992. John Palmer, professor of economics at the University of Western Ontario, condemned "tree-huggers" for failing to understand the mechanics of market forces. A flurry of replies followed from around the campus, and then I published a short reply to Palmer some weeks later (a revised version of which appears here).

TREE-HUGGERS WARPING MARKETS

John Palmer

We can continue to log our brains out, and we probably won't run out of wood for another 50 years. But we will run out, because current management is not sustainable.

The above quotation from a touchy-feely tree-hugger is pure and simple hogwash. Why? Because the writer has an incomplete understanding of economics.

Will we run out of timber for logging? Not likely. As current supplies are harvested, the decline in supply will cause prices to rise. Furthermore, as population and wealth increase, so will the demand for timber, also putting upward pressure on prices.

But these higher prices provide important signals. They encourage people who would like to earn some profits to plant more trees. And they encourage potential buyers to look for substitutes for timber and to cut down on their use of lumber.

We will not run out of timber, because, despite the warnings of naive tree-huggers, prices will rise, eliciting responses that promote conservation and more production.

If the tree-huggers really believe we will run out of timber, they should buy up lots of land and plant lots of trees. And they and their progeny will be rich beyond their wildest dreams, if their predictions of doom and gloom are correct.

But if they *do* plant more trees now, there will be more trees in the future, and their predictions will be wrong. And even if the doomsayers don't plant the trees, some people will; the anticipation of future profits will keep us from running out of timber.

There is a heavy shadow of doubt clouding this rosy picture, though. It comes from the spectre of government intervention in the timber market in two ways.

First, as the government gets involved in tree-planting and the leasing of timber lands, the incentive for lumber companies to practice conservation is diminished. "Why conserve," they reasonably ask themselves, "if the government is going to undercut our actions with their own programs?"

Second, government intervention designed to keep prices low will further deter private conservation efforts. "Why plant more trees," people will reasonably ask, "if we can't sell them for a price high enough to cover all our costs?"

And so the more the government tries to keep future prices down, the more it deters private conservation efforts.

Will we run out of timber? Only if we implement really stupid government policies that discourage private conservation.

[The letters in reply to Palmer are from *The Gazette*, March 19, 1992.]

Eco Prof Hit Nail on the Head

To the Editor:

John Palmer's article was a breath of fresh air (Mar. 13).

Palmer's polemic implied a fundamental truth which I felt deserved explicit statement. Government intervention in the marketplace—which interferes with the natural processes of price determination—is the principal threat to the continuing existence of natural resources.

Palmer's article detailed how government intervention in the timber market would actually lead to the destruction of the supply of trees. But what is true for trees is true for whatever resource you want to talk about.

So what would preserve the supply of resources—not just trees, but resources in general? The answer: greedy capitalists selfishly pursuing private profits in a free market.

Why, then, is it that environmentalists are anti-capitalist? I hope it's just because they don't know much about economics. Among those that do, I suspect there are motives operating whose sinister nature I shudder to imagine.

W.R. Minto
Philosophy

Tree Hugger Fights Back

To the Editor:

On March 13, an article by John Palmer, a professor of economics, appeared in *The Gazette*. He accused environmentalists (tree-huggers) of having an incomplete understanding of economics and of naivety. He pleaded for unencumbered markets to control forestry practices. Palmer's article affirmed that corporate North America is leading us down the path towards environmental degradation. The road to hell is paved with sickening rationalizations.

The Greek roots of economy and ecology are inextricably linked. Economy, from oikonomic, means the management of the household, whereas ecology, from the root oikos plus logos, means household.

But Palmer suggests that the free market will provide all that we need when it becomes profitable.

Palmer maintains that an incomplete understanding of economics has led to the naive view that trees are becoming endangered. The market will provide all that we need. Scientific reality maintains:

- The widespread destruction of trees for timber or farmland has contributed to global warming;
- Logging practices practically ensure soil destruction, harming future growth;
- Planting trees for short-term economic gain is an asinine proposition because trees take substantial time to grow;
- So much is wasted that demand-side economics just makes sense;
- One of the leading causes of animal species extinction is loss of habitat.

Has simple economics accounted for these factors or are they the "externalities" evoked by many economists when a model goes wrong? The presence of externalities means that economists don't understand all factors involved. I fail to see how Dr. Palmer's "complete" understanding of economics would preserve vital resources.

Palmer's article is guilty of the heinous crime of which he accuses environmentalists. Economists simply have an incomplete understanding of ecology and cannot begin to account for the infinite number of variables and nuances in an ecosystem. Physician, heal thyself.

Eugene Tan
Environmental Issues Commissioner
Mature tree-hugger

Eco Prof's Column Was Pure "Hogwash"

To the Editor:

In the Friday, March 13 edition of *The Gazette*, John Palmer's article in "The Academics" series was pure hogwash. Why? Because the writer has no understanding of silviculture, or biology in general.

Palmer puts a great deal of faith in the reliability of market forces to ensure a continuous supply of timber. The spectacular vistas of forests enticing us to visit "Super Natural British Columbia" are not reforested sections. I have seen the aftermath of forest fires that are more ecologically sound than current reforestation attempts.

I wonder if he thinks that his theory holds for harvesting of the Atlantic cod stocks, the ivory trade, or hunting passenger pigeons. After all, it was an economist that burdened us with the term "sustainable development."

Take heart Western, perhaps the *Maclean's* poll was based only on the department of Economics.

Fred Williams
Department of Microbiology and Immunology

THE ECONOMICS OF EXTINCTION

Kent A. Peacock

Professor John Palmer condemns "tree-huggers" for failing to understand economics. Don't worry about running out of trees, he tells us, market forces will guarantee that timber producers will do the right thing and make sure that there are lots of trees for the future. The only thing, he says, that could cause us to run out of timber would be government intervention in environmental management, since that would remove the incentive for private conservation.

I wish I could agree with this rosy picture of the magic of market economics; life would be so much simpler. But the relationships between market forces and ecological necessities are far more complex and problematic than Palmer is apparently aware. Of course there is an incentive to conserve a resource, or renew it if one knows how; that is elementary. However, the free-market boosters forget that all too often there are also enormous short-term *disincentives* to conservation and renewal. Sometimes it is highly economically advantageous to *wipe out* a resource rather than conserve it. This dismal process is known as the *economics of extinction*, and it is worthwhile, although unpleasant, to remind ourselves how it works.

As a resource (say timber, whales, cod, rhino horns) becomes more and more scarce, its market value approaches infinity. Market value often has little to do with the actual value of the resource for human welfare; we do need timber, but no one has any real need for pulverized rhino horns. Nevertheless, they command such a fabulous price on certain markets that poachers will risk death to hunt down the few remaining rhinos. No incentive to conserve can override the immediate gain to be made from cashing in the resource. Furthermore, any measure which could increase the supply (say, establishing a rhino ranch) would tend to lower its market value; the more effective the renewal method, the more it would tend to cancel out the scarcity value of the resource. Add to all this the fact that measures to renew and conserve a resource can be economically risky and have costs, often large, which may not be recoverable in the short term at all. Hence, when a resource is scarce there are positive *disincentives* to renew it. The scarcer the resource, the more it is in demand, and the harder it is to renew, the more these disincentives tend to operate. If nothing but pure market forces govern, the result (and this has happened time and again in history) is very often the extinction or commercial exhaustion of the resource, not its preservation.

Another practice that contributes to extinction is *discounting the future* when carrying out an economic cost-benefit analysis. This means that we often apply a discount to the value of a resource that we will not be able to profit from right away; the longer we will have to wait to use it, the more we discount it. This is just an academic way of saying that we often grab all of something for ourselves now, and let the future take care of itself. Sometimes people have even deliberately destroyed remaining stocks of a resource so that no one else can profit from it; butterfly collectors used to burn out the hillsides that were home to rare species so that they would have the only remaining specimens to sell (see Rolston 1989). The grab-it-all-now factor is especially likely to operate if the resource is very expensive or impossible to renew, if there is a very high immediate demand for it, or if its renewal is so slow that the money invested in the harvesting technology cannot be recovered if one waits for the resource to renew itself. (The latter is the case for whales; see Dobra 1978.) We need something like the **seventh-generation rule** of many Native North American peoples — before you act, consider the effect on the seventh generation to follow!

Nothing I have said here should be news to anyone familiar with economics or the long and tragic history of resource depletion. Let's talk about forestry, for instance, since Palmer brought the subject up; the eroded, desiccated area of the world now known as Lebanon is a very good example of what can happen if the needs of commerce are allowed to determine the fate of a resource. (To be sure, commercial exploitation is not the only reason for the deforestation of the Levant—but it was one of the major reasons.) Three thousand years ago, Lebanon had at least two million acres in timber, the famous cedars of Lebanon. (See the selection in this book by Carter and Dale, Chapter 4.) In fact, the topography, climate, and tree types were remarkably similar to those of British Columbia today. For several centuries, while the trees held out, forestry was the basis for the thriving Phoenician commercial empire. Eventually, though, the ecology collapsed, and with it the prosperity of the society it supported. Billions of tons of topsoil washed into the sea and the forests disappeared completely except for a few guarded sacred groves. The country today has only the remotest resemblance to its lush and fertile condition in biblical times.

And this is just a typical example; there is very little historical evidence to support the faith that market forces by themselves can guarantee adequate renewal and conservation of resources, and much evidence against it. What almost always seems to happen is that the immediate demand for a resource outweighs the perceived advantage to be gained by long-term measures. Many societies in the past have desperately attempted to reforest, to replenish topsoil, or conserve stocks of fish or game; only a few have succeeded, because the short-term pressure to exploit the resource was always too great.

Still speaking of forestry, Palmer also shows no sensitivity to the really tough biological and technical problems posed by reforestation. In fact, it is very unclear that we really know how to replace the forests that we are harvesting so rapaciously. Foresters would have us believe that they are competent to replace them with "managed" forests as good as or better than those that they clear-cut away. This, like the belief in the power of the "invisible hand" itself, is mostly an article of faith; there is insufficient evidence that present methods work, and some evidence that they do not (in the sense that they may lead to a long-term but inevitable decline in the vitality of the ecology). I am certainly not saying that sustainable harvesting of forest products is impossible, but I am saying that we have not yet found a completely reliable method, especially if we insist on continuing to be able to harvest at the rate and scale that we now find necessary.

The biggest problem we face right now is just the problem that Aldo Leopold identified many years ago: there is very little correspondence between the market value of a "resource" such as a plant or animal species and its real value to the health and functioning of the ecology. We must figure out how to devise an economic system that reflects ecological reality, or our hi-tech culture will go the way of all the other failed cultures whose ruins lie weathering in the deserts they created.

REFERENCES

See Dobra (1978) and especially Clark (1973) for much more detail on the economics of extinction.

Martin Lewis criticizes both environmentalists and anti-environmentalists for what he believes to be a failure to understand the real nature of economic development—and a failure to see that the much-debated cutting of old-growth forests is not really an instance of the market economy in action at all.

UNECONOMIC DESPOLIATION

Martin Lewis

As we near the end of the twentieth century, the rallying cry of American radical environmentalism is the call to halt the clear-cutting of old-growth forests in the Pacific Northwest. On this issue, I side firmly with the eco-extremists. But while lauding their nonviolent holding actions, I by no means condemn the capitalist system that they hold responsible. While old-growth logging is often highly profitable to individual firms, it is utterly inconsequential to the American economy as a whole. Where ecological costs are great and economic benefits modest, we must opt for preserving nature. But even in strictly economic terms, if we were fully able to tally the long-term costs entailed by such reckless logging, we might well discover that the final balance sheet is in the red. It is time to implement a new economic calculus that fully encompasses environmental variables. . . .

In many cases subtle calculations are not needed so much as honest reporting. Much of the old-growth logging in the United States is economic insanity even in the short term. In the Tongass National Forest of southeast Alaska, the clear-cutting of ancient forests is profitable only because loggers are given massive subsidies. In fact, in the majority of America's national forests, logging is an uneconomic activity that would wither away without continual federal handouts. Most of the environmentally destructive water projects in the American West are similarly sustained from the public trough, as is the massive overgrazing that occurs on almost all of the federal government's rangelands. Even tropical deforestation is often stimulated by state subsidies and other governmentally mandated economic distortions. In these cases avid proponents of capitalism ought to be just as incensed as the radical greens. That many self-proclaimed conservatives consistently support such subsidies may indicate that they care less about economic efficiency than they do for ensuring that key constituents are able to remain subsidized by the public purse.

In arguing against economically marginal and especially state-subsidized despoliation, one must recognize a hidden irony. Those who would clear the country's few remaining groves of uncut trees employ the same kind of romantic rhetoric commonly used by their antagonists. They argue, for example, that we are morally obligated to denude the slopes of southeast Alaska in order to save several hundred jobs and a few tiny communities. Most of the jobs will evaporate anyway, once the timber is depleted. But it is the rhetoric that is important; human communities come first, economic rationality be damned. Environmental protagonists and antagonists are thereby united in a mutual contempt for economics. It is in cases like this that hard heads are needed. If we embrace capitalism, we must accept that it necessarily involves what Schumpeter (1942) called "creative destruction." Old jobs will be lost, old communities with perish. A "soft-hearted" society would ease the transition of those persons affected, but it should be willing to let uneconomic—and intrinsically anti-ecological—industries fade into oblivion.

The ultimate irony of the late twentieth-century movement for environmental protection, however, is the fact that both the most strident greens and the most committed anti-environmentalists espouse a fundamentally similar—and thoroughly outdated—view of economic development. Both sides seem to believe that economic growth rests fundamentally on the exploitation of natural resources. The theory is the same, only the ethical positioning is reversed. Fortunately, the moral dilemma thus presented (should we opt for economic growth or environmental health?) is false, since the conceptual structure on which it rests is decrepit. Technologies, not natural resources, provide the essential motor of economic progress. If large segments of the American electorate continue to see forests and ore bodies, rather than research labs and product engineering centers, as the main repositories and wellsprings of national wealth, then we will seriously undercut our own well-being, and perhaps destroy the natural world in the very process.

While the claims of economic growth and environmental protection often do conflict, inefficiency in economic endeavors leads to its own severe forms of waste and degradation. Eventually we must realize, as economically oriented environmentalists are now telling us, that while the freedom to discharge wastes without cost into the environment may be a great boon to a given firm, it is remarkably destructive to the economy as a whole. Economic efficiency, at the most abstract level, is positively rather than negatively linked to most forms of environmental stewardship.

Hazel Henderson has for years been offering alternatives to conventional economic theory, which she has famously likened to "a form of brain disorder." We present here a short and refreshing excerpt from her latest book, *Paradigms in Progress: Life beyond Economics* (1991).

LET'S TAKE CREDIT FOR OUR INTELLIGENCE

Hazel Henderson

Arguments for using "the magic of market forces" to achieve social and regulatory goals has been a constant and sensible refrain in American politics. Our confusion was that we were blinded by economic dogma to *also* hold the contradictory belief that we did *not* actually create these markets, but rather that they were derived from some original state of grace or "human nature." As noted elsewhere, invoking "human nature" to buttress one's political beliefs or policy is a very old strategy. Furthermore, while it is true that, as Adam Smith said, humans have a propensity to barter—indeed we have been doing it since we came out of the caves—the social innovation of creating a nationwide system of markets as the primary resource-allocation mechanism is a fairly recent and brilliant human invention. It was only some 300 years ago in Britain that a package of social legislation to create this national system of markets was introduced and passed by Parliament. It rolled back ancient cultural customs of feudal obligations and right and the older resource-allocation methods still used by many societies (including ours and Britain's): reciprocity and redistribution. In fact, one of the most critical errors of economic theory has been the omission of the informal, unpaid sectors from its models (parenting, do-it-yourself, mutual aid, volunteering, food-raising, bartering, etc.), what I refer to as the "love economy," which all societies bogging down in "economism" are now rediscovering as the *unseen* half.

So, of course, we should create new markets to help eliminate pollution or keep it within Nature's regenerating tolerances. But let us *take credit* for our intelligence, rather than keeping up the pretense that these are "magic forces," or that the propensity of humans to barter was *invented* by Adam Smith, or that capitalism is the only context in which they are or can be used. And let us remember that all human societies depend on sets of explicit and implicit values, ethics, and morals—the more of which can be agreed to and inculcated as part of our *responsibilities* which go along with our rights, the less police and external enforcement will be needed. Indeed, we can use markets much more than we do now to shift our wasteful, unsustainable sector into the future and create whole new industries based on cleaning up and recycling, as well as future sustainability and even environmental enhancement and restoration.

The next item was a leaked internal memo at the World Bank, written by its then chief economist, Lawrence Summers. It offers a somewhat frightening glimpse into the mind of a person whose decisions could critically affect the lives of hundreds of millions of people.

LET THEM EAT POLLUTION

Lawrence Summers

Just between you and me, shouldn't the World Bank be encouraging *more* migration of the dirty industries to the LDCs? I can think of three reasons:

(1) The measurement of the costs of health-impairing pollution depends on the forgone earnings from increased morbidity and mortality. From this point of view a given amount of health-impairing pollution should be done in the country with the lowest cost, which will be the country with the lowest wages. I think the economic logic behind dumping a load of toxic waste in the lowest-wage country is impeccable and we should face up to that.

(2) The costs of pollution are likely to be non-linear as the initial increments of pollution probably have very low cost. I've always thought that under-populated countries in Africa are vastly *under*-polluted; their air quality is probably vastly inefficiently low [*sic*] compared to Los Angeles or Mexico City. Only the lamentable facts that so much pollution is generated by non-tradable industries (transport, electrical generation) and that the unit transport costs of solid waste are so high prevent world-welfare-enhancing trade in air pollution and waste.

(3) The demand for a clean environment for aesthetic and health reasons is likely to have very high income-elasticity. The concern over an agent that causes a one-in-a-million change in the odds of prostate cancer is obviously going to be much higher in a country where people survive to get prostate cancer than in a country where under-5 mortality is 200 per thousand. Also, much of the concern over industrial atmospheric discharge is about visibility-impairing particulates. These discharges may have very little direct health impact. Clearly trade in goods that embody aesthetic pollution concerns could

be welfare-enhancing. While production is mobile the consumption of pretty air is a non-tradable.

The problem with the arguments against all of these proposals for more pollution in LDCs (intrinsic rights to certain goods, moral reasons, social concerns, lack of adequate markets, etc.) could be turned around and used more or less effectively against every Bank proposal for liberalisation.

We conclude with Susan George's grim report on the realities of international development. George is a senior fellow of the Institute for Policy Studies.

FINANCING ECOCIDE IN THE THIRD WORLD

Susan George

Indebted countries have not just borrowed money; they have borrowed the future. Nature puts up the collateral. The environment is perhaps an unexpected victim of the debt crisis in the Third World, but one day we shall all pay for the damage this crisis does to ecosystems.

Many neoclassical economists still flatly deny even the theoretical possibility of limits to growth and refuse the notion that pollution and environmental destruction should figure in their equations. Anything difficult to quantify simply gets left out. Since the International Monetary Fund and the World Bank are peopled with neoclassical economists, it is not surprising that their loans and adjustment programs pay scant attention to ecological costs. It will be a long time before anyone can fully estimate exactly what those are—and by then it may well be too late. But there is already enough evidence to show clearly that the present road is not only wrong but stupid, even in economic terms. The price of cleaning up the mess now being made in the Third World will be horrendous, and it can only add to the present debt bill.

There are two debt/environment connections. The first is borrowing to finance ecologically destructive projects. The second is paying for those—and all the other elements of debt-financed "modernization"—by cashing in natural resources. Many of the grandiose projects that helped to put Third World countries on the debt treadmill are also environmental disasters, ones encouraged and financed by major development institutions like the World Bank. Huge undertakings such as large dams and other hydro-projects are part of the standard development model, paying no heed to future penalties for present recklessness.

For example, the Tucurui dam in Brazil's Amazonia, begun in 1976, is expected to cost at least $8 billion by the time it is completed. That figure does not reflect its true cost, merely that of the cement, steel, labor, etc., required to build it. Real cost includes losses of silt and fertility downstream, flooding of agricultural land and forests, destruction of wildlife, increased salinization of soils. Those are just a few of the physical effects—which have, of course, an immediate impact on people and their livelihoods.

People are hit directly by diseases (malaria, schistosomiasis, river blindness) that proliferate when water patterns are disturbed. They are also, sometimes forcibly, uprooted from their homes. Bruce Rich, former senior attorney of the U.S. Natural Resources Defense Council and now of the Environmental Defense Fund, claims that a 1984 World Bank internal document says, "[Large-scale hydroelectric and irrigation] projects approved by the World Bank in the period 1979–83 resulted in the involuntary resettlement of at least 400,000 to 450,000 people on four continents." One should add that "resettlement" is often an optimistic term, since many of those uprooted are simply left to fend for themselves without compensation.

The World Bank has been a major bulwark of Brazil's electric power program. By 1974, it had already made twenty-six loans to this industrial sector; in 1985–86 alone, bank energy-related lending to Brazil totaled more than $1.3 billion. The Tucurui dam is one of Brazil's many hydro-projects supported by the bank. It has flooded 216,000 hectares of forest land. Electronorte, the government company in charge, was in a hurry. Instead of clearing the forest, it left 13.4 million cubic meters of hardwood, from some 2.8 million trees, to rot under water, after having paid a private subcontractor to spray the forest cover with the infamous Agent Orange (containing dioxin), the devastating effects of which have been well known since the Vietnam War.

Some forty people are alleged to have died from the defoliant. The victims' families are unlikely to receive compensation, but even that is not the end of the story. According to *The Economist*'s monthly Development Report, "It seems a number of full drums of Agent Orange were never removed from the forest, and now nobody knows where they are. . . . They could easily burst under the pressure of water in the dam. The dam straddles the major water supply for the state capital of Belém, home to 1.2 million people."

A World Bank staff member who carried out an environmental assessment of the Tucurui project did not mention Agent Orange in a short description published in 1986; he did state, however, that Tucurui "entails the resettlement of five thousand non-Amerindian families, up to 30,000 people." Land previously owned by Indians in the region has already been significantly decreased by flooding, transmission lines, and a highway.

People are uprooted for purposes other than building dams. Indeed, ecological destruction seems wedded to contempt for ethnic minorities and for the basic needs of poor people. The best (or rather, worst) contemporary examples are provided by internal migration programs, the government-decreed resettlement schemes to move substantial numbers of citizens some place deemed more suitable. Both Brazil and Indonesia, among the largest debtors in the world, have instituted costly programs with the help of bilateral aid, multilateral development banks, and the World Bank. *The Ecologist*, a British magazine that consistently offers exhaustively researched articles on environmental questions, devoted an entire issue to Transmigrasi, the Indonesian Transmigration Program, in 1986.

In the initial, grandiose conception, Transmigrasi was intended to move nearly 70 million people from the "overcrowded" islands of Bali and Java to the so-called outer islands—Sumatra, Sulawesi, Kalimantan (formerly Borneo), Irian Jaya, and others—over a twenty-year period. Mercifully, this plan has been dramatically scaled back; Indonesia simply hasn't enough money to carry it out. Even so, by 1984, more than 3.6 million Indonesians had been moved, and the government seems to be shooting for a quarter to a third of its initial goal. Some 20 million people might ultimately be displaced.

The Transmigrasi budget for the five-year plan to 1989 is $3.5 billion. Indonesia's outstanding debt stood at $32.5 billion in 1984, making it the world's sixth most indebted nation. Transmigrasi absorbs about 6 percent of national spending. In 1985, the World Bank made its largest-ever loan to the program ($160 million), bringing its commitment since 1974 to over a half-billion dollars. As of June 1985, total foreign funding for the resettlement project, including substantial contributions from the Asian Development Bank, the United States, West Germany, and Holland, amounted to nearly $800 million, with $750 million more already in the pipeline.

The World Bank's rationale for this lending is that Transmigrasi will reduce population growth and soil erosion on Java, take advantage of unused or under-used land on the outer islands, and create 200,000 jobs a year. Supporters of the program stress that it gives poor, landless families a once-in-a-lifetime chance to own their own plots while improving living standards for the original inhabitants of the outer islands by its spillover effects. *The Ecologist*'s contributors demolish these claims and add evidence of gross abuse of both nature and human rights.

Theoretically, the settlers are supposed to receive a plot of cleared land, food aid, and agricultural inputs. In reality, *The Ecologist* reports,

> because of the lack of uninhabited land suitable for agriculture, most of the locations chosen are tropical rainforests. The forests have been cleared by private contractors . . . whose only concern is to

> complete the job as quickly and as profitably as possible. In many cases, only the commercially attractive trees have been felled, with large tree stumps being left behind. The transmigrants, who are moved in as soon as possible (often long before site preparation is completed), have not been able to finish the land clearance operations themselves.

Heavy machinery used for clearing land in the Transmigrasi program compacts and damages the soil; the promised houses are often not built, nor are roads or other infrastructure in place. Reports compiled from Indonesian newspapers and other sources indicate that the land is not suitable for growing most crops—certainly not rice, which is what Javanese settlers know best how to grow. What they do manage to grow may be eaten by rats and wild boar. Some settlers live close to starvation and in constant fear of the elephants and tigers that surround them, animals disturbed in their own natural habitats by the land clearing. The *Jakarta Post* reported in 1985 that on one site, in which 1,000 families had been settled, only twelve remained. They had been promised two hectares each, but received at most a quarter of a hectare, not enough for even bare subsistence.

Nicholas Guppy, who has been studying tropical rain forests for thirty-five years, explains concisely the ecological havoc wreaked by this program: "Visiting [cleared] areas, it is hard to view without emotion the miles of devastated trees, of felled, broken and burned trunks, of branches, mud, and bark crisscrossed with tractor trails—especially when one realizes that in most cases nothing of comparable value will grow again on the area. Such sights are reminiscent of photographs of Hiroshima.... *Indonesia might be regarded as waging the equivalent of thermonuclear war upon [its] own territories.*" [Emphasis added.]

In the course of all this devastation, the needs of the inhabitants of Indonesia's outer islands are swept aside, for the government sees tribal people as obstacles—"isolated and alien" is the official phrase. A national law makes quite clear that "the rights of traditional-law communities may not be allowed to stand in the way of the establishment of Transmigration settlements." The government also wants to regroup these people and subject them to the central administration they have hitherto largely escaped, using them as labor on cash-crop plantations. Since 1985, the Indonesian Army has been given a key role in enforcing Transmigrasi. Meanwhile, the objectives of the Department of Social Affairs with regard to tribal people include: "Developing a state of monotheistic religion ... by eliminating animistic traits. Developing their awareness and understanding of State and Government. Raising their capacity for rational and dynamic thinking. Developing and nurturing aesthetic concepts and values ... (so that they may) produce works of art and culture in tune with the values of Indonesian society." Any responsible anthropologist would readily characterize such attitudes and actions toward tribal people as ethnocide.

The World Bank has any number of internal directives and guidelines concerning the proper treatment of migrants, ethnic minorities, and the environment. Clearly, in the case of Transmigrasi, it is systematically flouting all of them. Some of the Bank's officials have expressed serious reservations about the program in draft reports, which are invariably rewritten and watered down in final versions, partly to satisfy the demands of the Indonesian government and partly to justify the enormous sums already invested by the bank. The bank admits that after three five-year plans (and half of a fourth), "an overall assessment of the program is not feasible" because "detailed evaluations" are unavailable. As Carmel Budiardjo, a longtime campaigner for human rights in Indonesia, says, "This gives the impression of a juggernaut hurtling toward some unknown destination, with no one pausing to consider the consequences."

The contributions of huge foreign loans to environmental plunder, widespread impoverishment, and ethnocide can no longer be denied. Numerous World Bank–sponsored ecological calamities are currently being perpetrated in Brazil—the Polonoreste project, for example, perhaps better described as the rape of Rondonia (a state in western Amazonia, on the Bolivian border), which at the present rate will deforest an area the size of Britain by the mid-1990s.

Farther east, the Grande Carajas iron ore project is said to be the world's largest single development scheme (the Tucurui dam is part of it and will provide electricity). Conceived by a Japanese team in 1980, Carajas will cost an estimated $62 billion and entail partial or total deforestation of an area larger than France and Britain put together. The European Community is contributing $600 million to the scheme. Carajas, with several billion tons of iron and half a dozen other mineral ore deposits, is described by the Brazilian government as a "national export project" and an answer to Brazil's crippling debt.

As of 1984, Indonesia owed $23 billion to public sources, plus $413 million to the I.M.F.; Brazil's publicly held debt was $66 billion and it owed the I.M.F. $4 billion. Thus, more than $93 billion in public money has been showered on those two countries alone. If taxpayers and World Bank bondholders in the creditor countries knew that they were indirectly financing ecocide, would the money flow so freely?

Ecologists in the United States are working to stem this flow and won major victories in 1985 and 1986, when Congress passed legislation aimed at forcing the multilateral development banks (M.D.B.s), including the World Bank, to walk a straight and narrow ecological path. Since the United States is the largest contributor to these banks, any restrictions it may impose upon them are of the greatest importance. Some of the major provisions of the legislation are:

- that the U.S. Treasury Department "regularly raise" the question of M.D.B. progress in "improving their environmental performance."
- that the U.S. Treasury and State Departments "propose formally" that each M.D.B. board "hold a special meeting within the next twelve months, focused specifically on environmental performance and better implementation of multilateral development policies designed to protect the environment and indigenous peoples."
- that the U.S. Treasury and State Departments undertake "diplomatic and other initiatives" to "insure cooperative implementation of the reforms."

Further provisions stipulate inclusion of environmental reviews in the entire "project cycle" of the M.D.B.s, regular ecological monitoring, active involvement of health and environmental ministers in borrowing nations during all phases of planning and execution, and "rehabilitation and management of the ecological resources of borrower nations on a sustained basis." Most innovative of all, the M.D.B.s are supposed to accept the participation of nongovernmental environmental and indigenous people's organizations "at all stages of project planning."

Given the M.D.B.s' penchant for secrecy, the provision for participation by nongovernmental groups may be one of the most difficult to implement. The World Bank usually hides behind a real or purported demand for confidentiality on the part of the borrower. When environmentalist Bruce Rich asked the bank why it was financing a project that was causing "rampant deforestation, invasion of Indian areas and destruction of natural lands unsuitable for agriculture in Brazil," the bank initially replied that it was "not at liberty to discuss the details of the implementation of the Polonoreste project because they are part of our ongoing discussions with the Brazilian government. These discussions are of a confidential nature." Senator Robert Kasten, Jr., then wrote to the president of the World Bank, complaining that the response was "a brushoff and an insult."

Money, fortunately, talks; and as Senator Kasten pointed out in his report that accompanied the 1986 legislation, "Funding for the M.D.B.s has been reduced because of their failure to address the Committee's critiques and proposals for reform." His colleague in the House, David Obey, made clear in his report that Congress is looking for real, substantial changes in policies and practices, "not just promises to do better."

So, the M.D.B.s may have to choose between opening their windows or closing their doors to significant funding. Congress recognizes, however, that it cannot force the necessary changes on a recalcitrant bank all by itself. The legislators hope that the requirement for diplomatic initiatives will cause other lending—and borrowing—nations to bring similar pressures to bear on the

M.D.B.s and insist that environmental protection become part of their standard operating procedures. The U.S. legislation could serve as a model for Green activists in other countries.

FURTHER READING

For more by Susan George, see her *A Fate Worse Than Debt* (1988b). Henderson (1981) and (1991) overflow with constructive suggestions, outspoken criticism, and a refreshing but guarded optimism that, these days, is a little unusual. Clark (1973) presents a very thorough mathematical analysis of the economics of extinction. Medvedev (1990) illustrates that the centrally planned Soviet economy fared little better in its environmental record than capitalist economies. See also Summers (1992b), in which he claims, "I, for one, feel the tug of the billion people who subsist on less than $1 a day in 1992 more acutely than the tug of future generations."

QUESTIONS TO CONSIDER

1. As an exercise, attempt to translate Summers's memo into plain English. Why might the inadvertent publication of this memo have caused some embarrassment for the World Bank? As a homework exercise, trace Summers's subsequent career at the World Bank.
2. Examine the parallels and differences between the shut-down of the East Coast fisheries in Canada and the impending end of old-growth logging, and consider the adequacy of market economics to resolve such crises.
3. How could one get around the dismal logic of the "economics of extinction"?
4. Consider the role of private property in the preservation of resources.

CHAPTER FIFTEEN

WHAT IS WEALTH?

In this chapter, Canadian writer Grant A. Whatmough presents a densely woven and challenging analysis of the complex relationships among environment, technology, and economy. In part, his topic is the nature and implications of a peculiarly modern variety of the macroparasitism described by William McNeill (see Chapter Seven), although he does not use quite the same terminology as McNeill. In part, also, he argues that if we could remind ourselves of just what the fundamental nature of wealth really is, then the apparently intractable problem of reconciling economic with environmental priorities simply dissolves—leaving us with the very real problem of constructing a culture that could be both humanly fulfilling and ecologically sustainable.

Grant Whatmough has had a rich and varied career as a naval architect, engineer, zoological researcher, sculptor, farmer, builder, and architectural designer. Throughout, his deepest concern has been the philosophy and rationality—either present or absent—in twentieth-century civilization as that unfolds.

MONEY, MACHINES, ENERGY, AND WEALTH

Grant A. Whatmough

The theories of the social sciences have become sacred, now treated as prophetic texts pointing the way towards a fuller and more affluent life for all. Amongst the most honoured, or worshipped, are those in the fields of economics and psychology; which is perfectly understandable. Together they have provided us with both a procedure and a justification by means of which vast numbers of people have come to be engaged in the distribution and exchange of products which none have actually produced, and of services that are largely composed of bookkeeping. They have allowed us to rise above the stigma which aristocratic societies attached to the notion of necessary work, and at the same time avoid the unpleasantness and immediacy of actual productive labour. Now we can all — or at least most of us — feel that we are personally involved in the exchanges and commitments that constitute the practical social process without having to face the rigours of extreme physical effort, or the consequences of inadequate skill and judgement.

Since the issues involved in this are not really moral issues — they are entirely practical matters though we customarily moralize about them — the only legitimate criticism of our current procedures would have to be that they involve some practical risk or limitation. And of course they do. When the central preoccupation of the economy narrows to an exaggerated emphasis of the processes of exchange and accountability, the quality of the things exchanged is of little importance. They become simply the tokens in some more abstract game in which numerical quantity is all that counts; and the means by which these quantities are acquired is not thought to be significant. We therefore eventually come to deprive and neglect our sources, cheating our prime producers and raping our ecology, in order to provide increasing quantities of basic materials to feed an exchange process which expands unchecked as fast as human ingenuity or political manipulation can invent the means for expansion. Eventually, unless some countering restraints are imposed, we must exhaust our supplies. We will not only have used everything that is immediately available but, while doing this, will have eliminated any possibility of regeneration, through our neglect of both human creative excellence and of the biological vitality of our physical world.

This understandable tendency towards bureaucratic expansion is as old as civilization, but has usually been controlled either by ethical traditions or by some immediate shortage of supplies. On those occasions when it has broken loose from its restraints it has sooner or later invariably destroyed itself by exhausting its own cultural base. In each of its reappearances it has been defended as a "higher order of civilization," and its supporters have earnestly believed that human knowledge and technology had reached a miraculous point where it could provide for the needs of mankind by overcoming all natural limitations. During such periods of confident positivism the process is invariably justified by a growing self-righteous morality, which opposes and condemns all factual limitations by claiming that they do not actually exist, that they are inventions of subversive and simplistic propaganda. Such periods usually end in a welter of bloodshed, privation, and misery, and with a total absence of effective morality of any sort.

Our present move in that direction probably began almost two centuries ago, but has accelerated most notably during the past fifty years. The earlier and more superficial of these recent attempts to speed up bureaucratic expansion were all short-lived and led to spectacular disasters — the collapse of the stock-market in 1929 and the failure of the Fascist dictatorships in the last World War — but we have learned from such mistakes and have proceeded on the basis of a more careful and thoughtful sophistry. By this means economic theory has established an incredible authority for itself during the past twenty or thirty years; a prestige so great that its practical failures are invariably believed to be unavoidable natural catastrophes. Hence our conviction that material shortages, ecological destruction, and climatic disasters result from our limited knowledge of the physical sciences; and that wars and revolutions are simply examples of political incompetence.

With its basic principles safely removed from the realm of practical criticism, economic theory now exhibits a fine-spun complexity as impenetrable as that of medieval theology. But since it is not supposed to be simply an exercise in blind faith or scholasticism — it is represented as a means for determining effective policy — this sort of ambiguous triviality is positively dangerous. It threatens to destroy our society by accident while exploring the purity of competing theoretical models, in a mood of experimental objectivity which seems oddly inappropriate where our actual survival is at stake. Bearing in mind that we now occupy most of the usable space in the world, and must therefore live with the consequences of any damage that we may do to it or to ourselves, such an attitude is madness. We have constructed our entire social system as a product of economic determinism, and have imposed both on the world at large; to a degree that makes it unlikely that either could survive any further erosion of economic common sense.

The most thoroughly mystical field in the entire "testament" of economic theory is that associated with the nature and function of money. This ought not to be so; the basic notions are not really complex and the practical functions can be clearly and directly inferred. But an enormously difficult terminology, together with a body of justifying theory, has developed within the last two centuries which seems designed to confuse the real issue and protect established procedures from the impact of rational criticism.

The original invention of money, in the form of interchangeable coinage, ranks in importance with the invention of written language with regard to the development of human culture. But from the beginning the value of both has been threatened by those who would misuse them for personal advantage. To be culturally effective and actually useful, money must function in exchange as a formal token of both human effort and accomplishment; it must represent not only the mechanical concept of a certain amount of work done but — as is also true in physics — some special quality in the effort applied. If money is allowed to represent either simple existence, a diffused generality, or the futile expenditure of energy to no productive purpose, it becomes *economically* worthless; a ritual token instead of a possible medium of exchange. Traditionally money has been referred to as "a repository of value"; which conceals this distinction, together with its attendant difficulties, by shifting the focus to the *process* of exchange — in short by reducing money to a mere social convention — and ignoring the consequent necessity of determining precisely what *economic* "value" can possibly be thus transferred. Of course this issue did not arise when gold and silver coinage was used; unless debased, the "value" was intrinsic in the coinage itself and hence such coinage did not function simply as a medium of exchange, but instead was a direct exchange or barter in itself. But from the beginning the chief threat to the value of money came from those who recognized that scarcity-value could be traded on; both the scarcity of certain artifacts and the scarcity of money itself. This produced usurious money-lending and the merchant trader; and while both were socially useful to a degree, their manipulations of the money supply invariably distorted its value. Its buying power, with regard to productive labour, was artificially increased to include a kind of "bonus" for the manipulator; and as long as precious metals limited the supply of money, the effects of usury and extortionate trading were to tax and to depress the actual exchange economy as a whole.

With time, three thousand years at least, the whole process became highly sophisticated and paper money came into use to allow further manipulation. It arose out of moneylending, by then dignified by the name of banking, and was simply a device by which the banker could collect interest on more money (gold) than he actually had. He issued promissory notes which circulated as money, on the assumption that only a limited number of these would have to be met with gold at any one time. With the invention of negotiable paper, money itself became inflated and its buying power was reduced; but this effect was confined to the country or kingdom of the banker since international exchange was still governed by gold. And it must be noted that the inflation of money could not offset the depressions of usury, since those effects were a depression of the actual physical economy; a matter of taking out of it goods and services for which no equivalent goods or services had ever been exchanged. The inflation of money was simply a monetary matter, the result of there being more money available; and while this expansion of the money-supply could provide capital to justify an increase of effective human effort it was also usuriously taxed (interest) and the economy continued to be drained proportionally. What our economists have called "stagflation," a depression of the actual physical economy accompanied by monetary inflation, has actually been with us for a long time.

And manipulative banking also allowed "credit"—an essentially political evaluation—to function with an economic power that, in practice, could eclipse the economic authority of effective productivity; since "credit" can always claim unlimited potential, and hence unlimited precedence, while productivity is necessarily confined to whatever may actually have been accomplished.

By the end of the eighteenth century the concept of economics was beginning to change. Until then it had traditionally been a philosophical matter, inextricably tied to ethics and political theory; a study of the proper exchange of goods and services amongst people, and the control of theft and tyranny. In this view the manipulation of money itself was simply one amongst many of the forms of theft; and it was from this position that Locke, Hobbes, and the earlier social philosophers framed their opinions. But then a new view arose, which held that the manipulation of money was dignified by tradition and custom, that it was in fact perfectly legitimate, and that the study of economics was essentially the study of manipulative techniques. Based on this innovation, economics broke loose from philosophical restraint and, as political economy, claimed status as a science in itself; a science of social manipulation and control. It spawned utilitarianism as a justifying polemic, and has continued in that form until today. As a result our real economy has been drained to the brink of destruction and that excellent invention, money, has been debased and reduced to the point of unusability—as sophistry and huckstering are now busily debasing our language.

While it is probably much too late to suggest that economics should once again be placed under the control of philosophy, or of any of its departments, it is not too late to demand responsible, or at least rational, behaviour from economists. If philosophical incompetence blinds them to the fallacy of assigning a central role to money—and to the logical absurdity of the concept of economic determinism—then they must improve their skills. They have claimed authority and they have achieved it; which now gives them an extraordinary power to make or break whatever we have left of our civilization.

But whatever we may ultimately be forced to do must be brought about from within the context of what we now call our urban industrial system; all of our older institutions have been destroyed or altered. That is not an easy undertaking. Our bureaucratic procedures have become so essential a part of our lives that any significant criticism of their industrial base appears as a threat to our personal security. We have profited enormously from our industrial myths and now, when our confidence is shaken by approaching austerity, we tend to defend them at all cost; hoping that they can somehow be made to transcend shortage and depletion, as they appear to have once overcome established moral and economic restraints. This is a dangerous delusion that owes a good deal of its credibility to our acceptance of the industrial process on faith; a non-critical belief in certain of its more persistent fables and pretensions.

The most secure of these is the vaguely-stated assumption that what we call the Industrial Revolution was brought about by an acceleration of technological advances arising out of the scientific accomplishments of the seventeenth and eighteenth centuries. In fact the reverse is true; it was the expansion of early industrialization that spurred technological advance and channelled public funds into the support of scientific inquiry. The industrial revolution was, and still is, essentially a technique for manipulating money; a device—we call it capitalism—by means of which a larger number of people could enjoy the financial advantages that would otherwise be confined to successful merchants and bankers. The technical equipment with which this process began had been around for centuries. Water and wind driven mills were common as were broad looms, lathes, and potter's wheels. The steam engine had first been invented and built by Hero of Alexandria more than two thousand years before James Watt was born, and had been abandoned as wasteful. The single factor that, more than any other, changed our world was the acceptance of money manipulation as an unavoidable and legitimate aspect of our economy.

As industrialism has expanded and other versions of unrestrained money-manipulation—confidence-rackets, public-funds swindles, and "social engineering"—have become a feature of our society, sporadic attempts have been made to re-examine the basic concepts. Innumerable books have been published on the general subject of "Man and the Machine," but they form a mixed reference; too many were written by people whose aim was to support and expand the system as it stood. The entire "futurist" movement which has been with us in one form or another since the 1920s is of this sort. Unfortunately the critical authors, those with a real concern, were themselves usually quite ignorant of the actual nature of machines and generally failed to make any clear case. The people who really understood at least the mechanical side of the matter, the engineers and technicians, have generally been either incoherent or uninterested in cultural implications, and have published nothing.

The essential point is to recognize that amongst the multitude of possible mechanical arrangements and assemblies there are a number of clear classifications, and at least two orders, of machines. The first, and simplest, of these orders—despite the apparent intricacy of some examples—are contrivances that are complete in themselves and serve simply as extensions of specific human capabilities. One of the more familiar classes of these are tools; devices that increase some particular human ability to act directly on an object so as to alter or control it in some way. They can be as simple as a lever or a skillsaw or a drill, but they can also be as complex as a bulldozer or a compound metal-working lathe; yet all will act in this direct way. When we describe some general assemblies as "tools," simply because we believe them to be useful, we tend to blur clear understanding and attach the notion of mechanical directness and inevitability to relationships that may not work that way at all. A second order of machines—and these may be further subdivided for other purposes—are compound arrangements in which the various parts interact to produce a multiplying effect. And in this second order of machines we also have our tools; examples of which would range from water-driven mills to modern factories and assembly-lines. These act not only on the objects that they are designed to affect; but with considerable force on their component parts—including the people who must serve them. In the case of the mill it is the driven millstone that is the first-order tool; the mill-as-a-whole serves not only to power it, but to supply it with raw materials and deal with its production. As a second-order machine it is immensely powerful and its production is relatively large; but its demands on those who serve it are proportionally relentless, and consequently its only possible social value depends upon whether it can show any actual material gains over alternative ways of accomplishing a corresponding production. In short it must produce the economic equivalent of some mechanical advantage; and in fact only a limited class of second-order machines can do that.

The original attraction was, of course, the sheer quantity of production; irresistible to a rising merchant class who had never doubted the value of unlimited quantities of tradable goods. And as a bonus there was the financial advantage that it gave to its owners. But there is every reason to doubt that any large number of those early second-order machines were actually capable of producing any real economic advantage. Certainly no English Midlands cotton mill of that time could possibly produce enough cloth to reimburse the general economy for all that it took out of it; the raw materials, fuel, buildings and machinery, the labour of all its employees plus all that they consumed, together with the vast quantities of things that were directly and indirectly used to support its profitable operation. In terms of the real economy as a whole it was not at all a productive facility, but amongst the largest of consumers; extracting an apparent profit by acquiring its raw materials for less than the real cost of producing them, and using productive energy—human labour—for which it paid less than replacement cost. No society can afford that sort of thing unless it has a sufficient excess of real assets to be able to squander them to indulge a taste for industrial products. Industry of that sort is not part of a possible economic system; it is simply a short-lived way of "cashing" accumulated economic capital.

The eventual result in England, where the volume of accumulated real economic assets was necessarily limited, became brutally apparent by 1900. As a consequence of little more than a century of increasing industrialization the real economy had been ruined and its agrarian base destroyed; with coal resources depleted, iron ore reserves exhausted, and the stands of merchantable timber almost wiped out. The general prosperity that had been slowly building up and diffusing over centuries had been replaced by a small number of excessively wealthy merchants and bankers, an expanding but severely rationed middle class, and a vast grinding poverty for the majority of the population. Had the total of real assets at that time been uniformly distributed it could barely have provided adequate clothing for them all; England's tangible prosperity had gone in the smoke of industrial-financial manipulation. Her gigantic Empire, her navy, and her merchant marine had all been pressed into the service of industrial ambition, and had in turn become additional charges on the real economy; while her expanding populations had been squandered in relatively unproductive subservience. By 1910 England was effectively bankrupt, her actual economic capital exhausted and the great bulk of her population demoralized, living on the Empire and on credit with all the self-assurance that any such collection of money-lenders and industrialists would feel at the conclusion of a successful foreclosure.

As social conditions degenerated during that period, our current political and social theories emerged as proposals for mitigating the damage. But most theorists apparently could not bring themselves to reject the myth of industrialism as a sort of productive miracle; and economists never seem to have understood the machine. With the exception of a few nostalgic reactionaries, all endorsed financial manipulation and sought other solutions; the socialists declaring their faith in enlightened public management, the communists their vision of the selfless army of the proletariat, while the various shades of conservatives were sure that the whole thing would resolve itself eventually as long as society remained resolute. Economic theory attained heights of irrelevant silliness which ultimately led J.M. Keynes (later Lord Keynes) to publish his famous *General Theory of Employment Interest and Money* in 1936; a book that has been hailed by social scientists as an intellectual triumph, and has significantly influenced economic policy since its publication. Lord Keynes's theoretical concepts were first applied without dilution or restraint in Great Britain during the last World War. Though they are declared to constitute an insight into inescapable truths as those govern our monetary system, and hence are supposed to be as inevitable as the laws of physics, it took the average small-time English profiteer very little more than a month to figure out how to beat them; and today England is still valiantly—or perhaps stubbornly—attempting to live with their consequences.

Fortunately our position is not now so hopeless as it appeared at the beginning of this century. While early industrialization was quite incapable of producing tangible goods to replace its excessive economic depletions, it did stimulate an acceleration of technological advances so great as to provide us with the means of possibly overcoming its destructive consequences. But if we are to accomplish this we will first have to get over our attachment to nineteenth century industrial fantasies, and come to a clear assessment of what we are left with from that desperate period. If we are to use our industrial technology effectively and productively we must learn how to separate it from financial manipulation, and how to defend the value of money as a medium of exchange. We must become familiar with the distinction between such industry as can actually show a real economic advantage, and that which simply produces large financial profits that have been extracted from the small reserves of economic capital that still remain.

Those second-order machines that now actually can produce more than they consume are mostly what we call primary industries; simple repetitive processes that produce standardized artifacts for use as the primary materials, or parts of some more specialized or singular production. The obvious examples are milled lumber and rolled or formed metals; but one should also include such things as nails and screws, paints and solvents, electrical and mechanical parts, electronic components, fabrics and papers, and a multitude of similar materials. In any highly technical society this class of artifacts should be considered as the actual raw materials of advanced production, while the ore from which we get the metals and the tree from which we get the lumber are simply resources. Primary industries of this sort should—together with farming, mining, fishing, and lumbering—be publicly assured of financial security, as essential social services; but given this support they should have their profits and their growth rigidly limited to the minimum necessary to make it possible for them to meet a spontaneous and unsolicited public demand.

It is by way of the secondary industries—the manufacture and distribution of consumer goods and the service sector of our economy, that the original manipulative tactics most threaten our survival. Here it is that the old predatory and extortionate instinct still rules, by means of "capital investment" and "providing jobs." Though the power-centre is now a technocracy, instead of an individual, the beliefs and convictions remain those of a century and a half ago. "Industry" or "business"—the terms have become synonymous as corporate chains come to dominate those fields—continue to claim their "right" to cash in our economic assets on the ground of acting in the best interest of the majority. And to ensure that these claims shall be enforced they have captured our public bureaucracies by intimidation, and compromised our politicians. It is this area of our economy that now provides a bureaucratic shelter for so many of us; and it is precisely here that the old nineteenth century fallacies most threaten our survival.

The fact is that the provision of services and the manufacture of finished products, for use in any highly developed civilization, *cannot* be effectively done by remote industrial means. When we attempt to do so we either degrade the quality of the product below levels acceptable to a critical and informed market, or we so distort the industrial process as to render it enormously wasteful of both materials and energy; the so-called "standard" product is simply one so compromised that it cannot conclusively "fit" any specific, or local, requirement at all—and there are few other sorts of actual needs. In practice we strike a compromise between apparent limitations, flooding our society with relatively degraded artifacts and wasting a huge proportion of our economic resources. By means of advertising we numb the critical faculties of the majority and coerce them into accepting that degree of degradation; and by a completely unrestrained exploitation of our resources we attempt to keep up with the waste. We have managed to produce a world distinguished by inappropriate and short-lived artifacts, arbitrary and inadequate services, and continuously changing purposes as our institutions are manipulated for the advantage of competing interests; a society requiring immeasurable quantities of energy and with garbage as its only enduring product. We have survived so far only because our world was so incredibly rich in resources when we began this insane policy.

The manufacture of finished products is simply a first-order tool-using process; commonly organized now as a second-order activity solely for financial advantage. And our technological advances of the past century have given us small, economically efficient, portable power tools of high quality that make any skilled artisan of today productively superior to the second-order machines (factories) of our earlier industrial tradition. The result has been to revolutionize manufacturing itself so that most of it—with the exception of a few highly specialized products—is now actually done by individuals using such tools; though they may work in shifts and in huge factories. In many cases, probably the majority, the so-called "economies of scale" are either a myth or a lie; at best a belief that justifies the preservation of the managing and distributing technocracy. In fact industrial production did not originally take over from local producers either because it was cheaper or better. It was almost invariably more expensive, and of lower quality. Its market appeal lay in the "snob" value of its "foreignness"—or in the simple fact that it was an exotic addition to the local economy. Now, with easy transportation and a general knowledge of techniques, the old manipulative industrial tradition is maintained only by limiting local credit and the supply of tools and primary components—or through advertising and the control of markets. Given free and equitable access to supplies, small local businesses could easily produce all that we could possibly use of appropriate artifacts of high quality, for a price equal to that charged at retail by our large industries for an inferior product—and need only a fraction of the energy now wasted in the industrial process. But some radical alteration would have to be made in our accustomed methods of distribution and public sales.

The profits and manipulative advantages—both political and economic—to be gained from the centralized industrial production of consumer goods are so great that these techniques have been expanded into the production of entirely redundant products and into the service sector of our economy. In fact they are even now being extended into agriculture, where "agribusiness" has already so altered procedures that farming is now a net consumer, drawing vast quantities of energy from our economic pool and returning only that small fraction which it has converted into food. Fossil fuels, timber, and hydroelectric power are used in enormous quantities to produce throw-away packaging, advertising handbills, disposable novelties, and misused metals—aluminum smelting is a simple case of converting raw electrical energy into a metal which is then largely wasted on trivial and redundant production. Our building "industry" now puts up structures whose life-expectancy is not sufficient to allow us to replace one half of the materials and labour that they consume. It is this kind of false-industry, an entirely misrepresented activity deriving power and profits from its expropriation of our labour and our energy supplies, that threatens to destroy our society.

Most of this misrepresentation is made possible by the failure, on the part of economists and participants alike, to understand the process. Such "industries" are created by bureaucrats who quite naturally believe that the bureaucratic method is their essential strength and, since technical terms and procedures are involved, then come to see themselves as technocrats. They defend the "mystique" of their method, as bureaucrats have always defended their rituals, and come to believe that their own characteristic incompetence reflects the complexity of a highly sophisticated technology. Decisions and judgements which a truly competent artisan would make correctly in moments now take weeks, months, or years of expensive planning and study—and are often wrong when made. Computers and research projects become necessary, and vast investments are made to keep the process running in spite of its management; all of which are described as "specialized experience and technical knowledge," and claimed to be essential to the running of such an enterprise.

Economists, totally ignorant of the realities involved, take all of this on face value and on faith, then defend it as our chief economic asset; declaring that above all else we must preserve and expand our technocracies, and contribute to their expenditures and investments.

For economists, politicians, and the general public alike, the accepted economic goal is adequate pay and full employment for our workforce; which ensures that the tactical strength of technocracies lies in their control over the supply of "jobs." Any policies or proposals which would weaken or limit their expansion and authority are met with a threat of loss of work for those already employed, or a lack of future work for the expanding population; and economists have been as timid as politicians in resisting this kind of distorted blackmail. This is inexcusable because it is obvious that, so far as the real economy of the country is concerned, these are empty threats; such "jobs" do not contribute in the slightest to the real economy—in fact they are a drain on it and now threaten to destroy it. If that entire segment of our "industry" were to be closed down tomorrow our actual economy would, as a consequence, become instantly wealthy, and well able to provide for the humane reorganization of its displaced populace. All that would have been lost would be our accustomed ways of providing incomes for their employees, the tax revenues to the government, and the anxieties that we now face with regard to the future. These false-industries contribute nothing to the needed or desired artifacts and valuable services of our society, they do not make life one bit more luxuriant but instead cheapen it and trespass on us all; though combined they are vastly the largest of consumers. Through their dominance of the market they have crippled and demoralized the artisan, the craftsman, and the small businessman, and have deprived our entire society of both excellence and uniqueness in our normal exchanges and acquisitions.

But it is certainly not the case that there is no practical escape from this. Bankers and technocrats could be restrained by law; though that probably would require a revised legal system to replace the one that now supports them. We certainly have a sufficient workforce—now squandered in bureaucracy—to replace false-industry with independent and productive local suppliers. The whole transition could be accomplished in a generation or two, if properly protected from reactionary attacks and deprivations. There need not be any sacrificial victims—if simple justice is legally imposed—and for that huge majority now facing the futility of wasted lifetimes of dependence and enslavement to a managerial technocracy, there could instead be the enjoyment of the authority and the rewards accorded to significant producers. Nor could there be any actual shortage of demand; in a technologically advanced society there could be no limit to the market for substantial products of real qualitative improvements—and as waste is eliminated, society could certainly afford them.

What we currently call the energy crisis is probably the most dramatic example we have of the impact of our industrial fallacy on the whole of our social fabric. In fact the entire issue has arisen out of nothing more than a sudden instability in international crude-oil prices. But since the petrochemical industries have been "cashing in" cheap oil for years—to dominate the market with synthetic fabrics, paints, and plastics—the impact on our economy is huge. Gigantic profits have made it possible for them to practically starve out competing suppliers of natural fibres, cellulose, and vegetable oils or gums, producing an inflated and dependent market precariously balanced on a single source; while simultaneously ignoring the fact that the entire enterprise was obviously a grotesque misuse of non-renewable supplies and chemical ingenuity. And when we added that to the waste entailed in promoting tourism to the status of a major international industry, and reducing the shipment of goods to a fumbling game played by incompetent bureaucrats, the consequences have been catastrophic. Of course in the panic that has resulted, the real issues have been kept obscure; and nobody has drawn attention to the fact that it is not Arab greed, but manipulative marketing and chemical synthesis, that now threatens our necessary fuel supplies. In fact it is a question of the fuel we need to heat us, give us light, and power our machines, that we refer to when we speak of the "energy crisis"; though I have heard one loyal and single-minded spokesman for the petrochemical industry declare that our industrial future rests on preserving fossil fuels for synthesis, and forcing the rest of society to find other supplies to meet its needs. He may be right; though if he is this idiotic process has gone farther, and is closer to a sudden end, than most of us would like to think.

It should be clear to us by now that no society can survive for very long if any large proportion of its energy supply is wasted. We not only have the remote examples of Egypt, Greece, and Rome—where labour and production both came to be directed to the expansion of administrative rituals—but the recent history of nineteenth century industrialism, in which the waste of timber, coal, and human energy so rapidly maimed European culture and brought it to the brink of suicide in two World Wars. No physical system—and any economic arrangement is precisely that—can survive a dissipation of the energies that bind its parts together; entropic decay cannot be overcome be deciding that it serves the greater glory of some special emphasis. Physical systems can expand but only coherently, and only if all such expansions entail the full use of any surplus energy available from whatever additions may come to be included in them—all other apparent expansions are no more than a concealed collapse.

Of course, in keeping with our present industrial tradition, the energy crisis has in itself been exploited to promote "conservation and control" as a growth industry. Flocks of specialists, consultants, and administrators have suddenly appeared to assist in imposing what is seen as an appropriate austerity. Luxuriant "research" projects—backed by entire academic departments—have been established. The repeated shuffling and replacement of heating and lighting systems, directed by conflicting opinions, has underwritten spectacular expansions for suppliers and installers. While manufacturers can now enjoy a whole new market for solar panels that consume more energy in their production and delivery than they can ever possibly produce; insulating and weather-sealing products whose excessive use not only threatens the endurance of the very structures in which they are installed, but consumes more energy than they can save; complex windows that are not only relatively ineffective, fragile, and short-lived, but are made almost entirely out of energy-intensive raw materials; and a multitude of other minor products whose production and continuous replacement is rapidly becoming a major drain on our resources. If our first fears of "shortage" were perhaps as bit exaggerated, there is little doubt that we will soon have justified them.

But as our industrial society is now organized we do, indeed, face a shortage of energy that threatens our actual production of real goods, limits needed services, and imposes some degree of austerity on most of us. And in an effort to meet what are supposed to be our "needs" the Appalachian highlands have already been irreversibly damaged, while huge areas of the northwestern Great Plains are now threatened with total destruction. Yet in fact it is simply false-industry, not real production or a natural domestic demand, that consumes more than 60% of all our energy; and in company with its associated bureaucracies will require the vast expansions planned for the next twenty years. If we could manage in some way to dispense with this as a form of habitual fraud, we would find that our present electrical energy capacity and petroleum reserves are together already so large that our populations would have to increase by one half at least before we could make full use of what we now have. It is neither patriotic nor rational for a populace to be deprived, or limited, in its possible prosperity and enjoyments for the sake of enhancing the power of special interests that already bear too heavily on it.

Supporting this exercise in irrationality, we still cherish those odd notions of the nature of wealth which the early nineteenth century economists concocted to support the legitimacy of money-manipulation. Though the various economic theories of that time might differ on every other point, they all agreed that wealth was simply a quantitative matter that translated directly into money, or money-earning capacity; a confused blurring of the distinction between wealth and profits. The original notion of wealth—involving the idea of prosperity as a fullness of life made possible by the possession of adequate and appropriate facilities—was altered to emphasize the possession of the means for productive volume, and hence that expansion of money which we call profit. It is this change which distinguishes all utilitarian economic theory from the older and more philosophical forms; a change in emphasis from the quality of life to be sought, to the acceptance of some simpler quantitative alternative. The political and social theories which followed in such numbers from this change inevitably reflected a similar confusion of primary concepts; all stumbling into the ancient fallacy of assuming that whatever can be shown to be desired has therefore been proven to be desirable.

This whole ridiculous distortion, with its pervasive Marxist obsessions, is completely unnecessary and avoidable if we simply admit that for several thousand years of history the human race had a perfectly clear understanding of the notion of wealth, which directly involved ideas both of prosperity and of personal wellbeing. Wealth is not and has never been a matter of surplus, or margin, or gain, or profit in any form; it is inescapably and factually a matter of sufficiency and of the enduring and life-enhancing value of that which is produced. Simple quantitative production can support only basic survival, to allow time for the development of such insights as may lead to wealth; but it can never constitute wealth in itself. The wealth of nations is not—as Adam Smith declared it to be in his book of that name—a function of the division of labour, nor a product simply of labour in any of its forms; these alone can provide only an austere, and perhaps genteel, poverty. The real wealth of any nation is the sum of the enduring quality of its artifacts, the good health of its ecology, and the creative vitality and abilities of its populations. Any economic system worthy of the name is one which not only allows, but leads to, the enhancement and expansion of these qualities which constitute the real wealth of the civilization.

The rise of modern technology does not alter in any way the real basis for wealth; it fact it emphasizes it. The essence of significant science or technology is effective skill and knowledge; both of which are manifestations of human individuality and wellbeing, and are not directly related either to cash investment or corporate organization. They are functions of the quality of thought, which follows from the quality of life itself; and are threatened, as life is threatened, by any imposed supremacy of simple quantitative aims. No modern civilization can long survive the imposition of self-denial or austerity on the majority of its citizens. Yet today, politicians and economists alike adopt the view that our society is nothing more than a single vast corporate entity in which private needs must be submerged in the interest of the State as a profitable whole. For the past hundred and fifty years — from the era in which Bismarck traded the German culture for an industrial Reich — this accountant's notion of civilization has dominated and impoverished all of our economies as completely as it has subjugated the Communist world, and kept us all on the brink of perpetual war.

This shopkeeping version of administration has strangely distorted the form of our governments, and has brought them excessively and improperly into the financial affairs of society as an active and competing participant. Their bureaucracies grow huge and blend imperceptibly into the machinery of expanding business technocracies; while the true responsibilities of government are neglected and denied. The only possible aim of proper government is to adopt and institute such policies and legislation as shall improve the quality of the relationship amongst people and to prohibit theft and trespass; and proper economic policy is simply that system of exchange which will best serve these ends. Instead we have unlimited increases in taxation to finance the growth of an omnipotent State bureaucracy, which imposes its own ambitious palliatives to offset the consequences of its own political failures. The notion of countervailing public force, grounded in a taxation of monetary surpluses, amounts to no more than the old dictum — "If you can't beat them, join them" — and a complete surrender to the consequences of manipulative policy.

But when all the arguments have finally been declared, when futurists are finished with their fevered dreams of "brave new worlds" devoted to unlimited consumerism, which science will apparently present to us, the truth remains that our ecology — which does include ourselves — is the ultimately limiting factor which will determine how, or whether, we survive. Society cannot persist in any form without resilient people, water, food, and oxygen, nor with capricious weather; in any sort of desert or with impoverished populations, it must die out. I certainly do not intend that anything that I have written above should be taken to mean that I seriously believe that it is probable that we will willingly make any essential choices. In fact I believe that collectivism, bureaucracy, and manipulative management are together so woven into the fabric of our society that our present policies and habits will almost certainly continue and intensify. We have become so attached to our sheltered corporate lives that we will continue to believe — because we want to believe — whatever Madison Avenue may tell us. After centuries of sophistic propaganda the habit of wishful gullibility is so entrenched — either as faith or optimism — as to be nearly incurable. But already we have destroyed at least one half of our ecological base and hence deprived ourselves of that prosperity that would have been possible with it. I think it likely that we will simply proceed until we have destroyed the remaining half. What I have described above is no more than what I believe we eventually *must* come to recognize. If we could miraculously find the strength to make rational judgements now, we could still salvage some real prosperity of an enduring sort out of what we have left. But these judgements will almost certainly not be made until they are forced on us; and then it will be far too late to hope for any comfort or prosperity out of it. All we could possibly have at that point is some sort of austere survival. The final "bottom line" of our entire economic balance sheet is dictated by the ecological vitality which we have allowed to *ourselves*, and to our world as we treat it.

FURTHER READING

For background on modern economics, see Galbraith (1973) and Keynes (1936). On "Man and the Machine," see Wright (1901) and Mumford (1934).

QUESTIONS TO CONSIDER

1. Describe in your own words Whatmough's account of the function of money in economic exchange, and the consequences entailed by our shift to a paper (or credit) economy.
2. Do you think that Whatmough's distinction between first- and second-order machines is valid?
3. Describe and evaluate the distinction Whatmough emphasizes between productive and parasitic (or opportunistically exploitative) economies.
4. Do you think that Whatmough's analysis of the misuse of energy by modern capitalism and his critique of the petrochemical industries are valid?
5. Whatmough in effect claims that our current industrialism is a kind of economic fraud, and imposed austerity little more than a supporting propaganda. Evaluate this claim, with reference to specific industrial practices.
6. Try to put Whatmough's definition of wealth in your own words. Is there any way to reflect this fundamental notion of wealth in our systems of credit and exchange?
7. Do you think that the pessimism Whatmough exhibits in his final paragraph is justified? (Note: this essay was written in 1975.)

CHAPTER SIXTEEN

SUSTAINABLE DEVELOPMENT: HYPOCRISY OR OUR BEST HOPE?

The concept of so-called *sustainable development* as a solution to the twin problems of environmental degradation and poverty was put forward in *Our Common Future*, the famous report of the World Commission on Environment and Development chaired by Norwegian Prime Minister Gro Harlem Brundtland. It has generated tremendous debate, and informs much current thought about the environment. Here we present the key sections of the Brundtland Report defining the notion of sustainable development, and two comments, one cautiously pro (Canadian political scientist Ted Schrecker) and one decidedly con (Larry Lohmann of *The Ecologist*).

TOWARDS SUSTAINABLE DEVELOPMENT

From the Brundtland Report

Sustainable development is development that meets the needs of the present without compromising the ability of future generations to meet their own needs. It contains within it two key concepts:

- the concept of "needs," in particular the essential needs of the world's poor, to which overriding priority should be given; and
- the idea of limitations imposed by the state of technology and social organization on the environment's ability to meet present and future needs.

Thus the goals of economic and social development must be defined in terms of sustainability in all countries—developed or developing, market-oriented or centrally planned. Interpretations will vary, but must share certain general features and must flow from a consensus on the basic concept of sustainable development and on a broad strategic framework for achieving it.

Development involves a progressive transformation of economy and society. A development path that is sustainable in a physical sense could theoretically be pursued even in a rigid social and political setting. But physical sustainability cannot be secured unless development policies pay attention to such considerations as changes in access to resources and in the distribution of costs and benefits. Even the narrow notion of physical sustainability implies a concern for social equity between generations, a concern that must logically be extended to equity within each generation.

I. The Concept of Sustainable Development

The satisfaction of human needs and aspirations is the major objective of development. The essential needs of vast numbers of people in developing countries—for food, clothing, shelter, jobs—are not being met, and beyond their basic needs these people have legitimate aspirations for an improved quality of life. A world in which poverty and inequity are endemic will always be prone to ecological and other crises. Sustainable development requires meeting the basic needs of all and extending to all the opportunity to satisfy their aspirations for a better life.

Living standards that go beyond the basic minimum are sustainable only if consumption standards everywhere have regard for long-term sustainability. Yet many of us live beyond the world's ecological means, for instance in our patterns of energy use. Perceived needs are socially and culturally determined, and sustainable development requires the promotion of values that encourage consumption standards that are within the bounds of the ecological possible and to which all can reasonably aspire.

Meeting essential needs depends in part on achieving full growth potential, and sustainable development clearly requires economic growth in places where such needs are not being met. Elsewhere, it can be consistent with economic growth, provided the content of growth reflects the broad principles of sustainability and non-exploitation of others. But growth by itself is not enough. High levels of productive activity and widespread poverty can coexist, and can endanger the environment. Hence sustainable development requires that societies meet human needs both by increasing productive potential and by ensuring equitable opportunities for all.

An expansion in numbers can increase the pressure on resources and slow the rise in living standards in areas where deprivation is widespread. Though the issue is not merely one of population size but of the distribution of resources, sustainable development can only be pursued if demographic developments are in harmony with the changing productive potential of the ecosystem.

A society may in many ways compromise its ability to meet the essential needs of its people in the future—by overexploiting resources, for example. The direction of technological developments may solve some immediate problems but lead to even greater ones. Large sections of the population may be marginalized by ill-considered development.

Settled agriculture, the diversion of watercourses, the extraction of minerals, the emission of heat and noxious gases into the atmosphere, commercial forests, and genetic manipulation are all examples of human intervention in natural systems during the course of development. Until recently, such interventions were small in scale and their impact limited. Today's interventions are more drastic in scale and impact, and more threatening to life-support systems both locally and globally. This need not happen. At a minimum, sustainable development must not endanger the natural systems that support life on Earth: the atmosphere, the waters, the soils, and the living beings.

Growth has no set limits in terms of population or resource use beyond which lies ecological disaster. Different limits hold for the use of energy, materials, water, and land. Many of these will manifest themselves in the form of rising costs and diminishing returns, rather than in the form of any sudden loss of a resource base. The accumulation of knowledge and the development of technology can enhance the carrying capacity of the resource base. But ultimate limits there are, and sustainability requires that long before these are reached, the world must ensure equitable access to the constrained resource and reorient technological efforts to relieve the pressure.

Economic growth and development obviously involve changes in the physical ecosystem. Every ecosystem everywhere cannot be preserved intact. A forest may be depleted in one part of a watershed and extended elsewhere, which is not a bad thing if the exploitation has been planned and the effects on soil erosion rates, water regimes, and genetic losses have been taken into account. In general, renewable resources like forests and fish stocks need not be depleted provided the rate of use is within the limits of regeneration and natural growth. But most renewable resources are part of a complex and interlinked ecosystem, and maximum sustainable yield must be defined after taking into account system-wide effects of exploitation.

As for non-renewable resources, like fossil fuels and minerals, their use reduces the stock available for future generations. But this does not mean that such resources should not be used. In general the rate of depletion should take into account the criticality of that resource, the availability of technologies for minimizing depletion, and the likelihood of substitutes being available. Thus land should not be degraded beyond reasonable recovery. With minerals and fossil fuels, the rate of depletion and the emphasis on recycling and economy of use should be calibrated to ensure that the resource does not run out before acceptable substitutes are available. Sustainable development requires that the rate of depletion of non-renewable resources should foreclose as few future options as possible.

Development tends to simplify ecosystems and to reduce their diversity of species. And species, once extinct, are not renewable. The loss of plant and animal species can greatly limit the options of future generations; so sustainable development requires the conservation of plant and animal species.

So-called free goods like air and water are also resources. The raw materials and energy of production processes are only partly converted to useful products. The rest comes out as wastes. Sustainable development requires that the adverse impacts on the quality of air, water, and other natural elements are minimized so as to sustain the ecosystem's overall integrity.

In essence, sustainable development is a process of change in which the exploitation of resources, the direction of investments, the orientation of technological development, and institutional change are all in harmony and enhance both current and future potential to meet human needs and aspirations.

II. Equity and the Common Interest

Sustainable development has been described here in general terms. How are individuals in the real world to be persuaded or made to act in the common interest? The answer lies partly in education, institutional development, and law enforcement. But many problems of resource depletion and environmental stress arise from disparities in economic and political power. An industry may get away with unacceptable levels of air and water pollution because the people who bear the brunt of it are poor and unable to complain effectively. A forest may be destroyed by excessive felling because the people living there have no alternatives or because timber contractors generally have more influence than forest dwellers.

Ecological interactions do not respect the boundaries of individual ownership and political jurisdiction. Thus:

- In a watershed, the ways in which a farmer up the slope uses land directly affect run-off on farms downstream.
- The irrigation practices, pesticides, and fertilizers used on one farm affect the productivity of neighbouring ones, especially among small farms.
- The efficiency of a factory boiler determines its rate of emission of soot and noxious chemicals and affects all who live and work around it.

- The hot water discharged by a thermal power plant into a river or a local sea affects the catch of all who fish locally.

Traditional social systems recognized some aspects of this interdependence and enforced community control over agricultural practices and traditional rights relating to water, forests, and land. This enforcement of the "common interest" did not necessarily impede growth and expansion though it may have limited the acceptance and diffusion of technical innovations.

Local interdependence has, if anything, increased because of the technology used in modern agriculture and manufacturing. Yet with this surge of technical progress, the growing "enclosure" of common lands, the erosion of common rights in forests and other resources, and the spread of commerce and production for the market, the responsibilities for decision making are being taken away from both groups and individuals. This shift is still under way in many developing countries.

It is not that there is one set of villains and another of victims. All would be better off if each person took into account the effect of his or her acts upon others. But each is unwilling to assume that others will behave in this socially desirable fashion, and hence all continue to pursue narrow self-interest. Communities or governments can compensate for this isolation through laws, education, taxes, subsidies, and other methods. Well-enforced laws and strict liability legislation can control harmful side effects. Most important, effective participation in decision-making processes by local communities can help them articulate and effectively enforce their common interest.

Interdependence is not simply a local phenomenon. Rapid growth in production has extended it to the international plane, with both physical and economic manifestations. There are growing global and regional pollution effects, such as in the more than 200 international river basins and the large number of shared seas.

The enforcement of common interest often suffers because areas of political jurisdictions and areas of impact do not coincide. Energy policies in one jurisdiction cause acid precipitation in another. The fishing policies of one state affect the fish catch of another. No supranational authority exists to resolve such issues, and the common interest can only be articulated through international cooperation.

In the same way, the ability of a government to control its national economy is reduced by growing international economic interactions. For example, foreign trade in commodities makes issues of carrying capacities and resource scarcities an international concern. If economic power and the benefits of trade were more equally distributed, common interests would be generally recognized. But the gains from trade are unequally distributed, and patterns of trade in, say, sugar affect not merely a local sugar-producing sector, but the economies and ecologies of the many developing countries that depend heavily on this product.

The search for common interest would be less difficult if all development and environment problems had solutions that would leave everyone better off. This is seldom the case, and there are usually winners and losers. Many problems arise from inequalities in access to resources. An inequitable landownership structure can lead to overexploitation of resources in the smallest holdings, with harmful effects on both environment and development. Internationally, monopolistic control over resources can drive those who do not share in them to excessive exploitation of marginal resources. The differing capacities of exploiters to commandeer "free" goods—locally, nationally, and internationally—is another manifestation of unequal access to resources. "Losers" in environment/development conflicts include those who suffer more than their fair share of the health, property, and ecosystem damage costs of pollution.

As a system approaches ecological limits, inequalities sharpen. Thus when a watershed deteriorates, poor farmers suffer more because they cannot afford the same anti-erosion measures as richer farmers. When urban air quality deteriorates, the poor, in their more vulnerable areas, suffer more health damage than the rich, who usually live in more pristine neighbourhoods. When mineral resources become depleted, late-comers to the industrialization process lose the benefits of low-cost supplies. Globally, wealthier nations are better placed financially and technologically to cope with the effects of possible climatic change.

Hence, our inability to promote the common interest in sustainable development is often a product of the relative neglect of economic and social justice within and amongst nations.

III. Strategic Imperatives

The world must quickly design strategies that will allow nations to move from their present, often destructive, processes of growth and development onto sustainable development paths. This will require policy changes in all countries, with respect both to their own development and to their impacts on other nations' development possibilities.

Critical objectives for environment and development policies that follow from the concept of sustainable development include:

- reviving growth;
- changing the quality of growth;
- meeting essential needs for jobs, food, energy, water, and sanitation;
- ensuring a sustainable level of population;
- conserving and enhancing the resource base;

- reorienting technology and managing risk; and
- merging environment and economics in decision making.

REVIVING GROWTH

As indicated earlier, development that is sustainable has to address the problem of the large number of people who live in absolute poverty—that is, who are unable to satisfy even the most basic of their needs. Poverty reduces people's capacity to use resources in a sustainable manner; it intensifies pressure on the environment. Most such absolute poverty is in developing countries; in many, it has been aggravated by the economic stagnation of the 1980s. A necessary but not a sufficient condition for the elimination of absolute poverty is a relatively rapid rise in per capita incomes in the Third World. It is therefore essential that the stagnant or declining growth trends of this decade be reversed.

While attainable growth rates will vary, a certain minimum is needed to have any impact on absolute poverty. It seems unlikely that, taking developing countries as a whole, these objectives can be accomplished with per capita income growth of under 3 per cent. Given current population growth rates, this would require overall national income growth of around 5 per cent a year in the developing economies of Asia, 5.5 per cent in Latin America, and 6 per cent in Africa and West Asia.

Are these orders of magnitude attainable? The record in South and East Asia over the past quarter-century and especially over the last five years suggests that 5 per cent annual growth can be attained in most countries, including the two largest, India and China. In Latin America, average growth rates on the order of 5 per cent were achieved during the 1960s and 1970s, but fell well below that in the first half of this decade, mainly because of the debt crisis. A revival of Latin American growth depends on the resolution of this crisis. In Africa, growth rates during the 1960s and 1970s were around 4–4.5 per cent, which at current rates of population growth would mean per capita income growth of only a little over 1 per cent. Moreover, during the 1980s, growth nearly halted and in two-thirds of the countries per capita income declined. Attaining a minimum level of growth in Africa requires the correction of short-term imbalances, and also the removal of deep-rooted constraints on the growth process.

Growth must be revived in developing countries because that is where the links between economic growth, the alleviation of poverty, and environmental conditions operate most directly. Yet developing countries are part of an interdependent world economy; their prospects also depend on the levels and patterns of growth in industrialized nations. The medium-term prospects for industrial countries are for growth of 3–4 per cent, the minimum that international financial institutions consider necessary if these countries are going to play a part in expanding the world economy. Such growth rates could be environmentally sustainable if industrialized nations can continue the recent shifts in the content of their growth towards less material- and energy-intensive activities and the improvement of their efficiency in using materials and energy.

As industrialized nations use less materials and energy, however, they will provide smaller markets for commodities and minerals from the developing nations. Yet if developing nations focus their efforts upon eliminating poverty and satisfying essential human needs, then domestic demand will increase for both agricultural products and manufactured goods and some services. Hence the very logic of sustainable development implies an internal stimulus to Third World growth.

Nonetheless, in large numbers of developing countries markets are very small; and for all developing countries high export growth, especially of non-traditional items, will also be necessary to finance imports, demand for which will be generated by rapid development. Thus a reorientation of international economic relations will be necessary for sustainable development.

CHANGING THE QUALITY OF GROWTH

Sustainable development involves more than growth. It requires a change in the content of growth, to make it less material- and energy-intensive and more equitable in its impact. These changes are required in all countries as part of a package of measures to maintain the stock of ecological capital, to improve the distribution of income, and to reduce the degree of vulnerability to economic crises.

The process of economic development must be more soundly based upon the realities of the stock of capital that sustains it. This is rarely done in either developed or developing countries. For example, income from forestry operations is conventionally measured in terms of the value of timber and other products extracted, minus the costs of extraction. The costs of regenerating the forest are not taken into account, unless money is actually spent on such work. Thus figuring profits from logging rarely takes full account of the losses in future revenue incurred through degradation of the forest. Similar incomplete accounting occurs in the exploitation of other natural resources, especially in the case of resources that are not capitalized in enterprise or national accounts: air, water, and soil. In all countries, rich or poor, economic development must take full account in its measurements of growth of the improvement or deterioration in the stock of natural resources.

Income distribution is one aspect of the quality of growth, as described in the preceding section, and rapid growth combined with deteriorating income distribution may be worse than slower growth combined with redistribution in favour of the poor. For instance, in many developing countries the introduction of large-scale commercial agriculture may produce revenue rapidly, but may also dispossess a large number of small farmers and make income distribution more inequitable. In the long run, such a path may not be sustainable; it impoverishes many people and can increase pressures on the natural resource base through overcommercialized agriculture and through the marginalization of subsistence farmers. Relying more on small-holder cultivation may be slower at first, but more easily sustained over the long term.

Economic development is unsustainable if it increases vulnerability to crises. A drought may force farmers to slaughter animals needed for sustaining production in future years. A drop in prices may cause farmers or other producers to overexploit natural resources to maintain incomes. But vulnerability can be reduced by using technologies that lower production risks, by choosing institutional options that reduce market fluctuations, and by building up reserves, especially of food and foreign exchange. A development path that combines growth with reduced vulnerability is more sustainable than one that does not.

Yet it is not enough to broaden the range of economic variables taken into account. Sustainability requires views of human needs and well-being that incorporate such non-economic variables as education and health enjoyed for their own sake, clean air and water, and the protection of natural beauty. It must also work to remove disabilities from disadvantaged groups, many of whom live in ecologically vulnerable areas, such as many tribal groups in forests, desert nomads, groups in remote hill areas, and indigenous peoples of the Americas and Australasia.

Changing the quality of growth requires changing our approach to development efforts to take account of all of their effects. For instance, a hydropower project should not be seen merely as a way of producing more electricity; its effects upon the local environment and the livelihood of the local community must be included in any balance sheets. Thus the abandonment of a hydro project because it will disturb a rare ecological system could be a measure of progress, not a setback to development. Nevertheless, in some cases, sustainability considerations will involve a rejection of activities that are financially attractive in the short run.

Economic and social development can and should be mutually reinforcing. Money spent on education and health can raise human productivity. Economic development can accelerate social development by providing opportunities for underprivileged groups or by spreading education more rapidly.

MEETING ESSENTIAL HUMAN NEEDS

The satisfaction of human needs and aspirations is so obviously an objective of productive activity that it may appear redundant to assert its central role in the concept of sustainable development. All too often poverty is such that people cannot satisfy their needs for survival and well-being even if goods and services are available. At the same time, the demands of those not in poverty may have major environmental consequences.

The principal development challenge is to meet the needs and aspirations of an expanding developing world population. The most basic of all needs is for a livelihood: that is, employment. Between 1985 and 2000 the labour force in developing countries will increase by nearly 900 million, and new livelihood opportunities will have to be generated for 60 million persons every year. The pace and pattern of economic development have to generate sustainable work opportunities on this scale and at a level of productivity that would enable poor households to meet minimum consumption standards.

More food is required not merely to feed more people but to attack undernourishment. For the developing world to eat, person for person, as well as the industrial world by the year 2000, annual increases of 5.0 per cent in calories and 5.8 per cent in proteins are needed in Africa; of 3.4 and 4.0 per cent, respectively, in Latin America; and of 3.5 and 4.5 per cent in Asia. Foodgrains and starchy roots are the primary sources of calories, while proteins are obtained primarily from products like milk, meat, fish, pulses, and oil-seeds.

Though the focus at present is necessarily on staple foods, the projections given above also highlight the need for a high rate of growth of protein availability. In Africa, the task is particularly challenging given the recent declining per capita food production and the current constraints on growth. In Asia and Latin America, the required growth rates in calorie and protein consumption seem to be more readily attainable. But increased food production should not be based on ecologically unsound production policies and compromise long-term prospects for food security.

Energy is another essential human need, one that cannot be universally met unless energy consumption patterns change. The most urgent problem is the requirements of poor Third World households, which depend mainly on fuelwood. By the turn of the century, 3 billion people may live in areas where wood is cut faster than it grows or where fuelwood is extremely scarce. Corrective action would both reduce the drudgery of collecting wood over long distances and preserve the ecological base. The minimum requirements for cooking fuel in most developing countries appear to be on the order of 250 kilogrammes of coal equivalent per capita per year. This is a fraction of the household energy consumption in industrialized countries.

The linked basic needs of housing, water supply, sanitation, and health care are also environmentally important. Deficiencies in these areas are often visible manifestations of environmental stress. In the Third World, the failure to meet these key needs is one of the major causes of many communicable diseases such as malaria, gastro-intestinal infestations, cholera, and typhoid. Population growth and the drift into cities threaten to make these problems worse. Planners must find ways of relying more on supporting community initiatives and self-help efforts and on effectively using low-cost technologies.

ENSURING A SUSTAINABLE LEVEL OF POPULATION

The sustainability of development is intimately linked to the dynamics of population growth. The issue, however, is not simply one of global population size. A child born in a country where levels of material and energy use are high places a greater burden on the Earth's resources than a child born in a poorer country. A similar argument applies within countries. Nonetheless, sustainable development can be pursued more easily when population size is stabilized at a level consistent with the productive capacity of the ecosystem.

In industrial countries, the overall rate of population growth is under 1 per cent, and several countries have reached or are approaching zero population growth. The total population of the industrialized world could increase from its current 1.2 billion to about 1.4 billion in the year 2025.

The greater part of global population increase will take place in developing countries, where the 1985 population of 3.7 billion may increase to 6.8 billion by 2025. The Third World does not have the option of migration to "new" lands, and the time available for adjustment is much less than industrial countries had. Hence the challenge now is to quickly lower population growth rates, especially in regions such as Africa, where these rates are increasing.

Birth rates declined in industrial countries largely because of economic and social development. Rising levels of income and urbanization and the changing role of women all played important roles. Similar processes are now at work in developing countries. These should be recognized and encouraged. Population policies should be integrated with other economic and social development programmes—female education, health care, and the expansion of the livelihood base of the poor. But time is short, and developing countries will also have to promote direct measures to reduce fertility, to avoid going radically beyond the productive potential to support their populations. In fact, increased access to family planning services is itself a form of social development that allows couples, and women in particular, the right to self-determination.

Population growth in developing countries will remain unevenly distributed between rural and urban areas. UN projections suggest that by the first decade of the next century, the absolute size of rural populations in most developing countries will start declining. Nearly 90 per cent of the increase in the developing world will take place in urban areas, the population of which is expected to rise from 1.15 billion in 1985 to 3.85 billion in 2025. The increase will be particularly marked in Africa and, to a lesser extent, in Asia.

Developing-country cities are growing much faster than the capacity of authorities to cope. Shortages of housing, water, sanitation, and mass transit are widespread. A growing proportion of city-dwellers live in slums and shanty towns, many of them exposed to air and water pollution and to industrial and natural hazards. Further deterioration is likely, given that most urban growth will take place in the largest cities. Thus more manageable cities may be the principal gain from slower rates of population growth.

Urbanization is itself part of the development process. The challenge is to manage the process so as to avoid a severe deterioration in the quality of life. Thus the development of smaller urban centres needs to be encouraged to reduce pressures in large cities. Solving the impending urban crisis will require the promotion of self-help housing and urban services by and for the poor, and a more positive approach to the role of the informal sector, supported by sufficient funds for water supply, sanitation, and other services.

CONSERVING AND ENHANCING THE RESOURCE BASE

If needs are to be met on a sustainable basis the Earth's natural resource base must be conserved and enhanced. Major changes in policies will be needed to cope with the industrial world's current high levels of consumption, the increases in consumption needed to meet minimum standards in developing countries, and expected population growth. However, the case for the conservation of nature should not rest only with development goals. It is part of our moral obligation to other living beings and future generations.

Pressure on resources increases when people lack alternatives. Development policies must widen people's options for earning a sustainable livelihood, particularly for resource-poor households and in areas under ecological stress. In a hilly area, for instance, economic self-interest and ecology can be combined by helping farmers shift from grain to tree crops by providing them with advice, equipment, and marketing assistance. Programmes to protect the incomes of farmers, fishermen, and foresters against short-term price declines may decrease their need to overexploit resources.

The conservation of agricultural resources is an urgent task because in many parts of the world cultivation has already been extended to marginal lands, and fishery and forestry resources have been overexploited. These resources must be conserved and enhanced to meet the needs of growing populations. Land use in agriculture and forestry should be based on a scientific assessment of land capacity, and the annual depletion of topsoil, fish stock, or forest resources must not exceed the rate of regeneration.

The pressures on agricultural land from crop and livestock production can be partly relieved by increasing productivity. But short-sighted, short-term improvements in productivity can create different forms of ecological stress, such as the loss of genetic diversity in standing crops, salinization and alkalization of irrigated lands, nitrate pollution of ground-water, and pesticide residues in food. Ecologically more benign alternatives are available. Future increases in productivity, in both developed and developing countries, should be based on the better controlled application of water and agrochemicals, as well as on more extensive use of organic manures and non-chemical means of pest control. These alternatives can be promoted only by an agricultural policy based on ecological realities.

In the case of fisheries and tropical forestry, we rely largely on the exploitation of the naturally available stocks. The sustainable yield from these stocks may well fall short of demand. Hence it will be necessary to turn to methods that produce more fish, fuelwood, and forest products under controlled conditions. Substitutes for fuelwood can be promoted.

The ultimate limits to global development are perhaps determined by the availability of energy resources and by the biosphere's capacity to absorb the by-products of energy use. These energy limits may be approached far sooner than the limits imposed by other material resources. First, there are the supply problems: the depletion of oil reserves, the high cost and environmental impact of coal mining, and the hazards of nuclear technology. Second, there are emission problems, most notably acid pollution and carbon dioxide build-up leading to global warming.

Some of these problems can be met by increased use of renewable energy sources. But the exploitation of renewable sources such as fuelwood and hydropower also entails ecological problems. Hence sustainability requires a clear focus on conserving and efficiently using energy.

Industrialized countries must recognize that their energy consumption is polluting the biosphere and eating into scarce fossil fuel supplies. Recent improvements in energy efficiency and a shift towards less energy-intensive sectors have helped limit consumption. But the process must be accelerated to reduce per capita consumption and encourage a shift to non-polluting sources and technologies. The simple duplication in the developing world of industrial countries' energy use patterns is neither feasible nor desirable. Changing these patterns for the better will call for new policies in urban development, industry location, housing design, transportation systems, and the choice of agricultural and industrial technologies.

Non-fuel mineral resources appear to pose fewer supply problems. Studies done before 1980 that assumed an exponentially growing demand did not envisage a problem until well into the next century. Since then, world consumption of most metals has remained nearly constant, which suggests that the exhaustion of non-fuel minerals is even more distant. The history of technological developments also suggests that industry can adjust to scarcity through greater efficiency in use, recycling, and substitution. More immediate needs include modifying the pattern of world trade in minerals to allow exporters a higher share in the value added from mineral use, and improving the access of developing countries to mineral supplies, as their demands increase.

The prevention and reduction of air and water pollution will remain a critical task of resource conservation. Air and water quality come under pressure from such activities as fertilizer and pesticide use, urban sewage, fossil fuel burning, the use of certain chemicals, and various other industrial activities. Each of these is expected to increase the pollution load on the biosphere substantially, particularly in developing countries. Cleaning up after the event is an expensive solution. Hence all countries need to anticipate and prevent these pollution problems, by, for instance, enforcing emission standards that reflect likely long-term effects, promoting low-waste technologies, and anticipating the impact of new products, technologies, and wastes.

REORIENTING TECHNOLOGY AND MANAGING RISK

The fulfilment of all these tasks will require the reorientation of technology—the key link between humans and nature. First, the capacity for technological innovation needs to be greatly enhanced in developing countries so that they can respond more effectively to the challenges of sustainable development. Second, the orientation of technology development must be changed to pay greater attention to environmental factors.

The technologies of industrial countries are not always suited or easily adaptable to the socio-economic and environmental conditions of developing countries. To compound the problem, the bulk of world research and development addresses few of the pressing issues facing these countries, such as arid-land agriculture or the control of tropical diseases. Not enough is being done to adapt recent innovations in materials technology, energy conservation, information technology, and biotechnology to the needs of developing countries. These gaps must be covered by enhancing research, design, development, and extension capabilities in the Third World.

In all countries, the processes of generating alternative technologies, upgrading traditional ones, and selecting and adapting imported technologies should be informed by environmental resource concerns. Most technological research by commercial organizations is devoted to product and process innovations that have market value. Technologies are needed that produce "social goods," such as improved air quality or increased product life, or that resolve problems normally outside the cost calculus of individual enterprises, such as the external costs of pollution or waste disposal.

The role of public policy is to ensure, through incentives and disincentives, that commercial organizations find it worthwhile to take fuller account of environmental factors in the technologies they develop. Publicly funded research institutions also need such direction, and the objectives of sustainable development and environmental protection must be built into the mandates of the institutions that work in environmentally sensitive areas.

The development of environmentally appropriate technologies is closely related to questions of risk management. Such systems as nuclear reactors, electric and other utility distribution networks, communication systems, and mass transportation are vulnerable if stressed beyond a certain point. The fact that they are connected through networks tends to make them immune to small disturbances but more vulnerable to unexpected disruptions that exceed a finite threshold. Applying sophisticated analyses of vulnerabilities and past failures to technology design, manufacturing standards, and contingency plans in operations can make the consequences of a failure or accident much less catastrophic.

The best vulnerability and risk analysis has not been applied consistently across technologies or systems. A major purpose of large system design should be to make the consequences of failure or sabotage less serious. There is thus a need for new techniques and technologies — as well as legal and institutional mechanisms — for safety design and control, accident prevention, contingency planning, damage mitigation, and provision of relief.

Environmental risks arising from technological and developmental decisions impinge on individuals and areas that have little or no influence on those decisions. Their interests must be taken into account. National and international institutional mechanisms are needed to assess potential impacts of new technologies before they are widely used, in order to ensure that their production, use, and disposal do not overstress environmental resources. Similar arrangements are required for major interventions in natural systems, such as river diversion or forest clearance. In addition, liability for damages from unintended consequences must be strengthened and enforced.

MERGING ENVIRONMENT AND ECONOMICS IN DECISION MAKING

The common theme throughout this strategy for sustainable development is the need to integrate economic and ecological considerations in decision making. They are, after all, integrated in the workings of the real world. This will require a change in attitudes and objectives and in institutional arrangements at every level.

Economic and ecological concerns are not necessarily in opposition. For example, policies that conserve the quality of agricultural land and protect forests improve the long-term prospects for agricultural development. An increase in the efficiency of energy and material use serves ecological purposes but can also reduce costs. But the compatibility of environmental and economic objectives is often lost in the pursuit of individual or group gains, with little regard for the impacts on others, with a blind faith in science's ability to find solutions, and in ignorance of the distant consequences of today's decisions. Institutional rigidities add to this myopia.

One important rigidity is the tendency to deal with one industry or sector in isolation, failing to recognize the importance of intersectoral linkages. Modern agriculture uses substantial amounts of commercially produced energy and large quantities of industrial products. At the same time, the more traditional connection—in which agriculture is a source of raw materials for industry—is being diluted by the widening use of synthetics. The energy-industry connection is also changing, with a strong tendency towards a decline in the energy intensity of industrial production in industrial countries. In the Third World, however, the gradual shift of the industrial base towards the basic material-producing sectors is leading to an increase in the energy intensity of industrial production.

These intersectoral connections create patterns of economic and ecological interdependence rarely reflected in the ways in which policy is made. Sectoral organizations tend to pursue sectoral objectives and to treat their impacts on other sectors as side effects, taken into account only if compelled to do so. Hence impacts on forests rarely worry those involved in guiding public policy or business activities in the fields of energy, industrial development, crop husbandry, or foreign trade. Many of the environment and development problems that confront us have their roots in this sectoral fragmentation of responsibility. Sustainable development requires that such fragmentation be overcome.

Sustainability requires the enforcement of wider responsibilities for the impacts of decisions. This requires changes in the legal and institutional frameworks that will enforce the common interest. Some necessary changes in the legal framework start from the proposition that an environment adequate for health and well-being is essential for all human beings—including future generations. Such a view places the right to use public and private resources in its proper social context and provides a goal for more specific measures.

The law alone cannot enforce the common interest. It principally needs community knowledge and support, which entails greater public participation in the decisions that affect the environment. This is best secured by decentralizing the management of resources upon which local communities depend, and giving these communities an effective say over the use of these resources. It will also require promoting citizens' initiatives, empowering people's organizations, and strengthening local democracy.

Some large-scale projects, however, require participation on a different basis. Public inquiries and hearings on the development and environment impacts can help greatly in drawing attention to different points of view. Free access to relevant information and the availability of alternative sources of technical expertise can provide an informed basis for public discussion. When the environmental impact of a proposed project is particularly high, public scrutiny of the case should be mandatory and, wherever feasible, the decision should be subject to prior public approval, perhaps by referendum.

Changes are also required in the attitudes and procedures of both public and private-sector enterprises. Moreover, environmental regulation must move beyond the usual menu of safety regulations, zoning laws, and pollution control enactments; environmental objectives must be built into taxation, prior approval procedures for investment and technology choice, foreign trade incentives, and all components of development policy.

The integration of economic and ecological factors into the law and into decision-making systems within countries has to be matched at the international level. The growth in fuel and material use dictates that direct physical linkages between ecosystems of different countries will increase. Economic interactions through trade, finance, investment, and travel will also grow and heighten economic and ecological interdependence. Hence in the future, even more so than now, sustainable development requires the unification of economics and ecology in international relations. . . .

IV. Conclusion

In its broadest sense, the strategy for sustainable development aims to promote harmony among human beings and between humanity and nature. In the specific context of the development and environment crises of the 1980s, which current national and international political and economic institutions have not and perhaps cannot overcome, the pursuit of sustainable development requires:

- a political system that secures effective citizen participation in decision making,
- an economic system that is able to generate surpluses and technical knowledge on a self-reliant and sustained basis,
- a social system that provides for solutions for the tensions arising from disharmonious development,
- a production system that respects the obligation to preserve the ecological base for development,

- a technological system that can search continuously for new solutions,
- an international system that fosters sustainable patterns of trade and finance, and
- an administrative system that is flexible and has the capacity for self-correction.

These requirements are more in the nature of goals that should underlie national and international action on development. What matters is the sincerity with which these goals are pursued and the effectiveness with which departures from them are corrected.

While enthusiastically embraced by many, the concept of sustainable development has also been derided as a self-serving evasion. None have put this more bluntly than Canadian naturalist and environmental philosopher John Livingston:

> The exotic ideology [of human domination] has been advanced in the last few decades under a variety of banners. The words may change, but the message is constant. "Resource management," of course, is now a centenarian; of more recent arrival was "resource development." This soon mutated into the lunatic term "ecodevelopment." . . . At roughly the same time we had "appropriate technology," which was perilously close to being internally contradictory. At the present moment we have "sustainable development," a full-blown oxymoron. What these slogans seem to say is "How to plunder Nature and get away with it." (Livingston 1994, pp. 59–60)

In our next selection, Larry Lohmann sets forth a scathing political critique of sustainable development.

WHOSE COMMON FUTURE?

Larry Lohmann

Partnership is what is needed in today's world, partnership between government and industry, between producers and consumers, between the present and the future. . . . We need to build new coalitions. . . . We must agree on a global agenda for the management of change. . . . We must continue to move from confrontation, through dialogue to cooperation. We must . . . embrace the notion of sustainable development. . . . We see the possibility for a new era of economic growth, a growth that is different, one that must be based on policies that sustain and expand the resource base. The time has come for a recommitment to multilateralism. . . . Collective management of global interdependence is . . . the only acceptable formula in the world of the 1990s. . . . The close integration of environmental concerns into our economies and into decision-making will continue to require political management and leadership at every level.

–Gro Harlem Brundtland

I feel pain and anger that our people, the indigenous peoples of this globe, have been so neglected in the mass rush towards what you now call development, but what you once, more honestly, called plunder. . . . I have heard grand talk of a new coalition of industry, scientists, governments and environmentalists from all over the world who will now finally work together to save the planet. But not once have I heard that indigenous peoples are to be included in this global alliance.

–Chief Ruby Dunstan, *Lytton Indian Band, British Columbia*

We don't believe that . . . ministers shall decide our future. Why should we believe that they, who have the power today, should want to change the world?

–Gunnar Album Alstad, *Norwegian environmental activist*

Never underestimate the ability of modern elites to work out ways of coming through a crisis with their power intact.

From the days of the American populists through the Depression, postwar reconstruction, the end of colonialism, and the age of "development," our contemporary leaders and their institutions have sought to turn pressures for change to their advantage. The New Deal, the Marshall Plan, Bretton Woods, multilateral lending—all in their turn have taken challenges to the system and transformed them into ways of defusing popular initiatives and developing the economic and political domains of the powerful.

Now comes the global environmental crisis. Once again those in high places are making solemn noises about "grave threats to our common security and the very survival of our planet." Once again their proposed solutions leave the main causes of the trouble untouched. As ordinary people try to reclaim local lands, forests, and waters from the depredations of business and the state, and work to build democratic movements to preserve the planet's health, those in power continue to occupy themselves with damage control and the containment of threats to the way power is currently distributed and held. The difference is important to keep in mind when listening to the calls to arms from the new statesmen and women of environmentalism.

Political Management of the Crisis

Two of the most prominent of these, former Norwegian Prime Minister Gro Harlem Brundtland and Canadian businessman Maurice Strong, newly-appointed Secretary-General of the 1992 United Nations Conference on Environment and Development (UNCED), were in Vancouver in March to reiterate the message that we all share a "common future" in environmental preservation and "sustainable development." Their speeches at the "Globe 90" conference and "green" trade fair gave valuable clues about how the more progressive global elites are organizing themselves for the political management of the environment crisis.

The first instinct of those in high places when faced with a problem is to avoid analyzing its causes if doing so would put the current power structure in an unfavourable light. In Vancouver, Brundtland averted her gaze from the destruction brought about through economic growth, technology transfer, and capital flows from North to South and vice versa, and instead rounded up the usual suspects of "poverty," "population growth," and "underdevelopment," without exploring the origins of any of them. She spoke of global warming, a declining resource base, pollution, overexploitation of resources, and a "crushing debt burden" for the South, but omitted mentioning who or what might be responsible. Environmental problems, she implied, were mainly to be found in the South. Admittedly the North had made some mistakes, she said, but luckily it knows the answers now and can prevent the South from making the same errors as it toddles along behind the North on the path to sustainable development.

Whose Security?

The stress of a crisis also tends to drive those in power to the use of vague code words that can rally other members of the elite. In Vancouver the word was "security." Brundtland and Strong warned of the "new (environmental) threats to our security" and dwelt on the ideas of a "global concept of security," a "safe future," and a new "security alliance" with an obsessiveness worthy of Richard Nixon.

What was all this talk of "security" about? In the rural societies where most of the world's people live, security generally means land, family, village, and freedom from outside interference. Had the ex-Prime Minister of Norway and the Chairman of Strovest Holdings, Inc. suddenly become land reform activists and virulent opponents of the development projects and market economy expansion which uproot villagers from their farms, communities, and livelihoods? Or were they perhaps hinting at another kind of security, the security that First World privilege wants against the economic and political chaos that would follow environmental collapse? In the atmosphere of Globe 90, where everyone was constantly assured that all humanity had "community security" interests, it was not always easy to keep in mind the distinction between the first, which entails devolution of power, and the second, which requires the reverse.

A third instinct of crisis managers in high places is to seek the "solution" that requires the least change to the existing power structure. Here Brundtland and Strong, as befits two contenders for the UN Secretary-Generalship, repeated a formula to be found partly in UN General Assembly documents relating to UNCED. This is:

1. reverse the financial flows currently coursing from South to North, using debt relief, new lending, and new infusions of aid possibly augmented by taxes on fossil fuels and transfers from military budgets;
2. transfer technology, particularly "green" technology, from North to South; and
3. boost economic growth, particularly in the South.

This scheme has obvious attractions for the world's powerful. For one thing, a resumption of net North–South capital flows would provide a bonanza for Northern export industries. Funds from the West and Japan would be sent on a quick round trip through a few institutions in other parts of the world before being returned, somewhat depleted by payoffs to elites along the way, to the coffers of Northern firms. Third World income freed up by debt relief would add immensely to corporate profits. Buoyed up by a fresh flow of funds, Southern leaders would become more receptive to the advice of Northern-dominated institutions and more dependent on Northern technology and aid. Injections of remedial technology, in addition, might well provide an incentive for the South to follow the strategy of dealing with the effects rather than the causes of environmental degradation. That would mean more money for both polluting and pollution-correcting industries.

The scheme also shores up the present industrial and financial system by suggesting that the solution to the environmental crisis lies within that system, or, in the words of Chief Ruby Dunstan, that "no basic change in consciousness is needed." It implies that environmental issues are technological and financial and not matters of social equity and distribution of power—discussion of which would call much of the system into question. The scheme invokes and reinforces the superstitions that it is lack of capital that leads to environmental crisis; that capital flows are going to "expand the resource base," replace soil fertility, and restore water tables and tropical forests lost to commercial exploitation; that poverty will be somehow relieved rather than exacerbated by economic growth; and that capital flows "naturally" in large quantities from North to South.[1]

Weighing up the Costs

Admittedly, the UNCED plan has costs for those in power. Bankers may not be overjoyed at the prospect of debt relief, but since the alternatives seem to be either continued insupportable and destabilizing South–North net financial transfers or the perpetuation of the process of servicing Third World debts with new loans, they may agree in the end. Northern countries will also have to spend massively on "green" technology now in order to be in a position to put pressure on the South to do the same later.[2] But this is not necessarily a bad thing for industry, which can "clean up" the mess it itself makes around the world, perhaps in the process creating new problems which will require further business solutions. As one of Globe 90's organizers put it, "a solution to most environmental issues is a business opportunity."[3] Another obstacle to the UNCED scheme is that it may stir resistance among its Southern "beneficiaries." Raul Montenegro, a veteran of the struggle against Canada's transfer of nuclear reactor technology to Argentina, speaks for many in the South when he says, "We do not need technology transfer. We need exchange of sustainable technologies."

Perhaps a bigger problem for the UNCED scheme is that it does not actually address the environmental crisis in either North or South. By tailoring solutions not to the problems but to the interests of those who created them, the plan is in fact likely to make things worse. As Chief Ruby Dunstan put it, "business as usual will not and cannot ensure global survival. Sustainable development is about life, not about economics." The UNCED plan will reinforce Southern dependence on environmentally-destructive models of development imposed by the North and increase the power of Southern elites over their societies. It will promote technology most of which, like the tree-planting machine on display at Globe 90, has only a spurious claim to being "green" and which will have to be paid for eventually by cashing in resources. It does not examine the effects of importing large amounts of capital into the South and endorses the continuing devastating economization of the natural and social heritage of both North and South. It is, however, probably as far as elites can go at present without challenging their own position. As for the future, there is always the hope that, as the brochure of one Japanese organization present at Globe 90 put it, the problems of global warming, ozone depletion, acid rain, desertification, and tropical forest destruction can someday be solved "through technological innovations."[4]

The "New Alliance"

A fourth tendency among elite crisis managers is to identify the executors of the solution with the existing power structure. This Brundtland and Strong did, but with an added twist that shows them to be real masters of their art.

The technical fixes of the UNCED agenda are to be promoted and implemented by a "new global partnership" or environmental quadruple alliance consisting of industry, government, scientists, and non-governmental organizations — "the most important security alliance we have ever entered into on this planet," according to Strong.

The composition of this projected alliance can probably be fairly guessed by glancing at the list of participants at Globe 90 itself. As one of the organizers put it, the event was "almost a working model of the kind of public and private sector partnership called for in *Our Common Future*."

Among corporate sponsors, advisers, and exhibitors at the meeting were Atomic Energy of Canada, Ltd., notorious for export of nuclear reactors and food irradiators to Third World countries; H.A. Simons, adviser for environmentally damaging plantations in Brazil and Southeast Asia; Dow Chemical; Mitsubishi; Esso; Imperial Oil; Hitachi; British Nuclear Fuels; B.C. Hydro; Weyerhauser; and a host of coal, electrical, nuclear, mining, oil, asbestos, and paper and pulp industry associations. On the government side were official representatives from Canada, the U.S., Japan, West Germany, the U.K., Austria, Norway, France, Finland, Italy, Australia, the Netherlands, Israel, and Hong Kong. Various universities and institutes bolstered the scientific end, and representatives of the World Bank and Asian Development Bank were also present.

Seasoned observers looking over this roster may wonder what is supposed to distinguish the new environmental alliance from the familiar sort of elite ententes that helped land the world in its current environmental mess — the old-boy networks and clubs typified by the military-industrial complex, the World Bank's web of clients, consultants, and contractors, the Trilateral Commission, and so on.

Co-opting the NGOs

The answer is non-governmental organizations (**NGO**s). Although few NGO names appeared on the official sponsors list for Globe 90, great emphasis was laid on "summoning" as many more as possible into the incipient global alliance. The Centre for Our Common Future, a small but well-connected Geneva-based organization, was delegated the responsibility of laying the groundwork for channeling NGO "input" into the 1992 UNCED.

Why the interest in NGOs? One reason is that they might be used to push business and government in a slightly less destructive direction. Another is that official or corporate environmental initiatives need credibility. Establishment political strategists have not failed to note the growing role of NGOs in recent popular movements from Latin America to South and Southeast Asia and Eastern and Central Europe. By 1992, the strategists realize, UNCED will probably have to claim support from many such organizations in order to be able to make any credible claim of broad popular support—particularly if the other members of the "new alliance" are notorious environmental offenders of the sort listed above. "New alliance" leaders are thus courting and manipulating NGOs, particularly tame NGO umbrella groups, groups with establishment links, and groups with jet-set ambitions, in the hope of being able to use their names to say that UNCED initiatives have the backing of environmentalists, youth, trade unions, women's groups, the socially concerned, and "all the nations and peoples of the world."

These manoeuvres, however, cannot conceal the fact that grassroots NGO "participation" in UNCED and other "new alliance" activities, to say nothing of the participation of ordinary people, is a fraud. That much should have been clear already from the wheeling and dealing on display in Vancouver and the spectacle of conference politicians from Ottawa or Geneva explaining glibly how "grassroots participation" from the "constituency outside government" could influence governments or be magically filtered upward through the complicated pipelines of the UNCED system. The General Assembly document setting out the role of NGOs, however, lays it out in black and white: the "form and manner of (NGO) participation in the preparatory process and in the Conference . . . can be determined in the light of the preparatory arrangements to be agreed upon by the (UNCED Preparatory) Committee." The NGO community is to be allowed at most to "enrich and enhance the deliberations of the Conference" and to "serve as an important channel to disseminate its results, as well as mobilize public support." Translation is hardly necessary. It is governments who decide who is allowed to say what, just as it is governments who will be signing agreements in 1992. NGOs are expected to carry governments' message to the people and help them stay in power.[5]

A Common Interest?

Outside official meetings, of course, it is business whose voice will inevitably carry above that of all others in the "new alliance." If Globe 90 is any indication, it is not likely to be a voice urging environmental and political sanity. Nor are grassroots-oriented environmental activists likely to be excited about joining a coalition carrying the industry agenda put forward at the Vancouver conference. At the conference's opening plenary session, for example, Earl Harbison of Monsanto launched into an emotional defence of the need to spread the use of corporate-controlled biotechnology throughout agriculture. If technologies such as BST (see Samuel S. Epstein, "BST: The Public Health Hazards," *The Ecologist*, Vol. 19, No. 5, September/October 1989) or crops genetically "vaccinated" against pests are judged on their "political acceptability," Harbison said, then "we are headed for trouble." The solution, he said, was to stop "polluting the scientific process with politics"—a recipe for technocratic dictatorship if ever there was one. Elsewhere, Adam Zimmerman of Noranda Forests phlegmatically defended his company's role in forest destruction in Canada, and a mining industry representative described coal as the "solution to our energy problems." The ideas of business about what "sustainable development" might consist of, meanwhile, ranged from "comfortable living" to "scientific and technological innovation."

Many environmentalists, nevertheless, will feel that joining the "new global alliance" can do no harm if it presents an opportunity for nudging business and government in a more "green" direction. Such a conclusion is questionable. It is one thing to pressure business and government into changing their ways with all the means at one's disposal. It is quite another to pledge allegiance in advance to a new elite coalition with a predetermined or unknown agenda which one will have little power to change.

Any alliance which tells us that we *must* seek consensus, that no opposition is to be brooked to Brundtland as Our Common Leader, or that there is a perfect potential community of interest between, say, a UN bureaucrat and a Sri Lankan subsistence fisherman, is one that deserves suspicion at the outset. Consensus-seeking is neither good nor necessary in itself—it may, after all, function merely to conceal exploitation—but only when it is agreed by all parties after full discussion to be possible and fruitful.

This is not to denigrate the ambitious professionals associated with the UNCED, but merely to state a fact. To seek genuine solutions it is necessary to accept, respect, and explore differences, to face causes, and to understand the workings of power. It may well be that parties with wildly divergent interests can come to agreements on the crisis confronting the planet. Come the millennium, we may all even be able to form one grand coalition. But until then, it is best to remember the lesson of history: that no matter how warmly it seems to have embraced the slogans of the rebels, the Empire always strikes back.

NOTES

1. Payer, C., "Causes of the Debt Crisis" in B. Onimode (ed.), *The IMF, the World Bank and Africa Debt: The Social and Political Impact*, Zed, London, 1989, pp. 7–16.

2. "Action for Whose Common Future?", *Solidarity for Equality, Ecology and Development Newsletter* 1, 1989. Torggt. 34, N-1083 Oslo 1, Norway, pp. 6–7.
3. Wiebe, J.D., Vice-President, Globe 90, Executive Vice-President, Asia Pacific Foundation, in *Globe 90 Official Buyers' Guide and Trade Fair Directory*, p. 13.
4. Global Industrial and Social Progress Research Institute brochure, p. 3.
5. United Nations General Assembly, A/CONF 151/PC/2, 23 February 1990, p. 8.

Finally, Canadian political scientist Ted Schrecker sets forth a cautiously optimistic view.

MISSING THE POINT ABOUT GROWTH

Ted Schrecker

For two decades now, sundry polemicists within and outside the academic community have been arguing about whether scarcities of natural resources are imminent, and what those scarcities might mean in terms of future national or global economic growth. Although there are obvious historical antecedents in the work of Malthus and Jevons, the contemporary debate began in earnest with the Club of Rome's 1972 report on *The Limits to Growth.*[1] The growth debate has now been rekindled by the World Commission on Environment and Development (the Brundtland Commission). The Commission's report, *Our Common Future*,[2] contains a sobering and sometimes alarming catalogue of environmental and resource-related problems. However, the report also differs from many previous global-scale analyses of environmental issues in its approach to the questions of limits to growth and carrying capacity.

The Commission states that biophysical limits may exist to certain kinds of economic activity. However, it stresses that many limits which appear to be in this category are, in fact, "imposed by the present state of technology and social organization,"[3] and are therefore not immutable. Further, *Our Common Future* points out, as part of its emphasis on meeting basic needs, that: "The most basic of all needs is for a livelihood: that is, employment. Between 1985 and 2000 . . . new livelihood opportunities will have to be generated for 60 million persons every year" in the developing countries. Consequently, the economic challenge is "to generate sustainable work opportunities on this scale and at a level of productivity that would enable poor households to meet minimum consumption standards."[4] In an admittedly rather vague manner, the Brundtland Commission points to existing and potential reductions in the materials requirements and pollution outputs of industrial production, as well as to the potential for dramatic increases in the efficiency of energy use, as ways of "producing more with less": continuing economic growth without fatally compromising the integrity of the natural systems on which, ultimately, all life depends.[5]

One might be tempted to take issue with this last assertion, which is reflected in claims like that of David Suzuki that "without a clean environment, we won't be around, and there can't be an economy."[6] The concept of the planet as a life-support system is itself a social construction with its own particular biases. The livelihoods of Edmonton lawyers or Hamilton steelworkers do not depend on the earth as a life-support system in the same way, and with the same immediacy, as those of Sahelian nomadic herders, Brazilian rubber-tappers, or even Saskatchewan wheat farmers. This is, however, quite the opposite of the approach taken by environmentalists who, taking the project of saving the planet seriously and uncritically, have rejected the Brundtland approach, and its presumption of the continued viability of economic growth.

Instead, they have become more or less explicit advocates of an economically steady state, either globally or at least in the richer industrialized countries. In the latter vein, Suzuki argues that industrialized nations "have to reduce our impact and free resources for the poor nations by cutting back on consumption."[7] In either case, the claim being made is based on the existence of biophysical limits to growth, often referred to in terms of the carrying capacity of the environment either regionally or globally.[8]

Several arguments can be advanced in reply. For reasons of space I cannot review the extensive body of scientific argument purporting to demonstrate the existence of biophysical limits to growth, but it should be pointed out that most of its literature ignores the flexible relations among technological change, economic growth, and sustainability. As an illustration of the relevance of this point, the environmental consequences of today's levels of industrial production would be devastating were it carried out using only the technology available at the start of the century, demanding the associated resource and energy inputs, and creating the associated levels of pollution. This is, in fact, exactly what has happened in eastern Europe, but it need not have occurred. Much of that region is now an environmental disaster area not because of industrialization *per se*; rather, the disaster arose because of a conspicuous, if readily explicable failure to realize the global benefits of technology transfer.

In other words, the root of the problem is not the level of industrial activity, however measured, but rather the technologies used in achieving that level. The Brundtland Commission is right to say that carrying capacity is socially and technologically, as well as biologically determined. Such observations are particularly important for meeting basic needs in poor countries because they suggest the potential for rapid, yet environmentally benign growth by way of "technological leapfrogging"[9] if ways can be found to ensure that developing economies adopt even current state-of-the-art technologies rather than the rich world's castoffs.

On a global scale, the Brundtland Commission points out that a "five- to ten-fold increase in world industrial output" would be needed to bring world-wide consumption of manufactured goods up to today's levels in industrialized countries, given predictable increases in worldwide population.[10] This may seem implausible, but it isn't necessarily so. After all, today's levels and patterns of economic activity would seem wildly implausible to an observer from the 1950s unacquainted with the last few decades' advances in areas such as micro-electronics and telecommunications.

We cannot, of course, reliably predict such developments, but neither should we presume the cessation of technological progress in the future as a basis for making far-reaching decisions about environmental policy and economic development. This leads us to the core of the Brundtland Commission's argument, which rests on three interrelated sociopolitical assumptions. First, "in most situations, redistributive policies can only operate on increases in income" at the national level; this is how the Commission links poor country growth to the prospects for reducing absolute poverty.[11] Second, in an increasingly inter-dependent global economy, it is unrealistic to project growth in the poorer countries of the world in isolation from growth in the rich ones, which serve simultaneously as markets and sources of investment.

This latter point is particularly important because of the urgent need to reverse the current pattern of North–South capital flows if sustained growth in the poor countries is to be achieved. The Brundtland report pointed out that because of the cessation of much new lending and direct investment combined with interest obligations on past borrowing, by the mid-1980s the rich countries were draining capital from the poor ones, to the tune of tens of billions of dollars a year.[12] Hence the third assumption, a corollary of the first two: in the absence of attractive returns from investments in poor countries, the drain of capital from the economic periphery to the centre can only be reversed by means of altruistic transfers in the form of development assistance. Such transfers are especially improbable when the economies capable of providing such assistance are themselves growing slowly.

Any reasonably observant Canadian will be able to confirm the strength of these assumptions about self-interest and sharing from everyday experience. For a micro-level example consider what happens when funds for government-supported universities are in short supply. Internal cutbacks do not seriously affect tenured faculty members' incomes and job security. They hit part-time and temporary faculty, support staff, and budget items like library acquisitions that are of most benefit to the less powerful and privileged members of the university community, who cannot readily afford the research trips and journal purchases needed to make up for the deficiencies in libraries as a common pool resource. This is a small-scale example of a process brilliantly described by Lester Thurow more than a decade ago. Thurow referred to a stagnant economy, or one whose future growth is uncertain as a "zero-sum society" because one person's or group's gain is perceived inevitably (and probably correctly) as another's loss.[13] Relatively affluent and well organized groups, said Thurow, will be able to protect and even expand their entitlements in such circumstances. They possess precisely those resources needed to work the political process to their advantage. The rest of us are likely to be left out in the cold, sometimes literally.

We can see the politics of zero-sum at work in Ontario, where a mildly social democratic (New Democratic Party) government was elected in 1990 at the start of a major recession. Ambitious plans developed by a previous government to expand and improve income support programs in the province, which (as elsewhere in Canada) leave recipients well below the poverty line, were largely abandoned;[14] so were brave words about progressive taxation. Shortly after taking office, the NDP increased basic welfare benefit levels by a sub-inflationary two percent, while awarding its highest paid civil servants a six percent pay increase. As record numbers of Ontarians relied on food banks, the most recent (1992) provincial budget announced a high-profile enforcement program aimed at the recurrent bogeyman of welfare fraud, while leaving untouched a variety of subsidies which benefit principally the middle class. At least some members of the government probably had genuine commitments to progressive taxation and spending, but these commitments have not been implemented. The political process just doesn't work that way when existing entitlements are at stake.

The lesson here is clear. Policies of progressive redistribution may be politically fragile in most situations, but they are especially unworkable in a steady state context. People who stand to lose simply will not let them happen, and when the prospect becomes sufficiently threatening the veneer of democratic civility shatters very quickly. Much of the propertied Chilean middle class at least tacitly supported the brutalities of the Pinochet regime in 1973, and its virtual destruction of Chilean civil society for a decade afterward, as preferable to the revival of the redistributive proposals that brought the Allende government to power.[15] Closer to home, the jury verdict that exonerated four white Los Angeles police officers in the videotaped beating of a black citizen, and led to riots of Spring 1992, reflected a similar dynamic. When people view an institution that protects their economic prerogatives as being threatened, they will do almost anything to maintain its political viability, whether the institution at stake is the Los Angeles Police Department or the Chilean armed forces.

The interaction of the national and global dimensions of the politics of privilege can be observed in national responses to the global "debt crisis" that has distorted the economic and environmental priorities of many poor countries. Administratively, this crisis would be amazingly easy to resolve. Rich-country governments could discharge the intergovernmental obligations of poor countries, either directly or by way of expanded contributions to multilateral institutions like the World Bank and the International Monetary Fund. They could also buy the debts owed to private sector banks on the secondary market, probably at a substantial discount, and discharge them. This would relieve poor countries of billions of dollars a year in interest obligations, payable in convertible currencies, that probably drive them to undertake a variety of unsustainable economic activities.[16] As suggested by the UNICEF-sponsored study of "adjustment with a human face," it might also create a political space for more humane, and possibly even more effective domestic economic policies.[17]

Yet what elected rich-country government would be willing to divert the necessary funds from domestic spending priorities to such an objective, or to raise taxes on its citizens to support a program whose contribution to global economic equity would be indisputable? How much would the securely employed academic proponents of the steady state, in the richest countries of the world, be willing to see their taxes go up or their salaries go down to support the retirement of Third World debt?[18] How much less rich is scientist and broadcaster Suzuki willing to be?

To ask the question in that form is to answer it. The same dynamic applies even to development assistance programs on a much more modest scale. As UNICEF points out, the conditions in which children live in the poor countries often constitute "passive atrocities,"[19] yet the international community has been singularly unsuccessful in mobilizing resources equivalent to one day's global military spending for programs that would save the lives of many of the 100 million children likely to die from illness and malnutrition in the 1990s.[20] However, development assistance is the only substantial category of government expenditure without an obvious or inherent domestic clientele. Critics of "tied aid" often miss the point: the contribution of development assistance programs to the incomes of some identifiable group in the donor country may distort the objectives of such programs, but it is a political precondition for their survival. The high and rising level of political support for restrictive immigration policies in Canada and various countries of the EEC is another illustration of this dynamic; there seem to be few altruists around when people are confronted with the prospect of actually sharing economic opportunities.

The various environmental and resource management problems identified in *Our Common Future*, and elaborated upon in a large and growing literature,[21] are indisputably threatening. Simply listing these problems, as Michael Clow does,[22] is not an argument for the steady state, or indeed an argument for anything. It is rather a way of avoiding argument; Ralf Dahrendorf has wisely identified those who adopt this style in environmental debates as "promoters of ethics by the force of things."[23] The preceding, necessarily sketchy discussion shows that Clow's position is indefensible. The contemporary growth debate is really about balancing the biophysical and technological uncertainties associated with the prospect of continued economic growth against the sociopolitical uncertainties and intensified distributional inequities that are almost certain to be associated with its absence. More sophisticated proponents of a steady state, like Canadian ecologist William Rees, acknowledge this point and argue the need for "special measures to be put in place to ensure that the burden does not fall unfairly on the poor."[24] They are conspicuously silent with respect to the political possibilities for accomplishing this latter objective. Their silence is tactically wise, for it is hard to envision a political situation in which such measures could actually be implemented in the context of a steady-state economy.

Rees further suggests that people who question the position "that we may be fast approaching absolute limits to material economic growth . . . have an obligation to refute the analysis."[25] I think he is wrong. Considerably less is known about the biophysical limitations to economic growth than about the behaviour of steady-state economies and societies. Once again, there is no disputing the environmental damage associated with the present quality of growth, and the need for effective measures to reduce it. However, until commentators with a preference for no-growth can explain convincingly how to avoid the deepening polarization of economic opportunity and political power that appear to go along with the steady state, no-growth should be counted as a non-starter.

NOTES

* A.M. Schrecker and John Wadland provided valuable comments on early versions of this chapter; they are blameless with respect to its content.

1. D. Meadows et al., *The Limits to Growth* (New York: Universe, 1972). For a critique of the assumptions and methodologies used in this study, see H.S.D. Cole et al. (eds.), *Model of Doom: A Critique of the Limits to Growth* (New York: Universe, 1972).
2. World Commission on Environment and Development, *Our Common Future* (New York: Oxford University Press, 1987).
3. Ibid., 8.

4. Ibid., 54; see also 44–46.
5. Ibid., 168–234.
6. D. Suzuki, "Why conventional economics spells doom," *Toronto Star*, March 2, 1991, D6.
7. Ibid.
8. For elaborations of this argument see *e.g.* H. Daly, "Carrying capacity as a tool of development policy: the Ecuadoran Amazon and the Paraguayan Chaco," *Ecological Economics* 2 (1990), 187–195; P. Ehrlich, "Environmental Disruption: Implications for the Social Sciences," *Social Science Quarterly* 62 (1981), 7–22; W. Rees, "A Role for Environmental Assessment in Achieving Sustainable Development," *Environmental Impact Assessment Review* 8 (1988), 273–291.
9. The term used in a particularly useful study of the potential for energy efficiency improvements in Brazil (and by implication in other developing countries) by J. Goldenberg et al., "Basic Needs and Much More with One Kilowatt Per Capita," *Ambio* 14 (1985), 190–200.
10. *Our Common Future*, 213.
11. Ibid., 50–51.
12. Ibid., 67–75.
13. L. Thurow, *The Zero-Sum Society: Distribution and the Possibilities for Economic Change* (New York: Penguin, 1980).
14. These plans are outlined in *Transitions: Report of the Social Assistance Review Committee* (Toronto: Ontario Ministry of Community and Social Services, 1988).
15. Cf. the comment of Alain Rouquié (in 1984) that: "The recollection of three years of Popular Unity government is still the surest foundation of the Chilean dictatorship." "Demilitarization and Military-dominated Polities in Latin America," in G. O'Donnell et al. (eds.), *Transition from Authoritarian Rule: Comparative Perspectives* (Baltimore: Johns Hopkins University Press, 1986), 131.
16. N. Myers, "Economics and Ecology in the International Arena," *Ambio* 15 (1986), 299–300.
17. G. Cornia et al. (eds.), *Adjustment with a Human Face*, vol. 1: *Protecting the Vulnerable and Promoting Growth* (Oxford: Clarendon Press, 1987). On the impact of the debt crisis on human welfare in debtor countries see also UNICEF, *The State of the World's Children 1989* (New York: Oxford University Press, 1989), 15–36.
18. I leave out of this discussion the emotionally attractive option of directly requiring private sector banks to absorb the entire cost of debt retirement. No government in the world is sufficiently independent from the international financial system to embark on this form of active expropriation, although some governments have made a partial and indirect effort to achieve broadly the same effect, by restricting banks' ability to carry non-performing developing country loans on their books as assets.
19. UNICEF, *State of the World's Children 1989*, 40.
20. UNICEF, *State of the World's Children 1990* (New York: Oxford University Press, 1990), 16–36.

21. For an overview, see *Managing Planet Earth: Readings from Scientific American Magazine* (San Francisco: W.H. Freeman, 1990). Particularly useful as a source of more detailed information on a global basis are the reports produced by the World Resources Institute, *World Resources* 1986, 1987, 1988–89 (New York: Basic Books) and *World Resources* 1990–91 and 1992–93 (New York: Oxford University Press); for Canada, see Government of Canada, *The State of Canada's Environment* (Ottawa: Supply and Services Canada, 1991).
22. M. Clow, "Sustainable Development Won't Be Enough," *Policy Options*, November 1990, 6–8.
23. R. Dahrendorf, *Law and Order* (London: Stevens & Sons, 1985), 170, n. 75.
24. W. Rees, "The Ecology of Sustainable Development," *The Ecologist* 20 (no. 1, January/February 1990), 21.
25. Ibid., 23.

FURTHER READING

The literature on sustainability and sustainable development is huge; here we can only indicate a few entry points. Carolyn Merchant very significantly links the concept of sustainability to the achievement of a human/land symbiosis; see her chapter on sustainable development in Merchant (1992). Robinson et al. (1990) explore the linkages between socio-political and environmental sustainability. Rees (1990) argues that the call for sustainable development threatens to become merely an excuse for more ordinary unsustainable development, and suggests that we may be now so close to biophysical limitations that the very possibility of further growth is untenable. Clow (1990) argues similarly that unconstrained economic activity "necessarily means killing the goose that lays the golden eggs." Nickerson (1993) outlines a concept of sustainability from an ethical viewpoint, and suggests that the achievement of sustainability would amount essentially to the maturation of human culture. Robinson et al. (1990) and Manning (1990) wrestle with various interpretations of sustainability. Peacock (1995) argues that any sustainable state must be symbiotic. See also Schrecker (1994) and Archubugi and Nijkamp, eds. (1989) for further perspectives.

QUESTIONS TO CONSIDER

1. Do you think that biophysical limits are the major barrier to further economic growth? Or are the major impediments socio-political? Or can these two kinds of problems really be separated?
2. Is "sustainable development" an oxymoron? Are we just trying to have our ecological cake and eat it too? Or do you agree that improvements in technology, energy efficiency, agricultural techniques, etc., can yield the kind of increases in productivity called for by the Brundtland Report without irreparably damaging the environment?
3. Schrecker argues that we should opt for economic growth (as environmentally friendly as possible, of course) in order to avoid the social polarization and inequities of a "zero-sum" society. Why does he believe this? Is this not merely putting off the

problem of inequity to a later date? If so, what would be wrong with doing that?

4. Do you think that Lohmann's worries about the motives behind the call for sustainable development are sound?
5. The Brundtland Report states, "Development tends to simplify ecosystems and to reduce their diversity of species." Is this necessarily the case? Bear in mind the observations of Hecht and Cockburn (Chapter Six) that certain kinds of skilful manipulation of the environment can actually increase biodiversity. Would such "development" be symbiotic?

PART SIX

Toward symbiosis

In our final part, we present several authors who give us glimpses of what it could mean for humans to approach a genuine mutualism with Gaia. The theme common to all the items presented here is that it might well be possible for the human species to interact with the environment in something other than an essentially parasitical manner. Not all environmental thinkers would agree with this. Both radical deep ecologists such as Christopher Manes (1990) and lifeboat ethicists such as Garrett Hardin (see his widely reprinted 1968 article) might well say (although they do not use exactly these terms) that all we can ever hope for is a sort of mitigated parasitism upon the planetary ecosystem; or as Whatmough calls it below, a sort of "endemic" relationship. It would be as if we were to aspire to make ourselves the forehead mites of Gaia. (See Wilson's account of the acarine mites in Chapter Seven.) Even those who insist that this is the only sort of possibility would tend to agree that it is a rather dismal prospect at best, except perhaps for a few (such, perhaps, as Manes) who seem to relish the prospect of a return to the Neolithic.

Here, then, is the problem we pose for consideration: Do we play out the ecological drama to the bitter end, or (to borrow Rachel Carson's phrase) seek another road?

CHAPTER SEVENTEEN

CAN SPECIES BE SAVED?

In the first chapter of this part, we consider a question of slightly more limited scope than the grand question itself of the possibility of human/land mutualism, but one that has a great bearing on that question. Faced with the cataclysmic wave of anthropogenic extinctions now under way, is there anything that can be done to save at least some species from oblivion? Is it simply inevitable that everything disappear under the steamroller of human expansion? And what problem, precisely, have we solved by saving some particular species?

Conservationists now sometimes undertake extraordinary measures to rescue species on the brink of survival. A familiar example, usually counted as a success story, is the whooping crane. It used to be said that if you had seen fifteen of them, you had seen them all; but careful and dedicated nurturing has increased their numbers to 150 or more (Freedman 1989, pp. 295–96). It can be argued that one has not really saved a wild species by such measures, but created a domesticated relict variant; so that it is questionable whether one has really succeeded in preserving natural biodiversity at all. In any case, it seems clear that such special measures as were successful with the whooping crane cannot help the thousands of species of birds, animals, insects, and plants (many but not all of which are tropical) that are threatened now by habitat loss and exploitation. The only measures that can save them, in all likelihood, would be preservation of their habitats and lessening of hunting pressure — things that do not seem likely to happen soon enough to save many species.

A more hopeful approach is to focus on protecting what ecologists call "keystone species." Edward O. Wilson recounts one encouraging success story.

REPLACING A KEYSTONE

Edward O. Wilson

The bald eagle, one species, flies above the Chippewa National Forest of Minnesota. A thousand species of plants compose the vegetation below. Why does this particular combination obtain rather than a thousand eagles and one plant? Or a thousand eagles and a thousand plants? It is natural to ask whether the numbers that do exist are governed by mathematical laws. If there are such laws, it follows that we can someday predict diversity in other places, in other groups of organisms. To master complexity by such an economical means would be the crowning achievement of ecology.

There are no laws unfortunately, at least none that biologists have hit upon yet, not in the sense ordained by physicists and chemists. But, as in any study of evolution, there are principles that can be written in the form of rules or statistical trends. The discipline formulating these weaker statements, community ecology, is still youthful and rapidly growing, which is a polite way of saying that it is a long way behind the physical sciences — but there is progress, and ambition.

Before us now is the overwhelmingly important problem of how biodiversity is assembled by the creation of ecosystems. We can address it by recognizing two extreme possibilities. One is that a community of organisms, like that occupying the Chippewa National Forest, is in total disorder. The species come and go as free spirits. Their colonization and extinction are not determined by the presence or absence of other species. Consequently, according to this extreme model, the amount of biodiversity is a random process, and the habitats in which the various species live fail to coincide except by accident. The second extreme possibility is perfect order. The species are so closely interdependent, the food webs so rigid, the symbioses so tightly bound that the community is virtually one great organism, a superorganism. This means that if only one of the species were named, say the Acadian flycatcher, marbled salamander, or goblin fern, the thousands of other species could be ticked off without further information about that particular community.

Ecologists dismiss the possibility of either extreme. They envision an intermediate form of community organization, something like this: whether a particular species occurs in a given suitable habitat is largely due to chance, but for most organisms the chance is strongly affected — the dice are loaded — by the identity of the species already present.

In such loosely organized communities there are little players and big players, and the biggest players of all are the keystone species. As the name implies, the removal of a keystone species causes a substantial part of the community to change drastically. Many other species decline to near or total extinction or else rise to unprecedented abundance. Sometimes other species previously excluded from the community by competition and lack of opportunity now invade it, altering its structure still more. Put the keystone species back in and the community typically, but not invariably, returns to something resembling its original state.

The most potent keystone species known in the world may be the sea otter (*Enhydra lutris*). This wonderful animal, large and supple in body, cousin to the weasels, whiskered like a cat, staring with a languorously deadpan expression, once thrived among the kelp beds close to shore from Alaska to southern California. It was hunted by European explorers and settlers for its fur, so that by the end of the nineteenth century it was close to extinction. In places where sea otters disappeared completely, an unexpected sequence of events unfolded. Sea urchins, normally among the major prey of the otters, exploded in numbers and proceeded to consume large portions of the kelp and other inshore seaweeds. In otter times, the heavy kelp growth, anchored on the sea bottom and reaching to the surface, was a veritable forest. Now it was mostly gone, literally eaten away. Large stretches of the shallow ocean floor were reduced to a desert-like terrain, called sea-urchin barrens.

With strong public support, conservationists were able to restore the sea otter and with it the original habitat and biodiversity. A small number of the animals had managed to survive at far opposite ends of the range, in the outer Aleutian Islands to the north and a few localities along the southern California coast. Some of these were now transported to scattered intermediate sites in the United States and Canada, and strict measures were taken to protect the species throughout its range. The otters waxed and the sea urchins waned. The kelp forests grew back to their original luxuriance. A host of lesser algal species moved in, along with crustaceans, squid, fishes, and other organisms. Gray whales migrated closer to shore to park their young in breaks along the kelp edge while feeding on the dense concentrations of animal plankton.

Efforts to save endangered species are sometimes tinged with bitter ironies. Often the only action we can take is "too little, too late." Sometimes we seem to be faced with intractable dilemmas that seem to force us to condemn to death the very thing we are trying to save. An example is the case in New Zealand of the weta versus the tuatara. The tuatara is an endangered lizard species, the last remaining representative of an entire order of reptiles. The weta is an exotic cricket-like flightless insect that can weigh up to 70 grams. Conservationists are struggling to save both, and yet the favourite prey of the tuatara is precisely the weta. What can one do when one endangered species is the main diet of the other? (See Diamond 1990 for details.)

To illustrate similar ironies in a Canadian setting, we present here a discussion by agricultural writer John D. Milton on the efforts to save the Canadian wood buffalo.

For sobering background on the systematic extermination of the North American bisons, see Farley Mowat's "The Passing of the Buff" (in Mowat 1984) and Freedman (1989), pp. 293–95. It is not generally realized that there were once at least four subspecies of buffalo native to North America. These were the plains buffalo, the wood buffalo, the Oregon, and the eastern. The eastern, which was the largest, once roamed all of the eastern part of the continent. It was an animal considerably more massive than the moose, which we now think of as the major native herbivore of the wooded parts of the continent. Its hide had a very high commercial value, and accordingly it was hunted so ruthlessly that it had already been wiped out through most of its natural range by 1720, except for a few scattered herds in the Appalachian Mountains. The last two survivors, a cow and a calf, were spotted in 1825 and, as Mowat puts it, "To find them was to kill them." The subspecies is now extinct—and forgotten.

THE RETURN OF THE WOOD BISON: THE IRONY OF SUCCESS

John D. Milton

Bison did at one time provide a major source of meat and hides for my people. Today we rely primarily on moose, bear, waterfowl, fish. Nevertheless, we consider it our right to have access to and hunt bison in northern Alberta.

–Chief Pat Marcel, *Athabasca Chipewyan Band*

As far as the cattle producers are concerned, while our primary objective is obviously the removal of any risk of disease spreading from the bison into domestic cattle, we are also committed to a solution that will mean the retention of the Park and of a herd of free-ranging disease-free bison in the Park. We have never advocated anything different.

–Gordon Mitchell, Assistant Manager, *Alberta Cattle Commission*

. . . To manipulate an organism of the ecosystem is to affect the environment as a whole. One only has to look at the disasters of the past for any supportive evidence. This absolute was obviously ignored when the bison were moved from Wainwright to Wood Buffalo National Park.

So today we now have a wildlife problem in the Park, and consequently, the Slave River Lowlands, that is artificial, recent, speaking historically, and man-made.

–Ken Herbert, Executive Director,
Northwest Territories Wildlife Federation

The small single-prop plane banked gently over the land. Below, Canada Wildlife Service (CWS) biologist Nick Novakowski could see the bison moving through the aspen forest. The excitement swelled within him. Could these be wood bison? And indeed they were. With Novakowski's discovery of this herd in a remote corner of Wood Buffalo National Park, there began an intensive recovery program to bring back the wood bison, thought by many to be extinct, to its historical range across mid-western Canada. Today, there are more than 3,000 wood bison roaming through the wilds of northern boreal forests and aspen parklands. But, once again, they are being threatened, this time by the legacy of history.

Disappearance and Rediscovery

Larger and darker-coloured than its prairie cousin, the wood bison once ranged throughout the northern boreal forests and aspen parklands where it could be found feeding in open grass meadows.

Hunting and several successive severe winters very nearly drove the wood bison to extinction in the late 1800s. By 1891, estimates placed their numbers at less than 300, concentrated between Great Slave Lake and the Peace-Athabasca Delta.

Conservation efforts designed to protect the bison had begun as early as 1877 with the passing of the Buffalo Protection Act. However, lack of enforcement made this law ineffective. The Act was strengthened in 1893, but actual enforcement remained minimal until assigned to the Northwest Mounted Police in 1897. By 1911, there were six full-time buffalo rangers patrolling the last ranges of the wood bison. Their efforts, and the creation of Wood Buffalo National Park in 1922 as a haven for wood bison, seemingly ensured the wood bison was on the road to recovery.

However, their recovery was to be dealt a serious, even fatal, blow with the introduction of a herd of prairie bison to Wood Buffalo National Park between 1925 and 1928. Just how the Canadian federal government came to own such a herd is itself a success story in this country's conservation history. At the turn of the last century, the final few herds of prairie bison were privately owned. The largest of these herds, the Pablo-Allard herd located in Montana, was threatened with eradication—its owners having lost the grazing rights to vast tracts of virgin prairies in favour of new settlers and permanent agriculture. The Canadian government bought it and shipped it to Wainwright, Alberta, in 1907.

By 1923, their numbers had swollen to the thousands and the herd was once again the centre of an intense, and often emotional, debate. Its rangeland was depleted, unable to sustain the growing numbers. Settlers and agriculture were pressing in.

The federal government was confronted with the same choice Pablo and Allard had faced nearly twenty years earlier — to either find a new home for the prairie bison or to slaughter many of the bison. Public opinion was overwhelmingly opposed to slaughtering what constituted the last great herd of prairie bison and, rather than face public wrath, the government elected to ship nearly 7,000 of these bison north to Wood Buffalo Park in northern Alberta.

This the government did despite the formal opposition of many biologists and their societies. The two subspecies, they argued, had evolved differently in subtle ways and had remained distinct because of their relative isolation from the other during breeding season. Wood bison tended to move further north into the boreal forests to breed while the prairie bison moved southwards. Forced together artificially, the two bisons would naturally interbreed.

A second concern was disease. Because of their close proximity to domestic livestock, the prairie bison had become infected with tuberculosis and most likely brucellosis. Hayes Lloyd, then park supervisor, voiced his concern, writing, "It is thought to be very bad epidemiology to ship buffalo from a herd known to be diseased and place them in contact with buffalo at Wood Buffalo Park which are not known to be diseased."

Despite these fears, 6,673 young prairie bison were moved northwards, travelling by rail from Wainwright to Waterways (now Fort McMurray) and then by barge down the Athabasca and Slave Rivers to Labutte Landing near Hay Camp where they were released. As feared, the two bison quickly interbred and disease took its toll on the wood bison. By 1934, wildlife biologists concluded that the wood bison were disappearing and were being replaced by a hybrid of wood and prairie bison. By 1940, it was generally believed pure wood bison had become extinct. It appeared political expediency had single-handedly erased nearly 50 years of conservation efforts and had succeeded in pushing the wood bison into memory.

Yet, there were some biologists who believed isolated herds of pure wood bison could still exist, particularly in the northwest portion of the park. Canadian Wildlife Service biologist Nick Novakowski shared this belief. It led him into that remote part of the park during an aerial survey in 1957 and his subsequent discovery of what he believed was a herd of 200 wood bison in the Nyarling River–Buffalo Lake region.

In 1959, five dead specimens were located and collected from the region. Tests confirmed these were, in morphological terms, wood bison. The first CWS round-up occurred in February 1963 near Needle Lake. Of the 77 live bison captured, 19 were found to be disease-free and were selected to form the nucleus of a breeding herd that the CWS hoped to repopulate the northern rangelands with. The captive herd was declared disease-free by Agriculture Canada in July 1964 following a second testing for both brucellosis and tuberculosis.

Disease soon threatened the wood bison again. A series of outbreaks of anthrax, a deadly and highly contagious respiratory disease, occurred in the hybrid populations. These outbreaks prompted the CWS to capture another 18 wood bison from the Nyarling River–Buffalo Lake region and, after being found free of disease, to move them 300 kilometres northwest to a range near Fort Providence, NWT. This range has since come to be known as the Mackenzie Bison Sanctuary, which today is the home for more than 2,000 wood bison.

A second general round-up near Needle Lake took place in February 1965. Twenty-four of these newly-captured bison were tested for brucellosis and tuberculosis, found negative, and moved to Elk Island National Park in the fall of 1965. Descendants of this herd number more than 300 head and have become the basic source breeding herd for relocation projects to re-establish free-roaming herds in northern Alberta and Manitoba, the Yukon, and the Northwest Territories.

Journey to Nahanni: Recovery Program Established

In 1975, a co-operative recovery program was formally initiated by the federal, provincial, and territorial governments in Western Canada. Its primary goal was to establish a minimum of three, and ideally five, free-ranging herds of wood bison in their historic range. Captive breeding herds were also to be created in zoos and wildlife parks to preserve the bison gene pool.

"Urban and agricultural development over the past half century have resulted in the loss of a major portion of prairie rangeland," says Hal Reynolds, CWS biologist in Edmonton and a moving force behind the Wood Bison Recovery Program. "Because of the incompatibility of free-roaming herds of bison with human development and agriculture in particular, and the potential for serious conflicts between man and bison, such wild populations on the prairies can never again be a reality. The more isolated and undeveloped rangelands in northern Canada are the only remaining areas where wild herds are possible."

The first transplant to the wild since the Mackenzie Bison Sanctuary was not successful. A small herd was transferred to Jasper National Park in the summer of 1978. Although suitable habitat was present where the herd was released, the bison travelled more than 160 kilometres in a month over mountainous terrain, onto provincial land and ultimately into a settled agricultural area. In the end, the wood bison had to be recaptured and removed from the area.

"A lot of study is necessary before such a release is attempted," Reynolds explains. "First, a potential area is identified. Then, forage availability is estimated using aerial, and later ground, surveys. From these, the carrying capacity of the region can be estimated. A blueprint outlining long-term management options is also prepared. All release programs are co-operative ventures involving federal, provincial, and territorial governments, native Indian Bands, and non-governmental wildlife organizations. Once released, full responsibility for the herd's management is transferred to a provincial or territorial management agency."

A second release was attempted in 1980, this time to the Nahanni region in the Northwest Territories. Reynolds was the CWS biologist in charge.

"Initially the herd separated and dispersed widely in the forests but by early winter, it appeared that two sub-herds had formed," Reynolds says. "One ranged along the Nahanni River between Yohin Lake in the Nahanni National Park to Nahanni Butte. The second, larger herd ranged from meadows near the mouth of the Netla River south to Fort Liard along both sides of the Liard River."

During the fall of 1980, a herd of eight wood bison from the Nahanni-Liard herd followed a winter road south to the Fort Nelson region of northern British Columbia. These have not been observed since 1983.

"It appears from our monitoring that the remaining bison are returning to previously foraged areas, establishing home ranges in the region," Reynolds says. "Although the Nahanni-Liard herds remain vulnerable to catastrophic environmental and chance demographic events because of their small sizes, the repopulation effort appears to have been successful. In 1989, a captive breeding herd was established at the Moose Jaw Wild Animal Park in southern Saskatchewan to further reduce these threats."

Bolstered by this success, efforts intensified to establish other free-roaming herds. Today there are similar programs in northern Alberta, the Yukon, and Manitoba.

The Manitoba project is unique due to its commercial aspect. Under a co-operative management agreement, the original stock is being managed by the Waterhen Indian Band–owned corporation, Wood Bison Ranches Ltd., for meat and other products.

"Commercial considerations must come into play," Reynolds says. "As agricultural development continues to push northwards, there is a corresponding loss of wildlife habitat. In the prairie provinces, bison ranching is profitable. In northern areas, development of such an industry should be encouraged using wood bison rather than prairie bison or cattle. The use of wood bison can be viewed as an alternative to conventional agriculture contributing to sustainable agriculture and offering economic, ecological, cultural, and aesthetic benefits."

Reynolds points to the other re-establishment projects as indicators of the recovery effort's success. In March 1986, 34 wood bison were released into an enclosure along the Nisling River about 80 kilometres west of Carmacks, Yukon. The herd has prospered under intensive management and the first 21 wood bison were released in March 1988. Additional animals were released in 1989 and 1990, bringing the total free-ranging herd to more than 60 head. The approved management plan sets a wild herd of 200 head by 1994 as its goal.

Another project, initiated in 1981 in co-operation with the Dene Tha Indian Band, is centred in northwestern Alberta. Although flooding conditions and severe winters have affected the project, the managers are still optimistic. However, the release program has been indefinitely postponed because of the risk of disease infection from, and interbreeding with, free-ranging hybrid bison in the region.

The Irony of Success

Progress is being made; a seemingly extinct species has been given second life. Wood bison numbers have grown at least five-fold, to nearly 3,000 head, since 1978 when the wood bison was first designated as endangered. Today there exist two geographically separated source herds of wood bison — in the Mackenzie Sanctuary and at Elk Island National Park. Four other herds are being nurtured through co-operative projects.

And yet, with such success, it is ironic that the wood bison is again being threatened, this time by history. As wood bison numbers increase, there is growing concern these herds will again come in contact with diseased hybrid bison in Wood Buffalo National Park where the twin threat of brucellosis and tuberculosis still exists. As the Wood Bison Recovery Team stated in its submission to the Northern Diseased Bison Assessment Panel, "The future productivity and viability of free-ranging herds of wood bison are jeopardized by the presence of the diseased bison herds in and around Wood Buffalo National Park. The Mackenzie herd is particularly at risk of acquiring brucellosis and tuberculosis present in the infected bison herds."

It is a legacy biologists wished never had happened. Despite three separate attempts in the past thirty years, efforts to eradicate these diseases have failed. Today there seems little hope of ever controlling the spread of these diseases short of slaughtering the hybrid herd and repopulating the park and adjacent lands with disease-free wood bison. To the ranchers who settled Alberta's Fort Vermilion district, and who now live near the park's borders, such a solution, although radical, is the only practical solution to a very serious threat.

Indeed, the Wood Bison Recovery Team concludes, "Elimination of the two diseases in the region would remove the largest single obstacle to the recovery of wood bison and would increase the potential for re-establishing healthy wood bison herds in an additional 54 per cent of their historic range. The expanded region includes the highest quality range for the subspecies and the core area of the historic range."

Eradication and repopulation with disease-free wood bison is supported by livestock producers. It took more than a billion dollars and 80 years to eradicate both these diseases from Canada's domestic herds. Nearly 400,000 head of cattle were slaughtered during this time. Naturally, the thought of either disease finding its way back into Canada's cattle industry is a concern shared by Agriculture Canada, ranchers, and dairymen across the country. At risk is Canada's international reputation as a disease-free exporter of livestock and meat products. The loss of this reputation, and access to crucial international markets, could cost cattlemen, and Canada, millions of dollars a year.

It is also supported by biologists and international conservation organizations. In a draft Action Plan for North American Bison, the Bison Specialist Group of the Species Survival Commission of IUCN suggests eliminating the diseased hybrid bison in Wood Buffalo National Park and the surrounding area and replacing them with disease-free wood bison. So, history has come full circle. Prairie bison were originally infected by diseased cattle. Now the rancher fears the bison.

The fate of the hybrid population has resurrected the debate of the late 1920s: to slaughter or not to slaughter. It is a difficult choice to make today, just as it was then.

In August 1990, the Northern Diseased Bison Environmental Assessment Panel submitted its report to the Ministers of the Environment and Agriculture. The Panel was to study possible ways to control and eradicate brucellosis and tuberculosis from the area. Solutions studied included the fencing of the Park, immunization of the bison populations, and slaughter. As part of the Panel's study, it conducted public hearings in Fort Vermilion, Fort Chipewyan, and Edmonton, Alberta, and at Fort Providence, Hay River, Fort Resolution, and Fort Smith, Northwest Territories, during January 1990.

The Panel concluded that "*eradication of the existing bison population is the only method of eliminating the risk of transmission of bovine brucellosis and tuberculosis from bison in and around Wood Buffalo National Park to domestic cattle, wood bison and humans.*" Consequently, the Panel recommended "that all free-ranging bison now living in Wood Buffalo National Park and surrounding areas be removed [i.e., slaughtered] and replaced by disease-free wood bison."

It is a radical solution to an extremely serious problem. It is a solution that cannot please everyone. However, as the Wood Bison Recovery Team concluded in their submission, "The frequently expressed idea of 'correcting past wrongs' is consistent with evolving public support for conservation, restoration, maintenance and wise use of natural resources. Public interest in the northern diseased bison debate is high. Not since the first two decades of this century has there been an opportunity to restore the wood bison to its former role within a healthy, productive and intact ecosystem in a broad section of the boreal forest. The consequences of failing to achieve this goal when it is within our reach would indeed be a sad legacy to leave for future generations."

So far (1994), the recommendations put forward by the Northern Diseased Bison Environmental Assessment Panel have not been acted upon. A stakeholders' group, the Northern Buffalo Management Board, was created in June 1991 to devise a management plan for the twin diseases and for the infected bison. It submitted its report in March 1993 in which it proposes an additional three-year study before finalizing a management plan. This report is still being considered by the federal government with a decision expected by the fall of 1994.

The process is cumbersome; the seriousness of the situation compounded by good intentions and aggravated by time. With so many stakeholders—including four federal government departments, provincial governments, agricultural and First Nation organizations—it is not surprising that progress has been slow. The goal set forth by the management board is to have a free-roaming disease-free wood bison herd in Wood Buffalo National Park by 2005. It would seem that this leaves ample time. The question is: Will the diseases remain isolated within this herd until action is initiated? Ironically, the number of bison in the park have fallen in recent years, hunted down by wolves. It would seem that nature is contributing to the solution as the diseased animals make easier prey for the wolves.

Unfortunately, procrastination is not the key to a solution. Although the park's herd remains isolated from the now larger Mackenzie Sanctuary herd, the danger of such contact increases with every passing year. The Sanctuary herd continues to grow in numbers, and as it does, it seeks to expand its range southwards. Already the vanguard of the northern herd have ventured southwards dangerously near the park's herd along the south shore of Great Slave Lake and have been forcibly pushed back into the Sanctuary. Experts wonder whether contact has not, in fact, already occurred.

Pressure for eradication has lessened somewhat from cattlemen. Canada's international reputation for being brucellosis- and tuberculosis-free is not perceived as being endangered; opinion on the international scene is ready to accept such isolated pockets of disease. However, even this carries a stiff price. Agriculture and Agri-Food Canada maintains a sharp eye on the diseases through a comprehensive testing program in the region so as to ensure the diseases are not shipped south with cattle going to market. That would be catastrophic.

And so the wood bison wait. Still, people remain strongly divided on what to do. Some believe that we should leave the animals alone and permit nature to run its course. Others still promote total eradication and re-introduction. Regardless of the course chosen, the repercussions will be felt for decades, just as those actions taken at the turn of this century are still being felt today.

FURTHER READING

Livingston (1981) is a controversial debunking of the conventional rationale for wildlife conservation. Mountford (1978) describes some successes in wildlife conservation, while Ryan (1992) is a very useful overview of the difficulties involved in conserving biodiversity in the coming "greenhouse century." See Mowat (1984) and Freedman (1989) for more detail on the fate of the bison. Kaufman and Mallory (1986) discuss extensively the problems of species conservation. Cohen (1992) examines the dilemmas of wildlife managers who seem to be forced to kill in order to save. For a challenging critique of the recommendation to slaughter the diseased buffalo herd, see Struzik (1990).

QUESTIONS TO CONSIDER

1. With reference to Milton's article about the wood buffalo, consider the pros and cons of slaughtering the diseased herd in order to protect the undiseased animals. What would you recommend?
2. Again with reference to the wood buffalo, should protecting the undiseased buffalo herd have a higher priority than protecting domesticated cattle?
3. To what extent can we avoid effectively domesticating species that we somehow do manage to save?

CHAPTER EIGHTEEN

THE ARTIFACTUAL ECOLOGY

In our first selection, Grant A. Whatmough argues that an "artifactual ecosystem" is, for humans, an evolutionary necessity, and properly constituted would be the essential modality of a human/Gaian symbiosis, if ever there can be such a thing. By an artifactual ecology, one means simply an environment that is, in part, an artifact — something that is *made*. One immediately thinks of relatively localized constructions such as beaver lodges, ant nests, or human homes, cathedrals, and office towers in this connection. But, in fact, an entire landscape or environment may be partially an artifact or "contrivance" (as Lovelock and Margulis put it in Chapter Eight); the concept is very broad. See also Hecht and Cockburn (Chapter Six in this volume) on the extent to which the Amazon rainforest was moulded by its native inhabitants, and Lovelock (later in this chapter) on the English landscape as an artifact.

THE ARTIFACTUAL ECOLOGY: AN ECOLOGICAL NECESSITY

Grant A. Whatmough

We must never lose sight of the evolutionary status of our species. We are at least as dependent as ants or termites or honeybees on the construction of a specialized environment as a necessary condition for our survival and well-being, with our civilization itself as our sheltering construction. Of course, we did not begin like that. Precisely because we are so much larger, metabolically extravagant, and ingenious (all genetic and evolutionary characteristics), we start with different limits than the social insects. We began *our* history as opportunistic predators who expediently became expansively parasitic as our species prospered and our numbers increased—with that parasitic phase predominant and intensifying over the last two or three millennia. And because we are ingenious we have been able to continue by way of parasitic mutations (now called commercial expansion and development) as our numbers have increased. This has expanded our "host" sector (after the killing off of the larger and more vulnerable post-glacial game animals) through limited and local areas of ecological devastation (North Africa, Asia Minor, the Indus Basin, parts of China), to a generalized invasion of the world at large. This expansion has been constrained only by the limitations of our own ingenuity. Of course, we can keep that going for some time yet; our ingenuity (as mutational technique), while clearly now driven more by desperation than by aspiration, can still invent new ways to feed upon the residue of structural vitality remaining in our "found" ecology. And that, in essence, is the basis of the so-called "life-boat ethic"; a proposal that accepts our present parasitic status as inherent, and thus suggests—as the only practical possibility—a limited and impoverished future as an "endemic" infestation of the entire world (with all due respect to Professor McNeill). This seems implausible (and unnecessary) to me; an essentially foolish and impractical notion that ignores the starkly reactive realities of desperation and privation, and presumes some infinite power for detached sophistic rationalism. It has a kind of Greek futility about it; advocating some sort of austerely intellectual sublimation, as our physical world winds down around us.

In fact, the real issue seems transparently clear. No parasitic species has ever, nor can ever, prosper expansively. Our species, like the ancient stromatolitic algae so long before us, must either accomplish a symbiotic adaptation, or perish as we "force" an ecological mutation (that process is called macroevolution). Thus the only *serious* question is whether we can actually manage any such adaptation within the context of those genetic features that distinguish our species. Amongst those is our uniquely receptive neurology—our "open" and experientially-structured synaptic system—that has given us our "minds," our "souls," our consciousness, and ingenuity. And already, in the last millennium of our history, that has—on two small islands with dense populations and limited resources (England and Japan)—created for a time a "horticulturally" modified ecology that proved itself well able to provide a prosperous abundance of food, clothing, and civilized shelter for substantial populations, *by way of an intensified ecology*. And that is the significant point, and the critical measure: the increase in the density and luxuriance of the whole spectrum of local flora and fauna, as an entailed consequence of the techniques by which those populations then produced their necessary supplies. Those were primarily artifactual ecologies (however accidental); ecologies that were not only regeneratively vital and expansive, but utterly dependent on the essential contribution of their human element (and so of course they are now unravelling rapidly). And they were artifacts as surely as the wheel is an artifact. It can only be by some such means that our species can possibly transform our present parasitic dependence on the found ecology to some kind of symbiotic alternative.

The concept of an artifactual ecology must apply specifically to whatever portions of the lands and waters of this earth that we intentionally exploit for our immediate advantage. Any notion — implicit or otherwise — of being able to "reach out of our ecology" to import supplies from elsewhere has been absurd for at least a century now. In fact, so far as ecological vitality is concerned, the entire planet is entailed as a single interdependent whole. Such special parts of it as the oceanic deeps, the rainforests, Antarctica, freshwater lakes, and mountain biospheres, demand undamaged protection just as the salmon rivers and the copses and lakes and streams of England were protected until industrialism and populism seized and destroyed them. This is an ecological fact that remains unaltered whether or not we like the privileged prerogatives that then protected them. Such pivotal elements are the essential fulcrums of any viable ecology at all. And since for any given species the very notion of alternative ecologies is an obvious absurdity, for us an artifactual ecology (or human symbiosis) cannot possibly entail alternatives to ecological vitality, only a humanly-induced intensification. And so it also follows that we should be pretty hesitant about the notion of "manipulation"— that can too easily be no more than a simplistic or sophistic argument for further damage — particularly if it is taken to imply anything much beyond some kind of careful stewardship. The whole point at issue here is that we have already been so intensely and exploitively destructive that the only possible way in which we can hope to become symbiotically coherent is to be ingenious enough to invent a restorative modality; alternatives won't do.

And this leads to a discussion of technological innovation itself, as "corporatism" has now suppressed it. In any such context it must certainly have virtually slowed to a halt, since significant change is the greatest of all possible threats to the very concept of corporate administration and control. Technocratic corporatism has now taken over all of our social institutions from government through academia to most commercial enterprises (we now call that capitalism). Trivial variations and interpolations are, of course, allowed and encouraged *ad nauseam*; but novel innovation — which implies significant change — is simply excluded now by various sophistic prohibitions. How many academics would endorse a completely novel interpretation or conception that could undermine the credibility of their achieved positions? What would their findings be as referees? How many engineers would choose to challenge codes of practice? How many scholastics would seriously criticize the opinions of accredited experts? How many physicists would challenge abstract quantification as the ground for physical conceptions?—and so it goes. Our real difficulty so far as ecological symbiosis is concerned is not a matter of some lack of technical ingenuity—that is hardly possible—but rather the entrenchment of socio/political authority.

And so, we might ask, what are our priorities now? Where do "we" begin? The very notion of priorities entails both power and authority; precisely the kind of "ordering" that has made us parasitic. The immediacies and diversity of individual perceptions have always been more adaptive than static—whenever actual facts (or knowledge) have not been concealed. It is not individuals, faced with stark reality, who are unteachable; but collectives, dependent upon abstractions, and driven by that minority of neurotics who seek controlled ordering as a shelter. (And this, of course, is the whole point of Churchill's comments [Chapter 5].) Any possible symbiotic future *must* depend upon some growing general awareness of our restrictive privation, and on the variety of individually reactive preferences that can yield the adaptive fragments of some vital balance.

Sir Albert Howard is regarded as one of the pioneers of the organic farming movement. Over a period of several years in central India, he developed a composting technique, which he called the Indore Process. This formed the lynchpin of an integrated system of farming involving a mutualistic cooperation at several levels among humans, farm animals, plants, soil fauna, and fungi. He argued that the basis of successful farming and indeed a flourishing human culture is soil fertility, and he insisted that the soil must be looked upon as a living thing—a symbiotic assemblage of plant roots, bacteria, fungi, etc.—and nurtured accordingly:

> Freshly prepared humus is perhaps the farmer's chief asset and must therefore be looked after as if it were actual money. It is also an important section of the live stock of the farm. Although this live stock can only be seen under the microscope, it requires just as much thought and care as the pigs which can be seen with the naked eye. (Howard 1943, p. 50)

Here is the concluding section of Howard's book (1943), in which he summarizes his position.

AN AGRICULTURAL TESTAMENT

Sir Albert Howard

The capital of the nations which is real, permanent, and independent of everything except a market for the products of farming, is the soil. To utilize and also to safeguard this important possession the maintenance of fertility is essential.

In the consideration of soil fertility many things besides agriculture proper are involved—finance, industry, public health, the efficiency of the population, and the future of civilization. In this book [*An Agricultural Testament*] an attempt has been made to deal with the soil in its wider aspects, while devoting due attention to the technical side of the subject.

The Industrial Revolution, by creating a new hunger—that of the machine—and a vast increase in the urban population, has encroached seriously on the world's store of fertility. A rapid transfer of the soil's capital is taking place. This expansion in manufacture and in population would have made little or no difference had the waste products of the factory and the town been faithfully returned to the land. But this has not been done. Instead, the first principle of agriculture has been disregarded: growth has been speeded up, but nothing has been done to accelerate decay. Farming has become unbalanced. The gap between the two halves of the wheel of life has been left unbridged, or it has been filled by a substitute in the shape of artificial manures. The soils of the world are either being worn out and left in ruins, or are being slowly poisoned. All over the world our capital is being squandered. The restoration and maintenance of soil fertility has become a universal problem.

The outward and visible sign of the destruction of soil is the speed at which the menace of soil erosion is growing. The transfer of capital, in the shape of soil fertility, to the profit and loss account of agriculture is being followed by the bankruptcy of the land. The only way this destructive process can be arrested is by restoring the fertility of each field of the catchment area of the rivers which are afflicted by this disease of civilization. This formidable task is going to put some of our oversea administrations to a very severe test.

The slow poisoning of the life of the soil by artificial manures is one of the greatest calamities which has befallen agriculture and mankind. The responsibility for this disaster must be shared equally by the disciples of Liebig and by the economic system under which we are living. The experiments of the Broadbalk field showed that increased crops could be obtained by the skilful use of chemicals. Industry at once manufactured these manures and organized their sale.

The flooding of the English market with cheap food, grown anywhere and anyhow, forced the farmers of this country to throw to the winds the old and well-tried principles of mixed farming, and to save themselves from bankruptcy by reducing the cost of production. But this temporary salvation was paid for by loss of fertility. Mother earth has recorded her disapproval by the steady growth of disease in crops, animals, and mankind. The spraying machine was called in to protect the plant; vaccines and serums the animal; in the last resort the afflicted live stock are slaughtered and burnt. This policy is failing before our eyes. The population, fed on improperly grown food, has to be bolstered up by an expensive system of patent medicines, panel doctors, dispensaries, hospitals, and convalescent homes. A C_3 population is being created.

The situation can only be saved by the community as a whole. The first step is to convince it of the danger and to show the road out of this impasse. The connexion which exists between a fertile soil and healthy crops, healthy animals and, last but not least, healthy human beings must be made known far and wide. As many resident communities as possible, with sufficient land of their own to produce their vegetables, fruit, milk and milk products, cereals, and meat, must be persuaded to feed themselves and to demonstrate the results of fresh food raised on fertile soil. An important item in education, both in the home and in the school, must be the knowledge of the superiority in taste, quality, and keeping power of food, like vegetables and fruit, grown with humus, over produce raised on artificials. The women of England—the mothers of the generations of the future—will then exert their influence in food reform. Foodstuffs will have to be graded, marketed, and retailed according to the way the soil is manured. The urban communities (which in the past have prospered at the expense of the soil) will have to join forces with rural England (which has suffered from exploitation) in making possible the restitution to the country-side of its manurial rights. All connected with the soil—owners, farmers, and labourers—must be assisted financially to restore the lost fertility. Steps must then be taken to safeguard the land of the Empire from the operations of finance. This is essential because our greatest possession is ourselves and because a prosperous and contented country-side is the strongest possible support for the safeguarding of the country's future. Failure to work out a compromise between the needs of the people and of finance can only end in the ruin of both. The mistakes of ancient Rome must be avoided.

One of the agencies which can assist the land to come into its own is agricultural research. A new type of investigator is needed. The research work of the future must be placed in the hands of a few men and women, who have been brought up on the land, who have received a first-class scientific education, and who have inherited a special aptitude for practical farming. They must combine in each one of them practice and science. Travel must be included in their training because a country like Great Britain, for instance, for reasons of climate and geology, cannot provide examples of the dramatic way in which the growth factors operate.

The approach to the problems of farming must be made from the field, not from the laboratory. The discovery of the things that matter is three-quarters of the battle. In this the observant farmer and labourer, who have spent their lives in close contact with Nature, can be of the greatest help to the investigator. The views of the peasantry in all countries are worthy of respect; there is always good reason for their practices; in matters like the cultivation of mixed crops they themselves are still the pioneers. Association with the farmer and the labourer will help research to abandon all false notions of prestige; all ideas of bolstering up their position by methods far too reminiscent of the esoteric priesthoods of the past. All engaged on the land must be brother cultivators together; the investigator of the future will only differ from the farmer in the possession of an extra implement—science—and in the wider experience which travel confers. The future standing of the research worker will depend on success: on ability to show how good farming can be made still better. The illusion that the agricultural community will not adopt improvements will disappear, once the improver can write his message on the land itself instead of in the transactions of the learned societies. The natural leaders of the country-side, as has been abundantly proved in rural India, are only too ready to assist in this work as soon as they are provided with real results. No special organization, for bringing the results of the experiment stations to the farmer, is necessary.

The administration of agricultural research must be reformed. The vast, top-heavy, complicated, and expensive structure, which has grown up by accretion in the British Empire, must be swept away. The time-consuming and ineffective committee must be abolished. The vast volume of print must be curtailed. The expenditure must be reduced. The dictum of Carrel that "the best way to increase the intelligence of scientists would be to reduce their number" must be implemented. The research applied to agriculture must be of the very best. The men and women who are capable of conducting it need no assistance from the administration beyond the means for their work and protection from interference. One of the chief duties of the Government will be to prevent the research workers themselves from creating an organization which will act as a bar to progress.

The base line of the investigations of the future must be a fertile soil. The land must be got into good heart to begin with. The response of the crop and the animal to improved soil conditions must be carefully observed. These are our greatest and most profound experts. We must watch them at work; we must pose to them simple questions; we must build up a case on their replies in ways similar to those Charles Darwin used in his study of the earthworm.

Other equally important agencies in research are the insects, fungi, and other micro-organisms which attack the plant and the animal. These are nature's censors for indicating bad farming. To-day the policy is to destroy these priceless agencies and to perpetuate the inefficient crops and animals they are doing their best to remove. To-morrow we shall regard them as Nature's professors of agriculture and as an essential factor in any rational system of farming. Another valuable method of testing our practice is to observe the effect of time on the variety. If it shows a tendency to run out, something is wrong. If it seems to be permanent, our methods are correct. The efficiency of the agriculture of the future will therefore be measured by the reduction in the number of plant breeders. A few only will be needed when soils become fertile and remain so.

Nature has provided in the forest an example which can be safely copied in transforming wastes into humus — the key to prosperity. This is the basis of the Indore Process. Mixed vegetable and animal wastes can be converted into humus by fungi and bacteria in ninety days, provided they are supplied with water, sufficient air, and a base for neutralizing excessive acidity. As the compost heap is alive, it needs just as much care and attention as the live stock on the farm; otherwise humus of the best quality will not be obtained.

The first step in the manufacture of humus, in countries like Great Britain, is to reform the manure heap — the weakest link in Western agriculture. It is biologically unbalanced because the micro-organisms are deprived of two things needed to make humus — cellulose and sufficient air. It is chemically unstable because it cannot hold itself together — valuable nitrogen and ammonia are being lost to the atmosphere. The urban centres can help agriculture, and incidentally themselves, by providing the farmers with pulverized town wastes for diluting their manure heaps and, by releasing, for agriculture and horticulture, the vast volumes of humus lying idle in the controlled tips.

The utilization of humus by the crop depends partly on the mycorrhizal association — the living fungous bridge which connects soil and sap. Nature has gone to great pains to perfect the work of the green leaf by the previous digestion of carbohydrates and proteins. We must make the fullest use of this machinery by keeping up the humus content of the soil. When this is done, quality and health appear in the crop and in the live stock.

Evidence is accumulating that such healthy produce is an important factor in the well-being of mankind. That our own health is not satisfactory is indicated by one example. Carrel states that in the United States alone no less than £700,000,000 a year is spent in medical care. This sum does not include the loss of efficiency resulting from illness. If the restitution of the manurial rights of the soils of the United States can avoid even a quarter of this heavy burden, its importance to the community and to the future of the American people needs no argument. The prophet is always at the mercy of events; nevertheless, I venture to conclude this book with the forecast that at least half the illnesses of mankind will disappear once our food supplies are raised from fertile soil and consumed in a fresh condition.

Finally, we give the last word to James Lovelock, co-creator of the Gaia hypothesis. Note his rueful confession of his one-time complicity in the destruction (that he now has come to deplore) of the English countryside. More important, note his description of the English landscape as "no natural ecosystem" but "a nation-sized garden . . . a great work of art." Could such a thing be possible again, in England, Canada, or anywhere else?

LIVING WITH GAIA

James Lovelock

I will not cease from Mental Fight,
Nor shall my sword sleep in my hand
Till we have built Jerusalem
In England's green and pleasant Land.
–William Blake, *Milton*

In letters and conversation, people often ask, "How should we live in harmony with Gaia?" I am tempted to reply, "Why ask me? All that I have done is to see the Earth differently; that does not qualify me to prescribe a way of life for you." Indeed, after nearly twenty years of writing and thinking about Gaia, it still seems that there is no prescription for living with Gaia, only consequences. Knowing that the question about how to live with Gaia is serious and that such a reply would be discourteous, as well as unhelpful, I will try to show what living with Gaia means to me. Then, perhaps, the questioner will discover something that we share in common.

My life, as a scientist-hermit, would suit very few. Most people are gregarious and enjoy the lively chattering of human company in pubs, churches, and parties. Living alone with Nature, even as a family unit, is not for them. So let me take you on a tour around the place where we live in north Devon, and as you walk with me I will try to explain why we prefer to live as we do. Then maybe you will see your own way to live with Gaia.

Soon after Helen and I came to live at Coombe Mill we adopted a peacock and a peahen. It was a delusion of grandeur coming from recollections of stately homes where peafowl strutted sedately and displayed their amazing colored tails. Coombe Mill is, in fact, a small cottage with thick mud-and-straw walls and a slate roof, an English adobe. But we did have 14 acres of land to start with, now grown to 30 acres. With the nearest neighbor about a mile away, it is room enough to keep the noisiest birds there are. Noisy they may be, but to us their triumphant trumpet sound at mating time is fitting and seems to usher in the spring. For the rest of the year, their extensive vocabulary ranges from a gentle clucking or purring sound to cries like a donkey braying. Then there is the sharp bark of their alarm call when, all too often, wild dogs stray onto our land. Helen, the dedicated gardener and keeper of our environment, calls them mobile shrubs, and we both have enjoyed their colorful company over the years. There is only one disadvantage—their habit, either through friendliness or the expectation of snacks, of gathering on the pavement outside the door. There they leave their smelly dung. I used to curse then when I trod in it unawares or had to clean it up. But then it came to me that I was wrong and they were right. Those ecologically minded birds were doing their best to turn the dead concrete of the path back to living soil again. What better way to digest away the concrete than by the daily application of nutrients and bacteria in the shedding of their shit?

Why should we need 30 acres to live on? We are not farmers. I think the purchase of a house with so large a garden was a reaction to the changes that took place in our last village, Bowerchalke, some 130 miles to the east. In the twenty years that we lived there, we saw a living village dispossessed of its country people, and its hinterland of seemly countryside destroyed. It was a quiet rape and pillage, no savage hordes swept upon us from the downs. The destruction was by a thousand small changes over the years, until the match between our model of what the countryside should be and the reality no longer coincided. To a casual visitor the village would have looked as beautiful as ever, but with each year that passed the farms underwent metamorphosis into agribusiness factories. Fields that in the summer were Wiltshire's glory, scarlet with poppies among the grain, became a uniform green sea of weed-free barley. Meadows that once had been gardens of wildflowers were plowed and sown with a single highly productive strain of grass. When we moved, we were determined to find a place where the environment was not likely to change so drastically again. The best way to achieve this seemed to be to find a house with enough land around it to allow us to control what happened to it.

I first saw Bowerchalke in 1936 on a journey by bicycle across southern England during a summer holiday from school. Of all the places between Kent and Cornwall that I traveled, none left so lasting a memory of perfection, and I resolved there and then that one day it would be my home. I had planned my journey with the single-mindedness of a general going to war. Like him,

I scrutinized ordnance maps, one inch to the mile. So detailed were these maps that they marked almost every house and tree, and finely drawn contour lines conveyed the lay of the land. I spent most winter evenings imagining the places I would visit. In those days there were few cars, and fewer still traveled on the minor roads I intended to use. With the aid of the ordnance maps, I traced a path through the network of winding lanes that joined in vertices at the villages and hamlets. Each country had its own style of architecture and its own accent. My journey was about 500 miles long and lasted for two weeks. The scale of life in England then made such a journey seem as much as expedition as does a trip to Australia now. It was not that we were diminished; it was the slower and more human pace of travel which enlarged the world.

As a novice scientist I was interested in things like wild plants, especially the poisonous ones like henbane, aconite, and deadly nightshade. I experimented once by chewing a fraction of a leaf of one of them and learnt the hard way the discomfort of atropine poisoning. Fossils too had a fascination, and the coastline of Dorset and Devon, where they lie as pebbles on the beaches, was part of my itinerary. I was led to Bowerchalke by the strange names of the Wiltshire and Dorset villages. I had to see what Plush, Folly, and Piddletrenthide looked like. I had to discover what Sydling St. Nicholas was, and hear the sonorous sounding Whitchurch Canonicorum. To reach these villages, my map showed that I had to follow the Ebble Valley that led through Bowerchalke in a gentle rising slope to the high downs of Dorset. The only tight-packed contour lines, marking a steep hill, were at the head of the valley just beyond Bowerchalke, an ideal road for a traveling by bicycle.

I can still remember passing up the road from Broadchalke, with the watercress beds on my left, and rounding a corner to see before me the small thatched village of Bowerchalke, the stage of an amphitheatre of green and shrubby downland hills. I arrived there at about four on a sunny Sunday afternoon in July. I was thirsty but, unusually, there were no signs outside the cottages offering teas. In those days walkers and cyclists were common enough to make it worth the while of villagers to sell refreshments. So remote was this region, and so few the travelers, that such efforts would have brought a poor return. I asked a man walking if there was anyone who would supply my needs, and he said, "Why, yes, Mrs. Gulliver in the white cottage over there sometimes will make you a tea"; and she did. It was the memory of the quiet tranquility of Bowerchalke then, when the countryside and the people merged in a natural seemliness, free from any taint of the city, that lingered in my mind and brought me back some twenty years later to make it our family home.

The recent act of destruction of the English countryside is a vandalism almost without parallel in modern history. Blake saw the threat of those dark satanic mills a century ago, but he never knew that one day they would spread until the whole of England was a factory floor. Humans and Nature had evolved together to form a system that sustained a rich diversity of species; something that stirred poets and even Darwin, who wrote about the mystery of the "tangled bank." It was so familiar, so taken for granted, that we never noticed its going until it was gone. Had anyone proposed building a new road through the close of Salisbury Cathedral the reaction would have been immediate. But farmers were paid by the Ministry of Agriculture to emulate the prairies, those man-made deserts in which nothing grows but grain, and nothing lives but farmers and their livestock. The yearly romp of vast and heavy machines and the generous spraying of herbicides and pesticides ensured that all but a few resistant plant and insect species were eliminated. The older-style farmers could not stomach it, and left the land to young agricultural college graduates working as managers for city institutions. One old farmer said to me, "I didn't do farming to be a mechanic in a factory." But it was wonderfully efficient, and soon England was producing far more food than could be eaten.

The destruction still goes on. Even here in Devon, the hedgerows and small copses still fall to the chain saws and diggers. Rachel Carson was right in her gloomy prediction of a silent spring, but it has come about not simply by pesticide poisoning, as she imagined, but by the attack on all fronts of the farmer's enemies, "weeds, pests, and vermin." Birds need a place to nest, and where better than the hedges, those marvelous linear forests that once divided our fields. Government, on the advice of negligent civil servants, paid handsome subsidies to farmers to root out the hedgerows, until the wildlife was destroyed, just as effectively as if the land had been sprayed with pesticide. The environmentalists, who should have seen what was happening and protested before it was too late, were much too busy fighting urban battles, or demonstrating outside the nuclear power stations. Their battle, whatever was claimed otherwise, was more against authority, represented by the monolithic electricity supply board, than for saving the countryside. They sometimes noticed poisonous sprays, for they were the products of the hated multinational chemical industries. But few were the friends of the soil who protested the agribusiness farms, or noticed the mechanized army of diggers and cutters working to make the landscape sterile for next year's planting of grain. There is no excuse for their neglect. Marion Shoard, in her moving and well-publicized book, *The Theft of the Countryside*, said all that I have said and much more.

To those who see the world in terms of a conflict between human societies and groupings for power, my personal view of the changing landscape must seem obsessional and irrelevant. They also are the vast majority everywhere, whether in the cozy comfort of air-conditioned suburban homes of the First World, or in the squalor of a Bidonville.

Who was most to blame for the destruction? Without doubt it was the scientists and agronomists who worked to make farming efficient. The experience of near starvation in the Second World War was a powerful stimulant to make Britain self-sustaining in food. Their intentions were good, it was just that they could not foresee the consequences. I know, because I was a small part of it. In my role of inventor, I helped friends and colleagues at the Grassland Research Institute near Stratford-upon-Avon in the 1940s. They were intent on improving the output of food from the small-scale English farms. I recall their sermons to young farmers on the inefficiency of hedgerows that hindered the free movement of machinery around a field; on the waste of meadows left as permanent pasture compared with a good crop of Italian rye grass grown as a monoculture. We never dreamt that the message would be so well heard that the government would be persuaded to pass the legislation that led to the removal of hedges and to the nurturing of agribusiness. Nor did we have the imagination to see that most young farmers share, with young males everywhere, a delight in mechanical toys. We, and through us the government, were giving them the money to buy, and the license to use, some of the most dangerously destructive weapons ever used. Weapons to fight the farmer's enemies, which were all life other than crops, livestock, hired help, and the farmer's family.

Should anyone think that I have got it wrong, that this was another example of heartless exploitation done by a government of capitalist nominees for the profit of a few multinationals, I would remind them that it started in the late 1940s during the period of the post-war Labor government, an administration secure in power, confident, and committed to its socialism. The destruction of the countryside was independent of politics; it was carried through by good intentions aided by the tendency of civil servants to apply positive feedback by subsidies, or a negative one through taxes. Farmers work on very small margins. They may own land worth up to a million pounds, but their returns may be very small compared with the returns from simple investment. A minuscule subsidy can turn a slight loss into a comfortable profit. The countryside has vanished from most of England, and what little remains here in the West Country is passing away because the government continues to pay farmers a subsidy which is just enough to make it worth their while to act as destroyers rather than as gardeners. The small subsidy to remove hedgerows has led to the loss of over 100,000 miles of them in the past few decades. An equally small subsidy would put them back again, although it would be generations before they served once more as the linear ecosystems and artistic landscape features of the countryside.

So what should we do instead? My vision of a future England would be like Blake's: to build Jerusalem on this green and pleasant land. It would involve the return to small, densely populated cities, never so big that the countryside was further than a walk or a bus ride away. At least one-third of the land should revert to natural woodland and heath, what farmers now call derelict land. Some land would be open to people for recreation; but one-sixth, at least, should be "derelict," private to wildlife only. Farming would be a mixture of intensive production where it was fit so to be, and small unsubsidized farms for those with the vocation of living in harmony with the land. In recent years, the overproduction of food by immoderate farming in the European Economic Community, including England, has been so vast that events have made my vision the basis of a practical plan for countryside management.

In their humorless despair, I have sometimes heard Greens parody Sir John Betjeman's verse, written near the beginning of the Second World War:

> Come, friendly bombs, and fall on Slough,
> To get it ready for the plough.
> The cabbages are coming now;
> The Earth exhales.

with

> Come friendly nukes and strike them down
> And blast their ever spreading town . . .

Even for the desperate, such an evil catharsis is not needed. Left to herself, Gaia will relax again into another long ice age. We forget that the temperate Northern Hemisphere, the home of the rich First World, now enjoys a brief summer between long, long periods of winter that last for a hundred thousand years. Even the nukes would not so devastate the land; nor would a "nuclear winter," if it could happen at all, last long enough to return the land to its normal frozen state. The natural state here in Devon has been, for most of the past million years, a permanent arctic winter. Even though close to the ocean, it was still as bitterly cold and barren as is Bear Island in the Arctic Ocean now. A mere 50 miles to the north or east of Coombe Mill were the great permanent glaciers of the "ice ages." These bulldozer blades of ice scraped off every vestige of surface life that had flowered in the brief interglacials like now.

So why should I fret over the destruction of a countryside that is, at most, only a few thousand years old and soon to vanish again? I do so because the English countryside was a great work of art; as much a sacrament as the cathedrals, music, and poetry. It has not all gone yet, and I ask, is there no one prepared to let it survive long enough to illustrate a gentle relationship between humans and the land, a living example of how one small group of humans, for a brief spell, did it right?

The little that is left of old England is still under threat. The donnish guardians of the landscape seem unaware of its existence. They see the countryside through romantic notions of scenic beauty. In my part of Devon they look only at the tundra of Dartmoor, and see it as something of inestimable value to be preserved at all costs. Tundra—the waterlogged bog, too wet and too cold for trees to grow—is a common place where the polar and temperate zones merge, a memory of what this region was in the last glaciation. In great contrast, the same guardians regard the land to the north of Dartmoor, with its small low-efficiency farms, rich wildlife, and village communities that have changed little since the Domesday Book, as of no account and expendable, a fit place for new schemes, such as a reservoir, a new road, or an industrial site.

I often think that those city planners who act so destructively have been misled by that great novelist Thomas Hardy. His writing deeply influenced my city-born and city-bred mother, a woman who easily saw the countryside through Hardy's distorting spectacles. My father, though, was born in Hardy's Wessex, and he showed me how very different was the reality. Hardy, for all the brilliance of his characterization, did not understand the countryside and used it merely as a background to act out his own tragic view of the human condition.

The England I knew as a child and a young man was breathtakingly beautiful, hedgerows and small copses were abundant, and small streams and rivers teemed with fish and fed the otters. It inspired generations of poets to make coherent the feelings we could not ourselves express. Yet that landscape of England was no natural ecosystem; it was a nation-sized garden, wonderfully and carefully tended. The degraded agricultural monocultures of today—with their filthy batteries for cattle and poultry, their ugly sheet-metal buildings, and roaring, stinking machinery—have made the countryside seem to be a part of Blake's dark satanic mills. I know it seems that way because I knew it as it was. Visitors come to Coombe Mill from the cities and abroad, and eulogize over the few glories that remain. They, and the planners of the countryside, do not understand that, unless we stop the ecocide soon, Rachel Carson's gloomy prediction of a silent spring will come true, not because we have poisoned the birds with pesticides, but because we have destroyed their habitats, and they no longer have anywhere to live.

Being a typical Englishman, I did not expect "them," the establishment, to change their ways. There was nothing for it but for my family to try to do our best with the land we owned at Coombe Mill; make it a habitat and a refuge for some of the plants and animals that agribusiness is destroying. This is how we, personally, choose to live with Gaia.

There are only three of us here, but 30 acres is not much more difficult to manage than a suburban garden. A garden lawn forever needs mowing, feeding, watering, and weeding; a ceaseless labor or a cost if someone else is to do it. Ten acres of our land is grass. It is no nightmare lawn requiring the ceaseless attention of an army of gardeners; it grows as meadows rich with wildflowers and small animals. The meadows divide and form a setting for the 20 acres of planted trees. It needs only to be enjoyed and cut once a year when the grass has grown long. Local farmers are glad to come and cut it; they use the grass for fodder and pay for it. The cost of keeping 10 acres of meadow is comparable with that of a well-kept suburban garden. The trees need more attention, but not so much as to be in any way a burden for the three of us.

The River Carey divides our land into two equal parts, which posed a problem. The river runs by the house, which was once a water mill, and is about 60 feet wide. It cannot easily be crossed by wading, and we soon discovered that to reach our new land involved a five-mile walk. Bridges across the Carey are widely spaced apart. Two years ago, we decided to build a bridge so that we could more easily tend the 10,000 trees that were newly planted on the west bank of the Carey. As metaphors go, building a bridge has almost become a cliché. But just try building a bridge in real life; it is amazing to experience, personally, the power of reducing a metaphor to practice.

As you will have gathered, we are solitary people and don't much mix with our neighbors. Yet in this part of west Devon we were welcomed as soon as we came and have experienced more spontaneous kindness than in any other place that we have lived. Helen and I and our son John are in various ways physically handicapped so that we add up to make one able-bodied person, not enough to run a place as large as this. It would not have flourished had it not been for the unstinting care and generous help of our friends from the village, Keith and Margaret Sargent. Our home and the buildings that go to make up the rest of this place are of mud and straw, with slate roofs. They would never have survived the winter storms but for the skillful repairs of our other village friends, and former occupants of Coombe Mill, Ernie and Bill Orchard. But it was not until we started to plan our bridge that we experienced the full vigor of the community in which we are immersed.

When these friends knew what was in our minds, the bridge began to form—first in the imagination as an exciting project, and then more solidly as the plans were drawn and the materials gathered. They had the skills needed to do with élan and enjoyment a challenging task, one that arose from no more than a passing personal thought. The project showed, in a Gaian way, how a thought became an act that brought personal and then local benefit.

Our bridge is made of steel; it was built by a blacksmith, Gilbert Rendall, and is in every way a mechanical construction. I am never quite comfortable with things mechanical. I well recall a conversation with my friends Stuart Brand, editor of *CoEvolution Quarterly*, and Gary Snyder, the poet. They were shocked and indignant when I said, "Chain saws are an invention more evil than the hydrogen bomb." To me a chain saw was something that cut down in minutes a tree that had taken a hundred years to grow. It was the means of destroying the tropical forests. To Gary Snyder it was a benign gardening tool with which he could carefully, like a surgeon, remove the scars of years of bad husbandry in his forests. It is not what you do but the way it is done; the more powerful the tool, the harder it is to use it right.

How, you may ask, do these rambling thoughts tell us about how to live with Gaia? I would reply that as a metaphor, Gaia emphasizes most the significance of the individual organism. It is always from the action of individuals that powerful local, regional, and global systems evolve. When the activity of an organism favors the environment as well as the organism itself, then its spread will be assisted; eventually the organism and the environmental change associated with it will become global in extent. The reverse is also true, and any species that adversely affects the environment is doomed; but life goes on. Does this apply to humans now? Are we doomed by our destruction of the natural world? Gaia is not purposefully antihuman, but so long as we continue to change the global environment against her preferences, we encourage our replacement with a more environmentally seemly species.

It all depends on you and me. If we see the world as a living organism of which we are a part — not the owner, nor the tenant; not even a passenger — we could have a long time ahead of us and our species might survive for its "allotted span." It is up to us to act personally in a way that is constructive. The present frenzy of agriculture and forestry is a global ecocide as foolish as it would be to act on the notion that our brains are supreme and the cells of other organs expendable. Would we drill wells through our skins to take the blood for its nutrients? If living with Gaia is a personal responsibility, how should we do it? Each of us will have a personal solution to the problem. There must be many simpler ways of living with Gaia than the one we have chosen at Coombe Mill. I find it useful to think of things that are harmless in moderation but malign in excess. For me these are the three deadly Cs: cars, cattle, and chain saws. For example, you could eat less beef. If you do this, and if the clinicians are right, your health might improve and at the same time you would ease the pressures to turn the forests of the humid tropics into absurdly wasteful beef farms.

Gaia theory arose from a detached, extraterrestrial view of the Earth, too distant to be much concerned with humans. Strangely, the view is not inconsistent with the human values of kindness and compassion; indeed it helps us to reject sentimentality about pain and death, and accept mortality, for us as well as for our species. With such a view in mind, Helen and I wish our eight grandchildren to inherit a healthy planet. In some ways, the worst fate that we can imagine for them is to become immortal through medical science—to be condemned to live on a geriatric planet, with the unending and overwhelming task of forever keeping it and themselves alive for our kind of life. Death and decay are certain, but they seem a small price to pay for the possession, even briefly, of life as an individual. The second law of thermodynamics points the only way the Universe can run—down, to a heat death. The pessimists are those who would use a flashlight to see their way in the dark and expect the battery to last forever. Better to live as Edna St. Vincent Millay advised:

> My candle burns at both ends;
> It will not last the night;
> But, ah, my foes, and, oh, my friends —
> It gives a lovely light!

FURTHER READING

Shoard (1980) surveys the tragedy of the English countryside. O'Hare (1988) cites grim facts and figures on its despoliation, and Hoskins (1955) recounts its creation. Bookchin (1990) defends human intervention in the environment. For more by Howard, see his 1943 and 1947 works. Lewis (1992) argues, in contrast to the symbiotic approach, that technology could allow humans to *decouple* from dependency on the environment. Giono (1985), although pure fiction, is an uplifting vision of what might be possible.

QUESTIONS TO CONSIDER

1. Lovelock tells us that there are no prescriptions for living with Gaia, "only consequences." Precisely what does this mean? (Hint: cf. Whatmough's remarks about the inappropriateness of managerial prioritizing.)
2. Central to Howard's method of organic farming was the use of livestock. Fresh manure was an essential ingredient in his composting process; he often cited the "manurial rights" of the soil. What concerns might an animal rights activist such as Tom Regan have about this? How would you respond to such concerns?
3. Consider Lovelock's "vision of a future England," with its small, densely populated cities, horticultural farming, and wilderness preserves. Would something like this really constitute a genuine symbiosis or mutualism, in any precise sense of the term, with the nonhuman members of the ecosystem?
4. Can we "live with the Earth" in some mutualistic way, or is all this just wishful thinking? If so, what is the alternative?

A PERSONAL NOTE, IN CONCLUSION

In this book, I have tended to give prominence to the impact of environmental degradation upon humans, and I have more than once suggested, or presented other authors who suggest, that human stewardship of the environment is a meaningful and desirable end. In the eyes of many, such views will be called "arrogant" and "anthropocentric." And in some circles these days, to be found out as anthropocentric is a very grave thing indeed. And yet (like Murray Bookchin — see his 1990 article), I resist being classified as either anthropocentric or biocentric exclusively. It seems to me that this categorization is beside the point if not harmful. I seek a view that recognizes both the special abilities and the special responsibilities of humans, and at the same time recognizes the dependency of humans upon nonhuman life and the relative insignificance of humans in the grand biotic scheme. To pretend that nonhuman life does not have intrinsic value, however philosophers may struggle to define such values, is indeed fatuous arrogance; to deny that humans do not have special capacities and a special place (for a while, at least) in nature on this planet is a simple abdication of responsibility. We have had enough of both, the arrogance and the abdication; now let's get on with the task of figuring out how to live with the Earth, instead of just on it.

GLOSSARY

active processes Biological or biochemical processes that expend free energy to construct or maintain a biological structure; they tend to operate against general thermodynamic gradients.

anthropocentric, anthropocentrism Placing human values first, or at the centre. Cf. biocentrism.

anthropogenic Literally, "caused by humans." For example, we speak of "anthropogenic climate change."

artifactual ecology An ecosystem that is partially an artifact: e.g., an ant hill, New York City.

atomistic Antonym of holistic, *q.v.*

biocentrism Rating life in general as of highest value. In general, biocentrists would regard human interests as no more privileged than the interests of other forms of life. Cf. anthropocentrism.

boom and crash A pattern in which a population of animals, plants, or humans grows exponentially for a period of time and then overshoots some resource limit, causing an abrupt fall in population numbers. Cf. exponential growth, logistic curve, overshoot.

carrying capacity The population that a particular ecosystem is capable of supporting. In general, it is a complicated function of many variables, and will vary with time. The sustainable carrying capacity of an ecosystem might be much smaller than the temporary carrying capacity that could be made possible by liquidation of biological resources that were capable of self-regeneration.

CFCs (chlorofluorocarbons) A class of organic compounds containing chlorine and fluorine. They are characterized by high chemical stability and are used for a variety of industrial and commercial purposes, the most important being refrigeration. CFCs are now known to be a major agent in the destruction of the ozone layer.

Chipko movement Literally, "tree-huggers"; grass-roots movement in India, frequently led by women, that seeks to protect trees as a source of sustenance from commercial exploitation.

clear-cutting The controversial practice of cutting an entire forest or stand of trees. Cf. selective forestry.

commensal, commensalism A relationship in which two or more organisms live in close proximity but in which one, the so-called *commensal,* benefits from the other without stressing it significantly. The commensal can be totally dependent on its host for the environment it needs to survive. Example: human forehead mites, which use our bodies as habitat but which (as far as we know) have no influence on our own well-being.

deep ecology A philosophical approach to environmental issues that stresses holistic and biocentric values and seeks to found regard for the environment on something beyond enlightened self-interest; deep ecologists are frequently activists and in extreme cases advocate **ecotage**, *q.v.*

dissipative system A physical system characterized by a stable coherent structure far from thermodynamic equilibrium; requires a generous external flow of energy for its maintenance. Living organisms are a class of dissipative systems. See **life**.

ecofeminism A multifaceted aspect of the women's movement that links exploitation of the environment with oppression of women.

ecology The science of the interrelations of organisms and their environment.

ecotage "Ecological sabotage" — sabotage of industrial activities believed to be harmful to wilderness or the environment in general; e.g., spiking old-growth trees.

entropy A term that has a technical definition within statistical mechanics, but that loosely can be thought of as a measure of the disorder within a physical system. Cf. second law of thermodynamics.

essentialism The notion that entities have an "essence," i.e., a set of definite **intrinsic** (*q.v.*) properties by which they may be defined once and for all.

ethics The word "ethic" is essentially a pun in ancient Greek, in which language the word for "habit" (*ethos*) differs only by a vowel from the word for character. Hence for Aristotle, to be ethical was, roughly speaking, to have habits that conduced to virtue or excellence of character. The notion of appropriate *habit* is very deeply built into the meaning of ethics in general.

exponential growth A type of change of a magnitude in which that magnitude increases in some definite proportion to its own size. The human population is currently growing at an exponential rate. Cf. boom and crash, logistic curve, overshoot.

extrinsic value A value of an entity defined only in relation to other entities or values. Cf. intrinsic, essentialism.

feedback, feedback loop A cause-and-effect relationship in which an outcome in turn has an influence on the original circumstances that brought it about. In *positive* feedback, the effect tends to increase or *amplify* the original cause; in *negative* feedback, the effect tends to decrease or *damp* the original cause. Unchecked positive feedback will destabilize a physical system, while negative feedback may tend to stabilize systems.

Gaia Ancient Greek term for the Earth Goddess; adopted by James Lovelock and Lynn Margulis as a term for the planet Earth considered as a unified symbiotic being.

Gaia hypothesis The scientific hypothesis, put forward by James Lovelock and Lynn Margulis, that the entire planet Earth is a single living being formed by a highly coherent symbiotic association of many or all other living beings on the planet. More precisely, it proposes that many critical biophysical parameters on the Earth (such as temperature, salinity, soil pH, etc.) are maintained within ranges favourable to life by the active responses of earthly organisms. The Gaia hypothesis is scientifically controversial, but gaining in respectability.

greenhouse effect The tendency of certain gases to trap heat in the troposphere.

holistic, holism The notion that some or all entities cannot be fully or accurately thought of or described without reference to some properties they possess as a totality or whole; such properties, according to holism, are not reducible to mere combinations of properties of isolable parts of the entity. Cf. **reductionism**. A tension exists between holistic and reductionistic ways of thought. The purpose of an organ in a body (e.g., the purpose of the heart, which is to pump blood) might well be considered a holistic property, since it is irreducible to any conjunction of facts about the biochemistry, cell structure, etc., of the heart itself, even though it is a function of those things (or *supervenes* upon them).

homeostasis Maintenance of a steady state by active biological processes.

humanism A value system that ranks human interests very highly or highest. Roughly synonymous with anthropocentrism, *q.v.*

intrinsic Cf. extrinsic. An intrinsic (or *inherent*) value is a value that an entity possesses in and of itself without qualification; in formal logic it would be represented by a monadic predicate. It is interesting that philosophers who insist that living beings have intrinsic value are often also those who argue against essentialism. Cf. essentialism.

life This term is so difficult to define that some philosophers have argued that there is no such thing — suggesting the obvious retort that those with such opinions should speak for themselves alone. Here is an attempt (which may please no one) at a rather abstract definition of life: a living being is a dissipative (*q.v.*) physical system that maintains by active cybernetic processes a high degree of internal order in spite of surrounding thermodynamic gradients. (The qualification "by active cybernetic" excludes some **dissipative systems** such as tornados and ball lightning as living systems, leaves viruses as borderline cases, but might include the entire planet Earth as a living being.) Cf. Gaia hypothesis, active processes.

lifeboat ethic A starkly simplified (some might say pathological) "ethic" characterized by triage (cutting losses) and exclusion. It tends to be practised almost inevitably in temporary conditions of very extreme survival pressure.

logistic curve A curve describing population growth in which a population increases exponentially for a while and then smoothly levels off to a steady state as it comes into equilibrium with its environment. Cf. boom and crash, exponential growth.

macroparasitism Term coined by historian William McNeill to denote the parasitical exploitation by one human group of some other human group or natural ecosystem.

mutualism A relationship between two or more organisms that is mutually beneficial. Cf. symbiosis, parasitism, commensalism.

naturalism This word has a variety of connotations. Usually it means any doctrine that seeks an explanation of the way things are in terms of natural as opposed to supernatural forces. In the context of environmental ethics, it is sometimes taken to be roughly an antonym for "humanism" and is, therefore, the ranking of nonhuman nature as a high or the highest ethical priority. "Ethical naturalism" is the attempt to derive ethical from natural categories or constraints.

naturalistic fallacy Ethical theory recognizes that it is a mistake (a "non sequitur") to attempt to derive an "ought" from an "is." For instance, the fact that childbirth can be painful and dangerous in no way entails that it ought to be painful and dangerous, even though such a belief once fuelled resistance to medical advances that made childbearing less so. Within environmental ethics, discussion of the naturalistic fallacy takes a peculiar twist, since we do attempt, in a variety of ways, to infer something about how things ought to be, or at least could be, from the way nature actually works.

NGO (non-governmental organization) An advocacy or activist group that is not sanctioned, supported, or appointed by any government. They can be as big as Greenpeace or as small as an informal gathering of neighbours to clean up trash on the street. NGOs (sometimes also called "grassroots" organizations) can have considerable, and sometimes decisive, influence in environmental affairs.

overshoot A process in which an activity has an impact upon a physical system, but in which negative feedback that could keep the effects of the activity within recoverable limits is so slow in coming that the system may suffer permanent damage; analogous to a speeding motorcycle running a stop sign and crashing because the driver is unable to react quickly enough to stop it. Many authors have argued that current ecological breakdown is a sign of overshoot. See Catton (1980), Meadows et al. (1991).

parasitism The tendency of one organism to exploit another, especially when it occurs to the detriment of that other. Cf. macroparasitism, mutualism, symbiosis, commensalism.

reductionism The notion that the properties of significant wholes are merely combinations, according to some definite rule, of the properties of definite parts. Cf. holism.

resourcism Pejorative term for the tendency to regard other forms of life as nothing more than resources to serve human ends.

second law of thermodynamics The statement that within a closed, isolated system the entropy must increase until it reaches a maximum. (A system is *closed* if it exchanges no matter with its surroundings. A system is *isolated* if it exchanges no radiant energy or matter with its surroundings.) A closed but not isolated system like Gaia can apparently violate the second law within its own boundaries because organisms within the system (like photosynthetic cells or human beings) can redirect some of the externally supplied flow of energy toward the creation and maintenance of orderly structures. Cf. entropy, life.

selective forestry The practice of cutting trees selectively from a forest. Cf. clear-cutting.

seventh-generation rule A Native North American ethical precept: consider the effect of your actions on the seventh generation — instead of just the next quarter!

shallow ecology Pejorative term coined by Arne Naess for an approach to environmental ethics that, although it may still advocate many environmentally friendly measures, is based on placing human values first. Cf. deep ecology.

social ecology An approach to environmental ethics pioneered by Murray Bookchin, which sees the exploitative dominance of nature as arising out of the exploitative dominance of persons by persons.

speciesism Pejorative term for the tendency to regard some species as in some way inferior or less worthy of consideration.

sustainable development A form of economic development that is supposed to increase human prosperity but that would at the same time be sustainable because it would not degrade our supporting ecosystems. Critics have argued that the very term is oxymoronic.

symbiosis Literally, "living together." The usage of this term varies. The most common sense of the term is a relationship between two or more organisms that is mutually beneficial; in this sense it means much the same as *mutualism* (*q.v.*). Some biologists refer to parasitism, mutualism, and commensalism as different types of symbiosis; others take mutualism and symbiosis to be more or less synonymous. Cf. parasitism, macroparasitism, mutualism. Symbiotic relationships can be to greater or lesser degrees *obligate* (not optional) or *facultative* (optional).

triage (From an Old French root meaning "to pick, sort.") This is used in two importantly different senses. In a modern hospital, triage means the practice of directing limited resources to those who need them most. In a battlefield or lifeboat, triage is the practice of cutting losses; medical resources would be limited to those most likely to benefit from them. Garrett Hardin and some radical "deep" ecologists have controversially advocated the practice of "eco-triage," meaning that better-off peoples in the world should not compromise their own survival by helping people on the edge of survival because of war or ecological breakdown.

Waldsterben Literally, "death of trees," a mysterious dying-off of forests in Europe. It is usually suspected to be due to industrial pollution, primarily in the form of acid rain, although some have suggested that inappropriate forestry practices may contribute as well.

BIBLIOGRAPHY

Anderson, G. Christopher. 1990. "'More Research Needed,'" *Nature* 343, February 22, 684.

Archubugi, F., and Nijkamp, P. (eds.). 1989. *Economy and Ecology: Towards Sustainable Development.* Dordrecht: Kluwer.

Armstrong, Susan J., and Botzler, Richard G. 1993. *Environmental Ethics: Divergence and Convergence.* New York: McGraw-Hill.

Beauchamp, Tom L. 1991. *Philosophical Ethics: An Introduction to Moral Philosophy.* Second Edition. New York: McGraw-Hill.

Bookchin, Murray. 1982. *The Ecology of Freedom: The Emergence and Dissolution of Hierarchy.* Palo Alto, CA: Cheshire Books.

———. 1987. "Thinking Ecologically: A Dialectical Approach," *Our Generation* 18(2), 3–40.

———. 1990. "Recovering Evolution: A Reply to Eckersley and Fox," *Environmental Ethics* 12(3), 253–74.

Bradley, Raymond, and Duguid, Stephen (eds.). 1989. *Environmental Ethics, Volume II.* Burnaby, BC: Institute for the Humanities, Simon Fraser University Publications.

Bromfield, Louis. 1950. *Out of the Earth.* New York: Harper.

Brookes, Warren T. 1989. "The Global Warming Panic," *Forbes*, December 25, 96–102.

Brown, Lester R. et al. 1990. *The State of the World 1990: A Worldwatch Institute Report on Progress toward a Sustainable Society.* New York and London: W.W. Norton.

Bryson, Reid A., and Murray, Thomas J. 1977. *Climates of Hunger: Mankind and the World's Changing Weather.* Madison: University of Wisconsin Press.

Burnett, J.A. et al. 1989. *On the Brink: Endangered Species in Canada.* An Environment Canada State of the Environment Report. Saskatoon: Western Producer Prairie Books.

Callicott, J. Baird. 1980. "Animal Liberation: A Triangular Affair," *Environmental Ethics* 2(4), 311–38.

———. 1987. "The Conceptual Foundations of the Land Ethic," in J. Baird Callicott (ed.), *Companion to A Sand County Almanac: Interpretive and Critical Essays*. Madison: University of Wisconsin Press.

———. 1989. "The Metaphysical Implications of Ecology," in Callicott and Ames (eds.) 1989.

Callicott, J. Baird, and Ames, Roger T. (eds.). 1989. *Nature in Asian Traditions of Thought: Essays in Environmental Philosophy*. Albany, NY: State University of New York Press.

Canadian Broadcasting Corporation (CBC). 1992. "The Wounded Sky," broadcast presentation on *The Journal*, July 20.

———. 1994. "Unpeopled Shores: The Unmaking of a Province," narrated by Rex Murphy, presented on *Prime Time News*, March 2.

Carson, Rachel. 1962. *Silent Spring*. Boston: Houghton Mifflin.

Carter, Vernon Gill, and Dale, Tom. 1974. *Topsoil and Civilization*. Revised Edition. (First Edition 1955.) Norman, OK: University of Oklahoma Press.

Catton, William R., Jr. 1980. *Overshoot: The Ecological Basis of Revolutionary Change*. Urbana: University of Illinois Press.

———. 1985. "On the Dire Destiny of Human Lemmings," in Tobias (ed.) 1985, 74–89.

Caudill, Harry M. 1963. *Night Comes to the Cumberlands: Biography of a Depressed Area*. Boston: Little, Brown.

———. 1976. *The Watches of the Night*. Boston: Little, Brown.

Charlton, Mark, and Riddell-Dixon, Elizabeth (eds.). 1993. *Crosscurrents: International Relations in the Post–Cold War Era*. Scarborough, ON: Nelson Canada.

Clark, C. 1973. "The Economics of Overexploitation," *Science* 181, 630–34.

Clow, Michael. 1990. "Sustainable Development Won't Be Enough," *Policy Options* 11(9), 6–8; reprinted in Charlton and Riddell-Dixon (eds.) 1993.

Cohen, Andrew Neal. 1992. "Weeding the Garden," *Atlantic Monthly* 270(5), 76–86.

Day, David. 1989. *The Eco Wars: True Tales of Environmental Madness*. Toronto: Key Porter Books.

Dehaas, David. 1987. "The Beavers of Starvation Creek," *Canadian Geographic*, February/March, 55–65.

Devall, Bill, and Sessions, George (eds.). 1985. *Deep Ecology*. Salt Lake City, UT: Peregrin Smith Books.

Diamond, Jared M. 1990. "Learning from Saving Species," *Nature* 343, January 18, 211–12.

Dobra, Peter M. 1978. "Cetaceans: A Litany of Cain," *Boston College Environmental Affairs Law Review* 7(1), 165–83; reprinted in VanDeVeer and Pierce (eds.) 1986.

Dotto, Lydia, and Schiff, Harold. 1978. *The Ozone War*. Garden City, NY: Doubleday.

Eckersley, Robyn. 1989. "Divining Evolution: The Ecological Ethics of Murray Bookchin," *Environmental Ethics* 11(2), 99–116.

Ehrlich, Paul R. 1971. *The Population Bomb*. Revised Edition. New York: Ballantine Books.

Ehrlich, Paul, and Ehrlich, Anne. 1981. *Extinction: The Causes and Consequences of the Disappearance of Species*. New York: Random House.

Ehrlich, Paul, Ehrlich, Anne, and Holdren, John P. 1973. *Human Ecology: Problems and Solutions.* San Francisco: W.H. Freeman.

Eliot, T.S. 1958. *Collected Poems 1909–1962*. London: Faber and Faber.

Environment Canada. 1991. *The State of Canada's Environment*. Ottawa: Government of Canada.

———. 1994a. "The Effects of Increased UV-B Radiation," Executive Summary of Report from the Workshop on the Effects of Increased UV-B Radiation (Toronto, April 1993), *Delta: Newsletter of the Canadian Global Change Program* 5(1), 5–8.

———. 1994b. "Stratospheric Ozone Depletion," SOE Bulletin No. 94-6, National Environmental Indicator Series.

Evernden, Neil. 1985. *The Natural Alien*. Toronto: University of Toronto Press.

Faulkner, Edward. 1943. *Plowman's Folly*. New York: Grosset.

Fausto-Sterling, Anne. 1993. "Is Nature Really Red in Tooth and Claw?" *Discover*, April, 24–27.

Fisher, David E. 1990. *Fire and Ice: The Greenhouse Effect, Ozone Depletion, and Nuclear Winter.* New York: Harper and Row.

Flader, Susan. 1974. *Thinking Like a Mountain: Aldo Leopold and the Evolution of an Ecological Attitude toward Deer.* Columbia: University of Missouri Press.

Fox, Warwick. 1989. "The Deep Ecology-Ecofeminism Debate and Its Parallels," *Environmental Ethics* 11, 5–25.

Freedman, Bill. 1989. *Environmental Ecology: The Impacts of Pollution and Other Stresses on Ecosystem Structure and Function.* New York: Academic Press.

Funk and Wagnalls. 1958. *Standard Dictionary of the English Language*. New York: Funk and Wagnalls Company.

Gaard, Greta (ed.). 1993. *Ecofeminism: Women, Animals, Nature*. Philadelphia: Temple University Press.

Galbraith, John Kenneth. 1973. *Economics and the Public Purpose*. New York: Houghton Mifflin.

Garlich, Carolyn. 1994. "Ethics and the Necessity of Population Reduction." Presented at the Conference on Sustainability and Distributive Justice at the University of Calgary.

George, Susan. 1988a. "Financing Ecocide in the Third World," *The Nation* 246(17), 601.

———. 1988b. *A Fate Worse Than Debt*. New York: Grove Press.

Giono, Jean. 1985. *The Man Who Planted Trees*. With Afterword by Norma L. Goodrich. Chelsea, VT: Chelsea Green Publishing Co.

Gladwell, Malcolm. 1995. "The Plague Year," *The New Republic* 213(3–4) (July 17 and 24), 38–46.

Goldsmith, Edward. 1993. *The Way: An Ecological World-view*. Boston: Shambhala Publications.

Gray, James H. 1967. *Men against the Desert*. Saskatoon: Western Producer Prairie Books.

Gribbin, John (ed.). 1986. *The Breathing Planet*. Oxford: Basil Blackwell.

Guha, Ramachandra. 1989. "Radical American Environmentalism and Wilderness Preservation: A Third World Critique," *Environmental Ethics* 12(1), 71–83.

Hanson, Philip P. (ed.). 1986. *Environmental Ethics [Volume I]: Philosophical and Policy Perspectives*. Burnaby, BC: Institute for the Humanities, Simon Fraser University Publications.

Hardin, Garrett. 1968. "The Tragedy of the Commons," *Science* 162, December 13, 1243–48.

———. 1974. "The Case against Helping the Poor," *Psychology Today*, September, p. 38.

Hecht, Susanna, and Cockburn, Alexander. 1989. *The Fate of the Forest: Developers, Destroyers and Defenders of the Amazon*. London and New York: Verso.

Henderson, Hazel. 1981. *The Politics of the Solar Age: Alternatives to Economics*. Garden City, NY: Anchor Press/Doubleday.

———. 1991. *Paradigms in Progress: Life beyond Economics*. Indianapolis, IN: Knowledge Systems.

Hoffman, John S. 1990. "Replacing CFCs: The Search for Alternatives," *Ambio* 19(6–7), 329–33.

Hoskins, W.G. 1955. *The Making of the English Landscape.* London: Hodder and Stoughton. (Penguin reprint, 1985.)

Howard, Sir Albert. 1943. *An Agricultural Testament.* New York and London: Oxford University Press.

———. 1947. *Farming and Gardening for Health or Disease.* Devin-Adair. (Published by Schocken Books, New York, 1972, as *The Soil and Health.*)

Immen, Wallace. 1993. "Researchers Confirm Link between Ozone, UV Levels," *The Globe and Mail* (Toronto), Friday, November 12, A8.

Inglis, Julian T. (ed.). 1993. *Traditional Ecological Knowledge: Concepts and Cases.* Ottawa: International Program on Traditional Ecological Knowledge and International Development Research Centre.

Israelson, David. 1990. *Silent Earth: The Politics of Our Survival.* Markham, ON: Viking (Penguin Books Canada).

Jacobs, Marius. 1987. *Tropical Rain Forest: A First Encounter.* Berlin and New York: Springer-Verlag.

Joseph, Lawrence E. 1990. *Gaia: The Growth of an Idea.* New York: St. Martin's Press.

Kaplan, Robert D. 1994. "The Coming Anarchy," *Atlantic Monthly,* 273(2), 44–76.

Karentz, Deneb. 1991. "Ecological Considerations of Antarctic Ozone Depletion," *Antarctic Science* 3(1), 3–11.

Kaufman, Les, and Mallory, Kenneth (eds.). 1986. *The Last Extinction.* Cambridge, MA: The MIT Press.

Keynes, John Maynard. 1936. *The General Theory of Employment, Interest and Money.* London: Macmillan.

Kheel, Marti. 1993. "From Heroic to Holistic Ethics: The Ecofeminist Challenge," in Gaard (ed.) 1993, pp. 243–71.

King, Ynestra. 1987. "What Is Ecofeminism?" *The Nation* 245(20), 702.

Laing, David. 1991. *The Earth System: An Introduction to Earth Science.* Dubuque, IA: Wm. C. Brown Publishers.

Leiss, William. 1986. "Instrumental Rationality, the Domination of Nature, and Why We Do Not Need an Environmental Ethic," in Hanson (ed.) 1986.

Leopold, Aldo. 1966. *A Sand County Almanac.* New York: Oxford University Press.

Levi, Barbara Goss. 1988. "Ozone Depletion at the Poles: The Hole Story Emerges," *Physics Today* 41(7), 17–21.

———. 1990. "Climate Modelers Struggle to Understand Global Warming," *Physics Today* 43(2), 17–19.

Lewis, Martin W. 1992. *Green Delusions: An Environmentalist Critique of Radical Environmentalism*. Durham and London: Duke University Press.

Lewontin, R.C. 1991. *Biology as Ideology: The Doctrine of DNA*. Concord, ON: Anansi.

Livingston, John. 1981. *The Fallacy of Wildlife Conservation.* Toronto: McClelland and Stewart.

———. 1985. "Moral Concern and the Ecosphere," *Alternatives* 12(2), 3–9.

———. 1989. "The Ecological Imperative," in Bradley and Duguid (eds.) 1989, 127–35.

———. 1994. *Rogue Primate: An Exploration of Human Domestication*. Toronto: Key Porter Books.

Lovelock, James. 1979. *Gaia: A New Look at Life on Earth*. New York: Oxford University Press.

———. 1988. *The Ages of Gaia: A Biography of Our Living Earth*. New York: W.W. Norton.

Lovelock, James, and Epton, Sidney. 1986. "The Quest for Gaia," in Gribbin (ed.) 1986.

Lovelock, James, and Margulis, Lynn. 1974. "Atmospheric Homeostasis by and for the Biosphere: The Gaia Hypothesis," *Tellus* 26(1–2), 2–9.

MacKenzie, Debora. 1995. "Polar Meltdown Fulfils Worst Predictions," *New Scientist* 147(1990), August 12, 4.

Manchester, William. 1988. *Winston Spencer Churchill, The Last Lion. Vol II: Alone, 1932–1940.* Boston: Little, Brown.

Manes, Christopher. 1990. *Green Rage: Radical Environmentalism and the Unmaking of Civilization.* Boston, Toronto, London: Little, Brown.

Manning, Edward W. 1990. "Presidential Address: Sustainable Development, the Challenge," *The Canadian Geographer* 34(4), 290–302.

March, George P. 1898. *The Earth as Modified by Human Action*. (Revision of *Man and Nature,* 1864.) New York: Charles Scribner's Sons.

McIntosh, Robert P. 1985. *The Background of Ecology: Concept and Theory.* Cambridge: Cambridge University Press.

McNeill, William H. 1976. *Plagues and Peoples*. Garden City, NY: Anchor Press/Doubleday.

Meadows, Donella H., Meadows, Dennis L., and Randers, Jørgen. 1992. *Beyond the Limits: Confronting Global Collapse, Envisioning a Sustainable Future.* Toronto: McClelland and Stewart.

Meadows, Donella H., Meadows, Dennis L., Randers, Jørgen, and Behrens, William W., III. 1972. *The Limits to Growth*. New York: Universe Books.

Medvedev, Zhores A. 1990. "The Environmental Destruction of the Soviet Union," *The Ecologist* 20(1), 24–29.

Meine, Kurt. 1988. *Aldo Leopold: His Life and Work*. Madison, WI: University of Wisconsin Press.

Merchant, Carolyn. 1992. *Radical Ecology: The Search for a Livable World*. New York and London: Routledge.

Mies, Maria, and Shiva, Vandana. 1993. *Ecofeminism*. Halifax: Fernwood Publications, and London and New Jersey: Zed Books.

Moorehead, Alan. 1959. *No Room in the Ark*. London: Hamish Hamilton. (Penguin reprint, 1962.)

Mountford, Guy. 1978. *Back from the Brink: Successes in Wildlife Conservation*. London: Hutchinson.

Mowat, Farley. 1972. *A Whale for the Killing*. Boston: Little, Brown.

———. 1984. *Sea of Slaughter*. Toronto: Seal Books (McClelland and Stewart).

Mumford, Lewis. 1934. *Technics and Civilization*. New York: Harcourt Brace.

Myers, Norman. 1992. *The Primary Source: Tropical Forests and Our Future*. New York and London: W.W. Norton.

Naess, Arne. 1985. "Identification as the Source of Deep Ecological Values," in Tobias (ed.) 1985.

Nance, John J. 1991. *What Goes Up: The Global Assault on Our Atmosphere*. New York: Morrow.

Nickerson, Mike. 1993. *Planning for Seven Generations: Guideposts for a Sustainable Future*. Hull, Quebec: Voyageur Publishing.

Odum, Eugene P. 1971. *Fundamentals of Ecology*. Third Edition. Philadelphia: W.B. Saunders.

———. 1989. *Ecology and Our Endangered Life-Support Systems*. Sunderland, MA: Sinauer Associates.

Oeschger, H., and Dütsch, H.U. 1989. "Ozone and the Greenhouse Effect," *Nature* 339, May 4, 19.

O'Hare, Greg. 1988. *Soils, Vegetation, Ecosystems*. Edinburgh: Oliver and Boyd.

Ophuls, William. 1977. *Ecology and the Politics of Scarcity: Prologue to a Political Theory of the Steady State*. San Francisco: W.H. Freeman.

Passmore, John. 1980. *Man's Responsibility for Nature: Ecological Problems and Western Traditions*. Second Edition. London: Duckworth.

Peacock, Kent A. 1992. "Can 'Bandaids' Close the Ozone Hole?" *Physics Today* 45(10), 140–41.

———. 1995. "Sustainability as Symbiosis: Why We Can't Be the Forehead Mites of Gaia," *Alternatives* 21(4), 16–22.

Pearce, Fred. 1994. "Not Warming, but Cooling," *New Scientist* 143(1933), July 9, 37–41.

Perlin, John. 1989. *A Forest Journey: The Role of Wood in the Development of Civilization*. New York and London: W.W. Norton.

Picard, André. 1989. "Greenhouse Effect Blamed for Deaths of One Million in Third World Last Year," *The Globe and Mail* (Toronto), November 24.

Piper, Alison. 1992. "Dusanka Ognjanovic-Filipovic, P.Eng," *Engineering Dimensions*, January/February, 37.

Plant, Judith (ed.). 1989. *Healing the Wounds: The Promise of Ecofeminism*. Philadelphia: New Society Publishers.

Postel, Sandra, and Heise, Lori. 1988. *Reforesting the Earth: Worldwatch Paper 83*. Washington, DC: Worldwatch Institute.

Rachels, James. 1986. *The Elements of Moral Philosophy*. Philadelphia: Temple University Press.

Radford, Tim. 1990. *The Crisis of Life on Earth: Our Legacy from the Second Millennium*. Wellingborough: Thorsons Publishing Group.

Raup, David M. 1991. *Extinction: Bad Genes or Bad Luck?* New York and London: W.W. Norton.

Rees, William E. 1990. "The Ecology of Sustainable Development," *The Ecologist* 20(1), January/February, 18–23.

Regan, Tom. 1985. "The Case for Animal Rights," in Singer (ed.) 1985.

Regan, Tom (ed.). 1984. *Earthbound: New Introductory Essays in Environmental Ethics*. New York: Random House.

Regenstein, Lewis. 1975. *The Politics of Extinction: The Shocking Story of the World's Endangered Wildlife*. New York: Macmillan.

Revelle, Roger, and Suess, Hans E. 1957. "Carbon Dioxide Exchange between Atmosphere and Ocean and the Question of an Increase of Atmospheric during the Past Decades," *Tellus* 9(1), 18.

Revkin, Andrew. 1990. *The Burning Season: The Murder of Chico Mendes and the Fight for the Amazon Rain Forest*. London: Collins.

———. 1992. *Global Warming: Understanding the Forecast*. New York: Abbeville Press.

Roan, Sharon L. 1989. *Ozone Crisis: The 15-Year Evolution of a Sudden Global Emergency*. New York: John Wiley and Sons.

Robinson, John, Francis, George, Legge, Russell, and Lerner, Sally. 1990. "Defining a Sustainable Society," *Alternatives* 17(2), 36–45.

Rolston, Holmes, III. 1989. *Philosophy Gone Wild: Environmental Ethics*. Buffalo, NY: Prometheus Books.

Rowland, F. Sherwood. 1990. "Stratospheric Ozone Depletion by Chlorofluorocarbons," *Ambio* 19(6–7), 281–92.

Runnels, Curtis N. 1995. "Environmental Degradation in Ancient Greece," *Scientific American* 272(3), 96–99.

Ryan, John C. 1992. *Life Support: Conserving Biological Diversity*. Washington, DC: Worldwatch Institute.

Sadik, N. 1989. *The State of World Population 1989*. New York: United Nations Population Fund.

Sale, Kirkpatrick. 1987. "Ecofeminism—A New Perspective," *The Nation* 245(9), 302.

———. 1988. "Deep Ecology and Its Critics," *The Nation* 246(19), 670.

Santayana, George. 1948. *The Life of Reason*. Second Edition. New York: Scribners.

Sapp, Jan. 1994. *Evolution by Association: A History of Symbiosis*. New York: Oxford University Press.

Schneider, Stephen H. 1989. *Global Warming: Are We Entering the Greenhouse Century?* San Francisco: Sierra Club Books.

Schneider, Stephen H., and Boston, Penelope J. (eds.). 1991. *Scientists on Gaia*. Cambridge, MA: The MIT Press.

Schrecker, Ted. 1993. "Missing the Point about Growth," in Charlton and Riddell-Dixon (eds.) 1993.

———. 1994. "Environmentalism and the Politics of Invisibility," *Alternatives* 20(2), 32–37.

Schrödinger, Erwin. 1944. *What Is Life?* Cambridge: The University Press.

Schweitzer, Albert. 1955. *The Philosophy of Civilization*. Translated by C.T. Campion. New York: Macmillan.

———. 1990 [1933]. *Out of My Life and Thought: An Autobiography*. Translated by A.B. Lemke. New York: Henry Holt.

Sears, Paul B. 1980 [1935]. *Deserts on the March: Fourth Edition*. Norman, OK: University of Oklahoma Press.

Shiva, Vandana. 1989a. *Staying Alive: Women, Ecology and Development*. London: Zed Books.

———. 1989b. *The Violence of the Green Revolution*. Dehra Dun: Vandana Shiva.

———. 1993. *Monocultures of the Mind: Perspectives on Biodiversity and Biotechnology*. London and New Jersey: Zed Books, and Penang: Third World Network.

Shoard, Marion. 1980. *The Theft of the Countryside*. London: Temple Smith. (Foreword by Henry Moore.)

Shukla, J., Nobre, C., and Sellers, P. 1990. "Amazon Deforestation and Climate Change," *Science* 247, March 10, 1322–25.

Simon, Julian. 1981. *The Ultimate Resource*. Princeton, NJ: Princeton University Press.

Singer, Peter (ed.). 1985. *In Defence of Animals*. Oxford and New York: Basil Blackwell.

Smith, R.C. et al. 1992. "Ozone Depletion: Ultraviolet Radiation and Phytoplankton Biology in Antarctic Waters," *Science* 255, February 21, 952–59.

Solow, Robert M. 1974. "The Economics of Resources or the Resources of Economics," *American Economic Review* 64(2), 1–14.

Soto, Suzanne. 1993. "Third World War: Thomas Homer-Dixon's Wake-Up Call," *University of Toronto Magazine* (Summer), 11–13.

Strauss, Stephen. 1994. "Study Finds Hope for the Ozone Layer," *The Globe and Mail* (Toronto), Thursday, August 25, A1.

Struzik, Ed. 1990. "The Last Buffalo Slaughter," *Canadian Forum* 69(794), 6–11.

Summers, Lawrence. 1992a. "Let Them Eat Pollution," *The Economist*, February 8, 66.

———. 1992b. "Summers on Sustainable Growth," *The Economist*, May 30, 65.

Sumner, L.W. 1986. "Review of Robin Attfield's *The Ethics of Environmental Concern*," *Environmental Ethics* 8, p. 77.

Swift, Jamie. 1983. *Cut and Run: The Assault on Canada's Forests*. Toronto: Between the Lines.

Taylor, Paul. 1990. "Thinning Ozone Layer Blamed for Eye Burns," *The Globe and Mail* (Toronto), January 17.

Thirgood, J.V. 1981. *Man and the Mediterranean Forest: A History of Resource Depletion*. London and New York: Academic Press.

Thompson, Janna. 1990. "A Refutation of Environmental Ethics," *Environmental Ethics* 12(2).

Tobias, Michael (ed.). 1985. *Deep Ecology*. San Marcos, CA: Avant Books.

Tuan, Yi-Fu. 1968. "Discrepancies between Environmental Attitude and Behavior: Examples from Europe and China," *Canadian Geographer* 12(3), 176–191.

———. 1974. *Topophilia: A Study of Environmental Perception, Attitudes, and Values.* Englewood Cliffs, NJ: Prentice-Hall.

United Nations Fund for Population Activities. 1991. *Population, Resources and the Environment: The Critical Challenges.* London.

VanDeVeer, Donald, and Pierce, Christine (eds.). 1986. *People, Penguins and Plastic Trees: Basic Issues in Environmental Ethics.* Belmont, CA: Wadsworth.

———. 1994. *The Environmental Ethics and Policy Book: Philosophy, Ecology, Economics.* Belmont, CA: Wadsworth. (This is a much-expanded version of VanDeVeer and Pierce 1986.)

Voytek, Mary A. 1990. "Addressing the Biological Effects of Decreased Ozone on the Antarctic Environment," *Ambio* 19(6–7), 52–61.

Ward, Peter D. 1994. *The End of Evolution: On Mass Extinctions and the Preservation of Biodiversity.* New York: Bantam Books.

Wavey, Chief Robert. 1993. "Keynote Address to International Workshop on Indigenous Knowledge and Community-based Resource Management," in Inglis (ed.) 1993.

Wells, H.G. 1920. *Outline of History.* London: Cassell.

Westphal, Dale, and Westphal, Fred (eds.). 1994. *Planet in Peril: Essays in Environmental Ethics.* New York: Harcourt Brace College Publishers.

White, Lynn, Jr. 1962. *Medieval Technology and Social Change.* London and New York: Oxford University Press.

———. 1967. "The Historical Dimensions of Our Ecological Crisis," *Science* 155(3767), 1203–7.

Will, Gavin. 1992. "Canada's Biggest Layoff: Inshore Fishery Could Be Sustainable." *This Magazine* 26(3), 4–5.

Wilson, Edward O. 1992. *The Diversity of Life.* New York and London: W.W. Norton.

World Commission on Environment and Development (WCED). 1987. *Our Common Future* (The Brundtland Report). New York: Oxford University Press.

Worster, Donald. 1977. *Nature's Economy: The Roots of Ecology.* San Francisco: Sierra Club Books.

———. 1979. *Dust Bowl: The Southern Plains in the 1930s.* New York: Oxford University Press.

———. 1990. "The Ecology of Order and Chaos," *Environmental Review* 14(1–2), 1–18.

Wright, Frank Lloyd. 1901. "The Art and Craft of the Machine." Lecture given at Hull House, Chicago. Reprinted in Frederick Gutheim (ed.), *On Architecture: Selected Writings by Frank Lloyd Wright*. New York: Duell, Sloan and Pierce, 1941.

Zimmerman, Michael E., Callicott, J. Baird, Sessions, George, Warren, Karen J., and Clark, John (eds.). 1993. *Environmental Philosophy: From Animal Rights to Radical Ecology*. Englewood Cliffs, NJ: Prentice-Hall.

CREDITS

The editors wish to thank the publishers and copyright holders for permission to reprint the selections in this book, which are listed below in order of their appearance.

Part One *Is There Really an Environmental Crisis?*

CHAPTER 1 **Crisis in the Skies: The Ozone Hole and Global Warming**

Barbara Goss Levi, "Climate Modelers Struggle to Understand Global Warming," excerpted from *Physics Today* 43(2), (1990), pp. 17–19. Reprinted by permission.

André Picard, "Greenhouse Effect Blamed for Deaths of One Million in Third World Last Year," *The Globe and Mail* (November 24, 1989), pp. A1, A2. Reprinted by permission of *The Globe and Mail.*

G. Christopher Anderson, "More Research Needed," *Nature* 343 (February 22, 1990), p. 684. Copyright © 1990 Macmillan Magazines Limited. Reprinted with permission from *Nature.*

CHAPTER 2 **Extinction Is So Final: The Crisis in Biodiversity**

"Two Extinctions," exerpted from Canadian Broadcasting Corporation, "Transcripts for March 2, 1994," *CBC Prime Time News.* Copyright © 1994 Canadian Broadcasting Corporation. Reprinted by permission of *CBC Prime Time News.*

Farley Mowat, "'The Seas Are Dying, As If You Didn't Know,'" excerpted from *Sea of Slaughter* (Toronto: McClelland and Stewart, 1984), pp. 174–79. Used by permission of the Canadian Publishers, McClelland and Stewart.

Les Kaufman, excerpted from "Why the Ark Is Sinking," in Les Kaufman and Kenneth Mallory (eds.), *The Last Extinction* (Cambridge, MA: The MIT Press, 1986), pp. 1–14. Copyright © 1986 Massachusetts Institute of Technology Press. Reprinted by permission of MIT Press.

Edward O. Wilson, "Hunters' Blitzkrieg," excerpted from *The Diversity of Life* (Cambridge, MA: The Belknap Press of Harvard University Press, 1992), pp. 243–51. Copyright © 1992 by Edward O. Wilson. Reprinted by permission of the publisher.

Peter Ward, "A Parent's Nightmare," in *The End of Evolution* (New York: Bantam Books, 1994), pp. 271–72. Copyright © 1994 Peter Ward.

Bill Freedman, "'What Do You Mean the Great Auk's Extinct?'" in *Environmental Ecology* (San Diego: Academic Press, 1989), p. 282. Copyright © 1989 Academic Press. Reprinted by permission.

CHAPTER 3 The Human Crisis: War, Disease, Poverty, and Overpopulation

Richard Preston, "The Earth Responds," from *The Hot Zone* (New York, NY: Crown Publishers, 1994). Copyright © 1994 by Richard Preston. Reprinted by permission of Crown Publishers, Inc.

Jared Diamond, "Easter's End," *Discover Magazine* 16(8) (August 1995), pp. 62–69. Copyright © 1995 The Walt Disney Co. Reprinted by permission of *Discover Magazine.*

Part Two "Those Who Cannot Remember the Past . . . "

CHAPTER 4 Soils and Forests

John Perlin, "A Forest Journey," excerpted from *A Forest Journey: The Role of Wood in the Development of Civilization* (New York, NY: W.W. Norton & Company, 1989), pp. 35–42, 93–101. Copyright © 1989 by John Perlin. Reprinted with the permission of W.W. Norton & Company, Inc.

Vernon Gill Carter and Tom Dale, "Lumberjacks in Lebanon," excerpted from *Topsoil and Civilization*, Revised Edition (Norman, OK: University of Oklahoma Press, 1974), pp. 68–75. Copyright © 1955, 1974 by the University of Oklahoma Press. Reprinted by permission of University of Oklahoma Press.

Jamie Swift, "'That's All Trees Are For . . . '" in *Cut and Run: The Assault on Canada's Forests* (Toronto: Between the Lines, 1983), pp. 91–92. Copyright © 1983 Between the Lines. Reprinted by permission of Between the Lines.

Gwaganad, "Speaking for the Earth: The Haida Way," in Judith Plant (ed.), *Healing the Wounds: The Promise of Ecofeminism* (Philadelphia: New Society Publishers, 1989), pp. 76–79. Copyright © 1989 Judith Plant. Reprinted by permission of New Society Publishers.

CHAPTER 5 Seeking a Perspective

George Perkins Marsh, "The Ravages of Man," excerpted from *Man and Nature* (Cambridge, MA: The Belknap Press of Harvard University Press, 1965), pp. 42–43. Copyright © 1965 by the President and Fellows of Harvard College. Reprinted by permission of the publishers.

Yi-Fu Tuan, "Discrepancies between Environmental Attitude and Behaviour: Examples from Europe and China," *The Canadian Geographer* 12(3) (1968), pp. 176–91. Reprinted by permission of The Canadian Association of Geographers.

W.G. Hoskins, "The Landscape Today," in *The Making of the English Landscape* (London: Penguin Books, 1955), pp. 298–303. Copyright © 1955 W.G. Hoskins. Reprinted by permission of Penguin Books Ltd.

Harry M. Caudill, "The Myth of Superabundance," in *The Watches of the Night* (Boston and Toronto: Little, Brown, 1976), pp. 269–70. Copyright © 1976 Harry M. Caudill.

The Editor, "The Gospel of Chief Seattle Is a Hoax," *Environmental Ethics*, 11(3) (Fall 1989), pp. 195–196. Copyright © 1989 Environmental Philosophy, Inc. Reprinted by permission.

Winston Churchill quotations from William Manchester, *The Last Lion: Winston Spencer Churchill Alone, 1932–1940* (New York: Dell Publishing, 1988), pp. 137, 189–90, and 677. Copyright © 1988 by William Manchester. Reprinted by permission of Little, Brown and Company.

Part Three What Is the Environment?

CHAPTER 6 Some Views of the Ecosystem

Eugene P. Odum, "Some Basics," excerpted from *Fundamentals of Ecology*, Third Edition (Orlando, FL: Saunders College Publishing, 1971), pp. 3–6, 8–9, 33–36. Copyright © 1971 by Saunders College Publishing. Reprinted by permission of the publisher.

Susanna Hecht and Alexander Cockburn, "Man-Made Nature," excerpted from *The Fate of the Forest: Developers, Destroyers and Defenders of the Amazon* (London: Verso, 1989), pp. 27–41. Copyright © 1989 Susanna Hecht and Alexander Cockburn. Reprinted by permission of Penguin Books Ltd.

Chief Robert Wavey, "Accept What Is Obvious," from "International Workshop on Indigenous Knowledge and Community-based Resource Management: Keynote Address," in Julian T. Inglis (ed.), *Traditional Ecological Knowledge: Concepts and Cases* (Ottawa: Canadian Museum of Nature, 1993), pp. 11–16. Copyright © 1993 International Program on Traditional Ecological Knowledge. Reprinted by permission.

Richard C. Lewontin, "There Is No 'Environment,'" *Biology as Ideology: The Doctrine of DNA* (Don Mills, ON: House of Anansi Press, 1991), pp. 83–97. Copyright © 1991 R.C Lewontin. Reprinted with the permission of Stoddart Publishing, Don Mills, Ontario, M3B 2T6.

Rachel Carson, "The Other Road," from *Silent Spring*. Copyright © 1962 by Rachel L. Carson, renewed 1990 by Roger Christie. Reprinted by permission of Houghton Mifflin Co. All rights reserved.

CHAPTER 7 **Symbiosis, Parasitism, and Commensalism**

Edward O. Wilson, "Varieties of Symbiosis," excerpted from *The Diversity of Life* (Cambridge, MA: The Belknap Press of Harvard University Press). Copyright © 1992 by Edward O. Wilson. Reprinted by permission of the publishers.

Anne Fausto-Sterling, "Is Nature Really Red in Tooth and Claw?" *Discover Magazine* 14(4) (April 1993), pp. 24–27. Copyright © 1993 The Walt Disney Co. Reprinted by permission of *Discover Magazine.*

William H. McNeill, "Macroparasitism and the Human Problem," excerpted from *Plagues and Peoples* (New York: Anchor Press/Doubleday, 1976), pp. 15–23. Copyright © 1976 by William H. McNeill. Used by permission of Doubleday, a division of Bantam Doubleday Dell Publishing Group, Inc.

Eugene P. Odum, "A Challenge for Humans," excerpted from *Fundamentals of Ecology*, Third Edition (Orlando, FL: Saunders College Publishing, 1971), pp. 222–23. Copyright © 1971 by Saunders College Publishing. Reprinted by permission of the publisher.

CHAPTER 8 **The Gaia Hypothesis**

James E. Lovelock and Lynn Margulis, "Atmospheric Homeostasis by and for the Biosphere: The Gaia Hypothesis," *Tellus* 26(1–2) (1974), pp. 2–9. Copyright © 1974 The Swedish Geophysical Society. Reprinted by permission.

James Lovelock and Sidney Epton, "The Quest for Gaia," in John Gribbin (ed.), *The Breathing Scientist* (Oxford, UK: Basil Blackwell & New Scientist, 1986), pp. 3–10. Copyright © IPC Magazines Ltd. Reprinted by permission.

Part Four *Environmental Ethics At Last*

CHAPTER 9 **Where Ecology Meets Philosophy**

Murray Bookchin, "The Immanence of Ethics," excerpted from the Epilogue in Murray Bookchin, *The Ecology of Freedom* (Palo Alta, CA: Cheshire Books, 1982), pp. 357–65. Copyright © 1982 Murray Bookchin. Reprinted by permission of Black Rose Books.

Aldo Leopold, "The Land Ethic," excerpted from *A Sand County Almanac: And Sketches Here and There* (New York, NY: Oxford University Press, 1949), pp. 217–41. Copyright © 1949, 1977 by Oxford University Press, Inc. Reprinted by permission.

CHAPTER 10 Is Anything Sacred?

Albert Schweitzer, "Reverence for Life," in *Out of My Life and Thought: An Autobiography* (New York: Henry Holt and Company, 1990), pp. 144–59. Copyright © 1933, 1949 Henry Holt and Co., Inc. Copyright © 1990 Rhena Schweitzer Miller. Translation copyright © 1990 Antje Bultmann Lamke. Reprinted by permission of Henry Holt and Co., Inc.

John A. Livingston, "Moral Concern and the Ecosphere," *Alternatives* 12 (2) (Winter 1985), pp. 3–9. Reprinted by permission of *Alternatives.*

William Leiss, "Instrumental Rationality, the Domination of Nature, and Why We Do Not Need an Environmental Ethic," in Philip P. Hanson (ed.), *Environmental Ethics: Philosophical and Policy Perspectives* (Burnaby, BC: Institute for the Humanities/SFU Publications, 1986), pp. 175–79. Copyright © 1986 Institute for the Humanities. Reprinted by permission of the Institute for the Humanities.

CHAPTER 11 "Deep" and "Shallow" Ecology

Arne Naess, "Identification as a Source of Deep Ecological Attitudes," in Michael Tobias (ed.), *Deep Ecology* (San Marcos, CA: Avant Books, 1988), pp. 256–71. Reprinted by permission.

Ramachandra Guha, "Radical American Environmentalism and Wilderness Preservation: A Third World Critique," *Environmental Ethics* 11(1) (Spring 1989), pp. 71–83. Copyright © 1989 Environmental Philosophy, Inc. Reprinted by permission.

CHAPTER 12 Hunting, Trapping, and Animal Rights

L.W. Sumner, "The Canadian Harp Seal Hunt: A Moral Issue," *Alternatives* 12(2) (Winter 1985), pp. 55–60. Reprinted by permission of *Alternatives.*

David Dehaas, "The Beavers of Starvation Creek," *Canadian Geographic* 107(1) (February/March 1987), pp. 55–60. Copyright © 1987 David Dehaas. Reprinted by permission of David Dehaas.

CHAPTER 13 Ecofeminism

Ynestra King, "A Sense of Urgency," from "What Is Ecofeminism?" in *The Nation* 245(20) (December 12, 1987), pp. 1702–1703. Copyright © 1987 The Nation Company, L.P. Reprinted with permission from *The Nation* magazine.

Stephanie Lahar, "Roots: Rejoining Natural and Social History," in Greta Gaard (ed.), *Ecofeminism: Women, Animals, Nature* (Philadelphia: Temple University Press, 1993), pp. 91–117. Copyright © 1988 Temple University Press. Reprinted by permission of Temple University Press.

Part Five The Environment and the Economy

CHAPTER 14 Should We Let the Market Decide?

John Palmer, "Tree-Huggers Warping Markets," *The University of Western Ontario Gazette* (March 13, 1992). Reprinted by permission of John Palmer.

W.R. Minto, "Eco Prof Hit Nail on the Head," *The University of Western Ontario Gazette* (March 19, 1992). Reprinted by permission of W.R. Minto.

Eugene Tan, "Tree Hugger Fights Back," *The University of Western Ontario Gazette* (March 19, 1992). Reprinted by permission of Eugene Tan.

Fred Williams, "Eco Prof's Column Was Pure 'Hogwash,'" *The University of Western Ontario Gazette* (March 19, 1992). Reprinted by permission of Fred Williams.

Martin Lewis, "Uneconomic Despoliation," in *Green Delusions* (Durham, NC: Duke University Press, 1992), pp. 20–22. Copyright © 1992 Duke University Press. Reprinted by permission of Duke University Press.

Hazel Henderson, "Let's Take Credit for Our Intelligence," excerpted from *Paradigms in Progress: Life beyond Economics* (San Francisco, CA: Barrett-Koehler Publishing Co., 1991), p. 101. Copyright © 1991, 1995 Hazel Henderson. Reprinted by permission of Hazel Henderson.

Lawrence Summers, "Let Them Eat Pollution," *The Economist* 322(7745) (February 8, 1992), p. 66. Reprinted by permission of *The Economist.*

Susan George, "Financing Ecocide in the Third World," *The Nation* 246(17) (April 30, 1988), pp. 6601–6604. Copyright © 1988 The Nation Company, L.P. Reprinted with permission from *The Nation* magazine.

CHAPTER 15 What Is Wealth?

Grant A. Whatmough, "Money, Machines, Energy, and Wealth" (Unpublished paper, 1976), pp. 1–13. Copyright © 1976 Grant A. Whatmough. Reprinted by permission of Grant A. Whatmough.

CHAPTER 16 Sustainable Development: Hypocrisy or Our Best Hope?

From the Brundtland Report, "Towards Sustainable Development," in *Our Common Future* (Oxford: Oxford University Press, 1987), pp. 43–66. Copyright © World Commission on Environment and Development, 1987. Reprinted from *Our Common Future* (1987) by permission of Oxford University Press.

Larry Lohmann, "Whose Common Future?" *The Ecologist* 20(3) (May/June 1990), pp. 82–84. Copyright © 1990 *The Ecologist*. Reprinted by permission of *The Ecologist.*

Ted Schrecker, "Missing the Point about Growth," in Mark Charlton and Elizabeth Riddell-Dixon (eds.), *Crosscurrents: International Relations in the Post–Cold War Era* (Scarborough, ON: Nelson Canada, 1993), pp. 535–41. Reprinted by permission of Ted Schrecker.

Part Six *Toward Symbiosis*

CHAPTER 17 **Can Species Be Saved?**

Edward O. Wilson, "Replacing a Keystone," excerpted from *The Diversity of Life* (Cambridge, MA: The Belknap Press of Harvard University Press, 1992), pp. 163–65. Copyright © 1992 by Edward O. Wilson.

John D. Milton, "The Return of the Wood Bison: The Irony of Success" (Unpublished paper, 1994), pp. 1–7. Reprinted by permission of John D. Milton.

CHAPTER 18 **The Artifactual Ecology**

Grant A. Whatmough, "The Artifactual Ecology: An Ecological Necessity" (Unpublished paper, 1994), pp. 1–3. Reprinted by permission of Grant A. Whatmough.

Sir Albert Howard, "An Agricultural Testament," in *An Agricultural Testament* (New York and London: Oxford University Press, 1943), pp. 219–24. Copyright © 1943 Oxford University Press. Reprinted from "A Final Survey" by Sir Albert Howard (1940) by permission of Oxford University Press.

James Lovelock, "Living with Gaia," from *The Ages of Gaia: A Biography of Our Living Earth* (New York: Bantam Publishing, 1988), pp. 225–37. Copyright © 1988 by the Commonwealth Fund Book Program of Memorial Sloan-Kettering Cancer Center. Reprinted with the permission of W.W. Norton & Company, Inc.

Edna St. Vincent Millay, "First Fig," in *Collected Poems* (Cambridge, MA: Harper Collins). Copyright © 1922, 1950 by Edna St. Vincent Millay. Reprinted by permission of Elizabeth Barnett, literary executor.

Reader Reply Card

We are interested in your reaction to *Living with the Earth: An Introduction to Environmental Philosophy*, by Kent A. Peacock. You can help us to improve this book in future editions by completing this questionnaire.

1. What was your reason for using this book?
   - ☐ university course ☐ college course ☐ continuing education course
   - ☐ professional ☐ personal ☐ other (specify) interest

   ____

2. If you are a student, please identify your school and the course in which you used this book.

3. Which chapters or parts of this book did you use? Which did you omit?

4. What did you like best about this book? What did you like least?

5. Please identify any topics you think should be added to future editions.

6. Please add any comments or suggestions.

7. May we contact you for further information?

   Name: ______________________________

   ____

   Address: ______________________________

   ____

   ____

   Phone: ______________________________

(fold here and tape shut)

Canada Post Corporation / Société canadienne des postes

Postage paid If mailed in Canada | **Port payé** si posté au Canada

Business Reply | **Réponse d'affaires**

0116870399 01

0116870399-M8Z4X6-BR01

Heather McWhinney
Publisher, College Division
HARCOURT BRACE & COMPANY, CANADA
55 HORNER AVENUE
TORONTO, ONTARIO
M8Z 9Z9